THE RIGHT TO SELF-DETERMINATION AND POST-COLONIAL GOVERNANCE

The Case of the Netherlands Antilles and Aruba

THE RIGHT TO SELF-DETERMINATION AND POST-COLONIAL GOVERNANCE

The Case of the Netherlands Antilles and Aruba

Steven Hillebrink

T·M·C·ASSER PRESS

Published by T·M·C·Asser press
P.O. Box 16163, 2500 BD The Hague, The Netherlands
<www.asserpress.nl>

T·M·C·Asser press' English language books are distributed exclusively by:

Cambridge University Press, The Edinburgh Building, Shaftesbury Road,
Cambridge CB2 2RU, UK,
or
for customers in the USA, Canada and Mexico:
Cambridge University Press, 100 Brook Hill Drive, West Nyack, NY 10994-2133, USA
<www.cambridge.org>

ISBN 978-90-6704-279-6

PREFACE

This book describes the international law concerning the right to self-determination of overseas territories with a colonial history. It provides the reader with a clearer picture of this area of international law and a better understanding of the position of the remaining overseas territories in the international system. It does not aim to analyse overseas policies thoroughly, nor to discuss in detail the various problems encountered in the administration of these islands, but it provides an overview of some of the most characteristic demands of post-colonial governance, particularly the obligation to respect the right to self-determination of the inhabitants of these small territories who wish to continue their dependence on a distant metropolis.

The case of the Netherlands Antilles and Aruba is discussed in more depth, because it represents an interesting form of decolonization, whereas their unique constitutional position within the Kingdom of the Netherlands is often misunderstood. The book – the first study on this subject to be written in English – reviews the structure of the Kingdom of the Netherlands, as well as provides an insight into the current process of the constitutional reform of the Netherlands Antilles.

This study is one of the results of the research programme 'Securing the rule of law in a world of multilevel jurisdiction' by Leiden University. Although I completed the book while working at the Dutch Ministry of the Interior and Kingdom Relations and the Ministry of Justice, the opinions expressed therein are my own and should in no way be construed as representing the opinions of the Dutch government.

Voorburg, July 2008

TABLE OF CONTENTS

LIST OF ABBREVIATIONS

AB	Administratiefrechtelijke beslissingen
ACP states	African, Caribbean and Pacific states
CAP	Common Agricultural Policy of the EU
CARICOM	Caribbean Community and Common Market
CEDAW	The Convention on the Elimination of All Forms of Discrimination against Women
DOM	Département d'outre-mer (overseas department of France)
EC	European Community
EEC	European Economic Community
ECHR	European Court of Human Rights
ECR	European Court Reports
ERNA	Eilandenregeling Nederlandse Antillen (Regulation for the Islands of the Netherlands Antilles)
EDF	European Development Fund
EU	European Union
GA	General Assembly of the United Nations
GAOR	General Assembly Official Records
HRC	Human Rights Committee
ICCPR	International Covenant on Civil and Political Rights
ICESCR	International Covenant on Economic, Social and Cultural Rights
ICJ	International Court of Justice
ILC	International Law Commission
ILO	International Labour Organisation
IMF	International Monetary Fund
JO	Journal officiel
LJIL	Leiden Journal of International Law
NAM	Non-Aligned Movement
NJ	Nederlandse jurisprudentie
NJB	Nederlands juristenblad

NSGT   Non-Self-Governing Territories

OAS   Organization of American States
OCT   Overseas Countries and Territories of the European Union

PE   Parlement européen

Res.   Resolution
RTC   Ronde Tafel Conferentie (Round Table Conference)

SEW   Sociaal-economische wetgeving: Tijdschrift voor Europees en
economisch recht
Stb   Staatsblad
Stcrt   Staatscourant

TOM   Territoire d'outre-mer (overseas territory of France)

UK   United Kingdom of Great-Britain and Northern Ireland
UN   United Nations
UNDP   United Nations Development Programme
UPT   Ultra-Peripheral Territories of the European Union
US   United States of America

WIAS   West Indies Associated States of the UK
WTO   World Trade Organization

FREQUENTLY USED TERMS

Administering States	Member States of the United Nations which are responsible for the administration of one or more Non-Self-Governing Territories in the sense of Chapter XI of the UN Charter.
Caribbean Countries	The Netherlands Antilles and Aruba.
Council of Ministers of the Kingdom	*Rijksministerraad* – The Council of Ministers of the Kingdom consists of the members of the Council of Ministers of the Netherlands and the Ministers Plenipotentiary of the Netherlands Antilles and Aruba.
Decolonization Committee	UN 'Special Committee on the Situation with Regard to the Implementation of the Declaration on the Granting of Independence to Colonial Countries and Peoples' also called the 'Special Committee', also sometimes referred to as the 'Committee of 24'.
Fourth Committee	'The Special Political and Decolonization Committee' of the UN General Assembly, which each year discusses the decolonization issues on the agenda of the GA.
Governor	*Gouverneur* – Representative of the King of the Netherlands in the Netherlands Antilles or Aruba and head of government in those Countries.
Handelingen	Minutes of the debates in the *Staten-Generaal*. *Handeling I* refers to the debates in the Senate and *Handelingen II* refers to the debates in the Lower House.
Island Territory	*Eilandgebied* – Administrative unit of the Netherlands Antilles. Each of the five islands constitutes a separate Island Territory.
Kamerstukken	Official records of the *Staten-Generaal* of the Netherlands.
Kingdom act	*Rijkswet* – A statute adopted jointly by the Kingdom government and the *Staten-Generaal*, and which regulates a Kingdom affair, or which contains an agreement between the Countries concerning an automous affair.
Kingdom affairs	*Koninkrijksaangelegenheden* – Common affairs of the three Countries, for which the Kingdom as a whole is responsible.

Kingdom Government   *Koninkrijksregering* – The King and the Council of
                          Ministers of the Kingdom.

Kingdom regulation   *Algemene maatregel van Rijksbestuur (AMvRB)* – A
                          regulation adopted by the Kingdom government, re-
                          garding a Kingdom affair, or containing an agreement
                          between the Countries concerning an autonomous af-
                          fair.

Lower House   *Tweede Kamer* – The politically leading house of the
                          parliament of the Netherlands (*Staten-Generaal*).

Metropolis   Refers to a (former) mother country of an overseas ter-
                          ritory, or the government of such a country.

Minister Plenipotentiary *Gevolmachtigde minister* – The representative of the
                          government of the Netherlands Antilles or Aruba in The
                          Hague. The Minister takes part in the meetings of the
                          Council of Ministers of the Kingdom and has the right
                          to participate in the debates of the *Staten-Generaal*.

Raad van State   The main advisory body of the government of the Neth-
                          erlands. The *Raad van State* of the Kingdom consists of
                          the members of the Dutch *Raad van State*, with the ad-
                          dition of two members who are nominated by the gov-
                          ernments of the Netherlands Antilles and Aruba.

Round Table Conference   A conference at which the Countries of the Kingdom
                          convene to discuss constitutional reform.

Senate   *Eerste Kamer* – the upper house of the *Staten-Gene-
                          raal*.

Staatsregeling   The regulation containing the internal constitution of
                          the Netherlands Antilles or Aruba.

Staten-Generaal   The parliament of the Netherlands, consisting of a
                          Lower House, which is politically leading, and a Sen-
                          ate.

Staten   The parliament of either the Netherlands Antilles or
                          Aruba.

Supreme Court   *Hoge Raad* – The highest court of law in the Nether-
                          lands, which also functions as the highest court for the
                          Netherlands Antilles and Aruba in some areas of the
                          law.

POLITICAL PARTIES REFERRED TO

ARP   Protestant Party (Netherlands – incorporated in the CDA in 1980)
AVP   Christian-Democratic Party (Aruba)
D66   Social-Liberal Party (Netherlands)
CDA   Christian-Democratic Party (Netherlands)
FOL   Labour Party (Curaçao)
KVP   Roman Catholic Party (Netherlands – incorporated in the CDA in 1980)
MEP   Party founded by Betico Croes (Aruba)
PvdA   Social-Democratic Party (Netherlands)
VVD   Liberal-Conservative Party (Netherlands)
SP   Socialist Party (Netherlands)

Chapter 1
INTRODUCTION

In 2005, a referendum was held on the island of Curaçao about its future political status. The results showed a preference for an autonomous position within
the Kingdom of the Netherlands, and local politicians claimed that the Netherlands had to cooperate in realizing the outcome of the referendum and could
not set conditions for the desired constitutional status of the island in relation to
the Netherlands. A surprised Dutch senator stated with dismay that 'there is
talk of a right to self-determination' and recommended that the Netherlands
should not accept the outcome of the referendum.[1]

Perceptions on the role of the right to self-determination tend to diverge
considerably in the Netherlands. The Charter for the Kingdom of the Netherlands, which regulates the constitutional relations between the Netherlands and
the two Caribbean Countries, the Netherlands Antilles and Aruba, does not
mention the right to self-determination, but when the Charter was promulgated
in 1954, it was hailed as the end of the colonial era for the Netherlands. Since
then, some have claimed that the right to self-determination simply does not
exist within the Kingdom, or that it only means that the islands may leave the
Kingdom and become independent if and when they want to. Others see it as
an absolute right for the islands to determine their constitutional position within
the Kingdom, which the Netherlands should simply accept.

In this study, I will look at what international law has to say about self-
determination in the context of decolonization in order to determine if – or to
what extent – the legal rules that emanate from this fundamental principle of
the international legal order might still have a bearing on the constitutional
relations between the Netherlands and the Dutch Caribbean islands.

To obtain a view of the general rules concerning decolonization and self-
determination, especially of small overseas territories with a colonial history
such as the Netherlands Antilles and Aruba, I have used some of the research
methods that are common in international legal research, by trying to deduce
rules of customary law from the practice of states and the organs of the United
Nations, in combination with statements that could be taken as evidence that

---

[1] *Handelingen I* 2004/05, p. 1029.

S. Hillebrink, The Right to Self-Determination and Post-Colonial Governance
© 2008, T·M·C·Asser Press, *The Hague, The Netherlands and the Author*

this practice is considered to be based on legal rules. This is not an exact science, for which reason the reader will often encounter phrases such as 'probably', 'perhaps' and 'it could be argued that'.

The first chapters will outline the development of international law in the area of decolonization since 1945, from the recognition that all overseas territories of the Western states should be 'decolonized', to the definition of three forms of self-government that can be chosen by the 'colonial peoples' when they exercise their right to self-determination. Then I will discuss whether this law can or should be applied to the constitutional relations between the Netherlands, the Netherlands Antilles and Aruba, and if so, which obligations could be derived from this law. These are the central questions this study will try to answer.

For this purpose, I will recount the historical debate on the nature of the Kingdom of the Netherlands, especially the part of the debate that took place in the UN General Assembly. I will also try to categorize the Kingdom as a form of government, from the perspective of constitutional theory and international law. Two additional questions will be dealt with in the final chapters; the right to self-determination of the individual islands of the Netherlands Antilles, and the role of this right in relations with the European Union. Since these two issues have played a prominent role in the status debates during recent decades, I consider it useful to see how the answer to the central question of this study could play a role in these debates.

I have found it necessary to study many of the cases that have been considered comparable to the situation of the Netherlands Antilles and Aruba, because the legal scholarship is not very developed in this area, and literature that has extracted general legal rules from the practice of states and the UN organs is rather scarce. I have looked into a number of precedents that might be important for the Kingdom of the Netherlands, and I have described some of them at considerable length, while explaining why they are relevant for the present case. The descriptions of these cases are usually entirely based on existing literature and the UN documents, since I have not been able to visit most of these islands. Since some of the sources I have used are difficult to come by in most parts of the world, and are simply not available in the Dutch Caribbean, I have included a number of purely descriptive paragraphs for the benefit of those readers who do not have access to a UN depository library or such interesting journals as the *Victoria University of Wellington Law Review*.

Chapter 2
THE RIGHT TO DECOLONIZATION AND SELF-DETERMINATION

This chapter describes the right to decolonization as it has developed in international law, and I will look at its relation to the right to self-determination.

2.1 THE RIGHT TO DECOLONIZATION

Since 1945, it has become uncommon to refer to overseas territories as 'colonies', because the term has become something of a fighting word. Instead of 'colony', the term 'dependent territory' is nowadays used to refer to the same category of territories. But the term 'decolonization' has remained in frequent use, to refer to 'the process that leads toward ending political dominion by colonial powers over overseas territories, and which intends to open possibilities for free political, economic, social and cultural development.'[1] The emphasis in the modern discourse on decolonization appears to be on the political dominance of the metropolis, which is no longer based on economic exploitation, violent repression or feelings of racial or cultural superiority. Instead, overseas relations are now treated by political science as a particular manifestation of the more common phenomena of dependence and core-periphery relations. The term decolonization therefore nowadays usually refers to the termination of political (and social) structures that give the metropolis a dominant position in relation to its overseas territories.[2]

At the United Nations, a system has been developed to supervise this process. Colonies are often equalled to Non-Self-Governing Territories (NSGTs) at the UN,[3] and this usage has been adopted in the legal litera-

---

[1] Verton 1990, p. 215.

[2] *Verton*, in his description of the decolonization of the Netherlands Antilles, claims that true decolonization also involves changes to the internal social structures, in order to redress the dominance of colonial elites within the territory (*see* Verton 1977).

[3] *See* GA Res. 1514 (XV), the Declaration on the Granting of Independence to Colonial Countries and Peoples of 1960 which applies to NSGTs (operative para. 5) and the yearly GA

S. Hillebrink, The Right to Self-Determination and Post-Colonial Governance
© 2008, T·M·C·ASSER PRESS, *The Hague, The Netherlands and the Author*

ture,[4] although doubts have been expressed whether the two terms really cover exactly the same categories of territories.[5] The GA has developed criteria to determine whether a territory is no longer a NSGT. If the concept of colonies should indeed be equalled to NSGTs, then these criteria should also be considered to determine when the process of decolonization is complete, at least in the eyes of the UN.

2.1.1   Chapter XI of the UN Charter

Chapter XI of the UN Charter, the 'Declaration Regarding Non-Self-Governing Territories', was a revolutionary statement, in that the colonial powers of 1945 promised that from then on, the interests of the colonial peoples would be of the first most importance in the administration of the NSGTs. Article 73 states that:

> Members of the United Nations which have or assume responsibilities for the administration of territories whose peoples have not yet attained a full measure of self-government recognize the principle that the interests of the inhabitants of these territories are paramount, and accept as a sacred trust the obligation to promote to the utmost, within the system of international peace and security established by the present Charter, the well-being of the inhabitants of these territories
> ....

The 'Administering Members' furthermore promised to develop the political, economic, social and educational advancement of the territories, and to develop self-government, while taking into account the political aspirations of the people. The Declaration does not refer to 'independence' (in contrast with Chapter XII, 'International trusteeship system') or 'self-determination.'

---

resolutions based on this Declaration. *See also* GA Res. 1541 (XV) which declares that NSGTs are territories that were known to be 'of the colonial type' in 1945. The identification of NSGTs with colonies is also found in the information provided by the UN Department of Public Information. *See for instance* the *Basic Facts about the United Nations* (New York: Department of Public Information 1998) which on p. 275 claims that the peoples of the NSGTs live 'under colonial rule.'

   [4] *See for instance* Kirchschläger 1961, p. 259, Cassese 1995, p. 71, Doehring 2002, p. 52, Fastenrath 2002, pp. 1089-90, Malanczuk 1997, p. 330, and Ermacora 1992, p. 665.

   [5] *Rigo Sureda* considers that on the basis of the criteria of 'salt water and skin pigmentation' (laid down in GA Res. 1541, *see below*) the UN continues to view the traditional colonies of 1945 as under 'colonial rule' as long as they have not become independent. Colonial status could perhaps also end through free association or integration, but in those cases a democratic form of government and a degree of political advancement of the population, and in case of integration also an amount of experience in self-government, is required. These criteria are not applied in case of independence, which leads *Rigo Sureda* to conclude that 'colonial rule' is akin to non-independence. *See* Rigo Sureda 1973, p. 261.

The colonial powers of 1945 probably intended Chapter XI to be no more than a code of good conduct,[6] but difference of opinion existed from the start among the Members of the UN on the legal character of Chapter XI. The colonial powers had insisted, at the San Francisco Conference, that the Chapter should be titled a 'declaration', to show that it was intended as a unilateral statement of principles, not merely the basis for a system of supervision by the United Nations. After the adoption of the UN Charter, the anti-colonial Members of the UN, supported by a majority of legal scholars,[7] argued that since the Declaration had been incorporated into a treaty, it was equally binding as any other Chapter of the Charter.

The Administering Members maintained that even though Chapter XI created far-reaching obligations and responsibilities, it should in no way infringe upon their domestic jurisdiction. Between 1945 and 1970 many states, including the Netherlands, claimed that Article 2, paragraph 7 prohibited the UN from interfering in the administration of their NSGTs. The 'colonial problem' should remain an internal affair of states. But as *Kelsen* had already pointed out in 1950, Article 10 of the Charter gives the GA the authority to discuss any subject within the scope of the Charter and make recommendations thereon. Under Article 6 of the Charter, the GA could, upon the recommendation of the Security Council, expel a member state that persistently violated the principles of the Charter. *Kelsen* states: 'If this is "supervision", the Charter indeed does provide organs for the supervision of application of Chapter XI.'[8] According to *Kelsen*, it is not impossible for states to invoke Article 2, paragraph 7 in this area, but an interpretation that places the administration of the NSGTs essentially within the domestic jurisdiction of states would make the provisions of Chapter XI illusory.

Which Territories were intended to fall within the scope of Chapter XI?

There is some disagreement among writers as to the categories of territories that the drafters intended to be covered by Chapter XI. *Kelsen* thought that it referred only to those colonies inhabited by 'relatively primitive aborigines with a backward civilization', or 'peoples which were not yet able to stand by themselves.'[9] *Engers* and *El-Ayouty* pointed out that only the UK expressed

---

[6] Kuyper & Kapteyn 1980, p. 155.
[7] *See* Engers 1956, pp. 200-10 for a comprehensive review of the contemporary scholarship on the legal status of Chapter XI.
[8] Kelsen 1950, p. 551, note 1.
[9] Kelsen 1950, p. 556. *See also* Ninčić 1970, p. 227, where it is claimed the drafters intended the 'areas of classical colonialism.'

itself in this sense during the drafting of the Charter.[10] *Fastenrath* thinks it reasonable to assume that the drafters intended the territories that were traditionally considered colonies in 1945. *Goodrich, Hambro & Simons* consider that the records of the San Francisco Conference do not shed much light on what the drafters had in mind.[11]

Whatever the real intentions of the drafters, the representatives at the UN assumed that Chapter XI had been intended to cover all of the Western overseas territories, and that it had not been intended for other dependent, backward, or disenfranchised population groups.[12] *Kelsen* pointed out that under Chapter XI it is possible that territories not traditionally considered colonies could be NSGTs, as long as they are not part of the 'metropolitan areas' of the Member states, as Article 74 of the Charter puts it,[13] but the UN has not made use of this possibility.

The early UN practice shows that all of the territories that were traditionally considered 'colonies' were considered to fall within the ambit of Chapter XI. During the first debates in the GA on this issue, Administering States such as Australia and the UK explicitly considered that Chapter XI dealt with the 'colonies.' The UK for instance spoke of 'the colonial or non-self-governing peoples.'[14] The correctness of the equation colony = NSGT has been called into question, most notably by the Belgian representatives at the UN. The so-called 'Belgian thesis' provides that Chapter XI of the Charter, dealing with the NSGTs, should also be applied to the backward or otherwise non-self-governing areas of the non-Western states.[15] This thesis has not been accepted[16] and

---

[10] *See* Engers 1956 and El-Ayouty 1971 for analyses of the *travaux préparatoires*.

[11] Goodrich, Hambro & Simons 1969, pp. 458-9. Fastenrath 2002, p. 1091.

[12] The representatives thought there had existed 'a measure of agreement' at the San Francisco Conference that dependent peoples living within the borders of the metropolitan areas of states were excluded from the scope of Chapter XI. *See* the summary of the debates on this issue in *Non-Self-Governing Territories: Summaries and Analyses of Information Transmitted to the Secretary-General during 1950*, New York: United Nations 1951 (UN Doc. ST/TRI/SER.A.5/Vol.I), pp. 51-2.

[13] Kelsen 1950, p. 556. *See also* Crawford 2006, pp. 610-12.

[14] Cited in Kelsen 1950, p. 555, note 5.

[15] *See* for instance, the speech by the Belgian representative in the Fourth Committee of the Fourth Session, GAOR (IV) Fourth Committee, 124th Meeting, par. 39-40. *See also* Claude 1975, p. 125 et seq.

[16] In the early years of the UN, it was also defended by France, *see for instance* the statement of the representative of France in the Special Committee on Information of 1949, UN Doc. A/AC.28/SR.2, p. 7. China (Taiwan) in 1963 requested the Decolonization Committee to declare that the Declaration on the Granting of Independence also applied to the European and Asian territories that were subjected to 'Soviet colonialism', especially the 'Chinese' territories that Russia had acquired during the nineteenth century through the conclusion of unequal treaties. *See* Barbier 1974, p. 165.

in fact increasingly aroused the anger of the Third World states, for which reason Belgium was requested by the other Administering Members not to defend it any more in the GA.[17]

2.1.2 Transmission of Information under Article 73(e)

Paragraph (e) of Article 73 is the only paragraph of Chapter XI that provides for a concrete and controllable obligation. It obliges the Administering Members to transmit regularly 'statistical and other information of a technical nature relating to economic, social and educational conditions in the territories for which they are ... responsible.' Political conditions were intentionally excluded, and the reports would serve 'information purposes' only. The paragraph does not state how and by whom it should be decided when this obligation to transmit information exists.

All of the Members that were considered to possess colonies, upon the request of the Secretary-General, had listed the NSGTs that they administered and had already started reporting on them.[18] The list included all of the Western 'colonies' (except those of Spain and Portugal, which were not yet members of the UN) and even included some European territories,[19] and a number of territories about which it might have been doubted whether they fell within the traditional category of colonies because their Administering States were not Western European powers.[20]

When Spain and Portugal joined the UN in 1955, they informed the Secretary-General that they did not consider their African and Asian 'overseas provinces' to be NSGTs, but a majority in the GA probably thought otherwise.[21] The non-Administering states wished to declare these territories NSGTs, but such a move by the GA would have been unprecedented since all of the other NSGTs had been voluntarily listed by the Administering Members. The GA had been working on a list of factors that should decide whether a territory was a NSGT or not, but this process had been consistently opposed by the Western states.[22]

The GA in 1959 made another attempt to reach consensus on the definition of NSGTs. It instituted a 'special committee of six on the transmission of in-

---

[17] During the final debates on the Netherlands Antilles and Surinam in 1955, the Netherlands delegation feared Belgium would again enrage the anti-colonial states, and asked the UK to request Belgium not to make a radical speech in the GA.

[18] GA Res. 66 (I) of 14 December 1946.

[19] Cyprus, Gibraltar and Malta.

[20] Australia, New Zealand and the United States.

[21] See El-Ayouty 1971, p. 180 and Wohlgemuth 1963.

[22] See El-Ayouty 1971 for a description of the extensive debates at the UN on this subject during the 1940s and 1950s.

formation under Article 73(e)', to study the 'principles' which should guide member states in determining whether or not an obligation existed to transmit information under Article 73(e).[23] The Committee was made up of three non-Administering States (India, Mexico and Morocco), and three Administering Powers (the UK, the US and the Netherlands[24]).

On the basis of the study of factors conducted in the early 1950s, and on the views on this issue that twenty-six governments had submitted to the Secretary-General,[25] the Committee unanimously drew up a list of twelve principles to be approved in the Fifteenth Session of the GA. This result, the Netherlands representative stated, was 'a shining example to the Fourth Committee of what members can achieve when united by common effort, good faith and perseverance, under the guidance of an inspiring chairman.'[26] These Principles would be adopted as GA Resolution 1541 (XV) on 15 December 1960.

The first Principle 'reaffirms' that Chapter XI applies only to territories which were known in 1945 'to be of the colonial type.' The GA thus explicitly connected Chapter XI to colonialism and thereby also rejected the Belgian thesis. The representatives were not entirely in agreement on the question of which territories were 'of the colonial type', as was shown by the attempt of the Ukraine to have the Canary Islands included in a list of territories on which Spain should transmit information.[27]

---

[23] GA Res. 1467 (XIV) of 12 December 1959, adopted by 54 votes to 5, with 15 abstentions. The Netherlands abstained, see GAOR (XIV) Plenary meetings, p. 726.

[24] The Netherlands at that time still administered West New Guinea as a NSGT. Because of the mounting political tensions concerning this territory, the Netherlands was keen to show its dedication to the cause of decolonization.

[25] Summarized in UN Doc. A/AC.100/L.1 (mimeographed only).

[26] Statement by Dingemans in the Fourth Committee on 2 November 1960, GAOR (XV) 4th Comm., 1032nd Meeting, para. 1.

[27] See UN Doc. A/C.4/L.651, introduced during the 1046th Meeting of the 15th Session of the GA (Fourth Committee), para. 20. The Soviet representatives claimed that this proposal was based on facts 'known to any schoolboy' (Soviet Union, 1034th Meeting, para. 30) and the Canary Islands 'had the same status as the other Non-Self-Governing Territories under Spanish administration' (Ukraine, 1046th Meeting, para. 20). Colombia responded that 'as every schoolboy knew, the Canary Islands, far from having ever been a colony, had been Columbus's last Spanish port of call on his way to America'(1047th Meeting, para. 39). Ireland (1049th Meeting, para. 9), Argentina (para. 31) and Haiti (para. 33) supported Spain, which considered the Ukrainian proposal 'a personal offence against all Spaniards' (1048th Meeting, para. 68). It seems that Spain had reached an agreement with representatives of a number of anti-colonial states, in which Spain would voluntarily consider a number of its territories as NSGTs. Spain in exchange obtained the guarantee that the Canary Islands would not be considered a NSGT (see BuZa 1961, p. 161). One possible reason why the African states were willing to negotiate with Spain was that Morocco objected against the listing of the Western Sahara, Ifni, Ceuta and Melilla as NSGTs because it considered them integral parts of its territory (1046th Meeting, para. 39). The proposal of the Ukraine was rejected by 42 votes to 15, with 16 abstentions (1048th Meeting, para. 71-77). Other

The second Principle refuted a position often defended by the Netherlands and other Western states until 1960, and which played an important role in the debate on the status of the Netherlands Antilles and Surinam. The Principle states that the obligation to transmit information continues to exist until a full measure of self-government has been reached, and not until the territory has become self-governing in the three fields mentioned in Article 73(e). Principle IV further clarifies the scope of Article 73(e): an obligation to transmit information exists *prima facie* when that territory is geographically separate and ethnically and/or culturally distinct from the state administering it. In combination with the first principle, this definition included all of the territories that were at that time considered Non-Self-Governing, and it presumably also included such territories as the French DOMs and TOMs, Puerto Rico, Hawaii, the Netherlands Antilles and Surinam, and the Spanish and Portuguese overseas provinces. Based on Principles I and IV there exists a presumption that all of these territories were NSGTs. The burden of proof probably lies with the presumed Administering State to show that Article 73(e) does not apply.[28]

Principle V offers further criteria that might strengthen or deny this presumption. These criteria were 'additional elements *inter alia* of an administrative, political, juridical, economic or historical nature', of which it was said that:

> If they affect the relationship between the metropolitan State and the territory concerned in a manner which arbitrarily places the latter in a position or status of subordination, they support the presumption that there is an obligation to transmit information under Article 73 e of the Charter.

It must be assumed that these additional elements could also lead to the conclusion that an obligation to transmit information does *not* exist, even though that obligation existed *prima facie* on the basis of the Principles I and IV. In that case, the additional evidence should prove that the territory is *not* arbitrarily subordinated to the metropolitan state. The Principle does not indicate how it should be determined whether a territory is 'arbitrarily' placed in a position of subordination, but the next Principle states that:

> A Non-Self-Governing Territory can be said to have reached a full measure of self-government by:
> (a) Emergence as a sovereign independent State;

---

states suggested that the Azores and Madeira should be included in the list of Portuguese territories, but this suggestion was not acted upon.

[28] Principles IV and V were interpreted in the Fourth Committee to place the burden of proof with the state, *see for instance* the statement by Pakistan (GAOR (XV) 4th Committee, para. 4).

(b) Free association with an independent State; or

(c) Integration with an independent State.

Strictly speaking, the Resolution does not state that a full measure of self-government can only be achieved in these three ways, nor that a territory which has not achieved any of these three statuses is arbitrarily placed in a position of subordination. The Principles do not explicitly exclude the possibility that the constitutional relations between a territory and a metropolitan state do not comply with the criteria for integration or association, as defined by Principles VII to IX, but still do not constitute an arbitrary subordination of the territory.

The Principles might also be used (more or less *a contrario*) to define the status of colony. Colonies, according to Principles IV and V, would be overseas territories, ethnically and culturally distinct from the people of the metropolis, and arbitrarily subjugated to the metropolis. The population of a colony has not voluntarily agreed to its political status, because it is a key element in free association and integration that the people should have freely adopted it (Principles VII and IX). Any political status that has not been clearly approved by the population therefore runs the risk of being branded 'colonial' on the basis of GA Resolution 1541.

Resolution 1541 constituted a large step towards consensus on the issue of decolonization among the Administering and non-Administering States. The main point of contention remained the competence issue, but besides that, most of the UN members agreed that the Principles represented an accurate picture of 'a full measure of self-government.'

For the most part, the Principles were generally supported in the GA, as 'logical and clear',[29] 'clear-cut basic principles',[30] which were 'extremely' satisfactory.[31] Some Third World representatives stated that the Principles were nothing new, because the GA had already agreed on everything they contained. Other Third World states thought it very important that the Principles were the result of a compromise between the Administering and non-Administering States. This would add to their status, especially if the GA were to adopt them unanimously. It was hoped that the Principles would compel the Administering States to change their interpretation of Chapter XI so that their behaviour would not be in violation of international law. The Netherlands stated there could be 'no doubt that the twelve principles set forth in the report will be a useful guide to all member nations represented here in determining whether or not an obligation exists to transmit information.'[32]

---

[29] The Netherlands (1032nd Meeting, para. 1).

[30] Ghana (1032nd Meeting, para. 16).

[31] Cambodia (1044th Meeting, para. 2).

[32] Statement by Dr Dingemans in the Fourth Committee, reproduced in BuZa 1961, p. 378. The Official Records of the GA report that Dingemans said: 'the Principles would be a useful

UN Supervision

The Fourth Committee made only one change to the proposals, albeit an important one. The Administering members of the Committee of Six had agreed to include in principle IX, which dealt with the processes by which a NSGT could integrate with a state, the following sentence:

> It is recognised that in certain circumstances United Nations supervision of such processes may be desirable.[33]

This sentence already represented a major change in the position of the Administering members, in that it allowed the possibility that the UN might play a supervisory role in the integration of territories with states, but it did not go far enough for a majority of the UN members.

The UN's supervisory role in these processes was one of the most contentious issues before the Fifteenth Session of the GA. In the Fourth Committee, the representatives of Tunisia and Togo submitted an amendment[34] which changed the final sentence of Principle IX to read: 'The United Nations could, when it deems it necessary, supervise these processes.'[35]

Tunisia and Togo were urged by many representatives to withdraw their proposal in order not to disrupt the wide but delicate consensus established through the carefully crafted compromise in the Committee of Six. It was feared that the amendment, if adopted, would lead to the Administering States abstaining from the vote on the Principles, which would lessen their value.[36] The amendment was nonetheless put to the vote and adopted by 38 votes to 24 (including the Netherlands and all the other Western states) with 26 abstentions,[37] showing how divided states still were on the subject of UN supervision.[38]

---

guide to the Fourth Committee in determining whether an obligation existed to transmit the information called for in Article 73 e of the Charter.' That would mean the Netherlands already considered the GA competent to decide when Article 73(e) applied (GAOR (XV) 4th Committee, 1032nd Meeting, para. 1).

[33] Report of the Special Committee of Six (etc.) of 3 October 1960, UN Doc. A/4526, p. 3.

[34] According to the Netherlands Ministry for Foreign Affairs, the amendment was inspired by the situation in Algeria (see BuZa 1961, p. 160). Algeria was one of the most contentious issues of the 15th GA, see below.

[35] Principle IX (b).

[36] GAOR (XV), 4th Committee, 1042nd–1046th Meetings. See also BuZa 1961, p. 160.

[37] 1045th Meeting, para. 28.

[38] It was shown during the same session of the GA that a majority of states were prepared to put Principle IX into practice with regard to Algeria (even though that territory was not consid-

Unity of Article 73

Most states considered that the obligation of Article 73(e) could not be isolated from the rest of the Article.[39] Chapter XI should be read as a whole and the obligation to transmit information could only end when the territory achieved a full measure of self-government. Only by studying the information transmitted by the Administering state could the UN judge whether a state had fulfilled its obligations under Article 73(a) to (d). This subject is of particular relevance to the status of the Netherlands Antilles and Aruba under Chapter XI (*see* chapter 6).

The text of Article 73(e) provides that the information is transmitted 'subject to such limitation as security and constitutional considerations may require.' Principle XI interprets this provision as follows:

> The only constitutional considerations to which Article 73 e of the Charter refers are those arising from constitutional relations of the territory with the Administering Member. They refer to a situation in which the constitution of the territory gives it self-government in economic, social and educational matters through freely elected institutions. Nevertheless, the responsibility for transmitting information under Article 73 e continues, unless these constitutional relations preclude the Government or parliament of the Administering Member from receiving statistical and other information of a technical nature relating to economic, social and educational conditions in the territory.

This suggests that it might be possible for territories to exist which do not possess a full measure of self-government, but on which the Administering State does not have to report to the Secretary-General. Difference of opinion existed among members of the Special Committee and the Fourth Committee on what the Principles actually meant to provide for such situations.

The idea that there could be NSGTs on which no information was transmitted was unpalatable for many non-Administering States. They stated that the GA had never accepted that 'fallacious argument'[40] which could be used as a pretext by colonial powers to provide no information on their colonies.[41] Some

---

ered a NSGT). Tunisia (together with 23 other states) submitted a proposal to have the GA 'decide' that a referendum should be conducted in Algeria, 'organized, controlled and supervised by the United Nations.' This proposal was adopted by the Fourth Committee by 38 to 33 votes, but the Committee also decided that this resolution required a two-thirds majority in the Plenary. Cyprus submitted a compromise proposal recommending that a referendum should be held under the auspices of the UN. This proposal received 53 votes in favour and 27 against, and was therefore not adopted. *See* the *Yearbook of the United Nations 1960*, pp. 132-6.

[39] Burma (1033rd Meeting, para. 7).
[40] Burma (1033rd Meeting, para. 8).
[41] Venezuela (1035th Meeting, para. 22) and Nigeria (1035th Meeting, para. 29).

members thought the situation purely hypothetical. Why should the constitution of a NSGT provide that it would not transmit information to the Administering State? Moreover, in a situation where only limited powers had been delegated to the NSGT, the final responsibility for the territory still lay with the Administering State.[42]

The debate also involved Principle X, which states that:

> The transmission of information on Non-Self-Governing Territories under Article 73 e of the Charter is subject to such limitation as constitutional and security considerations may require. This means that the extent of the information may be limited in certain circumstances, but the limitation in Article 73 cannot relieve a Member State of the obligations of Chapter XI. The 'limitation' can relate only to the quantum of information of economic, social and educational nature to be transmitted.

The UK representative in the Special Committee of Six only accepted Principle X 'on the understanding that there might be circumstances in which constitutional considerations of the kind referred to reduced to nil the amount of information which could be transmitted.'[43] A number of representatives in the Fourth Committee regretted that the UK had made this 'reservation', because it limited the value of the Principles, or could even make them void.[44] Venezuela stated that under no circumstances could the amount of information be reduced to nil, because Principle X stated that the constitutional considerations could not relieve a state of its obligations under Chapter XI, and the UK should have been satisfied with the last sentence of Principle XI. The UK answered that the statement had not been intended as a reservation but as a clarification, and agreed with Venezuela that Principle XI met the UK's position.[45] Principles X and XI were adopted unchanged by the GA.

Voting

The Principles were adopted in the Plenary of the GA by 69 votes to two (South Africa and Portugal) with 21 abstentions.[46] The Netherlands and most of the

---

[42] Nigeria (1035th Meeting, para. 29).

[43] Report of the Special Committee of Six (etc.), GAOR (XV), Annexes, Agenda item 38, para. 15 (UN Doc. A/4526).

[44] Venezuela (1035th Meeting, para. 21).

[45] UK (1035th Meeting, para. 24.

[46] GAOR (XV) Plenary, 948th Meeting, para. 88. In the Fourth Committee, there had been three negative votes. Spain had apparently changed its opinion and abstained in the Plenary. It explained its vote by stating that the Principles 'contain valuable ideas' but the draft resolution was 'confused, imprecise and open to erroneous interpretations' (GAOR (XV) Plenary, 948th Meeting, para. 95).

other Administering States abstained from the vote, but not because they did not agree to the principles which they had helped to draft. They stated that their reason for abstaining lay in the adoption of the amendment submitted by Tunisia and Togo, while the Principles were otherwise completely acceptable.[47] The Socialist states of Eastern Europe also abstained, because they still considered decolonization could only lead to independence.

During this same session of the GA, the representative of Spain announced that his government would start transmitting information on a number of Spanish NSGTs.[48] The government of Portugal refused to make a similar promise and the GA therefore decided to take the revolutionary step of declaring that it considered nine Portuguese territories to be non-self-governing, and that an obligation existed for Portugal to transmit information on these territories under Article 73(e).[49] The GA also issued a strong declaration regarding Algeria, a territory which France claimed was integrated with the metropolis.[50] By these two declarations, the GA showed that it considered itself competent to decide which territories fall within the scope of Chapter XI.

2.1.3   Subsequent attitudes towards Resolution 1541

A considerable number of GA Resolutions have referred to Resolution 1541 as one of the signposts for the decolonization process in almost all of the remaining NSGTs and similar territories. Administering States have treated Resolution 1541 as an authoritative document for the purpose of determining the acceptability of decolonization schemes falling short of independence. A clear example was the decolonization process of the Cook Islands and Niue, where New Zealand explicitly used the criteria of Resolution 1541 to guide its actions. The UK aimed at 'complete compliance' with Resolution 1541 in the creation of the Federation of Malaysia,[51] and with regard to its associated states

---

[47] For the Netherlands, *see* the statement by Dr Dingemans in the Fourth Committee (1046th Meeting), reproduced in BuZa 1961, p. 382. Belgium abstained because it did not think the GA was authorized to say anything on a matter that lay 'within the exclusive jurisdiction of sovereign States.' (1046th Meeting). Spain and Portugal (which voted against) stated that the Principles would be used against them, which showed that they were not properly formulated. South Africa did not explain its negative vote.

[48] GAOR (XV) Fourth Committee, 1048th Meeting. This announcement appears to have been the result of negotiations between Spain and the anti-colonial Third World countries, *see below* in the Paragraph on the Decolonization Committee.

[49] GA Res. 1542 (XV) of 15 December 1960, adopted by 68 votes to 6, with 17 abstentions. The Netherlands abstained.

[50] GA Res. 1573 (XV) of 19 December 1960.

[51] *See* Rapoport et al. 1971, p. 101.

in the Caribbean. Australia used Resolution 1541 in the decolonization of the Cocos (Keeling) Islands. *See further* in chapter 3.

The Netherlands considered Resolution 1541 as one of the most important resolutions with respect to self-determination and decolonization,[52] although since 1970 the Netherlands has attached more importance to the Friendly Relations Declaration (2625 (XXV)) in various official statements on self-determination. The Netherlands also claimed that its relations with Surinam and the Netherlands Antilles fulfilled the Principles of Resolution 1541, in the sense that those territories had become freely associated with the Netherlands (*see* chapter 6). The Netherlands government claimed that Resolution 1541 offered freedom of choice to the inhabitants of colonial territories. It vented this opinion, for instance, in the Security Council with regard to the Portuguese overseas territories,[53] and in the Fourth Committee of the GA with regard to Fiji,[54] and with regard to Gibraltar.[55] This attitude by the Netherlands was obviously influenced by the desire to obtain or maintain the support of states and UN organs for its ties with West New Guinea, Surinam and the Netherlands Antilles.[56] But it also shows that the Netherlands had accepted that the UN could lay down criteria for the administration of the overseas territories of the Netherlands, and that it considered that its relations with the Netherlands Antilles (and Aruba) should comply with the standards of Resolution 1541.

Resolution 1541 was emphatically used in the debate on New Caledonia in 1986.[57] It has also been invoked in many other (unsuccessful) attempts to have territories (re-) inscribed on the list of NSGTs.[58]

---

[52] *See* Kuyper & Kapteyn 1980, pp. 201-4.

[53] *See* statement by the Netherlands representative of 9 November 1965 in the Security Council, BuZa, No. 82, p. 195.

[54] *See* statement by the Netherlands representative of 6 December 1966 in the Fourth Committee, BuZa, No. 83, p. 343.

[55] *See* statement by the Netherlands representative of 16 December 1968 in the Fourth Committee, BuZa, No. 93, p. 298.

[56] Kuyper & Kapteyn 1980, p. 202.

[57] When the GA decided in 1986 that the situation in the French *territoire d'outre-mer* New Caledonia was one of international concern, it applied the Principles to reach the conclusion that 'New Caledonia is a Non-Self-Governing Territory within the meaning of the Charter' and that 'an obligation exists on the part of the Government of France to transmit information on New Caledonia under Chapter XI of the Charter.' On this occasion, an Administering State (New Zealand) and a former Administering State (Australia) used the Principles of Res. 1541 as the legal basis for their argument that New Caledonia was a NSGT. The other South Pacific states also referred to Res. 1541, 'which must guide the membership' in making a determination of the status of a territory. The representative of Fiji underlined that the Principles of Res. 1541 were 'drawn up carefully, deliberately and systematically', that they were 'overwhelmingly endorsed by the Assembly', and that 'their status in international law has been attested to by the International Court of Justice.' (GAOR (41), Plenary, 92nd Meeting, p. 7). Similar comments were made by the representatives of Thailand (91st Meeting, p. 93), and Ghana (92nd Meeting, p. 47).

Some authors have nonetheless belittled the importance of Resolution 1541,[59] usually from a viewpoint of the right of colonies to independence, in which context GA Resolution 1514 (XV) was, of course, much more important. When discussing integration and especially free association regimes, many authors are of the opinion that the criteria of Resolution 1541 are internationally accepted standards.[60]

2.1.4   Legally Binding Force of Resolution 1541

During the debate on the Principles in the Fourth Committee, many representatives said that the formulation of the Principles was a legal matter.[61] It could well be argued that the project of formulating the Principles intended to register the agreement among states on the interpretation of Chapter XI. After long and difficult negotiations on this subject during the first fifteen years of the UN, the members finally succeeded in reaching an agreement regarding a few essential principles to be taken into account when applying Chapter XI. The choice of words of the representatives sometimes revealed that the formulation of the Principles was thought to be akin to the drafting of a treaty.[62] If the main intent of the Resolution was to express an agreement among the member states, it could be regarded as having the same legally binding force as a treaty.[63] The

---

[58] *See* Lopez-Reyes 1996, Castanha 1996, Churchill 2002, and Pakaukau 2004 on appeals to have Hawaii re-inscribed as a NSGT. Barsh 1984 uses Res. 1541 to show that Alaska should perhaps not have been removed from the list of NSGTs.

[59] *See for instance* De Smith 1974, p. 71.

[60] *See for instance* Clark 1980, p. 71. *Keitner & Reisman* (2003) consider that Res. 1541 contains 'critical factors in determining the international lawfulness of an association.'

[61] *See for instance* the statement by Brazil (1037th Meeting, para. 17), Guinea (1038th Meeting, para. 5), and Mexico (1043rd Meeting, para. 37). A number of (Third World and Socialist) representatives thought that a legal debate was not necessary or desirable because the colonial problem should or would be resolved by political means, *see for instance* the statement by the representatives of Liberia (1034th Meeting, para. 3). These states attached much importance to the fact that the Report of the Committee of Six stated in its introduction to the Principles that the Charter was 'a living document' and that 'the obligations under Chapter XI should be viewed in the light of the changing spirit of the times', but a proposal to have GA Res. 1541 refer to this paragraph in the report of the Committee was not adopted. The Canadian representative remarked afterwards that the debate 'might well give the impression that the Fourth Committee was the legislative body of a world Government and that it was engaged in drafting the fundamental law or even the criminal code of that Government', although he immediately added that the Committee should realise it was *not* the world legislature (GAOR (XV), 4th Committee, 1046th Meeting, para. 2).

[62] *See for instance* the discussion about the British 'reservation' to Principle X, GAOR (XV) 4th Committee, 1035th Meeting.

[63] *See* Castañeda 1969, p. 150 et seq. and Sloan 1991, pp. 65-6 for GA Resolutions as agreements. *See also* Article 31 of the Vienna Convention on the Law of Treaties. The Vienna Conven-

main problem with this argument is that none of the Administering States voted in favour of the resolution, which would make it worthless as a treaty concerning the obligations of the Administering States.

It is perhaps better to see Resolution 1541 as a generally acceptable interpretation of a Charter provision.[64] Whether such an interpretation is binding upon the members depends upon the circumstances. The GA is not explicitly authorized to give authentic interpretations of the Charter. But the idea that the GA can – under certain circumstances – give binding interpretations of Charter provisions is generally accepted.[65] At the San Francisco Conference it was concluded that 'each organ will interpret such parts of the Charter as are applicable to its particular functions.' Combined with Article 10 of the Charter, the competence of the GA to interpret the Charter is considered to be very wide. In San Francisco it was also stated, however, that these interpretations of the Charter by an organ would not have binding force if they were 'not generally acceptable.'[66]

This statement has been interpreted to mean *a contrario* that GA Resolutions which interpret the Charter, and which are 'generally acceptable', are legally binding.[67] It has been suggested that all members of the UN should agree to such an interpretation,[68] or that 'an overwhelming majority' is needed,[69] or that the normal majority as provided by the Charter suffices,[70] or that the amendment procedure of the Charter should be applied analogously (two-thirds majority including the permanent members of the Security Council, *see* Article 108 of the Charter).[71]

---

tion does not apply to the UN Charter because the Charter predates the Convention (*see* Article 4 of the Convention) but its rules regarding interpretation of treaties were already part of international law in 1945.

[64] Some representatives stated that they considered the Principles a legal interpretation of the Charter, for instance Tunisia (1036th Meeting, para. 29), Brazil (1037th Meeting, para. 17), Guinea (1038th meeting, para. 5), and Sudan (1039th Meeting, para. 12).

[65] *See* Sloan 1991, p. 59.

[66] Report of the Rapporteur of Committee IV/2, UNCIO Doc. 933, IV/2/42(2), p. 7, 12 June 1945 (UNCIO Documents, Vol. 13, p. 703). Reproduced in Sloan 1991, p. 480.

[67] *See* Sloan 1991, pp. 59-60 for references to the works of *Schachter, Sohn, Šahović, Tunkin* and many others.

[68] Šahović 1972, p. 49.

[69] Asamoah 1966, p. 35.

[70] Castañeda 1969, p. 123. This seems illogical, as the decisions of organs are always supported by a majority. That the phrase 'generally acceptable' was added at the San Francisco Conference therefore would have to mean something more than a simple majority, otherwise it would be pleonastic. *Castañeda* himself adds that 'politically', the consent of the principal members involved in the case, will determine whether the interpretation 'is, or remains, binding' (Castañeda 1969, p. 218, note 10).

[71] Sloan 1991, p. 60 refers to *Akehurst*, with regard to a modification of the Charter by subsequent practice.

Despite these differing opinions, it may be concluded that a GA Resolution which clearly intends to interpret Charter obligations, and which is unanimously accepted, will have binding force on the member states.[72] If it is not unanimously accepted, then it may still have binding force if only a few states vote against it, especially if these do not include any of the permanent members of the Security Council. Special importance should also be attributed to the opinion of the states which should execute the obligations, especially in a case such as this, where only a few states are considered to have obligations.

Only two states voted against Resolution 1541, but one of these was an Administering State (Portugal). All of the other Administering States abstained, as did all of the permanent members of the Security Council (three of which were also Administering States). But it should be recalled that the abstentions of most of the Administering States were caused by the amendment which gave the GA the authority to consider when UN supervision was necessary in a territory contemplating integration with the mother country. Most Administering States wholeheartedly supported the rest of the Principles, which were not really contested by the other UN members either. The Resolution was used by Administering States in the decolonization of several small territories (*see above*). Only France has not yet explicitly recognized Resolution 1541 as a valid interpretation of the Charter, but during the debate on New Caledonia in the GA in 1986, it did not contest the legitimacy of Resolution 1541.[73]

For the Netherlands, it is important to remember that it was a member of the Committee of Six that unanimously submitted the draft for the Principles to the GA, which was adopted with hardly any changes. The Netherlands abstained

---

[72] Sloan 1991, p. 60.

[73] Curiously, the UK has recently denied the applicability of the Resolution to its NSGTs. On 12 November 2003, the Parliamentary Under Secretary of State for the Overseas Territories wrote to the Government Leaders of the Overseas Territories, stating: 'The UK did not vote for Resolution 1541 and is not bound by it.' He also asserted that the option of 'Free Association is unacceptable to the UK.' This statement should probably be considered as a mistake, or as irrelevant, since the UK cooperated in the drafting Res. 1541, and during the 1960s explicitly considered that it contained the international standards for the decolonization of NSGTs. The chairman of the Decolonization Committee, in a reaction to the UK, wrote that: 'If all UN members were to claim not to be bound by resolutions for which they did not vote, then the UN could not function. In fact, the UK was one of the authors of the resolution and in particular the concept of the three options. Its abstention during voting was only linked to disagreement with the issue of transmission of information. (…) It is unfortunate that the UK still wants to limit the options facing the territories to gaining independence or maintaining the status quo. We have pointed out and wish to emphasize that the "free association" option offers the flexibility to allow both parties – the territories and the UK – to achieve their objectives' (UN Doc. SC24/46/03). *See also* the paper presented by *Pineau and Ebanks* at the Cayman Islands Country Conference of 27–28 May 2004 at the University of the West Indies, entitled 'Self-Determination: The United Kingdom and the Overseas Territories.'

from the final vote because of the passage referring to the visiting missions, but it has confirmed on various occasions since 1960 that Resolution 1541 should guide the UN and member states in the area of decolonization.[74]

The main elements of Resolution 1541 were confirmed in 1970 by the unanimously adopted GA Resolution 2625 (XXV) which was intended to formulate a number of principles as the foundation of modern international law (*see below*). The legally binding character of Resolution 1541 was also confirmed by the Advisory Opinion of the ICJ on the Western Sahara of 1975.[75] The Court has in general been prepared to consider the resolutions of international organizations as valid interpretations of their constituting treaties, and has paid little attention to the question of whether these resolutions were unanimously adopted or not.[76]

Resolution 1541 could therefore be considered as a generally accepted, and therefore legally binding, interpretation of the Charter. Resolution 2625 would confirm the validity of the status options of Resolution 1541, and connect them explicitly with the exercise of the right to self-determination.

2.1.5 Reaffirmation of the Status Options: GA Resolution 2625 (XXV)

The 'Declaration on Principles of International Law concerning Friendly Relations and Cooperation among States in Accordance with the Charter of the United Nations'[77] was the result of a drafting process that started in 1961 when the GA asked its Legal Committee to study seven general principles of international law recognized in the UN Charter, among them the principle of equal rights and self-determination, and create new formulations of these principles in a draft declaration.[78]

The aim was to reaffirm these principles as the foundations of modern international law.[79] The Declaration represented a compromise between the Western states (and their supporters) and the rest of the world. The principles became the subject of 'a bitter struggle' between the jurists representing their governments,[80] but the end result was adopted unanimously by the GA as part of the festivities surrounding the 25th anniversary of the UN in 1970.

---

[74] *See* Kuyper & Kapteyn 1980, pp. 201-4.

[75] Advisory Opinion of 16 October 1975, *ICJ Reports* 1975, pp. 32-3. *See also* Cassese 1996, p. 356 et seq. and Crawford 2001.

[76] Sloan 1991, pp. 60-1.

[77] GA Res. 2625 (XXV).

[78] For the genesis of Res. 2625 (XXV) *see* Šahović 1972, Arangio-Ruiz 1979 and Mani 1993.

[79] The drafting of the formulations was delegated to a Special Committee, which was asked to strive for consensus so that the formulations might gain the status of international law (*see* Šahović 1972, p. 11, note 7).

[80] Šahović 1972, p. 12.

It was also proposed by Third World and Socialist states to have the GA declare colonialism contrary to international law, for which reason it should be eliminated in all its forms.[81] As this might be interpreted as declaring the entire system of Chapter XI of the Charter illegal, it was decided to declare instead that 'subjection of peoples to alien subjugation, domination and exploitation constitutes a violation of the principle [of equal rights and self-determination of peoples].' The proposal to include the phrase 'and other forms of colonialism' after the word 'exploitation' was not adopted, but it was decided to declare that: 'Every State has the duty to promote ... realization of the principle of equal rights and self-determination of peoples ... in order: ... (b) To bring a speedy end to colonialism.' Until this goal is achieved, the Declaration provides that:

> The territory of a colony or other non-self-governing territory has, under the Charter, a status separate and distinct from the territory of the State administering it; and such separate and distinct status under the Charter shall exist until the people of the colony or non-self-governing territory have exercised their right of self-determination in accordance with the Charter, and particularly its purposes and principles.

It is not entirely clear what was meant by 'colonies or (other) non-self-governing territories.' A number of Third World and Socialist states gave their opinion on how a colonial situation could be recognised. These states thought that the concept of colonies was much wider than the conception of NSGTs current at that time. Many states referred in general to situations of 'subjugation and exploitation' and 'alien domination.' These situations might include the importation of foreign settlers, trade agreements concluded with individuals who did not represent the people, and racism. Examples given of colonial situations were South Africa, Namibia, Southern Rhodesia, Vietnam, Israel, the Maldives, Cyprus, Angola and Mozambique. The Soviet Union listed as an example 'the so-called administrative arrangements between former colonial powers and their erstwhile colonies', which may have included the 1954 Charter of the Kingdom of the Netherlands.[82]

The representative of Ghana stated that colonial relationships demonstrated an 'arbitrary subjugation of the interests of a recognizable group to the interests of another recognizable group in which the power of government rested' and also that the colonial people lived in an area distinct from the 'ruling area.' In case of doubt, the representative of Ghana suggested that the ICJ should be empowered to decide whether the situation exhibited the basic features of co-

---

[81] *See* the several proposals cited in Mani 1993, p. 237.
[82] Statement by the Soviet Union (UN Doc. A/AC.125/SR.43, p. 13).

lonialism. The Court should consider 'all relevant factors such as geography, ethnic diversity, cultural differences, degree of self-government, history and tradition.'[83]

The Western states were not inclined to provide a material definition of 'colonies', but the proposals for the text on self-determination submitted by the UK and the US showed that these states considered colonies as a sub-category of the NSGTs.

The wording of the paragraph suggests that the category of NSGTs includes all colonies and perhaps also a number of territories that are no longer colonies. This would mean that any territory which is not a NSGT is not a colony either. It is not certain whether the GA was aware of this implication. Later resolutions contain the phrase 'Non-Self-Governing Territories and other colonies', which seems to imply that 'colonies' is the broader category, encompassing all NSGTs and some other territories.[84] This choice of words may relate to a real difference of opinion on the definition of colonies and NSGTs, which is also visible at other instances. The first definition was proposed by the US and the UK, and fits the notion that colonialism is something of the past, or to be found only in a very humane form in a few NSGTs that are too small for full self-government. The second definition is typical of resolutions proposed by the Non-Aligned countries, and relates to the wish to provoke outrage against the apartheid regime of South-Africa and against Israel, and also to keep open the possibility of adding new territories to the list of NSGTs.

Arangio-Ruiz, who represented Italy in the Committee, states that the paragraph was 'intended to discourage or neutralise ... the tendency of States to "dissimulate" the dependent condition of a people by promoting it to the status of province or overseas *département* or other municipal law subdivision, or to any other more or less autonomous status ' This intention certainly existed with some states that considered free association and integration unacceptable and thought the Declaration should refer to the obligation to grant independence without delay.[85]

However, 'informal negotiations' between the delegations during the final session of the Special Committee led to the inclusion of the other modes of exercising the right to self-determination.[86] The Declaration proclaims that:

---

[83] Statement by Ghana (UN Doc. A/AC.125/SR.68, pp. 18-19).

[84] *See for instance* GA Res. 35/118 of 11 December 1980, which contains the 'Plan of Action for the Full Implementation of the Declaration on the Granting of Independence to Colonial Countries and Peoples.'

[85] *See for instance*, the statement by Syria that 'concepts such as free association of a colonial territory with an independent State cannot be accepted because of their own inherent weaknesses' (cited in Mani 1993, p. 243), and the final Report of the Special Committee (GAOR (XXV) Supplement No. 18, p. 61), which refers to statements by delegations to this effect.

[86] Report of the Special Committee (GAOR (XXV) Supplement No. 18), p. 48.

The establishment of a sovereign and independent State, the free association or integration with an independent State or the emergence into any other political status freely determined by a people constitute modes of implementing the right to self-determination by that people.

It is therefore not justified to claim that the Declaration denounces or discourages autonomous regimes or forms of integration with the mother country, as long as those are 'freely determined by a people.'

It is not clear what the fourth option 'any other political status' means. It may have been intended merely to stress that self-government should be freely chosen by the population, whatever form it takes, as the ICJ appeared to think in the Western Sahara case. Seeing the absence of debate on this option during the drafting stage, it could also be considered as 'a mere slip of the pen.'[87]

The Friendly Relations Declaration is considered to be one of the most important resolutions of the GA. Its historical value was 'strongly emphasized by all the members of the United Nations who had taken part in the debate in the Legal Committee and in the plenary meeting of the 25th session of the General Assembly.'[88] It provides evidence for the existence of *opinio juris* among most states that self-determination is a legal right of peoples, the exercise of which can lead to independence, free association, integration, or any other status freely chosen by a people. In view of its aim to interpret and develop a number of basic principles of the UN Charter, its unanimous approval in the GA and the extensive legal debates and political negotiations among states which preceded it, the Declaration should be considered as an interpretation by the member states of their obligations under the Charter.[89] The section of the Resolution that deals with the freedom of choice is formulated to proclaim an existing right and a binding rule of law.

2.1.6 Who Determines Whether Chapter XI Applies?

Chapter XI does not state how and by whom it should be decided whether a territory is self-governing or not. During the debates on GA Resolution 1541 the question naturally arose about who is competent to apply these factors and principles. With respect to many of the remaining overseas territories of Western states, the answer to this question really decides whether these territories

---

[87] Clark 1980, p. 77.

[88] Šahović 1972, p. 48.

[89] In this sense, *see* Šahović 1972, p. 49, Macdonald 1981, pp. 243-4, and Ofuatey-Kodjoe 1995, p. 360. *See also above*, chapter 2.1.4, on the legally binding force of GA Res. 1541.

are NSGTs or not, as the majority of the UN member states probably differ in opinion with the Administering States on the status of these territories.[90]

The GA has claimed a large role in determining the meaning of the concept of 'a full measure of self-government', and has claimed to be competent to decide whether a territory is self-governing. GA Resolution 648 (VII) 'recognised' that the GA shared the authority to declare a territory self-governing with the Administering State. Resolution 742 (VIII) recommended that the GA and the Administering States would use the factors annexed to that resolution in determining whether a territory falls within the scope of Chapter XI of the Charter. Resolution 748 (VIII), on Puerto Rico, referred to the 'competence of the General Assembly to decide whether a Non-Self-Governing Territory has or has not attained a full measure of self-government',[91] as did Resolution 945 (X) on Surinam and the Netherlands Antilles.[92] The Administering States quite consistently opposed this opinion of the majority of states. Later resolutions avoided the subject in order to be able to reach unanimity.

This problem was one of the most divisive under consideration at the UN during the 1950s, as it determined whether the administration of the overseas territories of the Western states fell within their domestic jurisdiction or not.[93] Writers on the subject at the time varied in their opinions on this question, which was part of the uncertainty that existed from the start of the UN on the role of the GA in the 'supervision' of the application of Chapter XI.[94]

The GA has acted upon its claim of authority by declaring the Portuguese overseas provinces to be NSGTs in 1960,[95] and New Caledonia in 1986.[96] The GA has also adopted a number of resolutions in which it extended the application of Resolution 1514 to territories which were not previously considered to

---

[90] These would at least appear to include Puerto Rico, the French overseas territories, and the Netherlands Antilles and Aruba (see below).

[91] This paragraph of the Resolution was voted on separately and by roll-call. All Western states voted against it. The US nonetheless voted in favour of the resolution as a whole. Belgium and Australia voted against it. The other Administering States abstained (see GAOR (VIII), Plenary, 459th Meeting, paras. 159-60.

[92] In this case, the competence paragraph was also unanimously rejected by the Administering States, but this time, Denmark, France, the US and the Netherlands voted in favour of the resolution as a whole. Only Belgium voted against it. The other Administering States abstained.

[93] See Ninčić p. 219 et seq.

[94] Engers claimed that by the resolutions of 1953 and 1955, part of the Administering States' sovereignty has been taken away by a majority decision in the GA (Engers 1956, p. 159). Spits considered at the time that these decisions meant that the GA could now classify territories as non-self-governing that were not yet on the list of NSGTs, although he considered it doubtful whether the GA realized this, and whether it would ever take such a decision (Spits 1953, p. 110-11). See also Spits 1954, p. 444, where the author states with regard to a similar paragraph in the factors resolution of 1953 (GA Res. 742 (VIII), see below), that it is the GA which shall decide whether information should be transmitted under Article 73(e).

[95] GA Res. 1542 (XV) of 15 December 1960.

[96] GA Res. 41/41 A of 2 December 1986.

be NSGTs. In 1961, it adopted such a resolution on Algeria,[97] in 1962 on Southern Rhodesia,[98] in 1965 on Oman,[99] in 1966 on French Somaliland,[100] in 1973
on the Comoro Archipelago,[101] and in 1975 on Brunei.[102] All of these resolutions prompted the Decolonization Committee to involve itself with these territories, which is not entirely the same as declaring them to be NSGTs, but the
GA is rarely concerned with such legal niceties when decolonization is concerned.

Oppenheim considers that it was legitimate for the GA to establish suitable
procedures for the implementation of Chapter XI, but does not state whether
the GA is authorized to determine whether a territory is non-self-governing.[103]
Dahm thinks that the interpretation of Article 73 must be left to the organs of
the UN that are competent to receive the information under Article 73(e), and
these organs should also be allowed to insist on compliance with it.[104] According to *Thürer*, the organs of the UN are competent to demand that the obligations of Chapter XI are fulfilled, and states have a duty of loyalty to the
organization.[105] A number of authors consider that the GA has simply claimed
this authority in practice and has thereby acquired it.[106]

---

[97] GA Res. 1724 (XVI) of 1961. Earlier resolutions on Algeria were probably not yet examples of the GA using or extending its authority under Chapter XI or GA Res. 1514, *see* GA Res.
1012 (XI) of 1957, 1184 (XII) of 1957, and 1573 (XV) of 1960. All of these resolutions were
prepared by the First Committee instead of the Fourth Committee, which usually deals with
decolonization issues. None used such words as 'colonial', 'Territory' or 'administering power.'
Algeria was referred to by a number of states during the debate on Res. 1541 in 1960 as an
example of fake integration with a mother country. In 1960, Res. 1573 quoted a passage from
Res. 1514 ('the passionate yearning for freedom of all dependent peoples') and recognised the
right to self-determination of the Algerian people. Res. 1724 explicitly referred to Res. 1514,
thereby probably classifying Algeria as a colony, although not necessarily as a NSGT. The independence of Algeria (1962) came too soon for the Decolonization Committee to get involved with
the issue.

[98] GA Res. 1747 (XVII) of 28 June 1962.

[99] GA Res. 2073 (XX) of 17 December 1965.

[100] GA Res. 2228 (XXI) of 20 December 1966.

[101] GA Res. 3161 (XXVIII) of 14 December 1973.

[102] GA Res. 3424 (XXX) of 8 December 1975. The Decolonization Committee has also
placed Puerto Rico on the list, but this decision was not endorsed by the GA (*see below*)

[103] Oppenheim/Jennings & Watts 1992, p. 291. *Oppenheim* provides a list of instances in
which the GA has stretched its legal powers beyond the limits of the Charter in the area of
decolonization, but the unilateral claim of authority in determining NSGT is not on this list
(Oppenheim/Jennings & Watts 1992, p. 294).

[104] Dahm 1958, p. 579. The text of Article 73(e) provides that the Secretary-General should
receive the information.

[105] Thürer 1976, pp. 97-8. Islam 1989, pp. 10-12 considers the UN has a very broad and
varied jurisdiction to intervene in the event of a transgression of its purposes. *Islam* considers the
decolonization of the NSGTs as one of the purposes of the UN.

[106] *El Ayouty* considers the competence question was not answered by the Charter, but by the
GA, which resorted to a broad political interpretation of Chapter XI (El Ayouty 1971, pp. 230-2).

Castañeda has argued that unanimous approval is not necessary when the GA decides whether a particular territory is Non-Self-Governing. Even if the state concerned does not agree, the decision is nonetheless binding, because the organs of the UN interpret the scope of the obligations imposed on states by the Charter in the process of applying the Charter provisions in concrete cases.[107] Another way of considering the legal character of the GA Resolutions on Chapter XI is by treating them as 'true determinations of facts or concrete legal situations', as *Castañeda* calls them. This type of resolution provides 'the hypothesis or condition of the rules of law applied, or at times issued, by international organs in the performance of their activities.'[108] *Castañeda* differentiates between the condition (or hypothesis) and the consequence that is the result of the fulfilment of that condition. The consequence is determined by the law, but the existence of the condition must be determined by a person or an organ in the real world. As an example, *Castañeda* refers to the rule of Article 73(e), which provides that if a state administers a NSGT (condition), then it is obligated to transmit information (consequence). For the GA to observe the compliance with this rule (which, *Castañada* assumes, is within the competence of that organ) it must determine when this condition is fulfilled. This determination does not in itself create a legal obligation, it only makes possible the application of a rule established by the Charter.

In the South-West Africa cases before the ICJ in 1962, Judge Jessup considered that the discussions at the UN on the authority of the GA under Chapter XI should be seen as negotiations between the member states of the UN. The objections of the Administering States to the 'interference' of the UN in this area diminished considerably during the second half of the twentieth century. In 1960, most of the Administering States stated that the GA did not have the authority to list the NSGTs of Portugal and voted against the resolution in which the GA nonetheless did so.[109] But during the 1960s the Administering States changed opinion, or perhaps considered opposing the GA's policy less impor-

---

According to *Sloan*, the GA thus acquired through its own practice the authority to apply Chapter XI (Sloan 1991, p. 22). *Igarashi* maintains that self-government cannot legally be achieved without the explicit approval of the UN. When a state stops transmitting information under Article 73(e) without the approval of the GA 'it is in obvious violation of its duty under the United Nations Charter' (Igarashi 2002, p. 234). Another view has been to see the role of the UN in this area as a guarantor, while the Administering State acts as the obligee (Ofautey Kodjoe 1970, pp. 177-9). This view is also defended by Lopez-Reyes 1996, pp. 84-5.

[107] Castañeda 1969, pp. 122-3. This does not mean that the GA is authorized to give general authentic interpretations of the Charter. *Castañeda* therefore considers that GA Res. 742 (VIII) and 1541 (XV) are not binding.

[108] Castañeda 1969, p. 118 et seq.

[109] *See* GAOR (XV) 4th Committee, 1049th Meeting for the explanations of the negative votes cast by most Administering States on Res. 1542 (XV). The Netherlands abstained from the vote, but did not explain why.

tant. From 1971, a general paragraph was included in the yearly resolution on Article 73(e), which affirmed that:

> In the absence of a decision by the General Assembly itself that a Non-Self-Governing Territory has attained a full measure of self-government in terms of Chapter XI of the Charter, the administering Power concerned should continue to transmit information under Article 73 e of the Charter with respect to that Territory. [110]

At first, the Western states opposed this phrase, but the GA has continued to include it in its annual decolonization resolution. From 1986, these resolutions have been adopted unanimously, with only a small number of states abstaining from the vote.[111]

There are now a considerable number of arguments for concluding that the GA does indeed have the authority to declare a territory non-self-governing. The GA has supported this assumption in unanimously adopted resolutions for more than 20 years now, it has used its alleged authority with respect to a large number of territories since the 1950s, the Administering Powers (except France) have usually solicited a positive GA decision before or shortly after ceasing to transmit information on a territory that did not become independent, and most legal writers have concluded that the GA has the authority to decide when a full measure of self-government has been achieved.

It can therefore be concluded that the GA is competent to decide when a NSGT attains a full measure of self-government other than through independence. This does not necessarily mean that the GA is also authorized to decide when the transmission of information should *start*. But it seems logical that when an organ has the authority to decide whether a territory is still a NSGT because it does not possess a full measure of self-government, it also has the authority to decide that a territory has *become* a NSGT because it no longer possesses a full measure of self-government. The GA does, however, appear to feel itself bound by the 'colonial confession' of 1946, whereby the colonial powers voluntarily listed their NSGTs. GA Resolution 66 (I), which had taken note of this list, perhaps represents the maximum scope of application of Chapter XI of the Charter. Resolution 1541 in a sense acknowledged this by limiting the obligation to transmit information to territories 'of the colonial type.'

---

[110] GA Res. 2870 (XXVI) of 20 December 1971.

[111] *See for instance* GA Res. 41/13 of 31 October 1986. In 2003, the general decolonization resolution (including the usual statement of the GA's competence) was adopted by 163 votes to nil, with 6 abstentions (the US, the UK, France, the Federated States of Micronesia and Angola). *See* GA Res. 58/102 of 17 December 2003.

2.1.7   The Colonial Countries and Peoples of Resolution 1514

With regard to the implementation of GA Resolution 1514, the 'Declaration on the Granting of Independence to Colonial Countries and Peoples' of 1960, the GA has granted itself the unlimited authority to declare that territories fall under its application. This freedom of application was perhaps even one of the reasons for adopting the Declaration, and certainly for developing a system for its implementation.

The adoption of Resolution 1514 is considered to have been very important for the UN drive to obtain independence for all colonial territories. Looking at the GA Resolutions dealing with decolonization issues since 1960, the Declaration is referred to in each and every one. Indeed, in the eyes of the GA (and many observers[112]), the Declaration was the key legal instrument in the area of decolonization, at least during the 1960s and 1970s.[113] In that period, the UN involvement with the NSGTs was claimed to be based in the first place on the Declaration, which gave the GA the freedom to designate any territory as 'a territory to which the Declaration applies.' This freedom appeared to open the door to purely politically motivated decisions to declare certain areas 'colonial', but in practice it was almost only used with respect to territories that also fell within the ambit of Chapter XI of the Charter as interpreted by Resolution 1541.[114] When considering that Resolution 1541 also recognizes a right of independence for NSGTs, it could be wondered what addition Resolution 1514 has really made, in a legal sense, to Chapter XI and Resolution 1541 (*see below*). But one thing that the Declaration has definitely accomplished, is the establishment of the Decolonization Committee.

---

[112] *See for instance* De Smith 1974, p. 71, and Asamoah 1966.

[113] For the process of the adoption of Res. 1514, *see* Higgins 1963, pp. 100-1. For the legal significance of the Resolution during the early 1960s, *see* Asamoah 1966.

[114] Islam 1989, p. 10 considers that the actions of the GA in the area of decolonization suggest that NSGTs may also include other territories than the conventional colonies. But the GA has only four times applied GA Res. 1514 to territories that had not been on the first list of NSGTs (GA Res. 66 (I)), namely Oman, Algeria, the Portuguese overseas provinces, and a number of Spanish overseas territories. The GA has considered the situation in South Africa and Palestine in resolutions that also dealt with the application of GA Res. 1514 (*see for instance* GA Res. 35/28 of 11 November 1980 and 35/35 of 14 December 1980), but these situations were never discussed in the Decolonization Committee, nor placed on the list of territories to which 1514 applied. The wording of the resolutions on South Africa and Palestine suggest that the GA considers apartheid, racism, and the treatment of the Palestinians by Israel to belong to the same category of international crimes as colonialism.

The Relation between Resolutions 1541 and 1514

The Declaration on the Granting of Independence (Resolution 1514) portrays 'complete independence and freedom' as the Valhalla of all dependent peoples. The most important paragraph of 1514 in this respect is operative paragraph 5:

> Immediate steps shall be taken, in Trust and Non-Self-Governing Territories or all other territories which have not yet attained independence, to transfer all powers to the peoples of those territories, without any conditions or reservations, in accordance with their freely expressed will and desire, in order to enable them to enjoy complete independence and freedom.

All territories which have not yet attained independence should therefore be given the possibility to 'enjoy complete independence' as soon as possible. This does not mean, however, that the founding of an independent state should always be the end result.[115] Dependent peoples should be enabled to choose independence in a situation where they possess 'all powers', but they are not obliged to use this freedom to become an independent state.

The Declaration demands from the metropolitan states that they relinquish political control over their non-metropolitan territories, at least for a period long enough for those territories to reach a sovereign decision on their future.[116] The Declaration does not forbid the people of the territory to choose, as a sovereign people, to reaffirm its ties with the mother country, or to delegate certain of its sovereign powers to that mother country. This interpretation of the Declaration is in line with the demands the Decolonization Committee made from several Administering States during the 1960s and 1970s. It was also defended by the representative of the UK during the debate in the Decolonization Committee on the West Indies Associated States in 1967, when he stated that:

> That paragraph could have only one meaning: all powers must be offered to the people and those which they wished to assume and exercise for themselves directly must be transferred to them. In cases where they freely decided to request some other authority to exercise certain limited powers on their behalf, that fundamental recommendation in resolution 1514 (XV) was nevertheless satisfied, especially if, as in the present case, they had the opportunity to assume full powers themselves.[117]

---

[115] *See* in this sense Ofuatey-Kodjoe 1995, p. 359.

[116] For a similar view of what decolonization should entail, but from a sociological point of view, *see above* in the Paragraph on Colonies and Decolonization, with reference to the study by *Verton. See also* Korthals Altes 1999, p. 189 et seq.

[117] GAOR (XXII), Annexes, Addendum to agenda item 23 (part III), para. 787.

It might be wondered whether it is enough to merely 'offer' all powers to comply with Resolution 1514. Some authors interpret paragraph 5 to mean that the territory should be really *in possession* of all powers, and be a fully independent state, even if only for a second. Only at that moment can the population make a free choice to hand back certain powers to the former mother country.[118]

Most of the members of the Decolonization Committee considered, however, that even when the people of a territory had freely chosen to become associated with an independent state, Resolution 1514 could continue to apply, as in the case of the West Indies Associated States and the Cook Islands. Perhaps Puerto Rico is another example. In these cases, the Administering State might no longer have an obligation to report on the territory on the basis of Article 73(e) because the criteria of Resolutions 742 and 1541 had been met, and the territory could therefore perhaps no longer be considered a NSGT. But the GA could nonetheless decide to involve itself with the territory if the need arose, based on Resolution 1514, which continued to apply until the territory had achieved independence, many states thought.[119] The Resolution on the Cook Islands of 1965 specified this, and the debates on the West Indies Associated States and Puerto Rico also confirmed that this was the opinion of a majority of states.[120]

The question remains, then, whether a choice not to become independent, in compliance with Resolution 1541, should be considered final, or whether such a territory retains a right to decolonization. Resolution 1514 might be read to mean that decolonization can only really be considered complete after full independence has been achieved. Resolution 1541 suggests otherwise, as does Resolution 2625 for that matter.

Some authors consider that Resolution 1541 should take precedence over 1514. *Ofuatey-Kodjoe* calls 1541 'an even more authoritative definition of the

---

[118] *See for instance* the recitation by Harrop Freeman of 1979 cited in Macdonald 1981, pp. 249-50.

[119] *See for instance* the statement by Tanzania in the Decolonization Committee in 1967 (GAOR (XXII), Annexes, Addendum to agenda item 23 (Part III), para. 808. Similarly India in para. 927). During this debate on the West Indies Associated States, the UK repeatedly asked the anti-colonial states whether they rejected Res. 1541. India, in response, probably voiced the opinion of the majority of the Committee, when it agreed with the UK that 'Resolutions 1514 (XV) and 1541 (XV), both highly respected by his delegation, were not contradictory. By that his delegation meant that in a case where Resolution 1541 (XV) had been satisfied, Resolution 1514 (XV) might still apply, though not necessarily in every case.' (para. 919). The representative of Uruguay objected to this, and stated: 'If that interpretation was accepted, the integration of Greenland with Denmark, for example, and of Surinam with the Netherlands (...) would have to be considered invalid' (para. 860), but he was not supported by other representatives on this point.

[120] *See* chapter 3 on the Cook Islands, the West Indies Associated States and Puerto Rico. The Netherlands Antilles and Aruba perhaps also fall in this category (*see* chapter 6).

meaning of the right of peoples to self-determination' than 1514, because the Principles have 'furnished the basis of subsequent UN practices of self-determination.' In his view, Resolution 1541 'is more consistent with the practice of the United Nations throughout the era of decolonization.'[121] *Prince* thinks that 'Resolution 1541 should carry more weight because it reflects more of an attempt to interpret United Nations Charter provisions.'[122] *Macdonald* tries to reconcile Resolutions 1514 and 1541, 'these two embodiments of opposing political and philosophical positions', by interpreting them to create on the one hand 'an irrebuttable presumption' that with independence the right to self-determination would be satisfied, while on the other hand creating 'a rebuttable presumption *against* free association and integration' as forms of self-determination, because these status options 'possess more possibility for exploitation and denial of self-determination by the metropolitan country than independence.'[123] In the chapter on free association and integration (chapter 3), the finality of these options will be discussed further.

The interpretation of Resolution 1514, and the scope of its application, has been determined to a great extent by the Decolonization Committee.

The Decolonization Committee

The GA in 1961 instituted a Special Committee on the Situation with Regard to the Implementation of the Declaration (here referred to as the Decolonization Committee, but also called the Special Committee, or the Committee of 24).[124] The membership of this Committee was not based on parity between Administering and non-Administering States, as the previous committees which only dealt with Chapter XI had been. Consequently it quickly became a platform for the most radical anti-colonial states to attack the policies of the remaining Administering Powers.[125] The US, the UK, Italy and Australia all resigned from the Committee between 1969 and 1971,[126] and as France and Portugal had

---

[121] *Ofuatey-Kodjoe* considers that despite its dramatic impact, 'the Declaration's effect on the General Assembly's definition of the right to self-determination was more peripheral than at first believed' (Ofuatey-Kodjoe 1995, p. 359).

[122] Prince 1989, p. 44.

[123] Macdonald 1981, p. 244. In a similar sense, *see* Asamoah 1966, p. 166, and Prince 1989, p. 83.

[124] GA Res. 1654 (XVI) of 27 November 1961, adopted by 97 to nil, with 4 abstentions (France, South Africa, Spain and the UK). GA Res. 1810 (XVII) of 17 December 1962 provided further instructions for the Committee.

[125] Franck 1985 describes how the 'radicals' within the anti-colonial movement succeeded in 'hijacking' the Committee.

[126] The UK withdrew when the GA adopted Res. 2908 (XXV), the programme of action for the implementation of GA Res. 1514, which contained special recommendations for Southern

never cooperated, the only Administering Powers that remained willing to discuss their policies with the Committee were Spain and New Zealand.[127] After 1971, the anti-colonialists could freely express their opinions on decolonization through the resolutions of the Committee, since it was no longer necessary to keep the US, France and the UK 'on board.' But without the cooperation of the most important Administering States, the recommendations of the Decolonization Committee became slightly pointless.

From 1970, UN officials no longer hid their skepticism about the work of the Committee.[128] It found itself in a complete deadlock, faced on the one hand by Administering States which were unwilling to furnish the Committee with the most basic information, and on the other hand by territories that clearly did not wish to become independent. To make matters worse, the anti-colonial movement started using the small territories in the Caribbean, Pacific and Indian Ocean, which possessed some strategic importance for France, the UK and the US, to blackmail these states into cooperating with isolating South Africa and Portugal. The Administering States were told that the UN would continue to insist on independence for even the smallest overseas territories until the Western states would help to realize the decolonization of the Portuguese territories and Namibia, and a regime change in South Africa. The NSGTs obviously did not appreciate being used as 'spare change' in this way, and consequently became highly suspicious of any involvement of the Decolonization Committee.[129]

After the fall of the Berlin Wall, attempts were made to eliminate the Committee. A number of states, notably including a few Eastern European states which used to be among the most fervent supporters of the Committee, now argued in the Plenary of the GA that the Committee no longer served a useful purpose because it did not take into account 'the realistic interests of the re-

---

Rhodesia and other territories, and which convinced the UK that the Committee could no longer offer solutions to the problems of decolonization. The other Western states resigned because they considered the Committee no longer acted within the limits of its legal powers (Oppenheim/ Jennings & Watts 1992, p. 292-3. *See also* El Ayouty 1971, p. 236, Barbier 1974, p. 112 and Franck 1985, pp. 193-4, and the letters by the UK and the US to the Secretary-General, dated 11 January 1971 (A/8276 and A/8277).

[127] *See* Aldrich & Connell 1998, p. 156 et seq.

[128] Barbier 1974, pp. 630-1. According to *Barbier*, the Committee reached a peak in radicalism and dogmatism around 1970, and at the same time became very ineffective.

[129] Barbier 1974, p. 632 and Aldrich & Connell 1998, pp. 142 and 156 et seq. When the Administering States started inviting UN visiting missions to the NSGTs, these often did not receive a very warm welcome, especially in the small island NSGTs. *See* Drower 1992, pp. 44-5 for a description of how a visiting mission to Montserrat in 1975 was 'sent packing', and Aldrich & Connell 1998, p. 142 for similar unwelcoming reactions in the Cayman Islands in 1993. For a long time, the Decolonization Committee appeared to visit the islands 'just to check they haven't changed their minds!' (Drower 1992, p. 45).

maining colonial peoples.'[130] The Committee dealt out 'excessively harsh criticism' and used 'outdated formulas', the representative of Czechoslovakia claimed.[131] The Third World supporters of the Committee did not swerve, however. The GA instead declared the 1990s to be the 'Decade for the Eradication of Colonialism.' The campaign for the abolition of the Committee continued during the 1990s,[132] but the decade between 2000 and 2010 was nonetheless declared the 'Second Decade for the Eradication of Colonialism', probably ensuring the continued existence of the Committee, at least until 2010.

Since the fall of the Salazar regime in Portugal, which lead to the independence of the Portuguese overseas provinces (except East Timor) in 1975, and after the Western states agreed to isolate South Africa, the remaining NSGTs have received a more fair treatment by the Decolonization Committee. The Committee has discontinued its most controversial practice, of unilaterally setting a date for independence, or urging the Administering State to set a timetable for realizing 'the right to self-determination and independence', even with respect to such tiny territories as Pitcairn and St Helena.[133] The last case in which the Committee urged an Administering State to grant independence before a certain date was Belize in 1979.[134]

The Administering States have also changed their attitude towards the Committee. During the 1970s, Australia and the UK again started providing information, answering questions and inviting visiting missions to their territories.[135] Australia rejoined the Committee in 1973.[136] The Labour government that took office in the UK in 1974 decided that the irritating demands of the Committee might be lessened by cooperating with it. The Foreign and Commonwealth Office therefore started to invite visiting missions to the remaining British NSGTs.[137] New Zealand, the US and Spain already cooperated (to a differing

---

[130] Statement by the UK, UN Doc. A/45/PV.44, p. 71.

[131] UN Doc. A/45/PV.44, pp. 7-8, cited in Duursma 1996, p. 49.

[132] Corbin 2000, p. 9.

[133] UN Repertory of Practice, Suppl. No. 4, Vol. 2, para. 180 et seq. and Suppl. No. 5, Vol. 4, para. 221 et seq. This practice was started by the GA itself after the adoption of GA Res. 1514. By Res. 2189 (XXI) and 2326 (XXII) of 1966 and 1967 the GA asked the Committee to set a date for independence whenever it considered it proper and appropriate. *See also* Corbin 2000, p. 6.

[134] UN Repertory of Practice, Suppl. No. 6, Vol. 5, paras. 75 and 107.

[135] The UN Department of Political Affairs noted a remarkable increase in the cooperation of the Administering States after 1972, *see Decolonization* Vol. II, No. 6 (December 1975), p. 17. *See also* Franck 1985, p. 188.

[136] De Smith 1974, p. 69.

[137] Drower 1992, p. 44. In 1986, the British government (at that time Conservative) announced it would stop cooperating with the Committee, because it did not appreciate the anti-colonial wording of the annual resolution of the GA regarding the remaining NSGTs (most of which are British). The UK considered its NSGTs were no longer colonies, and that it would therefore serve no useful purpose to take part in the activities of the Committee. It advised the UN

extent), leaving only France as a persistent objector to the work of the Committee. The Committee's Regional Seminars, which have been held each year since 1990, either on a Caribbean or a Pacific island, during the 'Week of Solidarity with Peoples of All Colonial Territories Fighting for Freedom, Independence and Human Rights', are attended by an observer of France when the seminar is held in the Pacific, and by a delegation of the UK when the seminar is held in the Caribbean. In 2003, the seminar was held in Anguilla, which was the first time it was held in a NSGT. The UK participated in the debates at this seminars, as did some 40 other UN member states, representatives of the territories, and a number of NGOs.[138]

Even though the Administering States may not appreciate the work of the Committee, and have never hesitated to ignore its more radical recommendations, they have good reason to cooperate with the Committee, and to provide it with information. It has been pointed out by *Franck*, who is not exactly an enthusiastic supporter of the Committee's work, that the well-funded Committee creates a paper record through its reports and resolutions which is consulted by diplomats who often have no prior knowledge of the situation. Moreover:

> its distortions and half-truths have a way of becoming conventional wisdom. They reappear, buttressed with authoritative U.N. citations, in publications all over the world. No matter how often they are later refuted, these 'facts' take on a life of their own and frequently are cited to justify subsequent U.N. activities.[139]

Franck also points out that states cooperating with the Committee will usually find that it makes constructive contributions to solving problems in the territories. It conducts thorough research, and is usually more interested in maintaining a dialogue than in seeking a confrontation. The reports of the visiting missions the Committee sends to the territories usually note improvements and accomplishments in the territories, and commend the positive attitude of the Administering Power.[140] Once the Committee has drawn up its report, little can be done to prevent the GA from approving it. Adoption of the report of the Decolonization Committee is 'a sacred annual ritual', in the words of one US

---

to devote its time and resources to other more pressing matters (GAOR (41), Plenary Meetings, 92nd Meeting, pp. 71-3). The UK did not persist in this attitude.

[138] *See* the Report of the Decolonization Committee of 2003. *See* Tanoh-Boutchoue 2001 on the seminars in general. The Regional Seminars could be a useful addition to this process, but not in their present form. Their impact appears to be minimal. They may only be attended on a special invitation. Media attention is absent. By organizing these seminar in their present form, the Committee confirms its reputation as a 'traveling circus' that is not open to the public.

[139] Franck 1985, p. 197.

[140] *See for instance* the visiting missions to the US territories of the Virgin Islands and American Samoa in 1978 and 1980, reported in Franck 1985, pp. 188-9.

delegate, who also stated that it is 'virtually impossible for any country – particularly a Western country – to amend it from the floor.'[141] Also, 'very few of the NAMs will vote against a decolonization resolution, no matter how absurd, or how much they disapprove of its content.'[142] Only France still thinks it is worthwhile to resist UN involvement with its overseas departments and territories.[143]

The Committee has studied the question of the list of territories to which Resolution 1514 applies from its first session in 1961. In 1963, the Committee drew up a preliminary list of territories, which included Trust Territories, other NSGTs on which the Administering Powers transmitted information, the territories declared non-self-governing by the GA, and South West Africa (Namibia).[144] The Committee asked a Working Group to continue looking for other territories which should be on the list. This instruction is repeated every year, but in reality, the Working Group only acts when it is asked to study the situation in a particular territory, as in the cases of French Somaliland, Puerto Rico, and New Caledonia. This practice allows the Committee to discuss the situation in any territory that it finds 'colonial' for whatever reason.

The Committee and its Working Group sometimes seem reluctant to decide that a territory should be included in the list. Such a decision is often postponed for several years, and it is clearly not enough if the Committee is merely petitioned by inhabitants of an overseas territory with a request to include their territory on the list.[145] Considerable political pressure is needed to keep the wheels of the Committee in motion towards a decision to declare that the Declaration (Resolution 1514) applies to a territory. As the case of New Caledonia showed, the attempts by one small state did not convince the Committee to spring into action, and the collective action by all of the South Pacific states in

---

[141] Cited in Franck 1985, p. 199.

[142] Cited in Franck 1985, p. 202. The 'NAMs' are the member states of the Non-Aligned Movement.

[143] During a debate on New Caledonia in 1986, the representative of Vanuatu stated about this French policy: 'So much effort seems to have been put into providing disinformation on New Caledonia, one cannot help but wonder in amazement at how much easier it would have been for the administering Power simply to cooperate with the United Nations and regularly transmit information on the Territory as it is required to do.'GAOR (41), Plenary Meetings, 92nd Meeting, p. 40.

[144] Reproduced in Barbier 1974, p. 164.

[145] In 1970, for instance, an organization devoted to realizing the self-determination and independence of the Spanish territory of the Canary Islands petitioned the Committee to place the Canary Islands on the list. The Committee took no action. See Barbier 1974, p. 165. In the 1960 debate on GA Res. 1541, the Soviet Union, Bulgaria and Somalia had already claimed that Chapter XI applied to the Canary Islands and the Ukraine submitted an amendment to GA Res. 1542 to that effect which was not adopted (GAOR (XV) 4th Comm., 1046th Meeting, para. 20.

1986 only caused the Working Group to place the matter on the agenda of the next session. The case of New Caledonia also showed, however, that it is possible to bypass the Committee. The South Pacific states simply submitted a draft resolution in the GA, by which the territory was declared a NSGT.[146]

Despite its occasional reluctance to act, the Committee has added many territories to the list. At first, such a decision was preceded by a GA resolution declaring the territory a NSGT.[147] Later, the GA only adopted a resolution requesting the Committee to study the application of the Declaration to that territory,[148] after which the GA approved the recommendations of the Committee. From 1965, it was the Committee itself which took the initiative to add new territories.[149] The main difference between the Committee's approach, and that of its predecessors and the GA under the system of Chapter XI, is that the Committee considers itself authorized to study and discuss any territory that it considers colonial. It does not consider it necessary that a territory was on the original list of territories of GA Resolution 66 (I), nor can it be prevented from discussing a territory by a GA resolution that declared the territory self-governing. The main criteria for the Committee are those of geographic and ethnic separateness, as laid down in GA Resolution 1541 (XV), the absence of independence, and a strong political lobby at the UN to denounce the metropolitan state. How this works, will be discussed *below*, in the sections on Puerto Rico and New Caledonia.

The Committee has relinquished its radical and unrealistic insistence on independence for all territories, no matter how small or remote. It has been widely acknowledged at the UN that independence may not be a viable option for many small island territories. Secretary-General U Thant already expressed considerable scepticism about the independence of the smallest NSGTs during

---

[146] This procedure was also employed by the Arab states in the case of Oman, *see* Barbier 1974, p. 166.

[147] *See* the case of the Portuguese Territories, GA Res. 1542 (XV).

[148] In the case of Southern Rhodesia, the GA asked the Decolonization Committee to determine whether the UK should or could still transmit information under Article 73(e) of the Charter, and to pay attention to the question whether the self-government of the territory had been established through freely elected institutions, as required by Principle XI of 1541 (*see* GA Res. 1745 (XVI) of 23 February 1962). The Netherlands and the other Administering states voted against this resolution. After a Sub-Committee had discussed this question with the UK government, the Decolonization Committee considered Chapter XI still applied to Southern Rhodesia. The UK refused to report on Southern Rhodesia because it considered the territory had acquired full self-government and because it was constitutionally prohibited from requiring the information of Article 73(e) from the government of Southern Rhodesia. The GA declared Southern Rhodesia a NSGT (*see* GA Res. 1747 (XVI) of 28 June 1962). But the UK continued to disagree with the UN, until the unilateral declaration of independence by the Smith regime in 1965. *See* El-Ayouty 1971, pp. 202-6.

[149] For example with regard to French Somaliland and the Comoros.

the 1960s.[150] A UNITAR study of 1971 pointed out many of the specific problems that face small states and territories, and which make full independence a very unattractive option for them, but also for the world community.[151] The UN became increasingly worried about the proliferation of membership of the UN resulting from the process of decolonization during the 1960s and 1970s. It was feared that the new members would not be able to carry out their obligations as UN members and would thereby weaken the system as a whole.[152] Also, they would not be able to contribute to the UN, financially or otherwise, but they would receive an equal vote in the GA and other organs. Small states might also not be interested in participating in most of the affairs of the UN and the world community because their international interests would be limited to their direct surroundings. The Decolonization Committee appeared to remain blind to these fears, which were widely expressed in other UN bodies. Since the 1970s, however, it has started to pay some attention to the specific problems of these territories and suggested solutions other than independence. It approved the integration of the Cocos (Keeling) Islands with Australia in 1984, and has admitted that independence is not a viable option for tiny island territories. At present, the specific problems of small territories appear to be one of the main concerns of the Decolonization Committee.

The work of the Committee nowadays receives little attention in the media, and even less in the legal scholarship. According to *Aldrich & Connell* it has 'only the most trivial significance in metropolitan states, though considerable value is attached to the committee's deliberations in some territories as the sole international authority on decolonisation.'[153] Many attempts have been made by islanders and organizations to have their territories re-inscribed on the list of NSGTs,[154] also by Dutch Caribbean politicians (*see* chapter 5 in the section on anti-colonial discourse). The aims of many of these petitioners can probably be summarized in these words of a Hawaiian activist:

> We're not saying give Hawaii independence, we're just saying re-list Hawaii. Have the U.N. take a look at it, and give our people the opportunity to make a choice, which we never had in 1959.[155]

For most of the remaining overseas territories it is very difficult to gain attention from the metropolis for their problems, or to obtain the opportunity to

---

[150] Reported in Drower 1992, p. 45.

[151] Rapoport et al. 1971.

[152] Drower 1992, p. 45.

[153] Aldrich & Connell 1998, p. 161. Similarly, Leibowitz 1989, pp. 56-8.

[154] These territories include the Canary Islands (Spain), French Polynesia, Easter Island (Chile), West Papua (Indonesia), Bougainville (Papua New Guinea), and Hawaii (US).

[155] Cited in the *Honolulu Star-Bulletin* 11 August 1998.

choose a different political status. The Committee serves as one of the few means of gaining some attention. The Western attempts to put an end to the Decolonization Committee therefore led to considerable concern in several territories,[156] including a number of territories that were not even on the list, such as Hawaii.[157]

2.2   THE RIGHT TO SELF-DETERMINATION IN THE CONTEXT OF DECOLONIZATION

Chapter XI revolves around the concept of 'self-government', but at the UN a link was quickly made between this concept (and the process of decolonization) and the right to self-determination and other fundamental human rights, when the Third Committee of the GA started drafting the two Human Rights Covenants that would be signed in 1966. Much has been written on the development of the right to self-determination, and I refer the reader to the various excellent publications that are available on this subject.[158] Suffice to say that the self-determination of peoples has since the 1960s been considered an essential element of any decolonization process, as was confirmed by the Advisory Opinions of the ICJ on Namibia and the Western Sahara, the two UN Human Rights Covenants of 1966, GA Resolutions 1514 and 2625, and by the legal scholarship. It has often been considered to have the status of *jus cogens*, and to create *erga omnes* obligations.

For the purpose of this study it is important to note that the right to self-determination has been defined in international law as 'the need to pay regard to the freely expressed will of peoples.'[159]

2.2.1   Freedom of Choice

It could well be argued that decolonization is not complete until the population has had the opportunity to make a free choice, and until that choice has been realized as well as possible. When reviewing the notions and developments sketched above regarding decolonization and self-determination, it could be

---

[156] *See* Corbin 2000, p. 9, *In Motion Magazine* of 20 November 1997, the *Honolulu Star-Bulletin* of 12 August 1998, and the editorial in *Indigenous Affairs*, No. 1 (2000).

[157] In 1998, organizations in Hawaii circulated a petition to the UN to continue the mandate of the Decolonization Committee.

[158] *See for instance*, Crawford 2001, Musgrave 1997, and McCorquodale 2000.

[159] Advisory Opinion of the ICJ on the Western Sahara (16 October 1975), *ICJ Reports* 1975, p. 33. *See also* Cassese 1996, p. 358, and Crawford 2001, pp. 32-3.

concluded that the concept of freedom of choice has been central to most discussions. All states, except a number of the Communist states of Eastern Europe, agreed that decolonization cannot take place without respect for the freely made choices of the populations involved. According to the International Court of Justice, decolonization and self-determination go hand in hand, and should be defined, as noted *above*, as 'the need to pay regard to the freely expressed will of the people.'[160] In the literature, freedom of choice has also been considered the essence of self-determination.[161] It could be argued, however, that state practice has not always respected this, or that 'freedom of choice' has only been granted when and if it served metropolitan needs. As *Wesley-Smith* notes: 'Political freedom was returned to the colonial peoples in the 1960s and 1970s essentially for the same reason it was removed in an earlier era – to meet the needs of the colonial power.'[162]

If it were accepted that the right to self-determination indeed entails a right to choose in complete freedom any constitutional status within or outside of a state, total chaos might ensue. International law has therefore been very reluctant in granting populations the status 'peoples' entitled to self-determination, and has only developed the right to free choice for the benefit of decolonization. In order to 'eradicate all forms of colonialism', the populations of the overseas possessions of the Western states have been given an almost unconditionally formulated right under international law to choose their own political status.

Does this mean that the Administering State has to accept any outcome of the exercise of the right to self-determination by its overseas populations? This is something of a theoretical question, since no state would probably accept such an absolute or unconditional right for its overseas populations, and the international community would not be prepared to enforce it in such an absolute form with regard to the remaining overseas territories, which are all small and mostly of no international political importance. For the purpose of this study, it is nonetheless relevant to consider whether international law does indeed oblige states to respect the freedom of choice unconditionally, since this claim is sometimes defended in the Netherlands Antilles (*see* chapter 8).

The doctrine is silent on this subject and the UN instruments do not directly provide an answer either. The law is not developed on this point, for historical and political reasons, but I think some conclusions can be derived from the law of decolonization. The anti-colonial states were only interested in dissolving

---

[160] Western Sahara, Advisory Opinion, *ICJ Reports* 1975, p. 33.

[161] *See for instance,* Pomerance 1982, pp. 24-5, and Prince 1989, p. 45.

[162] Terrence Wesley-Smith, 'Australia', in: K. Howe et al. (eds.), *Tides of History. The Pacific Islands in the Twentieth Century*, Sydney: Allen & Unwin 1994, p. 221, cited in De Decker 1996, p. 360.

the colonial empires, and therefore wished to grant a right to freedom of choice because it was assumed that any people would choose independence when given the opportunity. The colonial powers after World War II initially wished to defend their overseas possessions, and proposed that decolonization could also take the form of a grant of full and equal democratic rights to the overseas populations, who could then freely decide to maintain their constitutional ties with the mother country.

These two opposing political drives could only find common ground in the tenet that the wish of the overseas population should be decisive, a consensus that was laid down in many UN Resolutions and other documents, and has become a part of international law, as was confirmed by the International Court of Justice.[163] Based on this consensus, the UN proceeded to define a number of forms of full self-government that could be seen as acceptable outcomes of the exercise of the right to self-determination. During the 1960s, when the UN discussed the possible negative consequences for the state community if even the smallest of the remaining 30 or so overseas territories were to become independent states (and members of the UN), it was emphasized by various committees, some of which were established specifically for this purpose, that the options of Resolution 1541 were especially relevant to small territories, and that there existed an obligation for states to make sure that the peoples of these territories were offered a real choice between the alternatives, and that they were not forced into an independent status they could not support.[164]

Paradoxically, this could be seen as limiting the freedom of choice, but since Resolution 1541 only lays down criteria that safeguard rights for the overseas populations and create obligations for the state, the Resolution must be considered as a form of protection for the overseas population against metropolitan domination. The early practice of decolonization had already convincingly shown that overseas territories were often the weaker party in negotiations concerning self-government. It is clear that in a situation where the Administering State still holds a dominant position in an overseas territory, it is often possible to obtain a certain 'consent' of the population for even a very onerous political status, or to frustrate the freedom of choice by stating that certain status options are 'out of the question' before the negotiations have even started.

---

[163] Advisory Opinion, Namibia, *ICJ Reports* (1971) 47, p. 31 et seq., and *see also* the Western Sahara case, cited *above*.

[164] *See for instance* GAOR (XIX) Annexes Part I, Annex No. 8, p. 493 (on the British Leeward & Windward Islands). The emphasis on the freedom of choice was frequently reiterated during the 1960s and 1970s, for instance during the debate on the West Indies Associated States, where many states made clear that *any* status that the population of a small territory would freely choose, should be acceptable to the UN. *See also* Thomas 1987, p. 145.

The freedom of choice has been recognized as a legal right, but this might not prevent Administering States from keeping overseas populations of small islands in a position of arbitrary subordination while on the surface appearing to respect their freedom, for instance, by offering them a choice between independence and the status quo. It was therefore necessary to create a 'black list' of forbidden, onerous or suspect clauses, to strengthen the position of the weaker party in these relations. Resolution 1541 should be seen as an attempt to create at least a minimum amount of internationally guaranteed freedom for the overseas populations, by restricting the state from creating forms of government that do not conform to these minimum standards.

Resolution 1541 does not really offer three options to the non-self-governing populations, but only prohibits states from creating forms of government that constitute 'arbitrary subordination.' The freedom of choice of the populations is not limited by Resolution 1541. Nor should the metropolitan government try to limit the options to those listed in Resolution 1541. In practice, this rule is not always observed by states. It would take a separate study to study all of the cases in which the mother country limited the possible choices to only one option (independence), or where integration or free association were excluded beforehand.[165]

Independence as the Destiny of All Overseas Territories?

During the 1960s, some states appeared to think that there existed a duty for all colonies to become independent, or at least a duty for all colonial powers to grant them independence. But a sense of realism – and a growing fear that the fragmentation of the state community might cripple the UN and other forms of international cooperation – led to a consensus among most states that independence was not a desirable outcome of the process of self-determination for the smallest and most remote territories. Difference of opinion existed about which territories were really too small to become independent, and some Communist and Third World states continued to press for the independence of *all* depen-

---

[165] Drower 1992 contains many examples of the UK's refusal even to discuss other options than the one actually desired by the UK, even when there were indications that the population favoured a different option than the UK government. De Smith 1968, p. 608 describes how one of the main political parties of Mauritius in 1965 opposed independence and favoured free association with the UK. The UK's Secretary of State for the colonies refused to hold a referendum that would offer a choice between independence and free association because that would prolong uncertainty and would 'harden and deepen communal divisions and rivalries.' France has never organized a referendum in which more than one or two options were on the ballot, as far as I am aware. The Dutch government chose to ignore the strong indications that the population of Surinam did not wish to become independent in 1975, and did not heed the calls for a referendum.

dent territories. Since 1970, most states seem to agree that the wishes of the local population should be paramount, including in small territories which do not wish to become independent.

Even the Decolonization Committee, which had pushed for the independence of all territories during the 1960s, acknowledged that small territories might freely choose to maintain ties with the mother country. The Chairman of the Committee stated in 1973 that: 'Independence or self-determination is a right and not a favour, and there can never be any question of imposing independence on a people against its wishes.'[166]

In spite of this quite generally held opinion, the consultation of popular opinion on independence has been a rather rare phenomenon in the mainstream of decolonization. Popular opinion was simply assumed to be in favour of independence, or it was considered not relevant once a policy decision had been made in the metropolis that it was no longer desirable to exercise sovereignty over overseas territories. As *Wesley-Smith* observes: 'Political freedom was returned to the colonial peoples in the 1960s and 1970s for the same reason it was removed in an earlier era – to meet the needs of the colonial power.'[167] The history of decolonization is full of examples of small territories being more or less pushed into independence without any evidence that the population desired independence, or where there was even strong evidence that the population did *not* want independence.[168]

In view of this practice, it could be wondered whether the right to self-determination of dependent peoples – in the sense of the freedom of choice – is even part of international law. To deny this, however, would mean dismissing

---

[166] UN Doc. A/AC.109/SC.22/SR.119.

[167] Terrence Wesley-Smith, 'Australia', in K. Howe et al. (eds.), *Tides of History. The Pacific Islands in the Twentieth Century*, Sydney: Allen & Unwin 1994, p. 221, cited in De Decker 1996, p. 360.

[168] *See* MacQueen 1997, p. 88 for the sudden achievement of independence of all the Portuguese territories in Africa. Houbert 1980, p. 154 et seq and De Smith 1968 describe the eagerness of the UK to get rid of Mauritius and the Seychelles as part of the termination of its strategic military role in the Indian Ocean, while ignoring calls for referendums and continued ties with the mother country. Drower 1992 contains many other examples of the UK ignoring local opinion in favour of its own desire to get rid of overseas territories. Laing 1979, p. 300 et seq, and Thomas 1987, pp. 280-2 describe the achievement of independence of the UK West Indies Associated States, including the ignored calls for referendums which were required by the Constitutions of these territories. This practice was obviously not consistent with the UK's statements at the UN in 1967 that the wishes of the populations should be paramount, and that referendums should be held before independence was achieved, to 'safeguard against hasty, arbitrary or ill-considered constitutional change' (GAOR (XXII), Annexes, Addendum to agenda item 23 (Part III), para. 783). The independence of Surinam was also realized in the face of strong opposition in the territory and vain calls for a referendum. It has often been noted that the population of Surinam was not involved in the decision to become independent, *see for instance* Ramsoedh 1993.

as meaningless the countless unanimously adopted UN Resolutions, several advisory opinions of the ICJ, and the international legal doctrine, which all hold that the populations of overseas territories that have not yet achieved full self-government have the right to choose their own future status. Also, the state practice does not contain many examples of outright denial of a choice made by an overseas people. Metropolitan states have always been eager to see their own choices realized, but in recent years they have certainly not been blind to the wishes of the overseas populations. Especially with regard to the smallest territories, there have been some regrets in the metropolitan capitals regarding the somewhat hasty or even forced independence of some of these territories, which did not increase the stability of the world community.[169]

If the concept of 'freedom of choice' were qualified to mean that overseas populations have a right to express their opinion and a right to be taken seriously, then it would certainly be supported by state practice. The metropolitan states have, since the 1950s, generally acted in the awareness that they are obligated to obtain some sort of evidence of popular support for the sovereignty that they continue to exercise over their territories, and to some extent also for the form of government of the territory.

While the metropolitan governments have hardly ever spontaneously offered a choice between more than two options, they have also often cooperated (albeit grudgingly) with overseas proposals for status changes, especially when these appeared to enjoy the support of the population. In fact the only cases where the metropolitan government has consistently refused to realize such proposals over a longer period of time are those where the population appears to be deeply divided on the future of the territory, such as in Puerto Rico, or where the proposals for status change are defended with little enthusiasm or lack of much outspoken support from the population. Outright denial of the outspoken wish of an overseas population has become a rare phenomenon during the past few decades.[170] Recent years have witnessed a remarkable increase in active metropolitan support for the freedom of choice.[171]

---

[169] Shortly after the UK had granted independence to the last of its West Indies Associated States in the 1980s, the UK government noted that: 'The last 20 years have witnessed the emergence of a large number of small independent states which are incapable of providing for their own economic or political security.' (Drower 1992, p. xii).

[170] Some of the initial Dutch reactions to the referendum on St Maarten in 2000 tended towards such outright denial, *see* chapter 8.

[171] *See for instance* the new Articles 72-1 and 72-4 of the French Constitution, which creates a possibility to submit proposals for status change. Two islands of Guadeloupe (a DOM), Saint-Martin and Saint-Barthélémy, have already used this opportunity. The new status of *POM* created for New Caledonia, the extended autonomy of French Polynesia, and the offer to the DOMs to improve their status, are also examples of the active support from Paris for the freedom of choice, as was the introduction of para. 7 in Article IV-4 of the Constitution for the EU, offering an easier

The metropolitan states may therefore not be very eager to cooperate with realizing the contents of the UN instruments in the sense that they would be obliged to stimulate the realization of an informed choice that would be binding on the government of the state, but otherwise the principles enshrined in the UN instruments are usually respected by and large, at least to the extent that once an overseas population does make a choice, metropolitan governments generally tend to take these choices seriously.

It could well be argued that there exists a consistent state practice in this area, to the effect that clearly expressed wishes of an overseas territory with a colonial past are respected by the metropolis and are often realized. In combination with the *opinio juris* expressed through such UN Resolutions as 1514, 1541 and 2625, it could be concluded that there exists a rule of customary international law which provides that the freedom of choice of the population with regard to the political status of NSGTs and similar territories should be respected by the metropolitan government.

Some territories are too small to petition the metropolis effectively for status change, or even to formulate an informed opinion on their ideal political status. In these cases, the metropolitan obligations of Chapter XI of the UN Charter are especially relevant, namely to provide information and to create awareness among the population of the various ways that might lead to the achievement of a full measure of self-government.

States have rarely done this, as far as I am aware, and it could therefore perhaps be argued that this obligation cannot be derived from customary law. But this does not really matter, since this obligation is specified in the UN Charter, at least with regard to NSGTs.

Whether a particular form of administrative subordination to the metropolis is too restrictive or 'arbitrary' can probably only be determined on a case-by-

---

procedure for status change in relation to the EU, which was introduced at the instigation of France and the Netherlands (*see* chapter 9). The referendum of 1984 in the Cocos (Keeling) Islands showed Australia's preparedness to offer all three of the options of Res. 1541 to the population. The granting of *status aparte* to Aruba could also be added to this list, as could the policy change of the Netherlands government in 2004 with regard to the breaking up of the Antilles and negotiating new status options for the individual islands. A remarkable example is the draft Treaty devised for the relation between New Zealand and its last NSGT, Tokelau. Article 11 of the Treaty provides that: 'New Zealand acknowledges that the people of Tokelau may at some time in the future wish to consider a status different from that of self-government in free association with New Zealand, including independence or integration with New Zealand. ... New Zealand and Tokelau shall negotiate in good faith the terms of any change of status.' The Treaty was put to a referendum in Tokelau in 2006, observed by the UN (Electoral Assistance Division and Decolonization Committee). It received 60 per cent of the votes, whereas a minimum of 66 per cent was required for its approval. In 2007, the Treaty was again put to a referendum, in which it received 64 per cent of the votes, again narrowly missing the threshold of 66 per cent. The parliament of Tokelau decided that a period of reflection was necessary. *See* <www.tokelau.org.nz>.

case basis, as the situation in the remaining dependent territories is immensely diverse and calls for creative solutions geared to tackle the specific problems of each territory. Principle V of Resolution 1541 suggests that the burden of proof is on the metropolis to show that it is not possible to realize the wishes of the overseas populations, or that these wishes are unreasonable in relation to the interests of the metropolitan part of the state.

In summary, a metropolitan state should respect the freedom of choice of its overseas territories, especially those that have not yet achieved a full measure of self-government. States have a wide margin of tolerance to decide how to implement this duty, because international law provides few rules on this subject. Political and other realities dictate that the metropolitan government in practice usually has a strong voice in the determination of the constitutional status of an overseas territory, and it is hard to prevent metropolitan governments from using their dominant position in order to realize a form of government that is geared more towards realizing their own wishes than those of the overseas population. As *Prince* has noted:

> A central purpose of the United Nations Charter provisions relating to non-self-governing territories is the prevention of exploitation by powerful nations. The line between the proper use of bargaining power and exploitation, however, is often difficult to define.[172]

For this reason a few minimum standards have been formulated in international law, which aim to protect the interests of the overseas populations and strengthen their position in the negotiations with the metropolis. In cases where these standards are not met, the UN may decide to supervise the process in order to ensure that 'a free and genuine expression of the will of the people' is realized[173] and that the choice of the population is respected. This does not mean that the metropolitan government is not allowed to take the interests of the metropolitan populations into account when dealing with a wish for status change. Rather, it has probably been assumed that governments will do this anyway, and practice has confirmed this assumption. Nevertheless, it is obvious that metropolitan states should fulfil their obligations towards their overseas territories in good faith and take into account the principle of equity.

Freedom to Choose Colonial Subordination?

Could the aspirations of a people also amount to remaining in (or returning to) colonial subordination? Some islands seem to harbour this wish, but it is not

---

[172] Prince 1989, p. 83, footnote omitted.

[173] Advisory Opinion of the International Court of Justice on the Western Sahara, *ICJ Reports* (1975) 12, p. 37.

certain whether international law would allow an Administering State to accept such a situation. The cases of Tokelau and American Samoa, territories which have rejected offers of full self-government, but instead have chosen to retain their subordinated status, show that this is not merely a theoretical question. The government of the island of Saba has also sometimes claimed it wishes to become a colony of the Netherlands. The Decolonization Committee is very reluctant to accept that a people does not want self-government, but does recognize that full self-government may not be attractive to very small territories.[174]

The situation of territories that appear to have freely chosen a status that does not meet the standards that the GA has set for 'a full measure of self-government' remains something of a legal puzzle. One solution could be that these territories (which may include the Netherlands Antilles and Aruba, *see* chapter 6) did exercise their right to self-determination, but did not achieve self-government. This may seem contradictory, but the UN doctrine of self-determination and self-government is itself potentially internally contradictory – what if a people makes a free and informed choice for a status that does not represent a full measure of self-government? Should such a choice be denied? Many of the state representatives struggled with this question in the discussion of the Netherlands Antilles and Surinam in 1955.

If all colonial peoples should be granted independence or some other form of full self-government, while at the same time the will of the people should be paramount, situations can arise that are impossible to solve in accordance with the UN doctrine, unless it is accepted that it is possible to exercise the right to self-determination *without achieving full self-government*.

In my view, self-determination should take precedence over self-government and the demands of decolonization. The freedom of choice of peoples should therefore also include the freedom to choose *not* to obtain 'a full measure of self-government.' At the same time, such a choice means that the obligations of the Administering State under Chapter XI of the Charter continue to apply.[175]

---

[174] After visiting Tokelau in 1976 and 1981, the Committee accepted that the island had freely chosen its current status, *see* De Deckker 1997, p. 84. But it continued to press New Zealand to develop the territory towards self-government. The Committee's Regional Seminar of 2004 was 'willing to support the choice of the people of American Samoa', even though that choice clearly did not represent a 'full measure of self-government.'

[175] According to Crawford 2006, pp. 636-7, populations of NSGTs should be able to express a wish to retain their status, in which case 'the territory remains subject to Chapter XI.' *Crawford* considers that such a choice could be seen as 'a phase in the process of self-determination.'

2.3 CONCLUSION

The UN has developed a mechanism to guide and speed up the process of decolonization, based on Chapter XI of the Charter and the Declaration on the Granting of Independence to Colonial Countries and Peoples (GA Resolution 1514 of 1960). According to Chapter XI, decolonization is completed when 'a full measure of self-government' is achieved. The GA has interpreted this Charter provision to mean that full self-government may take the form of independence, free association or integration with an independent state. The GA has created a number of criteria that must be met before free association or integration may be considered 'a full measure of self-government', the most important of which is that the population should freely choose such a form of government, in full awareness of the consequences.

The Declaration on the Granting of Independence demands that all powers be transferred to the population of the territory, in order for the population to make a sovereign choice on its political status. The GA has not excluded the possibility that a population might choose not to become independent. A problematic situation arises when a population also does not wish to achieve another form of full self-government besides independence. Based on the right to self-determination peoples should have freedom of choice. A choice for a form of subordination to the metropolis, if made freely and in the awareness of the consequences, cannot be dismissed as illegal and should be respected as much as possible. Nevertheless it may not release the metropolitan government from its obligation to promote self-government, and to try and achieve a form of political decolonization.

In the next chapter, three forms of self-government will be discussed that have been worked out in international law as acceptable forms of decolonization, as well as a few examples of self-government that may not comply with the international standards, but which are comparable to the status of the Netherlands Antilles and Aruba.

Chapter 3
DIFFERENT MODES OF
POLITICAL DECOLONIZATION

International law recognizes three types of political status as forms of decolonization if they are the outcome of a process of self-determination. According to General Assembly Resolution 2625 of 1970 it is also possible that self-determination and decolonization can lead to 'any other status freely chosen by the population.' This chapter will outline what these options mean and how they can be recognized, in order to be able to determine (in the next chapter) whether the constitution of the Kingdom of the Netherlands can be characterized as a form of decolonization.

3.1 INDEPENDENCE

The developments described in the preceding chapter have clearly led to the establishment of an unconditional right to independence for all territories that were once considered colonies, and that still maintain constitutional ties with their mother country,[1] except perhaps when these territories have become an integral part of the mother country (*see below*). This right has an uncontested status in international law and in Dutch constitutional law. Since independent statehood has already been the subject of an overwhelming body of legal scholarship, and since the populations of the Netherlands Antilles and Aruba are not interested in independence, at least not in the near future, it does not seem necessary to go into this subject at this point. The right to choose free association, integration or another form of continued metropolitan sovereignty has received much less attention in the literature, but seems more relevant to this study in view of the preference of the Caribbean populations for continued ties with the Netherlands. I will therefore try to describe these status options in order to be able to determine in the next chapters whether the present constitu-

---

[1] In a similar sense, *see for instance* Cassese 1996, p. 357, with reference to the Advisory Opinion of the ICJ on Namibia.

S. Hillebrink, The Right to Self-Determination and Post-Colonial Governance
© 2008, T·M·C·ASSER PRESS, *The Hague, The Netherlands and the Author*

tion of the Kingdom of the Netherlands could be classified in one of these categories, or whether these forms of decolonization might serve to complete the decolonization of the Dutch Caribbean.

3.2   FREE ASSOCIATION[2]

UN General Assembly Resolution 1541 of 1960, in Principle VII, provides:

> (a) Free association should be the result of a free and voluntary choice by the peoples of the territory concerned expressed through informed and democratic processes. It should be one which respects the individuality and the cultural characteristics of the territory and its peoples, and retains for the peoples of the territory which is associated with an independent State the freedom to modify the status of that territory through the expression of their will by democratic means and through constitutional processes.

> (b) The associated territory should have the right to determine its internal constitution without outside interference, in accordance with due constitutional process and the freely expressed wishes of the people. This does not preclude consultations as appropriate or necessary under the terms of the free association agreed upon.

The definition of this status option did not provoke much debate in the Committee of Six which drafted the Resolution. The representative of India cited Puerto Rico as an example of free association, which he described as a situation where a territory voluntarily renounced some aspects of its sovereignty while reserving the right to reconsider that decision.[3] This statement was not contested, and the GA accepted the Committee's proposal without much discussion.

The GA Resolutions on self-government and decolonization of the 1950s, which preceded Resolution 1541,[4] make clear that a majority of the GA considered that an associated territory should have complete self-government in internal affairs, including the right to make its own laws, elect its own representatives, and appoint the members of the judiciary, but Resolution 1541 does not state this clearly. It is not certain whether the right of the territory 'to deter-

---

[2] For this political status in general, *see* Broderick 1968, Clark 1980, Thomas 1987, Igarashi 2002, Keitner & Reisman 2003 and Crawford 2006.

[3] 'Study of the principles which should guide Members in determining whether or not an obligation exists to transmit the information called for in Article 73 e of the Charter of the United Nations', UN Doc. A/AC.100/SR.5, p. 11.

[4] GA Res. 567 (VI) and 648 (VII) of 1952, and 724 (VIII) of 1953.

mine its internal constitution' could perhaps lead to a voluntary decision to delegate certain aspects of the internal government to the independent state with which it is associated (the 'principal state'). This would lead to something less than complete internal self-government. It seems doubtful that the GA really intended to make this possible, and the Resolution is not usually interpreted in this way. The text certainly leaves open this possibility, however, and it does not appear unreasonable to grant the territory the freedom to limit its internal self-government in the same way that it can delegate its foreign affairs and defence to the principal state. It should therefore be possible, in my opinion, for such arrangements to comply with Resolution 1541, on the conditions that the associated territory can renounce them, and that they are based on clear popular support in the territory.

In order for such arrangements to be seen as a form of decolonization, it would also be important to take account of Paragraph 5 of Resolution 1514, which demands that 'all powers' should be transferred to the people of the territory. What this means is not entirely certain, but it has often been argued (even by anti-colonial states) that it only demands that the people should be in possession of all powers at some point, and that it does not mean that the people cannot decide to hand back certain powers to the principal state if such a decision were made freely and in the awareness of the consequences (*see* chapter 2).

The legal literature has shown little interest in the concept of free association. Some writers consider it as a valuable addition to the state system, others see it as a curious or anachronistic aberration. *Crawford* considers that associated status 'is a modern and, it might be thought, sanitised version of older arrangements whereby a territory retained internal self-government with responsibilities for international relations and defence assumed by another country.' The associated states are similar to the colonial protectorates as they existed before the Second World War, according to *Crawford*, with two essential differences; the population has voluntarily accepted the relation with the 'principal state' (the former mother country) and it possesses the freedom to choose another status.[5]

Broderick is much less optimistic. She doubts whether the concept of associated states will ever provide a successful solution to the problems of overseas government, because international law does not contain clear rules concerning the responsibility for and of 'subordinate entities', and because it does not provide for a real identity for associated states in the areas of treaty-making and international co-operation.[6] *Thomas'* criticism is less diplomatically worded –

---

[5] Crawford 1989, p. 282.
[6] Broderick 1968, pp. 402-3.

he concludes that the international community views associated states as colonies and treats them as such, in spite of Resolution 1541.[7]

Both these writers base their criticism mainly on the UK experience, but the associations entered into by New Zealand and the US show that it is possible to grant associated states a real international identity (which the UK chose not to do). *Crawford* maintains that it is untenable to maintain that associated states lack all international personality, and *Oppenheim* agrees that certain territories which are not fully independent, may have some international status.[8] The problem with the UK associations was that the islands continued to be considered as 'subordinate entities' by the UK and therefore also by the international community.

Most other writers on free association think that the concept could be a good alternative for many of the remaining dependencies.[9] In my opinion, it might be an attractive option for the Netherlands Antilles and Aruba, if the Kingdom partners and the international community are prepared to learn from the experiences of New Zealand and not to repeat the mistakes of the UK. In chapter 6 I will discuss the question of whether the Kingdom might not already be considered as a form of free association.

The state practice is rather limited. Three states have attempted to gain UN approval for what they explicitly considered as 'free association', but only the status of the Cook Islands and Niue has been recognized by the GA as free association. The associated states of the US in the Pacific have been accepted as a form of decolonization by the Trusteeship Council and the Security Council. The UK example is interesting because it fell just short of the UN standards and led to some further discussion on the concept of free association. I will discuss these cases briefly, and then try to determine a number of common characteristics, and see which criteria need to be met in order to obtain UN approval.

3.2.1 Three Cases

The Cook Islands and Niue

The Cook Islands and Niue are very small and isolated territories located in the South Pacific Ocean, about halfway between New Zealand and Hawaii.[10] The

---

[7] Thomas 1987, p. 318. *See also* Connell 1970, p. 344.

[8] Crawford 2006, p. 633, and Oppenheim/Jennings & Watts 1992, pp. 279-80. In a similar sense, *see* Keitner & Reisman 2003.

[9] *See for instance* Rapoport et al. 1971, pp. 181-8, Reisman 1975, p. 19, Macdonald 1981, p. 281, Gilmore 1982, pp. 17-20, and Igarashi 2002, pp. 298-301.

[10] The Cook Islands covers 240 km^2 spread out over 15 islands and atolls, and its population currently stands at 21,000. Niue consists of a single island which covers 260 km^2, with a steadily decreasing population (currently 2,000). Most Niueans live in New Zealand.

UK transferred its responsibility for the islands to New Zealand in 1900 and 1901. The islanders live off agriculture, fishing, tourism and economic aid from New Zealand. The islands have GDPs per capita that are about average for the region.[11] In 1965, New Zealand's aid amounted to 20 per cent of the total annual income of the territory, and it accounted for 75 per cent of government expenditures in the territory.[12] After the Cook Islands became an associated state, the aid more than doubled.[13] At present, the aid seems to make up some 10 per cent of the GDP. New Zealand aid constitutes some 35 per cent of the GDP of Niue.[14]

New Zealand voluntarily cooperated with the UN during the early 1960s when it decided it was time to fully decolonize the Cook Islands and Niue. It invited several UN visiting missions, and kept the UN informed of the developments.[15] Other Administering States were not happy with New Zealand's approach, because it disrupted the united front against UN involvement.[16] Most of the other Administering States would nonetheless soon afterwards follow New Zealand's example of cooperation with the UN, because it produced positive results.

When the GA discussed the new status of the Cook Islands in 1965, many states expressed enthusiasm about the way the Cook Islanders had been allowed to exercise their right to self-determination, and recommended the result to other small NSGTs. The Socialist states and a number of Third World states, however, thought that the Cook Islands remained a colonial territory because it had not become independent. As a compromise, the reference to Resolution 1541 was struck from the draft Resolution, and a paragraph was introduced which stated that Resolution 1514 continued to apply, in the sense that the UN remained responsible for assisting the Cook Islands 'in the eventual achievement of independence of full independence, if they so wish, at a future date.' The GA unanimously adopted this Resolution, which explicitly released New Zealand from its obligations under Article 73 of the UN Charter 'since the Cook Islands have attained full internal self-government', and because 'the people of the Cook Islands have ... control of their internal affairs and of their

---

[11] The GDP per capita of the Cook Islands is approximately US$ 5,000, and in Niue it stands at US$ 3,600 (according to the *CIA World Factbook* published on <https://www.cia.gov/library/publications/the-world-factbook/>).

[12] Stone 1966, p. 177. *See also* Kolff 1965.

[13] Leibowitz 1976, p. 145.

[14] According to the *CIA World Factbook*.

[15] The UN supervised the elections in which the free association with New Zealand was approved (GAOR (XX), Annexes, Agenda items 23 and 24), and the plebiscite in Niue (GAOR (XXIX) Supplement No. 23, Chapter XXII, Annex 1).

[16] Stone 1966, p. 169.

future.'[17] This last phrase was almost deleted, but the Fourth Committee voted 29 to 28, with 43 abstentions, to keep it in.[18]

The free association of Niue was received much more enthusiastically in 1974. The GA clearly appeared more convinced that the people of Niue had freely chosen its new status, and that consequently New Zealand had fulfilled its obligations under the Charter and Resolutions 1514 and 1541. No negative speeches were made during the debate, and the Resolution was unanimously approved without a roll-call.[19] The difference from the procedure involving the Cook Islands was probably due to the fact that a referendum was held on Niue, but not on the Cook Islands, but it may also be viewed 'to lend further support to the notion of an evolutionary development [of] the law of free association.'[20] Also, the high tide of anti-colonialism had passed. In any case, both territories were removed from the list of NSGTs.

The Cook Islands has full control over its Constitution, which is the supreme law of the Cook Islands. It can be amended by its parliament, except for the Articles that deal with the association with New Zealand, which also need the approval of two- thirds of the electorate of the Cook Islands in a referendum. New Zealand has no legislative power in the Cook Islands on *any* subject.[21] The situation is similar in Niue, although that territory can still request the New Zealand parliament to legislate for Niue, which it occasionally does.[22] In both territories some New Zealand laws and English common law still apply, because the territorial legislators have not used their power to provide new

---

[17] GA Res. 2064 (XX) of 16 December 1965, adopted by 78 votes to nil, with 29 abstentions. *See* Barbier 1974, pp. 601-2, and Igarashi 2002, pp. 107-10.

[18] Igarashi 2002, p. 108.

[19] GA Res. 3285 (XXIX) of 1974. For the voting, *see* GAOR (XIX), Plenary, 2318th Meeting. *See also* Clark 1980, p. 60.

[20] Macdonald 1981, p. 247.

[21] The New Zealand representative informed the UN in 1965 that New Zealand had 'legislated away' its authority to make laws that applied in the Cook Islands unilaterally, even though the New Zealand parliament had appeared to think differently when it approved the free association. During a conflict regarding civil aviation matters in 1969, it was settled that the New Zealand parliament could not legislate in the Cook Islands, not even in matters of external affairs or defence. (Frame 1987, p. 144 et seq.) This conclusion was confirmed by the exchange of letters between the Prime Ministers of New Zealand and the Cook Islands to clarify the free association. New Zealand's Prime Minister wrote: 'There are no legal fetters of any kind upon the freedom of the Cook Islands, which make their own laws and control their own Constitution' (letter of 4 May 1973, reproduced in Blaustein/Raworth 2001b, p. 99). In the 'Joint Centenary Declaration of the Principles of the Relationship between New Zealand and the Cook Islands' (11 June 2001), it was recalled that 'the Cook Islands has full and exclusive powers to make its own laws and adopt its own policies.'

[22] Townend 2003, p. 591. The same option used to exist for the Cook Islands, but it was abolished by that territory in 1981.

laws on all subjects. In some respects, these territories seem to be more closely connected with the metropolis than the Netherlands Antilles and Aruba, perhaps because they are economically more tied in with New Zealand. The Cook Islands and Niue, for instance, still use the New Zealand dollar.

Executive power in both these territories lies with a cabinet that commands the confidence of parliament.[23] New Zealand can only act on behalf of the Cook Islands or Niue in matters of foreign affairs or defence. In 1965, a few representatives in the GA criticized the arrangement because the High Commissioner of New Zealand in the Cook Islands also had powers in the internal affairs of the Cook Islands. Upon New Zealand's explanation that the Cook Islands were free to appoint whomever they wanted as High Commissioner, the GA decided not to condemn this fact, but to note that 'the people of the Cook Islands have ... control of their internal affairs and of their future.'[24]

With regard to internal affairs, the situation is clear – the Cook Islands and Niue are fully autonomous – but in foreign affairs, there exists some uncertainty. The Cook Islands has gradually achieved an apparently complete control over its foreign affairs, in a development similar to that of the dominions within the Commonwealth between the two World Wars. The original arrangement was laid down in Article 5 of the Cook Islands Constitution Act 1964, which states that: 'Nothing in this Act or in the Constitution shall affect the responsibilities of Her Majesty the Queen in right of New Zealand for the external affairs and defence of the Cook Islands, those responsibilities to be discharged after consultation with the Prime Minister of the Cook Islands.'[25] Based on this Article, New Zealand handled foreign affairs, including treaties, although it had no formal powers to ensure the Cook Islands' compliance with international obligations.

This arrangement was changed, or re-interpreted, when the Cook Islands government increasingly started to handle its own foreign affairs independently, from the 1960s onwards. A convention was created through 'the quiet growth of an acceptable practice' that 'Her Majesty the Queen in right of New Zealand' was advised on the foreign affairs of the Cook Islands by her ministers of the Cook Islands, and no longer by those of New Zealand – the British formula for expressing that the Cook Island had become fully self-governing in foreign affairs as well.[26]

---

[23] *See* Ntumy & Adzoxornu 1993 for further details.

[24] GA Res. 2064 (XX), *see also* UN Yearbook 1965, p. 572.

[25] Section 5 of the Cook Islands Constitution Act 1964. This New Zealand act contained the original Constitution of the Cook Islands as a schedule. It can now only be amended by the Cook Islands, *see* Article 41 of the Cook Islands Constitution.

[26] Frame 1987, p. 148. It seems that the negative reaction by the UN to the fact that the UK had retained some reserved powers under the West Indies Associated States played a role in

This development raised some questions with foreign states, who wondered, for instance, whether the Cook Islands had the capacity to sign international treaties. New Zealand, when requested by the US to clarify the situation in 1976, stated that: 'The Cook Islands Government is not restrained from initiating international negotiations or concluding agreements and there is no constitutional requirement for prior authority or approval from the Government of New Zealand.'[27] During the 1980s, New Zealand appears to have stopped ratifying treaties in the name of the Cook Islands.

The Cook Islands now appears to be very similar to an independent state. It has contemplated requesting UN membership, but it has not yet done so – probably because of the high costs involved.[28] This does make it more difficult for the Cook Islands to take part in international affairs.[29] *Ntumy* concluded in 1993 that 'the status of the Cook Islands as an independent state capable of entering into international relations is controversial', and that while many states dealt with the territory as an independent legal personality, it was not recognized as a sovereign state by some states, including Japan and the US.[30] *Blaustein* summarized the situation in 2001 by stating that 'strictly speaking' the Cook Islands and Niue are not dependencies of New Zealand, 'but they are normally regarded as such.' It seems doubtful whether this is still an accurate description of the situation.[31] The *United Nations Treaties Series* in 2005 lists 141 treaties that the Cook Islands has concluded with many different organizations and states (including New Zealand, indicating the international nature the relations

---

forming and maintaining the convention that New Zealand cannot use Article 5 to act on behalf of the Cook Islands, except at the request and with the consent of the Cook Islands (Frame 1987, p. 145).

[27] Cited in Frame 1987, p. 150. *See also* Ntumy & Adzoxornu 1993, p. 12. Upon this response, the US decided to enter into an agreement with the Cook Islands.

[28] Crocombe & Tuainekore Crocombe 1996, p. 180 write that the Cook Islands was considering UN membership in 1995. The authors think that the Cook Islands could join the UN, 'because several UN members are less independent than the Cook Islands.'

[29] The Cook Islands' membership of the International Maritime Organization, for instance, is still pending, because that organization requires that two-thirds of its members approve the membership of a state that is not a member of the UN. Currently, 57 members have expressed their support (including the Netherlands) but important states such as Japan and the US have not (*see* <http://www.imo.org>).

[30] Ntumy & Adzoxornu 1993, pp. 12-13. The author expected that the US might change its attitude because it would like the associated states of its former Pacific Trust Territory to be recognized as independent states as well. The US State Department still lists the Cook Islands and Niue under 'Dependencies and Areas of Special Sovereignty' with New Zealand as the sovereign. The US associated states are listed as 'independent states.' *See* <http://www.state.gov/s/inr/states/>. Japan still seems to refuse to recognize the independence of the Cook Islands, but does give economic aid to the islands directly (Crocombe & Tuainekore Crocombe 1996, p. 180).

[31] Blaustein/Raworth 2001c, p. 1.

have assumed).[32] It is a full member of a number of international organizations.[33]

Whether New Zealand is still internationally liable for the actions of the Cook Islands is not certain. *Frame* thinks that New Zealand is still responsible for the Cook Islands, even though that responsibility does not carry with it any legislative or executive authority,[34] but *Clark* considers that it is 'a little murky' what the responsibilities of New Zealand exactly entail.[35] In its response to the US, the New Zealand government stated that 'until the Cook Islands assumes sole responsibility for the conduct of its international relations, New Zealand will remain internationally responsible for the acts and obligations of the Cook Islands.'[36] In an exchange of letters with the Asian Development Bank, the Cook Islands and New Zealand convinced the Bank that the Cook Islands could be held internationally accountable for its loans, and not New Zealand (*see below* in the section on international personality). The restatement of the free association, entitled the 'Joint Centenary Declaration of the Principles of the Relationship between New Zealand and the Cook Islands' (2001), holds that 'responsibility at international law rests with the Cook Islands in terms of its actions and the exercise of its international rights and fulfilment of its international obligations.' This statement seems to conflict with Article 5 of the Constitution of the Cook Islands Act 1964 (cited *above*), which is still in force, as the Declaration did not aim to replace this Act. I am not certain as to how these two different texts should be brought in line with each other.

Since the 1980s, the Cook Islands has acceded to multilateral treaties that were originally ratified by New Zealand in the name of the Cook Islands. In these cases, the New Zealand has informed the UN Secretary-General that it no longer holds any state responsibility for the adherence to the treaty by the Cook Islands. It should probably be assumed therefore that New Zealand accepts that it still holds responsibility for the treaties and perhaps also the other actions that it has concluded or performed in the name of the Cook Islands, but this is not certain.[37]

---

[32] For Niue, the number stands at 116.

[33] For instance, the Cook Islands has joined the WHO (1984), the FAO (1985), and UNESCO (1989) as a full member.

[34] Frame 1987, p. 150.

[35] Clark 1980, p. 55.

[36] Cited in Frame 1987, p. 150.

[37] The uncertainty surrounding the continuing responsibilities of New Zealand for the Cook Islands is also visible in the New Zealand reports on the UN human rights instruments. New Zealand's initial report on the Cook Islands to the Human Rights Committee (CCPR/C/10/Add.13) was discussed in 1985, at which point the Cook Islands representative still held that New Zealand carried international obligations for the Cook Islands. But thereafter, New Zealand has only informed the HRC and other committees that it is unable to supply information, that 'the Cook

Niue takes a somewhat different approach to the relationship of free association, thereby providing evidence of the flexibility of the arrangement. Niue deliberately slowed down the process of decolonization between 1963 and 1972, and has not been as eager as the Cook Islands to limit New Zealand's role.[38] The association still takes the form that was devised in the 1960s. Niueans seem to find the influence of New Zealand less objectionable. There even appears to be some support for complete integration with New Zealand, but because of the virtual absence of recent literature on Niue, it is very difficult to gain a view of the actual situation. To some extent one can only agree with the writers of the *Lonely Planet* travel guide for the South Pacific, who write on Niue: 'Independence came in 1974, but Niue continues to operate in "free association" with New Zealand. Free association is usually something you do with your psychiatrist, so who knows what goes on in the corridors of power.'[39]

The scarcity of information available on Niue and the Cook Islands could be taken as evidence that the local situation is not very troublesome, or at least that the relation with New Zealand operates satisfactorily, as some authors assume.[40] *Drower* cites an interview with a New Zealander at the Commonwealth Parliamentary Association, who claimed that 'the Cooks' are happy with their status, and that the association 'has actually worked. If it hadn't the Cooks would merely have grabbed at independence.'[41] New Zealand also seems to have retained its faith in the concept of free association, as it recently offered free association to its last remaining NSGT, Tokelau. A treaty of free association was drafted, which was put to a referendum twice, but not approved by the population with the required two-thirds majority.[42]

Occasionally, however, some worrying reports are published on the government of the Cook Islands, which have earned it a somewhat disreputable reputation.[43] New Zealand sometimes seems worried about public spending in the

---

Islands is aware of its obligations', and that New Zealand supplies experts to help in the preparation of the reports. No further information appears to have been supplied to the committees on the human rights situation in the Cook Islands since the 1980s (according to the treaty body database, at <http://www.unhchr.ch/>).

[38] Chapman 1982, p. 137 attributes Niue's slow and somewhat reluctant acceptance of self-government to the 'overtly and absolutely egalitarian' and individualistic nature of Niueans, which will not accept that one of them should rule the other, and therefore they prefer the rule of neutral outsiders. The leader of the Niuean of government in 1973 explained to the UN that the people 'preferred what they believed to be the impartial rule of the New Zealand Administration for New Zealand had no stake in Niue' (cited in Chapman 1982, p. 138).

[39] Geert Cole et al. (eds.), *South Pacific*, [s.l.]: Lonely Planet 2003.

[40] *See for instance* Gilmore 1982, p. 18.

[41] Drower 1992, p. 35.

[42] *See* the 2005 working paper on Tokelau prepared by the UN Secretariat (UN Doc. A/AC.109/2005/3) and the website of the Tokelau government, <http://www.tokelau.org.nz/>.

[43] In 1995, it was discovered that the Cook Islands had enabled 'the largest tax evasion scam' in New Zealand's history, which had been perpetrated through trust companies established on the

Cook Islands. It has been speculated that this might cause New Zealand to cut back on the Cook Islands' privileges, to refuse to extend its nationality to the Cook Islanders in future, or to terminate the association altogether.[44] Whether New Zealand could lawfully take all of these steps seems uncertain.

It has been stated that, for the Cook Islands and Niue, self-government might well be meaningless as long as they remain economically so dependent on New Zealand.[45] If New Zealand were to apply the principle of 'who pays the piper, calls the tune' the self-government of the associated states would indeed be rather meaningless, but this does not seem to be the case.[46] In fact, the association devised for these islands seems to be a legally very flexible system, which can accommodate territories with very different ambitions such as Niue and the Cook Islands. To what extent this system is comparable to that of the Kingdom of the Netherlands, and whether it might serve as an example for the Dutch Caribbean, will be discussed in chapter 6.

The UK West Indies Associated States

Inspired by the example of New Zealand, the UK experimented with the concept of free association in six of its dependent territories; St Kitts-Nevis-Anguilla, Dominica, St Lucia, St Vincent, Grenada, and Antigua and Barbuda. These island territories are located in the eastern Caribbean and are comparable in size (and many other aspects) with the Netherlands Antilles and Aruba.[47] While their larger neighbours chose independence during the 1960s, these islands wished to stay with Britain. In 1967, the UK government considered that 'it

---

islands. Even though the scandal involved some of the largest financial institutions of New Zealand, at least part of the blame was placed with the Cook Islands, which had always maintained that its offshore sector was completely clean. Many New Zealanders felt 'ripped off' by a country that receives large amounts of New Zealand tax money, and public opinion for further concessions disappeared. Unpredictable and unreliable government practice seems to have 'deterred investors of integrity and attracted those who lack it.' The government continued to hire more and more personnel, while its efficiency decreased. It was unable to acquire any more private loans to finance its debts. The government abandoned the Cook Islands dollar and reverted to the New Zealand dollar. *See* Crocombe & Tuainekore Crocombe 1996, p. 176.

[44] Crocombe & Tuainekore Crocombe 1996, p. 180, and Clark 1980, p. 56.

[45] Kolff 1966.

[46] The UN did not criticize the economic dependence of the islands. In fact, it recommended to New Zealand to continue providing aid to Niue, when it approved the cessation of information on that territory in 1974 through GA Res. 3285 (XXIX).

[47] St Kitts-Nevis is located very close to St Maarten, St Eustatius and Saba, and maintains many historical and personal links with those islands. It originally also included the island of Anguilla. It covers 260 km^2 (excluding Anguilla) and had some 45,000 inhabitants around 1970. Dominica is 750 km^2 and had 70,000 inhabitants around 1970. St Lucia is 615 km^2 and 100,000 inhabitants, St Vincent 390 km^2 and 87,000 inhabitants, Grenada 310 km^2 and 90,000 inhabitants, and Antigua 440 km^2 and 65,000 inhabitants around 1970 (source: Thomas 1987, p. 2).

would be totally wrong to abandon them before they can stand on their own'
and offered free association to the islands, after briefly considering and reject-
ing the option of integration with Britain. The parliaments of the islands accepted the British proposals, but no referendums were held.[48]

The West Indies Act of 1967 attributed legislative and executive powers
almost completely to the elected organs of the associated states. The British
parliament lost its power to legislate for the islands without their consent, except with regard to foreign affairs, defence, and nationality.[49] The British government was no longer responsible to parliament for the internal affairs of the
islands.[50]

The Constitutions of the associated states were provided by an Order in
Council, which is a form of subordinate legislation created by the Privy Council (the Queen and her cabinet ministers). The Constitutions could be amended
by an Order in Council, upon the request and with the consent of the government of the associated state, or by a more difficult procedure to be followed in
the associated states, as provided in the constitutions themselves.[51] The UK
considered itself not principally obligated to cooperate with the amendment of
a constitution, but it remained unclear under which circumstances it would
withhold its cooperation.[52] It also remained somewhat unclear whether the UK
parliament would be allowed to amend the West Indies Act itself without the
consent of the associated states.[53]

---

[48] For the genesis of the West Indies Act, *see* Thomas 1987 and Broderick 1967.

[49] Section 3(1) of the West Indies Act 1967.

[50] The UK Secretary of State explained in 1966 that in the colonial system, 'The British
Government were held internationally responsible for matters which they had no effective means
of controlling. At the same time the British Government were constantly urged to try to interfere
in matters which the local Government regarded as their sole responsibility' (statement by the
Secretary of State at one of the Constitutional Conferences of 1966, cited in Spackman 1975,
p. 388). The bill for the West Indies Act was criticized in the UK parliament 'as a means of a
rather hasty sloughing off of colonial responsibilities and an end to ministerial responsibility in
the House' (Broderick 1968, p. 392). This abdication of responsibility was one of the reasons why
the UK preferred an association over the normal colonial system of government, but it was actually far from certain that the UK had also lost its responsibility for the islands under international
law. *Broderick* doubts whether the UK government could avoid international responsibility for
actions of the associated states, since it was responsible for those states' external affairs (Broderick
1968, pp. 382-3 and 402).

[51] Section 5 of the West Indies Act 1967.

[52] Memorandum in Appendix I to the Constitutional Proposals of 1965, reproduced in
Spackman 1975, p. 378. *See also* Forbes 1970, p. 86, who notes that these procedures, and the
procedures for terminating the association, indicated that the UK had 'continuing reservations
about the standard of political behaviour in the territories.'

[53] The West Indies Act contained no provision on its amendment, but the Constitutional
Proposals of 1965 stated that 'neither Britain nor the territory will be able to change the relationship ... without the consent of the other party', except through unilateral termination of the association (reproduced in Spackman 1975, p. 380).

The UK government remained responsible for any matter which – in the opinion of the UK government – was a matter relating to external affairs, defence or nationality.[54] The powers in these areas were attributed to the UK government, which could delegate them to the governments of the associated states.[55] The UK government concluded agreements with each of the associated states by which the associated states could be required either to provide legislation themselves, or to allow the UK to make legislation for them, if that was considered necessary in the interest of the UK's responsibilities for defence and foreign affairs. In case of a conflict, the agreement stipulated an obligation for consultation, but failing an agreement, the associated states had to accept the decision of the UK, or terminate the association.[56] The agreements obligated the UK to consult with the associated states before entering into international obligations with respect to those states, and required the associated states to keep the UK informed of developments that might be relevant to foreign affairs and defence.[57]

The UK was allowed to make changes to any law of the associated states (by an Order in Council), if these changes appeared necessary to the UK government in the interest of external affairs or defence.[58] According to *Broderick*, the Act thus created 'the competence of the United Kingdom Government, even without Parliamentary debate, to affect, at least in part, the Constitutions of the Associated States where, in the opinion of Whitehall, the matter is within the United Kingdom's reserved area of power.'[59] This caused some 'disquiet' among the governments of the islands, according to *Broderick*, because the limits of these powers were unclear,[60] and because the final word was unequivocally attributed to the UK, as *Clark* puts it.[61]

Broderick described the association as 'a precarious balance' between autonomy in internal affairs and UK responsibility for external affairs, and as a 'delicate fabric' which might well be 'ripped asunder' if 'any serious political

---

[54] Section 2 (1) of the West Indies Act 1967.

[55] The Secretary of State for the Colonies would send a dispatch to the associated state governments in which those governments were authorized to conclude treaties on a few subjects, and to apply for membership of international organizations of which the UK was a member. See for an example of such a dispatch, Spackman 1975, p. 400 et seq.

[56] *See for instance* the Antigua Agreement, reproduced in Spackman 1975, p. 397 et seq.

[57] Broderick 1968, p. 381 notes that there existed no obligation for the UK to inform the associated states of the international obligations that the UK had already entered into before 1967. And even if the UK were to do so, the legal divisions of the islands would not be capable of analysing the some 500 treaties that applied to the islands, and would perhaps 'proceed to legislate in ignorance', or to 'stumble into contradictions' with the UK's obligations.

[58] Section 7 of the West Indies Act 1967.

[59] Broderick 1968, p. 375. 'Whitehall' refers to the UK government, or its civil service.

[60] Broderick 1968, pp. 374-5.

[61] Clark 1980, p. 61.

collisions occur between [the associated states] and the metropolis.'[62] The extent of the reserved powers that the UK could fall back on was ultimately defined unilaterally by the UK government, and the associated states appear to have had no way of challenging a UK decision on legal grounds.[63] Similar to the relations within the Kingdom of the Netherlands, the extent of the self-government of the islands would ultimately depend on the decisions of the metropolitan government. The associated states did not have any constitutionally guaranteed means to influence UK decisions which concerned them, and they also did not have a right of veto in any matter.[64]

The relations clearly differed from those between the Cook Islands and New Zealand, in that New Zealand has no reserved powers to intervene in the Cook Islands under any circumstance.[65] The conflicts concerning civil aviation that occurred around the same time in the Cook Islands and Antigua were a clear example of the different position of these territories. Whereas New Zealand decided that the issue could only be resolved through mutual agreement even though it concerned external affairs, the UK government simply enforced its own views *because* civil aviation touched on external affairs.[66] The constitutional position of the Cook Islands after 1965 could well be compared with that of the Dominions under the Statute of Westminster, but the status of the West Indies associated states clearly fell short of this.[67]

Forbes wrote in 1970 that the association was not intended to create parity of political status in the relationship between the UK and the associated states. Instead: 'Associated statehood means essentially a decision to limit colonial-type controls to the areas of defence and external relations. Bearing in mind the openness of these small island economies and their dependence for survival on external contacts, British control of external affairs does have very serious political implications.'[68] For this reason, the West Indies Act was considered by some writers to be inconsistent with Principle VII of Resolution 1541.[69]

---

[62] Broderick 1968, p. 371.

[63] Gilmore 1982, p. 11.

[64] There was, for instance, no obligation for the UK to cooperate with the ratification or termination of economic and financial treaties for the associated states, similar to Article 25 of the Kingdom Charter, and the associated states also did not have any of the constitutional rights of participation in the ratification process (or other legislative processes) that the Caribbean Countries have under the Kingdom Charter.

[65] In the UK parliament, this difference was explained by stating that the Cook Islands are relatively close to New Zealand, whereas the Caribbean islands maintain close contacts with the American states. This created more occasions for political contradictions than in the Cook Islands. *See* Broderick 1968, pp. 391-2.

[66] Broderick 1968, pp. 378-9 describes a conflict that took place in 1967.

[67] Broderick 1968, p. 372 and Gilmore 1982, p. 11.

[68] Forbes 1970, p. 87.

[69] Crawford 2006, p. 631 and Gilmore 1982, p. 17. Clark 1980, pp. 61-2, however, thinks that the association seemed to comply with Res. 1541.

After the West Indies Act 1967 formalized the association, the UK government stopped transmitting information under Article 73(e) of the UN Charter. At the UN, the UK explained that it had attached much importance to making sure the association would comply with Resolution 1541, and repeatedly stated that all of the stipulations of Principle VII had been met.[70] The UK and the territories 'had carefully borne Resolution 1541 in mind while devising the new status',[71] and they had also made 'a careful study of the principal recent precedent of the Cook Islands.'[72]

Surprisingly, only a few of the members of the Decolonization Committee commented on this.[73] The Soviet Union claimed that the UK retained 'the right to direct interference in the domestic affairs of the Territories',[74] and that the territories had not even achieved internal self-government.[75] Syria criticized the fact that the UK would be authorized to legislate for the territories, at least in the fields of defence and foreign affairs, without their consent.[76] A few representatives regretted that the territories had no say in the appointment or removal of the Governor.[77] Sierra Leone considered that free association should take place on the basis of complete equality[78] and found the role of the associated states in the defence of their territories incompatible with that principle: 'One would expect an association which was based on absolute equality to require consultation rather than to place one partner in a position of subservience.'[79]

The UK did not really respond to these allegations, perhaps because this view did not appear to be shared by the more moderate members of the Committee, who stated that the association would have been acceptable as a form of decolonization, if only the populations of the territories had been consulted on it. The debate focussed almost entirely on the question of whether the UK should have ascertained the wishes of the population, which led to the conclusion that the decolonization of the islands was not complete and that the UK should continue reporting under Article 73(e). It remained unclear whether the arrangement complied with Principle VII in other respects.

---

[70] GAOR (XXII), Annexes, Addendum to agenda item 23 (part III), para. 787. *See also* Gilmore 1982, pp. 14-17.

[71] *Idem*, para. 830.

[72] *Idem*, para. 889.

[73] *See* De Smith 1974, p. 73.

[74] GAOR (XXII), Annexes, Addendum to agenda item 23 (part III), para. 734.

[75] *Idem*, para. 879.

[76] *Idem*, para. 789.

[77] Sierra Leone (para. 825), and Madagascar (843).

[78] The representative derived this phrase from the factors for association in Res. 742 (VIII) of 1953. But these factors really referred to *integration* with an independent state, in the sense of Res. 1541, and were therefore strictly speaking not applicable to the associated states.

[79] GAOR (XXII), Annexes, Addendum to agenda item 23 (part III), para. 827.

A majority of the members did not agree with the UK's contention that Article 73(e) of the Charter no longer applied. They considered that the arrangement might have fulfilled the criteria for free association (although the particulars were hardly discussed), if only the population had been consulted.[80]

After one month of debating the issue, and after a UK minister had visited New York for 'informal discussions', a compromise was reached. The anti-colonial states softened the tone of the draft resolution, which would no longer express 'deep regrets.' In return the UK stated that it was not opposed to further UN discussion of the case, and would cooperate with the Decolonization Committee and enable it to ascertain whether the wishes of the population had been realized. It also announced that it was prepared to consider arrangements for the territories similar to those adopted for the Cook Islands.[81]

In the Fourth Committee and the Plenary GA the UK again (at length) explained the West Indies Act and the way in which it had been drafted. The US and the Netherlands were the only states which supported the UK.[82] None of the anti-colonial states found it necessary to go into the matter. GA Resolution 2357 (XXII) of 19 December 1967 simply lumped the six territories together with the (other) NSGTs, noted that constitutional changes had taken place, and reiterated the customary recommendations for the Administering States. It was adopted by 86 votes to nil, with the abstention of most of the Western states and a few of the former colonies of the UK.

The Decolonization Committee continued to request that the UK would allow a visiting mission to the islands, while the UK repeated that it had supplied enough information. The GA 'strongly regretted' that the UK no longer reported on the islands.[83] The secession of Anguilla from the associated state of St Kitts-Nevis-Anguilla and the subsequent military intervention of the UK in 1969 inspired a number of member states to again reject the status of association as a form of colonialism.[84]

---

[80] Many representatives seemed to agree with Yugoslavia's statement that: 'No one could have questioned the new arrangements had the people of the Territories been [given] an opportunity, under United Nations supervision, to express their views.' (GAOR (XXII), Annexes, Addendum to agenda item 23 (part III), para. 764). A few representatives (Mali and the Soviet Union), however, maintained that the territories would have simply remained colonies.

[81] *Idem*, para. 933. The Decolonization Committee adopted a Resolution which reaffirmed that Res. 1514 continued to apply and requested a sub-committee to study the situation further (Resolution of 23 March 1967 (A/AC.109/235), adopted by 18 votes to 3, with 3 abstentions).

[82] The Netherlands considered that the UK had fulfilled its obligations under the Charter and Res. 1541, and that 'it was undeniable that the people had been sufficiently consulted' (GAOR (XXII), Fourth Committee, 1753rd Meeting, para. 4-6).

[83] *See* GA Res. 2422 (XXIII) of 18 December 1968, and GA Res. 2701 (XXV) of 14 December 1970.

[84] For the problems with Anguilla, *see further* chapter 8. According to *De Smith*, the Decolonization Committee was 'fortified in its conviction that associated statehood was a bogus form of decolonization' (De Smith 1974, p. 73).

A number of reasons have been identified to explain why the associated states quickly became dissatisfied with their new status. Firstly, the British resolution of the Anguilla problem bypassed the West Indies Act by removing the island from the associated state of St Kitts-Nevis-Anguilla without the consent of that state, which created a fear that when push came to shove, the UK still wielded unlimited powers in the associated states. Secondly there existed 'a certain inflexibility in British attitudes' when it came to an independent role for the associated states in external affairs.[85] Thirdly, the UK provided economic aid to the islands, but it also made it clear that the amount of aid would not change if the states should choose to become independent, while the states were under the impression that they would qualify for more aid from other states and international organizations if they became independent.[86] Fourthly, when the UK acceded to the EEC, the associated states had to become Overseas Countries and Territories, and it was feared this status would conflict with their participation in CARICOM, the members of which were all ACP states.[87] Finally, the right of abode of the inhabitants of the associated states in the UK was restricted during the 1960s, through British policies that 'were widely perceived as racist in intent and [which] caused obvious resentment.'[88] These policies would ultimately lead to the 'the truly immoral British Nationality Act 1981', through which most of the inhabitants of the remaining dependencies and associated states lost their UK citizenship.[89] Consequently, the associated states thought they stood to lose little, and perhaps might gain something from independence.

According to *Thomas*, 'independence in 1974 was no more realistic than in 1965',[90] when it was rejected as not viable by both the UK and the territories.

---

[85] Gilmore 1982, p. 13. The UK, for instance, demanded that the associated states should not cooperate with any CARICOM policies that concerned the foreign relations of the associated states, without the consent of the UK. For this reason, CARICOM decided to exclude the associated states from participation in a number of important areas.

[86] Thomas 1987, pp. 159-60. Gilmore 1982, p. 14 acknowledges that this perception existed, but also thinks that the association relationship did not make it impossible for the islands to receive aid from sources other than the UK.

[87] Thomas 1987, p. 162 et seq. The problem of the lack of independent representation of the OCTs in Brussels is discussed in chapter 9.

[88] Gilmore 1982, p. 14. The legal instruments by which the restrictions were realized were the Commonwealth Immigration Act 1962 and the Immigration Act 1971. When the UK acceded to the EC in 1972, it declared that 'nationals' in the sense of the EC Treaty did not include the inhabitants of the associated states and the other non-European territories of the UK (*see* European Court of Justice, judgment of 20 February 2001 (C-192/99, *Kaur* v. *UK*) in which this declaration was considered valid).

[89] Ritchie 1998, p. 6. By the time the Act came into force (1983), only one associated state, St Kitts-Nevis, had not yet become independent. *See also* Hintjens 1997, p. 39, and Aldrich & Connell 1998, pp. 21-2.

[90] Thomas 1987, p. 286.

The most important reason for choosing independence, in spite of the economic decline of the islands during the 1970s, was that the association did not offer an effective way of taking part in the international community. Also, the UN had dropped its initial reservations about the membership of micro-states. There was also pressure exercised by their independent neighbours, who apparently did not appreciate that the UK remained a factor in their attempts at regional integration, and did not consider the leaders of the dependent islands as equal partners. At the CARICOM conference of 1975, the associated states were called upon to terminate their relationship with Britain because the association no longer served the interests of their populations.[91]

Thomas also notes that the association did not offer some of the benefits of other forms of association, such as the right of abode in the metropolis.[92] The examples of the Cook Islands, Niue and the Netherlands Antilles indicate that this may have been a crucial factor, since the right of abode in New Zealand and the Netherlands respectively is considered one of the most important reasons for maintaining constitutional ties with the metropolis in those islands.

For the UK, the problems with Anguilla seem to have led to the conclusion that the West Indies Act gave it a responsibility for problems that were legally and politically beyond its control. It was therefore glad to cooperate with the independence of the associated states, and the experiment with free association was seen as a complete failure by many in the UK and the territories. *Gilmore* put the blame on the extensive authority that the UK retained in external affairs, the inflexibility of the West Indies Act, and a lack of mutual trust. He contrasted the British experiment with the Cook Islands scheme, 'which continues to prosper in the Pacific', and concluded that free association could still offer an attractive option for the UK's relations with its remaining dependencies.[93] But the UK has not been prepared to discuss free association as a method of decolonization, even though some of its dependencies have expressed an interest in it. It appears to be a steady UK policy since the 1970s that no more powers are transferred to the overseas territories, unless they choose independence.[94] *Drower* thinks that this is a wise policy, because 'associations with overseas territories could be more trouble than they were worth.'[95]

---

[91] Cited in Thomas 1987, p. 280. These conclusions were formulated with the agreement of the premiers of the associated states.

[92] Thomas 1987, p. 286, where a comparison is made with the Cook Islands, Puerto Rico and the Netherlands Antilles.

[93] Gilmore 1982, pp. 17-20.

[94] Drower 1992, p. 144 states that the Anguilla episode convinced the UK not to grant associated statehood to any other territory.

[95] Drower 1992, p. 36.

The Charter for the Kingdom of the Netherlands is somewhat similar to the associations created by the West Indies Act 1967. I will discuss these similarities in chapter 6.

The Associated States of the US in the Pacific

The US has entered into free association relations with Palau,[96] Micronesia[97] and the Marshall Islands.[98] These are tiny island states spread out over large stretches of the western Pacific. Their indigenous populations exist mainly on subsistence farming and fishing, although tourism is developing. The islands became part of the US Strategic Trust Territory of the Pacific Islands in 1945, together with the Northern Mariana Islands (which became a 'commonwealth' of the US in 1976, *see below*). After it was decided during the 1970s that the Strategic Trust Territory would not become independent as a whole, the US applied the example of the Cook Islands to those parts of the Territory that strove towards independence. Like the UK, however, it attempted to modify the Cook Islands model so that it would retain more formal control over the islands, especially in matters of defence.

The US was not prepared to grant the islands full independence, or at least not if that meant giving up its military control over the western Pacific. It had hardly any interest in the islands themselves, which are very poor and lacking in resources, but merely wished (and still wishes) to deny aggressive foreign states access to the area.[99] The Marshall Islands and Micronesia are among the poorest countries in the Pacific. Their GDP per capita, as calculated by the *CIA World Factbook*, is about ten times smaller than that of French Polynesia, and only slightly larger than that of the poorest country in the region, Kiribati.[100] Palau seems to do slightly better than the average Pacific micro-state.[101]

---

[96] Palau (or Belau) consists of more than 200 islands (460 km² in total), and has a population of 19,000 (*CIA World Factbook*, 2001).

[97] The Federated States of Micronesia consists of more than 600 islands (700 km²), spread out over a vast area of the Pacific Ocean. Its population is 135,000 (*CIA World Factbook*, 2001).

[98] The Marshall Islands consist of 5 islands and 29 atolls, some 180 km² in all. Its population is 70,000 (*CIA World Factbook*, 2001).

[99] Keitner & Reisman 2003, pp. 34-5, and Boneparth & Wilkinson 1995, pp. 66-7. The Marshall Islands used to be a test site for nuclear weapons (Bikini), and for intercontinental ballistic missiles (Kwajalein). It currently seems to play a role in the development of a missile defence system for the US (Aldrich & Connell 1998, p. 182).

[100] The *CIA World Factbook* estimates that in 2001/2002 the GDP per capita of the Marshall Islands was US$ 1,600 and US$ 2,000 for Micronesia. A number of independent states in the region seem to fare much better economically, for instance Fiji (US$ 5,900) and Samoa (US$ 5,600), and all of the territories which maintain constitutional ties with a Western state are considerably better off than these two associated states.

[101] The GDP per capita of Palau is estimated at US$ 9,000.

The US concluded 15-year Compacts of Free Association with Micronesia and the Marshall Islands that entered into force in 1986 after they had been approved in referendums. They were renewed in 2004 for another 20 years.[102] The Compact with Palau initially ran into trouble because it had adopted a constitution which provided that any bilateral agreement which allowed for the 'use, testing, storage or disposal of' nuclear and other toxic substances on Palau's territory required the approval of 75 per cent of the votes in a referendum. The Compact contained such provisions (at the wish of the US), but it failed to achieve a sufficient majority in seven subsequent referendums. The US continued to insist that its freedom to bring nuclear weapons into Palau was essential to its defence obligations. Eventually, Palau amended its Constitution so that a simple majority would be enough. The Compact was then adopted in 1993, in the eighth referendum. *Hinck* argues that the US position in this conflict violated the right to self-determination of Palau, and *Clark & Roff* criticize the US exploitation of Palau's dependency.[103]

Under the law of the associated states, their constitutions are the supreme law of the land,[104] which can only be amended by the legislature of these states themselves. The autonomy and self-government of the islands is thereby constitutionally guaranteed, and in principle unlimited. The constitutions give the governments of the states the authority to conclude treaties, and the Compacts are considered to be based on that authority.

Through the Compacts, the states have delegated a number of powers to the US government, some of which cannot be retracted. The US government has a right of veto over any action taken by an associated state that the US considers inconsistent with its obligation to defend the islands. The Marshall Islands, Micronesia and Palau must furthermore 'consult' with the US on foreign affairs,[105] and the Compacts provide that the US has full authority and responsibility for security and defence matters in or relating to the three states.[106] They shall refrain from actions that the US considers incompatible with its responsibilities for their defence.[107] This provision seems to give the US the right to interfere in the internal affairs of the associated states, if such interference is considered necessary – by the US – for defence purposes.[108] The US has also reserved the right to establish military bases in these states.

---

[102] Compacts of Free Association Amendments Act 2003, Public Law 108-188. This law covers 116 pages with many intertwining and excessively complicated provisions.

[103] Clark & Roff 1984, p. 5, and Hinck 1990.

[104] *See for instance* Article I, Section 1 of the Constitution of the Marshall Islands.

[105] Section 123 of the three Compacts of Free Association.

[106] Section 311 of the Compacts of the Marshall Islands and Micronesia, and Section 312 of the Compact of Palau.

[107] Section 313 of the Compacts.

[108] Igarashi 2002, p. 208.

The Compacts of the Marshall Islands and Micronesia contain certain 'survivability' provisions, which stipulate that the defence and security provisions of the Compact will continue in full force until 2024, even if the associated state or the US terminates the Compact.[109] Subsidiary agreements on defence, which provide (among other things) a 'right of denial'[110] for the US, can only be terminated by mutual consent and were intended by the US Congress to continue in perpetuity.[111] In the case of Palau, the provisions on defence and security continue for 50 years, that is to say until 2044, even if the Compact is terminated before that time.[112] The US right of denial also continues after the Compacts are terminated, and can only be ended by mutual consent.[113]

Keitner & Reisman admit that the survivability provisions may perhaps be questionable under contract law.[114] *Macdonald* doubts whether the clauses could be enforced after a unilateral termination 'since it might be argued with some force, that post-termination Micronesians are not bound, as a matter of law, to pre-termination agreements.'[115] Whether this is true seems to depend on whether one agrees that the Compacts are really treaties concluded between independent states. It could be argued that the associated states were not fully independent before they signed the Compacts, and that it should be determined by the law of succession whether certain onerous pre-independence obligations could still be enforced after independence. This argument is of course considerably weakened by the fact that Micronesia and the Marshall Islands have renewed their Compacts in 2004. The fact that the US and the associated states are very unequal partners does not automatically invalidate treaties concluded between them.[116]

The survivability clauses do seem to be inconsistent with Principle VII of Resolution 1541, in that they make it impossible for the associated states to choose full independence unilaterally.[117] It might seem strange to interpret this

---

[109] Sections 451 to 453 of the Compacts. These provisions were introduced in the Compacts after the Reagan administration refused to submit the Compacts (already signed by President Carter) to the US Congress (Leibowitz 1989, pp. 650-1).

[110] Right of denial means a right to deny other states military access to the territory of the associated states.

[111] Prince 1989, p. 55, note 212, and Leibowitz 1989, pp. 673 and 683 et seq.

[112] Section 453(a) of the Compact of Palau. The arrangement with Palau makes it possible for the US to occupy one-third of the land on the largest island, *see* Clark & Roff 1984.

[113] Section 453 of the Palau Compact.

[114] Keitner & Reisman 2003, p. 58.

[115] Macdonald 1981, p. 252.

[116] Brownlie 2003, p. 591.

[117] *Clark*, who had written in 1980 that the draft Compacts probably complied with the UN criteria for self-determination and decolonization, changed his opinion when the survivability provisions were introduced. *Clark* testified before the Trusteeship Council in 1986 that the provisions made the Compacts incompatible with 'a proper exercise of self-determination', and should be viewed as void for that reason (UN TCOR, 53rd Session (1986), 1604th Meeting, pp. 39-43).

Principle so as to forbid associated states to enter into non-revocable agreements. But when it concerns agreements with the mother country that limit the sovereignty of the associated states permanently for the benefit of the military interests of the mother country, it is probably justified to presume that the agreement was not fully voluntary on the part of the associate.[118] There is evidence, moreover, that the associated states were not happy with the survivability clauses during the negotiations, and that they were forced to accept them.[119]

The Trusteeship Council and the Security Council accepted the Compacts as compatible with the right to self-determination. The Western members of the Trusteeship Council (the US, the UK and France) approved the termination of the Trusteeship in 1986, even before the Compacts had entered into force. The only other active member of the Council, the Soviet Union, opposed the Compacts all the way. A Resolution was adopted which declared that the islands had exercised their right to self-determination in plebiscites observed by the UN in which they had chosen for free association (and in the case of the Northern Mariana Islands, for a commonwealth status similar to Puerto Rico).[120] Because the Soviet Union would probably have vetoed a similar resolution by the Security Council, the US waited until the fall of the Berlin Wall before it dared to submit the case to the Security Council. The termination of the Trusteeship was approved by the Security Council in 1990 and 1994.[121]

The US associated states are full members of a few international organizations.[122] *Macdonald* argued in 1981 that the associated states would not fulfil all of the criteria for UN membership because the defence arrangements with the US would not allow them to support the UN in each case as required by the Charter.[123] When the Marshall Islands and Micronesia subsequently applied for UN membership, their status became the subject of a behind-the-scenes debate. *Boneparth & Wilkinson*, two members of the US delegation to the UN during this time, write that 'some (mostly Western) diplomats and legal advisers questioned whether FSM and RMI delegations to the United Nations could vote freely or pursue their own national interests faithfully, given constraints

---

[118] Prince thinks it would be 'overly paternalistic, even in the Trusteeship context' to refuse to recognize the ability of the island governments to enter into such agreements. This would be true if the islands had been free to accept or reject the defence arrangements, which seems doubtful.

[119] De Smith 1974, p. 77.

[120] Trusteeship Council Res. 2183 (LIII) of 1986 (UN Doc. T/1901).

[121] Security Council Res. 683 of 22 December 1990 (Marshall Islands, Micronesia and the Marianas), and Res. 956 of 10 November 1994 (Palau).

[122] Keitner & Reisman 2003, p. 59 et seq. provides an overview of the international organizations of which these states are members.

[123] Macdonald 1981, p. 273.

built into the Compacts of Free Association.'[124] It was also doubted whether micro-states could contribute anything to the UN, and whether it was justified to grant such states full voting power in the GA, for which reason the Western states, including the US, had always opposed the membership of very small states.[125] This reluctance was abandoned, for some reason, when Liechtenstein (again) tried to become a member of the UN in 1988. Surprisingly, the princi- pality with 30,000 inhabitants was warmly welcomed as a valuable addition to the UN, and its application did not meet with any outspoken criticism at the UN.[126]

The issue was resolved purely on the basis of politics, with the US claiming membership for the associated states because it would lead to two extra votes for the US in the GA, while most other states were afraid to confront the US by raising 'the spectre of colonialism.'[127] The associated states were admitted to the UN as members.[128] Some authors think that the independence of the asso- ciated states was thereby established, but others continue to doubt whether the states really fulfil the criteria for independence.[129] *Duursma* considers that bi- lateral agreements such as the Compacts cannot prevail over the Charter obli- gations of member states, and that therefore the restrictions on the external powers of the associated states have no legal effect within the UN. The voting behaviour of the associated states is conspicuously in harmony with that of the US, which perhaps indicates that they do not (yet) really participate within the UN as fully sovereign states.[130] The associated states have concluded some international treaties,[131] and they have established diplomatic relations with a few foreign states.

---

[124] Boneparth & Wilkinson 1995, p. 65. 'FSM' stands for the Federated States of Micronesia, and 'RMI' refers to the Republic of the Marshall Islands. Drower 1992, p. 36 reveals that one of the states which opposed UN membership for Micronesia was the UK.

[125] Duursma 1996, p. 134 et seq.

[126] Security Council Res. 663 of 14 August 1990, and GA Res. 45/1 of 18 September 1990. *See also* Duursma 1996, p. 195 et seq. Liechtenstein's application to the League of Nations had been rejected in 1920, and it also failed to join the UN during the 1960s.

[127] Boneparth & Wilkinson 1995, p. 66.

[128] Security Council Res. 703 and 704, adopted without a vote on 9 August 1991, and GA Res. 46/2 and 46/3 of 17 September 1991, also adopted without a vote.

[129] Duursma 1996, p. 425. *See also* Boneparth & Wilkinson 1995, p. 75, note 15.

[130] The voting coincidence of the associated states with the US used to be 100 per cent or very close to that percentage, but it is declining. In 2002, the US State Department still noted with satisfaction that Palau's voting coincidence with the US was 98.5 per cent, which is the highest percentage of any UN member state. But Micronesia and Marshall Islands showed substantially lower percentages, although they still came third and fourth in the top 10 of friendly nations, *see* the Report to Congress Submitted Pursuant to Public Law, 101-246, June 17, 2002. The sympa- thetic voting behaviour of the associated states recently gained some international attention when they were virtually the only UN member states which continued to support the US and Israel in opposing the GA's conviction of Israel's building of the safety barrier.

[131] The *United Nations Treaties Series* contains 23 treaties signed by Micronesia, 94 by the Marshall Islands, and 33 by Palau.

The economic aid provided under the Compacts is probably the most important aspect of their relationship with the US. In the case of Micronesia, the US spent US$ 1.5 billion during the first 15 years of the Compact, nearly US$ 1 billion in the Marshall Islands, and around US$ 400 million in Palau. The Compact funding is currently estimated to contribute around 35 per cent of the GDP of Palau,[132] 40 per cent in the case of Micronesia,[133] and probably even more in the Marshall Islands.[134] The government budgets of these states almost completely consist of US money.[135] Especially the Marshall Islands and Micronesia seem to be unable to generate economic development of any substance. The aid is generally considered to have contributed little to the growth of the local economies,[136] but cutbacks in US support have in the past created serious social and economic problems, and were therefore reversed. The renegotiated Compacts provide for US$ 3.5 billion in aid to the Marshall Islands and Micronesia over the next 20 years.[137] A number of federal programmes and services assistance also apply to the associated states, such as rural development, supporting the postal system and assuring safe air transportation.

Joint committees, in which the US has a majority vote, will decide on the use of the Compact funds. This has led to accusations of 'neo-colonialism', which may seem exaggerated and unjustified,[138] but the reliance of the associated states on US funding has become so strong that the strict application of the principle of 'he who pays the piper calls the tune' would mean a severe restriction on the independence of the associated states. *Boneparth & Wilkinson* conclude that the independence of the associated states 'may mean little unless economic dependence can be decreased.'[139]

Free association 'compact style' is similar to the Cook Islands model in that it leaves the associated state free to determine its own policies, draft its own

---

[132] According to the information in Palau's Core Document for the UN human rights instruments, *see* HRI/CORE/1/Add.107, 10 January 2000.

[133] Dobbin & Hezel 1998.

[134] According to the magazine *Marianas Variety* of 18 August 2003, the US provided 61 per cent of the government budget of the Marshall Islands in 2004.

[135] Prince 1989, p. 79 states that US aid constituted 90 per cent of the budget of Micronesia.

[136] This was already noted by the UN visiting mission of 1976 to Palau, and in a staff report of the US House of Representatives of 1978, *see* Clark & Roff 1984, p. 9.

[137] *Pacific Islands Report* of 25 July 2003. Complaints about the misspending of the Compact funding and rumours about widespread corruption in the associated states prompted the US Congress in 2000 to request the US General Accounting Office to audit the spending of the Compact funding during the first 15 years in the associated states before it would be prepared to approve the granting of any new subsidies (*Pacific Islands Report* of 29 February 2000).

[138] *See* the response to these accusations by the head of the office that will implement the new financial assistance programme in the *Pacific Magazine* of June 2003.

[139] Boneparth & Wilkinson 1995, p. 71.

laws, and conduct its own foreign affairs, while receiving substantial financial aid from the principal state. It is different because of the military servitudes. The US associated states also appear to operate less independently in foreign affairs than the Cook Islands.

3.2.2   Characteristics of Freely Associated Territories

The examples discussed *above* exhibit a few common characteristics, which are supported to some extent by the criteria developed at the UN, as formulated in the Principles of Resolution 1541 of 1960.

Popular Consent

Principle VII of Resolution 1541 states that: 'Free association should be the result of a free and voluntary choice by the peoples of the territory concerned expressed through informed and democratic processes.' This has been the key criterion for the UN to determine whether a form of association can be considered as 'a full measure of self-government.' It places the burden of evidence on the principal state to show that the association was the result of a truly free choice by the overseas population. This proof can probably only be delivered through 'an affirmative showing supervised by the United Nations that the people of the territory do, in fact, desire the free association status.'[140]

UN supervision is probably indeed compulsory, but the UN has not excluded the possibility that peoples exercise their right to self-determination through elections, instead of a plebiscite. In the case of the Cook Islands, the UN approved the free association with New Zealand after a general election resulted in a parliamentary majority for political parties that supported free association.[141] This procedure has been criticized as obscuring the true wishes of the population.[142] All of the political parties which participated in the elections seem to have been in favour of free association.[143] Requests for a referen-

---

[140] Macdonald 1981, p. 280.

[141] GA Res. 2064 (XX) of 16 December 1965. The UN representative who observed the elections reported that 'there was, in a fairly large selection of the population, a fair degree of awareness of the significance of the elections' (UN Doc. A/5962, cited in UN Yearbook of 1965, p. 571). The fact that *all* of the political parties more or less supported the proposals for free association was not criticized.

[142] Mali, Yugoslavia and the Soviet Union in the GA criticized the fact that no referendum had been held (UN Yearbook 1965, p. 572). Northey 1965, p. 112 condemned the procedure as an attempt to launch the Cook Islands on the road to independence against its will. *See* Stone 1965 and Stone 1966 for a response to this allegation.

[143] Only an opposition party in New Zealand opposed free association. It unsuccessfully campaigned for a referendum on the Cook Islands (*see* Northey 1965).

dum were denied, and the population was therefore not given a direct – nor in fact an indirect – opportunity to express its preference. The GA was clearly more satisfied by the free association of Niue, which had been approved in a referendum. The GA considered the process in Niue as an expression of the right to self-determination that was 'in accordance with the principles of the Charter of the United Nations and the Declaration on the Granting of Independence to Colonial Countries and Peoples.' The Resolution on the Cook Islands did not declare this.[144]

The UN consideration of the West Indies Associated States in 1966 and 1967 led to a fundamental discussion on the meaning of 'popular consent.' A majority in the GA rejected the UK's position that the populations of the islands had consented to their new status. There had not been plebiscites, and in two of the territories there had not even been elections in which the new constitutional structure had been an issue. In 1966, the Decolonization Committee recommended that plebiscites should be held, and also requested (in vain) to be allowed to monitor the process.[145] A representative of the opposition in Grenada stated before the Decolonization Committee in 1967 that the people of Grenada had been demonstrating in large numbers 'also because [the government] had begun discussions with the United Kingdom Government on a new constitution without first consulting the people.'[146] According to this representative the people of Grenada were not opposed to an association *per se*, but objected to the way in which it was being realized.

In his dissertation, *Thomas* represents the West Indian perspective on the coming about of the association:

> The statehood idea was conceived in the UK without participation of the political leaders of the islands. It was only after the UK government had firmly decided on the new constitutional arrangement, including the specific conditions, [that] statehood [was] offered. It was packaged, gift-wrapped and presented with the compliments of the Colonial Office – and you do not look gift horses in the mouth![147]

The UK responded to these objections by arguing that during the constitutional conferences which had been held in England in 1966, and which had been

---

[144] Before New Zealand entered into a relation of free association with Niue in 1974, the Niue Island Assembly decided to hold a referendum on the new Constitution (UN Doc. A/9623/ Add. 5 (Part V), Chapter XXII, para. 86 et seq.). The UN was requested to supervise the referendum, and the GA afterwards considered that this process had allowed the people of Niue to use its right to self-determination, *see* GA Res. 3285 (XXIX).

[145] Thomas 1987, pp. 148-9.

[146] GAOR (XXII), Annexes, Addendum to agenda item 23 (part III), para. 655.

[147] Thomas 1987, p. 149.

attended by every political party that was represented in the parliaments of the six territories, 'full and unqualified agreement' had been reached on the basic objectives of associated statehood. The proposals were subsequently approved by the parliaments of the six territories without a single dissenting vote. The United Kingdom furthermore stated that referendums or special elections had not been deemed necessary, considering that the West Indies Act 1967 offered the Associated States the possibility to become independent without the interference of the United Kingdom.

The position of the UK on the ascertainment of the wishes of the people was rejected by all members of the Committee, except the US. The representatives of the other Western states agreed that it would have been preferable to hold referendums.[148] The representative of Italy stated that: 'The crucial element in decolonization, at least as far as small Territories were concerned, was self-determination, or the consultation of the populations of the Territories as to their future.'[149] All of the members (including the UK) agreed on this, but the UK stated that a referendum was not suitable for complex questions such as the adoption of a new constitution.[150]

Only a few members considered that the holding of a referendum was obligatory in each case of free association,[151] but a majority was convinced that the UK procedure had been insufficient. The fact that the UK had not allowed a UN visiting mission to observe the process appeared to be a crucial factor. Other cases have shown that the Decolonization Committee does not wish to rely on the information of the Administering State only,[152] and that it considers it an obligation of the UN to make sure that the populations are granted an opportunity to make a free choice.[153]

A majority of the Committee also did not accept the opinion of the UK that it was enough to conclude that the populations of the West Indian islands were not opposed to association with the UK, because there had been little or no outspoken opposition to the West Indies Act. The representative of Uruguay, who took a moderate position and supported the UK on many other points, stated: 'It was not enough to say that no opposition had been expressed to the

---

[148] Italy (GAOR (XXII), Annexes, Addendum to agenda item 23 (part III), para. 746), and Finland (para. 822).

[149] GAOR (XXII), Annexes, Addendum to agenda item 23 (part III), para. 809.

[150] *Idem*, para. 894.

[151] Poland (para. 772), and Venezuela (para. 888).

[152] The UK had not followed the examples of the Netherlands and New Zealand of including members of the territories in the UN delegation.

[153] The representative of Tanzania stated: 'Particularly in the case of small Territories, the United Nations should take appropriate steps to ensure that the people of the Territories were enabled to express themselves freely on their future status and in full knowledge of the options available to them' (para. 716).

proposed arrangements; General Assembly Resolution 1514 (XV) required not merely the absence of opposition but the existence of a positive desire for a particular arrangement.'[154]

Another point of criticism was that the population had not been given a real choice between the three options of Resolution 1541. Chile, for instance, regretted that the association 'had not been based on a referendum in which the peoples of the islands had specifically chosen association with the former administering Power in preference to independence or integration. If that procedure had been followed, the people would have exercised their right to self-determination.'[155] Australia stated that: 'It might be argued that a clearer choice should have been given between independence, integration and association.'[156] The UK responded to this that it had been impossible to realize a federation between the islands, and that independence had been rejected by the representatives of the islands. The only choice that could therefore have been offered, according to the UK, would have been between association and colonial status.[157] Apparently, integration with the UK was out of the question. The UK, the US and a number of other states added that the new status of the islands allowed them the freedom to unilaterally choose independence or integration with an independent member of the Commonwealth. According to the UK, 'self-determination would not cease when the new arrangements came into effect, since they provided a permanent machinery for its continuing exercise',[158] echoing New Zealand's phrase, 'continuous self-determination', that was used with some success in the Cook Islands case.[159]

The UN attitude in these case was perhaps not very consistent, and probably guided – at least partly – by the UK's unpopularity at the time. But the 1967 debate does seem to have set the standard for the future. This standard – free choice between different options in a UN supervised plebiscite – is in line with Resolutions 1514 and 1541. It might very well be wondered whether it is at all possible to ascertain the opinion of the population of a small island on a change in status through elections for the representative organs. The UK practice (as well as the Dutch) has long been to assume that the government speaks for the people, and that referendums 'are not the British way.' *Drower* has criticized this approach based on a review of the way six small UK territories achieved

---

[154] *Idem,* para. 723. *Similarly* Poland (para. 773).

[155] *Idem*, para. 743.

[156] *Idem*, para. 775.

[157] *Idem,* para. 756 The other members of the Committee did not refer to this option either, and interpreted 'integration' as the option of a federation with an independent state in the Caribbean, for instance Trinidad and Tobago (*see below* in paragraph 3.3 on integration).

[158] *Idem*, para. 785.

[159] The phrase was first used by New Zealand in 1964, *see* Stone 1966, p. 169.

independence, and states: 'In territories such as Grenada, Dominica, St Lucia and the Seychelles, election outcomes were as much influenced by the personal popularity of the leading contestants as they were by the inhabitants' views on decolonization.'[160] Moreover, elections sometimes offer no choice on the constitutional future of the territory. In the cases of the Cook Islands in 1965,[161] the West Indies Associated States in 1967,[162] the Netherlands Antilles during the 1950s and Aruba in the 1970s and 1980s, all of the parties that participated in the elections supported the proposal under discussion, or at least its main features. Under such circumstances, the electorate is obviously not given an opportunity to make a choice, and the right to self-determination – defined as the freedom of choice of the population – is effectively reduced to zero. Complete reliance on the assumption that the wishes of the population will be accurately represented through the party system was shown to be unjustified on at least one occasion in the Netherlands Antilles.[163] It was also criticized in the case of Puerto Rico.[164] This is not to say that plebiscites will always lead to a more accurate gauging of popular opinion, witness the approval of the Compacts of Free Association arrangements between the US and Micronesia, the Marshall Islands, and Palau.[165]

---

[160] Drower 1992, p. 133. *See also* Northey 1965, p. 113, who calls it 'an absurd assumption' that the future status of the Cook Islands was the main issue in the 1965 election: 'Personalities and policies will dominate this issue at the election.'

[161] Stone 1966, p. 171.

[162] The UK explained to the Decolonization Committee in 1967 that 'no political party had sought independence and all had agreed in supporting the new association agreements' (para. 709).

[163] The outcome of the referendum of 1993 on Curaçao had not been supported by any political party represented in the Island Council previously to the referendum (Van Rijn 1999, p. 42, and Pietersz 1993). Drower 1992, p. 133 contains a considerable list of UK territories in which the elected representatives of the people chose independence while the people themselves did not appear to desire it.

[164] *See below* 3.4.1.

[165] When the UK representative in the Trusteeship Council stated that: 'The people of Micronesia could have chosen whatever status they wished – be it independence, integration with the United States, or a relationship with some other state', he was probably being deliberately naïve (UN TCOR (XVI) 1669th Meeting (1989), pp. 7-8). The history of the negotiations shows that none of these options was really open to the territories, as far as the US government was concerned, except perhaps some sort of status similar to the Commonwealth status of the Marianas, which can be called neither integration nor association. The Compacts were the subject of UN supervised referendums on the islands, after the Trusteeship Council had urged the US to make sure that free association was really the status desired by the islanders. This was achieved by offering the population a choice of yes or no on the infinitely complex Compacts, and by including an 'advisory section' in which the voters were asked what kind of status they would prefer if the Compacts were rejected. The advisory section offered a choice between independence or another relation with the US which the voters could describe themselves. The UN visiting missions noted a high level of apathy among the inhabitants, and were surprised that such a major

It can be inferred from these cases that UN approval of a free association as a form of decolonization can only be obtained if UN observers are present to witness or supervise the exercise of the right to self-determination. There might be various ways of consulting the people that are acceptable, as long as it becomes sufficiently clear that the new status enjoys the support of the population.

In the cases of free association approved by the UN so far, there was no evidence that the population was given the opportunity to choose between different status options. In each case, the terms of the association were determined through negotiations between the principal states and representatives of the islands, after which the result was sometimes put to the people in a referendum in a single 'yes or no' vote, or made an issue in a general election. This obviously leaves much room for improvement. A simple 'yes or no' vote is rather a crude way of determining whether the new status enjoys the support of the population. In territories that have little experience with self-government, or where the population has not developed much political awareness, a referendum on a fully worked out association scheme can even be seen as confronting the people with a *fait accompli*.

International law offers little consolation here, and it is probably up to the population itself to make sure that it is not faced with a 'yes or no' vote on a form of full self-government that is not in line with its aspirations, and with no view to an alternative. It is therefore important to realize that in spite of the fact that the freedom of choice of these populations is recognized in international law, their full use of this freedom can still be annulled quite easily, with the approval of the UN. Attention should be focussed on the moment when it is decided to start negotiations with the metropolis on a form of association, given that most of the associations ('free' or not) discussed in this study have developed into a form of independence, without the population ever explicitly choosing it. The principal decision to pursue the goal of association instead of other options should therefore ideally be made by the population, with full aware-

---

political event inspired so little enthusiasm. This could indicate that the population felt it was confronted with a *fait accompli* which it did not understand. Despite the fact that interest groups distributed stickers with certain status options printed on them (including 'communism' which was used by one voter in the Marshall Islands), 20 per cent of the voters in Micronesia and over 70 per cent in the Marshall Islands did not fill in the advisory section. Both UN visiting missions considered the advisory part of the plebiscite as a failure. The information campaign had concentrated on the Compacts, and the other options were probably not properly understood by the voters, or 'did not excite much interest.' *See* the 'Report of the United Nations Visiting Mission to Observe the Plebiscite in the Federated States of Micronesia, Trust Territory of the Pacific Islands, June 1983' (UN TCOR, 51ˢᵗ Session, Supplement 1, UN Doc. T/1860), and the report on the Marshall Islands (*idem*, supplement 2).

ness that the end result is likely to be very close to independent statehood in the long run.

Continuing Self-Determination

According to Resolution 1541, the people of the associated state should have the right to choose another status 'through the expression of their will by democratic means and through constitutional processes.'[166] The legal doctrine considers this an essential attribute of associated statehood.[167] A choice for free association is in effect one of 'continuing self-determination', as the representative of New Zealand described it at the UN. This view was shared by the Netherlands during the drafting of Resolution 2625.[168] According to *Crawford*, 'it is clear that those territories which have so far achieved associated status have remained self-determination units, able both in international and municipal law to choose other more permanent forms of self-government.'[169]

The debates on the Cook Islands showed that New Zealand's promise that the territory had the freedom to proceed towards independence if it so desired was very important to many member states, as it had been in the cases of Puerto Rico and the Dutch Caribbean Countries. This freedom is considered by certain writers to be a right to choose another relationship with New Zealand, including integration.[170]

The GA Resolution on the Cook Islands insisted that the UN would have an obligation to assist the Cook Islands if it wanted to proceed to independence.[171] The Resolution of 1974 on Niue did not contain such a promise, which perhaps shows that the GA had become less suspicious of free association, or convinced that New Zealand would really not oppose a drive towards independence.[172]

---

[166] Principle VII of Res. 1541.

[167] *See for instance* Crawford 2006, p. 633, and Hannum 1996, p. 17. *Cassese* is the only writer (as far as I am aware) who thinks that a choice for free association terminates the right to self-determination. He bases this conclusion on a questionable interpretation of Res. 2625, which declares that 'the separate and distinct status' of colonial territories continues until the right to self-determination has been exercised (Cassese 1995, p. 73).

[168] The Netherlands considered that the right to external self-determination also applied to freely associated territories that had already exercised their right to self-determination but not necessarily for the last time (statement by the Netherlands in the Drafting Committee (UN Doc. A/AC.125/SR.107, p. 84), *see also* the Report of the Netherlands delegation, cited in Kuyper & Kapteyn 1980, p. 204). *See also* Wainhouse 1964, p. 72.

[169] Crawford 1979, p. 376. This passage was deleted from the second edition, *see* Crawford 2006, p. 633.

[170] The draft Treaty of Free Association for Tokelau granted the population the right to choose independence or integration with New Zealand.

[171] GA Res. 2064 (XX) of 1965.

[172] GA Res. 3285 (XXIX) of 1974.

The association arrangements discussed *above* contain a procedure which the associated state could follow towards terminating the association. A referendum is prescribed, as well as a qualified majority of the votes of the members of the representative body. The US Compacts of Free Association give the US the right to break off the association unilaterally, and the UK West Indies Act also made this possible for the UK.[173] The relationship between New Zealand and its associated states is usually regarded as 'a partnership from which each partner can withdraw at any time', although it is not certain whether New Zealand would really have the right to break off the relations unilaterally.[174]

This element of the free association arrangements has not been criticized, perhaps because so far none of the principal states has broken off the association without the consent of the associated state. It could be argued that such an action would be illegal under international law, and the respective clauses in the association agreements might be invalid, because unilateral termination without the consent of the associated people would violate their right to self-determination.[175] But it could also be argued that, if it is established that the associated state voluntarily agreed to the termination clause, with the consent of its people, it might not be unreasonable for the metropolitan state to hold the associated state to it, if it were clear that the metropolitan state would be severely affected by a continuation of the association.

Nelissen & Tillema write on this subject:

> If one argues now that once a territory is associated, in conformity with its rights and the administering power's duties under Article 73 [of the UN Charter] and subsequent developments, the obligations under Article 73 cease to exist, it would mean that one could do exactly that what [sic!] had been forbidden before: to force upon the people a political status they did not desire and to take not their interests, but one's own interests as paramount.[176]

---

[173] The UK had made clear in the Constitutional Proposals of 1965 that the termination of the association by the UK 'will not require the request and consent of the territory' (Spackman 1975, pp. 379-80). The Compacts of Free Association unequivocally create a right for the US to terminate them, although certain provisions will persist, mainly regarding the defence obligations of the US, and the obligation to donate to a Trust Fund for the islands.

[174] Fears that New Zealand might force the islands to become independent do exist in Niue and the Cook Islands, *see* Aldrich & Connell 1998, p. 141, and Clark 1980, p. 64.

[175] Brownlie 2003, p. 489. *See also* Crawford 1979, p. 376: 'Given that association relations are accepted in practice as satisfying the principle of self-determination, and are accepted on the basis of undertakings and arrangements to which the Metropolitan state is committed, it cannot be argued that association relations are, as a matter of international law, revocable at the will of the metropolitan State.' This passage was rewritten for the second edition of *Crawford*'s study, and now merely asserts that association agreements are binding under international law (Crawford 2006, p. 633).

[176] Nelissen & Tillema 1989, p. 190.

In any case, it could well be maintained that the procedure by which the UK's associated states achieved independence is hard to reconcile with the right to self-determination. The governments of the states requested independence, but they did not want to follow the prescribed procedure including a referendum, probably for fear that the population would vote against independence. The West Indies Act made it possible for the UK government to end the association by a simple Order in Council.[177] All of the West Indies Associated States became independent between 1974 and 1983, but no referendum was held in any of them. Instead, the UK chose to avoid confrontations with the governments of the associated states, and ended the association by Orders in Council in the face of strong opposition to independence in most of the territories. This procedure denied the associated populations their right of 'continuing self-determination', while there appeared to be no pressing need for the UK to break off the relations.

Should an associated territory also be able to choose integration with the principal state? This question, which might be of some relevance to the Netherlands Antilles or Aruba in the future, has never been answered clearly (or even asked) at the UN, although some statements indicated that the freedom of choice of Principle VII should perhaps not be limited to independence (*see below* in section 3.3 on integration).

International Personality

It is far from clear what the international legal consequences should be when a territory enters into a free association with an independent state, apart from the fact that the reporting obligation under Article 73(e) of the UN Charter probably ceases. For an associated state to be able to exercise rights, or to take on obligations, under international law, it is often entirely dependent on the recognition of the international community that it has the capacity to do so. This recognition can only be obtained on a case-by-case basis as long as general international law does not clearly define the position of associated states in the

---

[177] This procedure had obviously not been intended to be used in this way. In 1967, the UK had expected the association to be permanent because the territories were too small for independence, and they should not be allowed to make the mistake of choosing independence too easily. According to Drower 1992, p. 135, the Order in Council procedure was intended to protect the UK from 'unwelcome behaviour' by the associated states. Forbes 1970, p. 87 writes on the difficult procedure for independence to be followed by the associated states: 'The inference, quite clearly, is that a high probability of impulsive authoritarian behaviour does exist and must be taken into account. In contrast, the United Kingdom Government can be entrusted, without any legal procedural restraints, to proceed with maturity of judgment in terminating the association by the purely ministerial device of an Order in Council.'

international system, and international organizations do not make allowance for the existence of associated states as a separate category of international persons that are neither independent states nor dependencies.[178]

Some attempts at clarification of the status of associated territories have been made. The International Law Commission debated whether the Vienna Convention on the Succession of States in Respect of Treaties should include a reference to the special situation of associated states, but the debate merely revealed that the members were confused about the exact meaning of associated status, and whether the existing examples could be treated as a single category. The confusion was caused (among other things) because the Special Rapporteur also discussed the Netherlands Antilles and Surinam in this category, as well as other overseas territories that do not conform to the UN criteria at all.[179] The ILC decided to recommend not including a reference to associated states, which is unfortunate, because the current situation with regard to territories such as the Cook Islands is rather in need of some clarification.

It has been up to the associated states themselves, with the help of their principal, to force an entrance onto the international scene. States and organizations often continue to demand from associated states that they exhibit all the characteristics of independent states before they can participate in international relations independently of their principal. The territories sometimes attempt to pose as independent states. Some fare better at this than others, for reasons which are not always clear, but the principal states appear to play an important role in this process.

New Zealand has taken considerable effort to enable the associated states 'to gyrate on the international scene.'[180] New Zealand and the Cook Islands have had to explain the special status of the associated states on numerous occasions, in order to convince states and organizations that the Cook Islands was no longer a colony or a dependency, and was capable of entering into international relations in its own name. These attempts have become increasingly successful as the status of the Cook Islands developed. In 1981, the Lomé Council refused a request by the Cook Islands to be allowed to the second Lomé Convention,[181] but in 2000, it was allowed to sign the Cotonou agreement and became part of the group of ACP states (along with Niue). During the 1970s and 1980s, New Zealand and the Cook Islands also tried to realize a

---

[178] In a similar sense, *see* Macdonald 1981, pp. 281-2, and Broderick 1968, p. 402.

[179] Igarashi 2002, pp. 150-2.

[180] Gilmore 1982, p. 18.

[181] According to Crocombe & Tuainekore Crocombe 1996, p. 179 only the African bloc objected.

provision in the UN Convention on the Law of the Sea which would make it possible for associated states to become a party to the Convention. This campaign was finally successful in 1982 when the Prime Minister of the Cook Islands signed the Convention and received 'a loud ovation and applause from delegates, particularly from the small island states.'[182]

The Asian Development Bank also changed its opinion during this period. When the Cook Islands became a member of the Bank in 1976, it was agreed between New Zealand, the Cook Islands and the Bank that New Zealand would be responsible for debts incurred by the Cook Islands, under Article 3, paragraph 3 of the Charter of the Bank, which refers to dependencies.[183] In 1992, the Cook Islands and New Zealand informed the Bank that, in view of the fact that the Cook Islands had assumed responsibility for its foreign affairs, it would also take on responsibilities for its loans. The Bank accepted this.[184] In spite of this, the New Zealand government still appears to fear that it may be held responsible if the Cook Islands should fail to satisfy its creditors.[185] The international community now seems to have accepted the Cook Islands and Niue as entities capable of exercising international functions independently, even though some doubts continue to exist. New Zealand, for instance, has had to explain repeatedly to the UN human rights monitoring bodies why it no longer reports on the Cook Islands and Niue, which are described by various committee members as 'dependencies', and are compared to, for instance, the British Virgin Islands (a NSGT). The explanation by New Zealand that the associated states

---

[182] Igarashi 2002, p. 282. New Zealand at first also defended the interests of the Dutch territories. The final text of the Convention however only allows the signature of self-governing territories 'recognized as such by the United Nations', and 'which have competence over the matters governed by this Convention, including the competence to enter into treaties in respect of those matters' (Article 305(e)). The Netherlands Antilles and Aruba might claim to fulfil the first criterion, but the Kingdom Charter clearly precludes them from concluding treaties in their own name. The Caribbean Countries are therefore not allowed to become parties to the Convention.

[183] Article 3, para. 3 of the Charter of the ADB provides: 'In the case of associate members of the United Nations Economic Commission for Asia and the Far East which are not responsible for the conduct of their international relations, application for membership in the Bank shall be presented by the member of the Bank responsible for the international relations of the applicant and accompanied by an undertaking by such member that, until the applicant itself assumes such responsibility, the member shall be responsible for all obligations that may be incurred by the applicant by reason of admission to membership in the Bank and enjoyment of the benefits of such membership.

[184] *The Cook Islands. A Voyage to Statehood* (Occasional Paper prepared by the Ministry of Foreign Affairs and Immigration of the Cook Islands, July 1998).

[185] Crocombe & Tuainekore Crocombe 1996, pp. 174-5 recount how four foreign swindlers almost bankrupted the Cook Islands by a failed scheme that involved a sum 21 times the annual income of the government. New Zealand pressed for an investigation. The report described the Cook Islands government as 'a gullible victim.'

are fully responsible for the implementation of the human rights treaties and the reporting thereon, now does seem to be accepted by the monitoring bodies.[186]

The US has taken a different approach by presenting its associated states as independent states with a special relation with the US. This approach has been successful, in the sense that the Marshall Islands, Micronesia and Palau have been accepted as UN members. For this reason they are now sometimes viewed as more independent than the Cook Islands and Niue, even though they clearly appear to be less active on the international scene and are still very dependent on the US.[187] The UN membership of the US associated states may help to make the concept of associated statehood more acceptable to states and international organizations. If it means that associated statehood will be equated with independence, however, it may lead to elimination of the concept as a real option separate from independence.

Nationality and Access to the Principal State

Resolution 1541 does not provide anything on the subject of nationality and citizenship, but in practice this has been an important aspect of association relations. It should probably be assumed that the principal and the associated states are free to choose whether to establish a separate nationality for the inhabitants of the associated territory or not.[188] The practice of the UK, the US and New Zealand varies considerably.

The inhabitants of the Cook Islands and Niue are New Zealand nationals with unrestricted right of access to New Zealand (and Australia). Only 28 per cent of the Cook Islanders actually live in the Cook Islands. Most of the others live in New Zealand and Australia. New Zealanders do not have the right of

---

[186] The EU also exhibits a somewhat ambiguous attitude towards the situation. After the Cook Islands and Niue were allowed by the EU to sign the Cotonou development agreement of 2000 in their own names, the website of the Directorate-General for the Development Commission of the EU explained that: 'In practical terms, the Cook Islands acts as an independent country and the government has full executive and legislative powers.' (*See* the Country Overview on the Cook Islands at <http://europa.eu.int/comm/development/body/country/.>) Even though the two states have thus been allowed into the group of ACP states, which otherwise consists entirely of independent states (*see* chapter 9), the EU still appears reluctant to accept the independence of the Cook Islands and Niue, other than 'in practical terms.'

[187] Witness for example the number of international treaties in which they have participated, according to the *United Nations Treaties Series* (Cook Islands 144 versus Micronesia 23, *see above*).

[188] According to Igarashi 2002, p. 249 it is not in contention that territories which are not independent states may have their own separate nationality.

abode in the Cook Islands and Niue, which hardly ever grant permanent residence to any outsider.[189]

Japan and other countries have refused to recognize the Cook Islands and Niue as independent states because their inhabitants have New Zealand nationality.[190] It has been pointed out by several authors, however, that this is not really a valid reason for withholding recognition.[191] Citizenship used to mean an allegiance to the head of state, which would conflict with the idea of establishing a separate state, but this appears to be an outdated view.[192] Anyway, it did not prevent the UN from welcoming several former French and British colonies as members during the 1950s and 1960s while they did not have a separate nationality.[193] The Cook Islands has established a separate citizenship for its inhabitants, and seems to contemplate issuing its own passports.[194]

The inhabitants of the UK associated states also did not have a separate nationality. They were considered 'citizens of the United Kingdom and Colonies' until 1983, but this did not entitle them to unrestricted access to the UK. The UK's immigration policies became more strict during the 1960s, in order to restrict 'the immigration into the country of coloured people from the British colonial territories.'[195] Most UK citizens who lived in the Caribbean lost their right of abode in the UK in 1962, and the British Nationality Act 1981 would

---

[189] *See* Crocombe & Tuainekore Crocombe 1996, p. 180, who consider that there are 'limits to how much cake New Zealand will allow the Cook Islands Government to eat and keep at the same time.' Broderick 1968, p. 389 cites a New Zealand minister as saying in 1967 that it was impossible to deport Cook Islanders who had committed crimes in New Zealand, because no distinction could be made between New Zealand citizens, wherever they were from.

[190] Ntumy & Adzoxornu 1993, p. 13. It seems that one of the reasons why the Cook Islands were refused accession to the Lomé II Convention in the early 1980s was because it did not have its own nationality (Igarashi 2002, p. 265). As a result of this, the Cook Islands Constitution was amended (among other things) to create the status of 'permanent resident of the Cook Islands' (Igarashi 2002, p. 239), which might be considered as a form of citizenship that co-exists with New Zealand nationality. It seems doubtful that this operation was the reason why the Cook Islands was allowed to sign the Cotonou agreement of 2000, seeing that Niue, which did not change its Constitution, was also allowed to sign it.

[191] *See* Keitner & Reisman 2003, p. 9.

[192] According to Townend 2003, pp. 595-6, New Zealand citizenship is not dependent on allegiance to the head of state of New Zealand, and could be extended by statute to inhabitants of foreign territories.

[193] The inhabitants of the French West African states that remained part of the *Communauté* retained French nationality after independence, *see* Reisman 1975, pp. 57-8. Thirteen of these African states were nonetheless admitted as members of the UN. *See also* Igarashi 2002, p. 292.

[194] Crocombe & Tuainekore Crocombe 1996, p. 180. This could bring in money for the government, as the sale of passports to wealthy stateless persons seems to be a profitable business in Tonga and the Marshall Islands. *See also* footnote 190, *above*.

[195] J.M. Evans, *Immigration Law*, Sweet & Maxwell: London 1983, p. 94, cited in Igarashi 2002, p. 250.

strip them of their UK citizenship to replace it with a 'Dependent Territory Citizenship.'[196]

The US associated states do have their own nationality. With the entry into force of the Compacts, they gained an essentially unrestricted access to the US,[197] which was followed by a considerable increase of migration, especially to Hawaii and other US territories in the Pacific, because there were more job opportunities on those islands, and the US provided better health care and social services in those territories.[198] According to the US State Department, there was concern over 'migrants who have communicable diseases, criminal records, or are likely to become a public charge as a result of chronic health or other problems.' Hawaii and the other US territories claimed compensation from the US federal government for the costs incurred.[199] The amendments to the Compacts in 2004 terminated the unrestricted access to the US, and made clear that US immigration laws would apply to Micronesians and Marshall Islanders as they do to other foreigners, with certain exceptions.[200]

It may be concluded that nationality is an important aspect of association arrangements, but that the legality of the association is not affected by a choice for separate nationality or not.

Capacity to Comply with International Human Rights Standards?

Keitner & Reisman consider that the legality of any association agreement essentially depends on the consent of the population, and the 'extent to which the association conduces to a better fulfilment of the human (including economic and social) rights deemed under contemporary prescriptions to be minimum international standards.'[201] There is abundant evidence that the first factor is indeed essential, but it seems doubtful whether the second factor is indeed relevant to the legality of association schemes.

If the situation with regard to the UN human rights treaties is any indication, serious questions could be raised as to the legality of the associations described *above*, assuming that *Keitner & Reisman's* opinion is correct. Only one of the

---

[196] *See above*, in the paragraph on the West Indies Associated States.

[197] Ntumy & Adzoxornu 1993, p. 107.

[198] Grieco 2003.

[199] Paper presented by John Fairlamb of the US State Department at a conference in Hawaii, June 2001 (published on the website of the government of Micronesia, <http://www.fsmgov.org>).

[200] Section 141(a) of the Compacts of Micronesia and the Marshall Islands, as amended in 2004. The Compact with Palau is not up for renegotiation until 2009, but the US government has announced that it wants to restrict immigration from that state as soon as possible along the same lines.

[201] Keitner & Reisman 2003.

associated states of the US and New Zealand has acceded to more than one of the UN human rights treaties in its own name,[202] and only three of them have ever reported on the implementation of these treaties independently,[203] whereas their principal states are parties to three and eight of these treaties respectively and report regularly on them (or in the case of the US, occasionally).

Might not the human rights of the inhabitants of these territories be better served if the principal states were directly responsible for them? Clearly, the governments of the associated states are not able to realize the material standards of living in the principal states. In the Marshall Islands and Micronesia, standards appear to be very much lower than in the US. While this is obviously an area of legitimate concern, the fact that the US territories are nonetheless internationally accepted as states makes it likely that the legality of these association arrangements does not depend – at least not essentially – on their capacity to ensure respect for human rights.

3.2.3   Conclusion

Free association is a form of full self-government and decolonization that has been accepted by the UN as a legitimate outcome of the process of self-determination and decolonization, at least for small territories. In the view of the UN, an associated territory remains sovereign in the sense that it voluntarily delegates certain tasks to the metropolitan state, but retains the right to make another choice in the future.

The UN criteria for free association could be summarized as follows: the associated state should have full self-government, although it may voluntarily

---

[202] The associated states have only acceded to the Convention on the Rights of the Child, except Micronesia, which is also party to the CEDAW. New Zealand used to extend the application of human rights treaties to the Cook Islands and Niue, but these territories have not used the possibility to accede (or succeed) to them in their own name, nor do they report on these treaties. The reports of New Zealand used to contain paragraphs on the Cook Islands and Niue, but no longer do. One of the members of the CEDAW asked New Zealand in 2003, 'What to do with the Cook Islands.' New Zealand answered that the Convention applied in the Cook Islands and Niue, but: 'Following the act of self-determination by the Cook Islands and Niue, New Zealand had no residual powers in regard to the two territories, he added. New Zealand did not have the power to require the Cook Islands and Niue to take any particular action. In that respect, it would not be appropriate for New Zealand to report to the Committee on matters to which it had no direct knowledge. In his view, it would be appropriate for the Committee to approach the Cook Islands regarding its outstanding reports. The Government encouraged the Cook Islands and Niue to submit reports. The matter was no longer in the hands of New Zealand.' (CEDAW, 14 July 2003, 624th & 625th Meetings.) A similar debate took place during the discussion of New Zealand's report on the CESCR in 2003 (E/C.12/Q/NZE/1 (List of Issues) and E/C.12/2003/SR.11.).

[203] Micronesia, the Marshall Islands and Palau have reported on the implementation of the Convention on the Rights of the Child in their territories.

delegate certain tasks to the metropolitan state, especially in the fields of foreign affairs and defence; the association should be embraced by the population
in an act of free choice observed by the UN; and the territory should retain the
guaranteed right to choose another status in the future.

The practice of New Zealand and the UK indicates that free association may
be a satisfactory form of decolonization if the metropolitan state is prepared to
relinquish its legislative and administrative control over the territory and to
promote its capacity to enter into international relations independently. The
attempts by the UK to retain control and to maintain a unified foreign policy
were an important reason why the relations with the West Indies Associated
States quickly turned sour. The US has granted its associated states more freedom in foreign affairs than the UK, but remains a strong factor in the territories
through its responsibilities for defence, and through substantial financial aid.[204]

State responsibility for associated states remains a little murky (*see below* in
section 3.5 on state responsibility). It seems logical to assume that when an
associated territory is not limited by its relations with the principal state from
entering into international relations independently, it ought to be treated as
such by states and organizations. In practice, however, freely associated territories still tend to be treated as dependencies of their principal states. Some
progress has been realized through the initiatives of New Zealand and the Cook
Islands. But the Cook Islands seems to have been forced to modify its relations
with New Zealand to such an extent that the differences with full independence
are now almost indiscernible.

If the concept of free association is to have a future, states and international
organizations should relinquish their hesitance to accept associated states as
participants in the international arena. The development of the concept of free
association places an obligation on states to recognize entities which the UN
has determined to have achieved 'a full measure of self-government.' One of
the factors for full self-government adopted in 1953 by the GA provides that
the associated territory should be able to enter into relations with foreign states
and international organizations. If the metropolitan state grants this freedom to
the territory with the approval of the UN, the international community should
not try to annul this development by ignoring the existence of associated states
as international persons.

Associated states are allowed to go their own way, and make their own
mistakes, which may also mean that they descend into poverty. The US, the
UK and New Zealand have shown considerable financial solidarity with their
associated territories, but full internal self-government inevitably entails certain risks for small territories, which have become very visible in territories

---

[204] *See* Macdonald 1981, p. 252.

such as the Marshall Islands. Associated territories also tend to disappear beneath the radar of international human rights supervision once it becomes clear that the metropolitan state cannot be held responsible any longer.

3.3   INTEGRATION

Integration of an overseas territory into a metropolitan state is generally interpreted to mean that the territory becomes part of that state and loses most or all of its separate status and personality under international law. The territory is incorporated in the normal constitutional structure of the state on an equal footing with the metropolitan administrative subdivisions of that state.

There are three elements of integration that distinguish it from association. First, the metropolitan state is fully responsible for every aspect of the government of its integrated territories, whereas associations may exonerate the metropolitan government from such responsibilities. Secondly, integration means that the overseas population should have the same status as the metropolitan population, with equal rights and obligations. In practice this does not mean that, for instance, social security benefits will always be exactly the same as in the mainland, not even in a unitary state such as France, but as a rule there should be equality, while exceptions will have to be clearly motivated by the demands of the local circumstances of the overseas territory itself. Thirdly, integration is usually assumed to be a definitive choice which extinguishes the separate position of the territory under international law.

GA Resolution 1541 recognizes integration as a valid form of full self-government.[205] Principles VIII and IX lay down the basic principles for integration, which were accepted almost without opposition in the GA:

Principle VIII

Integration with an independent State should be on the basis of complete equality between the peoples of the erstwhile Non-Self-Governing Territory and those of the independent country with which it is integrated. The peoples of both territories should have equal status and rights of citizenship and equal guarantees of fundamental rights and freedoms without any distinction or discrimination; both should have equal rights and opportunities for representation and effective participation at all levels in the executive, legislative and judicial organs of government.

---

[205] 'Self-government' is in this case perhaps a misnomer, since integration does not mean that the territory gains the right to govern itself but only a right to participate in the government of the entire state.

Principle IX

Integration should have come about in the following circumstances:

(a) The integrating territory should have attained an advanced stage of self-government with free political institutions, so that its peoples would have the capacity to make a responsible choice through informed and democratic processes;

(b) The integration should be the result of the freely expressed wishes of the territory's peoples acting with full knowledge of the change in their status, their wishes having been expressed through informed and democratic processes, impartially conducted and based on universal adult suffrage. The United Nations could, when it deems it necessary, supervise these processes.

The Resolution clearly creates higher standards for integration than for association, both with regard to the content of the status and the procedure by which it is achieved. This reflects a critical attitude towards integration among states, which originated in the 1940s and 1950s because of the assimilation policies of France and Portugal. Many states feared the colonial powers would use integration as a legal façade behind which colonial rule would simply continue.

Mere references to constitutional provisions that guarantee the equality of the overseas departments or provinces were quickly dismissed during the debates on the Portuguese overseas provinces and several French territories. Many representatives insisted that in these cases, practice was as important as law.[206] With regard to the Portuguese territories the representatives discussed such questions as racial discrimination, labour conditions, under-nourishment, infant mortality rate, and the fact that there was only one indigenous inhabitant of Mozambique with a university degree.[207] In the debate of 1986 on New Caledonia, representatives attached much importance to the French policy of stimulating migration of Francophone people to New Caledonia in order to ensure that the indigenous Kanaks would not represent a majority of the population in the territory.[208] It could be deduced from these debates that the equality of the overseas population should be real, and not merely symbolic, and that integration should not lead to forced assimilation or repression of the indigenous population.[209]

---

[206] *See for instance* the statement by the representative of Jordan during the debate on Res. 1541 in 1960, GAOR (XV), 4th Comm., 1033rd Meeting, para. 17.

[207] *See for instance* the statements by Iraq (GAOR (XV) 4th Comm., 1036th Meeting), Byelorussia (1037th Meeting), Guinea (1038th Meeting), India (1040th Meeting), Ukraine (1042nd Meeting).

[208] *See* paragraph 3.4.2 on New Caledonia.

[209] *Oppenheim* concludes that 'in particular, the adoption of a constitutional structure by which overseas territories, however distant, are constituted as provinces or departments of the

During the 1960s and 1970s, integration was not considered a valid way of exercising the right to self-determination by many states. An important reason for the unpopularity of integration was that it eliminated the possibility of independence for the future, and that it was expected to bring the territory fully under the domestic jurisdiction of the metropolitan state. The UN would therefore not be allowed to involve itself with the territory anymore. A majority of states thought that the UN should always send visiting missions to supervise elections or referendums which might lead to integration of the territory. The representative of Tunisia expressed this sentiment in the Fourth Committee in 1960:

> The Committee must therefore be mindful of the immense harm it could cause the Non-Self-Governing Territories if it decided that the United Nations did not have the right to scrutinize rigged elections which would sanction for all time an 'integration' which the population of the Non-Self-Governing Territory concerned had not really wanted.[210]

It was never explicitly agreed that integration would put an end to the international status of an integrated territory, but Resolutions 1541 and 2625 suggest that this is the case. Some writers such as *Crawford*[211] and *Cassese*[212] think that a choice for integration is final, at least where international law is concerned. *Pomerance*, on the other hand, writes that any alternative to independence is deemed to be inherently reversible.[213] This latter position is supported by Resolution 1514, which applies to any territory which has not yet become independent. It is also supported by GA Resolution 742 (VIII) of 1953, which states that the population of territories that achieved self-government as an integral part of a state should still be able to choose freely 'to modify this status through the expression of their will by democratic means.'[214] But perhaps this

---

parent state, on an equal footing with provinces or departments in the metropolitan territory of the state, may not be sufficient in itself to render them any the less in substance colonial territories.' (Oppenheim/Jennings & Watts 1992, p. 277).

[210] GAOR (XV) 4th Comm. 1044th Meeting, para. 7. Morocco agreed that integration was indeed 'an indissoluble marriage and an irrevocable procedure' (*idem*, para. 27). The UN visiting mission to the Cocos [Keeling] Islands answered several questions by the islanders whether a choice for integration was final that: 'The act of self-determination could not be held again in the future' (Report of the visiting mission (17 September 1984), UN Doc. A/39/494, para. 189).

[211] Crawford 2001, p. 17.

[212] Cassese 1995, p. 73. *Cassese* bases this conclusion on para. VI of GA Res. 2625 (XXV) of 1970, which declares that the separate status of overseas territories continues until they have exercised their right to self-determination.

[213] Pomerance 1982, p. 25.

[214] Factor A.2 of the Third Part of the Annex to Draft Resolution I (GAOR (VIII) Annexes, Agenda item 32, p. 13) and to GA Res. 742 (VIII) of 27 November 1953.

criterion was included in this list because the distinction between associated and integrated territories had not yet fully crystallized in 1953.

The UN Charter and Resolution 1541 suggest that an acceptable form of integration means that the relations between the metropolis and the overseas territories are from then on 'essentially within the domestic jurisdiction' of the state in the sense of Article 2, paragraph 7 of the Charter. The population would thereby lose its legal right to choose another status unilaterally. Of course, it would probably be politically very difficult for a democratic state to hold on to an overseas territory in which the majority wished to secede from the state, no matter what international or domestic law dictates.

It might be that the question of legal finality can only really be answered in the abstract by giving preference to either the anti-colonial doctrine laid down in Resolution 1514, or the law based on Chapter XI and Resolution 1541. It might also be that these two doctrines can be brought into conformity with each other by concluding that integration ends the applicability of Chapter XI and 1541, but that 1514 continues to apply, meaning that the UN could still involve itself with the case, and the population retains its right to self-determination. This is consistent with the fact that during the drafting of the ICCPR and ICESCR there appeared to be a consensus that self-determination was a permanent right.[215] This conclusion is not supported (nor contradicted) by the practice of the GA in cases of integration. There is simply too little practice, and states and UN organs have never really spoken out on this issue. The question of finality will probably remain unresolved until the GA is faced with a case of a fully integrated overseas territory that wishes to change its relation with the metropolis.[216]

3.3.1 State Practice

Most of the colonial powers have at one time or another contemplated integrating their remaining overseas territories into the state on a basis of equality, but only a few have actually realized this. Since 1946, the French overseas departments and Hawaii have been the main examples of integration as a serious alternative to independence or association.

---

[215] *See for instance* the statement by the chairman of the Working Party that drafted the text of Article 1 of both Covenants, GAOR (X), 3rd Comm., 668th Meeting, par. 3.

[216] The UN involvement with Algeria in the early 1960s is not really an example of such a case, because the GA had never explicitly accepted it as a case of decolonization through integration with France. The case of New Caledonia (and the other *territoires d'outre-mer*) is not a good example either, because the GA did not consider their relation with France as a form of integration in the sense of Res. 1541.

The Overseas Departments of France

The local leaders of Martinique and Guadeloupe – the 'old' French colonies in the Caribbean – had been petitioning for integration with the mother country since the nineteenth century.[217] In 1946, this request was granted when the islands became *départments d'outre-mer* (DOM). France immediately stopped transmitting information on the DOMs (and a number of other territories) under Article 73(e) of the UN Charter, which led the GA to request a reason for this decision.[218] France replied that the peoples of the DOMs had requested 'complete assimilation.' The peoples would 'receive all the civic freedoms, duties and faculties which belong to the inhabitants of metropolitan France: all political differentiation in their regard disappears within a single legal and moral community.' Although the status of the DOMs would only be 'largely identical' to that of the metropolitan departments, the inhabitants of the DOMs would enjoy exactly the same status as the metropolitan French, or so France claimed.[219]

Although the French territories were removed from the list of NSGTs, the majority of the UN member states do not consider the events of 1947 as conclusive *per se*, witness the re-listing of New Caledonia in 1986. Some of the other French territories were also re-listed in the 1960s and 1970s (*see below*), but these all concerned territories that were far less integrated with France than the DOMs. Whether the GA could also decide to re-list the DOMs has never been discussed, as far as I am aware, and it would probably depend on the estimation of the GA whether DOM status represents a full measure of self-government and a completed form of decolonization in the sense of Resolutions 1541 and 1514.[220]

The DOM status means that all French legislation applies, unless the legislator explicitly decides it does not, as Article 73 of the French Constitution provides:

> *Dans les départements et les régions d'outre-mer, les lois et règlements sont applicables de plein droit. Ils peuvent faire l'objet d'adaptations tenant aux caractéristiques et contraintes particulières de ces collectivités.*

---

[217] Oostindie & Klinkers 2003, p. 34.

[218] GA Res. 222 (III) of 3 November 1948. *See also* GAOR (IV), Annual Report of the Secretary-General on the Work of the Organization, Supplement No. 1, p. 127.

[219] Translation by the Secretary-General of a letter by the French government of 29 April 1949 (UN Doc. A/915). France also included a large collection of applicable laws and decrees to the Secretary General.

[220] The independence movement on Guadeloupe attempted to have the territory re-listed as a NSGT during the 1980s, but without success. *See* Aldrich & Connell 1992, p. 239.

Such adaptations are made by the legislator, or by the local authorities if they have been legally authorized to do so. In theory, this system could lead to 'arbitrary subordination' because it is entirely up to the French legislator to decide which rules and benefits are extended to the DOMs. But the *Conseil Constitutionnel* has interpreted the legislator's freedom restrictively, and only accepts exceptions for the DOMs if they are necessary and motivated by the particular circumstances of the territory itself. Also, the adaptations should not distort the nature of the DOM, for instance, by turning it into something more like a TOM.[221]

Since World War II, the financial contributions of France to the DOMs have been huge, and they have transformed their backward rural communities in almost every respect. Infrastructure, health care, education, housing, etc. are all supposed to be at French levels, but in 1981 it was still estimated that '*la protection sociale*' was 43 per cent to 49 per cent lower than in the metropolis. The professed reason for this was that the unemployed population of the DOMs should be stimulated to migrate to metropolitan France.[222] This policy seems to have been abandoned during the 1990s. Increased efforts have been made to integrate the DOMs with the European Union. As 'ultra-peripheral territories', they have received large amounts of European funding to develop their economic ties with Europe, and to to tackle their specific problems (*see* chapter 9).

Political parties in Martinique and Guadeloupe have campaigned for more local autonomy and exceptions from the metropolitan legal regime.[223] An independence movement has also developed, which could never count on much popular support, but which instead resorted to violence, even in metropolitan France.[224] In 1982, France increased the competences of the local organs, and the DOMs were allowed to develop more of a separate identity. Since then, the independence movement has gradually been pacified, although it remains active.

France only seems prepared to fully integrate territories into the Republic that are already very French. After the failed experiment with Saint-Pierre-et-Miquelon during the 1970s (*see* chapter 9), the French have become reluctant to create any new DOMs. The integration of Mayotte has been held off by Paris, in spite of an overwhelming vote in favour of *départementalisation* in a referendum on the island in 1976. The French government instead announced that the issue would be put to a second referendum, which was frequently postponed during the next 25 years. This French refusal may have been influenced

---

[221] Miclo 1989, p. 104 et seq.
[222] Blérald 1989, p. 266.
[223] Constant 1992, p. 55.
[224] Aldrich & Connell 1992, p. 237.

by international pressure to reunite Mayotte with the Comoros (*see* chapter 8), but also by the fact that Mayotte is much less French than the existing DOMs. French is not widely spoken and the population is mainly Muslim. Another important factor is that the island is very poor.[225]

In 1986 France placed Mayotte on a par with the DOMs for development purposes, and it has invested considerable sums since the late 1980s, increasing the social standards and improving the infrastructure. In 2000, an agreement was reached between the French government and the political parties of Mayotte on a new status, called *collectivité départementale*, which entailed an increase in autonomy for the island government and more French financial contributions, and which offers full departmental status as a possibility in some distant future. The inhabitants approved the new status in a referendum.

The United States

The US is the only metropolitan state that has developed some explicit conditions under which a request for integration would not be denied. These conditions were based on the Northwest Ordinance, by which the US Congress in 1787 spelled out the criteria that should be met by the western territories before they could enter the Union as states equal to the old states. It also provided that the settlers of the new territories would become equal citizens of the US.

Three main criteria are currently identified in the literature: (1) the inhabitants of the territory should embrace the principles of democracy 'as exemplified in the American form of government'; (2) they should desire statehood; and (3) the territory should have sufficient population and resources to support state government, and to take a share in the cost of the federal government.[226] Geographic separation and cultural differences have been considered problematic in the case of Puerto Rico, and in the case of Hawaii statehood was held off for a long time because of racist sentiments in Congress,[227] but according to *Leibowitz* it is now possible for a non-English speaking territory to become a state.[228]

The practice shows that Congress requires a long period of sustained petitioning, mainly because the existing states are not keen on sharing power with new states, but also perhaps to make sure that the territory really wants to become American. Alaska and Hawaii campaigned for statehood for 50 years, with three plebiscites being held in Alaska and two in Hawaii, all showing a

---

[225] Aldrich & Connell 1998, p. 228 et seq.
[226] Leibowitz 1989, p. 70.
[227] Daws 1974, p. 388.
[228] Leibowitz 1989, p. 76.

clear majority for statehood. The third criterion has often been used to oppose new states, but if the political will exists to admit a territory as a state, the issue of small size can be resolved. *Leibowitz* considers that requests by small US territories such as Guam or the US Virgin Islands could not be refused on this ground, 'once it is accepted that the Nation should be responsive to the citizens of the United States in their status preference.'[229]

These criteria were applied in the cases of Hawaii and Alaska, both NSGTs which became states in 1959. The US government informed the UN that it would no longer report on the territories. The Fourth Committee briefly debated the issue.[230] It was stated that NSGTs could achieve self-government primarily through independence, but integration could also be acceptable, if it was realized on the basis of absolute equality with the metropolis, and in concurrence with the freely expressed wishes of the population. There was unanimous agreement that Alaska and Hawaii had achieved a full measure of self-government on the basis of equality with the other states of the US, and that they had exercised their right to choose their own form of government.[231] The GA expressed the opinion that 'the people of Alaska and Hawaii have effectively exercised their right to self-determination and have freely chosen their present status', and it congratulated them and the US upon the achievement of a full measure of self-government.[232]

In recent years there have been quite a few publications in which it is claimed that Hawaiians did not really enjoy a free choice in 1959, mainly because the only option on the ballot was integration with the US, and because the franchise was based on US citizenship.[233] In 1999, a UN Special Rapporteur on the human rights of indigenous peoples suggested that Hawaii should be re-inscribed on the list of NSGTs because its annexation by the US in 1897 had been a violation of international law at the time.[234] Authors such as *Lopez Reyes*,

---

[229] Leibowitz 1989, p. 82.

[230] GAOR (XIV), Fourth Comm., 981st–983rd Meetings.

[231] Repertory of Practice of UN organs, Supplement No. 2 (1955-59), Vol. 3, para. 101.

[232] GA Res. 1469 (XIV) of 1959, adopted without a roll-call.

[233] The indigenous Hawaiians were already a numerical minority in 1959, and a number of them had not chosen to become US citizens (although they did have that option) and were therefore not allowed to vote.

[234] *See* 'Human Rights of Indigenous Peoples. Study on treaties, agreements and other constructive arrangements between States and indigenous populations. Final report by Miguel Alfonso Martínez, Special Rapporteur' of 22 June 1999, UN Doc. E/CN.4/Sub.2/1999/20. Para. 163-4 read: 'the 1897 treaty of annexation between the United States and Hawaii appears as an unequal treaty that could be declared invalid on those grounds, according to the international law of the time. It follows that the case of Hawaii could be re-entered on the list of non-self-governing territories of the United Nations and resubmitted to the bodies of the Organization competent in the field of decolonization.'

Castanha, *Churchill*, and *Pakaukau* conclude that the Hawaiian 'people' was not given a chance to exercise its right to self-determination, even though the GA in 1959 explicitly stated otherwise.[235]

The case really concerns the rights of indigenous minorities, or lack of respect for those rights,[236] but the arguments for re-inscription do not appear to be very strong. The process of 1959 did have some flaws, because the plebiscite was not observed by the UN and did not offer a choice of options other than integration or continued non-self-governing status. The authors cited *above* do not, however, provide proof that the overall population of Hawaii desires some other status or is unhappy with its current status. The argument some of these authors explicitly use is that only those Hawaiians are entitled to participate in the process of self-determination whose ancestors lived on the islands before the first Europeans arrived.[237]

At least some members of the UN appeared to be sensitive to this argument in the case of New Caledonia, which is somewhat similar in this respect to Hawaii. To some extent it was also accepted by the HRC and the ECHR in the case of *Py* v. *France*, where the Committee and the Court admitted that a process of self-determination could justify the exclusion of newcomers from the exercise of voting rights in referendums on the future of the island (*see below* in section 3.4.2 on New Caledonia).

Other Cases

The option of integration was discussed in the UK during the 1950s and 1960s, most seriously with regard to Malta. In 1956, the government of that island, which had an autonomous status in association with the UK, requested the British government to consider the integration of Malta into the UK. At first, the UK was not opposed to integration, apparently because of Malta's value as a military strongpoint. At a parliamentary conference in London, a plan for

---

[235] *See* Castanha 1996, Lopez-Reyes 1996, Churchill 2002, and Pakaukau 2004.

[236] Merry 2000, p. 23 writes that: 'For the Native Hawaiian descendants of the once-sovereign Hawaiian nation ... statehood exacerbated a long-term slide into political powerlessness, economic fragility, and cultural dispossession.'

[237] This argument leads to a far-reaching form of distinction based on descent which is unacceptable. Similar views appear to be held by some people in the Netherlands Antilles, especially on St Maarten, where the population has grown exponentially during the past few decades through an influx of migrants, demoting the indigenous (or 'real' as they tend to call themselves) St Maarteners to a minority, albeit a powerful one. The debate on 'St Martin culture' sometimes seems to be aimed at excluding a large part of the inhabitants of the island from participating in decisions concerning the future of the island. *See for instance* the claim by the St Martin Nation Building Foundation that only the 'real' St Maarteners have the right to self-determination (*Amigoe*, 7 November 2005).

integration was drawn up. It was put to a plebiscite on the island in 1956, where it was supported by a substantial majority, although the largest opposition party boycotted it. It seems the UK government was subsequently taken aback by the estimated costs of creating 'economic parity' for Malta. Because the plan also caused some controversy in the British media, Britain decided not to guarantee the financial solidarity that Malta requested. The plan was abandoned and the island became independent in 1964.[238]

The British willingness to discuss integration quickly disappeared thereafter. A former British Parliamentary Under-Secretary explained in an interview why a similar request from the Seychelles had been rejected: 'It is simply – to our way of thinking – impossible to imagine a tiny island, thousands of miles away, being just like a county of England.'[239]

Wainhouse writes that the UK did sound out a few territories 'for which integration seemed appropriate' around the time when the integration of Malta was contemplated, but the French model seemed a regressive step to the British dependencies.[240] *Leibowitz* writes that the British islands in the eastern Caribbean were not enthusiastic about the idea, because they feared that their interests would not be served by a House of Commons in which they would have only one seat. According to *Leibowitz* the most important factor was 'the extra burden that would have fallen on Great Britain to introduce the benefits of the welfare state and the higher educational standards', as *Leibowitz* writes.[241] Whatever the reasons, the idea had been abandoned by the UK in 1966, when the West Indies Associated States were discussed in the Decolonization Committee, and the UK explained that the only imaginable status options for these islands were independence, integration into any other state than the UK, association with the UK, or colonial status.

The UK has also refused to integrate such tiny territories as St Helena, which appear to be very British already,[242] and which are clearly too small ever to become independent. The financial argument could not have played much of a role in these decisions, but perhaps the UK was led by the fear that the integration of these tiny outposts might have tempted larger territories to hold out for this option instead of independence.[243]

---

[238] Drower 1992, p. 22, and Aldrich & Connell 1998, p. 31.

[239] Cited in Drower 1992, p. 144. The request was made in 1971.

[240] Wainhouse 1964, pp. 72-3.

[241] Leibowitz 1976, p. 182.

[242] *See* Ritchie 1998 for a description of life on St Helena and other small British outposts.

[243] This theory was defended in an editorial entitled 'Small States and Left-Overs of Empire' in *The Round Table* (1984), no. 292, p. 128.

Australia offered integration to the Cocos (Keeling) Islands[244] in a plebiscite in 1984.[245] The option of integration was defined by Australia in a paper distributed among the islanders. It would entail 'the full rights, privileges and obligations of other Australian citizens', including social security, health care, and the application of other 'appropriate' Australian legislation. Integration also meant that taxation would be introduced, but it was estimated that the indigenous population's income was currently below the threshold for income tax. The Australian government would take measures to bring the level of services and the standard of living to Australian levels within 10 years, but it would consult closely with the locally elected representatives about any proposed measures, with the aim of preventing 'overly-rapid change.'[246]

Upon a request by the Cocos (Keeling) Islands, Australia invited a visiting mission to observe the plebiscite.[247] The mission reported that the preparations by Australia for the plebiscite were beyond reproach, although the full implications of the three options were not completely understood by the people. On voting day, only 9 islanders voted for independence, 21 voted for free association, and 229 chose to become integrated with Australia. The turnout was a remarkable 100 per cent.[248] The visiting mission concluded that the choice for integration was made in complete freedom, and that the people of the islands had exercised their right to self-determination, which conclusion was adopted by the GA without comment.[249]

---

[244] This minute and extremely isolated island territory is located in the Indian Ocean, approximately half-way between Australia and Sri Lanka. The nearest country is Indonesia, 960 kilometres away. Its total surface is 14 km^2 and its population in 1983 stood at 559. The main economic activity in the islands is the production of coconuts (Report of the UN visiting mission of 1984, UN Doc. A/39/494, para. 15 et seq.).

[245] The plebiscite offered a choice between independence, free association with Australia, or integration with Australia.

[246] See the options paper distributed on the islands, reproduced in the Report of the visiting mission, pp. 46-8 See also the explanation of the Minister for Territories and Local Government to the Australian parliament in 1984, cited in Brown 1991, p. 180. It seemed that the voters were somewhat encouraged by Australia to choose for integration, but Australia never made its preference clear. One of the inhabitants of the islands complained to the UN that Australia wished to annex the islands in order to turn it into a military base. This was denied by the Australian government, and so far Australia has lived up to its promise. The complainant (a descendant of Captain John Clunies-Ross, who acquired the islands in the nineteenth century) was perhaps motivated by the fact that Australia was trying to expropriate him in order to terminate his control over the islands, see the Report of the visiting mission, para. 25, 41-2 and 66.

[247] Brown 1991, p. 180. The members of the visiting mission were appointed by the Chairman of the Decolonization Committee.

[248] Report of the UN visiting mission, para. 184 and 192. The Referendum Ordinance provided for compulsory voting.

[249] The Decolonization Committee only briefly considered the report (UN Doc. A/AC.109/PV.1269, para. 37). The GA approved it without discussion, and adopted a Resolution that con-

There is one other case of integration that was approved by the GA, that of Greenland. This was a special case that did not inspire much debate at the UN, perhaps because Greenland was not considered part of the Third World. The fact that Denmark was not unpopular at the UN, unlike the Netherlands and the other real 'colonial powers', must also have played a role, as well as the fact that Greenland was considered of strategic importance to the US. [250] The GA did not discuss any of the particulars of the situation, and in 1954 expressed a conviction that Greenland had freely decided on its integration with Denmark 'on an equal constitutional and administrative basis.' The territory had thereby achieved self-government and Chapter XI of the Charter ceased to apply. The Resolution made no explicit or implicit criticism of Denmark and included all the elements which the GA would refuse to include in the Resolution on the Netherlands Antilles the next year; self-determination, full self-government, compliance with Resolution 742, and the termination of the applicability of Chapter XI. [251]

Portugal integrated all of its overseas territories as 'provinces' into the metropolis, but this was rejected by the GA as a fake form of decolonization because the overseas populations were clearly not treated equally to the Portuguese in Europe. [252] The integration of the Azores and Madeira into Portugal, and the Canary Islands into Spain, could be considered as successful forms of integration, but they were not discussed at the UN because these territories were consciously excluded from the application of GA Resolution 1541 (*see* chapter 2, footnote 27). New Zealand seriously considered the concept of integration around 1950, and has offered it to several of its overseas territories. [253] This means that the Netherlands is one of very few metropolitan states – or perhaps even the only one[254] – which never contemplated integrating any of its overseas territories, up till now. The new status developed for Bonaire, St Eustatius and Saba may amount to a form of integration (*see* chapters 4 and 6).

---

firmed that the islanders had exercised their right to self-determination, and that Article 73 of the Charter no longer applied, *see* GA Res. 39/30 of 5 December 1984, adopted by consensus (GAOR, 39th Session, Plenary, 87th Meeting). The Cocos (Keeling) Islands were removed from the list of NSGTs.

[250] *See* GAOR (IX), Suppl. 18, part 1 of section IX.

[251] GA Res. 849 (IX) of 22 November 1954.

[252] GA Res. 1542 (XV) of 1960.

[253] New Zealand considered integration as a likely long-term result of the decolonization of its overseas territories after World War II, but it abandoned this idea in favour of free association around 1955 because it expected 'disastrous social effects' for the islands (*see* Stone 1965, p. 366). It has nonetheless offered this option to the Cook Islands and Niue, and included integration as a possible choice for the future in the draft treaty with Tokelau.

[254] I do not know whether this option was ever on the table with regard to the Belgian territories.

Cases such as Hong Kong, Goa, West New Guinea, East Timor and the Western Sahara could also be considered under the heading of integration, but since it is uncertain whether the principles of Resolution 1541 should be applied in these cases, where the territory did not integrate with the mother country, but with a neighbouring state, I will not discuss them here.

3.3.2 Conclusion

In practice, metropolitan states have interpreted integration to mean that a territory becomes fully part of the state, with equal status for its inhabitants, and a duty for the state to ensure that public services, human rights, and other conditions are up to the standards applied in the metropolitan territory. It is a rare form of decolonization of overseas territories. The most important reason why it has not been used more often seems to have been that the metropolitan governments are not prepared to pay for it. Another inhibiting factor has been the resistance in the territories to what is perceived as 're-colonization.' But in those cases where the metropolis offered integration as a real option to the population of small overseas territories, it was rarely refused. The benefits to the population are obvious, and support for it has remained very firm in all of the integrated territories discussed *above* (except Greenland), despite all sorts of economic, social and cultural problems that have accompanied this status option.

GA Resolution 1541 demands that the government of the state should treat the inhabitants of an integrated overseas territory the same as the metropolitan population. In practice, many exceptions are made, mainly with an eye to protecting the interests of the overseas territory and its economic, social and cultural distinctness, but sometimes also for the benefit of the metropolis. How far these exceptions may go, and which grounds for unequal treatment are acceptable, is hard to say on the basis of the law of decolonization and self-determination. In general, it may be assumed that exceptions are not in line with the principles of Resolution 1541 and the UN Charter if it seems to place the interests of the metropolis before those of the overseas population without good cause. If such a situation leads to a form of 'arbitrary subordination' it could perhaps even invalidate the integration as a form of decolonization and revive the non-self-governing status of the territory.

Under the international law of decolonization and self-determination, integration should be considered as a valid way of ending non-self-governing status, if it is the result of a free and informed choice by the population. It is uncertain whether integration definitively ends the international status of the territory and extinguishes the separate right to self-determination of the population. Full assimilation of the territory in every respect is not necessary, and perhaps not allowed if the overseas population does not want it, in view of the rights of minorities and indigenous peoples.[255] It does seem reasonable, or perhaps even inevitable, that the overseas population is prepared to adopt the national identity of the metropolitan state, at least to some extent. France and the US have even used this criterion as an essential pre-condition for integration, and the UK also seems only to have contemplated the integration of territories which exhibit a sufficient amount of 'British-ness', but this is not a legal criterion.

Metropolitan states have considered themselves authorized to set criteria before offering integration as an option to an overseas territory. In many cases they have simply rejected integration beforehand as impractical or too expensive. Metropolitan policies sometimes also seem to be guided by strategic military considerations. It might well be wondered whether such policies are consistent with the principle that due account should be taken of the wishes of the population. These metropolitan governments should perhaps have taken their obligations under the Charter more seriously, especially their duty to try and realize the political aspirations of the population as well as possible. The alternatives to independence were considered of special relevance to small territories in the debates between the Administering States and the anti-colonial states during the drafting of Resolution 1541, and in the Decolonization Committee since the 1960s. In spite of this, no examples of integration were realized after 1960, except by Australia in the tiny Cocos (Keeling) Islands.

When a territory consistently demands integration over a longer period of time, with clear support from the population, such a demand has not been refused, although there are only a few examples of this. States probably did not act out of awareness of an international obligation to realize the wishes of the population. On the contrary, it seems that most metropolitan governments think they can exclude integration as a possible form of decolonization, which practice is hardly consistent with the right to self-determination. But all of the states studied here are democracies, where it is uncommon that the wishes of the population would go unheard over a prolonged period of time.

In the few territories that were integrated into the mother country during the 1940s and 1950s, the population remains very attached to that status, although there are small but very active groups which still strive for independence and claim that decolonization has not been completed. In some territories there are also problems with disfranchised indigenous peoples. Full integration can also lead to severe economic and social problems, and if the living standards are

---

[255] Van Rijn 2005b, p. 161 considers that the right to self-determination means that a choice for integration does not mean that the islands should automatically give up all of their individuality.

raised to a level substantially higher than is common in the region, an increase in economic migration can obviously be expected.

3.4 OTHER OPTIONS

Resolution 2652 (XXV) of 1970 recognizes that dependent territories may not only exercise their right to self-determination by choosing for free association or integration, but also for 'any other political status freely determined by a people.' I will discuss the cases of Puerto Rico and New Caledonia to see how the UN looks at such cases, and whether they could nevertheless be regarded as 'a full measure of self-government' in the sense of Article 73 of the UN Charter.

3.4.1 **Puerto Rico**

Puerto Rico was a Spanish colony until 1898, when it was conquered by the US during the Spanish-American war. By the Treaty of Paris of that same year, Spain ceded Puerto Rico to the United States. The Treaty differed from other treaties of cession that the US had concluded during the nineteenth century[256] as it made no mention of a possible future incorporation of Puerto Rico into the US. Article IX of the Treaty read: 'The civil rights and political status of the territories hereby ceded to the United States shall be determined by the Congress.' Some US Senators wondered whether the US Constitution allowed Congress to hold territories without the intention of granting them statehood, but the Treaty was ratified, and became the legal basis for US sovereignty over Puerto Rico.

When in 1900 Puerto Rico became the first 'unincorporated territory' of the US, the autonomy enjoyed under Spanish rule was significantly reduced. Unincorporated territories (also called 'possessions') are annexed overseas territories of the US that are subject to exclusive Federal control under the so-called Territorial Clause of the US Constitution.[257] This Clause reads:

> The Congress shall have Power to dispose of and make all needful Rules and Regulations respecting the Territory or other Property belonging to the United

---

[256] *See for instance* the treaties with France (regarding Louisiana, 1803), Spain (Florida, 1819), and Russia (Alaska, 1867).

[257] *See* Leibowitz 1989, p. 17 et seq. for a discussion of the development of the concept of unincorporated territories.

States; and nothing in this Constitution shall be so construed as to Prejudice any Claims of the United States, or of any particular State.[258]

Based on this clause, the unincorporated territories come under the direct control of Congress and the Federal executive, and do not enjoy the autonomy of the states of the US. By the 'Insular Cases', a series of cases decided in 1901, the US Supreme Court decided that, in the case of an unincorporated territory, the US Constitution only applied with respect to those fundamental rights which were essential to the citizens of the US. The Constitution did not apply fully in these territories because, contrary to incorporated territories, they were not intended to become states.

In Puerto Rico, there already existed a strong movement for full autonomy at the start of US rule over the island. This movement did not strive for independence, but for Puerto Rican self-government in association with the US. It opposed any measures that would integrate Puerto Rico into the US. In 1917, when the Jones Act granted US citizenship to Puerto Ricans, the autonomist movement protested, as US citizenship might 'undermine the foundation of the Puerto Rican nation.'[259]

The Commonwealth of Puerto Rico

In 1950 the US Congress adopted Public Law 600,[260] which offered Puerto Rico the opportunity to adopt its own constitution. The Law stated in its preamble that it was adopted 'in the form of a compact', and it would only enter into force after it had been approved in a referendum in Puerto Rico. The Puerto Ricans approved Public Law 600, and a Constitutional Convention in Puerto Rico drew up a Constitution that would establish the *Estado Libre Associado* of Puerto Rico. The choice of this name, which literally translates into 'Associated Free State', shows that it was the intention of the framers of the Constitution to transform Puerto Rico into an autonomous unit associated with the US. Realizing that this objective could not be achieved at that time, the Spanish term was translated instead into 'commonwealth', a term that has been used to describe a wide variety of political entities, and offered the opportunity (it was hoped) that the relation between the US and Puerto Rico could evolve into the desired form of association.[261]

---

[258] Article IV, section 3, clause 2.

[259] Reisman 1975, p. 28.

[260] Act of 3 July 1950, ch. 446, 64 Stat. 319. For the legislative history of PL 600, *see* Leibowitz 1989, p. 162 et seq.

[261] *See* Leibowitz 1989, p. 162, note 127.

The Constitution was modified on a number of points by the US Congress. Most importantly, the freedom of Puerto Rico to amend the Constitution was limited, as any amendment should be in accordance with the Congressional resolution that approved the Constitution, the Puerto Rican Federal Relations Act (PRFR, an act of the US Congress[262]), the applicable provisions of the US Constitution, and Public Law 600.[263] The modified Constitution was approved in another Puerto Rican referendum.

A number of elements of the US-Puerto Rico relationship did not change with the creation of the Commonwealth in 1952. Puerto Ricans did not obtain the right to vote in US Presidential elections, nor did the Puerto Rican Resident Commissioner obtain the right to vote in the US Congress. Puerto Rico remained exempt from Federal taxation,[264] but the official currency on the islands remained the US dollar. Puerto Ricans can be, and have been. drafted for the US armed forces, and the US Federal government has retained full control over foreign affairs and defence. Puerto Rico only has very limited freedom to operate on the international scene.[265]

Puerto Rico's autonomy is not defined negatively, by enumerating the subjects that fall within the jurisdiction of the Federal authorities (as in the Kingdom Charter), but positively, by enumerating all the subjects which fall within the autonomous jurisdiction of Puerto Rico. All other subjects must be considered to fall within the jurisdiction of the Federal authorities of the US. The Puerto Rican Constitution of 1952 gives Puerto Rico the right to choose or appoint all members of its executive, judiciary and legislative branches. In matters of education, criminal law and civil law, the Puerto Rico legislature enjoys full autonomy, and it also determines its own budget. The Supreme Court of the US has decided that the Supreme Court of Puerto Rico is the final authority on the interpretation of Puerto Rican law, unless its interpretation is 'inescapably wrong' and the decision 'patently erroneous.'[266]

Federal Powers in Puerto Rico

Difference of opinion exists on the limits to the exercise of US Federal power in Puerto Rico. One interpretation holds that the relation has the character of a

---

[262] The PRFR is a collection of legal provisions that were created for Puerto Rico during the first half of the twentieth century. Part of these provisions were withdrawn to make room for the Constitution of Puerto Rico. The remainder of the Act contains provisions with respect to the fiscal and economical relationship between the US and Puerto Rico, on the US citizenship of Puerto Ricans, and on a few other subjects.

[263] Section 3 of Article VII of the Puerto Rican Constitution.

[264] Duany & Pantojas-García 2005, p. 23.

[265] Reisman 1975.

[266] *See* Reisman 1975, p. 35.

compact, which can only be amended or terminated by mutual consent. This would mean that Federal power has been limited by Public Law 600, the PRFR, and the Constitution of Puerto Rico. Adherents of this interpretation point to the procedure that led to the commonwealth status of Puerto Rico, which was similar to the procedures followed when territories became states of the Union or independent states, i.e. when territories achieved a status that could not be annulled or changed unilaterally by the US Congress.

The Constitutional Convention, which drew up the Constitution of Puerto Rico in 1952, considered that 'when this Constitution takes effect, the people of Puerto Rico shall thereupon be organized into a commonwealth established within the terms of the compact entered into by mutual consent.'[267] After the Constitution had come into force, the Governor of Puerto Rico concluded in a letter to President Eisenhower, dated 17 January 1953, that 'Our [Puerto Rico's] status and the terms of our association with the United States cannot be changed without our full consent.'[268] This interpretation was adopted by the US representative at the UN during the debate on the cessation of transmission of information with respect to Puerto Rico, when he described the new relationship as 'a compact of a bilateral nature whose terms may be changed only by common assent.'[269]

Although the US may be bound under international law by this statement at the UN,[270] the legal validity of the compact argument has nonetheless been questioned.[271] Congress did not support the statements made on behalf of the US government at the UN.[272] With the adoption of Public Law 600, Congress appears to have acted in the conviction that the Law would not 'preclude a future determination by Congress of Puerto Rico's ultimate political status.'[273]

---

[267] *See* the final declaration of the Constitutional Convention of Puerto Rico (Res. 23), cited in Reisman 1975, p. 42.

[268] Cited in Reisman 1975, p. 43.

[269] Statement by the US representative in the Fourth Committee of the Eighth session (1953) of the GA, cited in Reisman 1975, p. 44.

[270] Clark 1980, p. 45.

[271] Leibowitz 1989, p. 163, note 131 presents an extensive list of articles on this issue. *See also* Cabán 1993, p. 21. Stein 1961 and Helfeld 1952 concluded that PL 600 did not change Congressional power over Puerto Rico.

[272] *See* Leibowitz 1976, p. 48 et seq.

[273] Statement by Interior Secretary Oscar Chapman during the debate in the House of Representatives, cited in Trías Monge 1997, p. 112. This statement was followed in both the House or Representatives and the Senate Committee Reports on the bill, *see* Leibowitz 1989, p. 166. At the time of the enactment of Public Law 600 and the resolution approving the Constitution of Puerto Rico by the US Congress, there existed difference of opinion about the legal consequence of these acts. Congress seemed convinced that it did not relinquish its authority to legislate for Puerto Rico or to annul Puerto Rican legislation. To reaffirm the powers of Congress under the Territorial

In Congress, it has often been argued since 1952 that Public Law 600 has not changed the nature of US-Puerto Rico relations, and that Congress still possesses its unlimited authority to legislate with respect to Puerto Rico under the Territorial Clause of the US Constitution. Some lower Federal courts have assumed that there exists a compact, but the Supreme Court has not gone farther than to state that Puerto Rico is a commonwealth, and that is has a unique status, without defining that status.[274] The US courts consider Congress authorized to decide whether a US law is applicable in Puerto Rico, but they have occasionally refused to apply Federal legislation which 'conflicts with, or attempts to modify the Puerto Rican Constitution.'[275]

During the 1990s, some attempts were made by Congress to clarify the status of Puerto Rico. In 1996, the Chairmen of the several committees of the US House of Representatives which deal with Puerto Rico sent a letter to the Puerto Rican parliament, stating:

Although there is a history of confusion and ambiguity on the part of some in the U.S. and Puerto Rico regarding the legal and political nature of the current 'commonwealth' local government structure and territorial status, it is incontrovertible that Puerto Rico's present status is that of an unincorporated territory subject in all respects to the authority of the United States Congress under the Territorial Clause of the U.S. Constitution. As such, the current status does not provide guaranteed permanent union or guaranteed citizenship to the inhabitants of the territory of Puerto Rico, nor does the current status provide the basis for recognition of a separate Puerto Rican sovereignty or a binding government-to-government status pact... In addition it is important to recognize that the existing Commonwealth of Puerto Rico structure for local self-government, and any other measures which Congress may approve while Puerto Rico remains an unincorporated terri-

---

Clause, an amendment to the resolution approving the Constitution of Puerto Rico was submitted to Congress, which stated: 'That nothing herein contained shall be construed as an irrevocable delegation, transfer or release of the power of the Congress granted by Article IV, section 3, of the Constitution of the United States' (98 *Congressional Record* 6203, cited in Leibowitz 1989, p. 168). This amendment was rejected, but it was not clear why. It may have been rejected merely for technical reasons, or because it was considered unnecessary. In the end, the difference of opinion in Congress was not resolved, and the Constitution of Puerto Rico was approved while its legal status remained unclear.

[274] 'The Supreme Court has stated [that] the Commonwealth has a status in American Jurisprudence "unique in American history" but has yet to accord this unique status great significance. (...) no court has held that Commonwealth status requires mutual consent before a particular statute comes into effect.' (Leibowitz 1989, p. 66.)

[275] Reisman 1975, p. 36, note 75. For a discussion of the cases in which Federal courts were faced with the question of whether a Federal statute applied to Puerto Rico, *see* Leibowitz 1989, pp. 190-2.

tory, are not unalterable in a sense that is constitutionally binding upon a future Congress. [276]

This denial of the compact argument was upheld two years later by the House of Representatives when it approved H.R. 856, the 'United States-Puerto Rico Political Status Act.'[277] It can safely be assumed that in the view of the US Congress, Puerto Rico is still an unincorporated territory, which means that Congress' authority to legislate for Puerto Rico is unlimited, and that it can repeal the commonwealth status of Puerto Rico, including the US citizenship of the Puerto Ricans. Perhaps Congress could indeed retract at least some of the legislation in which it has defined the relation with Puerto Rico, but whether the Congress would really be authorized to set aside the Constitution of Puerto Rico seems uncertain in view of the way it was adopted. As it is, the US has considerable legislative powers in Puerto Rico, while it is uncertain whether Congress will respect the right to self-determination of the people of Puerto Rico.

A Full Measure of Self-Government?

There seems to exist little doubt in the legal literature and otherwise that Puerto Rico's status does not represent a full measure of self-government or a form of complete decolonization. Even *Reisman*, in his optimistic account of Puerto Rico's potential role in international relations, has to admit that in the light of Resolution 1541 'there are obvious imperfections in the association status of Puerto Rico', namely the reserved Congressional powers, the application of US Federal law in Puerto Rico, and the relative absence of Puerto Rico as an actor in international politics.[278] *Crawford* considers that there are substantive defects in the terms of the association of Puerto Rico, and he sees it as an unsatisfactory model of association because the territory has few means of participating in international and metropolitan affairs, and because its internal

---

[276] Letter to The Honorable Roberto Rexach-Benitez, President of the Senate, and the Honorable Zaida Hernandez-Torres, Speaker of the House of the Commonwealth of Puerto Rico, dated 29 February, 1996, reproduced on <http://www.puertorico51.org>.

[277] H.R. 856, 105th Cong. (1998). This bill was not adopted by the Senate, *see below.* According to this bill, Puerto Ricans only have US citizenship 'by statute', as opposed to citizenship on the basis of the US Constitution, which other American citizens posses. US citizenship of Americans born in one of the states is protected by Amendment XIV, section 1 of the US Constitution, *see* Roman 1998, p. 3. This would mean that the citizenship of Puerto Ricans is not based on the US Constitution, and that Congress could repeal the Jones Act of 1917 which conferred US citizenship on Puerto Ricans.

[278] Reisman 1975, p. 49.

autonomy is restricted.[279] Several sources do not hesitate to call the status of Puerto Rico colonial.[280]

The US has often presented Puerto Rico as a form of free association,[281] but Congress has recognized that the status of Puerto Rico is not a full measure of self-government. Resolution H.R. 856, which was adopted by the House of Representatives in 1998, not only claims that Puerto Rico does not have the status of free association with the US 'as that status is defined under United States law or international practice', but also that Puerto Rico has not become fully self-governing. Puerto Rican politicians also do not think a full measure of self-government has been achieved. When the Governor of Puerto Rico testified before the Decolonization Committee in 1989 and 1991 he stated that the status of Puerto Rico 'must be declared colonial by this Committee because it does not meet the minimum parameters for ... free association',[282] but in 1953, the GA had already decided otherwise.

The UN Debate on the Cessation of Transmission of Information on Puerto Rico

In 1953, Puerto Rico and the US agreed that the US should cease transmitting information on Puerto Rico under Article 73(e) of the UN Charter. Puerto Rico hoped that when the US was called upon by the UN to defend its position that Puerto Rico had achieved 'a full measure of self-government', the US would be forced to recognise that its grant of self-government to Puerto Rico could not be repealed unilaterally by Congress, and that Congress had limited its authority to legislate for Puerto Rico. The US wished to obtain the international recognition that Puerto Rico was no longer a colony of the US.[283]

The debate in the UN revealed a considerable degree of scepticism among a number of non-Western states about the measure of self-government Puerto

---

[279] Crawford 2006, p. 627.

[280] *See* Cabranes 1978, Duany & Pantojas-García 2005, and also the statements of Governors of Puerto Rico at the UN in 1978 and afterwards (*see below*).

[281] The US State Department has also defended it as a form of integration, *see* the *Digest of United States Practice in International Law* (1975, p. 104). *See also* Dempsey 1976, p. 297, who contradicts this claim.

[282] *See* the verbatim reports of the Special Committee's meetings of 1989 and 1991, UN Doc. A/AC.109/PV. 1357 (1989) and A/AC.109/PV. 1390 (1991).

[283] The Representative of the US at the UN informed the Secretary-General that 'in the light of the change in the constitutional position and status of Puerto Rico' the US considered it 'no longer necessary or appropriate for the United States to continue to transmit information on Puerto Rico under Article 73e.' Letter from the United States Mission to the UN, dated 19 January 1953, reproduced in *Non-Self-Governing Territories: Summaries and analyses of information transmitted to the Secretary-General during 1953*, p. 33 (UN Doc. ST/TRI/SER.A/8).

Rico had obtained. Opposition by the Communist states and a number of Asian states had been expected by the US, but the opposition was enlarged by a number of Latin American and Middle Eastern states, which found that the commonwealth did not meet the standards for full self-government. Puerto Rico did not appear to be associated with the US, and it had clearly not been integrated into the US.

Many states objected to the fact that Puerto Rico was partly governed by legislation enacted by organs in which it was not properly represented. Criticism was also directed at the US control over defence and foreign affairs, the seemingly arbitrary way in which Congress decided whether Federal legislation would apply to Puerto Rico or not, the jurisdiction of the US Supreme Court over Puerto Rico, the lack of economic independence, and the absence of a right of secession.[284]

During the lengthy debates in the Fourth Committee of the GA of 1953, the US representatives used the compact argument to convince states of the voluntary character of the relations and of the inviolability of the Puerto Rican autonomy, even though this interpretation of the Commonwealth was probably not supported by the US Congress. Most of the opponents of the US voiced doubts about the validity of the compact argument. Several Members were convinced that the relation between Puerto Rico and the US could be altered by the latter without the consent of the former, as the compact did not prevail over the laws of Congress, and had never intended to do so, since it was subject to the limitations established by those laws.[285]

Shortly before the final vote in the Plenary, the representative of the US announced on behalf of President Eisenhower that if at any time the legislative assembly of Puerto Rico should choose 'more complete or even absolute independence', the President would immediately thereafter recommend to Congress that such independence be granted.[286] The decision on the independence of Puerto Rico (let alone a choice for any other status) thus continued to lie with Congress.

The resolution approving the cessation of transmission of information could only be adopted in the Plenary of the GA after it had been decided by a very slim majority that the resolution did not require a two-thirds majority.[287] The

---

[284] BuZa 1954b, p. 142.

[285] *See for instance* the statement by the Iraqi representative, GAOR (VIII) Fourth Committee, 356th Meeting, p. 257.

[286] *See* statement by US Representative during the 459th Plenary Meeting of the Eighth Session of the GA on 27 November 1953 (A/PV.459, Par. 66). According to Clark 1980, the US government is probably bound by this promise as a matter of international law.

[287] A Mexican proposal, which was adopted by 30 votes to 26 (Par. 36 of the 459th Plenary Meeting of the Eighth GA), provided that under Article 18, para. 3 of the UN Charter a simple

resolution was adopted by 26 votes to 16, with 18 abstentions,[288] with the crucial support of eight Latin American states[289] that had disapproved of the cessation of transmission of information with respect to the Netherlands Antilles and Surinam only a few minutes earlier. The representatives of these states explained their vote by saying that Puerto Rico had achieved a larger measure of self-government than the Dutch territories. It was stated that Puerto Rico had drafted its own Constitution, the people of Puerto Rico had approved its new status in a plebiscite, and its governor was elected through elections in Puerto Rico.

Resolution 748 declared that 'Chapter XI of the Charter can no longer be applied to the Commonwealth of Puerto Rico', which meant that Puerto Rico had achieved a full measure of self-government and was no longer a Non-Self-Governing Territory. The resolution also declared that 'the people of Puerto Rico have effectively exercised their right to self-determination.'[290]

Interestingly, this conclusion was contested by the Dutch Ministry of Foreign Affairs in its report of the Eighth Session of the GA. The plebiscites of 1952 could not be considered a real exercise of the right to self-determination, as the population of the territory did not have the possibility to choose independence or integration in those plebiscites. In the view of the Dutch Ministry, the Puerto Rican general elections of 1948, in which status was an issue, and during which the political party that promoted the commonwealth received 61 per cent of the votes, could not be put on a par with a plebiscite, as the outcome of these elections were undoubtedly influenced by other issues as well.[291]

UN Involvement after 1953

The adversaries of the US came to consider Puerto Rico as its Achilles heel. Puerto Rico's status could be used to 'expose' the US as a colonial power and 'the enemy of Latin American freedom.'[292] From 1965, Cuba tried to have the 'colonial question of Puerto Rico' entered in the agenda of the Decolonization Committee. Cuba, and a majority of the Non-Aligned Movement[293] (supported

---

majority would suffice to adopt the resolution (or *all* resolutions dealing with Chapter XI of the UN Charter – there existed difference of opinion among the delegations about what had been voted upon exactly, *see* Par. 74-148 of the 459th Plenary Meeting of the Eighth GA).

[288] GAOR (VIII), Plenary, 459th Meeting, para. 160.

[289] Bolivia, Brazil, Chile, Colombia, Cuba, Haiti, Nicaragua and Uruguay.

[290] GA Res. 748 (VIII) of 27 November 1953.

[291] BuZa 1954b, p. 140.

[292] *See* Carr 1984, p. 348.

[293] In 1964, the final communiqué of the Cairo Conference of the Heads of State or Government of Non-Aligned Countries requested the Decolonization Committee to consider the case of Puerto Rico.

by the Communist bloc) viewed the mandate of the Decolonization Committee as including all territories which had traditionally been considered colonies of the Western states, and which had not yet achieved full independence. This certainly included Puerto Rico.[294] Resolution 748 of 1953 was only concerned with Chapter XI and could not decide on the application of the Declaration on the Granting of Independence (1514) of 1960.

In 1966, Puerto Rico was included in the agenda of the Decolonization Committee for the next year. The US announced that 'it would view very seriously any attempt to discuss the matter since that would question Puerto Rico's self-governing status.'[295] The GA nonetheless approved the report of the Decolonization Committee, including its decision to discuss the question of Puerto Rico at its next session.[296] The Committee, however, decided to postpone discussion of the matter *sine die.*

The US successfully foiled an attempt by Cuba to insert 'the colonial case of Puerto Rico' into the agenda of the GA in 1971.[297] After the US and the UK had resigned from the Decolonization Committee, however, that body felt itself more free to pursue anti-Western objectives, and Cuba succeeded in re-introducing the issue on the agenda of the Committee.[298] A Resolution was

---

[294] The first petition the Committee received from a territory therefore came from the Puerto Rican Pro-Independence Movement (reproduced in GAOR 26th Session, Annexes, Agenda item 8, p. 10-12 (UN Doc. A/8441/Add.1)). Puerto Rican independence organizations had requested hearings at the UN since 1953, but these had always been denied. Ironically, in 1953, the pro-independence parties represented the second largest political movement of Puerto Rico, while in 1973 when they were finally recognised by the Decolonization Committee as representatives of the Puerto Rican opposition, they had been reduced to splinter parties, which together received no more than 5 per cent of the votes, *see* Cabranes 1978, p. 80 for Puerto Rican election results.

[295] GAOR 21st Session, Annexes, Addendum to Agenda Item 23, (UN Doc. A/6300/Rev.1), Report of the Decolonization Committee on the Situation with regard to the Implementation of the Declaration on the Granting of Independence to Colonial Countries and Peoples, paras. 265-69.

[296] GA Res. 2189 (XXI) of 13 December 1966, operative para. 4. The Western states were of the opinion that by considering Puerto Rico to fall within its jurisdiction, the Committee would act counter to the GA's findings in 1953, and as a subsidiary body of the GA, it was not allowed to do so. The Committee should therefore limit itself to stating its lack of competence in the matter (GAOR 22nd Session, Annexes, Addendum to Agenda Item 23, (UN Doc. A/6700/Rev.1), Report of the Decolonization Committee on the Situation with regard to the Implementation of the Declaration on the Granting of Independence to Colonial Countries and Peoples, paras. 171-256).

[297] Letter dated 17 August 1971 from the Permanent Representative of Cuba to the Secretary-General, GAOR 26th Session, Annexes, Agenda item 8, p. 10, UN Doc. A/8441, Par. 41. The proposal was defeated by 10 votes to 5, with 8 abstentions (GAOR 26th Session, General Committee, 192nd Meeting, Item 104, UN Doc. A/BUR/SR.192).

[298] Letter dated 25 March 1972 from the Permanent Representative of Cuba to the United Nations addressed to the Chairman of the Decolonization Committee, GAOR 27th Session, Supplement 23 (Report of the Decolonization Committee), Annex III B, p. 93 (UN Doc. A/8723/Rev.1).

adopted, by 12 votes to none with 10 abstentions, which recognized the 'inalienable right of the people of Puerto Rico to self-determination and independence in accordance with General Assembly resolution 1514 (XV) of 14 December 1960.'[299] The Committee did not, however, recommend to the General Assembly that Puerto Rico should be included in the list of territories to which the Declaration is applicable.[300] Instead, it decided to continue discussing the issue at its next sessions.[301]

In 1978, the Governor of Puerto Rico and the leader of the largest opposition party announced they wanted to testify before the Decolonization Committee. In Puerto Rico many people had become disillusioned by the failure of Congress to implement any of the proposals for a stronger commonwealth after the plebiscite of 1967, and feared that the growing power of the Federal government would cause 'a relapse into colonialism.'[302] The pro-statehood party intended to use the UN to convince Congress to make Puerto Rico the 51st state.

The US Government made several attempts to prevent the Governor from testifying. In July of 1978, President Carter issued a proclamation to the Puerto Rican people in which he affirmed the US commitment to the principle of self-determination, and pledged to urge Congress to support whatever status the Puerto Ricans might choose in the referendum that was scheduled for 1981.[303] According to *Cabranes*, this proclamation was hailed in Puerto Rico as 'a milestone of considerable significance', but many Puerto Ricans still saw the Decolonization Committee as 'the only authoritative and disinterested body capable of guaranteeing the integrity and fairness of any process for political

---

Cuba also circulated a letter by the Political Committee of the Central Committee of the Puerto Rican Socialist Party (Pro-Independence Movement), which complained about the repression of the independence movement in Puerto Rico by US federal agencies, GAOR 27th Session, Supplement 23 (Report of the Decolonization Committee), Annex III C, pp. 97-100 (UN Doc. A/8723/Rev.1). In 2000, these accusations were shown to have had a basis in fact, when FBI director Louis Freeh 'stunned' a congressional budget hearing by conceding that his agency had for over 40 years pursued a secret campaign of surveillance, disruption and repression against Puerto Rico's independence movement (*New York Daily News*, 5 May 2000).

[299] Resolution (A/AC.109/419), as adopted by the Decolonization Committee at its 890th Meeting on 28 August 1972, see GAOR (XXVII), Supplement 23 (A/8723/Rev.1), *Report of the Decolonization Committee on the Situation with regard to the Implementation of the Declaration on the Granting of Independence to Colonial Countries and Peoples*, Vol. I, p. 31.

[300] It did make such a recommendation with respect to the Comoro Archipelago earlier that same session, by 17 votes to none with 2 abstentions See GAOR (XXVII), Supplement 23 (A/8723/Rev.1), *Report of the Decolonization Committee*, Vol. I, pp. 28-9.

[301] From 1973, the Decolonization Committee has each year received representatives of the Puerto Rican Socialist Party and the Puerto Rican Independence Party, two splinter parties.

[302] Carr 1984, pp. 354-5.

[303] Proclamation by President Carter, 25 July 1978, distributed at the UN in a statement by Ambassador Young on 28 August 1978, see Leibowitz 1989, p. 231, note 398.

change.'[304] The US Government, however, was not prepared to accept the Decolonization Committee as a forum for discussing the issue of the status of Puerto Rico, and perhaps more importantly, it wished to avoid appearing 'soft on Cuba.' Disappointed with the US attitude, the leader of the pro-Commonwealth party testified before the Committee that:

> If one takes into account that the United States has not recognised the will of the people of Puerto Rico, as expressed in the 1967 plebiscite, and that the President's assurances[305] depend upon his re-election in 1980 and that in the federal Government the power to decide upon the status of Puerto Rico resides in Congress, one still wonders if the exercise of the right to self-determination of the Puerto Rican people is properly guaranteed.[306]

The pro-statehood Governor of Puerto Rico testified that the relation of the US with Puerto Rico 'retains vestiges of colonialism', but also considered that the people of Puerto Rico should be free to continue such a semi-colonial relation. It can safely be assumed that a majority of the Committee did not agree, and this use of the 'forbidden word' (colonialism)[307] by the Governor of Puerto Rico added to the already large 'mass of negative testimony', which in the view of the US State Department 'materially undercut our position in the committee to defer the issue.'[308]

The Committee adopted a resolution which declared that the Committee deemed that: 'Any form of free association between Puerto Rico and the United States must be in terms of political equality in order to comply fully with the provisions of the relevant resolutions and decisions of the General Assembly and of applicable international law, and must recognize the sovereignty of the people of Puerto Rico.'[309] The resolution made no mention of the option of integration with the US as a valid exercise of the right to self-determination. Similar resolutions were adopted in 1979[310] and 1980,[311] in which the US was also asked to present a plan for the decolonization of Puerto Rico.

---

[304] Cabranes 1978, p. 85.

[305] To respect the outcome of the plebiscite of 1981 (see above).

[306] Verbatim record of the 1125th Meeting of the Decolonization Committee on the Situation (etc.) on 28 August 1978, UN Doc. A/AC.109/PV.1125, p. 26.

[307] See Cabranes 1978, p. 68 et seq.

[308] See Eric Swenden's article in Open Forum, No. 20 (Spring/Summer 1979), pp. 21-7, cited in Carr 1984, pp. 359-60.

[309] Operative para. 6 of the Resolution adopted by the Decolonization Committee at its 1133rd Meeting, on 12 September 1978, UN Doc. A/AC.109/574.

[310] Resolution adopted by the Decolonization Committee at its 1160th Meeting, on 15 August 1979, UN Doc. A/AC.109/589.

[311] Operative para. 2 of the Resolution adopted by the Decolonization Committee at its 1179th Meeting, on 20 August 1980, UN Doc. A/AC.109/628.

In 1981, the US State Department became seriously worried about the developments at the UN, because the Decolonization Committee had recommended to the GA to examine the issue of Puerto Rico as a separate item.[312] As long as the anti-colonialists had limited their activities to the Decolonization Committee, they had been tolerated as a 'nasty nuisance' to the US,[313] but if the GA should act upon the recommendation of the Committee, the issue would be considered a real political threat. The US feared it would be depicted by Third World countries as 'a South Africa of the Western Hemisphere.'[314] According to *Carr*, the issue of Puerto Rico also threatened to strain the relations with the Latin American states. In his view, states such as Venezuela, while loath to support Cuban initiatives, used the exhibition of 'support for the independence of Puerto Rico [as] a cheap way to display Venezuela's freedom, as a Third World power, from United States' pressure and its fidelity to the legacy of Bolívar the Liberator.'[315]

During the meetings of the GA, the US took considerable pains 'to rally America's friends and threaten its enemies', and made it clear to the Non-Aligned countries that a vote against the US on this matter would 'carry penalties.'[316] In the General Committee, the US obtained a victory of 11 votes to 7, with 8 abstentions.[317] Cuba complained that the US had used political pressure and even threats to convince several UN Members to vote against the Cuban proposal.

In the Plenary of that year, Cuba made a final attempt to convince the GA to take up the agenda item of Puerto Rico.[318] The US had invited the Mayor of

---

[312] Operative para. 3 of the Resolution adopted by the Decolonization Committee at its 1201st Meeting, on 20 August 1981, UN Doc A/AC.109/677.

[313] Statement by a member of the US Mission to the UN in the *Washington Post* of 21 August 1981, cited in Carr 1984, p. 361.

[314] Carr 1984, p. 361.

[315] Carr 1984, p. 362.

[316] One US diplomat described the diplomatic effort by saying that 'behind the scenes we raised holy hell with the NAMs' (cited in Franck 1985, p. 199, 'NAM's' refers to the members of the Non-Aligned Movement). The Netherlands and other Western states actively supported the US, *see* GAOR (XXXVI), 72nd and 73rd Plenary Meeting. US ambassadors vociferously pressed for a sympathetic vote in many Third World capitals, threatening explicitly to retaliate through economic measures or cutting back military aid. Allegedly, the ambassadors also threatened that the US would oppose World Bank loans to uncooperative countries. *See* Franck 1985, pp. 202-3.

[317] The president of the GA, after 'consultations with numerous delegations concerned', decided that a vote in favour of the Decolonization Committee's Report would not mean the automatic inclusion of Puerto Rico in the agenda of the next session (GAOR (XXXVI), 79th Plenary Meeting). Cuba was thereby forced to ask the General Committee to include an item entitled 'Question of Puerto Rico' in the agenda of the next session. This proposal was rejected by 11 votes to 7, with 8 abstentions (GAOR (XXXVII), General Committee, 2nd Meeting, para. 50-72 and 123-125, UN Doc. A/BUR/37/SR.2).

[318] GAOR (XXXVII), 4th Plenary Meeting, 24 September 1982, para. 21-32.

San Juan (the capital of Puerto Rico), to address the GA on this issue. The Mayor reiterated in Spanish the traditional US position that Puerto Rico was governed democratically and that the Puerto Ricans had the right to change their relation with the US at any time: 'Puerto Rico is not an international problem and does not wish to be one.'[319] The Cuban proposal was rejected by 70 votes to 30, with 43 abstentions, but not before a large number of representatives explained their vote at length.[320] The President of the GA reminded the representatives on two occasions that they should limit their comments to the procedural aspects, but many representatives nonetheless discussed the autonomy of Puerto Rico and the question whether the Puerto Rican people's right to self-determination was respected by the US, thereby in fact granting the Cuban request for a plenary discussion of the 'Question of Puerto Rico.'[321]

The US representative considered this result the greatest US victory at the UN that year, together with defeating the attempts to expel Israel from the UN.[322] *Trías Monge* describes it as 'a remarkable diplomatic feat, given the general opinion as to Puerto Rico's subordinate condition.'[323] The GA's repeated refusal to discuss Puerto Rico must be ascribed for a large part to the political and economic power of the US. For a majority of states it is obviously very unattractive to take sides with Cuba against the US on an issue which is of special importance to the US and of little importance to most other states. For many Third World countries this means repudiating a position which they have taken (and still take[324]) in the summits of the NAM and in the Decolonization Committee.[325]

---

[319] GAOR (XXXVII), 4th Plenary Meeting, 24 September 1982, para. 33-55.

[320] Curiously, many of the Members voting against the Cuban proposal were present at the summit of non-aligned countries in 1978, which issued a final communiqué in which it was reiterated that the UN should consider the case of Puerto Rico, and which condemned the fact that the US continued to exercise sovereignty over Puerto Rico. These states defended their apparent change of opinion by stating that the people of Puerto Rico had freely chosen their present status, and that GA Res. 1541 (XV) accepted free association and integration as modes of implementing the right to self-determination (*see for instance* the statements by the representatives of Uruguay and Zaire, GAOR (XXXVII), 4th Plenary Meeting, 24 September 1982, para. 65-77 and para. 131-135).

[321] GAOR (XXXVII), 4th Plenary Meeting, 24 September 1982, para. 57-145.

[322] Reported by *The New York Times*, 22 December 1982.

[323] Trías Monge 1997, p. 139. Franck 1985, p. 195 describes it as 'a textbook success in US diplomacy.'

[324] The final document of the thirteenth summit of the Non-Aligned Movement in 2003 declares: 'The Heads of State or Government once again reaffirmed the right of the people of Puerto Rico to self-determination and independence on the basis of Resolution 1514 (XV) of December 1960 by the United Nations General Assembly. The Movement took note of the resolution on Puerto Rico adopted by the Special Committee on Decolonization by consensus in 2000, 2001 and 2002, which, inter alia, urged the United States Government to order the immedi-

The Decolonization Committee remains a forum for Puerto Ricans to express their dissatisfaction with their present status, and perhaps also to provoke the US government into action and granting Puerto Rico a real choice between the status options of Resolution 1541. Every year approximately 20 Puerto Rican organizations send representatives to the UN in New York to be heard by the Committee. The Committee still accedes to these requests, but other than that, it has done little more since 1991 than postpone discussion of the issue until next year.

Proposals for Reform

Since 1953, many attempts have been made to clarify or modify the relation between Puerto Rico and the United States, partly, it seems, to prevent further UN involvement. To this end, several bills have been introduced in Congress, but none were approved.

In 1967, a plebiscite was held upon the recommendation of a Congressional Commission, in which the people of Puerto Rico were offered a choice between independence, integration with the United States, and improved Commonwealth status, which, according to the Commission, would 'remain to be based on the principles of mutual consent and self-determination.'[326] The Commonwealth option received almost 60 per cent of the votes, but Congress refused to take any further action.

Discussions between the US and Puerto Rico on the implementation of the results of the plebiscite continued until 1976, when President Ford announced that he believed Puerto Rico should become a state of the US. This statement sparked outbursts of violence in Puerto Rico and in the US. It took until 1988 before Congress again started to discuss the status of Puerto Rico. Several bills were introduced that proposed to organize another plebiscite on the issue. By now, it was expected Puerto Rico might opt for statehood. Popular support for commonwealth status had waned, as it was felt that this status only benefited a small group of industrialists who profited from Puerto Rico's exemption from Federal taxes. More than 50 per cent of Puerto Ricans continued to live below

---

ate halt of its armed forces military drills and manoeuvres on Vieques Island and to return the occupied land to the people of Puerto Rico.' (Final Document of the XIIIth Summit, Kuala Lumpur, 20-25 February 2003, para. 61).

[325] According to Franck, the NAM sometimes takes a radical anti-colonial stance as 'some left-NAMs enjoy a degree of influence out of all proportion to their numbers because they work harder and more relentlessly than the rest ... This means, generally, that as midnight comes and goes in the councils of the NAM and more delegates drift away, the few dedicated moderates often find themselves hopelessly manipulated.' (Franck 1985, p. 191).

[326] Trías Monge 1997, p. 130.

the poverty line, and they would profit from the social benefits associated with statehood.

Congress was unwilling to organize a plebiscite which might lead to statehood, however, as the integration of Puerto Rico into the Union was expected to be a multi-billion dollar operation. In 1993 the PNP, which at that time governed Puerto Rico and which favours statehood, decided to organize a plebiscite under Puerto Rican law, which offered a choice between independence, commonwealth status and statehood: 48.6 per cent of the voters chose for the continuation of the commonwealth, 46.3 per cent statehood, and 4.4 per cent independence.[327] It was generally assumed that statehood failed to win a majority vote because Congress had not expressed the willingness to implement that choice.

The Clinton administration, supported by the statehood party of Puerto Rico, urged Congress to authorize a binding referendum on the status of Puerto Rico with the promise that the results would be respected, even if it meant accepting Puerto Rico into the Union. The Democratic minority in the House of Representatives, which was in favour of such a referendum, was supported by a small number of Republicans to produce a one-vote majority.[328] In the Senate there was less support for the proposals. Most Republican Senators were not ready to accept into the Union a poor, Spanish- speaking state that would most likely send Democratic representatives to Congress. The bill was not put to a vote, and instead the Senate adopted a resolution which confirmed that Puerto Rico had the right to express itself on its future status, and to communicate its views to the President and Congress.

The government of Puerto Rico decided to hold a plebiscite in 1998. The ballot presented five options. Commonwealth, statehood, independence and free association were presented in the definitions that the House of Representatives had approved. A fifth option was added, which was entitled 'None of the Above', to satisfy the opposition of the pro-commonwealth party, the PPD. During the referendum campaign, the PPD advised the Puerto Ricans to vote for the 'None of the Above' option, and it gave its own interpretation of what such a vote would mean; increased and guaranteed autonomy in internal affairs, the right to seek membership of international organizations, continued citizenship of the US and full Federal social benefits for Puerto Ricans. Just

---

[327] The deadlock between these options could have been resolved by a provision that if none of the options gained an absolute majority, a second round should decide which of the two most popular options should be declared the winner. Such a provision has been included in referendum ordinances in the Netherlands Antilles.

[328] The bill was passed by 209 to 208 votes (*The New York Times*, 5 March 1998). President Clinton hailed the vote as 'victory for democracy and against exclusion.' *See* David Briscoe, 'House Votes to Allow Puerto Rico Referendum' (article for the Associated Press, 5 March 1998).

over 50 per cent of the votes went to 'None of the Above', and just over 46 per cent to statehood.[329] This result of course did not resolve the stalemate on the status issue, but it did reveal that the population is not happy with the current status of the island. Only 0.1 per cent voted for the status quo 'commonwealth' option, and the turn-out of 75 per cent showed that the issue is considered important by Puerto Ricans. In spite of this, the US merely took note of the outcome.

Conclusion

Puerto Rico has a considerable amount of internal autonomy and self-government, although it is certainly smaller than that of the recognized examples of free association discussed *above*. It is unclear to what extent Puerto Rico's autonomy is protected against interference by the US Congress. It is also unclear whether the US could unilaterally change the status of Puerto Rico, although it seems unlikely that Congress would attempt to do so.

The current status of Puerto Rico does not comply with the norms for free association or integration as defined by the UN. The GA Resolution of 1953 which declared that the US no longer needed to report under Article 73(e) was circumvented by the Decolonization Committee, on the basis of the reasoning that the Declaration on the Granting of Independence (Resolution 1514) still applied. Cuba's campaign to have Puerto Rico re-introduced to the list of territories to which the Declaration applies was not fully successful because of a powerful diplomatic effort by the US. Many political parties on Puerto Rico have supported Cuba's campaign, and even Puerto Rico's Governor has testified before the Decolonization Committee that the territory's relationship with the US retains elements of colonial rule.

The involvement of the UN has stimulated various initiatives from the US President and Congress to develop Puerto Rico's status into something that could be called a full measure of self-government. Two main directions are supported, both in the US and in Puerto Rico; integration with the US as the 51st state, or transforming the commonwealth status into a free association that complies with Resolution 1541. Internal dissensions, both in the US and in Puerto Rico, have frustrated these initiatives. No clear path for the future is

---

[329] In more detail: 50.2 per cent of the voters chose the option 'None of the Above', 46.5 per cent voted for statehood, 2.5 per cent for independence, 0.3 per cent for free association, and 0.1 per cent for 'commonwealth', as defined on the ballot. Governor Roselló interpreted the results as a victory for statehood, as none of the other defined options had attracted nearly as much votes. He saw the vote for 'None of the Above' as an expression of discontent with his internal policies, and not as a vote against statehood.

visible, since neither the Puerto Rican population nor the US Congress seem to be able to make a clear choice for integration or free association. A stalemate has continued for many years now, in spite of the fact that the 1998 plebiscite resulted in only 0.1 per cent of the votes for the option of retaining the *status quo*.

The UN has not played a very helpful role in resolving the status issue of Puerto Rico. Its acknowledgment in 1953 of the commonwealth as a full measure of self-government, and the process instigated by Public Law 600 as an exercise of the right to self-determination, satisfied the US that no further steps were necessary to develop the commonwealth into a truly self-governing unit. The unwillingness of the GA to apply its own standards for decolonization to Puerto Rico or to even discuss the issue of Puerto Rico during any of its subsequent sessions has also not fostered respect for those standards. This passive attitude of the GA must be explained by the considerable political support the US can still muster in the GA in times of need. The attitude of the GA towards Puerto Rico 'depends less on what the United States does in Puerto Rico than on its policies elsewhere, particularly in Latin America.'[330] The Decolonization Committee's actions with respect to Puerto Rico did convince the US government during the 1970s that Puerto Rico's status was a problem that needed attention, but the radical anti-colonialism of the Committee discredited it in the eyes of the US as a platform for discussing the issue of the status of Puerto Rico.

3.4.2   New Caledonia

The French policies of decolonization were quite different from those of the Netherlands and the English-speaking colonial powers. Instead of gradually devolving powers to the colonies in preparation for independence, France attempted to assimilate its overseas territories. After World War II, France retained its full legislative and administrative powers in most of its overseas territories, and granted the populations of these territories French nationality and the right to vote in French elections.[331] France's attitude was also different in that it adamantly refused any sort of UN involvement in the process of decolonization. This did not mean, however, that France has not been prepared to recognize a right to self-determination of its overseas territories, but this right is considered to be guaranteed by municipal law, more specifically, the French Constitution.

---

[330] Carr 1984, p. 364.
[331] Aldrich 1993, p. 159 et seq.

The French legal debate on the self-determination of the overseas peoples has focussed on French municipal law, and largely ignores the existence of the international law of self-determination, or denies its application to the French overseas territories.[332] One of the reasons for this might be the argument that the French overseas territories have all become integrated with France, and therefore no longer possess a separate right to self-determination. The overseas departments (DOM) are fully integrated with France, and the other territories were given a one-time option to choose another status in 1958, after which the Republic became indivisible.[333]

In the cases of French Somaliland, the Comoros and New Caledonia, this argument was summarily rejected by the GA, with no state except France speaking in defence of this interpretation. If one assumes that the GA is the final authority in determining whether a territory has achieved a full measure of self-government (*see* chapter 2), then its decisions on the French overseas terri-

---

[332] *See for instance* Pimont 1992, who in his paragraph on the self-determination of New Caledonia pays no attention to international law. Similarly, Maestre 1976 on the question of the self-determination of the TOMs entirely ignores international law. Autin 1997 mentions the UN Charter (on p. 265), and Dormoy 1997 briefly outlines the international right to self-determination and its application to New Caledonia (similarly Breillat 1993, p. 15). Gohin 1997, p. 72 considers that the international law of decolonization did not apply to the Comoros (nor presumably to the other TOMs), because the islands were decolonized in 1946, and the population became part of the people of France in 1959. *See also* Agniel 1997. Goesel-Le Bihan 1998 is an exception in that she discusses the Nouméa Accord with extensive reference to foreign examples and UN developments. Dormoy 1997 is the only French author (as far as I know) who refers to the decisions of the GA and the Decolonization Committee to reach the conclusion that the TOMs have a right to self-determination, including the right to choose independence, free association or integration.

[333] France put the Constitution of 1958 to a referendum in all of the overseas territories. All of the territories voted 'yes', except the West African territory of Guinea. France transferred sovereignty to Guinea only two days after the referendum, on 30 September, *see* Maestre 1976, p. 434. The Territorial Assemblies of the remaining *territoires d'outre-mer* (TOM) now had the option under Article 76 of the Constitution to choose, within four months after the promulgation of the Constitution, to become DOM, remain TOM, or become a member state of the new *Communauté*, which was a construction similar to the Dutch Kingdom order. Autin 1997, pp. 269-70, and Breillat 1993, pp. 6-9, describe this unsuccessful adventure of France into the realm of federalism. All of the larger African TOMs chose to become members of this new construction and quickly thereafter chose full independence. The smaller TOMs remained TOM, after which the French Republic became indivisible again. The French Prime Minister confirmed in 1959 that the transformation of DOMs or TOMs into member states of the *Communauté* or independent states was not constitutionally possible, *see* Maestre 1976, pp. 435-6. Secession from the Republic would require amending the Constitution, *see* Maestre 1976, p. 455 et seq. Some authors therefore considered the referendums on self-determination that were held in several TOMs and in Algeria after 1960 as unconstitutional, because they threatened the indivisibility of the Republic. *Maestre* even considers De Gaulle's offer of self-determination to Algeria in 1959 clearly contrary to the Constitution because the President is charged with guaranteeing the integrity of the territory of France (p. 455).

tories mean that their status does not qualify as a form of self-government under Chapter XI of the Charter, and that these territories have remained NSGTs. If this is correct, then the peoples of these territories do have an internationally guaranteed right to self-determination and decolonization.

The French government has consistently opposed this view, and it is hardly supported in the French legal literature. The French *Conseil Constitutionnel* considers that the TOMs have a right to self-determination, and that their populations constitute separate peoples from the people of France, but this conclusion was derived from the preamble and Article 53 of the Constitution, and not from international law. The *Conseil Constitutionnel* confirmed in a decision on Mayotte in 2000 that France is not bound by a choice of the population of a territory for a form of 'statutory evolution' short of independence, even though the *Conseil* does consider such a choice as an exercise of the right to self-determination.[334] It could be argued that French constitutional law is thus in conflict with international law, at least potentially, as it gives the French government the right to ignore the wishes of the overseas populations on their political status.

Article 72-4 of the Constitution, which was recently introduced, recognizes that it is possible for an overseas territory to change its status. The new status needs to be approved by a referendum in the territory, and by the French legislator. The initiative for such a status changes lies with Paris, according to Article 72-4. The Article has already been applied in Saint-Martin and Saint-Barthélémy, two islands that are part of the *département d'outre-mer* Guadeloupe. The islanders were offered a choice between remaining part of Guadeloupe or becoming separate *collectivités d'outre-mer*. A large majority of the voters in 2004 chose to be separated from the main island, a choice that France announced it would respect.[335]

---

[334] Décision 2000-428 DC of 4 May 2000. Since 1966, the French government and a majority of the French legal writers consider that the secession of an overseas territory (not being a DOM) is possible under Article 53 of the French Constitution, which provides (*inter alia*) that '*Nulle cession, nul échange, nulle adjonction de territoire n'est valable sans le consentement des populations intéressées.*' According to such authors as *Capitant*, *Luchaire* and *Prélot*, this provision also applies when an overseas territory expresses the wish to secede from the Republic (cited in Maestre 1976). Such a secession is constitutionally possible if the population of the territory agrees to it (preferably in a referendum) and the French legislator also approves of it, because para. 1 of Article 53 provides that the transfer of territory should be approved by law (cited in Maestre 1976, pp. 444-5). *See also* Pimont 1992, pp. 1689-96. *Maestre* considered that this so-called 'doctrine Capitant' involved an acrobatic interpretation of Article 53, but it was applied by the French Government in the cases of French Somaliland, the Comoros, and to some extent in New Caledonia. It is considered not to apply to the DOMs, although it has been argued in the French parliament that any territory, including the *départements* of metropolitan France, could use it to become independent (Maestre 1976, p. 447).

[335] The French government would, however, oppose the creation '*de "paradis fiscaux" comme il en existe dans la partie hollandaise de Saint-Martin*' (*Libération*, 8 December 2003). For the

French government practice has recognized to an increasing extent the freedom of the overseas populations to choose between different status options.
France has been prepared to discuss all sorts of status changes when the representatives of the departments or territories requested it, or when international
pressure mounted. This attitude led to the independence of some TOMs, with
Mayotte remaining a French *collectivité d'outre-mer*, to Wallis and Futuna becoming a TOM, and to the widening of French Polynesia's and New Caledonia's
autonomy during the 1990s. France has also campaigned for an addition to the
EU draft Constitution which makes it easier for an overseas territory to change
its relationship with the EU.[336]

A striking element of French practice is the readiness to organize a plebiscite almost as soon as dissatisfaction appears to exist in a territory. In this
respect, the French approach is entirely different from that of the UK and the
Netherlands. On the other hand, the French plebiscites usually offer very few
options. Often, the question put to the electorate has been: 'independence, yes
or no?', with a vote for 'no' being interpreted as a vote for unlimited French
control. France has also been accused of manipulating the outcome of referendums by an unwarranted limitation or widening of the franchise, or by tamper-
ing with the electoral districts. The process of decolonization in the French
TOMs has revolved to an exceptionally large extent around the issue of the
right to vote in referendums. French policies in this respect have not been consistent, except in the sense that only the *'populations intéressées'* should have
the right to vote.[337] It is also remarkable that almost none of these numerous
plebiscites were ever observed, assisted or supervised by the UN or other international organizations.[338]

It may be concluded, therefore, that even though French legal thought does
not generally recognize the application of the international law of self-determination and decolonization to the French overseas territories, French municipal
law and practice does at present recognize the principle of the freedom of choice
of the overseas populations, but the exercise of that freedom is still subject to
approval by the French legislator.

---

genesis of the new status, *see Saint-Martin: Objectif Statut. Repères pour l'Espoir. Recueil d'Études
sur l'Évolution Statutaire de Saint-Martin*, St Maarten: House of Nehesi 2002.

[336] *See* chapter 9.

[337] Pimont 1992, p. 1693, deplores the fact that France has not developed a consistent policy
with regard to plebiscites. He cites a number of different criteria used through the years, and
concludes that France has been led by local political conditions, instead of principles. Chenal
1976 thinks French policy *has* been consistent, in the sense that it always served short-term
French political interests.

[338] The 1977 referendum in French Somaliland is probably the only French referendum to be
observed by a UN visiting mission. At that time, France was eager to grant independence to the
territory, which probably explained its cooperative attitude.

Background of the Conflict[339]

The recent history of New Caledonia is characterized by bloody conflicts between the 'Kanaks', descendants of the indigenous Melanesian population, and the European French 'Caldoches', who started to arrive in the territory after France annexed it in 1853. The French colonial government concentrated the Kanak clans on arid and uncultivable areas, while the Caldoche settlers obtained ownership of most of the land.[340] Manual labour was imported from other Pacific and Asian countries, and through the establishment of a penal settlement.

New Caledonia's nickel deposits are estimated to be 25 per cent of the world reserves. Because of the growing importance of nickel, and the wish to maintain a strong French presence east of Suez, France remained very attached to New Caledonia after the Second World War. French workers were encouraged to move to New Caledonia and migration by English-speaking people was discouraged.[341] The mainly francophone immigrants have consistently supported the continuation of French sovereignty over the islands.[342]

French policies have led to the disfranchisement of the Kanak population, which, apart from becoming a minority, also do not participate substantially in the major economic activities in the territory, which are controlled by European French companies and Caldoche landowners.[343]

As a *territoire d'outre-mer* (TOM), New Caledonia remained under the legislative and administrative control of France (and its Governors, who were

---

[339] New Caledonia is located in the South Pacific, 1700 kilometres north of New Zealand and 1500 kilometres east of Australia. Its other neighbours are Vanuatu (formerly the condominium of the New Hebrides) and Fiji. Its area is 19,000 km^2 (consisting of the island of Grande Terre and the small Loyalty Islands), which is almost 25 times the area of the Netherlands Antilles, but its population is the same in size, approximately 215,000 (2002, estimate). The population consists of 43 per cent Kanaks, 37 per cent French settlers (called Caldoches), and 20 per cent immigrants from several Pacific and Asian countries. According to the *CIA World Factbook* of 2003, New Caledonia has a higher GDP per capita than any of the independent Pacific states that campaigned for its re-inscription as a NSGT, except New Zealand and Australia. Its estimated GDP per capita in 2002 (US\$ 14,000) is comparable to that of the Netherlands Antilles (US\$ 11,400), but three times higher than that of Fiji (US\$ 4,800) and eight times higher than that of the Solomon Islands (US\$ 1,700).

[340] Berman 1998, pp. 294-9.

[341] Requests by the governments of Tonga, the Gilbert and Ellice Islands, and Fiji for their citizens to be allowed to work in the nickel mining industry were denied. *See* Connell 1987, p. 217.

[342] *See* the chapter entitled 'The politics of population' in Connell 1987, p. 210 et seq. for figures and French policy statements. *See also* the statement of Papua New Guinea, GAOR (41), Plenary Meetings, 91st Meeting, pp. 9-11.

[343] Connell 1987, p. 122 et seq.

later called High Commissioners), until the 1980s.[344] The French socialist government elected in 1981 denounced 'the colonial character of New Caledonia',[345] but its attempts to increase local autonomy were overshadowed by the ethnic violence that erupted at this time. The Kanaks started to boycott elections and referendums, and sought support for their cause with the independent Pacific states, with international organizations such as the South Pacific Forum and the Non-Aligned Movement, and in fact with anyone that would offer support. Ultimately, this would lead to the re-listing of New Caledonia as a NSGT.

UN Involvement

In 1946, France decided to stop transmitting information under Article 73(e) on a number of territories, among them New Caledonia.[346] France never cooperated with the Decolonization Committee or its predecessors. It consistently defended a very restrictive interpretation of the UN's mandate on issues of decolonization, which repeatedly put it in an isolated position when its territories were discussed. Combined with its unwillingness to grant the TOMs an irrevocable form of self-government, this led to some of the TOMs being re-listed as NSGTs by the GA during the 1960s and 1970s.[347]

The Kanak independence movement started petitioning the Decolonization Committee in 1975, but initially without any success.[348] The Melanesian members of the South Pacific Forum[349] had been susceptible to the Kanak complaints since the 1970s. From 1980, when the group was reinforced by the

---

[344] Agniel 1997, p. 55.

[345] Aldrich 1993, p. 241 reports the words of the French Secretary of State for the DOM-TOMs in 1981.

[346] For this decision, and the UN response, *see above* in the paragraph on the integration of the French DOMs.

[347] For the case of French Somaliland (currently Djibouti), which was re-listed through GA Res. 2228 (XXI) of 1966, *see* Chenal 1976 and Franck & Hoffman 1976. The Comoros were re-listed as an NSGT by GA Res. 3161 (XXVIII) of 1973. The organization Pacific Action and an independence party in Te Ao Maohi (French Polynesia) have been pleading with the South Pacific Forum and other organizations in recent years to gain support for the re-inscription of 'French-occupied Polynesia' (as well as Ka Pae'Aina (Hawaii) and West Papua) on the list of NSGTs, *see* the website of Pacific Action at <http://www.planet.org.nz/pacific_action/action/tahitipet.html> (visited on 4 February 2004).

[348] Kircher 1986, p. 8.

[349] The South Pacific Forum was founded in 1971 and renamed the Pacific Islands Forum in 1999. It is the most important regional organization of the Pacific, and meets annually for the purpose of discussing joint political action and economic co-operation. In 1986, it counted 13 members. Seven were members of the UN (Australia, New Zealand, Fiji, Papua New Guinea, Samoa, Solomon Islands and Vanuatu), the other six were the Cook Islands, Niue, Nauru, Tonga, Tuvalu, and Kiribati.

independence of Vanuatu, these states started to lobby at the UN to have New Caledonia re-inscribed on the list of territories to which GA Resolution 1514 (XV) applies, and to have the GA declare that New Caledonia was still a NSGT.[350] The other members of the South Pacific Forum found it more important to maintain good relations with France, and were hopeful that the French government would implement changes in the government of the territory.[351] Fiji, New Zealand and Australia were not inclined to jeopardize their trade relations with the European Community and many Pacific countries saw France as an ally against possible Soviet influence in the region.[352] It was also feared that France would be able to block an attempt to classify New Caledonia as a NSGT, which would damage the Kanak cause.[353]

After the French elections of 1986, in which the troubles in New Caledonia were an issue, the right-wing alliance led by Jacques Chirac won a majority in the National Assembly. A new policy towards New Caledonia was instituted, which was clearly pro-Caldoche.[354] It was announced that a referendum would be held in 1987 on the question of whether New Caledonia should become independent.[355] The franchise for the referendum would be based on the same rules that applied in elections, which meant that all French citizens with domicile in New Caledonia, or who had resided for six months in the territory, were allowed to vote. Based on this franchise, a victory for the independence movement would be highly unlikely.

---

[350] These Melanesian states were Papua New Guinea, Vanuatu and the Solomon Islands. Fiji, which has a partly Melanesian population, did not actively support the Kanak movement for independence. Australia and Fiji were members of the Decolonization Committee when Papua New Guinea made its first requests, but did not take action (*see* Connell 1987, p. 398).

[351] *See for instance* the statements by Fiji and New Zealand in the GA of 1986, in which they explained why they had not brought the issue before the UN earlier (GAOR 41, Plenary Meetings, 90th and 91st Meetings).

[352] Connell 1987, p. 385 et seq. and p. 398 claims that these possible motives to support France were not strong, but did lead to a cautious attitude, even with Vanuatu, the strongest supporter of Kanak independence.

[353] The Australian Foreign Minister, Bill Hayden, stated at a press conference in 1985 that: 'France is in a position to call up quite a lot of IOUs at the United Nations, including from Third World countries, most particularly in Black Africa.' (cited in Connell 1987, p. 398).

[354] The authority of the French High Commissioner was increased, and the funds of the regional councils, some of which were controlled by Kanak majorities, were frozen, while the authority of the territorial congress, controlled by the Caldoches, was increased. More French troops were brought in, which started to patrol the Kanak regions (Aldrich 1993, p. 249 et seq. and Aldrich & Connell 1992, p. 222 et seq).

[355] The Socialist government had developed a plan in 1984 to hold a referendum in which a choice would be offered between independence, increased autonomy, or maintaining the status quo. In 1985, this was changed into a referendum with two options: a simple yes or no against a form of free association with France.

All of the members of the South Pacific Forum had now become convinced that international pressure on France should be increased, also because of the sinking of the *Rainbow Warrior* and nuclear testing in French Polynesia.[356] In August 1986, they unanimously[357] decided to request the Decolonization Committee to recommend to the GA the re-inscription of New Caledonia, 'to ensure regular review by the United Nations of the Territory's progress towards self-government and independence.'[358]

Debate at the UN

The Decolonization Committee decided to postpone discussion of the issue to the next session,[359] but to the surprise and dismay of some of the members of the Committee, the South Pacific states were not prepared to have the issue simmer on the backburners of the working groups and the sub-committees for years to come, as was the practice of the Committee. The South Pacific states simply brought up the question of New Caledonia in the plenary debate on the implementation of the Declaration on the Granting of Independence, bypassing the Fourth Committee on the way.[360]

The South Pacific states claimed that New Caledonia had always remained a NSGT, even though France had ceased to report on it in 1947. The GA had never explicitly approved this French decision, which meant that the obligations of Article 73 were still in force with respect to New Caledonia, it was stated. As an overseas territory that was culturally, historically and ethnically different from the metropolis, *prima facie* there existed an obligation to transmit information. This assumption was confirmed by the constitutional history of New Caledonia, which showed a consistent status of subordination to Paris. The South Pacific states concluded that under Principles IV and V of Resolu-

---

[356] Connell 1987, pp. 398-9.

[357] The Cook Islands abstained from the vote.

[358] GAOR 41st Session, Supplement No. 23 (A/41/23), Annex I, p. 53 et seq.

[359] GAOR 41st Session, Supplement No. 23 (A/41/23), para. 41-42. Earlier requests by Papua New Guinea to put the issue on the agenda of the Committee had been treated similarly.

[360] A number of states uttered their misgivings about this unprecedented promptness of action, which had also been inspired by the support of the NAM, which in September of that year, announced that it 'welcomed and supported the decision by the members of the South Pacific Forum (...) to seek the re-inscription of New Caledonia (...) and strongly urged the forty-first session of the United Nations General Assembly to re-inscribe New Caledonia on the list of Non-Self-Governing Territories.' *See* the Conclusions of the Eighth Conference of Heads of State or Government of Non-Aligned Countries in Harare, in September of 1986 (UN Doc. A/41/697, p. 75, para. 150, and p. 76, para. 151). The Commonwealth Heads of Government meeting 'stressed the need to secure the early independence of New Caledonia' (UN Doc. A/40/817, p. 15, para. 31).

tion 1541, New Caledonia was still a NSGT and 'continues a colonial relation with France.'[361]

With some feeling for drama, Fiji posed a question to the representatives:

> Do they [the representatives] believe that a European Power, a colonial Power, has the right in today's world to decide the future of people 20,000 kilometres away, under conditions worked out by that colonial Power alone? Or do they believe that the people of New Caledonia have the right to a proper act of self-determination, in accordance with the normal processes of the United Nations?[362]

A number of states tried to apply Resolution 1541, but none found it necessary to discuss whether Principles VIII and IX (on integration) applied, either because they thought the territory was clearly not integrated with France,[363] or because they thought integration was not a valid method of decolonization in the first place.[364]

New Zealand discussed at some length why it thought the situation represented a form of 'arbitrary subordination' in the sense of Principle V of Resolution 1541. New Zealand referred to the pre-eminent position that France had maintained throughout all of the changes in the administration of the territory, and especially in the fact that France had retained the right 'to promulgate arbitrary change', which it had used it in 1986 to abolish the devolutionary reforms implemented by the previous French government. 'No consultation; no agreement; a simple display of power', according to the representative of New Zealand.[365]

---

[361] A background paper was circulated among the UN members, which is annexed to a letter dated 2 October 1986 from the permanent representative of Fiji to the Secretary-General (UN Doc. A/41/668).

[362] GAOR (41), Plenary, 92nd Meeting, p. 56.

[363] Thailand considered Principle V applied because 'New Caledonia has not relinquished its status of dependency to France' (91st Meeting, p. 93). Ghana also called New Caledonia a dependency of France (92nd Meeting, p. 51). The Solomon Islands also limited its analysis to Principles IV and V, and simply stated that New Caledonia had been 'under colonial control and domination for 133 years' (92nd Meeting, p. 7). New Zealand also considered that Principle V 'was the crux of the matter.'

[364] Australia stated: 'France … used to maintain that about Algeria too. We all know that in 1986 this attitude seeks to perpetuate a myth and to sustain a legal fiction – a myth and a fiction which future historians may find as bemusing as King Canute's attempt to stem the oncoming tide. France cannot indefinitely resist, in New Caledonia, the wave of decolonization which has already washed over most of this earth.' (90th Meeting, p. 43). Curiously, Australia had only two years earlier decolonized its last NSGT, the Cocos (Keeling) Islands, through integration, with the unanimous approval of the UN (*see above*). A statement by Ghana also showed some evidence of a selective memory: 'The present claim that the Territory is part of metropolitan France is one of those peculiar postures which France takes when it comes to its own colonial Territories but which has no basis in international law or United Nations practice.' (92nd Meeting, p. 48).

[365] 92nd Meeting, p. 27.

France also used Resolution 1541, but it argued that New Caledonia was not a NSGT, because it was fully integrated with metropolitan France. Its inhabitants were French citizens and enjoyed 'fully the rights and freedoms attached to that status.' They participated in the elections for the president of France and had 'the same representation in Parliament as all other citizens.'

Fiji responded that French citizenship and the right to vote in French elections did not necessarily mean that the territory was integrated with France. Fiji referred to the situation in the French West-African territories before 1958, when those territories had representatives in the French parliament, but France nonetheless considered them NSGTs. New Zealand added another argument against the French position. The status of New Caledonia had remained one of 'arbitrary subordination' because the regional organs of New Caledonia held their authority 'only at the pleasure of Paris.'[366] The French Constitution in 1986 indeed did not contain any real checks on the power of the French legislature to change the status of New Caledonia as it saw fit, but it would seem to me that this is an inherent characteristic of the status of integrated territories. The GA, however, chose to view New Caledonia as not integrated into France at all.[367]

Should the status of New Caledonia be seen as compatible with the criteria for integration? The status of the population was not entirely the same as that of the metropolitan French, because many French laws did not apply in the TOMs, and these territories certainly were not as integrated with France as the DOMs. Since France is not a federal state, it could easily be argued that the integration of New Caledonia was incomplete, but whether it did not comply with Resolution 1541 is hard to say. The criteria for integration are rather vague and the GA did not attempt to make them more precise in the case of New Caledonia. Perhaps a conclusion could be drawn that a constitutional arrangement that places an overseas population in a substantially different position from the metropolitan population authorizes the UN to discuss the situation and declare that Resolutions 1514 and 1541 still apply. But a number of other factors obviously influenced the decision of the GA as well; firstly, the apparent repression of an indigenous non-white population, which had a long history of disfranchisement, and secondly, France was very unpopular in the region for its nuclear tests in Polynesia.

In view of the attitude of the vast majority of the GA, any arguments France could put forth in its defence were really immaterial. The French representa-

---

[366] 92nd Meeting, p. 27.

[367] Article 74 of the Constitution provided that the TOMs had their own particular organization *'tenant compte de leurs intérêts propres dans l'ensemble des intérêts de la République.'* The organization of the government in the TOMs was determined by an organic law, which was not adopted until after the local parliaments had been consulted.

tive nonetheless gave it a try. He stated that the Caledonians had the right to secede from France, if they so desired, but the representative organs of the territory had never expressed such a wish. France considered that the Pacific states distorted the principle of self-determination, because they wanted New Caledonia to become independent, even though the population did not want this. The Pacific states were attempting to force France to organize 'a slanted referendum whose outcome would be determined in advance.'[368] By insisting that only the Kanaks had the right to determine the future of New Caledonia, the Melanesian states had introduced 'a novel principle: "two men, one vote", which if applied to Australia or the US would mean that there were very few Australians or Americans.'[369] According to Australia, the franchise should be concentrated in the hands of those who have a long-term residence in, and a commitment to, New Caledonia.[370] France probably took this criticism to heart, because in 1988 it agreed with the Kanaks and Caldoches that the franchise for future referendums would be strictly limited to those persons with long-term residence in the territory, or strong historical ties to it (*see below*).

The GA adopted a resolution that declared New Caledonia was still a NSGT and that France should report on it.[371] The Netherlands explained its negative

---

[368] This reproach was perhaps justified with respect to Papua New Guinea, Vanuatu and the Solomon Islands. In the communiqué that these states had issued earlier, they had declared that 'the referendum scheduled for mid-1987 ... should lead to independence' and that only the Kanaks should have the right to vote. The representative of the Solomon Islands stated in the GA that France should make it possible 'to hold a fair and just referendum to decide on New Caledonia's future independent status' (92nd Meeting, p. 8). One might wonder how such a referendum could be relevant if New Caledonia was to become independent anyway. *Islam* writes that the non-Kanak population of New Caledonia does not come 'within the perview [*sic*] of "dependent peoples" of "territories which have not yet attained independence"' in the sense of GA Res. 1514. The colonial peoples do not include 'citizens of the colonisers and other independent States.' This does not mean that these persons would not have the right to become citizens of an independent New Caledonia, but 'the right of the Kanaks to colonial self-determination and the right of the settlers and their descendants to be citizens of independent New Caledonia are not the same but somewhat different and there need not be any conflict between these two rights' (*see* Islam 1989, p. 20). This attitude towards settlers of Western descent can also be found in other Pacific territories such as Hawaii (*see above*). It denies the legitimate rights of people who have lived in the islands for a long time, and in some cases even descend from settlers who arrived in the islands during the nineteenth century.

[369] 91st Meeting, pp. 60-9. Papua New Guinea and Vanuatu had issued a communiqué earlier that year in which they had declared that only the Kanaks should have the right to vote in the referendum. When confronted by France with this statement, they did not wish to repeat it, but Vanuatu stated that 'the colonized people of New Caledonia, the Kanaks, are not French.' (91st Meeting, p. 138).

[370] 90th Meeting, p. 47. Zimbabwe considered that only the 'colonized' should have the right to vote. People 'without roots or permanence in the territory cannot be included among the colonized.' (91st Meeting, p. 108).

[371] The resolution was adopted by 89 votes to 24, with 34 abstentions as GA Res. 41/41 A. The negative votes came from most of France's neighbours in Europe (including the Nether-

vote by stating that it considered UN action premature. It favoured waiting for the recommendations of the Decolonization Committee and 'had no reason to doubt that France will ensure that [the] referendum is held in a free and democratic manner.'[372] This statement seemed to imply that the Decolonization Committee was allowed to discuss the issue. Canada explained its abstention by stating that it would only seek to compel a state to transmit information if there was 'sufficient evidence that the administering Power was seeking actively to frustrate or deny self-determination.' It trusted that France would actively seek to ensure that the act of self-determination scheduled for 1987 would provide 'a meaningful and representative basis for determining the course of New Caledonia's future political process.'[373]

France did not take the GA decision lightly.[374] It expelled the Australian Consul-General from New Caledonia, and briefly broke off ministerial contacts with Australia.[375] Development aid was reduced for the countries that supported Kanak independence (and opposed French nuclear testing), whereas aid to the Cook Islands was increased, because it generally supported the French presence in the Pacific.[376]

Subsequent UN Involvement

In the GA debate, New Zealand and Australia had pointed out to France that the UN involvement with their own NSGTs in the Pacific had been beneficial.

---

lands), nine of its former colonies, and seven other small Third World states. Most of the Western states (including the US and the UK) abstained, as did a number of Arab, African and Caribbean states (92nd Meeting, p. 76).

[372] 93rd Meeting, p. 7.
[373] 93rd Meeting, pp. 2-3.
[374] Many of the Pacific states also noted 'with dismay the reports that many Governments have been subjected to economic and political pressure to keep them from doing what is right.' (statement by Papua New Guinea, 91st Meeting, p. 12). *See also* the statement by the Solomon Islands, 92nd Meeting, p. 16. The representative of Vanuatu stated that: 'Many of us have been pressured in ways never previously experienced, none more so than Vanuatu. In some instances, those pressures have been so great as to constitute nothing less than threats. Some of us have been reminded of our economic vulnerabilities. Some of us have been the recipients of rather unusual proposals and propositions.' (92nd Meeting, p. 39). *See also* the statements by Samoa (91st Meeting, p. 31), and the Solomon Islands (92nd Meeting, p. 39). Aldrich & Connell 1992, p. 224, state that the French campaign was aimed particularly at Australia, which was possibly threatened that its policies towards the indigenous Australians would be attacked by France in retaliation for its support of the Kanaks. In the GA debate it was stated that France had also threatened to take economic measures against certain states. It seems France had already uttered such threats in 1981, when it urged Fiji to use its influence in the South Pacific Forum to the benefit of the French presence in the Pacific, because Fiji sold sugar to the European Community based on the Lomé agreement (*see* Connell 1987, p. 396).
[375] Berman 1998, p. 322, note 202.
[376] Aldrich & Connell 1992, p. 224.

New Zealand stated that it had found the contributions of the UN had always been positive, helpful, and often conciliatory, providing 'sensible and often imaginative advice to all concerned.' It commended the thought to France that 'there is a place in the resolution of most conflicts for an impartial third party.' 'We thus ask no more of France than we have been prepared to do ourselves.'[377] New Zealand and Australia criticized France's consistent refusal to participate in any of the work of the Decolonization Committee or to allow UN visiting missions into its territories, and its refusal to supply information or attend hearings on French Somaliland after that territory had been declared a NSGT.[378] Ghana reminded the GA that by not providing any information on New Caledonia to the UN and by not allowing visiting missions, France made it impossible for the UN to determine whether the territory had attained a full measure of self-government.[379]

France has remained opposed to UN involvement with New Caledonia.[380] It has also refused to transmit information under Article 73(e). It does, however, annually provide the Secretary-General with information on New Caledonia, and it explains its policies with regard to New Caledonia in the Fourth Committee and it maintains informal contacts with the Decolonization Committee.[381] The Nouméa Accord of 1998 (*see below*) provides that the UN 'will be advised that New Caledonia's emancipation is under way.'[382] France still does not cooperate with the Decolonization Committee formally, but it sent an observer to the Pacific Regional Seminar of the Committee in 2002 and 2004.[383]

The Decolonization Committee, since 1986, has reviewed the situation in New Caledonia annually, heard petitioners from the territory, and drafted resolutions (always adopted by the GA) which have become increasingly detailed, outlining which developments in the territory are positive and which 'merit concern.'[384] The international criticism has become less severe since France,

---

[377] 92nd Meeting, pp. 18-20.

[378] 91st Meeting, p. 128 (New Zealand) and p. 133 (Australia).

[379] 92nd Meeting, p. 52.

[380] Berman 1998, p. 331.

[381] Goesel-Le Bihan 1998, pp. 28-9.

[382] Para. 3.2.1 of the Nouméa Accord. Goesel-Bihan 1998 pp. 55-6 sees this as an example of where France through constitutional processes has taken on an obligation that it has consistently opposed internationally. Another example is found in para. 5 of the Accord, where it is laid down that New Caledonia can only achieve independence as a whole, even though France has never accepted that it is obliged to respect the principle of *uti possidetis* when granting independence to a colony.

[383] UN Doc. A/AC.109/2003/7, para. 47.

[384] *See for instance* GA Res. 58/106 of December 2003, which has a preamble of 6 paragraphs, followed by 16 operative paragraphs, which note, for instance, the positive developments in mapping the marine resources within the economic zone of New Caledonia.

the Caldoches and the Kanaks signed agreements on the process of self-determination in 1988 and 1998.[385] A representative of the Kanak FLNKS stated at the Pacific Regional Seminar of 2002 that the close attention of the UN to the decolonization process has been 'a determining factor in the struggle of the indigenous people for freedom and independence.'[386]

The Nouméa Accord: A Procedure for Future Self-Determination

In 1998 a broad agreement on the future of New Caledonia was signed by France and representatives of the Kanaks and Caldoches, the Nouméa Accord.[387] It provides for a gradual development towards independence or free association with France, the decision on which is postponed. Between 2013 and 2018 a referendum is to be held in which the New Caledonians can choose between free association, independence or *status quo*. If the electorate should vote for *status quo*, two further referendums could be held on the same question.[388]

The Nouméa Accord was approved in a plebiscite in New Caledonia, and the French Constitution was changed to include a chapter devoted specifically to the territory (which was renamed a *pays d'outre-mer*).[389] It provides that France will delegate '*de façon définitive*' a number of powers to New Caledonia. It does not state which powers they are, nor in what way the delegation should become 'definitive.' But the preamble to the Nouméa Accord states that the delegated powers may not revert to France, 'reflecting the principle of irreversibility governing these arrangements.'[390] It must be assumed that France is

---

[385] Berman 1998, p. 331.

[386] Statement by the representative of the FLNKS during the Pacific Regional Seminar organized by the Decolonization Committee in 2002, *see* the Working Paper prepared by the Secretariat on New Caledonia (26 March 2003), UN Doc. A/AC.109/2003/7, para. 49. The case of New Caledonia appears to have inspired people and organizations from other Pacific territories to attempt to have their territories inscribed as NSGTs as well. Searching the internet for 'list non-self-governing territories' in combination with names of Pacific dependent territories such as Wallis and Futuna, Hawaii, French Polynesia, Bougainville, Easter Island or Alaska reveals many examples of such attempts, which generally appear to be inspired by alleged violations of indigenous rights. The UN records do not as yet indicate that the Decolonization Committee is willing to take up any of these cases, nor has the South Pacific Forum been prepared to support their cause in the way it supported the Kanaks.

[387] The text of this agreement is reproduced in UN Doc. A/AC.109/2114, annex.

[388] Para. 5 of the Nouméa Accord. This paragraph also stipulates that New Caledonia can only achieve independence as a whole, and that the results of the referendum(s) will be considered as a whole, and not by province. This provision appears to be inspired by the situation in the Comoros

[389] The amendment to the Constitution was approved by the *Congrès de la République* by 827 votes to 31, with 27 abstentions (*see* Goesel-Le Bihan 1998, p. 30).

[390] Para. 5 of the preamble of the Nouméa Accord. The translation used here is an 'informal translation' by the Pacific Community translation services, made available through the web site of the French embassy in Australia (<www.ambafrance-au.org>).

bound by this agreement, and that the autonomy of New Caledonia can no longer be retracted unilaterally by France. The Nouméa Accord also provides that if the New Caledonians do not vote in favour of devolution (free association) or independence in the referendum(s) of 2013–2018, the political organization set up by the Nouméa Accord will remain in force without there being any possibility of reversal, and this irreversibility will then be guaranteed by the Constitution.[391]

The new relations with New Caledonia are regulated by a French organic law,[392] which grants the *pays* the authority to promulgate 'laws of the country' ('*lois du pays*') which have the full force of law and can only be annulled by the French *Conseil Constitutionnel*.[393] The powers which are still exercised by France are external affairs, secondary and higher education, entry and stay of foreign nationals, law enforcement, penal and private law, public order, financial affairs, and a number of other smaller subjects.[394] The territory is competent in the areas of labour and social conditions, it can levy a number of local taxes, it controls some elements of foreign trade, and it can request (associated) membership of some international organizations (with the approval of France). The French government can authorize the President of the territorial government to negotiate and sign treaties with Pacific states.[395] A few of the remaining powers of the state will be transferred to New Caledonia during the period 2004–2014.[396] A new element is the incorporation of some elements of Kanak traditional law and institutions into the constitution of New Caledonia.[397]

The highly contentious issue of the franchise for the referendum(s) of 2013–2018 was settled by providing that only those persons will be allowed to vote who have French nationality, reside in New Caledonia, and were eligible to vote in the referendum of 1987, or who had not yet reached the required age in 1987. Other French nationals who have lived in New Caledonia continuously for 20 years in 2013, or who can prove specific links with the territory, either by birth, family ties, or other connections, will also be allowed to vote.[398] People

---

[391] Para. 5 of the Nouméa Accord.

[392] Organic Law No. 99-209 of 19 March 1999.

[393] This is considered to be a fundamental innovation of French constitutional law. *See* Goesel-Le Bihan 1998, p. 47 et seq. on the question whether the Nouméa Accord may have created a federal or confederal form of government, or whether it is simply a form of regionalization.

[394] Organic Law No. 99-209, Article 21-2. *See also* the Working Paper prepared by the Secretariat on New Caledonia (26 March 2003), UN Doc. A/AC.109/2003/7, para. 23-25.

[395] Articles 28-29 of the Organic Law. *See* Touboul 1997 for the external relations of the TOMs and New Caledonia.

[396] Article 26 of the Organic Law.

[397] *See* para. 1.2–1.4 of the Nouméa Accord, providing for the establishment of a Customary Senate, which must be consulted on 'subjects relating to Kanak identity', legal protection for sites that are sacred in Kanak tradition, and increased use of Kanak languages in school curricula.

[398] Para. 2.2 of the Nouméa Accord.

fulfilling these criteria can also apply for New Caledonian citizenship, to which the country may attach certain rights and obligations, and which may be transformed into New Caledonian nationality after 2013.

The franchise for the plebiscite to approve the Nouméa Accord was based on these rules (*mutatis mutandis*), which led to the exclusion of 8 per cent of the French inhabitants of New Caledonia who were on the electoral roll. A number of these French citizens lodged a complaint with the Human Rights Committee, claiming that Article 25 (right to vote) and 26 (prohibition of discrimination) of the ICCPR had been violated by the criteria for the referendums of 1998 and of 2013 or beyond.[399] The claimants considered the periods set for length of residence were excessive, and the criteria used to determine the electorate discriminated between French citizens on the basis of ethnic origin, place of birth, family ties, etc. France responded that as these referendums were 'part of a process of self-determination', and as this process might lead to independence, it required the 'consent of the population concerned', as Article 53 of the French Constitution stipulates.[400] According to France, the persons 'concerned' were those who prove that they have particular ties to the territory whose fate is in question.[401]

The HRC agreed with France that self-determination inevitably involved some form of exclusion, and it did not find the rules applied to be excessively exclusive.[402] The applicants also took their case to the European Court of Human Rights, which agreed with the HRC in its judgement of 2005 that restrictions to the right to vote were allowed in a process of self-determination.[403] The reasoning of the Committee and the Court, while understandable in the violent and extremely problematic case of New Caledonia, has perhaps created a precedent for other self-determination processes, legitimizing the exclusion of migrants from democratic rights, and may come to play an important role in

---

[399] Communication No. 932/2000 (CCPR/C/75/D/932/2000), submitted by Ms. Marie-Hélène Gillot et al., 25 June 1999.

[400] *See above* on the interpretation of Article 53. *See* Maestre 1976, p. 453 and Gohin 1997, p. 74 et seq. for the possible interpretations of the phrase '*populations intéressées.*'

[401] Communication No. 932/2000 (CCPR/C/75/D/932/2000), State party's observations on the merits, para. 8.14.

[402] In spite of the HRC's opinion that the Optional Protocol does not authorize it to receive complaints concerning violations of the right to self-determination, the HRC in this case considered that it should take Article 1 into account in interpreting Article 25 of the ICCPR. It noted, 'without expressing a view on the definition of "peoples" as referred to in Article 1, that it was not unreasonable to limit the self-determination decision in this case to the population "concerned", as the French Constitution provides' (Examination of the merits, para. 14.7). It agreed with the conclusion of the Senior Advocate General in the case before the French *Cour de Cassation*: 'Limitations to the electorate were legitimised by the need to ensure a sufficient definition of identity.'

[403] Judgment of 11 January 2005 (Application No. 66289/01, *Py* v. *France*).

the latent conflicts between indigenous populations and newcomers, which also exist in the Netherlands Antilles and Aruba.

In the meanwhile, the increased autonomy of New Caledonia has been a mixed success. The Caldoches and Kanaks have been forced to cooperate in administering the territory. There have been occasional violent incidents, but on the whole, the territory has become more stable, and attracts more foreign investors and tourism. The social problems remain largely unsolved, and the wealth of the country still appears to be divided very much along ethnic lines, thereby continuing to pose a threat to future stability.

Conclusion

France and the UN disagree on whether the international law of self-determination and decolonization still applies to the French overseas territories. French law and practice does at present recognize the principle of the freedom of choice of the overseas populations, but the exercise of that freedom is subject to approval by the French legislator. The power of Paris to change the status of the overseas territories unilaterally without the consent of the population was much criticized by UN members because of the way it was used in the 1980s in New Caledonia. Since then, the French Constitution has been amended to reflect the practice, which has grown since then, that status changes are no longer realized without the consent of the overseas populations.

France considered that New Caledonia was integrated with France in the sense of Principles VIII and IX of Resolution 1541, but no other state appeared to share this view. The GA decided that the territory is a NSGT, and that the Decolonization Committee should concern itself with the case. France at present informally cooperates with the UN involvement with New Caledonia, and the international pressure may have stimulated the French government to find a peaceful resolution of the ethnic conflict in New Caledonia. In contrast with Puerto Rico, the Decolonization Committee is not merely used as a platform to attack France, and it seems to play a positive role in this case.

3.5 STATE RESPONSIBILITY FOR OVERSEAS TERRITORIES

A general problem in many of the autonomy regimes described in this chapter is the issue of international responsibility for wrongful acts committed by the territory. It concerns such questions as who is responsible for the non-payment of debts or the default of other contractual obligations by a territorial government, the maltreatment of aliens in the territory, other violations of internationally protected human rights or other obligations created by international treaties that apply in the territory.[404] In many of the more or less autonomous territories described here – and certainly in the Netherlands Antilles and Aruba – the territorial government is fully self-governing in most areas where international obligations apply, and the government of the state may only intervene under very specific circumstances.

Nonetheless, when international obligations are violated in such territories, the state to which the territory belongs is fully responsible under international law. The ILC's Draft Articles on state responsibility for wrongful acts provide that: 'The responsible State may not rely on the provisions of its internal law as justification for failure to comply with its obligations' (Article 32). The Vienna Convention on treaties in Article 27 similarly states that: 'A party may not invoke the provisions of its internal law as justification for its failure to perform a treaty.' International courts such as the ECHR, and supervisory organs such as the HRC, the CEDAW and the CPT have made it clear in their dealings with states such as the Netherlands, that the state party is fully responsible for the upholding of international obligations in its overseas territories.[405]

Given the fact that the territories are usually located thousands of kilometres away from the metropolis, as well as the fact that the mere threat of interventions by the metropolis will raise the spectre of colonialism, metropolitan administrators are not always prepared or even able to prevent acts that violate international law in the territories. This creates a very unattractive situation for metropolitan governments, which are fully responsible for acts over which they have little control, and of which they may not even be aware. This situation has influenced the decision of most of the metropolitan governments to push for the independence of their remaining dependencies, or when failing to achieve that, to cling to a number of essential powers in the territories, thereby making themselves vulnerable to the reproach that their territories have not achieved a full measure of self-government.

State responsibility for the overseas territories is probably one of the main reasons for the difficult relations which often exist between a metropolis and its territories. The division of powers between the metropolis, the territorial government and in some cases the representative of the metropolitan government in the territory is often a source of turf wars and leads to uncertainty as to where the responsibility actually lies, as a former Governor of Montserrat, David

---

[404] The National Audit Office of the UK made an interesting inventory of these risks, or 'contingent liabilities', for the UK in the overseas territories: 'Managing Risk in the Overseas Territories.' Report by the Comptroller and Auditor General, HC 4 Session 2007-2008, 16 November 2007.

[405] *See for instance* the judgment of the ECHR in the case of *Mathew* v. *The Netherlands* of 29 September 2005 (Application No. 24919/03) or some of the concluding observations of the various treaty bodies in recent years.

Taylor, has noted with regard to the relations between the UK and its Carib-bean territories.[406] I will describe some of the turf wars that have taken place in the Kingdom of the Netherlands in chapter 4, in the section on international responsibility.

While this issue is one of domestic law in most of the relations discussed in this study, with regard to associated territories it may be one of international law. Some associated territories have the capacity to conclude treaties and per-form other international acts, and it seems logical to assume that the principal state is no longer responsible for the consequences of these acts. But this is not generally accepted, as was discussed in the section on international personality *above.*

The ILC did not go into the question of whether associated states could be considered as states in the sense of the Draft Articles, which seems to be the crucial question. The Commentary on the Draft Articles dismissed any possi-bility of dependencies being internationally responsible for the wrongful acts they may commit, even if the dependency has the capacity to conclude interna-tional treaties in its own right,[407] but at the same time the Commentary seems to consider that protected states and suzerainties – which were somewhat simi-lar to the present concept of associated states – could have been considered as States in the sense of the Draft Articles. As was noted *above*, this area of inter-national law is rather underdeveloped. The concept of associated statehood in international law, and especially the case of the Cook Islands, deserves further study, since it may offer an attractive solution to both the wishes of some terri-torial governments for a more independent role in international affairs, and the wishes of some metropolitan governments to be less responsible for the territo-ries.

---

[406] Taylor 2000.

[407] The commentary on Draft Article 17 states that: 'In most relationships of dependency between one territory and another, the dependent territory, even if it may possess some interna-tional personality, is not a State. Even in cases where a component unit of a federal State enters into treaties or other international legal relations in its own right, and not by delegation from the federal State, the component unit is not itself a State in international law. So far as State responsi-bility is concerned, the position of federal States is no different from that of any other States: the normal principles specified in articles 4 to 9 of the draft articles apply, and the federal State is internationally responsible for the conduct of its component units even though that conduct falls within their own local control under the federal constitution.' Commentary on Article 17 of the Draft Articles on Responsibility of States for Internationally Wrongful Acts, *Yearbook of the International Law Commission,* 2001, Vol. II, Part II.

3.6 DECOLONIZING SMALL OVERSEAS TERRITORIES – BEST PRACTICES

The state practice discussed in this chapter offers a basis for the identification of a number of best practices in the decolonization of small territories. It should be realized first, however, that there exists considerable difference of opinion on the question of what is 'good' with regard to decolonization and self-determination. This question should best be divided into two aspects, namely (1) what are the best results of a process of decolonization and (2) which are the best ways to conduct such a process.

The focus is often on the first aspect, the *results* of the process. It concerns questions such as: Is independence to be preferred because it offers better guarantees for the protection of the cultural identity of a territory, or stimulates the development of a local culture? Would the economy of a territory profit from its incorporation in the EU? And would that be good? Such questions concerning the desirability of the outcome of a process of decolonization lie outside of the scope of this study, since they cannot be answered on the basis of legal arguments.

International law does provide criteria to determine whether the results of a process of decolonization can be considered as 'a full measure of self-government.' But as was shown in this chapter and in chapter 2, such a determination ultimately depends on the question whether a free choice has been made by the population in the awareness of the ramifications of its choice, which brings us to the second aspect, *the process itself*.

Legal arguments could and should play an important role in determining whether a process of self-determination conforms to international standards, as I argued in chapter 2. The state practice discussed in this chapter (and also a few cases discussed in the following chapters) may provide some insight into the practices which have proven to be conducive to an optimal realization of the legal principles concerning self-determination in relations between a Western 'mother country' and its last remaining 'colonies.' An important caveat here is that I have only studied a limited number of the cases, and most of them only through the scholarly literature and UN documents. The list below should therefore be seen as no more than an indication of a few practices which might possibly be classified as 'best practices.' Further research would certainly be required before any firm conclusions could be drawn.

1. All of the cases of status change since the 1960s have at some point in the process involved a *referendum*, except those cases which led to independence. Referendums clearly decrease the chances of a territory achieving independence. If it is correct (as is often assumed) that the population of the remaining overseas territories do not want independence, then referendums have contrib-

uted to the realization of the right to self-determination of these populations. Holding a referendum does not automatically mean, however, that the opinion of the population is given a place in the decision making process in a way that conforms to the demands of international law. Nor does it seem to improve the likelihood of a successful status change *per se*. If a referendum is to play a useful role in the exercise of the right to self-determination and decolonization, attention should be devoted to the following points.

2. The option(s) which may reasonably be presumed to be the favourite(s), should be on the ballot. This point may seem too obvious to include, but in the past, referendums have been held on two options which clearly were not the favourite options of a large majority of the population, and there have also been referendums held where the population was asked to say 'yes' or 'no' to a proposal which clearly did not represent an improvement in the eyes of most voters, while the status quo was also undesirable. Such referendums may very well serve a short-term political purpose, but they make a mockery of the right to self-determination.

3. At least one of the options should be worked out in some detail. Some of the cases show that holding a referendum at a point in time when none of the options had been worked out in any detail decreases the chance that the outcome of the referendum will be realized. If it is realized, it will take many years to work out the details, at which point it may often be wondered whether the population still supports the idea, including the way it has been worked out. In some of the more successful cases, a proposal was drawn up in a transparent process in which there was room for the population to voice its opinion during the drafting process. Such a process has the added advantage that more people will have an informed opinion about the proposal when a referendum is organized.

4. If a proposal is developed by the government of the territory without the participation of the opposition, there is obviously a risk that the population will use the referendum to punish an unpopular government. Successful referendums were usually held at a moment when a basic form of agreement existed between the government of the territory and the metropolitan government on one of the options on the ballot, while there was no strong political opposition in the territory to the agreement reached.

5. All of the successful referendums – in the sense that the population was offered a fair choice, sufficient information was provided, and the outcome was realized – were observed by the UN. It seems reasonable to assume that a UN presence raises the status of the referendum and thereby increases the likelihood of its implementation. The prospect of international monitoring will probably also increase the efforts made to ensure that the referendum confirms to international standards. But it should be noted that the UN has also observed

a number of unsuccessful referendums, which means that a UN presence is not an absolute guarantee of success.

Even though referendums have become a firm part of state practice in these cases, it could probably not be proven that it is *impossible* to complete a process of self-determination successfully without holding a referendum. The status change of the Cook Islands in 1965 seems to have been an example of a successful exercise of the right to self-determination, but this may the proverbial exception which confirms the rule. In any case, a few other factors seem to contribute to the chances of a successful process, as discussed in the following paragraphs.

6. Successful cases of status change rarely drag on for years without intermediate results. Speed may therefore perhaps be considered as a success factor. Of course, in many cases speed is a direct result of the fact that there exists broad consensus on the status change, and vice versa, which makes it uncertain whether speed should be seen as an independent success factor.

7. It has been suggested that small territories should resort to violence in order to realize their wishes.[408] The cases discussed in this study do not confirm this proposition. Rather, the use of violence creates chaos and causes panic reactions which make it more difficult to conduct an orderly process of self-determination in which the population makes a free and informed choice. Violence, or the threat of violence, tends to push a territory in the direction of independence, whether the population wants it or not. The Nouméa Accord in New Caledonia is a successful example of how to pacify a violent situation without ignoring the international standards for self-determination and decolonization.

Another way of classifying successful cases of decolonization is by looking at the list of NSGTs, or rather, how territories are removed from the list. Independence has been the most common reason a territory was removed from the list, but in this study I have mainly looked at those processes of self-determination and decolonization that did not lead to independence. Leaving aside the cases from before 1960 – because these are generally considered to contain a number of examples which did not conform to the standards formulated during the 1950s – it is remarkable that only New Zealand and Australia have succeeded in removing territories from the list of NSGTs without granting them independence. Their practice differs most from the other metropolitan states in that they have actively involved the UN in the process and have clearly tried to comply with the UN standards. Probably the least successful mother country in this respect has been France, which is the only state that has been confronted with a UN decision to re-inscribe a territory on the list of NSGT (French

---

[408] Brison 2005.

Somaliland, the Comoros and New Caledonia). Not surprisingly, France has always strongly resisted UN involvement and it does not recognize the UN standards as binding.

Even though France has rejected the application of international law to its overseas territories and departments, it has in recent years found interesting ways to grant its territories some room to choose their own position within the Republic. The draft treaty between New Zealand and Tokelau creates a wide freedom of choice for Tokelau (*see above* in footnote 42) which would certainly be a bridge too far for most other metropolitan states, but which can hardly be improved from the perspective of the right to self-determination and decolonization.

3.7   CONCLUSION

It can be concluded from the interminable debates on self-determination and decolonization at the UN that alternative forms of self-government can only be accepted as a 'full measure of self-government' and a completion of the legal process of decolonization if the wishes of the population with regard to the political status of their territory are respected. The freedom of choice of the population has often been the focal point of the debates, but in spite of this, the UN has only formulated two alternatives to independence: free association and integration. The possibility of other options that could qualify as full self-government has never been excluded, and was recognized in Resolution 2625 of 1970, but in practice such options are viewed at the UN with even more suspicion than free association and integration, and are only accepted as temporary solutions at best.

Only a very forceful diplomatic campaign by the US prevented the GA from re-inscribing Puerto Rico on the list of NSGTs in 1981, even though the GA had declared in 1953 that Puerto Rico had achieved full self-government and had exercised its right to self-determination. The GA generally considers the Declaration on the Granting of Independence to Colonial Countries and Peoples (GA Resolution 1514 (XV)) sufficient legal basis for re-evaluating its involvement with any territory 'of the colonial type' that has not yet become independent. Therefore each year it approves the Decolonization Committee's report, which always includes a discussion of the situation in Puerto Rico. The case of New Caledonia showed that France could not prevent the GA from reviving its involvement with a territory that had not been on the list of NSGTs for almost thirty years.

The cases of Puerto Rico and New Caledonia, while hugely different to each other in most respects share at least one common characteristic: there exists considerable and long-standing dissatisfaction regarding their current political status, which is somewhere in between association and integration. One of the causes of this dissatisfaction appears to be the 'in-betweenity' of their status, because it suggests a partial responsibility of the metropolis for the internal problems of the territory, which is resented by some, and considered insufficient by others. There is internal disagreement both in the territories and in the metropolis on the political future of the territory, which creates a deadlock or stalemate situation that hampers the political development of the territory. In New Caledonia a way out of this predicament may have been found by explicitly deciding that the decision on the future of the territory ultimately rests with the population, while limiting the franchise for future plebiscites to those people that may be assumed to have a real and lasting connection with the territory.

Free association can be a satisfactory form of decolonization for small territories, if the metropolitan state is prepared to relinquish all of its legislative and administrative controls over the territory, and to actively promote the territory's capacity to enter into international relations independently. The population of a territory should be aware that the option of free association often ends up being very close to independent statehood. While the US and New Zealand have been prepared to support their associated states with substantial financial aid, they are not obligated to do so under international law, nor does international law compel the principal states to extend their nationality to the inhabitants of associated states.

International law also recognizes the possibility of integrating overseas territories into the mother country as a form of complete decolonization. Most metropolitan governments have not been very willing to discuss this option since the 1960s because of the fear that it would entail huge costs and cut off the road to independence for the territories. But the few territories that have been allowed to integrate completely into the metropolis do seem to be relatively happy with it.

The UN is generally rather suspicious of integration as a form of decolonization. It has re-listed a number of cases of incomplete integration as NSGTs. It should probably be assumed that a status which does not represent complete integration, but does continue to grant some jurisdiction to the metropolitan state in the internal affairs of the overseas territory may authorize the UN from considering that Chapter XI of the UN Charter and GA Resolutions 1514 and 1541 continue to apply.

Chapter 4
SELF-GOVERNMENT UNDER THE CHARTER FOR THE KINGDOM OF THE NETHERLANDS

In this chapter, I will briefly describe the self-government that the Netherlands Antilles and Aruba have achieved under the current constitution of the Kingdom of the Netherlands, before categorizing this form of self-government in the next two chapters. First, a very brief overview is given of some relevant facts and figures concerning the Netherlands Antilles and Aruba.

4.1   FACTS AND FIGURES

4.1.1   Geography and Demography

Aruba is a single island located 25 kilometres off the coast of Venezuela. The Netherlands Antilles consists of five islands; Curaçao, St Maarten, Bonaire, St Eustatius and Saba. Curaçao and Bonaire are located some 70 kilometres off the coast of Venezuela. St Maarten, St Eustatius and Saba are located some 900 kilometres to the north, close to Puerto Rico, Anguilla and St Kitts. St Maarten is the Dutch side of an island that is called Saint-Martin on the French side.

Table 4.1 Population statistics for Aruba and Netherlands Antilles

	area (km²)	*population[1]*
Aruba	*193*	*100,000*
Netherlands Antilles	*800*	*186,000*
Curaçao	444	136,000
Bonaire	288	11,000
St Maarten (Dutch)	34	35,000
St Eustatius	21	2,600
Saba	13	1,400

[1] The statistics for the Netherlands Antilles and its islands are based on a recent estimate by the *Centraal bureau voor de statistiek* of the Netherlands Antilles (*see* <www.cbs.an>). The figure for Aruba is derived from estimates reported by various newspapers.

S. Hillebrink, *The Right to Self-Determination and Post-Colonial Governance*
© 2008, T·M·C·ASSER PRESS, *The Hague, The Netherlands and the Author*

In Aruba, Bonaire and Curaçao, the local language, Papiamentu, is used most often. In St Maarten, St Eustatius and Saba, English and Caribbean English are dominant. Dutch is taught in schools. Laws and many other government documents are still written in Dutch.

All of the islands are quite diverse when it comes to the religious, ethnic and national background of the population. Catholicism is widespread in the southern islands, but less so in the northern islands, where the Methodist and Anglican churches, and many other religions, are present. Some of the islands are inhabited by more than 50 different nationalities, although Dutch nationality is still prevalent.

4.1.2 History and Economy

The islands were occupied by the Dutch West India Company (WIC) during the seventeenth century. Most of the indigenous population had already been exterminated before that time. Slaves were brought in from Africa to work in the plantations and salt ponds. Curaçao and St Eustatius became important trading posts. After the WIC became bankrupt near the end of the eighteenth century, the islands came under the control of the Dutch state. The islands gradually obtained a restricted form of self-government. Slavery was abolished in 1863. In the twentieth century, oil refineries in Curaçao and Aruba gave these islands an economic boost that lasted until after World War II. In recent decades, the economy of most of the islands has depended heavily on tourism from the US, Latin America, and Europe. Curaçao, on the other hand, derives substantial parts of its income from its harbour, oil refinery, and financial services.[2]

4.2   A New Legal Order

The Kingdom Charter of 1954 claims to create 'a new legal order'[3] which prevails over the Constitution of the Netherlands.[4] This new order consists of

---

[2] For more information in English on the history of the Netherlands Antilles and Aruba I refer the reader to Oostindie & Klinkers 2003 and Oostindie 2005. In Dutch, there exists an encyclopedia on the Netherlands Antilles and Aruba (Palm 1985). An analysis of the economy of the Netherlands Antilles is provided by Haan 1998. Sluis 2004 provides an accurate overview of the troubled relations between the islands of the Netherlands Antilles, and their relations with the Netherlands. More literature can be found in the *Caribbean Abstracts*, published yearly by the Koninklijk Instituut voor Taal-, Land- en Volkenkunde <www.kitlv.nl> in Leiden.

[3] *See* the Preamble of the Charter.

[4] Article 5 proclaims the primacy of the Charter over the Constitution.

three autonomous Countries ('*landen*') which together form a single state, called the Kingdom of the Netherlands. One of the Countries is also called the Netherlands. The other two Countries were originally Surinam[5] and the Netherlands Antilles. In 1986, one of the islands of the Netherlands Antilles, Aruba, became a separate country. The Netherlands Antilles and Aruba are therefore part of the *Kingdom* of the Netherlands, but not of the *Country* of the Netherlands.

The Charter leaves it to the Countries to determine their own constitutions in most areas. In this respect, the Netherlands has a different position than the other two Countries. Article 44 of the Charter provides that the Caribbean Countries may not amend their constitutions with regard to a number of subjects without the approval of the Kingdom government. The Kingdom government can therefore block certain amendments to the internal constitutions of the Caribbean Countries, mainly those concerning the protection of basic human rights, the powers of parliament and the courts, and the authorities of the Governor. Amendments to the Constitution of the Netherlands do not require the approval of the Kingdom government, unless they concern Kingdom affairs.[6]

It was the intention of the drafters of the Charter to grant self-government to Surinam and the Netherlands Antilles within a single constitutional structure, while changing as little as possible the constitution of the European part of the Kingdom. For that reason, the Charter has delegated many constitutional subjects to the Constitution of the Netherlands. The Charter only provides a number of basic elements of the Kingdom order and a few procedural rules. This means that the Charter has not really replaced the Dutch legal order as it existed before 1954, but merely added something to it. It also means that the Charter and the Constitution have become interwoven and should be read together.

The 'interwovenness' of the Charter and the Constitution is perhaps too complicated to function correctly in practice. It is also true that the limited political importance of Surinam, the Netherlands Antilles and Aruba to the Netherlands has meant that Dutch politicians and lawyers have usually not found it worthwhile to invest the time and effort that is needed to understand 'the many labyrinthine and twisting paths of the Charter.'[7] In fact, Dutch politi-

---

[5] Surinam became an independent state in 1975.

[6] According to Article 5, para. 3 of the Charter such amendments concerning Kingdom affairs have to follow the procedure prescribed for Kingdom acts in Articles 15 to 20 of the Charter. Article 45 of the Charter furthermore provides that amendments to the Constitution on certain important subjects are considered to affect the Netherlands Antilles and Aruba in the sense of Article 10 of the Charter, which means that such amendments have to be discussed in the Council of Ministers of the Kingdom.

[7] This description derives from a speech by Dutch Minister for Justice, Van Oven, in the Senate, *Handelingen I* 1956/57, pp. 29-30.

cians are often not aware of the contents of the Charter, and they are sometimes unpleasantly surprised that the Caribbean governments or parliaments should be consulted on certain 'Dutch' affairs. This Dutch attitude was already predicted in 1948 by *Van Helsdingen*, who suggested that the quasi-federal structure of the Kingdom could only work if the common affairs were kept to an absolute minimum. He suggested that the federal organs should be the same as the organs of the Netherlands, with the addition of Caribbean representatives when a subject was of real importance to the Caribbean Countries.[8] These principles have become the cornerstones of the Kingdom.

4.2.1   Equivalence and Voluntariness

According to the Preamble of the Charter, the three Countries administer their common affairs on the basis of equivalence. The term 'equivalence' was intended to convey the idea that Surinam and the Netherlands Antilles would no longer be subordinated to the Netherlands and that they would be involved in decisions regarding the common affairs of the Kingdom.[9] The Charter does not, however, treat the Countries entirely equally. Apart from the general rule that the Countries are autonomous in all affairs except those that the Charter reserves for the Kingdom, the Netherlands and the Caribbean Countries are treated differently in many respects.[10] The term 'equivalence' does have a symbolic function, meaning that the interests of one Country should not automatically outweigh those of another. The Charter is the result of an attempt to realize the principle of the equivalence of unequal partners, as *Borman* puts it.[11]

The principle of equivalence is sometimes used by politicians in the Netherlands Antilles and Aruba to support a claim that the Netherlands violates the Charter when it tries to enforce its policies against the will of the Caribbean Countries. In this interpretation, it seems to mean that all decisions that affect the Kingdom as a whole should be based on consensus between the Countries,[12] but the Charter does not prescribe this. In the Netherlands, the idea of

---

[8] Van Helsdingen 1957, p. 163.

[9] Res. I of the RTC of 1948, cited in Borman 2005, p. 20. *See also* Van Helsdingen 1957, p. 33, and Van der Pot-Donner/Prakke et al. 2001, p. 829.

[10] *See* Article 44 of the Charter, and also *below* for other examples. *See also* Ooft 1972, p. 197. De Jong 2002, p. 31 describes the practice of the Kingdom (especially since 1990) under the title 'Splits of inequality' (*'Spagaat van ongelijkheid'*).

[11] Borman 2006, pp. 20-1.

[12] Fernandes Mendes 1989, p. 27 describes that during the negotiations on the Charter, the Netherlands government stated that the overseas territories confused equivalence with equality, for which reason they made 'wrong' demands regarding rights of co-decision.

equivalence is sometimes rejected as a fiction,[13] or described as no more than a matter of etiquette[14] or psychology.[15]

The *voluntariness* of the Kingdom order was intended to express that the relations between the Countries are based on mutual consent, and will not be continued against the wishes of a Country. Its main function in 1954 was probably to convince the world – both in and outside the Kingdom – that the era of colonial domination had ended. It also means that the Kingdom organs cannot act outside the limited area of Kingdom affairs unless the Countries voluntarily accept the Kingdom's authority to do so.

4.2.2   Autonomous Affairs and Kingdom Affairs

The Countries are autonomous except with regard to the affairs of the Kingdom, which are listed exhaustively in the Charter. These are foreign affairs, defence, nationality, extradition and a number of other subjects.[16] The Kingdom is also charged with safeguarding fundamental human rights and freedoms, legal certainty and good governance in the entire Kingdom.[17]

The Countries are autonomous in all other affairs. They create their own legislation and policies for these areas autonomously. The Countries can decide to create additional Kingdom affairs, but this has never happened.[18] The Countries can also choose to handle a non-Kingdom affair jointly, which they have done, for instance to combat international terrorism. The economic development of the Netherlands Antilles, its public debt, and the problems with youth crime (both in the Netherlands and in the Netherlands Antilles) have also become somewhat of a common affair since the late 1990s. This does not mean that the Countries can no longer develop their own policies on these subjects, it merely means that their efforts are to some extent coordinated.

---

[13] *See for instance* the statement by member of the Lower House Herben (*LPF*) that the Netherlands and the Netherlands Antilles 'are not equivalent ... We should normalize the relations as soon as possible. We are in charge.' (*HP/De Tijd*, 12 September 2003).

[14] De Jong 2002, p. 53. Boersema 2005, p. 92 argues that the *raison d'être* of the Charter is the un-equivalence of the Countries.

[15] Munneke 1993, p. 858.

[16] The other Kingdom affairs are the regulation of knighthoods and royal decorations; the nationality of ships and safety standards for seafaring vessels; the supervision of the rules regarding the admission and expulsion of Dutch nationals to and from the Countries; the general conditions for the admission and expulsion of aliens; and the regulation of the functioning of the Kingdom organs (*see* Article 3, para. 1 of the Charter).

[17] Article 43, para. 2.

[18] Article 3, para. 2 of the Charter demands that the procedure for amendments to the Charter is followed when new Kingdom affairs are created.

The delineation of Kingdom affairs has sometimes caused difficulties, especially in the area of foreign affairs and law enforcement. A prominent example of a delineation issue was the establishment of a coast guard for the Netherlands Antilles and Aruba.[19] A number of other conflicts are described in a study of 2003 conducted by the Ministry for Foreign Affairs in order to evaluate its handling of the foreign affairs of the Netherlands Antilles and Aruba. The study notes that there exists a grey area between autonomous and Kingdom affairs which forces the parties involved to find pragmatic solutions in individual cases.[20] The implementation of treaties concerning the safety of seafaring ships has also caused some differences of opinion.[21]

The Caribbean Countries are allowed to maintain contacts with foreign states and international organizations more or less independently, as long as the position of the Kingdom as a whole is not at stake.[22] It is up to the Kingdom government to decide when this is the case. The Caribbean Countries are members of several international organizations, as full or associated member, or as observer.[23] They cannot join such organizations against the will of the Kingdom government, which sometimes creates conflicts.[24]

---

[19] The Netherlands government considered this to be a Kingdom affair (defence), but the Caribbean Countries, supported by an advice of the *Raad van State* of the Kingdom (*Bijvoegsel Stcrt.* 1996, no. 31), considered it to be an autonomous affair of the Countries (law enforcement). The *Raad van State* changed its opinion in 2005, based on the idea that different circumstances now meant that the coast guard had an important task in defending the sea borders of the Kingdom, and in fulfilling the international obligations of the Kingdom in the areas of crime control and the safety standards for seafaring vessels (*Kamerstukken II* 2005/06, 30531 (R 1810), no. 4). The Kingdom government chose to give the coast guard a dual legal foundation, both in the Kingdom affair of defence, and in the joint administration of a number of autonomous affairs (*Kamerstukken II* 2005/06, 30531 (R 1810), no. 2).

[20] IOB 2003, p. 3.

[21] According to a letter by the Minister for Transport, Public Works and Water Management, the delineation of the Kingdom affair of 'safety and navigation of seafaring vessels' should be based on the situation of 1954, because the official explanation to the Charter gives a description of this subject which is clearly based on the international standards as they were in 1954. The minister states that it is therefore an autonomous affair of the Countries whether they wish to adhere to additional international standards for ships which have been formulated since then, for instance with regard to the protection of the environment (*Kamerstukken II* 2003/04, 29 200 XII, no. 136, p. 3-4).

[22] *See* Articles 12 and 26, and the official explanation to Article 7 of the Charter.

[23] The Netherlands Antilles and Aruba are full members of Parlatino, the Universal Postal Union, and the World Meteorological Organization. They are associated members of the Association of Caribbean States, UNESCO, and the UN Economic Commission for Latin America and the Caribbean, and they are observers at CARICOM (Van Rijn 1999, p. 124, and Hoogers & De Vries 2002, pp. 202-3). The Kingdom as a whole is observer at the Organization of American States, but in practice this role is performed by the Caribbean Countries. The Netherlands Antilles has expressed the intention to pursue separate membership of the WTO.

[24] *See* IOB 2003, p. 85 et seq. for the difficult procedure leading up the associated membership of the Caribbean Countries of the ACS.

The Countries cannot conclude international treaties, because this capacity is exclusively attributed to the Kingdom. The Charter does provide that the Caribbean Countries will be involved in the conclusion of treaties which affect them.[25] Such treaties are sent to their parliaments, but not for their consent. Treaties that need to be approved by parliament before being ratified are always approved by the *Staten-Generaal* only.[26]

The Caribbean Countries can negotiate international agreements with foreign states, and then request the Kingdom to conclude such an agreement on their behalf. The Countries make use of this opportunity, especially in the area of trade agreements. Requests from the Caribbean governments for the conclusion (or termination) of a certain treaty are complied with by the Kingdom, unless the treaty conflicts with 'the unity of the Kingdom.'[27] The Caribbean Countries have a right of veto on the application of financial and economic treaties to their territory if they expect to be negatively affected.[28] The Kingdom usually leaves it to the Caribbean Countries to decide whether a treaty should be applied to their territory. The Kingdom government can decide that a certain treaty should apply to the entire Kingdom if it is of the opinion that the unity of the Kingdom would not tolerate a partial application of that treaty.[29]

The autonomy of the Caribbean Countries is not revocable without the consent of the parliaments of these Countries. It is legally guaranteed by the Kingdom Charter in Articles 3 and 41. *Ooft*, in his thesis on Surinam's constitutional law, nonetheless concluded that 'the autonomy is surrounded by so many restrictions and guarantees that it depends upon the good will and tolerance of the parties involved.'[30] To what extent the reserved powers of the Kingdom

---

[25] Article 28 of the Charter.

[26] Article 24 of the Charter and Article 91 of the Dutch Constitution.

[27] Article 26 of the Charter. This Article formally only applies to financial and economic treaties, but in practice it is also applied to other treaties, *see* Sondaal 1986, p. 191 ct seq., and Van Rijn 2005a, p. 95.

[28] Article 25 of the Charter.

[29] This situation occurs when a treaty concerns a Kingdom affair that affects all of the Countries. According to *Sondaal*, human rights treaties should always apply to the entire Kingdom (Sondaal 1986, p. 193, *idem* Van Rijn 2005a, p. 95 who claims that this rule also applies to other treaties that concern constitutional subjects). While this interpretation could certainly be defended on the basis of the text of the Kingdom Charter, it has not been adopted explicitly in practice. In the ratification process of the ICCPR and ICESCR the Kingdom government stated that the 'the Kingdom as a whole' should become a party to these Covenants. Perhaps it intended to declare that the Covenants should apply to the entire Kingdom, but since it left it to the Netherlands Antilles to decide whether and how the Covenants should apply to that Country, this seems unlikely (*Kamerstukken II* 1975/76, 13932 (R 1037), no. 3, p. 12). This ambiguous practice is often followed with regard to human rights treaties. As the Antilles and Aruba have not opposed the application of most of the important human rights treaties to their territories, it remains somewhat unclear how the Kingdom government (and the *Staten-Generaal*) really views this situation.

[30] Ooft 1972, p. 190.

could indeed be used to annul the autonomy of the Caribbean Countries is discussed *below*.

Since the 1990s, there has been increasing criticism, mainly in the Netherlands, but also in the Caribbean Countries, of the way in which the Caribbean Countries have made use of their autonomy. It is often stated (in increasingly plain terms) that the Caribbean governments are not able to effectively maintain the rule of law, provide good government and protect the human rights of their inhabitants.[31] Much criticism has also been directed at the economic policies and the public spending of the Antillean government, an area in which the Country is fully autonomous.[32]

4.2.3   The Organs of the Kingdom

The quasi-federal structure of the Kingdom requires that it has its own organs. The most important organ is the Kingdom government, which is composed of the King and the Council of Ministers of the Kingdom. The Council of Ministers consists of the ministers of the Country of the Netherlands, and one Minister Plenipotentiary for each Caribbean Country.[33] The Kingdom government is responsible for the administration of the Kingdom, and usually initiates Kingdom legislation. Article 2, paragraph 1 determines that the King is inviolable and the ministers shall be responsible. This means that the ministers are politically responsible to parliament (except the Ministers Plenipotentiary, *see below*), also with regard to Kingdom affairs. This means that the powers of the government are vested in the ministers, not the King.

The Ministers Plenipotentiary are voting members of the Council of Ministers, but they can always be outvoted by the Dutch ministers.[34] The Council strives towards consensus, but the fact that the Netherlands commands a majority obviously influences the decision-making process. The position of the Ministers Plenipotentiary is not the same as the Dutch ministers. They cannot submit bills for Kingdom legislation to parliament and they cannot countersign

---

[31] *See* Broek & Wijenberg 2005 for a brief overview of recent criticism by *Verton, Oostindie, Munneke, De Jong*, and others.

[32] *See for instance* Haan 1998, and the letter by the Dutch Minister for Administrative Reform and Kingdom Affairs to the Lower House, dated 24 August 2005 (*Kamerstukken II* 2004/05, 29 800 IV, no. 29).

[33] Article 7 of the Charter.

[34] In case the Council of Ministers of the Kingdom takes a decision with which one or both Ministers Plenipotentiary do not agree, they can ask for a continued session of the deliberations in which only they, the Dutch premier and two other Dutch ministers take part. The Ministers Plenipotentiary can also be joined by special delegates appointed by their governments, but the Dutch ministers will in each case constitute a voting majority during these sessions. *See* Article 12 of the Kingdom Charter

Kingdom acts, regulations, or other decisions by the Crown. For this reason, it could be questioned whether they are really part of the Kingdom government. As representatives of the governments of the Caribbean Countries, they are not responsible to the *Staten-Generaal*, but only to their respective governments. They also perform a number of duties comparable to ambassadors.[35]

The government of the Country of the Netherlands is represented in each of the Caribbean Countries by a representative of the Netherlands, who acts as a liaison between the government of the Netherlands and the governments of the Caribbean Countries.[36]

The King is the head of state of the Kingdom, but also presides over the governments of each Country. In the Netherlands Antilles and Aruba, the King is represented by a Governor (one for each Country). The Governors are appointed by the Kingdom government for a period of six years.[37] The government of the Country concerned recommends candidates to the Kingdom government. According to *Borman*, it would he hard to imagine that a candidate would be appointed against the wishes of the Country government concerned, although this has happened once.[38] The Governors have always been persons of Antillean and Aruban descent since the 1960s.

The Governor has a dual capacity, he heads the government of the Country, but at the same time, he represents the Kingdom in his Country. In his first capacity, he is an organ of the Country, and his powers are determined by the Constitution of the Country. The Governors have a similar position in the governments of the Netherlands Antilles and Aruba as the King in the government of the Netherlands, which means that only the ministers are responsible to parliament for the government's actions.[39] In the Netherlands Antilles and Aruba, the ministers are responsible to the parliaments of those Countries, which are called the *Staten*. When the Governor acts as an organ of the Kingdom, however, he is only responsible to the Kingdom government[40] and the Antillean

---

[35] Borman 2005, pp. 87-9, and Hoogers & De Vries 2002, p. 45.

[36] Borman 2005, p. 101. The Representatives of the Netherlands should not be confused with the Governors, who do not represent the Country of the Netherlands, and who have quite a different function.

[37] Article 2, para. 3 of the Charter, and Article 1, para. 2 of the Regulation for the Governor of the Netherlands Antilles (*idem* for Aruba).

[38] Borman 2005, p. 99. After the riots in Willemstad in 1969, the Kingdom government in 1970 appointed a different candidate than had been recommended by the government of the Netherlands Antilles (*see* Reinders 1993, p. 86).

[39] Article 11 of the Constitution of the Netherlands Antilles and Article II.1 of the Constitution of Aruba. *See also* Hoogers & De Vries 2002, p. 97 et seq. and Van Rijn 1999, p. 211.

[40] Article 15 of both the Regulation for the Governor of the Netherlands Antilles and the Regulation for the Governor of Aruba. These Regulations are enacted by the Kingdom in the form of Kingdom acts.

and Aruban ministers do not have to give an account of their actions to the *Staten*. The Governor's most important powers as representative of the Kingdom are in the area of supervision of the legislation and administration of the Caribbean Countries. The Netherlands Antilles during the 1950s in vain attempted to have some of these powers – which mainly date from the colonial era – removed, but the Netherlands refused.[41] In practice, these powers have only rarely led to conflicts between the Governor and his ministers.[42]

There is no constitutional court for the Kingdom. The Countries can bring some of their conflicts before the civil courts of the Netherlands or the other Countries, but they have so far done this on only one occasion.[43] It has been noted in the legal literature that the civil courts are not really equipped to settle these conflicts, and it has been recommended that a constitutional court should be created.[44] Recent history shows a number of examples where a Caribbean Country has been taken to court by an individual because an underlying conflict between the Netherlands and the Caribbean Country had remained unresolved.[45] The *Raad van State* of the Kingdom[46] and *ad hoc* committees are sometimes used to arbitrate in conflicts, but their non-binding recommendations are not always carried out, at least not fully. Most conflicts are eventually settled through compromise or by a trade-off, but some conflicts are simply left to fester. As a result, the constitutional law of the Kingdom remains contested and unclear in some areas.

---

[41] Oostindie & Klinkers 2001b, p. 41. The Netherlands Antilles claimed that the right of the Governor to refuse to ratify a decision of his ministers, and to refer the decision to the Kingdom government, constituted a form of *preventive* supervision. This was claimed to be in contradiction with the Charter, which only creates a form of *repressive* supervision in Article 50. The Netherlands government did not agree, and the conflict remained unresolved.

[42] Articles 15 to 26 of both Regulations for the Governor specify the functions of the Governor as Kingdom organ. *See also* Borman 2005, p. 99 et seq. *See* Oostindie & Klinkers 2001c, pp. 396-400 on the functioning of the Governors in recent practice. The Governor's authority to refuse the appointment of a minister led to a conflict in 1998 when the Governor of Aruba initially refused to appoint Glenbert Croes because of a criminal investigation that was conducted against him at the time. The issue was raised in the Council of Ministers of the Kingdom, which instituted a committee (*'Commissie Biesheuvel'*) to investigate the matter. The committee recommended the Kingdom government to use its authority with restraint, and the Aruban organs to make sure that the Kingdom would not need to use its authority.

[43] Judgment of the Supreme Court (*Hoge Raad*) of 10 September 1999 (*AB* 1999, 462), concerning an Antillean request to forbid a Dutch minister to vote in favour of the mid-term revision of the EU OCT Decision of 1997, *see* chapter 9.

[44] *See for instance* De Werd 1997 and De Werd 1998.

[45] Examples are the cases of *Oduber & Lamers* v. *Aruba* (HR 13 April 2007, Nr. R05/139HR), and *Matos* v. *The Netherlands Antilles* (HR 21 november 2000, *NJ* 2001, 376).

[46] In its function as advisor of the Kingdom Government, the *Raad van State* of the Kingdom was asked to provide an advice on the interpretation of Article 25 of the Kingdom Charter (W01.98.0081) in order to settle a conflict between the Countries. *See further* chapter 9 on the sugar and rice conflict.

A 'Democratic Deficit'

There exists no Kingdom parliament, although it could be argued that the Dutch parliament, the *Staten-Generaal*, functions as such, because it approves Kingdom acts and international treaties, including when these apply to the Netherlands Antilles and Aruba. In practice, it exercises political control over the Kingdom government, because the Dutch members of the Council of Ministers of the Kingdom are also members of the Dutch cabinet, and as such responsible to the *Staten-Generaal*.[47]

In spite of this, it was decided in 1952 that the inhabitants of the Netherlands Antilles and Surinam should not have the right to vote for the *Staten-Generaal*. The Netherlands Antilles and Surinam expected that the election of representatives in the *Staten-Generaal* (as proposed by the Netherlands in 1950) would lead to few results and would have several disadvantages. It was expected that the other proposed forms of participating in the drafting and approval of Kingdom acts (*see below* in paragraph 4.2.5 on Kingdom legislation) would be more effective.[48]

In the meetings which are regularly held between members of the parliaments of the three Countries (the *Contactplan*, which was renamed the *Parlementair Overleg Koninkrijksrelaties* (POK) in 2006), a debate was started in 1997 about a so-called 'democratic deficit' of the Kingdom, which is usually interpreted to mean that the influence of the Caribbean *Staten* and the populations of the islands on the decisions of the Kingdom is not strong enough, or that the influence of the Netherlands is too strong.[49] Various suggestions have been made to improve the input of the Netherlands Antilles and Aruba, but so far no changes have been made. In December 2007, the Dutch Secretary of State for the Interior and Kingdom Relations and the Minister of Justice informed the Lower House of a number of options that exist to improve the situation, namely the establishment of a Kingdom Parliament, the granting of the right to vote in the election of the members of the *Staten-Generaal*, or changes in the powers of the *Staten* or the special delegates of the *Staten*.[50]

In the meantime, two Aruban politicians (Messrs. M.G. Eman and O.B. Sevinger) attempted to address the perceived democratic deficit by claiming

---

[47] The Ministers Plenipotentiary are probably not responsible to any parliament, but the governments of the Netherlands Antilles and Aruba, which they represent, are responsible to the *Staten* for their actions.

[48] *See* the explanation to point 11 of the draft for a Charter of 1952 (Werkstuk 1952, p. 19). *See also* Van Helsdingen 1956, p. 156.

[49] For a summary of these discussions, *see* Nap 2003a, p. 68 and p. 115 et seq., and De Werd 1996.

[50] *Kamerstukken II* 2007/08, 30 945, no. 8.

the right to vote in the Lower House elections. They referred to Article 3 of Protocol 1 to the ECHR, which provides that: 'The High Contracting Parties undertake to hold free elections at reasonable intervals by secret ballot, under conditions which will ensure the free expression of the opinion of the people in the choice of the legislator.' The Arubans claimed that the 'legislator' of the Kingdom is the Kingdom government acting together with the *Staten-Generaal*, and they lodged an appeal with the Administrative Jurisdiction Division of the *Raad van State* against the decision that they were not eligible to vote in the Lower House elections of 2006. The Division rejected their appeal on the grounds that the procedure by which Kingdom legislation is created also includes the *Staten* and the Minister Plenipotentiary of Aruba (and the Netherlands Antilles), as provided by Articles 10 to 19 of the Kingdom Charter, while the two Arubans had the right to vote in the election of the *Staten*, and were thereby also indirectly involved in the appointment of their Minister Plenipotentiary.

Eman and Sevinger also claimed that they should be treated equally with Dutch citizens who live outside of the Kingdom, and who do have the right to vote in the election of the Lower House. They pointed to the curious situation that an Aruban who lives in Aruba – and is thereby bound by the Kingdom legislation which applies in Aruba – does not have the right to vote in the parliament which approves bills for Kingdom legislation, but when that same Aruban moves to Venezuela, he or she obtains the right to vote in the Lower House.[51] The Division also rejected this argument, because the situation of Dutch citizens abroad was not the same as Dutch citizens living in Aruba, who have the right to vote for the Aruban parliament, and are thus involved in the procedure for creating Kingdom legislation.[52]

The two Arubans lodged a complaint against this judgment with the European Court of Human Rights, but the Court unanimously considered their complaint inadmissible, because it was 'manifestly ill-founded' in the sense of Article 35, paragraph 4 of the ECHR. With regard to the claimed violation of Article 14 (protection against discrimination), the Court considered that the situation of the applicants 'is not relevantly similar to that of other Netherlands nationals who are not residing in Aruba or the Netherlands Antilles and who are thus not eligible to vote' for the *Staten* of these Countries. With regard to the alleged

---

[51] A similar argument was successful in the appeal lodged by the same two Arubans against the decision that they were not eligible to vote in the election of the European Parliament of 2004. *See* the judgment of the Administrative Jurisdiction Division of the *Raad van State* of 21 November 2006 in cases 200404446/1 and 200404450/1 and the corresponding pre-judicial decision of the European Court of Justice of 12 September 2006 in Case C-300/04, *Eman & Sevinger*.

[52] Judgment of the Administrative Jurisdiction Division of 21 November 2006, in cases 200607567/1 and 200607800/1. On this judgment, *see further* Hillebrink & Loeber 2006.

violation of Article 3 of the first Protocol to the EHCR, the Court considered that:

Netherlands nationals residing in Aruba are able to influence decisions taken by the Lower House of the Netherlands Parliament concerning Kingdom affairs. Having regard to the relatively small amount of Kingdom affairs in comparison with the amount of Netherlands internal affairs, the Court is of the opinion that it cannot reasonably be said that Netherlands nationals residing in Aruba are affected by the acts of the Lower House of the Netherlands Parliament to the same extent as Netherlands nationals residing in the Netherlands.[53]

Given the fact that States have been granted a wide margin of appreciation in electoral matters, the Court concluded that the Dutch Electoral Act could not be regarded as unreasonable or arbitrary, and was therefore compatible with Article 3 of the first Protocol.

From a material point of view, the decision of the Court is understandable, but the fact remains that the representatives of the inhabitants of the Netherlands Antilles and Aruba are not allowed to vote on bills for legislation which will apply in their Countries. The decision of the Court has so far not inspired any reactions in the Caribbean Countries, nor in the Netherlands, but some observers had expected a different outcome of the case.[54]

4.2.4 Supervision by the Kingdom

The Kingdom is obligated to safeguard fundamental human rights and freedoms, legal certainty and good government in each of the Countries. This obligation is aimed mainly at securing the rule of law and democracy in the Caribbean Countries. The Kingdom and the Country of the Netherlands contributes to this aim in various ways, but the Kingdom Charter only provides for two concrete powers of the Kingdom government in this area. It is authorized to annul legislative or administrative acts by the overseas countries if they are considered to be in violation of the Charter, an international treaty, a Kingdom act or regulation, or with the interests that the Kingdom has to look after or safeguard (Article 50).[55] The Kingdom government can also adopt Kingdom regulations to provide for situations when an organ of the Netherlands Antilles

---

[53] Decision of 6 September 2007 as to the admissibility of applications nos. 17173/07 and 17180/07 (*Sevinger and Eman* v. *The Netherlands*).

[54] *See* Besselink 2007 and Kortmann 2007.

[55] It is also possible for the Kingdom government to provide instructions to the Governor on how he should guard the 'general interest of the Kingdom.' *See* both Articles 11 of the Regulation for the Governor of the Netherlands Antilles and the Regulation for the Governor of Aruba.

or Aruba does not live up to its duties under the Charter, a treaty, a Kingdom act or a Kingdom regulation (Article 51). These are potentially very broad powers, and it is the Kingdom government itself that decides when they should be used.[56] The official explanation of the Charter states, however, that these powers should be used only as an *ultimum remedium*.

These powers have never been used, although since 1990 it is no longer uncommon for members of the Dutch parliament to speculate on whether the Kingdom government should use them to rectify an overseas situation that is considered unacceptable in the Netherlands, most pertinently with regard to the conditions in the prison of Willemstad – the Bon Futuro prison, formerly called Koraal Specht (*see below*). Dutch ministers have rarely admitted that a situation might be bad enough to justify an intervention. It is often assumed that an intervention would incur high costs for the Netherlands and that it would encounter considerable opposition in the Caribbean,[57] and that it would generate few positive effects. Former Antillean Governor Debrot was cited as saying in 1973 that if the Netherlands should try to guarantee legal certainty, human rights and good governance in the Netherlands Antilles, there would be big trouble.[58] Despite the reluctance to use them, however, the existence of these unused Kingdom powers must have had an effect on the Kingdom relations,[59] although it is hard to determine how large this effect really is.

An agreement signed between the Netherlands, Curaçao and St Maarten in 2006 provides for a new way of fulfilling the obligation of Article 43, paragraph 2 of the Charter. It was agreed that the Dutch Minister of Justice, in his capacity as member of the Council of the Ministers of the Kingdom, could instruct the public prosecutor of the future Countries Curaçao and St Maarten in order to safeguard human rights, legal certainty and/or good government on the basis of Article 43, paragraph 2.[60] This agreement became the subject of much controversy in Curaçao, because it was considered an unacceptable inroad on the autonomy of the future Country government (*see below* in the paragraph on the dismantling of the Netherlands Antilles).

---

[56] Articles 50 and 51 state that the Kingdom government 'could' intervene, and therefore do not appear to create an *obligation* to intervene.

[57] *Ooft* claims that the Kingdom did not use this power because of 'the internationally accepted principle of decolonization', Ooft 1972, p. 270.

[58] Cited in Oversteegen 1994, p. 263. *See also* Dip 2004, p. 329. Debrot also claimed that Article 43, para. 2, had become defunct and could no longer be considered as law.

[59] Borman 2005, p. 183.

[60] Final declaration (*Slotverklaring*) of the conference of the Netherlands, the Netherlands Antilles, Curaçao and Sint Maarten of 2 November 2006, *see Kamerstukken II* 2006/07, 30 800 IV, no. 9. The declaration itself was not published in the *Kamerstukken*, but it was published on <www.curacao-gov.an and www.minbzk.nl>.

The supervision by the Kingdom also pertains to amendments to the Constitutions of the Netherlands Antilles and Aruba (concerning a number of subjects),[61] the Islands Regulation of the Netherlands Antilles (*Eilandenregeling Nederlandse Antillen*, ERNA),[62] and the articles concerning the judicial and legal system in the joint regulation concerning the cooperation of the Netherlands Antilles and Aruba.[63] The Kingdom cannot change these provisions, but the amendments adopted by the Netherlands Antilles and Aruba cannot be promulgated without the approval of the Kingdom government.

In the Netherlands Antilles, there exist additional means for intervention by the Kingdom, which *have* been used. Based on Article 93 of the Constitution of the Netherlands Antilles, the Kingdom government can adopt a regulation to redress a situation of gross neglect in the government of one of the island territories.[64] According to *Borman*, this form of supervision is different from Articles 50 and 51 of the Charter, because there is supposed to be an unwritten rule that this power can only be used with the approval of the central government of the Netherlands Antilles.[65] The Constitution of the Netherlands Antilles and the ERNA furthermore make it possible for the Antillean Governor to annul or suspend decisions by the Executive Council and the Island Council of an island territory. This authority has more frequently been used than the other forms of supervision.[66]

4.2.5 Kingdom Legislation

Legislation regarding affairs of the Kingdom is provided by Kingdom acts and regulations.[67] When it concerns legislation which will only apply to the European part of the Kingdom, the legislator of the Country of the Netherlands is

---

[61] Article 44 of the Charter.

[62] Article 88 of the Constitution of the Netherlands Antilles and Article 44, para. 2 of the Charter.

[63] Article 74, para. 4 of the Joint regulation (*Samenwerkingsregeling*).

[64] In 1959, the Kingdom government, upon a request by the government of the Netherlands Antilles, dismissed the members of the Executive Council of Curaçao, who had refused to step down after the Island Council had requested their resignation. In 1992 the Kingdom decided that the Governor (and from 1994 the government) of the Netherlands Antilles should approve beforehand any important decision of the Executive Council of St Maarten, in order to restore the adherence to principles of good government. *See* Van Rijn 1999, p. 404 et seq.

[65] Borman 2005, p. 188.

[66] *See* Hoeneveld 2008 for a review of the practice of the Governors of the Netherlands Antilles.

[67] The Kingdom government has the power to promulgate legislation without the participation of a parliament, in the form of a regulation based on Article 14, para. 2 of the Charter. On the extent of this power *see* Hillebrink & Nap 2002.

authorized to provide this legislation itself, but this authority does not exist *vice versa* for the Caribbean Countries. The Netherlands makes ample use of this option. When it is desirable to create legislation on Kingdom affairs that will apply only in one or both of the Caribbean Countries, this can only be realized through a Kingdom act or regulation, which occasionally happens.[68]

Kingdom regulations are adopted by the government of the Kingdom, which means that the Ministers Plenipotentiary will be able to vote on the proposal in the Council of Ministers of the Kingdom. When a Minister Plenipotentiary thinks that a Kingdom act or regulation should not apply to his Country, he has a right of veto, which can only be overruled by the Council when 'the unity of the Kingdom' requires the application of the act or regulation in the Country concerned.[69] What this clause means is uncertain. The official explanation to the Charter only states that the Council decides in which cases the 'unity of the Kingdom' is at stake.[70] There is no evidence that the Council of Ministers has often used this reasoning to force a Caribbean Country to accept a certain Kingdom act or regulation.

The procedure for the adoption of Kingdom acts by the *Staten-Generaal* follows the same procedure as acts of the Dutch legislator, but with a few adaptations. Bills for Kingdom acts are sent to the *Staten* of the Netherlands Antilles and Aruba for their comment before they are considered by the *Staten-Generaal*. The Ministers Plenipotentiary may attend the debates in the Lower House and the Senate, and furnish such information as they may find desirable. The *Staten* of the Caribbean Countries can send delegates to participate in the debates. The Ministers Plenipotentiary may request the Lower House to initiate Kingdom legislation,[71] and they, or the special delegates, may propose amendments to bills. The Ministers Plenipotentiary and the special delegates do not have the right to vote in the Lower House or the Senate, but they can force the Lower House to postpone the vote on a bill until the next meeting, unless the House approves the bill by at least three-fifths of the number of votes cast.[72]

The Caribbean *Staten* sometimes use their right to comment on bills for Kingdom acts, and they have occasionally sent delegates to participate in Lower

---

[68] For example: extradition (a Kingdom affair) is regulated in the Netherlands by an act of parliament of the Country of the Netherlands (*Uitleveringswet*) and in the Netherlands Antilles and Aruba by a Kingdom regulation (*Nederlands-Antilliaans Uitleveringsbesluit*).

[69] Article 12, para. 1 of the Charter.

[70] A first draft for the Charter provided that it should concern a situation where 'the well-being of the Kingdom demands that each part of the Kingdom is bound by the regulation.' (Werkstuk 1952, p. 17).

[71] The Ministers Plenipotentiary may not submit bills to parliament on behalf of the Kingdom government. They can merely request the Lower House to adopt a bill for a Kingdom act, which would subsequently have to be approved by the Senate and the Kingdom government.

[72] Articles 15 to 18 of the Charter.

House debates. Most of the other means for participation have never – or very rarely – been used.[73] It is not really clear why so little use has been made of these rights of participation.

The Kingdom legislator is obliged to observe the Charter – and the Dutch Constitution as far as the Charter has delegated the establishment of rules concerning Kingdom legislation to the Constitution – but the courts are not allowed to annul Kingdom acts if they violate the Charter.[74] Other forms of Kingdom legislation (regulations issued by the Kingdom Government or a minister) can probably be tested against the Charter.[75] The courts have never been asked to do this, which can be explained from the limited body of existing Kingdom legislation and the fact that this legislation contains few provisions that are directly binding on the inhabitants of the Kingdom.

4.2.6 Ambiguities

The constitutional relations between the Netherlands and the Caribbean territories have always been full of ambiguities and contradictions.[76] The islands belong to the Netherlands, but at the same time they are not *part* of the Netherlands. They are part of the *Kingdom* of the Netherlands, but not of the *Country* of the Netherlands. This creates an ambiguous situation, since the Kingdom and the Country of the Netherlands are largely the same thing. This reflects a long-standing wish to treat the constitution of the metropolis as a closed system 'which only needs a short appendix about those peculiar and distant extensions that disrupt the beauty of the system', as *Van Vollenhoven* complained in 1934. He referred to 'a curious formula that is sometimes encountered, whereby these territories and their populations belong to the state internationally, but not nationally.'[77] This 'curious formula' became the basis for the Kingdom order in 1954.[78]

---

[73] *See* Nap 2003a, p. 71 et seq. on these methods for participation. In 2007, the Minister Plenipotentiary of the Netherlands Antilles used his right to propose an amendment to a bill in the Lower House. As far as know, it was the first time this right was used. The amendment was adopted. *See Kamerstukken II* 2007/08, 30 531, no. 11.

[74] *See* the judgment of the *Hoge Raad* of 14 April 1989, *AB* 1989, 207 (*Harmonisatiewet*).

[75] The judgment of the *Hoge Raad* of 7 November 2003 (*Nederlands-Antilliaans Uitleveringsbesluit*, No. R02/037HR JMH/AT) suggests that a Kingdom regulation is not impervious to judicial review. This is consistent with the rule of Dutch constitutional law which stipulates that acts of parliament cannot be tested against the Constitution, but regulations and other lower forms of legislation can be.

[76] Some of the uncertainties described here also exist (or existed) in British overseas constitutional law, *see* Roberts-Wray 1966, and with regard to the overseas territories of the US (*see* chapter 3 on Puerto Rico). *See also* Hillebrink 2005.

[77] *See* Van Vollenhoven 1934, pp. 343-4, who describes and rejects the 'appendix theory.'

[78] *See* Hoogers & De Vries 2002, p. 38: '*in reality* the Netherlands Antilles and Aruba are mainly a constitutional appendix of the Kingdom in Europe.'

It means that the Netherlands Antilles and Aruba are distinct and separate territories from the Netherlands, but at the same time share a single, indivisible nationality with the Netherlands, and represent a single state under international law. The three Countries sometimes present themselves outwardly as united, but more often as three entities that have little to do with each other. This occasionally leads to criticism or lack of understanding among foreign governments and international organizations.[79] The Countries are not independent, and according to the Charter depend on each other for support, but nonetheless sometimes seem to aim to do as little together as possible. The Kingdom consists of three – or seven, if one considers each island separately, which many people do – very different worlds that hardly connect, except through the narrow legal corridor that the Kingdom has created.

There have always been many connections between the islands (especially Curaçao) and the Netherlands based on personal contacts and initiatives which do not involve the governments. On this level, it could be said that there exists a limited amount of communality, and that the islands are actually more Dutch than they might appear at first sight. At the same time, the more than 100,000 Antilleans and Arubans who are currently living in the Netherlands have made that Country a little bit Caribbean as well.

The Kingdom does not have a single national identity.[80] The only national symbol that the Countries share is the monarchy, the house of Orange. The Countries compete separately in sporting events, they have their own flags, national anthems, stamps and currencies. The shared Dutch nationality has been invoked in calls for solidarity between the Kingdom partners and equal protection of fundamental rights for all citizens of the Kingdom,[81] but in practice it seems to mean little more than that Antilleans and Arubans have a Dutch passport.

The existing ambiguities reflect two different views on the Kingdom. The first stresses that the Kingdom is one, and should therefore be based on solidarity and common goals for the entire Kingdom. It emphasizes that the Kingdom is a single state under international law, with a single nationality and the obligation to uphold its international obligations in all parts of its territory.[82] The

---

[79] *See for instance* the discussion between a member of the Human Rights Committee and representatives of the Netherlands concerning the initial state report of the Netherlands on the ICCPR, UN Doc. CCPR/C/SR.321, para. 27 and SR.325, para. 3.

[80] Logemann 1955, p. 57 already noted that the overseas territories had developed their own national consciousness, and 'the people of the Caribbean territories do not feel that their societies are parts of the Dutch nation in the sociological sense.'

[81] *See for instance* the advice of the *Raad van State* of the Kingdom on the occasion of the 50th anniversary of the Kingdom Charter (*Kamerstukken II* 2005/06, 30 300 IV, no. 26). *See also* Broek & Wijenberg 2005, who make an appeal for an 'undivided Netherlandership.'

[82] This view is defended, for instance, by the *Raad van State* of the Kingdom, and by the *Comité 2004* that was formed to celebrate the 50th anniversary of the Kingdom Charter. The

other view of the Kingdom stresses that there are three Countries which are autonomous in almost all affairs, which have their own separate territories, governments, and legislators, and which do not necessarily share the same moral standards and values. Politicians on either side of the Atlantic often do not adhere to either view consistently, but can easily switch from one view to the other depending on the circumstances. It is possible (in each Country) for politicians to push unanimously for measures based on the reasoning 'that we are still a single Kingdom', and the next day promote policies of self-reliance, or give precedence to regional integration.[83]

In the *Staten-Generaal* there is often evidence of an ambiguous or even internally contradictory attitude towards the Kingdom relations. On the one hand, almost all of the Dutch political parties participate in the mantra of overseas self-reliance that is an invariable part of any parliamentary debate on the subject, but at the same time the Dutch government is often exhorted by parliament not to sit back and let the Caribbean Countries make their own mistakes.[84]

The Kingdom changes its shape depending on the perspective of the viewer. The Charter often does not favour or exclude one perspective or the other. When two different views collide, the text of the Charter often does not provide a solution, forcing those involved to seek a political compromise, or to accept a stalemate. Thus, the ambiguities of the Kingdom remain unresolved, which means that any analysis of the structure of the Kingdom or a labelling of its character can only be a tentative one, with a large allowance for the Kingdom to shift shape from time to time.[85]

The somewhat unclear division of power, which is a corollary of this situation, is not uncommon in overseas constitutional relations.[86] This could be considered undesirable, since it places the weakest partner in a situation of having to beg for things to which it might or might not be entitled, and leaves

---

Comité consisted of various prominent Kingdom citizens and presented its final report, entitled *Investing in Togetherness* ('*Investeren in gezamenlijkheid*') on 15 December 2005. An English version of this report is available on <www.comite2004.org>.

[83] In a similar sense, *see* Matos 2002.

[84] This attitude is accurately summarized in the current policy of the Dutch political party VVD regarding the Kingdom: 'The Netherlands Antilles are responsible for all their actions, but in view of the situation that has arisen the Netherlands cannot take a passive attitude.' *See* the website of the VVD, <http://www.vvd.nl>.

[85] In a similar sense, *see* Kranenburg 1955, p. 88. *See also* Croes 2006 for an analysis of the ambiguities of the Kingdom Charter.

[86] *Leibowitz*, in his study on the overseas territories of the US, provides an analysis which could also be applied to some extent to the Caribbean Countries of the Kingdom: 'There is a tendency to assume that their uncertain status is a necessary consequence of their demographic, geographic and cultural circumstance. But it is not. The status uncertainty results primarily from Federal decision ... combined now with institutional forces in the Federal government and in the territorial governments which make status change unusually difficult.' (Leibowitz 1989, p. 69).

doubts about the extent of the powers of the stronger partner. This uncertainty probably stimulates an atmosphere of distrust, and has been analysed as reinforcing 'colonial' elements in the Kingdom relations.[87]

Also, if the Kingdom Charter is to be considered as a form of association between the three Countries, it should provide the terms of the association 'clearly and fully' and 'in a form binding on the parties', as *Crawford* writes.[88] The Charter is clearly binding on the Countries, but it could be doubted whether it clearly sets down the terms of the 'association'. The Charter is intertwined with the Constitution of the Netherlands to create a legislative maze in which only a few people can find their way. Some of the crucial articles of the Charter use open terms and leave it to the Kingdom government and legislator to interpret them. Because this power of interpretation is only rarely used expressly, it could be argued that the precise terms of the relation are not clearly and fully set down.

4.2.7 State Responsibility for the Netherlands Antilles and Aruba

One of the reasons for the Netherlands' continued involvement with the internal affairs of the Netherlands Antilles and Aruba is the responsibility under international law for the Netherlands Antilles and Aruba, which rests on the shoulders of the Kingdom government. In chapter 3, I have discussed this issue in general, as it plays a role in all overseas dependency relations, and also in relations of free association.

Because of the local circumstances on the islands (their proximity to many other states, their dependence on tourism and international trade, etc.) the actions of the local governments will often have an international aspect. If it were accepted that the fulfilment of international obligations is always a task of the Kingdom, the autonomy of the Caribbean Countries could be very substantially reduced. For this reason it is usually assumed that the task of the Kingdom government in this area is limited to conducting the international affairs of the Kingdom, which includes the concluding of international treaties, but which does not include the implementation of those treaties in the national legal order, nor otherwise includes the fulfilment of international obligations in the Countries.

Under the constitutional law of the Kingdom, the responsibility therefore lies with the governments of the Caribbean Countries, but this does not change the rule that internationally, the Kingdom is responsible for the fulfilment of its

---

[87] Broek & Wijenberg 2005. *See also below* in chapter 5, section 5.4.6 on anti-colonial discourse.

[88] Crawford 2006, p. 632.

international obligations (*see* chapter 3). As Justice J. *Wit* recently warned his audience on Curaçao:

> The Kingdom, and more particularly the mother country as its flag bearer, is liable under international law for every violation of international law. This means that even if a Caribbean country in the Kingdom violates international law within a sphere that would normally be an internal affair the violation would automatically amount to a Kingdom affair. The Kingdom, read: the mother country, cannot have a contingent liability (as it is called) without in some way being able to intervene in the process that triggered the liability. Our politicians should be aware of this.[89]

This international responsibility is one of the reasons why the Netherlands insisted that the Kingdom Charter should include powers for the Kingdom to intervene in the internal affairs of the Caribbean Countries. These powers are relatively vaguely defined (*see above*), which makes it not very difficult to claim that the Kingdom should intervene when problems occur in a Caribbean Country. It has often been claimed – both in the Caribbean Countries and in the Netherlands – that the Kingdom should intervene in order to guarantee the fulfilment of international obligations, for instance with regard to the prisons, the oil refinery of Willemstad, and various social problems.[90]

Such calls for interventions by the Kingdom are occasionally triggered by international organizations, such as the European Committee for the Prevention of Torture and Inhuman or Degrading Treatment or Punishment (CPT), which has visited the prisons of the Caribbean Countries on five occasions since 1994.[91] In 2007, the Lower House of the *Staten-Generaal* adopted a motion which requested the Dutch government to take action so that the Kingdom government would give imperative instructions ('*een dwingende aanwijzing*') to the responsible authorities to take adequate measures in order to put an end to the structural problems in the prisons on Curaçao and St Maarten, or to make Justice a Kingdom affair, based on the Kingdom's role of guarantor as provided by the Charter.[92]

It is of course very common for states to give decentralized bodies or states of a federation a responsibility for the fulfilment international obligations. What makes the situation of the Kingdom remarkable is that the state (i.e. the King-

---

[89] Speech by Justice J. Wit of the Caribbean Court of Justice at a meeting of the *Vereniging Bedrijfsleven Curaçao*, 19 December 2007, p. 7.

[90] *See for instance* George 2003, p. 73 et seq. who argues that the Kingdom has an obligation to close down the oil refinery of Willemstad because it pollutes the environment.

[91] *See* Munneke 1999 and Oostindie & Klinkers 2001c, p. 267 et seq. for a discussion of the earlier visits of the CPT.

[92] Motion introduced on 5 December 2007, *Kamerstukken II* 2007/08, 31 200 IV, no. 17.

dom) takes an exceptionally hands-off approach to – perceived – violations of international obligations in parts of its territory.[93] This approach can be explained from a number of factors. Firstly, the Caribbean Countries are autonomous in almost all affairs, which makes the Kingdom different from federal or decentralized states. Secondly, the Kingdom has very little formal authority to intervene in the autonomous spheres of the Caribbean Countries. Thirdly, the Kingdom has few other ways of influencing the situation in the Caribbean Countries, given the fact that the Netherlands is located 8,000 kilometres from its Caribbean partners, and the fact that there are hardly any economic or other ties between the Countries. Fourthly, because of the enormous difference in size between the Countries and the fact that the Kingdom is by and large the same as the Country of the Netherlands, it is difficult for the Kingdom to take action in the Caribbean Countries without destroying the carefully nurtured fiction of a post-colonial Kingdom consisting of three equivalent Countries, and thereby seriously damaging the relations between the three governments.[94]

4.2.8 Amending the Charter

The procedure for amending the Charter was made relatively simple, to facilitate the constitutional development of the Netherlands Antilles and Surinam.[95] Amendments are first approved by the *Staten-Generaal* in a single reading, unless they are inconsistent with the Dutch Constitution. In that case the procedure for amendments to the Constitution is followed (two readings with an

---

[93] This approach is also visible in the Kingdom's practice of reporting on the implementation of human rights treaties. Human rights organizations in the Netherlands recently published a condemnation of this approach. The NGOs wrote that: 'The Netherlands structurally refuses to take responsibility for the implementation of the UN Human Rights conventions in all parts of the Kingdom of the Netherlands. It does not structurally include information on Aruba and the Netherlands Antilles in its periodic reports. Furthermore representatives from the Netherlands Antilles and Aruba usually do not participate in its constructive dialogue with the UN human rights bodies. ... We recommend the Human Rights Council to remind the Netherlands that it has the full responsibility for the implementation of the UN Human Rights instruments in all parts of the Kingdom. As a result the Netherlands will have to make sure its periodic reports cover all parts of the Kingdom of the Netherlands. The Netherlands must also ensure the participation in the future of representatives from the Netherlands Antilles in its constructive dialogue with the UN human rights bodies.' *See* pp. 8 and 9 of the Dutch NGOs' contribution to the First Universal Periodic Review of the Netherlands by the UN Human Rights Council of November 2007. The UPR was planned to be discussed at the UN in April 2008.

[94] In an editorial of the *NJCM-Bulletin* (a journal published by the Dutch section of the International Commission of Jurists) it was therefore proposed that the Kingdom Charter should include more proportional measures for the Kingdom to insure that international obligations are met (7 *NJCM-Bulletin* (2007), pp. 955-957).

[95] *See* the official explanation to Article 55.

intermediary dissolution of the Lower House) but with the proviso that a simple majority will be sufficient in both readings. Both the *Staten* of the Netherlands Antilles and of Aruba must then adopt the proposal as well, in two readings. The second reading is not necessary if the proposal is supported by more than two-thirds of the votes cast in the first reading.[96]

The Charter has so far been amended five times, three times to accommodate a status change of a Caribbean Country,[97] and twice to facilitate minor constitutional changes in the Netherlands.[98] Since the 1960s, it has often been said that the Charter should be modernized. A thorough modernization of the text of the Charter was drafted in the early 1990s, but the result was not submitted to parliament.[99] In 2004, the Netherlands government announced another attempt to realize such a modernization.

The process of the disintegration of the Netherlands Antilles could ultimately require changes in the Charter to realize a new status for the five remaining islands of the Antilles.[100] The Netherlands government has expressed its willingness to cooperate with breaking up the Netherlands Antilles, if it gains assurance that the new Countries (and/or other entities that might be created) will meet certain requirements in the areas of government finance and law enforcement, over which the Kingdom currently has little or no control.[101]

4.2.9   The Right to Secession

The Charter provides for a procedure for the secession of Aruba.[102] The *Staten* of Aruba can choose for independence by adopting a regulation, which must be supported by at least two-thirds of the members. Such a regulation should then

---

[96] Article 55 of the Charter.

[97] These concerned the independence of Surinam (1975), the *status aparte* of Aruba (1985), and the decision that Aruba would not become independent in 1996 (1994). *See* Borman 2005, pp. 41-2.

[98] These concerned the introduction of the right to vote for Dutch nationals abroad (1985), and to bring the Charter in line with the new procedure for amendments to the Dutch Constitution (1998).

[99] The '*Proeve van een nieuw Statuut*' as it was called, was never published.

[100] *See* the report by the Jesurun Commission of 2004 ('*Nu kan het... nu moet het!*'). *See also* my analysis of the proposals in the light of the international law of decolonization and self-determination (Hillebrink 2005).

[101] Letter by the Minister for Government Reform and Kingdom Relations (De Graaf) to the Lower House, dated 17 December 2004 (*Kamerstukken II*, 2004/04, 29 800 IV, no. 18). This position was repeated in several letters to the Lower House and statements in 2005 and 2006. *See also* the Outline Agreement (*Hoofdlijnenakkoord*) of 22 October 2005 and the Closing statement of the Round Table Conference of 26 November 2005 in Willemstad, Curaçao (available in an English translation on <www.minbzk.nl>).

[102] Articles 58 to 60 of the Charter.

be put to a referendum, in which at least 50 per cent of the total number of persons eligible to vote should support it. This is a high threshold, which deviates from the international practice of decolonization, in which independence was usually based on a simple agreement between the metropolis and the government of the overseas territory, or some other entity or person that could reasonably be assumed to represent the territory. If Aruba has the right to independence under international law, the procedure of the Charter might be too strict.[103] It should be assessed whether the people of Aruba really want independence before the Kingdom could legally agree to the secession of the island. Such an assessment could be made through a referendum, but international practice does not indicate that it would be necessary for at least 50 per cent of the Arubans entitled to vote to support independence. Rather, a simple majority of the votes should be enough, as long as there is a reasonably high turnout of the voters.[104]

The Charter contains no procedure for the secession of the Netherlands Antilles, other than through an amendment of the Charter. When the procedure for Aruba was introduced in the Charter, at the request of Aruba, the Netherlands Antilles stated that it saw no need for such a procedure for the Netherlands Antilles.[105] It is generally assumed that this Country also has a right of secession, because the Netherlands government has since 1971 consistently stated that it would cooperate with realizing a desire of the Netherlands Antilles to become independent.[106] If the Netherlands Antilles possesses some sort of

---

[103] In response to questions in the Lower House, the Dutch government stated that the conditions for independence of Articles 58 to 60 were indeed more strict than international law, but they were included because Aruba wished to make sure that a choice for independence would be made in a responsible manner (*Kamerstukken II* 1992/93, 22 593 (R 1433), no. 8, pp. 10-11). Hoeneveld 2005, p. 66, simply considers Articles 58 to 60 as void, because the Kingdom Charter cannot set conditions to a right that Aruba derives from international law. *See also* the remarks by the representative of Uruguay in the Decolonization Committee concerning a similar provision in the UK West Indies Act, that 'the decision might be in the hands of minorities and the freedom of the peoples concerned might be restricted', and that the provision 'would tend to protect the *status quo* and limit the possibility of self-determination.' The representative of Italy agreed with this statement (GAOR (XXII), Annexes, Addendum to agenda item 23 (part III), para. 696, 722, and 746). Australia considered a two-thirds majority acceptable, as it could 'prevent precipitate and irrevocable action on important questions' (para. 776, and similarly, the UK in para. 783).

[104] In the 2004 and 2005 referendums in the Netherlands Antilles the UN Electoral Assistance Division recommended that at least 50 per cent of those eligible to vote should turn out. If one of the options received more than 50 per cent of the votes, the referendum should be considered valid. These recommendations were followed by the referendum committees on the islands.

[105] Borman 2005, p. 40.

[106] In 1952, the Dutch minister, Kernkamp, had already written to the governing Council of Surinam that the Netherlands would not have a right of veto if Surinam should decide to leave the Kingdom. The minister was furthermore of the opinion that a country that wished to secede from the Kingdom should properly consult the opinion of its population (*see* Van Helsdingen 1957, p. 198). This promise has been repeated on countless occasions since then.

international personality, which it probably does (*see* chapter 5), it could be argued that pursuant to the ICJ's decisions in the *Nuclear Tests Cases* the Netherlands has created an international obligation with regard to the Netherlands Antilles which it should perform in good faith. It should therefore probably cooperate with the secession of the Netherlands Antilles, and it cannot unilaterally retract its promise. Of course, the right to self-determination could put limits on the Netherlands' ability to cooperate, if it were clear that the 'peoples' of the Netherlands Antilles did not support the move towards independence of their government.

The right of secession of the Caribbean Countries is not a full representation of the right to self-determination, because it only creates a right to independence, not a right to choose other status options such as integration or association.

4.2.10 The Right to Self-Determination

The drafting of the Charter suffered a two-year delay, mainly, it seems, because of a conflict of opinion on the right to self-determination, which was brought to light by the Surinam delegation at the Round Table Conference of 1952.[107] Surinam took offence at a statement by the Netherlands Minister of Justice that the Charter proceeded from the historical ties between the three countries, which suggested that the ties were not voluntary. The Surinam delegation replied that this proposal offered no guarantees that the new legal order would not be a *colonial* order. The Surinam delegation thought that the preamble of the Charter should express that the acceptance by Surinam and the Netherlands Antilles of the new legal order amounted to an exercise of their right to self-determination.[108] The Charter should not cut short any further constitutional development of Surinam and the Netherlands Antilles, and it should not be an obstacle to a redefinition of the relation between the constitutional partners, should the need arise.[109] The Netherlands delegation was not prepared to recognize this.

Surinam used the upcoming debates at the UN on the cessation of transmission of information on Surinam and the Netherlands Antilles. It threatened that Surinam and the Netherlands Antilles would not join the Dutch delegation to the UN to defend the Dutch position. Surinam claimed that its participation in the UN debates had been based on the assumption that the Netherlands recog-

---

[107] *Van Helsdingen*, who participated in the negotiations on the part of the Netherlands, and wrote an authoritative commentary on the Charter, describes the debates on self-determination as 'completely superfluous, useless, fruitless, time-consuming and causing serious delays.' (Van Helsdingen 1957, p. 189).

[108] Speech by Kernkamp in the Second Chamber, *Handelingen II* 1952/53, p. 503.

[109] Kasteel 1956, p. 267.

nized its right to self-determination. In the UN debates that took place shortly before the RTC, the representative of the Netherlands Antilles had expressly stated, with the approval of the head of the delegation, that: '*Las Antillas Neerlandesas sí poseen la auto-determinación*', which was translated in the Official Records as: 'The Netherlands Antilles were, however, entitled to self-determination.'[110]

The Netherlands government decided that the Charter should recognize the right of self-determination.[111] A letter was sent to Surinam and the Netherlands Antilles, requesting that Surinam and the Netherlands should participate in the UN delegation, to which was added that the representatives could declare at the UN that they 'defended the ongoing negotiations with the Netherlands at the RTC on the basis of the right to self-determination.'[112]

Surinam was not satisfied. Together with the Netherlands Antilles, it issued a statement in which the Netherlands government was requested to clarify its interpretation of the right to self-determination. Surinam and the Netherlands Antilles defined it as follows:

> The right to self-determination gives the people the freedom to determine its relation to other countries, whereby it has the right to choose between independence, association with the mother country or with another state, and incorporation.[113]

Pressed for time because the Seventh session of the GA was about to start, the Netherlands sent two cabinet ministers (Luns and Kernkamp) to New York in order to reach an agreement with Surinam and the Netherlands Antilles. A joint Memorandum was drafted,[114] which stated in point five that the right to self-

---

[110] GAOR (VI), Fourth Committee, 242nd Meeting, 10 January 1952, p. 277. The remarks of Debrot went unchallenged in the Netherlands, perhaps because the report of the Netherlands ministry of Foreign Affairs of the Sixth GA translated the Spanish phrase 'auto-determinación' with a non-existent Dutch word 'auto-determinatie', thus avoiding the controversial term 'zelfbeschikking', which is the usual translation. *See* Min. BuZa 28, p. 56 and 61.

[111] This decision was taken in September or October during a Cabinet meeting, but it was not made public until January the next year, when Prime Minister Drees explained the course of events before and after the Memorandum of New York. *See Handelingen I* 1952/53, p. 107.

[112] Speech by Kernkamp, Minister for Overseas Territories, during the deliberations on the budget of 1953, *Handelingen II* 1952/53, p. 504.

[113] Statement by the Governing Council of the Netherlands Antilles and the Surinam mission, cited in Van Helsdingen 1957, p. 197. According to *Van Helsdingen*, this definition was derived from a statement by the US representative at the Sixth GA of the UN.

[114] Minister Kernkamp stated during the debate in the Second Chamber on the budget of 1953, that he and Foreign Affairs Minister Luns, after they had reached agreement with the delegates of Surinam and the Netherlands Antilles, obtained by telegram the consent of the Netherlands premier and vice-premier on the text of the Memorandum. The delegates of Surinam and the Netherlands Antilles in New York were prepared to view this telegram as a decision of the Netherlands government. *Handelingen II* 1952/53, pp. 505-6.

determination would be expressed in the preamble of the Charter. The right was not defined in the Memorandum, and it quickly appeared that there still existed a conflict of opinion on its meaning, but the ensuing discussion centred entirely on the right of secession, and it is therefore not very relevant anymore.

Surinamese and Dutch politicians involved in the negotiations had hoped that a Charter based on the right to self-determination would weaken the position of the nationalist 'extremists' in Surinam. The Surinam government would strike a much better figure if it could claim that Surinam had been offered a choice between independence and a continuation of the ties with the Netherlands. In The Hague, the recognition of the right to self-determination was part of the difficult process of 'mental decolonization' after the independence of Indonesia.[115] The debates in the Netherlands parliament reflected differences of opinion about the future of the Netherlands as a colonial power, and were intensified by feelings of resentment and disappointment about the speed at which the Dutch colonial empire was dissolving. In the Netherlands Antilles, there was some sympathy for the wishes of Surinam to recognize the freedom of the overseas territories to determine their own future, but it was also feared that a guaranteed right of secession might at some point threaten the continuation of the ties with the Netherlands, which was considered very undesirable.

In the Netherlands parliament it appeared that a majority of the members agreed that the Netherlands Antilles and Surinam did have a right to self-determination, or at least that the Netherlands could not prevent them from exercising it.[116] Two right-wing members of parliament did think that the Charter would terminate this right, but a majority of the members did not appear to share this view.[117] Minister Kernkamp, in a letter to the governing Council of Surinam, explained that Surinam would not 'use up' its right to self-determination if the Charter referred to this right.[118]

The Netherlands government proposed in 1953 that the Charter would declare that Surinam and the Netherlands Antilles accepted the Charter on the

---

[115] *See* Blok et al. 1982, p. 439.

[116] In the Lower House, the *KVP* stated that the Kingdom Charter could recognize the concept of the right to self-determination. This concept should however conform to the right to self-determination as it was laid down in the Charter of the UN, and in the official interpretation of that right by the UN, which was generally accepted. The *PvdA* was of the opinion that the cabinet should declare before the resumption of the RTC that the Netherlands recognized the right to self-determination of Surinam and the Netherlands Antilles and all of its consequences (*Handelingen II* 1952/53, p. 481 et seq.).

[117] Senator Algra (*ARP*), for instance, stated that he did not think the right to self-determination would be extinguished by the Charter. He pointed out that territories such as Surinam could not be compared with regions such as Friesland, because Surinam had never been an integrated part of the Netherlands, and had never had any say in the government of the Netherlands.

[118] Van Helsdingen 1957, p. 198.

basis of their right to self-determination, but the official explanation of the Charter should state that secession could only take place through the procedure for amendments to the Charter.[119] Surinam accepted this offer, but in 1954 stated that it would prefer that the right to self-determination not be mentioned in the Charter at all, for reasons unknown. During the debates about the final version of the Charter the subject of self-determination was 'anxiously avoided',[120] and the text of the Charter therefore does not contain any explicit reference to self-determination.

It had been established, however, that the Netherlands Antilles and Surinam had a right to self-determination, which was re-confirmed by the three Countries at numerous occasions. At the Round Table Conference of 1961 it was concluded that the bond between the Countries was based on the right to self-determination.[121] During the debate on the ICCPR and ICESCR in the Lower House in 1978, in which delegates of the Netherlands Antilles took part, it became clear that most MPs, as well as the Kingdom government, considered that the two Covenants granted a right to self-determination to the Netherlands Antilles, which – it was stressed – should not be equated to independence. It also included the right to choose for free association or integration. Reference was made several times to GA Resolution 2625 (XXV).[122]

Since the 1960s, the common view has been that the populations of the Caribbean Countries have a right to self-determination,[123] although it has remained controversial what this right entails. The Netherlands has adopted the policy that it will not object to the independence of any island of the Netherlands Antilles or Aruba, but it has reserved the right of co-decision concerning choices that would lead to a different status within the Kingdom. The Caribbean Countries on the other hand, have sometimes claimed that their right to self-determination should mean that their choice of another status should always be respected by the Netherlands. How these differing interpretations should be assessed in the light of international law is discussed in chapter 8 in the

---

[119] Van Helsdingen 1957, pp. 239-40.

[120] Van Helsdingen 1957, p. 247.

[121] 'Slotcommuniqué' of the RTC, reported in Meel 1999, p. 373.

[122] See for instance the statement by Minister Van der Stee, Handelingen II 1978/79, p. 158.

[123] This view was also defended internationally, for instance, during the discussion of the Kingdom's state reports on the ICCPR. The members of the HRC seemed to agree that the Netherlands Antilles and Aruba were entitled to a right to self-determination and decolonization (see CCPR/C/SR.862 to 864). A member of the Lower House, Van Middelkoop (GPV and later ChristenUnie), was like 'the voice of one crying in the desert' during the 1990s, when he repeatedly questioned whether the islands of the Netherlands Antilles really had a right to self-determination including a right of secession (see for example Kamerstukken II 1998/99, 26 404, no. 3, p. 2).

context of the right to self-determination of the island territories of the Netherlands Antilles.

Might Independence be Imposed by the Netherlands?

Ever since the Caribbean possessions of the Netherlands stopped being profitable during the colonial era, the question has arisen of whether the Netherlands should abandon or sell the territories. This discussion continued even after the Netherlands had recognized the right to self-determination of the overseas populations.

In 1980, the Netherlands' representatives in a Working Group that had been charged to study the constitutional future of the Netherlands, stated that the Netherlands 'has the right to participate in a decision about its relation with those islands that prefer to maintain constitutional ties with the Netherlands.'[124] This statement was interpreted to mean that, the Netherlands Antilles having entered the so-called intermediate phase on the way to independence, the Netherlands could force any island to become independent.[125] If one or more islands would express a wish to maintain constitutional ties with the Netherlands, this could only be achieved after negotiations with the Netherlands, during which the Netherlands would reserve a right to break off the relations.

Kapteyn, who had been a member of the Working Group, wrote an influential article on this subject in 1982. On the basis of GA Resolution 2625 (XXV) of 1970, and the Advisory Opinion of the ICJ in the *Western Sahara* case, *Kapteyn* concluded that the essence of the right to self-determination of non-independent overseas territories such as the Netherlands Antilles lay in the need for the mother country to respect the freely expressed will of the population.[126] International good faith entailed that the Netherlands should also respect this will if it was aimed at maintaining the constitutional ties, unless 'serious political implications of an international or internal Antillean nature … might cause damage to the Netherlands or the Netherlands Antilles if the constitutional ties were maintained.' It would not be enough if the continued ties with the Netherlands Antilles would merely put the Netherlands in a 'difficult position.' At the RTC of 1981, *Kapteyn* referred to the situation of Comoros and Mayotte as an example of such serious international problems.[127]

---

[124] Report of the Kingdom Working Group 1980, p. 47.

[125] Gorsira 1988, p. 59. *See also* Post & Van der Veen 1980, p. 155 for a report of a discussion on this subject at a conference in 1980.

[126] Kapteyn 1982, pp. 17 and 24-5.

[127] Report of the RTC 1981, p. 24-5. Three out of the four islands of the French overseas territory of the Comoros had chosen independence in 1974, but one (Mayotte) chose to stay with

Nelissen & Tillema concluded in 1989 that the Netherlands Antilles had 'a continuing right to associate with the Netherlands.' The Netherlands had to respect this right 'as this is their obligation under international law.' The authors reached this conclusion after interpreting the UN law of self-determination on the basis of the principle 'that legal provisions should be so construed as to be effective and useful.' Pushing the islands into independence 'might be considered a colonial attitude.' The authors nonetheless think that under certain extreme circumstances, the Netherlands might have a right to sever its ties with the islands. As 'no right is absolute', the Netherlands Antilles had to take into account the legitimate interests of the Netherlands. A 'persistent forsaking of duties by the Antilles' might justify a breaking off of the constitutional relations by the Netherlands.[128]

Croes & Moenir Alam[129] and *Janus*[130] think that the right to self-determination simply forbids the Netherlands from forcing the Caribbean populations to leave the Kingdom. *Van Rijn* similarly considers that the Netherlands is not allowed to break off the ties unilaterally. It has a duty to respect a choice made by the Antillean population with respect to their political status, including a choice for continued association or integration with the Netherlands.[131]

Jessurun d'Oliveira is the only author who maintains that the Netherlands has a right to abandon the Netherlands Antilles and Aruba. He agrees that the Caribbean populations have a right to self-determination, which he describes as an unconditional right, but he also thinks that the population of the European part of the Kingdom has a similarly unconditional right to self-determination, including a right to secede from the Kingdom and choose 'independence.'[132] This is a somewhat absurd proposition, since the right to self-determination is always invoked by peoples as protection against more powerful nations. The Netherlands, as a Country which is 50 times larger than the Netherlands Antilles and Aruba, has many other ways of making sure its interests are protected in its relations with the Caribbean Countries.

Jessurun d'Oliveira's proposition also seems to ignore that the self-determination of the Antillean and Aruba peoples is part of a process of decolonization,

---

France. Based on the principle of *uti possidetis* the international community demanded that France should grant independence to the Comoros as a whole. France was forced to use its veto in the Security Council to prevent the adoption of a condemnatory resolution.

[128] Nelissen & Tillema 1989, p. 190.

[129] Croes & Moenir Alam 1990, pp. 89-90.

[130] Janus 1993, p. 49.

[131] Van Rijn 1999, p. 58 and 73.

[132] Jessurun d'Oliveira 2003a. *Jessurun d'Oliveira* also expounded this opinion in a number of letters to the editors of Dutch newspapers. *See also* my reaction to *Jessurun d'Oliveira's* article (Hillebrink 2003), and his postscript (Jessurun d'Oliveira 2003b). Van Rijn 2004, p. 2278 also rejects *Jessurun d'Oliveira's* proposition.

which makes all the difference under international law. But according to *Jessurun d'Oliveira*, a 'second round of decolonization' should allow the metropolitan states to force their territories to become independent. At present, international law clearly does not allow such forceable actions, since decolonization under international law means freedom of choice for the dependent peoples, and an obligation for the metropolitan government 'to pay regard to the freely expressed will of peoples.'[133] The Netherlands would therefore violate international law if it were to abandon the Netherlands Antilles and Aruba.[134]

4.2.11   The Constitutions of the Caribbean Countries

The Country of the Netherlands Antilles originally consisted of six islands (Curaçao, Aruba, St Maarten, Bonaire, St Eustatius and Saba), each forming a separate administrative unit, called an '*eilandgebied*' (island territory). Aruba became a separate Country in 1986, after which the Country of the Netherlands Antilles consisted of the five remaining island territories.

The constitution of the Netherlands Antilles is called the *Staatsregeling*. It was originally (in 1950) introduced by the Dutch legislator, but it can only be amended by the *Staten* of the Netherlands Antilles. Amendments regarding a number of important subjects can only be realized with the approval of the Kingdom government.[135] The same is true for the *Staatsregeling* of Aruba.

The Countries make their own legislation on all subjects which are not Kingdom affairs. This legislation is often materially quite similar to Dutch legislation. According to Article 39 of the Charter, the Countries are obligated to strive towards concordance of legislation on a number of important subjects, but there are other – more important – reasons for the similarity of legislation. Because the legal system of the Caribbean Countries is based on Dutch law, and since the Countries lack the capacity to develop much new law themselves,

---

[133] Advisory Opinion of the ICJ on the Western Sahara (16 October 1975), *ICJ Reports* 1975, p. 33. *See also* Cassese 1996, p. 358, and Crawford 2001, pp. 32-3.

[134] Article 41 of the proposals on state responsibility of the International Law Commission calls on states not to recognize the results of such an act. Self-determination is one of the 'peremptory norms' referred to by Article 40 and 41 of the proposals which are presumed to codify customary international law (Crawford 2002, p. 246). According to Malanczuk1997, p. 334, a state which is the result of a violation of the right to self-determination, is 'probably a nullity in the eyes of international law.' According to the ICJ, self-determination creates *erga omnes* obligations, which means that they are the concern of all states, and not just those directly affected (judgment of 30 June 1995 (the *East Timor* case)).

[135] Article 44 of the Charter. It concerns amendments regarding fundamental human rights, the powers of the Governor, the government, and the *Staten*, the administration of justice, the allocation of *Staten* seats to the island territories, and the provisions which deal with the island territories.

it is often considered a practical option to copy or emulate Dutch laws. Also, the judicial system of the Netherlands Antilles and Aruba depends to a large extent on lawyers from the Netherlands. If Antillean and Aruban law should start to deviate too much from Dutch law, it would become more difficult for Dutch lawyers to work in the Caribbean Countries.

Judges are appointed by the Crown and are usually European Dutch. The public prosecutors are appointed by the Countries and are often Antilleans or Arubans. In civil law and penal law, the Supreme Court of the Netherlands functions as the final instance. In administrative law, the Joint Court of the Netherlands Antilles and Aruba functions as such.

The Caribbean Countries have a parliamentary system similar to the Netherlands, with an executive branch composed of the Governor and a council of ministers, who depend on the support of a majority in parliament (the *Staten*). All Netherlanders who are registered as inhabitants of the Country have the right to vote in elections for the *Staten*. The Countries have an electoral system based on proportional representation, but in the *Staten* of the Netherlands Antilles, each of the five islands has a fixed number of seats. Curaçao has a majority of 14 seats in a total of 22 seats. St Maarten and Bonaire each have three seats, and Saba and St Eustatius have one seat each. The *Staten* represent the population of the Country as a whole, but because all of the existing political parties have their power base in only one of the islands, the members of the *Staten* are usually considered to represent their own island first and foremost.

The Islands Regulation of the Netherlands Antilles (ERNA) provides that the island territories are autonomous in all areas except civil, penal and labour law, the police, prisons, monetary affairs, health care, social security, taxation, and partly in education, and some other minor subjects.[136] The populations of the island territories elect an Island Council, which appoints a number of Commissioners. Together with the Lieutenant Governor[137] (who is appointed by the Kingdom government), the Commissioners form an Executive Council.[138] The island territory of Curaçao has a special position under the ERNA, with a slightly larger amount of autonomy and more authorities than the other island territories.

---

[136] The *ERNA* lists the areas in which the island territories are not autonomous, and which must be handled by the Netherlands Antilles (Articles 2 and 2A).

[137] '*Gezaghebber*' is usually translated in English as 'Lieutenant Governor', although this could cause confusion with the function of '*waarnemende Gouverneur*' ('acting Governor'), who replaces the Governor when he is incapacitated. The current *Gezaghebber* of St Maarten prefers to be called 'Governor' (*see* his website at <http://www.governorsxm.com>), in which case the Governor of the Netherlands Antilles should probably be referred to in English as the 'Governor General.'

[138] *See* Duzanson 2000 for further information on the functioning of the organs of the island territories.

4.2.12   The Kingdom in Practice

The first 15 years of implementation of the Charter passed relatively uneventfully. The Kingdom existed of three Countries 'that had rather little to do with each other, and therefore enabled a somewhat inconsequential respect for each other's autonomy', as *Oostindie & Klinkers* put it.[139] The fear that the Netherlands might become involved in maintaining order in the Caribbean Countries, inspired by the economic decline of the Netherlands Antilles and the incidents of 30 May 1969 in Willemstad,[140] or that the Netherlands might become embroiled in border conflicts between Surinam and British Guyana, were some of the main reasons why the Netherlands started to push for the independence of Surinam and the Netherlands Antilles. Dutch politics were quite suddenly gripped by the sentiment that overseas possessions were a thing of the past, obviously also inspired by the international wave of decolonization that had decimated the Western empires during the 1950s and 1960s. Surinam agreed to leave the Kingdom in 1975, but the Netherlands Antilles refused.

Around 1990, Dutch politics again unanimously changed direction. The Netherlands Antilles and Aruba no longer needed to become independent if they did not want to. But the Netherlands now insisted that more care was needed to ensure that the principles of good government, legal certainty and human rights would be adequately respected in the Caribbean Countries. The Netherlands government was no longer content merely to respect the autonomy of the overseas Countries, provide aid, and hope that the Antillean economy would take a turn for the better. More attention was paid to the Kingdom affairs, and the involvement of the Kingdom with the autonomous affairs of the Caribbean Countries was increased. A few examples of this new policy were the administrative supervision on St Maarten, the establishment of a coast guard for the Caribbean Countries, and the refurbishment of the Caribbean prisons after the visits by the European Committee for the Prevention of Torture and Inhuman or Degrading Treatment or Punishment (CPT).[141] This new policy led to numerous conflicts between The Hague and the Caribbean governments,

---

[139] Oostindie & Klinkers 2003, p. 218.

[140] The historic centre of Willemstad was looted and partly burned to the ground during a labour conflict in the oil refinery. Dutch marines assisted in restoring order, *see* Croese 1998 and Oostindie 1999.

[141] *See* Oostindie & Klinkers 2001c for a description of the conflicts between the Netherlands and the Netherlands Antilles and Aruba on these issues. Oostindie & Klinkers 2003, p. 219 summarize the situation as follows: 'Since the 1990s, the transatlantic relations have indeed been characterized by constant political bickering, sparked by the Dutch, regarding the boundaries between local autonomy on the one hand and overall responsibility of the Kingdom on the other.'

whereas such conflicts were rare before 1990. One of the solutions which have been proposed is the establishment of a Constitutional Court or some other organ which could be charged with the task of settling disputes between the Countries.[142]

At present, the financial situation of the Netherlands Antilles is of the greatest concern to the Kingdom. The Antillean debt grew exponentially during the 1980s and 1990s, reaching a level of more than 100 per cent of the GDP in 2005. It was established during the 1990s that the Antilles would no longer be able to solve this problem on its own, most authoritatively by a committee chaired by E. van Lennep, which recommended a structural solution, to be realized jointly by the Antilles and the Netherlands. The committee's recommendations were only partly executed, and the Antillean economy continued to decline.[143] The help of the IMF was enlisted, which recommended drastic cutbacks and a thorough liberalization of the Antillean economy, while the Netherlands should provide financial aid to soften the blow. The Antilles implemented at least a number of the IMF's recommendations, but the Netherlands refused to supply the financial impulse because it considered the Antillean effort insufficient. This decision was vehemently resented in Willemstad, and considered a betrayal of trust.

The economic recession on Curaçao continued, and coupled with the steady growth of the Dutch economy this caused a substantial part of the population of Curaçao to move to the Netherlands, or to seek resort in drugs smuggling through the flight connection between Willemstad and Amsterdam.[144] The constitutional bond with the autonomous Netherlands Antilles came to be perceived as causing concrete problems in the Netherlands when Antillean youngsters with little education, and hardly any command of the Dutch language, started to feature prominently in the Dutch crime statistics. To make things worse – from the perspective of the Dutch media and politics – the perceived anti-Dutch labour party *FOL* won the elections in the Netherlands Antilles in 2002, and formed a coalition government while some of its leaders had been indicted or were serving prison sentences for fraud. The Netherlands Antilles was found at the forefront of Dutch media attention for the first time in the history of the Kingdom, and gained a distinctly notorious reputation in the Dutch public eye.

Whether the short-lived media attention really changed the long-standing Dutch policy of treating the Netherlands Antilles and Aruba as 'posteriority

---

[142] *See for instance, Kamerstukken I/II* 1999/2000, 27 198, no. 1, pp. 6 and 30.

[143] Korthals Altes 1999, p. 163 et seq.

[144] In 2004, it was estimated that some 130,000 inhabitants of the Country of the Netherlands were of Antillean – mainly Curaçaoan – descent. At that time, Curaçao itself had some 140,000 inhabitants.

number one',[145] seems uncertain. There are few policies developed for the Kingdom in The Hague, and those that are developed, are often easily abandoned or forgotten. In political terms, Dutch cabinets do not need to develop coherent or productive policies for the Kingdom, because the Dutch Lower House has never seriously challenged a Dutch minister for his policies with regard to the Caribbean Countries.[146]

4.2.13   Dismantling of the Netherlands Antilles

The lively status debate in the Netherlands Antilles has not focused just on the relation with the Netherlands, but also – and probably more importantly – on the relations between the islands and the dominant position of the largest island, Curaçao. Throughout history, there has never been much cohesion between the islands of the Netherlands Antilles in any sense.[147]

After the six Dutch islands in the Caribbean were united as a single colony in 1845, the unity of the territory was continually threatened by centrifugal forces. The rivalry between Curaçao and Aruba came to play an increasing role in the history of the colony after the establishment of oil refineries on both Curaçao and Aruba, which led to a substantial increase of the population on both islands. After World War II, Aruba demanded an equal position in the government of the territory, but Curaçao held on to its dominant position, with the support of the Netherlands. A federal system of government was introduced, in which all powers rested with the islands, except those enumerated in the Islands Regulation of the Netherlands Antilles (*see above*). In practice, the Netherlands Antilles continued to exhibit many traits of a centralized form of government.

When the Dutch government decided in the early 1970s that the Netherlands Antilles should become independent, Aruba insisted that it would not become independent as part of the Netherlands Antilles. It would rather become independent on its own.[148] The determination of Aruba and its leader Betico Croes convinced the Netherlands and the Netherlands Antilles that there was no future for a Netherlands Antilles which included Aruba. In 1981, the Countries and the six islands convened a Round Table Conference, at which

---

[145] This description was used in an editorial of the *NRC Handelsblad* of 11 June 2005.

[146] The limited political importance of the Caribbean 'headache dossiers' can also be gauged from a remark by the Dutch minister charged with Kingdom affairs (among other subjects), who admitted in 2005 that he spent no more than one day a week on the relations with the Netherlands Antilles and Aruba (*NRC Handelsblad* of 21 March 2005).

[147] Dalhuisen et al. 1997, pp. 145-54.

[148] For the backgrounds of the Aruban drive for independence, *see* Van Benthem van den Bergh et al. 1978.

they recognized that each of the islands should determine its own political future, based on the right to self-determination (*see* chapter 8).

In 1983, the Netherlands and the Netherlands Antilles agreed that Aruba could leave the Netherlands Antilles, and it was decided that Aruba would become independent in 1996. During an intermediate phase, which started in 1986, Aruba obtained a *status aparte* as a separate Country within the Kingdom, in preparation of independence. After it had acquired Country status, Aruba successfully pleaded to stay part of the Kingdom. Its separate status within the Kingdom was made permanent in 1995.[149]

After Aruba had left the Antilles, the prediction of Antillean premier Evertz that 'six minus one equals zero' seemed to come true quickly. St Maarten took the place of Aruba as the antagonist of Curaçao in the federation, while the central government continued unable to get a firm grip on the problems of the Country. While the economic recession of the 1970s and 1980s continued on Curaçao, Aruba boomed, supporting the argument that the federal structure of the Netherlands Antilles impeded an effective government of the Country. During the 1990s, the GDP per capita of Aruba quickly outgrew that of the Netherlands Antilles.

The political parties of Curaçao unanimously decided that the island should obtain a similar status as Aruba. A referendum was held on the island in 1993, which surprisingly showed that a large majority of the population disagreed, and wanted to keep the Antilles together. Referenda on the other four islands in 1994 showed a similar outcome.[150] A new central government made an attempt to restructure the Antilles, but failed.

In 2000, a second series of referenda was started. Perhaps crucially, this second series was started on St Maarten. The population of St Maarten chose to leave the Antilles and become a separate Country. The Netherlands refused to cooperate with this outcome, but in 2004 the populations of Bonaire and Saba also chose a future outside of the Antilles, which effectively sealed the fate of the Netherlands Antilles.

The only factor that kept the Antilles together was the refusal of the Netherlands to cooperate with realizing the desired new status of the islands. But in 2004, the outcome of the referenda, the enormous public debt of the Antilles, the problems in the area of law enforcement, the large-scale migration of Antilleans to the Netherlands, and the media attention these issues generated in the Netherlands, convinced The Hague that drastic changes were necessary to change the tide. In 2005, an agreement was signed which started the process of

---

[149] The genesis of Aruba's *status aparte* is described in Oostindie & Klinkers 2001c, p. 75 et seq.

[150] *See also* section 6.4.1 on these referenda.

breaking up the Netherlands Antilles into five separate entities.[151] The Netherlands offered to take over a large part of the public debt of the Antilles, but in return demanded a number of guarantees in the areas of law enforcement and public spending.

An administrative agreement was signed on 2 November 2006 by the Netherlands, the Netherlands Antilles, Curaçao and St Maarten. It formulated in some detail a number of aspects of the continuation of the Common Court of Justice of the Dutch Caribbean, guarantees regarding criminal prosecution, cooperation in the areas of police, prisons, immigration, combating of cross-border crime, the fulfilment of international obligations, a restructuring of the public debt, supervision of public spending both during an interim phase and in the new constitutional structure, and a common central bank of Curaçao and St Maarten. Most of these points of agreement will be worked out in the form of Kingdom legislation based on consensus (Article 38, paragraph 2 of the Charter).

At the same time, an agreement was reached between the Netherlands and the three remaining smaller islands of the Netherlands Antilles: Bonaire, St Eustatius and Saba. Based on an advice by the *Raad van State* of the Kingdom,[152] the Netherlands and the islands agreed that the three islands should become part of the constitutional structure of the Country of the Netherlands in the form of special public entities. The Antillean legislation will be gradually replaced by Dutch legislation, but deviations from Dutch legislation will remain possible in light of the small scale of the islands, their location in the Caribbean, and other factors.[153] The new status of Bonaire, St Eustatius and Saba had not yet been fully worked out at the time of writing of this study, but it was clear that the agreement of October 2006 aims to create a situation in which the government of the Netherlands will be directly responsible for the government of the three islands, which represents a fundamental departure from the equivalent relation that currently exists between the Netherlands and the Netherlands Antilles.

In 2007 a time frame was adopted which envisioned the final break-up of the Netherlands Antilles in December 2008. The Netherlands set aside some 2.2 billion euros for the restructuring of the Antillean debt. A number of committees were established to work out the details of the agreement and prepare

---

[151] *See* the Outline Agreement (*Hoofdlijnenakkoord*) of 22 October 2005, and the Closing statement of the Round Table Conference of 26 November 2005 in Willemstad, Curaçao (available in an English translation on <www.minbzk.nl>).

[152] *Voorlichting* by the *Raad van State* of the Kingdom dated 18 September 2006, *Kamerstukken II* 2006/07, 30 800 IV, no. 4.

[153] Final declaration of the conference between the Netherlands, Bonaire, St Eustatius and Saba of 11 October 2006, *Kamerstukken II*, 30 800 IV, no. 5.

the necessary legislation, and the dismantling of the Netherlands Antilles seemed at hand.

The agreements with the Netherlands then encountered considerable opposition on one Antillean island, namely Curaçao. In the Island Council, a majority rejected the agreement, mainly because two aspects of the agreement were considered an unacceptable infringement of the autonomy of the future Country of Curaçao. First, the agreement stipulated that the Dutch Minister of Justice – in his capacity as member of the Council of Ministers of the Kingdom – could give instructions to the public prosecutor of Curaçao and St Maarten in order to safeguard good government, legal certainty and fundamental rights and freedoms, based on Article 43, paragraph 2 of the Charter. Secondly, the financial supervision on the budget of the future Country was also considered an unacceptable Dutch interference in internal affairs.

After the elections for the Island Council of April 2007, the newly elected Island Council approved the agreement with the Netherlands, and Curaçao joined the process of dismantling of the Netherlands Antilles which had continued in the mean time. Due to the complicated nature of this process – involving five very different islands and the Netherlands and Aruba – and the different expectations of the future relations, it seems unlikely that the constitutional reform will be completed by the agreed date of 15 December 2008.

4.3   CONCLUSION

According to the Charter for the Kingdom of the Netherlands, the Netherlands, the Netherlands Antilles and Aruba have voluntarily chosen to create a structure in which a number of affairs are handled jointly on the basis of equivalence. They form three separate Countries which are autonomous in all affairs, except those which are listed in the Charter as affairs of the Kingdom (most importantly: foreign affairs, nationality and defence). The Kingdom has very limited powers to intervene in the autonomous affairs of the Countries.

The Kingdom is a somewhat ambiguous structure, since the islands are part of the Kingdom, but not of the Country of the Netherlands, while the Kingdom is often identified with the Country of the Netherlands. The islands have the right to leave the Kingdom, based on the right to self-determination, but there exists difference of opinion on the question whether they also have the right to choose free association or integration, or some other political status in relation to the Netherlands. The Netherlands does not have the right to terminate the relations unilaterally.

During the first decades after 1954, the self-government of the Caribbean Countries was virtually unchallenged, but since the 1990s, the Netherlands has become more concerned with the government of the islands, demanding respect for the principles of good government, especially in the areas of law enforcement and public spending. Aruba left the Netherlands Antilles in 1986 to form a separate Country within the Kingdom, and in 2005, negotiations were started to dismantle the Netherlands Antilles entirely.

Chapter 5
CHARACTERIZATION OF THE KINGDOM OF THE NETHERLANDS IN CONSTITUTIONAL THEORY

The structure of the Kingdom under municipal law determines, to some extent, how international law looks at the Kingdom. In the context of the law of decolonization, the standards determining whether 'a full measure of self-government' has been achieved differ depending on whether the state presents itself as an integrated whole, or as an association of states, or as something else. It is therefore important to determine how the form of government of the Kingdom could be characterized, although it should of course be remembered 'that the various classifications of territories are primarily a matter of convenience and ... the designation given to a territory as a matter of internal or constitutional law may not reflect its proper characterisation in international law.'[1]

The official explanation to the Charter of 1954 states the Charter is a legal document with its own special character. Most Dutch authors agree that the constitutional order of the Kingdom does not fit any of the traditional forms of government. The Kingdom order is often described as a composite state with a unique, or *sui generis* character.[2]

It may not be possible to categorize the Kingdom with more precision, but I will discuss some of the attempts and see if the structure really does not resemble any of the established forms of government.

5.1 FEDERATION

Many authors have noted that the Charter has some federal traits,[3] most importantly the division of power between the Kingdom and the Countries, based on

---

[1] Oppenheim/Jennings & Watts 1992, p. 277.

[2] *See for instance* Kranenburg 1955, pp. 23-33, Jonkers 1960, p. 1323, Van Aller 1994, p. 306, Van Rijn 1999, p. 72, and Hoogers & De Vries 2002, pp. 36 and 41.

[3] Logemann 1955, p. 439, Munneke 1993, and Van Aller 1993, p. 305. Some authors even simply consider it as a federation, *see* Belinfante & De Reede 1997, p. 301 et seq., and Bongenaar 1987, p. 242. Hirsch Ballin 1989, p. 464 describes it as 'a curious, somewhat limping federal structure.'

S. Hillebrink, The Right to Self-Determination and Post-Colonial Governance
© 2008, T·M·C·ASSER PRESS, *The Hague, The Netherlands and the Author*

the exhaustive list of subjects in the Charter, which is one of the basic characteristics of federations according to *Bernier.*[4] It could be questioned, however,
to what extent this division of power really exists, and whether it should not be
considered as mere constitutional make-up.

The federal elements in the Charter were part of a compromise reached
between the Netherlands and Surinam during the negotiations on the Charter.
At first, a structure had been designed in which the Kingdom would become a
fully functioning federation with its own legislature, executive and judiciary.
This 'strong' Kingdom would guarantee that the interests of the overseas Countries were properly represented, but it was also feared there would not be enough
work for full-time institutions, and that a federal structure would make too
large a demand on the limited resources of the overseas Countries. After Indonesia had become independent, the draft for a federal 'Constitution for the
Realm' (*Rijksgrondwet*) of 1948 was considered too burdensome by the Netherlands, also because a large part of the constitutional law of the Country of the
Netherlands would have to be incorporated into it. [5]

In 1950, the Netherlands presented a 'Draft for a Charter' (*Schets van een
Statuut*), followed in 1952 by a Working Paper (*Werkstuk*), both of which abandoned the idea of a real federation and replaced it with a structure in which
there would be no separate federal level, but merely cooperation between the
Countries. No new institutions would be created, and it was proposed that the
common affairs of the Countries would be handled largely by the organs of the
Netherlands.

At the request of Surinam, the final text of the Charter represents a return in
some respects to the federal language of the original Constitution for the Realm.
The Charter seems to create a number of federal institutions, such as a Council
of Ministers of the Kingdom, a *Raad van State* of the Kingdom, and a Kingdom legislature. *Van der Hoeven* has argued convincingly, however, that the
Charter, despite its federal language, remained true to the concepts of the Draft
and the Working Paper.[6] The structure of the Kingdom remained the same. The
new organs that the Charter creates should not be considered new institutions,
Van der Hoeven argues. There are no institutions of the Kingdom, except perhaps the Kingdom government. The existing institutions of the Netherlands are
merely attributed new functions by the Charter, and the existing institutions of
the Netherlands Antilles and Surinam are given the right to influence the
fulfilment of these functions by the Netherlands. When a Dutch institution acts
as a Kingdom organ, it has the duty to follow the procedures of the Charter, but

---

[4] Bernier 1973, p. 5.
[5] Van Helsdingen 1957, p. 154 and 156, and Jonkers 1955, p. 54.
[6] Van der Hoeven 1959. In a similar sense, *see* Borman 2005, pp. 22-4.

it does not change its character because of this, in *Van der Hoeven's* view, which I think is correct. This means that the Kingdom cannot really be considered as a federation. There is no true division of power between the Kingdom organs and the organs of the Country of the Netherlands.

Most writers on Dutch constitutional law agree that the Kingdom is fundamentally different from a federation.[7] This opinion is based especially on the fact that there is no real equality or equivalence of the constituent parts of the Kingdom, and that the Kingdom government hardly functions as a separate level of government. In 2005, the Minister for Administrative Reform and Kingdom Relations responded to questions from the Lower House, that in his view the Kingdom was not a federation.[8]

5.2 CONFEDERATION

The Kingdom has occasionally been compared to a confederation. *Gastmann* detected a number of confederal elements in the structure of the Kingdom.[9] *Bijkerk* in one of his pleas for a federal interpretation of the Charter, complains that 'the worthy politicians on both sides of the [Atlantic] ocean have considered it opportune to interpret and apply the constitution of our Kingdom confederally.'[10] Government statements have occasionally confirmed *Bijkerk's* claim.[11]

Oppenheim described confederations as 'several fully sovereign states linked together for the maintenance of their external and internal independence by a treaty into a union with organs of its own, which are vested with a certain power over the member states, but not over the citizens of these states.'[12]

Some elements of *Oppenheim's* definition more or less apply to the Kingdom. It is a union of three entities that operate rather independently, and which have some international personality.[13] The union established by the Charter

---

[7] *See for instance* Luiten 1983, p. 69, Janus 1993, p. 36, Borman 2005, p. 23, Hoogers & De Vries 2002, p. 38, and Nap 2003a, p. 17. Bergamin & Van Maarseveen 1978, p. 432, and Matos 2002 call it a 'pseudo-federation.'

[8] *Aanhangsel Handelingen II*, 2005/06, no. 396.

[9] Gastmann 1968, p. 115.

[10] Bijkerk 2003, p. 1862. *Bijkerk* considers that it would not be allowed to radically change this interpretation without first consulting the populations of the Netherlands Antilles and Aruba in a referendum.

[11] *See for instance* the explanation of the Kingdom order by the Dutch representative during the discussion of the report of the Netherlands on the ICESCR in 1998, E/C.12/1998/SR.15.

[12] Oppenheim/Jennings & Watts 1992, pp. 246-7.

[13] It is usually assumed by writers on Dutch constitutional law that only the Kingdom has international legal personality, whereas only the Countries have legal standing under municipal

has very little direct control over the citizens of the Countries.[14] *Oppenheim* furthermore notes that the chief organ of a confederation 'is one where the member states are represented by diplomatic envoys; its power ... is essentially nothing else than the right of the body of the members to use various forms of coercion against such a member as will not comply with the requirements of the Treaty of Confederation.'[15] This description somewhat resembles the practice of the Council of Ministers of the Kingdom, which more or less functions as a procedure for conferring with the ministers plenipotentiary as ambassadors of their Countries. Decisions of the Kingdom are almost always based on consensus between the Countries.

The powers of the Kingdom government to intervene in the administration and legislation of the Caribbean Countries do not conform to this description of confederations, but these powers have so far been left unused. Other Kingdom powers are usually only employed with the consent, or even at the request, of the Countries.

The comments of the representative of India (and some other states) during the UN debates of 1955 suggest that the Kingdom was viewed in some quarters as a confederal structure linking an independent state with two colonies. India also claimed that the Kingdom as a whole should not be considered as a state under international law, but this conclusion is not shared by any writer, as far as I am aware, and it is also not supported by the international practice, which accepts that the Kingdom is authorized to conclude treaties and to perform other functions of independent states.

An important difference with confederations is that the Kingdom Charter is not an international treaty and that the Countries are not sovereign states. The Charter does bear some resemblance to a treaty (it is based on voluntariness

---

law (*see for instance* Borman 2005, p. 25, and Hoogers & De Vries 2002, p. 192). But if the Netherlands Antilles and Aruba do not possess a full measure of self-government, they can still exercise at least one right under international law, namely the right to self-determination, as part of their process of decolonization. This suggests that the Countries, or their 'peoples', have a form of international personality. GA Res. 2625 (XXV) of 1970 declares that territories such as the Netherlands Antilles and Aruba have 'a separate status' under international law. If it is assumed that the Charter creates an imperfect form of free association between the Countries, than they should also be viewed as having international personality. Only when the Netherlands Antilles and Aruba are considered as integrated with the Netherlands – an interpretation of the Charter which I will reject in the next chapter – could it be argued that only the Kingdom has legal standing under international law.

[14] The authority of the Kingdom legislator is mainly limited to subjects which usually have no direct impact on the life of its citizens. A few exceptions are the laws and regulations concerning Dutch nationality, extradition, and royal decorations. But on these subjects, the Kingdom legislator may sometimes choose to apply different standards in different Countries, for instance with regard to extradition.

[15] Oppenheim/Jennings & Watts 1992, p. 246.

and can only be amended with the approval of the 'state parties'), and the Countries are proto-states in the sense that they can perform most of the functions of states and they can choose to become independent (except the Netherlands).

It could therefore be argued that the Kingdom is somewhat similar to a confederation.[16] But the fact remains that the Kingdom relations are not based on a treaty concluded by independent states.[17] It would also be hard to deny that the Kingdom is considered a state under international law. For those reasons, *Oppenheim* does not discuss the Kingdom under the heading of 'Confederated states' (but under 'Colonies', *see below*).[18]

5.3   CONSTITUTIONAL ASSOCIATION

The term 'constitutional association' was used by *Janus* to describe the Kingdom, to make clear that the relations are determined (mainly) by the municipal law of the Kingdom, and not by international law (as is probably the case with free association).[19]

The term 'association' in this context refers to the voluntary and cooperative structure that the Kingdom intended to create. It is often used to describe the constitutional structure of the Kingdom, even by the Kingdom government.[20]

Van der Hoeven, in his insightful article on the relation between Kingdom law and the constitutional law of the Netherlands, coined the phrase 'the cooperative Kingdom', in which the Netherlands performs certain tasks for the Caribbean Countries after consulting with them.[21] This interpretation, which *Van der Hoeven* defends on dogmatic grounds, rejects the idea of the Kingdom as a separate, superimposed layer of government, and is more in line with the idea that there exists a 'constitutional association' between the three Countries. This

---

[16] This would spell doom for its present constitution, because confederal systems tend to be regarded as unsatisfactory and are usually not long-lived. In time, they always seem to be dissolved or transformed into real states, *see* Oppenheim/Jennings & Watts 1992, pp. 246-8.

[17] *Similarly, see* Meel 1999, p. 62.

[18] Oppenheim/Jennings & Watts 1992, pp. 280-1.

[19] Janus 1993, p. 36. *Janus* does think the relations have an international aspect, because the Netherlands Antilles and Aruba can claim a right to self-determination as long as they are not independent. Van Rijn 1999, pp. 57-8 also considers the relations with the Netherlands as a form of association, and on p. 72 he writes that these constitutional relations are also determined by the international right to self-determination.

[20] *See for instance* the Core Document which serves as the basis for the Kingdom's reports on its compliance with the UN human rights treaties to which the Kingdom is a party (UN Doc. HRI/CORE/1/Add.66, par. 32).

[21] Van der Hoeven 1959, p. 388.

interpretation is also confirmed by the practice of the Kingdom, at least before 1990, in which the Kingdom has functioned as a procedure for Dutch organs to consult with the Netherlands Antilles and Aruba before acting on their behalf. *Borman* therefore considers the Kingdom could be described as a cooperative structure governed by constitutional law.[22] I think that terms such as 'cooperative structure' or 'constitutional association' reflect the essential characteristics of the Kingdom – as it has operated in practice – quite well. But this is perhaps not a very meaningful conclusion since these terms are not defined in the general doctrine concerning constitutional law. Also, they do not reflect the fact that the relation between the Kingdom and the Caribbean Countries is still hierarchical, as evidenced by Articles 43 to 51 of the Charter (*see* chapter 4).

5.4   OTHER FORMS OF OVERSEAS RELATIONS

5.4.1 Dominions

The status of the Caribbean Countries has also been compared to that of the dominions within the British Commonwealth between 1926 and World War II, a status that also 'defies classification.'[23] The dominions (Australia, Canada, South Africa, New Zealand, Newfoundland and Ireland) were 'autonomous communities within the British empire, equal in status ... and freely associated as members of the British Commonwealth of Nations.'[24] As determined by the Statute of Westminster of 1931, the dominion parliaments became equal in status to the UK parliament, and the dominions themselves decided to what extent they wished to cooperate with the UK. The UK could only legislate for the dominions if they so desired. This status was therefore (broadly speaking) similar to that of the Cook Islands and Niue.

According to *Kranenburg,* the Kingdom is tied together more strongly than the pre-War Commonwealth was, by the acceptance of a common area of legislation and administration, and by a certain right of supervision by the Kingdom government, which did not exist for the dominions.[25] *Logemann* considered that these differences were necessitated by the fact that Surinam and the Netherlands Antilles considered themselves 'not yet well enough equipped' to exercise all of the functions of a state, whereas the dominions were already developed

---

[22] Borman 2005, p. 24.
[23] According to the Commission on Inter-Imperial Relations (1926), cited in Kranenburg 1955, p. 23. Klinkers 1999, p. 427 gives an historical overview of the use of the term 'dominion' in the debates on the status of Surinam and the Netherlands Antilles.
[24] The Balfour Declaration adopted at the Imperial Conference of 1926.
[25] Kranenburg 1955, p. 33. *See also* Van der Pot 1946, p. 110.

enough 'to stand by themselves under the strenuous conditions of the modern world' in 1926.[26]

Baker considered the dominions as separate persons under international law because they were 'capable of practically every international relationship of which "sovereign states" are capable.'[27] The Netherlands Antilles and Aruba have not reached this point. The Kingdom Charter does not explicitly prohibit the Countries from developing their 'proto-dominion status'[28] into something more akin to independence. The Charter in fact requires the Kingdom to involve the organs of the Countries as much as possible with Kingdom affairs, including foreign affairs and defence.[29] The only limit that the Charter places on the independent operation of the Countries is the conclusion, approval and ratification of treaties, which the Charter attributes to the King and the *Staten-Generaal*.

The potential for a more independent role of the Caribbean Countries on the international scene has not been developed fully (*see also* in chapter 6, section 6.2 on free association), and the status of the Netherlands Antilles (and Aruba) has largely stayed the same since 1954, for which reason the Kingdom is essentially different from the pre-War Commonwealth.

5.4.2 Puerto Rico

The commonwealth status of Puerto Rico has also been compared to the status of the Netherlands Antilles and Aruba.[30] The constitution of Puerto Rico may also be considered as a constitutional appendix to the US Constitution, and the island also has a slightly ambiguous and uncertain status in relation to the US that dates from the same time as the Kingdom Charter.

But commonwealth status seems to mean more metropolitan involvement and interference. The US Congress has retained its authority to legislate for Puerto Rico, and considers this authority as principally unlimited. The legislative and executive powers of the Kingdom in the Caribbean Countries are more restricted than those of the US in Puerto Rico. The Caribbean Countries also have more formal ways of influencing metropolitan decisions than Puerto Rico, and the Kingdom is not allowed to revoke the autonomy of the Countries, except temporarily and as a last resort. The nationality of the Caribbean Dutch is

---

[26] Logemann 1955, pp. 55-6.

[27] Baker 1929, p. 353.

[28] This description was used by a Surinam politician (Pengel) during the negotiations on the Charter (cited in Klinkers 1999, p. 427) and during the debates on the approval of the Charter in the *Staten* of Surinam by representative Karamat Ali, cited in Meel 1999, p. 77.

[29] Article 6, para. 2 of the Charter.

[30] Hintjens 1997, p. 538, and Van Aller 1996.

guaranteed by the Kingdom Charter. All this indicates that the Kingdom Charter has created more equivalent relations than the US relation with Puerto Rico.

5.4.3 New Caledonia

The new status of *pays d'outre-mer* of New Caledonia is comparable to the status of the Netherlands Antilles and Aruba in the sense that New Caledonia also has a separate identity within the Republic – tied to France, but not entirely a part of France in every respect. But French metropolitan control over various aspects of the government of the islands still appears to be considerably stronger. French citizens in New Caledonia also still possess several rights that they can claim from the French government directly, which means that New Caledonia is probably more integrated into the mother country than the Dutch Caribbean Countries. Another important difference is that France seems never to have contemplated refusing its overseas citizens access to the metropolis, as the Dutch government has done.[31]

The participation of New Caledonia in the exercise of the reserved powers of France is different from that of the Netherlands Antilles and Aruba. New Caledonia votes for the president and the parliament of France, but it does not have a representative comparable to the Ministers Plenipotentiary of the Dutch Caribbean Countries. The French government is obligated to request the advice of the local institutions in a number of situations, but for the most part it is constitutionally allowed to proceed on its own in the affairs that are not part of the autonomy of New Caledonia. Again, this points more to a form of integration into the mother country than the status of the Netherlands Antilles and Aruba.

5.4.4 Cook Islands and Niue

The Cook Islands and Niue are part of the Realm of New Zealand, but they are not part of New Zealand, which makes their status similar to that of the Netherlands Antilles and Aruba. However, the New Zealand government has no authority whatsoever to legislate for the Cook Islands, and for Niue only when that island requests it and consents to it. New Zealand also lacks any other authority to intervene in their affairs. These territories also have full control over their constitutions, which are the highest laws in the territories. The au-

---

[31] In 2006, the Dutch government presented a bill to enable the expulsion of unemployed Antillean and Aruban youngsters with insufficient education. At the time of writing, it was still uncertain whether the bill would become a law. Klinkers 1999, p. 327 et seq. describes the migration policies of France and the US, as compared to those of the UK and the Netherlands.

tonomy of these territories therefore exceeds that of the Netherlands Antilles and Aruba considerably. Curiously, a considerable part of the law in force in the Cook Islands, and even more so in Niue, consists of English common law and New Zealand laws that date from before the period of free association. The territorial parliaments are allowed to replace these foreign sources of law by indigenous legislation, but have not done so in many areas.[32] In this respect, they seem to be more closely connected with the metropolis than the Netherlands Antilles and Aruba, even though their legislative powers are formally larger than those of the Dutch territories.

For the same reason, the Netherlands Antilles and Aruba are essentially different from other associated territories such as the Federated States of Micronesia. The debate on the relations between the US and the associated states of Micronesia and the Marshall Islands, and between New Zealand and the Cook Islands and Niue is nonetheless somewhat reminiscent of the status debate in the Kingdom, especially regarding the relation between the Netherlands Antilles and the Netherlands. The fact that all of these islands depend to a considerable extent on support from the metropolis probably has a strong influence on the character of the relations, at least in the public debate.

5.4.5 West Indies Associated States

The closest parallel to the Kingdom relations is probably the British West Indies Associated States (WIAS), which no longer exist. Similar to the Kingdom Charter, the system of the WIAS was characterized by a limitative list of affairs that were attributed to the UK government, which was largely identical to the list of Kingdom affairs in the Charter. All other subjects were exclusively attributed to the governments of the associated states. The UK only had a right of intervention in case the foreign affairs or the defence of the associated state were at stake. The way in which the associated states were allowed to play a limited role in international affairs is also mirrored rather closely in the situation of the Netherlands Antilles and Aruba.

The West Indies Act did not create a superstructure similar to the Kingdom, and the associated states did not have representatives that took part in the deliberations of the government in London. Another difference was the absence of a right of abode in the UK for the citizens of the associated states. But this does not really change the basic constitutional structure, as well as the practice based on it, which appears to have been very similar.[33]

---

[32] *See* Ntumy & Adzoxornu 1993, p. 3 et seq. for the Cook Islands, and p. 158 et seq. for Niue.

[33] In a similar sense, *see* Oostindie & Klinkers 2003, p. 237, note 18. *See also* Broderick 1968, p. 400, who considers the only major distinction between the UK association and the Kingdom

5.4.6 **Colonies**

The term 'colonies' was never clearly defined in Dutch constitutional law. The overseas territories were originally considered to be possessions of the colonial trading companies, and from 1813 possessions of the Dutch state, which were administrated by the King without any constitutional restrictions. During the course of the nineteenth century, parliament extended its authority to the colonies and at the start of the twentieth century, the colonies were no longer considered possessions, but part of the territory of the Dutch state. The precise nature of the legal relation between the metropolis and the overseas territories remained somewhat murky.[34]

The end of the colonial era was celebrated more than once in the Netherlands. In 1922, the term 'colonies' was deleted from the Dutch Constitution to enable the development of the constitutional status of the Dutch East Indies.[35] Doubts persisted in the legal scholarship whether Curaçao was still a colony. The criterion used in this discussion was whether the overseas territories were subordinated to the Netherlands. Some writers claimed the territories were 'coordinated' on an equal footing with the other parts of the Kingdom. These writers claimed that the Kingdom consisted of four separate parts which were all equally subordinated to the state, and each of which had its own legislature.

Others rejected this interpretation as unrealistic, because the legislature for the overseas territories was ultimately still the Dutch *Staten-Generaal* and government, even though the Constitution of 1922 introduced the principle that the internal affairs of the overseas territories should be handled by the organs of those territories. This principle meant a decentralization of authorities from the metropolitan to the overseas organs, but it did not affect the subordination of the overseas territories to the metropolis. Also, the Netherlands could still unilaterally decide to change the Constitution. Some authors therefore continued to describe the position of the overseas territories as subordinated to the Netherlands.[36] *Van der Pot* and others saw the relation as developing from subordination into something else (perhaps 'sub-coordination' as *Eigeman* called it), because of which the relation could not yet be categorized.[37]

---

relations (a 'satisfactory solution by a Country with a similar problem to the United Kingdom') to be the absence of a right of secession for the Dutch Caribbean Countries. As was explained in chapter 4, the Countries have obtained this right. *See further* chapter 3 for a description of the WIAS and the reasons why these territories all became independent during the 1970s and 1980s.

[34] *See* Van Vollenhoven 1934.

[35] Kranenburg 1930, pp. 132-3. In 1936 the word 'colony' was dropped from the name of 'Curaçao and dependencies', *see* De Gaay Fortman 1947, p. 37.

[36] Oud 1967, pp. 14-15.

[37] Van der Pot 1946, p. 110.

One of the aims of the Kingdom Charter of 1954 was to end all remaining doubts regarding the status of the Dutch Caribbean territories.[38] In The Hague, it was expected that the Charter would easily succeed in achieving this goal, and the Charter was therefore hailed as the end of the colonial era in the Dutch West Indies. Dutch premier Drees stated during the final conference that: 'The colonial relation is ended; the intensive consultations alone are proof of that; those would have been out of the question during colonial times.'[39] In the Dutch Lower House, it was stated that a colonial relation was terminated by independence, but also when the 'unlimited supremacy of the mother Country' ended. In the opinion of many members of parliament, the Charter had transformed the colonial relation of subordination into a relation based on equivalence.[40] Only the communist members maintained that the colonial status of the Netherlands Antilles and Surinam would be continued under the Charter.[41]

Kranenburg described the Charter as a radical breach with the colonial situation,[42] and *Oud* wrote that the Charter ended the subordination of the Netherlands Antilles and Surinam.[43] But some writers on constitutional law were less certain. *Ooft*, while accepting that the Charter had created equivalent Countries, found Articles 41 to 51 to be colonial, as well as the regulations for the Governor.[44] *Van Haersolte* compared the Charter to the draft Constitution for the Realm of 1948, and concluded that it represented less of a radical breach with the old structure of the colonial era.[45] Much of the international literature also continued to consider the Netherlands Antilles and Surinam as colonial or dependent territories (*see* chapter 6).

The continued doubts may be explained partly from the fact that the Charter was born from the desire to make as few changes to the constitutional order of the colonial era as were necessary to realise a substantial amount of autonomy for the overseas Countries at relatively low costs, both in man power and financially. Surinam and the Netherlands Antilles were mainly interested in economic autonomy. The Netherlands was not prepared to create a really federal structure that would give the Caribbean Countries a say in Dutch affairs, and also not prepared to relinquish all constitutional control over the territories.

---

[38] Kranenburg 1955, p. 9.

[39] Cited in Klinkers 1999, p. 131. *See also* Van Helsdingen 1957, p. 586 for the opinion of the government of the Netherlands as expressed in parliament.

[40] *See* Van Helsdingen 1957, p. 584 and Klinkers 1999, pp. 209-10.

[41] Klinkers 1999, p. 130.

[42] Kranenburg 1955, p. 92. Kranenburg 1958, pp. 48-9 placed the breach with the colonial era in 1950-1 when the Interim Measures went into force.

[43] Oud 1967, p. 22. *In a similar sense, see* Van der Pot-Donner/Prakke et al. 2001, p. 822.

[44] Ooft 1972, pp. 197-9.

[45] Van Haersolte 1988, p. 158.

Because of this, the new order still exhibited elements of subordination, in spite of the Charter's claim that the Countries were equivalent.

Definition of Colonial Status by Foreign Writers

In the Netherlands, the essence of colonialism was therefore considered the element of subordination to the mother country, which was formally ended in 1954. But it may be interesting to see how colonial status has been defined by foreign writers. In the international literature the word 'colony' originally referred to an overseas territory where a group of settlers had occupied an uninhabited area or subdued the indigenous population, which was used as a trading post or to accommodate a population surplus in the home country of the settlers.[46] During the nineteenth and twentieth centuries, the term gained a negative connotation, describing a situation where a foreign white elite deprives the non-white masses of self-government and human rights in order to 'extract immense riches for their own profit.'[47] The term was still also used in a less disapproving way simply to refer to 'distant territories that remain, in some way, politically dependent on the metropolitan power', as *Aldrich & Connell* put it.[48]

In the older legal literature the concept of 'colonies' was sometimes considered not to be a legal concept, because the classification as a colony did not in itself create any rights or duties in international or domestic law.[49] This changed after the right to self-determination of colonial peoples became a generally recognized part of international law during the 1960s, and the need arose to find an accurate legal definition of colonies. A definition based on the usage in the legal literature should probably take account of the following six elements.

1. Subordination
According to *Ermacora*, in the *Encyclopedia of Public International Law*, colonial relationships were characterized by 'subordination and supremacy.' Colonies might obtain some delegated powers of government or be integrated in the state to some degree, but the colonial power remained 'a kind of *Oberstaat.*

---

[46] Wesel 1999. Under British constitutional law it meant 'any part of Her Majesty's dominions exclusive of the British Islands, and of British India' (Interpretation Act, 1889, section 18 (3)). This definition excluded the protectorates and protected states, and is narrower than the all-encompassing term 'possessions', *see* Roberts-Wray 1966, pp. 37-44. British law also distinguished between settled and conquered colonies, *see* Davies 1995.

[47] Aldrich & Connell 1998, p. 3.

[48] Aldrich & Connell 1998, p. 1.

[49] In this sense, *see for instance* Kirchschläger 1961, p. 256-7.

The colony is subordinated but without creating a confederation.'[50] *Fastenrath*, in Simma's commentary on the UN Charter, also sees the 'subjection' of the territory as a characteristic, although a colony could also be integrated into the state, but 'without the status of equal rights, or without its free decision.'[51] *Kirchschläger* speaks of an '*Unterwerfungsverhältnis*' (relation of subjection or subjugation).[52] *Crawford* also considers that colonial territories are subordinate to a metropolitan state.[53]

2. Separateness

Another characteristic to be found in the legal literature is that the territory of a colony is not part of the metropolitan area of the state. There is always a certain distinctness from the mother country, not only geographical but in other senses as well.[54] The separateness of colonies is connected to the historical goals of colonization, namely conquest and exploitation. The pursuit of these goals meant that the population of the colony could not be considered part of the nation or people of the mother country.[55]

3. No full citizenship rights

A characteristic which has been noted in the literature is the absence of full citizenship rights. After the abolition of slavery and the formalization of the concept of nationality in Europe, it was common practice to grant the population of colonies a status which entailed subservience to the state, but which did not grant them the fundamental rights and freedoms that were formulated in the European capitals during the nineteenth and twentieth centuries.

After the Second World War, the concept of fundamental rights and freedoms was gradually introduced in the government of all of the overseas territories, but in most of them, the rights and freedoms of the population were defined in a territorial constitution, and the inhabitants were not granted the protection of the metropolitan constitution. It has therefore become an aspect of the separateness from the metropolis that today's dependencies have their own constitutionally protected fundamental rights and freedoms, which may differ from those of the metropolitan population.

---

[50] Ermacora 1992, p. 663.

[51] Fastenrath 2002, p. 1090. Kirchschläger 1961, p. 257 also considers that there are colonies which are incorporated in the mother country or associated with it.

[52] Kirchschläger 1961, p. 257.

[53] Crawford 1997. The Dutch legal literature of the early twentieth century also used subordination as a defining characteristic of colonialism, *see* chapter 5.

[54] Oppenheim/Jennings & Watts 1992, p. 281. Crawford 1997 only refers to geographical separateness.

[55] Wesel 1999, p. 241-4.

4. Substantive metropolitan powers in the territory

Writers have also often noted that the government of the mother country has a final say in the colony. If the colony possesses a measure of autonomy, the mother country will always command 'reserved powers', either to intervene in the internal affairs of the territory, or to revoke the autonomy. *Oppenheim* considers that the internal autonomy which colonies often possess is a revocable delegation of the state's powers, at least from the metropolitan point of view.[56] In the first edition of *International Law* (1905), *Oppenheim* stated that the determining factor for colonial status was 'that their Governor, who has a veto, is appointed by the mother country.'[57] The fact that the metropolitan legislator is authorized to legislate for a colony is seen as the decisive criterion by *Belle Antoine.*[58]

5. Not voluntary

It is also sometimes stated as a characteristic of truly colonial relations that they are not voluntary on the part of the colony, or at least that they have originally come about against the wishes of the overseas populations.[59]

6. Dependence

All of the territories dealt with in the comprehensive study *The Last Colonies*[60] depend on the metropolis for financial support, or some other form of assistance, usually in the area of international relations and defence.[61] The assistance lent by the metropolis to the territories is felt by many, both in the territories and in the metropolises, to be indispensable.

Where the dependence results from extreme remoteness and smallness, external assistance of some form can indeed be called indispensable. Tristan da Cunha and Pitcairn exhibit this form of inevitable dependence.[62] The dependence of, for instance, Puerto Rico is of an entirely different nature. Its size,

---

[56] Oppenheim/Jennings & Watts 1992, p. 275-6. In 1905, *Oppenheim* wrote: 'the mother country could withdraw self-government from its Colonial States and legislate directly for them' (p. 103).

[57] Oppenheim 1905, p. 103.

[58] Belle Antoine 1999, p. 10, where it is claimed that the UK dependent territories are colonies for this reason. The author adds that 'there is, however, a non-enforceable convention which prescribes that the UK parliament should not legislate for the colonies without their consent.'

[59] *See for instance* Fastenrath 2002, p. 1090.

[60] Aldrich & Connell 1997, which discusses some 40 small overseas territories of Western states, including the Netherlands Antilles and Aruba.

[61] Aruba, Bonaire and Curaçao are clear examples of this feature, being located only a few kilometres off the South American mainland of Venezuela and Colombia, and almost 8,000 kilometres from The Hague.

[62] *See* Gorelick 1983 on the right to self-determination of Pitcairn.

population, and location do not clearly preclude it from being an independent state or from functioning without assistance by the US. Its dependence is not a fact of nature, but must be explained from historical and political factors.

Most of the other remaining dependencies do not clearly fall either in the category of Puerto Rico or Pitcairn. In most of these cases, including the Netherlands Antilles and Aruba, it is difficult to determine whether the dependence should be considered as a fact of nature, or whether it is the result of historical developments, political choices, or from such factors as 'aid addiction.' Sometimes these territories will choose to remain dependent because they (perhaps incorrectly) assume that they will not be able to survive as independent states. In other cases, the choice appears to be governed by the desire to continue to benefit from the advantages of being able to depend on a Western state.[63]

Many authors currently use 'dependent territory' or 'dependency' as a euphemistic[64] synonym of colony, although that is not strictly speaking correct.[65]

---

[63] Cf. Davies 1995, p. 2, with regard to the British overseas territories: 'Certain factors make independence difficult for some and undesirable for others.' Former Governor of Montserrat, David Taylor, writing about the OTs of the UK in the Caribbean, states that: 'Independence is available if a substantial majority of the voters want it but there seems to have been a tacit agreement between politicians and their electorates not to ask for it. Most politicians might like it in their heart of hearts but they know that people would not in general vote for it. The people, I suspect, regard continuing dependence as a safeguard against weak or corrupt government though history and sentiment play their part. The cynical might say that the present constitutional arrangements suit the political leaders well, enabling them to take the credit for good things and blame Britain for the bad ones, relying on Britain in times of emergency.' (Taylor 2000, p. 338).

[64] Perhaps because of this euphemistic usage, the term has gained a somewhat negative connotation itself. Roberts-Wray 1966, p. 60 notes that it 'does not find favour in some of the territories.' He also found that 'the term "dependent territories" does not appear to have acquired the same degree of unpopularity.' In 1999, the UK introduced the term 'overseas territories' to replace the 'outdated terms such as "dependent territories" or "colonies".' (Explanatory Notes to British Overseas Territories Act 2002, Chapter 8, para. 4), because 'today's territories are energetic, self-governing, and anything but dependent' (statement by the Foreign Secretary, Robin Cook, in the House of Commons, 17 March 1999). One wonders how long it will take for the term 'overseas territories' to gain a negative meaning in the UK as well, and by which term it will be replaced. Perhaps by 'non-independent territories', which is sometimes used in the present-day literature despite the double negative.

[65] See for instance, Crawford 1997, Ofuatey-Kodjoe 1970, p. 290, Davies 1995, pp. 1-5. Ermacora 1992, p. 663 finds the use of the term 'colonies' no longer justified. It should be replaced by the term 'dependent territories', even though he claims there still exist dependent territories which are colonies (p. 662). See also for instance, the analysis by the UN representative of Thailand in 1986 of the situation in New Caledonia, GAOR (41), Plenary Meetings, 91st meeting, p. 93. Under the domestic law of the UK and other metropolitan states, 'dependency' simply indicated a territory that was separate and subordinate to a larger territory, and the term is still sometimes used in that sense. See Roberts-Wray 1966, pp. 60-1, which uses 'dependent territories' to refer to all of the places in the Commonwealth that are not independent states when

It seems the term 'dependent peoples' is used in order to avoid giving offence, whereas the term 'colonial peoples' is used when the aim is to provoke or indict. The phrase 'dependent peoples' is quite common at the UN to indicate NSGTs, Trust Territories, and other territories that are – or were – considered colonial, such as Algeria.[66] In the context of the right to self-determination, UN usage often refers to the right to self-determination of dependent peoples, most importantly in GA Resolution 1514 (XV), the Declaration on the Granting of Independence to Colonial Countries and Peoples, which despite its title does not once use the phrase 'colonial peoples' but frequently speaks of 'dependent peoples.'

In *Blaustein's* collection of *Constitutions of Dependencies and Territories*, dependencies are described as 'those territories that are not part of a particular nation but tributary[67] to it.' *Blaustein* distinguishes them from 'national territories' which 'are an integral part of a particular nation.' The editors of the collection consider that the criterion of being an integral part of the state determines whether an overseas territory is a dependency or not.[68] But this does not explain why, for instance, Corsica, Hong Kong, the Faeroe Islands and Greenland

---

'precision is not important.' GA Res. 66 (I) of 1946 lists many NSGTs with dependencies. The Comoros were a dependency of Madagascar. Even tiny territories such as St Helena and Pitcairn have their 'dependencies', *see* Roberts-Wray 1966, p. 61. This meaning of 'dependency' corresponds to the Dutch concept of '*onderhorigheid*'. The Netherlands Antilles were called '*Curaçao en onderhorigheden*' before 1948.

[66] *See* the report of the Committee of Six which prepared the Principles of GA Res. 1541 (*see below*) which states that Chapter XI of the UN Charter 'expressed international concern for the welfare and freedom of dependent peoples', while the first Principle declares that Chapter XI was intended to cover all territories 'of the colonial type' (GAOR (XV) Annexes, Agenda item 38, para. 17). *See also for instance* GA Res. 1573 (XV) of 19 December 1960 on Algeria, which refers to 'the passionate yearning for freedom of all dependent peoples.' *See also* the *Yearbook of the United Nations 1960*, p. 504. According to a UN brochure entitled, 'A Sacred Trust. The Work of the United Nations for Dependent Peoples' (1957), the category of 'dependent territories' consists of Trust Territories and NSGTs (p. 2). A similar brochure, published in 1963 by the Office of Public Information, entitled 'From Dependence to Freedom. The United Nations Role in the Advance of Dependent Peoples towards Self-Government or Independence', explains that dependent peoples live in Trust Territories or NSGTs, which are colonies governed by distant metropolitan countries (p. 3). 'Dependent territories' is also used by the specialized agencies when reporting on their efforts to implement GA Res. 1514 (*see for instance,* UN Doc. E/2000/68 of 15 June 2000). It is also sometimes used at the UN to refer to the Netherlands Antilles and Aruba.

[67] The role of the tributary has been entirely reversed in the course of history. None of the territories literally pay tribute (an ancient form of taxation) to the metropolis anymore. On the contrary, most *receive* public funding from the mother country.

[68] *See also for instance*, the introduction to the section on the 'Netherlands Dependencies', which states that: 'Exceptionally in the case of dependencies, these territories are accorded special rights under the Dutch National Constitution. However, they are not an integral part of the Netherlands and thus cannot be considered national territories.' (Blaustein/Raworth 2001a, p. 1).

are categorized as national territories,[69] whereas Guadeloupe, Réunion, Martinique and the Cocos (Keeling) Islands are dependencies.[70]

Rather, the criterion (perhaps subconsciously) appears to be whether the territory was once considered a colony or is still considered as such, and has not yet become independent or integrated with a Third World state.[71] This is also indicated by *Blaustein's* remark with respect to dependencies that 'the degree of independence from colonial control varies.'[72]

Summing up, a tentative conclusion could be formulated that the present-day literature defines 'colonies' as separate territories of a Western state, which are subordinated to the metropolis. If the territory possesses a form of autonomy, this will either be revocable by the mother country, or be subject to 'reserved powers' to intervene in the autonomy of the territory. The metropolis is authorized to legislate for the colony, although this authority may be constitutionally restricted. Politically, the government of the mother country is still a dominant factor in the government of the colony, which is dependent on the mother country.

A number of aspects of the constitution of the Kingdom are indeed similar to forms of colonial government.

1. The constitutional institutions of the European part of the Kingdom continue to handle the Kingdom affairs for the overseas Countries, although the influence of the Caribbean Countries increased in these areas after 1954. The Ministers of the Netherlands and the Dutch *Staten-Generaal* can still take unilateral actions (in the form of Kingdom legislation, or other decisions) that can be made binding on the Caribbean Countries against their will, when it con-

---

[69] Some of these territories can be perhaps be considered integral parts of an independent state, but at least Greenland and the Azores have relations with Denmark and Portugal that appear to be closer to association than integration. The constitutional position of Corsica appears to be rather similar to that of the French 'dependencies' in the Caribbean or Pacific.

[70] These four territories are examples of colonies that have become integrated parts of the mother country (France and Australia), *see* chapter 3. The US State Department also include them in a list of dependencies, but explain that 'French Guiana, Guadeloupe, Martinique and Reunion are departments (first-order administrative units) of France, and are therefore not dependencies or areas of special sovereignty. They are included in this list only for the convenience of the user.' *See* the web site of the State Department: <http://www.state.gov/www/regions/dependencies.html> (visited on 3 March 2004).

[71] This does not explain why the Channel Islands and the Isle of Man are classed as dependencies, but the reason for this could be that these islands were for a long time called 'dependent territories' under UK law. The fact that Greenland is called a national territory is clearly a mistake. It is not an integral part of Denmark, and it used to be considered a colony, at least at the UN.

[72] Blaustein/Raworth 2002, p. 2.

cerns Kingdom affairs, or when the Netherlands considers that the interests of the Kingdom as a whole are at stake. The Netherlands Antilles and Aruba need to be consulted and may voice their opinion, but they do not have a right of veto, except when it concerns the application of economical or financial treaties to their territories.

2. The power of interpretation of the Charter ultimately lies with the Netherlands, without – in many cases – the possibility of judicial review, since the courts are not allowed to test Kingdom acts against the Charter.[73] This means that an interpretation of the Charter laid down in such forms of legislation is final, unless it violates international law.[74]

3. The Kingdom government appoints the Governors and some other officials for the Netherlands Antilles and Aruba. In the first edition of *Oppenheim*, it was considered to be the determining factor for colonial status 'that their Governor, who has a veto, is appointed by the mother Country.'[75] The Governors are always native Antilleans or Arubans, and they are proposed for appointment by the government of the Country concerned. The Governors nowadays function mainly as organs of their Countries, and not so much as representatives of the Kingdom government.[76] But the Governor does still have the duty to report decisions of the local government to the Kingdom government if he considers them to be in violation of international treaties, the Charter, other Kingdom legislation or if he thinks they conflict with the interests that the Kingdom has to observe or safeguard.

4. The Netherlands Antilles and Aruba cannot change certain parts of their constitutions without the consent of the Kingdom government.

5. There are a few less fundamental aspects of the Kingdom relations that essentially date from the colonial era.[77]

---

[73] HR 14 April 1989, *AB* 1989, 207 (*Harmonisatiewet*).

[74] An act of parliament which does not conform to self-executing provisions of international treaties can be challenged in the courts, *see* Article 94 of the Constitution. Besselink et al. 2002, p. 46 and Hoogers & Nap 2005, pp. 81-4 think that this provision does not apply to Kingdom acts. Other writers think it does, *see for instance* Van Rijn 2005a, p. 106, which seems the correct interpretation of the Charter and the Constitution.

[75] Oppenheim 1905, p. 103.

[76] *Borman* has proposed that the Governor should become entirely an organ of the Countries (Borman 1988, p. 18).

[77] For instance: the 'colonial clause' of the European Convention on Human Rights of 1950 (Article 56, para. 3) is considered to apply to the Netherlands Antilles and Aruba. This clause, which is also a part of each protocol to the Convention, intended to allow a 'different' level of human rights protection in 'certain colonial territories whose state of civilisation did not, it was thought, permit the full application of the Convention' (*Tyrer* v. *UK*, judgment of the ECHR of 25 April 1978 (Series A, no 26). It provides that:'The provisions of this Convention shall be applied in such territories with due regard ... to local requirements.' The Court of Human Rights has interpreted the phrase 'local requirements' very restrictively. In 2005, it accepted that the pacifi-

There are also a number of fundamental *differences* from colonial forms of government.

1. The Charter lists the Kingdom affairs exhaustively, and since the Charter cannot be amended without the consent of the Netherlands Antilles and Aruba, the powers of the Kingdom in the Caribbean are constitutionally limited.
2. The legal order of the Charter is based on consultation, cooperation and consensus, at least in practice. The Ministers Plenipotentiary participate in the decision making of the Council of Ministers of the Kingdom. The Charter does leave some room for decisions in which the Dutch ministers overrule the Ministers Plenipotentiary, and which can be made binding on the Netherlands Antilles and Aruba. But as a rule, the Kingdom only acts with the consent of all three Countries when it concerns affairs which affect the Countries.
3. The Kingdom relations are voluntary on the part of the Netherlands Antilles and Aruba. There has been little to no evidence in the twentieth century that the population of the islands would wish to sever the ties with the Netherlands. Rather, the islands have resisted the wish of the Dutch government to dissolve the Kingdom relations.

These differences probably outweigh the resemblances and should lead to the conclusion that the legal order of the Kingdom is essentially different from traditional colonial forms of government. The Kingdom Charter does still put the Netherlands Antilles and Aruba in a formally somewhat subordinate position in relation to the Netherlands. This does not, however, make them colonies. In view of their size, it would not be reasonable to expect the Netherlands to accept a fully equal position for the Caribbean Countries within the Kingdom, including a right of veto on decisions which affect the Kingdom as a whole. It has often been noted that the Caribbean Countries have a stronger voice in the government of the Kingdom than a Dutch city of comparable size. But the Netherlands Antilles and Aruba are not Dutch cities, and they cannot but be aware of the possibilities that the Charter offers to the Netherlands in

---

cation of the conflict in New Caledonia as well as the exercise of the right to self-determination of the local population required far-reaching restrictions on the right to vote, which were not in violation of Article 3 of the first protocol, read in conjunction with Article 56, para. 3 (*Py* v. *France*, judgment of the ECHR of 11 January 2005 (Application No. 66289/01)). Another colonial relic can be found in the decision of the Supreme Court of the Netherlands to accept that the principle of legality does not apply to the Kingdom order, as far as extradition is concerned. The decision concerned a regulation (similar to an order in council) dealing with extradition, which was not based on delegation by the Kingdom legislator, and which only applied to the Netherlands Antilles and Aruba. This situation dated from before the Kingdom Charter. *See* HR 7 November 2003, *NJ* 2004/99, m.n. Koopmans, who called this a 'colonial remnant' for which the Kingdom legislator 'ought to be ashamed.'

case of a conflict. This has created a considerable body of anti-colonial discourse on the Kingdom relations.

Anti-Colonial Discourse Concerning the Kingdom

The colonial history of the Kingdom relations still clearly plays a role in the public debate on the political relations between the Countries, and on the situation of the Caribbean Countries. There still exists a general perception in the Netherlands, the Netherlands Antilles and Aruba that the process of decolonization is somehow incomplete.[78]

The word 'colony' and its derivatives are often simply fighting words, used out of anger over incidents in which the Netherlands was perceived to act dominantly or to have shown a lack of respect for the Netherlands Antilles and Aruba. They are sometimes used to convey more profound dissatisfaction with the Kingdom order.

Social scientists still tend to recognize various influences of the colonial system in the societies of the Netherlands Antilles (and to a lesser extent Aruba), and often see the decolonization of the Netherlands Antilles and Aruba as incomplete. *Verton* considers that the Charter was the starting point for a process of decolonization that would meet with considerable resistance from the colonial system in the colonies itself. In his view, the introduction of general suffrage and autonomy for the Netherlands Antilles hailed the beginning of the 'late colonial phase', which has not yet been completed.[79] The effects of the Dutch policies of decolonization unintentionally led to 'political disintegration, an unproductive political system, and a stagnant socio-economic development process', *Verton* wrote in 1990. He rejected the Dutch insistence on independence as 'pseudo-decolonization', because it would lead to more dependence and fewer opportunities for development, which is the opposite of what decolonization should aim to achieve.[80]

Broek & Wijenberg consider the present relations between the Netherlands and the islands cultivate a significant 'colonial' element, because of the dominant role of gifts. The financial support of the islands by the Netherlands is still considered as a gift and not as a legal obligation. According to *Broek & Wijenberg*, the receiving of gifts by the islands from the Netherlands fits the

---

[78] *See for instance* the title of John Jansen van Galen's review of the Kingdom relations (2004): *De toekomst van het Koninkrijk. Over de dekolonisatie van de Nederlandse Antillen* ('The Future of the Kingdom. On the Decolonization of the Netherlands Antilles').

[79] Verton 1977, p. 234. *Verton* stresses that colonialism is not merely a relation between a mother country and an overseas territory, but also consists of relations within the colony itself, namely between the 'colonial elites' and the 'colonized'.

[80] Verton 1990, p. 215.

social and psychological relations between master and slave. An unequal relation based on gifts and the absence of legal certainty creates mutual distrust and makes cooperation difficult.[81]

Historians such as *Oostindie* describe the decolonization of the Dutch Caribbean as 'incomplete' or 'unfinished.' *Oostindie* has also written about a 'stagnant' decolonization process. In this case, he explains that this description derives from others, and that it suggests that decolonization should always lead to independence, which suggestion *Oostindie* rejects.[82]

In the Netherlands Antilles and Aruba, the relations with the Netherlands are still described in terms of decolonization. *Gorsira* considers the Kingdom as an intermediate phase in the process of decolonization.[83] Other Antillean and Aruban writers simply describe the relations as a form of colonial subordination. *Duzanson*, in his introduction to the public law of St Maarten, states that the constitution of the Kingdom and of the Netherlands Antilles makes it possible for St Maarten to be brought into a subordinate or colonial position, and that this possibility is occasionally used.[84] *Lake* describes St Maarten as 'one of the last colonies of the Caribbean.'[85] *Croes* thinks the relation of Aruba with the Netherlands is one of subordination.[86] *Brison* thinks his fellow Antilleans are suffering from a colonial complex which prohibits them from taking charge of their own destiny.[87]

There are also a few foreign authors who seem to have little doubt that the Netherlands Antilles and Aruba are still colonies. *Connell*, for instance, considers that only Great Britain and the Netherlands 'formally retain colonies.'[88] *Nowak*, in his authoritative commentary on the ICCPR, places the Arubans in the category of 'peoples living under colonial rule or comparable alien subjugation.'[89] *Oppenheim* discusses the Kingdom in his paragraph on colonies, although he considers the Kingdom relations as not 'fully colonial.'[90] Occasionally, the Kingdom is faced with the fact that foreign states view the Caribbean Countries as colonies, but these views are rarely expressed in public.

The word 'colonial' is still used in the Netherlands, the Netherlands Antilles and Aruba by politicians, activists and writers as a way of generating outrage

---

[81] Broek & Wijenberg 2005.
[82] Oostindie 1994, p. 13.
[83] Gorsira 1988, p. 60.
[84] Duzanson 2000, pp. 55-6.
[85] Lake 2000, p. 35.
[86] Croes 2005, p. 66.
[87] Brison 2005, p. 35 et seq.
[88] Connell 1987, p. 411.
[89] Nowak 1993, p. 21, note 87.
[90] Oppenheim/Jennings & Watts 1992, p. 280.

and decrying the Kingdom relations as a form of repression of the Netherlands Antilles and Aruba. Sometimes the anti-colonial doctrine that overseas territories should always become independent is used as a hidden argument, in which case it is easy to reach the conclusion that the Kingdom relations are colonial. But the anti-colonial discourse is also used by people who think the autonomy of the Netherlands Antilles and Aruba is absolute and should always be respected by the Netherlands, in which case 'colonialism' refers to Dutch interference or domineering behaviour. A recent example occurred when the Antillean Minister of Economic Affairs, Errol Cova, visited Venezuela, where he explained that the Dutch colonizers had forced a colonial complex on the Antilleans which was 'clever and very thorough' because 'it makes you feel that you are worthless because you can do nothing.'[91] Anti-colonial discourse can also be used in situations where the Netherlands refuses to grant the wishes of a Caribbean Country, as in the case of the sugar and rice conflict with the EU.[92]

These accusations of colonialism have been called 'colonitis', and they are sometimes used very effectively as a way of influencing the behaviour of politicians or entrepreneurs from Holland who are perceived as a threat to the autonomy of the Netherlands Antilles or Aruba.[93] Occasionally 'colonialism' is also used by the Dutch to criticize their own government's policies with regard to the Netherlands Antilles and Aruba, in which context it often seems to mean simply 'wrong.'[94]

The debate on constitutional reforms has inspired Antillean and Aruban politicians to address pleas to the Decolonization Committee, to visit New York (with the hope of being received by the Committee), or to threaten such actions, or to consider asking an independent neighbouring island to ask the GA to revise its decision of 1955.[95] The idea that the Decolonization Committee

---

[91] Reported in *Amigoe* (9 May 2005) and *NRC Handelsblad* (13 May 2005). The minister was soon after forced to resign by the *Staten* because of this statement, among other things. Premier Ys considered Cova's statements damaging to the Kingdom and a snub to the Queen. A similar statement was made soon afterwards by Eduardo Cova (a nephew of minister Errol Cova and one of the Commissioners of Curaçao) during a memorial of 30 May 1969, *see Amigoe* (31 May 2005). Errol Cova later stated that Curaçao had started 'a process of decolonization' that no-one should hinder (*NRC Handelsblad,* 8 August 2005).

[92] *See* chapter 9.

[93] De Jong 1998, p. 59 et seq. describes several outbreaks of 'colonitis' as deliberate attempts to scare off the Dutch, or to force them to comply with Antillean demands.

[94] *See for instance,* the remarks by a member of the Lower House, Van Bommel, in reaction to the announcement that the Netherlands would start restricting the access to its territory of unemployed and uneducated youngsters from the Antilles and Aruba (reported in *De Telegraaf,* 11 May 2005).

[95] Aruba sent a delegation to the Decolonization Committee in 1977. Croes, the Aruban leader, claimed that the vice-president of the Decolonization Committee and several members received the Aruban delegation, and were very curious to know why the Netherlands would not

could discuss the Netherlands Antilles is based on the assumption that the UN should not have accepted the cessation of transmission of information on the Netherlands Antilles in 1955,[96] or on the idea that Resolution 1514 (XV) of 1960 (the Declaration on the Granting of Independence to Colonial Countries and Peoples) applies to all overseas territories that have not yet become independent.

The colonial history of the Kingdom relations continues to cast a dark shadow over the present relations. Whether this will ever change is hard to predict, and is not really a subject of legal research anyway. But constitutional law could make a contribution by making sure that the constitution of the Kingdom is no longer vulnerable to accusations of colonialism. From a legal point of view, this could only be achieved by reforming the Kingdom in a way that would make clear that the political status of the Dutch Caribbean Countries has taken a shape that is freely chosen by their populations, as I will discuss in the next chapters.

5.5 Conclusion

The Dutch literature on constitutional law has not succeeded in categorizing the Kingdom order into one of the existing forms of government. It is usually called a construction *sui generis*, but it could also be called a 'constitutional association' or a 'cooperative structure governed by constitutional law.' The

---

grant Aruba independence (*see* Paula 1989). The governing party of Aruba (*MEP*) addressed a letter to the UN in 2003, in which it claimed that the Netherlands intended to stop Aruba from becoming independent (*Amigoe*, 18 November 2003). Errol Cova, as a minister of the Netherlands Antilles, shortly thereafter contacted the Decolonization Committee for advice on the meaning of the right to self-determination and the possibility of holding UN-supervised referendums (*Amigoe*, 20 November 2003). This news was discussed with some concern in the Senate of the Netherlands, but the Dutch Minister for Kingdom Affairs, De Graaf, stated that Cova had asked legitimate questions to the Committee, and that the Netherlands had not minded it when representatives of Saba had visited the UN headquarters in 2001 (*Kamerstukken I* 2003–04, 29 200 IV, B, p. 6). A delegation from the Island Council of Saba again visited New York in August of 2005 to inform the Committee of the ongoing talks on the constitutional restructuring of the Netherlands Antilles, and to complain about Dutch Minister for Kingdom Affairs, Pechtold, who allegedly delayed this process by laying down new demands (*NRC Handelsblad* (internet edition), 10 August 2005). *The Daily Herald* reported on 12 August 2005 that Saba would ask a UN member state (probably St Kitts and Nevis) to ask the GA to place the Netherlands Antilles on the list of NSGTs. Curaçaoan novelist Frank Martinus Arion in 2004 wrote that he supported those people who campaigned to have the UN referee between the Netherlands and Curaçao (*Amigoe*, 4 November 2004). *Munneke* proposed that the decolonization committee should send observers to the referendum of 2005 on Curaçao (*Amigoe*, 16 August 2003).

[96] *Bijkerk*, an adviser of the *UPB* of Bonaire, claims the Netherlands provided false information to the UN in 1955 in order to convince the member states that Surinam and the Netherlands Antilles were no longer colonies (Bijkerk 2003, p. 1862).

Charter has created a legal order that leaves the three Countries free to pursue their own policies in most areas, while establishing common organs for cooperation and some supervision over the Caribbean Countries. The Netherlands took on most of the common tasks of the Kingdom, with a right of consultation for the Caribbean Countries on subjects that concerned them, and a right of veto on the application of economic and financial treaties to their territories, and on amendments to the Charter. The Kingdom is substantially different from the other overseas forms of government discussed in this study, except perhaps the former British West Indies Associated States, which were considered by some to be freely associated with the UK, but by others – including the UN – to be Non-Self-Governing Territories (*see* chapter 3).

The Kingdom is not a nation state in the traditional sense. There have so far been few indications of the development of a trans-Atlantic community of interests that could lead to the birth of a nation.[97] The federal and unitary traits exhibited by the text of the Charter, are at present no more than constitutional make-up. The Kingdom functions more like a confederation, although it cannot be called that either, because it is not based on a treaty, the Countries are not independent states, and the organs of the Kingdom do have some – albeit very limited – power over the citizens of the Countries. The structure of the Kingdom also does not fit any of the other traditional forms of government.

Because of the large difference in size between the Netherlands and its Caribbean territories, combined with the firm desire to change as little as possible the constitution of the Kingdom as it existed before 1954, the drafting of the Charter resulted in a structure that was not a radical breach with the colonial era, but offered a practical way of realizing most of the basic wishes of the governments of the Netherlands, Surinam and the Netherlands Antilles at the time. But even though the Charter was intended to create a flexible system that could accommodate the constitutional development of the Caribbean Countries, it rather seems to have chained the three Countries together in a relationship that hardly anyone appears to be happy with at present.

It could be argued that some of the characteristics of colonial government, as they were defined before World War II, still exist (at least potentially) in the Kingdom order. The question whether the changes to the colonial order were substantial enough to warrant the title of a complete form of decolonization has not really been a subject in the Dutch literature on constitutional law. It has, however, been the subject of some discussion in the literature on international law, which I will discuss in the next chapter.

---

[97] Hirsch Ballin's plea for the creation of such a community is probably evidence that it does not yet exist, *see* Hirsch Ballin 2003. Logemann 1952, pp. 311-15 already noted that the Netherlands, Surinam and the Netherlands Antilles shared no common interests and that its citizens did not form a community. *See also* Croes 2005.

Chapter 6
CHARACTERIZATION OF THE KINGDOM ORDER UNDER INTERNATIONAL LAW

Between 1951 and 1955 the UN discussed the relationship between the Netherlands and its Caribbean territories in some detail, and a number of authors have written about the Kingdom Charter in English, French, and German, for which reasons the formal aspects of the relationship are well known among the experts on overseas territories and autonomy regimes.[1] Nonetheless, the Kingdom of the Netherlands is categorized in many different ways in the foreign literature. Three main strands of reasoning are prevalent, namely that the Caribbean Countries are integral parts of the Kingdom, associated with the Netherlands or non-self-governing. I will discuss these views, and the UN debate of the 1950s, and try to determine how the Kingdom could be characterized under international law on the basis of the conclusions drawn in the previous chapters.

6.1 INTEGRAL PART OF THE KINGDOM

A number of writers on international law explicitly or implicitly consider the relations of the Netherlands Antilles and Aruba with the Netherlands as a form of integration, and categorize the Kingdom as a federal, or even as a unitary state.[2] None of these sources really explain why the Caribbean Countries should

---

[1] The Explanatory Memorandum to the Kingdom Charter, which was submitted to the General Assembly in 1955 by the Netherlands government (UN Doc. A/AC.35/L.206) continues to be an important source for many writers, as well as *Van Panhuys*, who is cited by virtually all authors writing in English on the Kingdom, sometimes as their only source.

[2] Rapoport et al.1971, pp. 70-1, De Smith 1970, p. 32, and Hannum 1996, p. 347 et seq. Others consider the Caribbean Countries as incorporated into the metropolis in the same way as Alaska or Hawaii, or the French DOMs, but these writers must be considered simply misinformed. *See for instance,* Crawford 2006, p. 623, Ince 1974, p. 43, Lopez-Reyes 1996, p. 74, and Quane 1998, p. 553, note 82. Pakaukau 2004, p. 305 even speaks of 'The literal absorption (rather than decolonization) of several territories by colonizing powers in the 1950s – e.g., Surinam by the Netherlands.'

S. Hillebrink, The Right to Self-Determination and Post-Colonial Governance
© 2008, T·M·C·ASSER PRESS, *The Hague, The Netherlands and the Author*

be seen as integrated into the Netherlands, although the most convincing element for most writers seems to be the federal traits of the Charter.

Most of these authors base their opinion on the text of the Kingdom Charter, and on an article by *Van Panhuys* from 1958. This article compared the Kingdom structure to those of federal states, and to 'colonies of other States on their way to self-government.'[3] *Van Panhuys* considers that 'as to their standing under municipal public law, it may be concluded ... that Surinam and the Netherlands Antilles have been incorporated as autonomous units – on a basis of equality with the Netherlands – into an *ensemble fédératif.*'[4]

Van Panhuys' article has for a long time been the only legal analysis of the Kingdom order of any substance in English, and it has exercised a great deal of influence on international opinion regarding the Kingdom. Foreign readers of *Van Panhuys* may not be aware that some of the Charter's elements which are most indicative of the integration of the Caribbean Countries into the Kingdom have rarely been used, and some not at all. The federal elements of the Charter are furthermore mainly constitutional make-up, as I explained in chapter 5.

The Kingdom is clearly not similar to the internationally accepted examples of integration described in chapter 3. The Kingdom Charter does not make it impossible to realize a form of integration of the three Countries into a single community by jointly creating additional Kingdom affairs, or by creating common legislation and policies based on Article 36 of the Charter, but this possibility has only rarely been used. As a result, the three Countries have their own legislation and pursue their own policies on virtually all subjects, and the Kingdom remains very far removed from any notion of an integrated state.

This is not in debate in the Kingdom. There is a long history of Dutch and Caribbean proposals to integrate the Dutch Caribbean islands into the Netherlands, but these proposals have never been received with much enthusiasm by the governments of the Countries, and they are of course in themselves evidence that the islands are not an integral part of the Netherlands.

In recent years, the idea of full integration has gained more popularity, especially with regard to the Netherlands Antilles. It is usually based on the idea

---

[3] Van Panhuys 1958, p. 22. This sentence should not be interpreted to mean that the author considers Surinam and the Netherlands as colonies, or as not possessing self-government. *Van Panhuys* considers them to be 'self-governing former colonies' (p. 30).

[4] Van Panhuys 1958, p. 21. Near the end of his article, *Van Panhuys* calls Surinam and the Netherlands Antilles 'freely associated with the metropolitan country.' It must be remembered, however, that GA Res. 742 (VIII) of 1953, which was the most recent UN instrument on the status of (former) colonial territories at the time when *Van Panhuys* wrote his article, still referred to integrated territories as 'Free Association of a Territory on Equal Basis with the Metropolitan or other country as an Integral Part of That Country or any Other Form.' It seems likely that *Van Panhuys* was thinking of this category.

that the grave social and economic problems of that island are caused by the autonomy of the Netherlands Antilles, or at least that the autonomy is blocking a solution to the problems.[5]

The idea of integration has cropped up in many publications in the Netherlands, and also on Curaçao, especially during the rise to power of the radical Curaçaoan labour party *FOL*, and the short-lived Antillean cabinet of Mirna Louisa-Godett (2003–2004). During this time, public opinion in the Netherlands became convinced that Antillean politicians were not able to provide good government for the islands, and that the Netherlands should take charge, also because the problems of Curaçao were spilling over into the Netherlands.[6] Some Dutch politicians proposed the full integration of the Netherlands Antilles into the Netherlands, as a province or a municipality, usually as part of a 'take-it-or-leave-it' offer, where 'leave it' clearly meant independence.[7]

Recent statements and publications by individual members of the Dutch political parties *CDA, PvdA, SP* and *LPF*[8] and a recent debate in the Senate suggests that it can no longer be simply assumed that a majority in the *Staten-Generaal* would instantly reject the integration of the Netherlands Antilles into the Netherlands.[9] The policies of the Dutch political parties are not very devel-

---

[5] *See for instance,* the Winter 2005 issue of the journal *Christen-Democratische Verkenningen,* which was dedicated to the Antilles and Aruba, and which contained a special section on the integration option. *See also* Broek & Wijenberg 2005.

[6] *De Volkskrant,* in an editorial of 11 March 2005, concluded that some form of integration with the Netherlands was the best option for all of the islands of the Antilles. Another newspaper, *NRC Handelsblad,* in a special supplement of 15 November 2003, presented the future of the Netherlands Antilles as a choice between independence or integration.

[7] *Fortuyn's* column on this subject (*see* Fortuyn 2002) was emblematic of this view. According to *Fortuyn,* the autonomy of the Antilles should be abolished, and a small army of Dutch civil servants should be flown in to set things straight. 'Of course, we will not talk or negotiate this with the corrupt political elite of the Antilles, no, it is simply "take it or leave it".' *See also* the article by CDA members Pikeur and Lamers of 2005. Herben (*LPF*) defended the idea of integration, writing in *NRC Handelsblad* (15 November 2003) and *HP* (12 September 2003) (The proposal of his *LPF* colleague Eerdmans to abandon the Antilles was part of Eerdmans' application for membership of the new political movement of Wilders, *see de Volkskrant* of 8 January 2005). Van Bommel (*SP*) defended the idea of integration in an article in *Amigoe* (6 November 2004, co-authored by J. Wijenberg) and proposed that this option should be offered in a well-prepared referendum to the populations. Schrijer and Dijsselbloem (*PvdA*) proposed that a referendum should be held on the Antilles in which only two choices would be offered; integration or independence. According to these two politicians, the Netherlands should respect the choice of the population, which would 'choose for integration *en masse*' (*de Volkskrant,* 6 July 2004).

[8] These statements, some of which were cited *above,* mostly derive from individual party members. Official party policies are usually unclear on this point, or simply non-existent.

[9] In a debate in the Senate on 14 February 2006, many Senators appeared to have a preference for closer ties with the Netherlands Antilles and Aruba, perhaps even in the form of full integration of the islands (at least the smaller ones) into the Netherlands. *See Handelingen I* 2005/06, p. 18-850 et seq.

oped on this subject, and there has been little public debate on it. It might well be that The Hague would baulk at the costs of integrating the islands fully into the Netherlands, or recoil from the negative economic effects for some of the islands.[10] There does currently seem to be a consensus in the *Staten-Generaal* that the Kingdom should play a stronger role in the supervision of the internal affairs of the Netherlands Antilles (and possibly also Aruba).[11]

Antillean and Aruban politicians usually do not react to the Dutch proposals.[12] There are currently no political parties represented in the *Staten* or in the island councils that support the full integration of Aruba or the Netherlands Antilles into the Netherlands. The words '*provincie*' and '*gemeente*' (municipality) are more or less taboo in Caribbean politics, and such a status is considered shameful and colonial by many people, at least on Curaçao, Aruba and St Maarten. Politicians on the smaller islands do not seem to oppose a larger role for the Netherlands. Opinion polls show that the population is not opposed *per se* to more Dutch control over the local governments, even though the status of '*provincie*' or '*gemeente*' remains unpopular.[13]

In referenda held on all of the five islands of the Netherlands Antilles in 2000, 2004 and 2005, the option of full integration was only on the ballot on Curaçao and St Eustatius, where it received 25 and 2 per cent of the vote respectively. The options of direct link with the Netherlands that carried the vote on Bonaire and Saba could perhaps be seen as a choice for integration, although the precise ramifications of these status options were uncertain at the

---

[10] *See* Smeehuijzen & Ziekenoppasser 2005 for a rough estimate of the costs (to the Dutch Treasury and the economy of the islands) of introducing Dutch levels of social security in the Netherlands Antilles and Aruba. The authors admit that a reliable estimate cannot yet be made for lack of research into the costs of all of the different aspects and possible side-effects of full integration.

[11] *See for instance* the motions adopted by the Senate and by the Lower House in February 2006 (*Kamerstukken I* 2005/06, 30 300 IV, B and no. 32).

[12] Exceptionally, statements by *CDA* member of the Lower House Van der Knaap in favour of integration (*see de Volkskrant*, 25 June 2002, and *Algemeen Dagblad*, 12 June 2002) inspired a dismissive response by the Antillean premier Etienne Ys. Member of the Lower House De Graaf (*D66*) then asked the Secretary of State for Kingdom Affairs (De Vries, *VVD*) to react to Van der Knaap's proposals. De Vries avoided the question whether integration would be a good idea, but stated that he did not expect much support for this option in the Netherlands Antilles (*Aanhangsel Handelingen II* 2001/02, no. 2010211680). When De Graaf himself became Minister for Kingdom Affairs shortly thereafter, he stated that integration was 'relatively unthinkable' (*NRC Handelsblad*, 4 March 2004).

[13] *See* Oostindie & Verton 1998. An opinion poll on Curaçao in March of 2005 indicated that a majority of the voters was still in favour of Dutch supervision over the public finances and law enforcement of the island. In 2007, a poll during the elections on Curaçao showed a similar result (*see Antilliaans Dagblad*, 30 August 2007).

time the referendums were held.[14] The island government of Saba referred to Anguilla (a NSGT of the UK) as a model for the relationship they preferred to have with the Netherlands, but the three islands together declared in 2006 that they strove towards an integration model (*see further below*).

The new status of Bonaire, St Eustatius and Saba may turn out to be a form of integration, but it is also important to see whether the status of Country within the Kingdom can be characterized as a form of integration, since the other islands of the Netherlands Antilles (Curaçao and St Maarten) and Aruba wish to continue this arrangement.

6.1.1 Applying the Criteria of Resolution 1541

The Netherlands Antilles and Aruba are clearly not integrated into the Netherlands, but they are an integral part of the Kingdom. On that level one could apply Principles VIII and IX of GA Resolution 1541, which contain the criteria for a form of integration that constitutes a full measure of self-government. Some of the writers on international law who characterize the Kingdom as a form of integration also conclude that it does not comply with Resolution 1541.[15] It should be remembered that integration has always been considered a suspect form of self-government at the UN. Since 1960 only one case of integration has been accepted as 'a full measure of self-government.'[16]

Resolution 1541 does not demand that an integrated territory should be completely assimilated or incorporated into the mother country. Principle VIII merely demands that the integration should be based on 'complete equality' between the territory and the mother country, and should create 'equal status and rights of citizenship and equal guarantees of fundamental rights and freedoms without any distinction or discrimination' for the inhabitants.

It would be hard to argue that this is the case within the Kingdom. 'Complete equality' between the three Countries was not envisaged, nor realized in 1954. The citizens of the Kingdom are not mentioned in the Charter,[17] which

---

[14] This means that the requirements for integration of Res. 1541 were not fully met, because the population was not (and could not be) accurately informed about the consequences of its choice.

[15] De Smith 1970, and Hannum 1996. One source considers that this does not create legal problems as long as the population is happy with its current status (Rapoport et al. 1971).

[16] The Cocos (Keeling) Islands in 1984, *see* chapter 3.

[17] Articles 31 and 32 mention the inhabitants of the Netherlands Antilles and Aruba, and provide that they cannot be forced to serve in the armed forces of the Kingdom, except on the basis of a regulation adopted by their own Country's legislature.

does not contain a catalogue of fundamental rights,[18] but attributes the realization of these rights to the Countries.

In one respect the citizens of the Kingdom have equal status, because they are all Dutch nationals. However, the right of access and abode in the Countries is regulated by the Countries themselves. The Charter does not guarantee the freedom of movement of persons within the Kingdom. The Netherlands Antilles and Aruba have created regulations that limit the right of abode and the right to work for Dutch nationals who do not originate from that Country, although these restrictions have been eased in recent years, due to political pressure from the Netherlands and economic advice from organizations such as the IMF. The Netherlands has not put restrictions on the right of abode for Antilleans and Arubans, but such measures have been contemplated on several occasions since the early 1970s, and were recently requested by the Lower House.[19]

Equal rights of citizenship and equal protection of fundamental rights would be very hard to realize within a state where almost all government affairs are attributed to three autonomous governments, and which functions almost entirely as three separate legal orders. The three Countries have, moreover, not made this goal a top priority, which has resulted in the current situation where human rights are guaranteed differently in the constitutions of the Countries, and interpreted differently in practice, and where the inhabitants are entitled to

---

[18] An exception is the right to vote in elections, but even this right is not realized 'without any distinction or discrimination' between the citizens of the Countries. The inhabitants of the Country in Europe have the right to vote for the Lower House, and indirectly elect the Senate of the *Staten-Generaal*, which is the parliament of the Country of the Netherlands, but which also functions as the parliament of the Kingdom. Inhabitants of the Caribbean Countries only have the right to vote for the Lower House if they have previously lived in the European part of the Kingdom for at least 10 years (Article B 1 of the *Kieswet*, *see also* the decision of the *Raad van State* of 21 November 2006 in cases 200607567/1 and 200607800/1 which upheld this rule). The same rule currently applies in the elections for the European parliament, but this rule was challenged in 2004 before the *Raad van State* by two Arubans (Eman & Sevinger, *see* ABRS 13 July 2004, *Jb* 2004, 308). The Administrative Jurisdiction Division of the *Raad van State* decided to request a preliminary ruling by the Court of Justice of the EC on the meaning of European citizenship in relation to the right to vote for the European parliament (case C-300/04). The Court answered that member states were not obligated to accord the right to vote in the European elections to the inhabitants of OCTs, but considered the Dutch election law in breach of the principle of equality, because it differentiated between Dutch citizens abroad on the one hand, and in the OCTs on the other hand (Decision of 12 September 2006). The *Raad van State* decided that it was up to the Dutch legislator to somehow rectify this situation (judgment of 21 November 2006 in cases 200404446/1 and 200404450/1).

[19] *Kamerstukken II* 2004/05, 29 800 VI, no. 79. At the time of writing this study, the government was preparing an amendment to the Elections Act. *See* Oostindie & Klinkers 2001c, p. 340 et seq. for an overview of previous discussions on this subject.

very different levels of government protection and services.[20] To list all of the differences would require a separate study. It would perhaps even be easier to list the areas in which the three Countries treat their inhabitants in the *same* way, which sometimes happens when a Caribbean Country copies a European Dutch model or adopts norms and standards that the Netherlands applies in a certain area.

Resolution 1541 also sets criteria for the procedure by which a territory may choose to become integrated with an independent state. Principle IX states that the population should be politically developed and should have experience with self-government, and that it should choose integration through 'informed and democratic processes', and 'with full knowledge of the change in their status.' The process which led to the adoption of the Kingdom Charter can hardly be considered to conform to these criteria. Self-government was introduced in the Netherlands Antilles in 1951, when the negotiations on the Charter were already underway. There was therefore little experience with self-government. Whether the population was aware of the decisions being made and of the consequences these would have for their future, would probably require more historical research, but it seems very unlikely that this was the case. In any event, the Charter was adopted without a referendum, and it was not a major subject in any election in the Netherlands Antilles. If, therefore, the Kingdom is seen as a form of integration, it was not arrived at through a proper procedure.

Dutch politics seem to become increasingly enamoured of the idea of full integration of the islands into the Country of the Netherlands, but the populations of the islands – at least of the larger ones – do not appear to support the idea of full integration into the Netherlands. This can only be a tentative conclusion since the Netherlands never used to be prepared to discuss this option, for which reason many Antilleans and Arubans probably always assumed that the Netherlands would not agree to realize it anyway. The perception that most people in the Netherlands would prefer the islands to become independent obviously influences the opinion of Antilleans and Arubans with regard to the closeness of their ties with the Netherlands.

Summing up, it can be concluded that the Netherlands Antilles and Aruba are not integrated with the Netherlands in the sense of Resolution 1541. They are an integral part of the Kingdom, but this is probably not a meaningful form of integration with regard to Resolution 1541.

---

[20] During the discussion of the Netherlands report on the ICESCR in 1998, one member of the Committee noted with some concern that the level of protection of economic, social and cultural rights appeared to be much lower in the Netherlands Antilles than in the Netherlands. The representatives of the Netherlands responded that this was the responsibility of the Country governments (E/C.12/1998/SR.15).

6.1.2   Integration of Bonaire, St Eustatius and Saba into the Netherlands?

After the referendums of 2005, negotiations were started between the three smaller islands (Bonaire, St Eustatius and Saba) and the Netherlands to determine their new status in case the Country of the Netherlands Antilles should be abolished, which became increasingly likely.

The *Raad van State* of the Kingdom in September of 2006 recommended that the three islands should become part of the Country of the Netherlands, and that the Dutch Constitution would apply. The Council recommended that the islands should obtain a status as special public entities of the Netherlands under Article 134 of the Dutch Constitution – a provision which has been used in the past in order to facilitate the integration of newly impoldered territory, and two towns that were annexed from West Germany after World War II.[21] This would entail full responsibility of the government of the *Country* of the Netherlands for the three islands, and thereby represents a fundamental departure from the existing relation of equivalence between the Netherlands and the Netherlands Antilles and Aruba.

Confusingly, the *Raad van State* at the same time considered that the new status of the islands could be classified as a free association under international law. The new status which the Council outlined points to a much closer relation, in which the Netherlands has more control over – and responsibility for – the government of the islands than seems compatible with the UN's criterion that an associated territory has the right to determine its own constitution without outside interference, nor is it at all comparable to the internationally accepted forms of free association.

In October 2006, the recommendation of the *Raad van State* was adopted by the Netherlands and the three islands, and it was agreed that the islands will become part of the constitutional structure of the Country of the Netherlands, and that – in time – all Dutch legislation will apply in these islands, except those laws which cannot be applied due to the small size of the islands, the fact that they are located more than 8,000 kilometres from The Hague, or other factors.[22] The new status was not identified as a form of free association, nor as a form of integration. It was merely agreed that the islands would become special public entities on the basis of Article 134 of the Dutch Constitution.

---

[21] *See* the advice of the *Raad van State* of 18 September 2006, which was not published in the official records of the *Staten-Generaal* but which can be found on <www.raadvanstate.nl>. (*Voorlichting overeenkomstig artikel 18, tweede lid, van de Wet op de Raad van State inzake de hervorming van de staatkundige verhoudingen van de Antilliaanse eilanden binnen het Koninkrijk*).

[22] Final declaration of the mini-conference of 10 and 11 October 2006 (*Slotverklaring van de mini-conferentie*).

The Dutch government emphasized, however, that this did not mean that Dutch levels of public services would be introduced, since this might disrupt the local economy and attract large numbers of fortune-hunters from poorer countries in the region.

At the time of writing of this study, little information had yet been made public about the precise intentions of the Netherlands and the three islands regarding the constitutional position of the islands. But the agreement of October 2006 suggests that the goal for these three islands is a form of integration into the Netherlands. The inhabitants of the islands will obtain the right to vote in the elections for the Dutch Lower House, and in the final situation, Dutch legislation will apply (on principle). These elements point to a form of integration in the Country of the Netherlands, although the Dutch government also continued to emphasize the importance of self-reliance for the islands. The word 'integration' has so far been avoided in statements by the Dutch government, as have the words 'free association.'[23]

The island government of Bonaire explicitly advocated the island's integration into the Netherlands, but the government of Saba in 2007 voiced dissatisfaction with the direction the negotiations were taking. The Island Council adopted a motion which considered that the island had chosen a free association with the Netherlands, and not integration.[24] The island feared it would lose its autonomy and its right to self-determination, whereas the Netherlands was not prepared to raise the public services to Dutch levels. Either the island should become associated with the Netherlands and retain the right to self-determination and the freedom to organize its own tax system (among other things), or it should become fully integrated in the Netherlands, including the Dutch public services. In November of 2007, consultations between the three islands and the Dutch Secretary of State for Kingdom Relations were cut short when Bonaire and Saba demanded discussion of the level of public services in the new situation.[25]

It is not yet possible to determine whether the new status of these three islands would conform to the criteria of Resolution 1541, since this new status has not yet been defined. But if the new status of these three islands should be seen as a form of integration, then special attention should be given to the criterion that the status change should be freely accepted by the population, in the awareness of the consequences. The referenda of 2004 and 2005 are of

---

[23] A press bulletin (in English) published on <www.minbzk.nl> on 3 November 2006 explained that 'the status of these three islands within the Dutch constitutional system will be comparable to that of a municipality (*gemeente*). Their inhabitants may vote in general and European parliamentary elections and will be subject to the laws of the Netherlands.'

[24] Motion of the Island Council of Saba of 21 August 2007.

[25] See *Amigoe*, 10 November 2007.

course insufficient evidence of such approval, since the new status of the islands was not yet clear at that time, and in St Eustatius the option of integration
moreover received only 2 per cent of the votes. The Netherlands and the three
islands agreed in 2007 that the islands' right of approval of the new status of
the islands would be realized by their acceptance of the amendment of the
Kingdom Charter.[26]

6.2   ASSOCIATED WITH THE NETHERLANDS

The Kingdom relations clearly bear some resemblance to the West Indies Associated States of the UK, which were intended by the UK to comply with the
UN criteria for free association (*see* chapter 3). The Netherlands government
in the 1960s also considered the Kingdom to be a form of free association.
Shortly after Resolution 1541 had been adopted, the Dutch Ministry of Foreign
Affairs explained that Surinam and the Netherlands Antilles had entered into a
free association with the Netherlands based on Principle VI of 1541.[27]

However, it was probably clear to the Netherlands government that some of
the essential characteristics of the Kingdom relations did not conform to the
UN criteria. The government has tried a number of times to transform the relations into a free association that would comply with the international criteria,
and – probably more importantly – which would make clear that the Netherlands was no longer responsible for the internal affairs of the Caribbean Countries.

The first time this happened, it was sparked by Surinam's wish to have a
more independent role in international affairs, which was uttered at a Round
Table Conference in 1961. Surinam wished to create a 'basic Charter' that would
affirm the Queen as head of state, and would require the Kingdom to guarantee
the defence, legal certainty and good governance in the Countries, but would
leave Surinam free to pursue its own future in all other matters. At the RTC the
Netherlands rejected this proposition as impossible and internally contradictory.[28]

---

[26] *See* the list of decisions reached at the political consultations of 20 June 2007, (*Kamerstukken
II* 2007/08, 30 800 IV, no. 30).

[27] BuZa 1961, p. 158.

[28] *See* Meel 1999, pp. 325-400, and Oostindie & Klinkers 2001b, pp. 49-62. Minister for
Foreign Affairs Luns stated at the outset that if Surinam wanted a more independent role in
foreign affairs, the Netherlands would require a 'radical solution', meaning the full independence
of Surinam. It was concluded that the existing potential of the Charter would be maximized, for
instance, by establishing a Bureau for Foreign Affairs in Surinam that would operate under the
control of the premier of Surinam. Such a Bureau was created for the Netherlands Antilles as
well, in 1973.

The Netherlands government thereafter quickly changed its opinion. It started to develop a plan for a 'basic Charter' that would make it possible for the Caribbean Countries to handle their foreign affairs themselves, while maintaining constitutional ties with the Netherlands. It would be up to Surinam and the Netherlands Antilles to decide when this new phase in the relations would commence. The plan also specified that it would be possible for Surinam and the Netherlands to voluntarily proceed to a third phase, namely independence. The plan, which might have led to a form of free association between the Netherlands and Surinam and/or the Netherlands Antilles, was not offered to the Caribbean Countries after Surinam seemed to have lost interest in the idea.[29]

In 1973, a Dutch proposal for a 'light' Charter that would have substantially decreased the Kingdom's reserved powers, and which would have created a possibility for unilateral termination, was rejected by Surinam and the Netherlands Antilles. The Netherlands saw the proposal as an intermediate phase towards independence, and a way of freeing the Netherlands government from its unwanted role as guarantor of the Caribbean governments. The Caribbean negotiators seem to have feared that the new Charter would authorize the Netherlands to leave the Caribbean Countries to fend for themselves, while it was clear that the overseas populations were not keen on this at all.[30]

More recently, the Netherlands government seems to have offered the status of 'free association with the Kingdom' to Aruba, as an alternative to independence or Country status, at various points during the 1980s and 1990s.[31] Aruba refused these offers for reasons unknown. The proposals were not discussed publicly.

The Dutch government therefore must have viewed free association as substantially different from Country status under the Charter during this period. But in the Netherlands Antilles, the status of Country within the Kingdom was recently considered to be a form of free association by the island governments of Curaçao and St Maarten, and also by the Antillean central government.[32] Proposals to include the option of free association on the ballot of the referen-

---

[29] Oostindie & Klinkers 2001b, pp. 59-60.

[30] The Dutch proposal would have deleted Articles 43, 50 and 51 from the Charter. *See* Oostindie & Klinkers 2001b, pp. 111-2, Bos 1976, p. 137, and Kapteyn 1982, p. 24.

[31] *See* 'Rapport Gemengde commissie toekomst Antillen' (1982), p. 65 et seq., Janus 1993, p. 86, and Munneke 1990. The discussions between Aruba and the Netherlands on a possible 'commonwealth' between the Kingdom and Aruba also tended towards a form of free association.

[32] *See* the Report of the Antillean committee of preparation for the Round Table Conference of 2005 ('*Toekomst in zicht*'), dated 12 August 2005, p. 8. *See also* the legal advice of the Directorate for Legislation of the Netherlands Antilles to the prime minister, made public around 6 September 2005. The joint Dutch-Antillean Jesurun Committee seemed to start from the assumption that the status of the Caribbean Countries will have to comply with Principle VII of Res. 1541 (free association), *see* p. 42 of the report '*Nu kan het... nu moet het!*' of 8 October 2004.

dum in St Maarten (2000) and Curaçao (2005) were rejected by the local authorities, one of the reasons apparently being that Country status would be the same as free association.

Quite a number of legal writers also see the Kingdom as a form of association. Almost none of them, however, explicitly consider it to comply with Resolution 1541.[33] *Clark*, writing about the concept of free association, considered it arguable that the GA in 1955 considered the Kingdom relations as a form of association.[34] At the same time, *Clark* thinks the Kingdom Charter does not comply fully with Resolution 1541, and he treats the Dutch case as an example where the GA apparently applied lower standards.[35]

Kapteyn also came to the conclusion that the autonomy of the Netherlands Antilles was not up to the standards of Resolution 1541, at least not on paper. The author points to the reserved powers of the Kingdom. Because of the strong position of the Dutch ministers in the Kingdom government and of the Dutch parliament in the Kingdom legislation, *Kapteyn* wonders whether the Kingdom Charter does not create 'a position of subordination' in the sense of Principle V of 1541. The fact that certain changes to the *Staatsregeling* (constitution) of the Netherlands Antilles need the approval of the Kingdom government means that the Caribbean Countries are not free to determine their internal constitution without outside interference.[36]

The elements listed by *Kapteyn* are indeed inconsistent with Principle VII of Resolution 1541, seen in the light of the UN debates on the Cook Islands and the UK West Indies Associated States. The practice of the Charter has revealed the existence of a convention that the Netherlands always seeks consensus with

---

[33] *Broderick*, writing about the British West Indies Associated States, found the example of the Kingdom of the Netherlands 'most instructive' as it was 'indicative of a satisfactory solution reached by a country with a similar problem to the United Kingdom' (Broderick 1968, p. 400). *Hintjens* considers that 'the whole arrangement resembles a form of free association' (Hintjens 1997, p. 538). Other writers who see the Kingdom as a form of association are Logemann 1955, p. 51, Janus 1993, p. 36, Van Rijn 1999, p. 57, Tillema 1989, and Blaustein/Raworth 2001, p. 1. *See also* the paragraph on Constitutional Association in the previous chapter. During the discussion of the second periodic report of the Netherlands to the HRC, Mr. Wilms, representative of the Netherlands (Aruba), called the relationship an 'association.' Corbin 2006, p. 12 is an exception in that he considers the Kingdom relations as form of free association that complies with 'the criteria of present-day standards under Resolution 1541', although on p. 5 the author states that 'a review of the Kingdom Charter under the criteria of 1960 could have arguably revealed possible adjustments'.

[34] Some representatives did indeed use the term 'association', but in 1955, this concept had not yet been developed very clearly at the UN and was also sometimes used to refer to forms of integration with the mother country.

[35] Clark 1980, p. 48.

[36] Kapteyn 1982, p. 19-22.

the Caribbean Countries before using its powers in the Caribbean, but this does not mean that the Netherlands has relinquished its reserved powers.

I think the Kingdom order partly satisfies the criteria for free association. The practice of the Kingdom is to a large extent in line with Principle VII of Resolution 1541. A number of powers attributed to the Kingdom organs by the Charter do not, however, conform to the UN standards. The reserved powers of the Kingdom government with respect to the legislation and administration of the Caribbean Countries' internal affairs, its authority to appoint a number of key officials in the Caribbean Countries, its power of veto over certain elements of the constitutions of the Caribbean Countries, and its power to legislate for the Caribbean Countries in certain affairs without their consent, are not in line with the concept of free association as defined by the UN. Also, the lack of express popular approval of the Country status of the Netherlands Antilles and Aruba makes the Kingdom Charter vulnerable to criticism if it were presented as a form of free association.

If the Kingdom relations were really transformed into a free association, the Netherlands Antilles and Aruba would obtain more freedom in foreign affairs and full control over their own constitution, if they should aspire to achieve those things. Free association does not necessarily mean loss of Dutch nationality, but the people of the islands should realize that free association has been used by metropolitan states to distance themselves from territories for which they no longer want to be responsible, and that a choice for free association often leads to a status which closely resembles full independence.

Also, in order for the Kingdom of the Netherlands to be considered as a form of free association in international law, the Netherlands Antilles and Aruba would probably need international recognition of that status.[37] The cases of the Cook Islands and the other examples of association discussed in chapter 3 even show that UN recognition of freely associated status is not enough to guarantee that the territories will be able to function independently in international affairs, but that such recognition will have to acquired almost on a case-by-case basis, in which the assistance of the principal state is indispensable.

6.3   ANOTHER FORM OF FULL SELF-GOVERNMENT?

On the basis of the criteria for integration and free association of Resolution 1541, it is not possible to conclude that the Netherlands Antilles and Aruba

---

[37] *Macdonald* considers that for non-state subjects such as associated territories *Crawford's* view applies, that 'Recognition, while in principle declaratory, may thus be of great importance in particular cases' (Macdonald 1981, p. 239 cites Crawford 1979, p. 74).

have achieved a full measure of self-government. This could mean that they are still 'arbitrarily subordinated' in the sense of Principle V of 1541, but it is also possible that they have achieved another form of full self-government. This question was discussed at some length at the UN during 1951 and 1955, and since the GA has the final authority to decide when a territory has achieved a full measure of self-government, it is necessary to take a closer look at how the GA viewed the Kingdom Charter.

6.3.1   The Netherlands Antilles as a NSGT between 1946 and 1951

In 1946, the Netherlands Antilles (at that time still including Aruba[38]) was listed as a Non-Self-Governing Territory (NSGT) in GA Resolution 66 (I). The Netherlands had informed the Secretary-General that it administered three Non-Self-Governing Territories; the Netherlands East Indies (Indonesia), Surinam and Curaçao (as the Netherlands Antilles was then still called).[39] This is an important observation, because the application of Chapter XI has been virtually limited by the GA to those territories that were voluntarily listed by the Administering powers in 1946.[40]

In 1946, Surinam and the Netherlands Antilles were governed similarly to the Crown Colonies of the British empire.[41] With respect to the 'internal affairs' of the territories, the Governors could make laws together with the *Staten* which consisted of 10 members elected on the basis of limited suffrage, and 5 members appointed by the Governor. The Netherlands legislature had in principle an unlimited right to legislate for the territories 'should the need arise'

---

[38]   The position of Aruba is slightly different from that of the Netherlands Antilles. It was part of the colony of Curaçao in 1946, but it became a separate Country within the Kingdom in 1986. This change in status probably does not affect Aruba's position with respect to the UN Charter. Leaving aside the reluctance of international law to recognize the breaking up of colonies before independence, changes in the administrative divisions have usually been treated as immaterial to the application of Chapter XI of the Charter. What is important for the application of Chapter XI to Aruba, is the measure of self-government it possesses in relation to the metropolitan government. The GA has not expressed itself on the present status of Aruba, but seeing that this status is similar to the constitutional position of Surinam and the Netherlands Antilles at the time when these territories were discussed by the GA, the opinion of the GA on the Netherlands Antilles and Surinam can probably be applied analogously to Aruba.

[39]   Some member states challenged the competence of the Netherlands to transmit information on the Netherlands East Indies because that territory had declared its independence in 1946. The Netherlands rejected this challenge by stating that it felt obligated to provide information as long as it exercised sovereignty over the archipelago.

[40]   The only exception is Oman, which was not listed in 1946, but was discussed at the UN as if it were a NSGT, and perhaps also Algeria. *See* chapter 5.

[41]   Logemann 1955, pp. 48-9.

('*zoodra de behoefte daaraan blijkt te bestaan*').[42] The budget of the territories needed the approval of the Crown. In case of budget deficits (which were common), the budget was determined by a Dutch act of parliament, which gave rise to considerable interference by the Netherlands parliament with the affairs of the territories.[43] All of the territory's legislation could be suspended by the Crown and annulled by the Dutch legislature if it conflicted with the Dutch Constitution, a Dutch act of parliament, or with public interest ('*algemeen belang*').[44] If the Governor and the Staten could not reach agreement on a legislative issue, the Netherlands government could settle the issue by a regulation ('*Algemene maatregel van bestuur*').[45] The executive powers of the Netherlands government with respect to Surinam and the Netherlands Antilles were no longer unlimited, but existed only when the Dutch Constitution or a Dutch act of parliament provided for them. The Netherlands government was, however, authorized to give instructions to the Governors.

In 1948, universal suffrage was introduced in Surinam and the Netherlands Antilles, and the autonomy of the territories was strengthened. Most importantly, the Netherlands legislature could no longer intervene in the budgets of the territories if they were not balanced.[46] After the Dutch Constitution had been amended to allow for a new relation between the Netherlands and its overseas territories, the Interim Orders of Government ('*Interimregelingen*') of 1950 (Surinam) and 1951 (Netherlands Antilles) provisionally filled in this new relation.[47] The Interim Orders listed the areas of government for which the Netherlands remained responsible, and established the principle that the Netherlands Antilles and Surinam were autonomous in all other affairs. The executive powers in the territories were entrusted to the governments of the countries, which consisted of the Governor and a council of ministers. The ministers became responsible to the *Staten*.

6.3.2 The Netherlands Decides to Stop Transmitting Information under Article 73(e)

As was described in chapter 2, Article 73 of the UN Charter creates an obligation for the Administering State to supply annually to the Secretary-General

---

[42] Article 63 of the Constitution of 1938.

[43] *See* De Gaay Fortman 1947, p. 30. In 1929, Curaçao managed to present a balanced budget. The Lower House of the Netherlands was not prepared to accept that it could no longer discuss the situation in the colony, which was therefore discussed during the debate on the budget for the Ministry of Colonies.

[44] Article 64 of the Constitution of 1938.

[45] *See* De Gaay Fortman 1947, p. 37 et seq. and Van Rijn 1999, p. 30 et seq.

[46] Oostindie & Klinkers 2001a, pp. 105-6, Van Helsdingen 1956, p. 7 et seq, and Van Helsdingen 1957, pp. 65-8.

[47] *See* Van Helsdingen 1956, p. 14 for a discussion of the Interim Orders of Government.

'statistical and other information of a technical nature relating to economic, social, and educational conditions in the territories.' In 1951, the Netherlands government decided that the transmission of such information on Surinam and the Netherlands Antilles was no longer necessary because these territories had become 'quite autonomous as regards domestic affairs', as the Dutch government claimed in an 'Explanatory Note' sent to the Secretary-General. The new constitutional order did not allow the Netherlands government to collect information on the subjects enumerated in Article 73(e), as these subjects now belonged to the internal affairs of Surinam and the Netherlands Antilles.[48]

It appears from the records of the Council of Ministers of the Netherlands that there existed a firm conviction that the Netherlands could present a strong case, because the Netherlands would really not be able to transmit the information of Article 73(e) due to the autonomy of the Netherlands Antilles and Surinam.[49] Besides, in 1948 the UK, the US and France had unilaterally decided to stop transmitting information on some of their NSGTs as well, which decisions had only met with half-hearted criticism by a few states. Since then, however, the mood had already changed considerably at the UN, and perhaps the Netherlands should have realized that the anti-colonial members of the UN might try to seize the opportunity and make an example of the Netherlands, a small and at that time unpopular state, by applying Chapter XI of the Charter strictly to the Netherlands Antilles and Surinam.

Before informing the Secretary-General, the Netherlands government had asked the opinion of the governments and the *Staten* of Surinam and the Netherlands Antilles, which agreed that the transmission of information by the Netherlands government was incompatible with the new status of the territories, and that the territories would not co-operate with the gathering and transmitting of information, as this would constitute an infringement of their autonomy. Curiously, the Netherlands seems to have informed the Secretary-General of its decision before it had received the answers of these overseas organs.[50]

The Netherlands government expected that some states would not readily accept the Dutch decision.[51] The participation of the Netherlands Antilles and Surinam themselves in the defence of the Dutch position was therefore expected to be very important. If the Netherlands could show that the overseas

---

[48] Explanatory Note by the Government of the Netherlands of 31 August 1951, UN Doc. A/AC 35/L 55, reprinted in BuZa 1952a, p. 40.

[49] *See* Oostindie & Klinkers 2001a, p. 303.

[50] The *Staten* of Surinam expressed surprise at this turn of events, and wondered why its opinion had been asked at all. See the secret letter of Governor Klaasesz to Peters, the Dutch Minister of Union Affairs and Overseas Territories, of 5 July 1951, cited in Oostindie & Klinkers 2001a, p. 302, note 19.

[51] Spits 1952b, pp. 239-40.

countries considered they had achieved a full measure of self-government and wholeheartedly supported the cessation of transmission of information, it would become much more difficult for states to oppose it.[52] For the overseas countries to make a convincing case, it would be important that they could show that they had freely accepted the new legal order, or even better, that they had been granted the freedom to choose between independence and their present status.[53] However, the Netherlands government was not prepared even to discuss the independence of the territories, and feared that the Netherlands Antilles and Surinam would use this situation as leverage in the negotiations on the new structure of the Kingdom which were being conducted at that time.[54]

Another political factor which complicated the Dutch position was the so-called Monroe doctrine,[55] which had been reaffirmed at the Inter-American Conference of 1948, at which the Organization of American States was established.[56] The Conference declared that 'the emancipation of America will not be complete so long as there remain on the continent peoples and regions subject to a colonial regime, or territories occupied by non-American countries.'[57]

6.3.3 Preliminary UN Debates on Surinam and the Netherlands Antilles[58]

In line with GA Resolution 448 (V) the Secretary-General in 1951 referred the communication of the Netherlands government to the 'Special Committee on

---

[52] See Oostindie & Klinkers 2001a, pp. 301-2 (note 19) for a discussion of the role of the representatives of Surinam and the Netherlands Antilles (Pos and Debrot).

[53] Logemann 1955, p. 51.

[54] See the code telegram of the Netherlands Antilles Governor, Struycken, cited in Oostindie & Klinkers 2001a, pp. 301-2, note 20. In 1952, the Caribbean governments would indeed exploit this situation during the negotiations on the Kingdom Charter, see chapter 4, in the section on the right to self-determination.

[55] This doctrine was named after US President James Monroe, who stated in 1823 that the United States would regard any attempt by European powers to extend their system to any part of the Western hemisphere as being dangerous to the peace and safety of the US. The statement was a warning to the colonial powers of Western Europe, which were at that time rapidly expanding their empires in Africa and Asia, not to attempt to conquer new territories in America. See generally Martin 1978.

[56] Kasteel 1956, p. 179, and Van Aller 1994, p. 272.

[57] Reproduced in BuZa 1952a, p. 95. At the Conference, Venezuela unofficially interpreted the Monroe doctrine to mean that Aruba, Bonaire and Curaçao really belonged to Venezuela. Reported by the Surinam observer at the Conference, Mr. L.A.H. Lichtveld, see Kasteel 1956, p. 180 and Keesings Historisch Archief, No. 891, 7671 A. The Netherlands representative at the UN reported in 1951 that the Latin American states would be guided by this doctrine when considering the case of the Netherlands Antilles and Surinam, BuZa 1952a, p. 24. This expectation was partly inspired by the fact that the Cuban representative cited the first four paras. of Res. XXXIII in the Fourth Committee of the Sixth GA.

[58] For these debates see generally BuZa 1952a, BuZa 1954b, BuZa 1956a, Gastmann 1964, pp. 225-32, Hasan Ahmad 1974, pp. 311-30, Paula 1986, Te Beest 1988, Oostindie & Klinkers

Information transmitted under Article 73 *e* of the Charter.' It soon became clear to the Dutch delegation that a majority among the non-Administering members of the Committee (*i.e.* the Socialist, Latin American, African and Asian states) were not at all inclined to accept the cessation of transmission of information. In the eyes of the Dutch delegation, this attitude sprang from three main reasons. First, a general feeling of distrust towards the Administering States. Second, a lack of understanding of Dutch constitutional law. And third, the fact that the Netherlands government had translated only parts of the Interim Orders of Government, which created suspicion.[59] To these reasons might be added that the Netherlands had gained a bad reputation among the non-Administering states because of its attitude in the Indonesian conflict.[60]

The debates in the Special Committee and subsequently in the Fourth Committee of the General Assembly (which deals with issues of decolonization) in 1951 also revealed that a number of states feared that the autonomy granted to the territories might only be of a temporary nature, as the new constitutional structure was laid down in *Interim* Orders. Article II of the Interim Orders increased suspicion among the non-Administering States, as it contained a long list of subjects that remained within the exclusive competence of the Netherlands government. Questions were also raised on the subject of the appointment of the Governors by the Crown, on the powers of the Governors, on the appointment of members of the judiciary, on the relation between the executive and the legislative branch, and on the possibility of reversal of Surinam and Netherlands Antilles legislation by the Netherlands government.[61]

According to the member of the Dutch delegation for Surinam, a number of states had already prepared a sharp draft resolution condemning the Dutch decision, but he convinced them not to submit it.[62] Instead, the representatives of the non-Administering states argued that consideration of the Netherlands communication should be postponed until the constitutional reforms within the Kingdom of the Netherlands had been completed.[63]

In 1953, the issue was discussed at the UN on the basis of a letter by the Netherlands which formed an addition to the Explanatory Note of 1951, and

---

2001a, pp. 129-32 and the seven contributions by Spits to the journal *Indonesië* listed in the Bibliography.

[59] BuZa 1952a, p. 17

[60] Cf. Oostindie & Klinkers 2001a, p. 129,

[61] *See* Te Beest 1988 for a discussion of the debates in the Special Committee.

[62] Report of Mr. Pos to the Netherlands Council of Ministers, 29 October 1951, cited in Oostindie & Klinkers 2001b, p. 301, note 19.

[63] Furthermore, it was deemed impossible to assess the relation between the Netherlands and its overseas territories until the GA had formulated the factors which should decide whether a full measure of self-government had been reached. *See* GA Res. 568 (VI) of 18 January 1952.

which offered a slightly different legal underpinning of the Netherlands' decision.[64] The Explanatory Note had claimed primarily that Surinam and the Netherlands Antilles had become fully autonomous with regard to their domestic affairs. The letter of 1953 stressed that the new constitutional relation between the Netherlands and its overseas territories no longer allowed the Netherlands government to collect and transmit the information under Article 73(e) because this information regarded subjects that were now fully within the autonomous area of Surinam and the Netherlands Antilles. The letter steered away from the subject of the precise extent of the autonomy of the territories, and called attention to the 'constitutional considerations clause' of Article 73(e). The Netherlands stated that the factors which should decide whether a full measure of self-government had been achieved should not be applied to this case, as the Dutch cessation of transmission of information was due to constitutional considerations, and not to the achievement of full self-government of the Netherlands Antilles and Surinam. The Netherlands thus tried to separate the obligation under Article 73(e) from the question of self-government, just as the British government had done in 1949 with respect to Malta.[65]

In the *ad hoc* Committee on Factors the representative of Guatemala suggested a solution to the constitutional obstacles on which the Netherlands based its decision of 1951: the Governors could fulfil the duties of the Netherlands under Article 73(e), since they were charged under Article 52 of both Interim Orders with supervising the observance and implementation of treaties and agreements with international organizations in Surinam and the Netherlands Antilles. On the basis of this Article, and as representatives of the King, the Governors could transmit the information required by the UN Charter, the Guatemalan representative argued. The Netherlands delegation did not respond to this suggestion, but the representative of Surinam in the Netherlands delegation observed that the Netherlands government would in any event be unable to act on any recommendations the GA might make, as the subject matter of the reports fell entirely within the autonomous powers of Surinam and the Netherlands Antilles.[66]

During the discussions in the Committee it became clear that the non-Administering members considered the autonomy of the Dutch Caribbean territo-

---

[64] UN Doc A/AC.67/3. Reprinted in BuZa 1954b, p. 65-68. The letter also made much of a comparison with Article 35 of the Constitution of the International Labour Organisation, a specialized agency of the UN. Article 35 of the ILO Constitution (as amended in 1946) frees states from the obligation to apply conventions to their non-metropolitan territories if 'the subject-matter of the Convention is within the self-governing powers of the territory.'

[65] *See* El-Ayouty 1971, p. 151 et seq.

[66] Summary of the debate in the *ad hoc* Committee, UN Doc. AC.67/SR. 6 and 7 (mimeographed only), cited in Engers (1956) p. 178 and in BuZa 1954b, pp. 15-19.

ries insufficient to be termed 'a full measure of self-government.' These members also thought that paragraph (e) of Article 73 should be read in conjunction with the other paragraphs of that Article, which meant that the Netherlands government should continue transmitting reports until Surinam and the Netherlands Antilles had achieved 'a full measure of self-government.' The defence of the Netherlands based on the 'constitutional considerations' clause was rejected. The Netherlands position was supported, however, by the other Administering members, and because the Committee was established on the basis of parity between Administering and non-Administering members, it was unable to reach any conclusion on the matter.[67]

The Dutch delegation soon realised that a majority of the UN members did not approve of the cessation of transmission of information. The Netherlands had hoped to profit from the fact that the GA appeared willing to approve the cessation of transmission of information on Puerto Rico by the US which was expected during this same session.[68]

In the Fourth Committee of the GA, the Netherlands representative implicitly acknowledged that Surinam and the Netherlands Antilles had not achieved a full measure of self-government. He stated that the territories had not been fully integrated in the sense of Resolution 648 of 1952 (which was a precursor to Resolution 1541) but that constitutional considerations precluded the Netherlands from transmitting information under Article 73(e).

The representatives of Surinam and the Netherlands Antilles were allowed to address the Fourth Committee. They again supported the claim that the Netherlands could not provide the information under Article 73(e) because of the autonomy of the Netherlands Antilles and Surinam. If the Countries themselves would provide it, the Netherlands could not be held responsible for it, nor for the situations which it regarded. The Antillean representative suggested that states might consult the publications that the Netherlands Antilles issued annually on the subjects covered by Article 73(e), but the Netherlands Antilles could not be asked to transmit that information to the Netherlands for communication to the UN, as such an action would suggest that the Netherlands government still had jurisdiction over these affairs.[69]

During the subsequent debate, the constitutional relation between the Netherlands and the overseas countries did not play an important role, probably because the Netherlands had not claimed that a full measure of self-govern-

---

[67] Report of the Ad Hoc Committee on Factors (Non-Self-Governing Territories), GAOR (VIII), Annexes, Agenda item 33, p. 7 (UN Doc. A/2428).

[68] Cf. Spits 1954, pp. 450-51, Engers 1956, pp. 190-193, and BuZa 1954b, pp. 20-21.

[69] GAOR (VIII), Fourth Committee, 343rd Meeting, pp. 178-81. The full text of the speeches is reproduced in BuZa 1954b, pp. 85-90.

ment had been achieved. The relations were nonetheless clearly misrepresented by a number of representatives,[70] most strikingly by the Indonesian delegate, who stated that the inhabitants of Surinam and the Netherlands Antilles could not vote in the elections for the *Staten*, nor be appointed to the Governing Council, as members of those bodies must possess Dutch nationality.[71]

Only five states spoke in defence of the Netherlands position.[72] A majority of states was convinced that the Netherlands could find some way to transmit the information required by 73(e) in order to fulfil its obligations under the UN Charter. Some states also expressed surprise at the attitude of the Netherlands Antilles and Surinam; UN involvement with their territories would be beneficial and would help them develop their self-government. Why would these territories refuse to be helped? Besides, the objections by the overseas countries to the transmission of information could not release the Netherlands from its international obligations.[73]

Many representatives considered that the Netherlands Antilles and Surinam had not achieved a full measure of self-government,[74] and that the Netherlands itself had conceded this.[75] Most states doubted whether the Interim Orders really gave a substantial amount of autonomy to the overseas countries. The

---

[70] According to the representative of the Soviet Union, Surinam and the Netherlands Antilles were administered by Governors with extensive powers, who were not responsible to the parliaments of the territories. The legislative authority 'was entirely vested in the Parliament and Government of the Netherlands', the Governor appointed the members of the Governing Council and the president of the Staten, and the Supreme Court of the Netherlands had jurisdiction in the overseas countries. Although most of these observations were in correct in themselves, they also showed that the Soviet Union was not prepared to discuss the issue on the merits. *See* GAOR (VIII), Fourth Committee, 344th Meeting, p. 183.

[71] *See* GAOR (VIII), Fourth Committee, 345th Meeting, p. 191. The representative of Byelorussia also raised this point (345th Meeting, p. 193). Antilleans and Surinamese were in fact already citizens of the Netherlands at this time (as was pointed out by an 'astonished' Dutch representative) and the members of the Governing Councils of both countries already existed entirely of 'members belonging to the indigenous population' (347th Meeting, p. 208).

[72] Sweden, Denmark, Belgium, New Zealand, Australia, and the US. The UK and Canada explained their vote against the draft resolution by stating that the UN should have accepted the Dutch decision to stop transmitting information. France also explained its negative vote, but did not go into the question whether the Dutch cessation was justified. Pakistan stated it would be easy to take a decision on the matter (*i.e.* to decide that transmission of information should continue), but preferred to wait until the negotiations on the new constitutional order were completed. Cuba considered a full measure of self-government had not been achieved, but might be achieved after the negotiations on the new Charter had been completed. The Dominican Republic also preferred to wait.

[73] *See for instance* the statement by Brazil (GAOR (VIII), 346th Meeting, p. 198).

[74] Brazil, Poland, Liberia, Cuba, Soviet Union, Byelorussia, Yugoslavia, Iran, Iraq, India, Mexico and Chile.

[75] India, Mexico, Yugoslavia and Iraq.

fact that there continued to be 'Governors', appointed by the Dutch Crown and not directly responsible to the *Staten*, was an eyesore to many representatives. The Constitutions and the Interim Orders also appeared to place many important powers in the hands of the Governor, and it was not clear to the representatives that the executive and legislative powers had really been attributed to the ministers and the parliaments. The change in the position of the Governor after 1950/51 had in reality been quite drastic. It was described by one observer as: 'from tsar to servant' (*'van tsaar tot dienaar'*),[76] but this revolution had been expressed in words that were only comprehensible to those well versed in Dutch constitutional law.

The Plenary of the GA decided by 33 votes to 13 with 8 abstentions that the Netherlands should continue to report (Resolution 747 (VIII) of 1953). The Netherlands stated that it would not carry out the Resolution.[77] The next year, the Netherlands was accused in the GA of violating the Charter, but after the Netherlands had promised it would inform the UN next year on the Kingdom Charter which had been drafted, no further actions were taken.[78]

6.3.4 The Netherlands Presentation of the New Constitutional Order

In 1955, the Netherlands informed the UN that the Kingdom Charter had officially come into force. In compliance with Resolutions 222 (III) and 747 (VIII), the Netherlands transmitted an English and a Spanish translation of the Kingdom Charter, and an Explanatory Memorandum, also in English and in Span-

---

[76] Reinders 1993, p. 11.

[77] GAOR (VIII) 459th Plenary Meeting, p. 319. Eight Latin American states that disapproved of the cessation of transmission of information with respect to the Netherlands Antilles and Surinam only a few minutes later approved the US decision to stop transmitting information on Puerto Rico. These states explained their vote by saying that Puerto Rico had achieved a larger measure of self-government than the Dutch territories under the Interim Orders. It was stated that Puerto Rico had drafted its own Constitution, the people of Puerto Rico had approved its new status in a plebiscite, and its governor was elected through elections in Puerto Rico. The representative of India opposed this position because Puerto Rico was not as autonomous in economic affairs as the Netherlands Antilles and Surinam, and there had been true opposition among the people of Puerto Rico against the new status, which had been absent in the Dutch territories.

[78] During the ninth session of the GA, many non-Administering states called on the Netherlands to resume transmitting reports. The representative of the Soviet Union accused the Netherlands of violating the UN Charter. The other non-Administering states were willing (for the time being) to refrain from further actions, as the Netherlands representative had informed the Fourth Committee that agreement had been reached on a Kingdom Charter, which had been approved during 1954 by the parliaments of the Netherlands, Surinam and the Netherlands Antilles. The Netherlands representative promised to report to the Secretary-General within six months after the Kingdom Charter had come into force. *See* BuZa 1956a, pp. 7-12.

ish.[79] In the letter accompanying these documents, the permanent representative of the Netherlands (i.e., the Kingdom) stated that 'the Netherlands Government regard their responsibilities according to Chapter XI of the Charter with regard to [Surinam and the Netherlands Antilles] as terminated.' In other words, Surinam and the Netherlands Antilles had achieved a full measure of self-government, in the view of the Netherlands, even though the autonomy of Surinam and the Netherlands Antilles under the Kingdom Charter was hardly larger than under the Interim Measures. In case the UN should still think that Chapter XI applied, the Netherlands also stated that the constitutional considerations which had prevented the transmission of information since 1951 had 'become even stronger under the new Charter.'

The Netherlands expected the Caribbean Countries to join in the defence of the Kingdom Charter at the UN, and some political pressure was exerted to obtain their support.[80] Shortly before the UN was to discuss the case, a conflict between the governing council and the Governor of the Netherlands Antilles led the governing council to announce that the Netherlands delegation would not include an Antillean member, and that the Antilles would only send a representative to New York to discuss the problem with the Latin American states.[81] The Netherlands expressed its concern, and the Governor and the governing council soon settled their differences. The Netherlands Antilles issued a declaration to the UN that:

> [the Netherlands Antilles] do not feel like a colony or a dependent territory anymore, they feel like a country, small but proud of its rights and its quality to anyone. The Netherlands Antilles are satisfied with this unique relationship and the Netherlands Antilles in this phase of their political development consider themselves selfgoverning.[82]

The delegation of the Netherlands to the Committee on Information and the GA included representatives of the Netherlands Antilles and Surinam. In the Committee on Information, they were members of the delegation, in the GA they were 'special advisers' to the representatives. This posed an interesting

---

[79] UN Doc. A/AC.35/L.206. Reproduced in BuZa 1956a.

[80] The permanent representative of the Netherlands at the UN, Mr. Schürmann, went to Willemstad to convince the Netherlands Antilles, see Te Beest 1988, p. 53 and Oostindie & Klinkers 2001a, pp. 130-1. The pressure from the Netherlands created some suspicion in the Netherlands Antilles as it feared the Netherlands wished to force the Netherlands Antilles to declare at the UN that all of its constitutional wishes had been fulfilled by the Charter. The Netherlands might later use such a declaration in case the Netherlands Antilles should wish to change the Charter. See Oostindie & Klinkers 2001a, p. 304, note 27.

[81] Te Beest 1988, p. 53.

[82] Cited in Oostindie & Klinkers 2001a, p. 130.

problem from the perspective of international law and the constitutional law of the Kingdom. Did the members of the delegation speak on behalf of their countries or the Kingdom? The Netherlands representative stated that all members of the delegation represented the Kingdom. This was probably correct, for the Kingdom constitutes the state in international law, and the Kingdom is a member of the UN.[83] In this sense, all of the statements by all of the members of the delegation must be ascribed to the Kingdom, and the Kingdom must also be considered to be bound by statements of the representatives of Surinam and the Netherlands Antilles, inasmuch as statements at the UN are binding under international law. Apart from the fact that the special advisers sometimes appeared to think that they did speak on behalf of their country,[84] there was the problem that the delegation did not really speak with one voice. The members of the delegation differed in their interpretation of the new constitutional order of the Kingdom, and the role of the UN, although they did not emphasize these differences.[85] Nonetheless, it must have been notable to the other delegations at the UN that the Netherlands did not present a completely unified front.

The Netherlands somewhat misrepresented the new constitutional order at the UN. It exaggerated the legal autonomy of the overseas countries and the role of the those Countries in the legislation of the Kingdom. The Netherlands representative, for instance, claimed that during the 'continued deliberations' after a Minister Plenipotentiary has indicated that he has serious objections to a preliminary opinion of the Council of Ministers of the Kingdom (*see* Article 12 of the Charter), the Netherlands and the Caribbean Countries would be represented by an equal number of ministers, so as 'to prevent the possibility of the Ministers Plenipotentiary being outvoted or overruled.'[86] Mr. Ferrier, prime minister of Surinam, claimed in the Fourth Committee that the Ministers Plenipotentiary 'could block any proposed legislation of a general and binding na-

---

[83] The representatives of India and Ecuador thought differently (*see below*). India considered the delegates of Surinam and the Netherlands 'special advisers of the Netherlands delegation.'

[84] Mitrasing 1959, p. 281 et seq. refers to Ferrier and Van Ommeren as representatives of Surinam.

[85] *See for instance* the different views Schürmann (the representative of the Netherlands) and the special advisers on the right to self-determination and the right of secession. Schürmann uttered some misgivings to the Netherlands Government about certain remarks by Ephrain Jonckheer, the Prime Minister of the Netherlands Antilles, in the Fourth Committee. Jonckheer, on the other hand, is quoted to have said in 1957, during a conflict with The Hague on some other issues, that he would regard his defence of the Kingdom at the UN 'as a show' and that he would 'feel personally betrayed' if The Hague were now to decide against him. *See* Oostindie & Klinkers 2001, p. 131 and p. 305, note 29.

[86] GAOR (X), Fourth Committee, 520th Meeting, pp. 282-3.

ture if they considered it detrimental to the country.'[87] Neither speaker mentioned the crucial fact that the prime minister of the Netherlands also takes part in the continued deliberations, so that the Netherlands can in fact always 'outvote or overrule' the Caribbean Countries.[88]

The Netherlands also attempted to influence the opinion of the UN by translating the text of the Charter in a way that emphasized that the new constitutional order was based on mutual consent. The important phrase '*op voet van gelijkwaardigheid*' in the Preamble was translated as 'on the basis of equality' (in Spanish: '*en pie de igualdad*').[89] This was not correct, as '*gelijkwaardigheid*' translates as 'equivalence' ('*equivalencia*' in Spanish), whereas 'equality' or '*igualdad*' translates as '*gelijkheid*' in Dutch.[90] It is true that these terms are occasionally used interchangeably (for instance, in mathematics), but in relation to the Kingdom order a conscious choice was made to use the term equivalence instead of equality.[91]

The Explanatory Memorandum and the representatives of the Netherlands in the UN debates nonetheless repeatedly used the term 'equality', or even 'absolute equality',[92] which probably explains, at least partly, why so many states' representatives found it necessary to point out that the countries were *not* equal under the Kingdom Charter. Many representatives detected evidence of inequality between the three countries in matters of legislation and administration. It was wondered how the countries could conduct their common interests 'on the basis of equality' in view of the great disparity in the size of the populations of the three countries. Egypt stated there existed no equality between the countries because of the preponderance of the Netherlands in the procedure for Kingdom legislation, and because of the restrictions on the legislative powers of the overseas countries, in particular under Article 44 of the Charter. Many other states agreed the countries were unequal in a legal sense.[93]

---

[87] GAOR (X), Fourth Committee, 526th Meeting, p. 319.

[88] Except when Article 26 of the Kingdom Charter applies. In reply to a question by the representative of Venezuela, Jonckheer, Prime Minister of the Netherlands Antilles, admitted that the Netherlands always commanded a majority in these deliberations, as it would 'clearly be unjust' if Surinam and the Netherlands Antilles could impose their will on the Netherlands. But, Jonckheer added, the Prime Minister of the Netherlands 'by his very position, was able to judge a case impartially.'

[89] '*Igualdad*' is usually translated as 'equality'.

[90] In a similar sense, *see* Bos 1976, p. 134, and Munneke 1993, p. 62. *See also* Van Rijn 1999, p. 73. Logemann 1955, p. 51 translates '*gelijkwaardigheid*' as 'equality of status'. The English translation currently provided on the website of the Ministry of the Interior and Kingdom Relations still uses the phrase 'on a basis of equality', as does the translation in Besselink 2004.

[91] *See* chapter 4, in the section on equivalence and voluntariness.

[92] Statement by Ephrain Jonckheer, Prime Minister of the Netherlands Antilles, GAOR (X), Fourth Committee, 520th Meeting, p. 285.

[93] Iraq, Lebanon, India, Poland, Soviet Union, Ecuador, Venezuela, Yemen, Liberia, Indonesia, and Burma.

On the other hand, the states supporting the Dutch position often defended the Kingdom Charter by referring to the 'equality' it created between the countries. Israel, for instance, stated that 'by including the words "on a basis of equality" in the preamble to the Kingdom Charter, the Netherlands had declared an end of the colonial system and had subscribed to the general principle of equality among nations.'[94]

6.3.5 Debate on the Kingdom Charter

In the Committee on Information from Non-Self-Governing Territories of 1955, the Minister Plenipotentiary of Surinam (Mr. Pos) and the Lieutenant Governor of Curaçao (Mr. Gorsira), expounded on the new constitutional structure of the Kingdom and as a gesture of goodwill they submitted 'General Reviews' of the situation in their countries with respect to social, economic and educational affairs. The Netherlands had requested the governments of the Netherlands Antilles and Surinam to prepare these general reviews for the UN,[95] thereby in fact demonstrating how easy it might be for the Kingdom to fulfil the obligations under Article 73(e), but no state representative commented on this fact.

The representatives of Brazil, Burma, China, Guatemala and India posed a large number of rather critical questions on the extent of the autonomous powers of Surinam and the Netherlands Antilles and the procedure for creating Kingdom legislation. These were answered by the representatives of Surinam and the Netherlands Antilles.[96] To the question whether the inhabitants of Surinam and the Netherlands Antilles had been consulted with respect to their new constitutional status, it was answered that this had not been deemed necessary, 'since *all* political parties had supported the constitutional changes.'[97] The questions of Guatemala followed the scheme of the third part of the list of factors of GA Resolution 742 (VIII),[98] which dealt with the integration of a NSGT with the mother country. Guatemala therefore wanted information on the ethnical make-up of the population of Surinam and the Netherlands Antilles, the political development of the territories, the voting rights of illiterate persons, and a number of other subjects. The Guatemalan representative was also interested to know whether the opinion of the populations of the territories had

---

[94] GAOR (X), Fourth Committee, 523rd Meeting, p. 302. *See also* the statement by Mexico, 521st Meeting, p. 291.

[95] Te Beest 1988, p. 53, with reference to a letter by the Dutch Minister for Overseas Affairs.

[96] These questions and answers are summarized in BuZa 1956a, p. 103 et seq.

[97] Report of the Committee on Information from Non-Self-Governing Territories, GAOR (X) Supplement No. 16, pp. 7-10. UN Doc. A/2908.

[98] This Resolution was a precursor to Res. 1541 of 1960.

been freely expressed by informed and democratic processes. The Netherlands delegation answered that:

> The freely elected Parliaments in Surinam and the Netherlands Antilles had unanimously accepted the Charter of the Kingdom of the Netherlands. Negotiations with respect to the Charter had been under way for a number of years, and the questions at issue had been freely discussed in the local press. As a consequence, the population of Surinam and the Netherlands Antilles had been kept fully informed with respect to the constitutional changes which had subsequently been enacted.[99]

When asked whether the territories had the right to modify their present status, Mr. Pos replied that the Ministers Plenipotentiary of Surinam and the Netherlands Antilles had the right to introduce a bill to amend the Charter, which would have to be approved by the parliaments of the Netherlands, Surinam and the Netherlands Antilles. Mr. Pos furthermore assured the Committee that it would be 'contrary to the established policy of the Netherlands to prevent a partner from leaving the Kingdom if that partner desired to do so.'[100] This statement probably left the Members wondering how and when this Dutch policy had been 'established', but it was accepted as a promise with regard to the future policies of the Netherlands, and as such it played an important role in the debate in the Fourth Committee.

The Netherlands were convinced that the attitude of the Latin American states would be crucial. The other non-Administering members of the Committee would follow them, as the issue was considered to be of most importance for Latin America. The diplomatic offensive that the Netherlands had deployed during the adjournment of the Committee turned out to have been unsuccessful because none of the Latin American members were now prepared to submit the draft resolution approving the Dutch cessation of transmission of information that the Netherlands had circulated among the members.[101]

Finally, Brazil was found willing to defend the Dutch decision, but in a more marginal way than the Netherlands had hoped. The Netherlands draft resolution had declared that Article 73 no longer applied to the Netherlands Antilles and Surinam. The resolutions on Puerto Rico and Greenland had also declared this, but Brazil estimated that a majority of the Latin American states

---

[99] Report of the Committee on Information from Non-Self-Governing Territories, Addendum, GAOR (X) Supplement No. 16A, p. 1. (UN Doc. A/2908/Add.1.) The report does not indicate which member of the Netherlands delegation answered these questions.

[100] Report of the Committee on Information from Non-Self-Governing Territories, Addendum, GAOR (X) Supplement No. 16A, p. 1. UN Doc. A/2908/Add.1.

[101] Te Beest 1988, pp. 57-9 describes the diplomatic efforts by the Netherlands.

would not be willing to draw a similar conclusion with regard to the Netherlands Antilles and Surinam. Together with the US, it submitted a draft resolution, of which most important paragraph stated that the Committee was of the opinion that:

> The transmission of information under Article 73 *e* of the Charter in respect of Surinam and the Netherlands Antilles is no longer necessary or appropriate.[102]

The draft resolution did not declare that Article 73 in its entirety no longer applied to Surinam and the Netherlands Antilles, nor that those countries had obtained a full measure of self-government, or that they had exercised their right to self-determination, all of which had been declared in the Resolution on Puerto Rico.

The representatives of Brazil did state in the Committee that it considered Surinam and the Netherlands Antilles to be 'self-governing countries.' According to *Te Beest* this statement only referred to self-government in the affairs governed by Article 73(e), and not to 'a full measure of self-government.'[103] This might be true. The well-nigh impossible situation in which some non-Western states must have found themselves led to some creative use of language.

The Netherlands delegation, however, interpreted the statement by Brazil to mean that Brazil considered that Chapter XI no longer applied to Surinam and the Netherlands Antilles, and therefore regretted that the draft resolution did not make this explicit. It stated that:

> The Netherlands delegation, in order to avoid unnecessary controversy, was prepared to accept that omission because the conclusion reached in the draft resolution that transmission of information was no longer necessary or appropriate implied that those countries were no longer non-self-governing.

This implication was of course not all that obvious, as the Dutch case in 1953 had been based almost entirely on the constitutional considerations clause of Article 73(e), which makes it possible that information is no longer transmitted, even though a full measure of self-government has not been achieved.

The representative of Peru voiced the opinion of many Latin American states and other non-Administering states when he explained why his delegation would abstain from voting on the draft resolution. He conceded that the two territories

---

[102] UN Doc A/AC.35/L.216. *See* Report of the Committee on Information from Non-Self-Governing Territories, Addendum, GAOR (X) Supplement No. 16A, p. 3. (UN Doc. A/2908/Add.1.)

[103] Te Beest 1988, p. 59.

'had advanced considerably towards full self-government', and he expressed the hope that they would in the future attain full self-government 'through the exercise of the right of self-determination.' He regretted however that the draft resolution implied that the cessation of information was a consequence of the achievement of full self-government. Even though the territories enjoyed autonomy in the specific fields to which Article 73(e) of the Charter referred, it was clear that Surinam and the Netherlands Antilles 'remained ... in a state of dependency in important respects within the juridical system and under the authority of the State which had been administering them.' Peru accepted that the Netherlands might be unable to transmit the reports under Article 73(e), but Chapter XI contained other obligations which would continue to exist until the Territory had attained a full measure of self-government, at which point the entire Chapter became inapplicable.[104] The Brazilian-American draft resolution was adopted by the Committee on Information by seven to one votes, with five abstentions.

The Netherlands sent a large delegation to the subsequent debate in the Fourth Committee of the GA. It consisted of a representative of the Netherlands (whether the Country or the Kingdom was not made clear) and, as 'special advisers', the prime ministers of Surinam and the Netherlands Antilles and the presidents of the *Staten* of the Caribbean countries. The presence of these four representatives of the Netherlands Antilles and Surinam, which eloquently defended the new constitutional order of the Kingdom, appears to have made a considerable impact on the Fourth Committee. Many states, especially those which were not enthusiastic about the Dutch decision to stop transmitting information, commended the Netherlands on the composition of its delegation.

As in the Committee on Information, the debate in the Fourth Committee mainly consisted of a large number of questions posed by non-Administering states.[105] This was an indication of a greater willingness on the part of states to judge the issue on its merits. The Latin American states especially seemed determined to obtain an accurate impression of the measure of autonomy obtained by Surinam and the Netherlands Antilles, although Brazil, Mexico and Cuba stated at the start of the debate that they were satisfied with the results laid down in the Kingdom Charter and were prepared to release the Netherlands from its duties under Article 73(e) without further discussion. This was a clear sign of the changed situation in the GA, as these three states had explicitly declared in 1953 that the Netherlands Antilles and Surinam had not achieved

---

[104] Report of the Committee on Information from Non-Self-Governing Territories, Addendum, GAOR (X) Supplement No. 16A, p. 3. (UN Doc. A/2908/Add.1.)

[105] These debates took place in eight meetings on seven days, *see* GAOR (X), Fourth Committee, 520th-527th Meeting.

a full measure of self-government. A cynical observer might have concluded afterwards that the large number of questions by non-Administering states was only intended to justify the fact that most of these states abstained or voted in support of the Netherlands position, which needed to be defended to the anti-colonial movement in the UN and elsewhere. The fact remains that the debates revealed how states looked at the new constitutional order of the Kingdom and what they considered to be the obligations of the Kingdom under the UN Charter and other international law.

Confusion Created by the Charter

Many states complained that the Kingdom Charter was hard to understand. The representative of Haiti complained that 'it was easy to lose one's way in the tangle of those rather contradictory provisions' (concerning an amendment to the Charter that conflicted with the Constitution of the Netherlands).[106] One of the reasons for this was that some of the elements of the new order were not regulated by the Charter itself, but by other legislation of the Kingdom and the Countries. A number of representatives therefore asked for the text of the Kingdom act for the Governor ('*Reglement voor de gouverneur*'), the regulations of the countries with respect to the powers of the Governor, and the paragraphs of the Constitution of the Netherlands that were relevant to the Kingdom, 'to dispel certain doubts which still existed.'[107] The Netherlands representative did not consider it necessary to supply these documents as 'all provisions directly affecting relations between the countries were contained in the Charter.'[108] A number of representatives protested that the Charter clearly delegated legislative powers to the Constitution of the Netherlands (*see* Article 5, para 1 of the Charter). Schürmann could not deny that the Netherlands Constitution to a large extent determined the composition of the Kingdom organs, but still did not think it necessary to provide the UN with the text of the relevant Articles.

The US agreed that the 'the ingenious arrangement' between the Netherlands, Surinam and the Netherlands led to many misunderstandings and disagreements, for instance on the difference between the *Country* and the *Kingdom* of the Netherlands.[109] Pakistan asked whether it had been the Country that had transmitted information on the Netherlands Antilles and Surinam under Article 73(e).[110] Mr. Schürmann replied that the difference between the Country and

---

[106] 522nd Meeting, p. 297.

[107] Venezuela, Liberia, Thailand, Iraq, Peru, Guatemala and Ecuador.

[108] Statements by Schürmann, GAOR (X), Fourth Committee, 520th and 521st Meeting, pp. 286 and 292-3.

[109] *See for instance* the statement by Ecuador, 524th Meeting, p. 311.

[110] GAOR (X), Fourth Committee, 526th Meeting, p. 325.

the Kingdom had only existed since 1954, but that it had been the *Kingdom* government that had transmitted the text of the Charter and the Memorandum to the Secretary-General. The representative of Indonesia then pointed out that this communication had been received from the Netherlands government, which to her apparently meant the country of the Netherlands. Pakistan suggested striking out the word 'Kingdom' from the phrase 'the communication ... by which the Government of the Kingdom of the Netherlands transmitted to the Secretary-General the constitutional provisions (etc.)' in the preamble of the Brazil-US draft resolution.[111] India, Ecuador, Liberia, Lebanon and Syria spoke in support of this suggestion,[112] which was subsequently adopted by the sponsors of the draft resolution and thus found its way into the final text of the Resolution.

It was thereby impossible that the GA might seem to express its approval of the new structure of the Kingdom, or that the GA might seem to agree to the contention that the administration of the Netherlands Antilles and Surinam would be subsumed under the domestic jurisdiction of the Netherlands, and that Article 2, paragraph 7 of the UN Charter would prevent the GA from discussing the situation in the future. This discussion, and others like it, also showed that the representatives of non-Western states were not readily inclined to accept that the government institutions of the Netherlands could act in two different capacities, or that the Kingdom was not really the Netherlands. Many states considered the Kingdom a legal fiction which bore no resemblance to the real division of power between the Netherlands and the Caribbean countries.

Powers of the Kingdom

The representatives of Iraq and Indonesia stated that Article 44 of the Kingdom Charter gave the Netherlands veto power over matters which fell outside Kingdom affairs, and which should belong to the domestic affairs of Surinam and the Netherlands Antilles.[113] Iraq considered the legislative and executive bodies of the Netherlands were in fact, though not in name, the governing organs of the Kingdom as well, and hoped the Caribbean countries would eventually be granted a more effective representation in the parliament of the Netherlands and in the conduct of Kingdom affairs. A number of representatives also ob-

---

[111] GAOR (X), Fourth Committee, 527th Meeting, p. 326.
[112] GAOR (X), Fourth Committee, 527th Meeting, pp. 327-8.
[113] GAOR (X), Fourth Committee, 521st Meeting, p. 289, and 526th Meeting, p. 323. Article 44, para. 1 of the Kingdom Charter provides that changes to the constitutions of the Caribbean countries ('*Staatsregelingen*') which relate to fundamental human rights and freedoms, the powers of the Governor, the powers of the *Staten*, or the judiciary, should be approved by the government of the Kingdom.

jected to Articles 50 and 51 of the Charter, as it allowed the Kingdom Government to interfere with the internal affairs of Surinam and the Netherlands Antilles.[114] Questions were raised about the powers of the Governors, and whether the legislation regulating the position of the Governor had been promulgated already. Egypt stated that 'political control was reserved to the central government of the Kingdom', by which it meant the government of the country of the Netherlands.

Why No Independence?

Many states uttered their surprise or even disbelief at the contention that the Netherlands Antilles and Surinam did not want to become independent. Some simply stated that the Netherlands Antilles and Surinam did strive to become independent.[115] The Philippines wondered why there had been any need for the Kingdom Charter, seeing that the countries could conduct their internal affairs and make their own constitution, which were attributes of a sovereign state. Why had the countries not become fully independent?[116] The Soviet Union stated that 'it was scarcely credible … that the peoples of the two Territories who had struggled for centuries for independence really did not wish to rid themselves of colonialism and attain independence' and proposed to send a visiting mission in accordance with GA Resolution 850 (IX) of 1954.[117]

Mr. Yrausquin, president of the *Staten* of the Netherlands Antilles, assured the Fourth Committee that his country would have no difficulty in realizing a change in its existing status, in view of the principles laid down, and the understanding shown by the other parts of the Kingdom.[118] The Prime Minister of the Netherlands Antilles, Ephrain Jonckheer, seemed to think that his country had already acquired its independence,[119] but that it would not hesitate to apply to the UN should its relations with the Netherlands develop in a way that was

---

[114] Articles 50 and 51 give the Kingdom government the power to annul any legislative or executive decision of the Caribbean countries that is in violation of the Kingdom Charter or other Kingdom legislation, an international agreement, or with other interests that are entrusted to or guaranteed by the Kingdom. If an organ of a Caribbean country does not live up to its obligations under the Kingdom legislation or an international agreement, the Kingdom government can decide how these obligations will be met.

[115] For instance Czechoslovakia.

[116] 521st Meeting, p. 289.

[117] 524th Meeting, p. 308.

[118] 520th Meeting, p. 286.

[119] Statement by Jonckheer, 520th Meeting, p. 286 (full text reproduced in BuZa 1956a, p. 133): '*Nos sentimos y somos independientes*', which was translated in the GAOR as: 'The country had acquired its independence', and again during the 522nd Meeting ('two independent countries managing their own affairs').

not in conformity with the will of the people. Jonckheer reminded the Fourth Committee of the telegram he and other Antilleans had sent in 1948 to ask the UN and the Pan-American Union (now called the OAS) to support Curaçao in its struggle to obtain democratic rights and to rid itself of the colonial yoke.[120] The Netherlands representative reported back to the Netherlands government that he feared Jonckheer had recognized the competence of the UN to continue its involvement with the Kingdom relations by these remarks.[121]

Mr. Van Ommeren, president of the *Staten* of Surinam, also spoke of 'the acquired independence' of the countries, and of their feeling of complete autonomy, even though 'no formal provision with regard to the subject of secession has been formulated in the Statute (*sic*).'[122] Dr Johan Ferrier, Prime Minister of Surinam, was the only representative of the overseas countries who did not claim the countries were or felt independent. He admitted that Surinam had not achieved complete autonomy, but that it had freely done so and for good reasons.[123] The Netherlands representative did not go into this question, but the Explanatory Memorandum stated that none of the countries could unilaterally change the existing constitutional order.

Opinion of the People

Many states asked whether the opinion of the Antilleans and Surinamese had been requested. Dr Ferrier answered that 'the peoples concerned had accepted the Charter for the Kingdom.' The discussions on the proposed Charter had been followed by the press in Surinam, so there had been 'no point' in consulting the people directly.[124]

The representative of Liberia did not consider this consultation very democratic,[125] and stated that a referendum was essential.[126] A few other states agreed.[127] Many other states were satisfied, however, that the populations of the Netherlands Antilles and Surinam had expressed their opinion, albeit indirectly, on the Charter. Thailand for instance considered that there had been

---

[120] *Keesings Historisch Archief*, No. 876, 7535. The GAOR contains no reference to this telegram, but *The Washington Post* reported on it in the edition of 5 March 1948 under the heading: 'U.N. Is Asked to Intervene for Independence of Curaçao.' The telegram was at the time widely condemned in Curaçao, *see* Kasteel 1956, p. 179.

[121] Oostindie & Klinkers 2001a, p. 131.

[122] Statement by Van Ommeren, 520th Meeting, p. 284. Full text reproduced in BuZa 1956a, p. 127.

[123] 520th Meeting, p. 284.

[124] 522nd Meeting, p. 295.

[125] 522nd Meeting, p. 296.

[126] 525th Meeting, p. 317.

[127] Afghanistan, Guatemala and Burma.

'indirect plebiscites' because the authorities had clearly stated the issue of approval of the Charter during the elections.[128] The fact that no resistance was perceived to have existed against the new constitutional order in the Caribbean countries appeared to be an important factor for many representatives.[129]

Right of Secession?

The Minister Plenipotentiary of Surinam asked the Netherlands government before the start of the debate in the Committee on Information to issue a declaration similar to US President Eisenhower's declaration of 1953, in which he had promised that he would support a Puerto Rican request for independence. The Netherlands refused, because the Netherlands parliament had not been willing to recognize the right of self-determination (including the right of secession) of Surinam and the Netherlands Antilles in the Charter. It would not be acceptable if the government of the Netherlands would now recognize it in an international forum so that the Kingdom would be bound by it.[130]

The states which supported the Netherlands referred to a speech made by the Queen of the Netherlands at the promulgation of the Kingdom Charter, in which she stated that it was 'impossible, that an agreement such as this, would not be based on *complete voluntariness.*'[131] The interpretation of this speech changed during the debates. At first it was stated by the supporters of the Netherlands that the Netherlands would properly consider any reasonable request by the Netherlands Antilles or Surinam, and that states should simply trust the Netherlands.[132] Later, the speech was stated to have created a legal right of secession for the Caribbean countries.[133] Many other states were not satisfied

---

[128] The historical sources actually do not reveal that the negotiations on the Kingdom Charter had been an important issue in the parliamentary elections in the Netherlands Antilles (*see for instance* Reinders 1993, p. 23).

[129] The only act of resistance of which the representatives may perhaps have been aware was by a consortium of Surinamese organizations in the Netherlands, which sent a letter to the Secretary-General of the UN in November of 1955 in which they stated that Surinam should continue to be treated as a NSGT. It is not clear whether the Fourth Committee was aware of the letter. The GAOR does not contain a reference to it. In the press in Surinam, the telegram was denounced as 'treacherous' and the senders as 'parias' who were probably influenced by Communists. *See* Mitrasing 1959, pp. 281-2.

[130] Te Beest 1988, pp. 53-4.

[131] Speech of 15 December 1954, reproduced in *Schakels*, No. 54 (January 1955), p. 3. Mr. Pos, Minister Plenipotentiary of Surinam, first directed the attention of the members of the Committee on Information to this speech. In Dutch, this text read: '*onbestaanbaar, dat een overeenkomst als deze, anders dan op* volledige vrijwilligheid *gegrond zou zijn.*'

[132] *See for instance,* the statements by the US (521st Meeting, p. 290) and Mexico (521st Meeting, p. 291).

[133] *See for instance,* the statements by Lebonon (523rd Meeting, p. 304) and Liberia (525th Meeting, p. 317).

that the Queen's speech was sufficient guarantee for the countries' right of secession.[134]

Right to Self-Determination

The representatives of the Netherlands Antilles claimed that the 'peoples' of the Netherlands Antilles, Surinam and the Netherlands had exercised their right to self-determination in accepting the Charter for the Kingdom and that the Charter recognised the right to self-determination of the countries.[135] The Prime Minister of Surinam stated that the Charter was directly based on the principle of self-determination.[136] The Netherlands representative did not go into this subject, nor did the Explanatory Memorandum.

Some states agreed that the Netherlands Antilles and Surinam had exercised their right to self-determination,[137] or that the countries had been granted the possibility to exercise that right in the future.[138] Others thought that this right had not yet been exercised because the populations had not been granted the freedom to choose another political status than that laid down in the Kingdom Charter, and feared that the Charter might make it impossible in the future for the populations to exercise that right.[139] Most representatives, however, did not explicitly refer to the right to self-determination.

Characterization of the New Legal Order of the Charter

In fact, most states used the term 'association' to refer to the new Kingdom relations.[140] Unfortunately, the meaning of the term 'association' was in a state of flux in 1955. It did not necessarily refer to what is now known as associated statehood or free association. The third part of Resolution 742 (VIII) of 1953 used the term 'free association' to refer to what would be called 'integration' in Resolution 1541. Mexico and other states referred to this third part of Resolution 742, and perhaps thought the Kingdom should be classified as a form of integration, in today's language.[141] On the other hand, the debate focussed to a

---

[134] Egypt, Poland, Soviet Union, Czechoslovakia, Liberia and Afghanistan.

[135] Statements by Jonckheer and Yrausquin, GAOR (X), Fourth Committee, 520th Meeting, p. 284 and 286.

[136] GAOR (X), Fourth Committee, 520th Meeting, p. 284.

[137] Belgium and Colombia.

[138] Dominican Republic.

[139] India, Ecuador and Greece.

[140] The US, for instance, considered that the Kingdom had become a 'voluntary association of peoples' (521st Meeting, p. 290). Mexico referred to 'the association between the Netherlands, Surinam and the Netherlands Antilles' (521st Meeting, p. 291).

[141] Egypt and Venezuela also referred to the third list of factors (and concluded that the Kingdom relations were not yet up to par).

large extent on the right of secession of the Caribbean Countries and on the question whether the Kingdom organs could exert influence on the internal affairs of the Countries. This suggests that the representatives judged the Kingdom to be a form of free association.

A number of states claimed that Surinam and the Netherlands Antilles were still NSGTs. India stated that the position of the Netherlands Antilles and Surinam did not fulfil the criteria for full self-government, and that their position was not one of partnership but of dependence. In connection with this, India considered that the member state of the UN was not the new Kingdom, but 'the State of the Netherlands, a European country.' India did not accept that the Kingdom Charter had created a superstructure which exercised the sovereign powers of a state.[142] Ecuador agreed that the Kingdom was not the member state of the UN.[143] It explained that 'the tripartite association [of the Kingdom] was between a sovereign State on the one hand and two "countries", which were not states, on the other.'[144] Liberia and Syria also appeared to agree with this interpretation of the Kingdom structure.[145] The Soviet Union and Czechoslovakia stated that the Netherlands Antilles and Surinam were still colonies,[146] but no other states dared draw this conclusion in such unequivocal terms.[147]

A number of other representatives indicated that they thought a full measure of self-government could only be achieved when the 'Territories' acquired sovereignty or some other form of international personality, after which they might perhaps choose to delegate part of their sovereign powers to another state, or even to integrate with a state on an equal basis with other parts of that state (i.e. as a province, state, department or other form of administrative subdivision). The main point of these representatives was that the peoples of Surinam and the Netherlands Antilles had not acquired sovereignty under the Kingdom Charter, and were therefore not yet fully decolonized.[148] The thesis that the Netherlands had defended since 1951 that sovereignty had 'spread out' over the Netherlands Antilles, Surinam and the Netherlands remained controversial.

The discussion on who exactly had provided the information on the Kingdom Charter to the UN (see above) revealed that many of the anti-colonial

---

[142] 527th Meeting, p. 327. The Indian representative also maintained that Queen Juliana was only Queen of the Netherlands, not of Surinam or the Netherlands Antilles (524th Meeting, p. 309).

[143] 527th Meeting, p. 328.

[144] 524th Meeting, p. 310. The Caribbean countries were not states, according to Ecuador, because they did not possess the right to self-determination.

[145] 527th Meeting, p. 328.

[146] 525th Meeting, p. 316.

[147] Egypt, Venezuela and Ecuador also applied the third list of factors and concluded that the factors had not yet been fulfilled.

[148] Uruguay, Argentina, Peru,

states thought the Kingdom was little more than a paper construction to satisfy the UN, while the real form of government of the Netherlands was that of a state administering two NSGTs.

Lebanon appeared to think that the Kingdom was intended as a federal state when he commented that in most states with 'a pluralistic structure' the constitutionality of statutes was decided by the supreme judicial organ, whereas in the Kingdom that role was exercised by the King (based on Article 50).[149] Most supporters of the Netherlands did not try to pin a name on the structure of the Kingdom, but merely commended the partners for finding a unique solution to their problems.

A Full Measure of Self-Government?

All states agreed that the Netherlands Antilles and Surinam had achieved *some* measure of self-government, but only a few stated they had achieved a *full* measure, and of these states, at least some used this phrase (confusingly) to refer only to the subjects of Article 73(e).[150] Of the non-Administering states, some were unwilling to indicate exactly whether they thought the self-government of the Netherlands Antilles and Surinam was sufficient to warrant the title 'a full measure of self-government.' A considerable number of representatives stated that this was not the case,[151] and others, while not explicitly reaching this conclusion, left little doubt that they considered the autonomy of Surinam and the Netherlands insufficient.[152]

Application of the Other Paragraphs of Article 73

The representative of Yugoslavia asked Brazil and the US whether the adoption of their draft declaration would mean that the other paragraphs of Article 73 would no longer apply to the Netherlands as well, in which case Yugoslavia would vote against it. The US and Brazil answered that the resolution deliberately did not address the question whether Chapter XI still applied to Surinam and the Netherlands Antilles. The US representative stated that 'the proposal

---

[149] 522nd Meeting, p. 297.
[150] For instance China.
[151] Iraq, Poland, Soviet Union, India, Venezuela, Ecuador, Guatemala, Uruguay, Yemen, Czechoslovakia, Liberia, Indonesia, Hungary, Byelorussia, Ukraine, Poland, and Romania. According to Ecuador the administrative autonomy of the countries was less than that enjoyed by municipal governments in many Latin American states (524th Meeting, p. 311).
[152] Egypt, Greece, Argentina, Peru, Iran, Afghanistan and Yugoslavia.

left each representative free to vote on the draft resolution without prejudice to his interpretation of the Chapter as a whole.'[153]

This statement offered many non-Administering states a way out of their predicament. They did not wish to vote against a US proposal,[154] but they also did not wish to declare that the Netherlands Antilles and Surinam were self-governing. Many representatives stated in the Fourth Committee that they considered that Paragraphs (a) to (d) of Article 73 would remain to apply to Surinam and the Netherlands Antilles, and that the GA could resume the discussion on these territories at any given time.[155]

A number of representatives were not satisfied with the assurances of the US and Brazil, nor with the assurances of Jonckheer that the Netherlands Antilles and Surinam would find their way to the UN should the Netherlands oppose the will of the peoples of those countries. Ecuador stated the problem clearly:

> If it was agreed that all the other obligations [of Article 73] ceased with the obligation to transmit information, the relationship between the Netherlands and the United Nations in respect of its administration of Surinam and the Netherlands Antilles would also cease. The Netherlands, the Netherlands Antilles and Surinam would form a sovereign unit, and obviously any interference in that unit would come under the restrictions laid down in Article 2, paragraph 7, of the Charter of the United Nations. Thus, the doors of the United Nations would be closed to Surinam and the Netherlands Antilles.[156]

The Netherlands delegation became aware that India contemplated an amendment that requested the Netherlands to inform the UN of any changes to the Kingdom Charter in the future. The Netherlands undertook 'serious attempts' to convince India not to submit the amendment which was, according to the Netherlands delegation, 'utterly unacceptable' to the Administering States.[157] The attempts were apparently successful as India submitted an amendment which merely stated that the present GA Resolution would not prejudice 'the

---

[153] GAOR (X), Fourth Committee, 524th Meeting, p. 307. The US delegate later stated that: 'He hoped that the differences of opinion among members of the Committee about the interpretation of Chapter XI of the Charter would not prevent the Committee form declaring itself unequivocally on the more limited question before it.' (GAOR (X), Fourth Committee, 525th Meeting, pp. 317-18).

[154] In 1955, the era of US dominance of the UN had not yet ended (see Luard 1982), although the era of decolonization was about to start (see Luard 1989).

[155] Cf. for instance the statements by the delegates of India (GAOR (X), Fourth Committee, 524th Meeting, p. 308), Ecuador (GAOR (X), Fourth Committee, 524th Meeting, p. 311), Peru (GAOR (X), Fourth Committee, 525th Meeting, pp. 316-17) and Yugoslavia (GAOR (X), Fourth Committee, 526th Meeting, p. 324).

[156] 524th Meeting, p. 311.

[157] BuZa 1956a, pp. 28-9.

position of the United Nations as affirmed by GA resolution 742 (VIII), and such provisions of the Charter as may be relevant.'[158] In the Fourth Committee, India however explained this amendment by stating that it intended to declare that the decision of the GA only related to Article 73(e) and that paragraphs (a) to (d) 'remained in force and could be invoked by the GA at any time.'[159] The amendment aimed to make it possible for some states at least to abstain from the vote on the draft resolution.[160] The Netherlands (Schürmann) stated that it did not agree with the explanations of India, but that it did not seriously object to the wording of the amendment, and that it would therefore abstain from the vote on it. The Indian amendment was adopted by 27 votes to 7 with 18 abstentions.[161]

Resolution 945 Adopted

Nine states considered the draft resolution simply unacceptable and announced they would vote against it because the Netherlands Antilles and Surinam were still non-self-governing and the Netherlands should transmit information on them.[162] Their arguments were that the autonomy of Surinam and the Netherlands Antilles was restricted by the authorities of the Kingdom organs, which were exercised by the Netherlands and the Governor, who was appointed by the Netherlands. The socialist states maintained that Surinam and the Netherlands Antilles could not secede from the Kingdom and that the population had not been given the opportunity to express its opinion on the Charter.[163]

An amendment by Uruguay that reaffirmed 'the competence of the GA to decide whether a Non-Self-Governing Territory has attained the full measure of self-government referred to in Chapter XI of the Charter' was adopted by 29

---

[158] UN Doc. A/C.4/L.423.

[159] According to Pakaukau 2004, p. 316, this amendment 'prevented the Dutch from finalizing their 1954 incorporation of Surinam and vested the colonial people with a permanent right to alter their relationship to the Netherlands.'

[160] 524th Meeting, p. 309.

[161] 527th Meeting, p. 328.

[162] Afghanistan, Hungary, Liberia, Poland, Romania, Czechoslovakia and the three Soviet Republics.

[163] The Soviet Union painted a picture of the new Kingdom order, which left no room for any autonomous decisions by the parliaments of the Netherlands Antilles and Surinam, which was nonetheless almost entirely based on the text of the Charter. The only assertion that was not supported by any Article of the Kingdom Charter was that the Governors could reverse court decisions. The Governors are in no way authorized to do this. The only essential element of the new order that the Soviet Union neglected to mention was the responsibility of the Country ministers to the *Staten* for the decisions of the Governor as head of the Country government. The Soviet presentation nonetheless made clear that the reserved powers of the Kingdom were indeed impressive, at least on paper.

votes to 13, with 12 abstentions.[164] The representative of Uruguay had explained that he submitted this amendment because the Netherlands Antilles and Surinam were still not fully self-governing. The amendment was intended to offer the peoples of the Netherlands Antilles and Surinam 'a safeguard, an opportunity of coming at a later date to knock at the door of the United Nations, should the need arise.'[165] This could be interpreted as evidence that the majority of the Fourth Committee considered the decolonization of the Netherlands Antilles and Surinam as incomplete, and that the UN remained authorized to discuss the situation under Chapter XI of the UN Charter.[166]

The amendment forced the representatives of Belgium to vote against the Brazil-US draft resolution as a whole, and the representatives of Australia and the United Kingdom to abstain. The Brazil-US draft resolution was adopted by 18 votes to 10, with 27 abstentions.

During the 557th Plenary meeting of the GA on 15 December 1955, the draft resolution was adopted as Resolution 945 (X) by 21 to 10 votes, with 33 abstentions.[167]

6.3.6   What does Resolution 945 Mean for the Status of the Netherlands Antilles and Aruba?

Resolution 945 is an anomaly in the decolonization practice of the GA, since it released an Administering State from its obligation under Article 73(e) without declaring that the territories in question had become fully self-governing. This conflicts with the annually repeated rule that:

> In the absence of a decision by the General Assembly itself that a Non-Self-Governing Territory has attained a full measure of self-government in terms of Chapter XI of the Charter, the administering Power concerned should continue to

---

[164] UN Doc. A/C.4/L.422, GAOR (X), Annexes, Agenda item 32, p. 11.

[165] 525th Meeting, p. 315.

[166] Only Liberia stated in so many words that the Netherlands Antilles and Surinam were still NSGTs (525th Meeting, p. 317). The states which considered that a full measure of self-government had not yet been achieved (*see above*) of course thereby implied that Surinam and the Netherlands Antilles were still NSGTs.

[167] In favour voted: Brazil, Canada, China, Colombia, Cuba, Denmark, Dominican Republic, France, Iceland, Israel, Luxembourg, Mexico, Netherlands, Nicaragua, Norway, Pakistan, Philippines, Sweden, Thailand, Turkey, and the US. Opposed were: Afghanistan, Belgium, Byelorussia, Czechoslovakia, Hungary, Liberia, Poland, Romania, Ukraine, and the Soviet Union. Abstaining: Argentina, Australia, Bolivia, Burma, Ceylon, Chile, Costa Rica, Ecuador, Egypt, El Salvador, Ethiopia, Greece, Guatemala, Haiti, Honduras, India, Indonesia, Iran, Iraq, Jordan, Lebanon, New Zealand, Panama, Paraguay, Peru, Saudi Arabia, Spain, Syria, United Kingdom, Uruguay, Venezuela, Yemen, and Yugoslavia.

transmit information under Article 73 e of the Charter with respect to that Terri-tory. [168]

As far as I can see, there is only one way to resolve this conflict, and that is by interpreting Resolution 945 to mean that the Netherlands was released from its reporting obligation because of the 'constitutional considerations' mentioned in Article 73(e). The Netherlands claimed that it could no longer collect the information required, and transmitting it would suggest a responsibility for subjects that fell within the autonomy of the Caribbean Countries. The Carib-bean Countries themselves agreed, and the Netherlands presented this argu-ment as the most important reason why it had stopped reporting, and many states accepted this. [169]

This interpretation is consistent with the fact that, while voting on Resolu-tion 945, the representatives were under the assumption that 945 would not prejudge the question whether Chapter XI of the UN Charter and Resolution 742 still applied to the Netherlands Antilles and Surinam and whether those Countries had achieved a full measure of self-government. A number of amend-ments to the draft resolution intended to make this clear.

It is not certain whether the Principles of Resolution 1541 meant to leave open the possibility that the information transmitted under Article 73(e) would be reduced to zero. The UK thought that it did, but other states denied this (*see* chapter 2). No reference was made to Resolution 945 during the debate preced-ing Resolution 1541, and it must be assumed that it was not the intention of the GA to retract or reinterpret 945 through the adoption of 1541.

According to a contemporary observer, *Engers*, Resolution 945 meant no more than that the Dutch territories had achieved self-government in the three areas mentioned in Article 73(e) of the UN Charter. The status of Surinam and the Netherlands Antilles remained unchanged (at least *in politicis*) and the GA probably continued to consider itself authorized to take up the issue at a later date if the Kingdom relations should develop in a negative way. [170] According to *Engers*, the Resolution recognized the existence of an intermediary status between self-government and colonial status, because it did not link the cessa-

---

[168] This sentence was first included in GA Res. 2870 (XXVI) of 20 December 1971, and from 1986 it is adopted unanimously during each session of the GA.

[169] An advice to the Prime Minister of the Netherlands Antilles (published informally around 6 September 2005) claimed that the Netherlands had ceased transmitting information based on the 'constitutional considerations' mentioned in Article 73(e). According to the advice, Chapter XI of the Charter and Res. 1514 simply continued to apply.

[170] Engers 1956, p. 187. In a similar sense, *see* Kapteyn 1982, p. 20, and Hoeneveld 2005, p. 54.

tion of the transmission of information to the achievement of full self-government.[171]

This may indeed have been the intention of the GA. There have been other examples of unclear or intermediate status where the GA accepted that the Administering State no longer reported, even though the GA did not explicitly declare that a full measure of self-government had been achieved. Even in the case of the Cook Islands, where the GA *did* declare that full self-government had been achieved, it also declared that it remained competent to discuss the situation under Resolution 1514 if the need arose. These cases show that the GA has not always distinguished very sharply between NSGTs and self-governing territories, and it can be concluded that the Netherlands Antilles and Aruba take up a place somewhere in between these two categories.[172]

6.3.7   Could the UN Recommence its Involvement with the Netherlands Antilles and Aruba?

The reason why the GA accepted the Dutch decision to stop reporting was that the Netherlands Antilles and Surinam appeared happy with the amount of autonomy they had been granted, and that the Netherlands seemed to have promised that it would respect the right to self-determination of the Caribbean populations in the future. It might therefore be assumed that if one of the Caribbean Countries was prevented from achieving independence, or if it otherwise became apparent that the population of a Caribbean Country was no longer happy with its status in the Kingdom, the UN could decide to resume its dis-

---

[171] Engers 1956, p. 193. *See*, in a similar sense, Oppenheim/Jennings & Watts 1992, p. 280.

[172] Most of the UN organs appear to think that the Netherlands Antilles and Aruba are no longer NSGTs, although doubts are occasionally visible, for instance, among the treaty bodies that supervise the various UN human rights treaties. *See for instance,* the confusion that arose among the members of the CERD on the question whether the Netherlands Antilles and Aruba were NSGTs, when the Committee wished to include a specific observation regarding the Netherlands Antilles and Aruba in its concluding observations on the Netherlands (CERD/C/SR.1272). After a Committee member, Van Boven, had studied the matter, he recommended that all states should be requested to submit information on their NSGTs, and 'given the doubts over the status of Puerto Rico, New Caledonia, Aruba and East Timor, for example, the Committee should not seek to identify the States concerned specifically.' (CERD/C/SR.1286, para. 38). The Committee decided to direct this request to the states parties which are administering NSGTs 'or otherwise exercising jurisdiction over Territories.' (A/54/18, para. 553 et seq.). Similar doubts were also expressed by members of the HRC during the discussion of the initial report of the Kingdom on the ICCPR (UN Doc. CCPR/C/SR.321 and 322). During the discussion of the Second Periodic Report (1988), it was asked how Aruba could be considered self-governing if good governance was a Kingdom affair, and in relation to this, some members also wondered what the role of the Kingdom was in the safeguarding of human rights and fundamental freedoms (CCPR/C/SR.861, para. 44 and 52).

cussion of the situation under Chapter XI of the Charter (or under Resolution 1514). The debate preceding Resolution 945 made clear that a majority in the GA considered the decolonization of the Dutch Caribbean incomplete.

Apart from the absence of a clear recognition of the continuing right to self-determination, the questions and criticism of the representatives indicated that a number of aspects of the Kingdom Charter were inconsistent with full self-government, namely: the appointment of the Governor and his seemingly wide authorities; Articles 44, 50 and 51; and the dominant position of the Netherlands in the organs of the Kingdom, which have the authority to legislate for the Caribbean Countries without their consent.

Representatives also wondered whether the political status of Surinam and the Netherlands Antilles was really what the populations wanted, but this was insufficient reason to continue the reporting obligation, most states considered. This was somewhat surprising, as the GA had decided only a year earlier that decisions to stop transmitting information under Article 73(e) should be examined 'with particular emphasis on the manner in which the right of self-determination has been attained and freely exercised.'[173] In that same resolution the GA had also decided that (if the GA deemed it desirable) a UN mission should visit the territory 'in order to evaluate as fully as possible the opinion of the population as to the status or change in status which they desire.' Only the Soviet Union wondered despairingly why the Fourth Committee would not even consider sending a visiting mission to the Netherlands Antilles and Surinam. In 1967, when the West Indies Associated States of the UK were discussed, the GA decided the UK should continue reporting until the UN had been able to determine – through a visiting mission, or UN supervised plebiscites – that the population really supported the new status. Other cases also showed that after 1960, the GA became more strict in demanding clear evidence of popular support for forms of self-government that fall short of independence.

For this reason, it has often been assumed that Resolution 945 would not have been adopted after 1960.[174] Even shortly after 1955, it was already doubted whether the GA would stick to its decision.[175] *Clark* wrote in 1980 that 'the continuing validity of the Netherlands decision is dubious in the light of the changed political forces in the GA.'[176] *Barbier* calls it '*remarquable*' that the Dutch territories were not inserted in the Committee's list of 1963.[177] There

---

[173] GA Res. 850 (IX) of 22 November 1954.

[174] In this sense, *see* De Smith 1974, p. 71, Hannum 1996, p. 347 et seq, and Igarashi 2002, p. 62. Kapteyn 1982, p. 21 'seriously doubts' whether the GA would have approved of the Dutch cessation of transmission of information if it had taken place after 1960.

[175] Engers 1956, p. 187 and Van Panhuys 1958, p. 30.

[176] Clark 1980, p. 49.

[177] Barbier 1974, p. 163. According to *Barbier*, the reason why the Netherlands Antilles and Surinam (and a number of territories of France, the UK and Denmark) were not on the list, was

are quite a number of other authors who similarly think Chapter XI of the UN Charter does (or should) still apply to the Kingdom, or that the GA might not confirm its decision of 1955 if it had been asked to do so after 1960.[178] *Oppenheim* simply puts the Caribbean Countries in a special class of territories whose international status is somewhere in between NSGT and independence, such as Puerto Rico and the British WIAS.[179] *Blaustein* also has difficulty categorizing them.[180]

The UNITAR study of 1971, on the other hand, considers that the decision of 1955 would have been upheld after 1960 as well, as long the GA was satisfied that the Kingdom Charter really represented the clearly expressed wish of the population.[181] This may well be true, because the GA has never gone against the clearly expressed will of the people in these cases. But the GA would probably not have approved the situation without a referendum or a visiting mission.

Could the GA retract its decision of 1955? The case of Puerto Rico indicates that the GA will probably not consider Resolution 945 as prohibiting it from discussing the Netherlands Antilles and Aruba as a case of incomplete decolonization, should the need arise. With regard to Puerto Rico, the GA had declared that the territory had become fully self-governing and that it had exercised its right to self-determination, but the US still needed to wage a fierce diplomatic battle to prevent the GA from discussing Puerto Rico in the context

---

the method used by the Working Group charged with drawing up the list. It created four categories of colonial territories; Trust Territories, other NSGTs on which the administering powers transmitted information, the territories declared non-self-governing by the GA, and South West Africa (Namibia). The Netherlands Antilles and Surinam did not appear to fall into any of these categories, but this did not necessarily mean that the Committee considered the Declaration did not apply to them.

[178] *See* Rigo Sureda 1971, p. 261, De Smith 1974, p. 71, Hannum 1996, p. 333 and 347 et seq., and Igarashi 2002, pp. 34-44 and p. 62.

[179] Oppenheim/Jennings & Watts 1992, p. 280.

[180] In *Blaustein's* collection of *Constitutions of Dependencies and Territories*, the Netherlands Antilles and Aruba are placed in the category of dependencies which 'have complete internal self-government and operate without interference from the colonial power.' Other territories in the 2002 edition of this list are New Caledonia, Puerto Rico, the Cook Islands, and the US Virgin Islands. *Blaustein's* categorization is somewhat hard to understand in light of the fact that two or three of these territories are treated as NSGTs by the UN (Puerto Rico is a special case, *see* chapter 3). Furthermore, calling the metropolitan state 'colonial power' obviously means that these territories should be considered colonies (*see* Blaustein/Raworth 2002, p. 2). *Blaustein's* section on the 'Netherlands Dependencies' states: 'Both are self-governing territories in close association with the Netherlands. Exceptionally in the case of dependencies, these territories are accorded special rights under the Dutch National Constitution. However, they are not an integral part of the Netherlands and thus cannot be considered national territories.' (Blaustein/Raworth 2001, p. 1).

[181] Rapoport et al. 1971, p. 26.

of decolonization, and it could not prevent the Decolonization Committee from discussing Puerto Rico. The Netherlands will obviously not be able to exercise the kind of political pressure that the US exercised, and its legal position is also much weaker. The case of New Caledonia furthermore showed that the GA considered itself authorised to revive its involvement with a territory that had not been on the list of NSGTs for 40 years.

But these cases also show that before the GA might take such a step with regard to the Netherlands Antilles or Aruba, it will have to be clear that at least a substantial part of the local populations actively opposes the status quo, and a number of UN members will have to have a good reason for attacking the Netherlands. Puerto Rico was a popular subject for the enemies of the US during the Cold War, and the case of New Caledonia was partly created to punish France for its nuclear tests in the Pacific.

If the GA, for whatever reason, decides to review the status of the Netherlands Antilles or Aruba, it would probably use the criteria for free association of Resolution 1541, since the debates of 1955 showed that most representatives tended towards considering the Kingdom as a form of association. As I explained in the previous paragraphs, the Kingdom order does indeed bear more resemblance to free association than integration, although it fulfils the criteria for neither form of self-government.

This would mean that criticism could be expected with regard to the constitutionally guaranteed influence the Netherlands still has in the Netherlands Antilles and Aruba. But the most important question would undoubtedly be whether the population is happy with the current political status of their islands, and whether they have the possibility of exercising a form of 'continuing self-determination.' If the answer to both these questions would be 'yes', then the practice of the UN suggests that the discrepancies between the Kingdom Charter and Principle VII of Resolution 1541 will be glossed over. This would be justified in view of the principle that the right to self-determination should take precedence in any process of decolonization, as I explained in chapter 2.

The current discussions on a constitutional reform of the Netherlands Antilles raise one other question, since the option is being discussed that one or more of the islands of the Netherlands Antilles might in the future obtain a status in which some or all of the responsibilities that are currently held by the Netherlands Antilles would revert to the Netherlands, because some of the islands consider themselves too small to handle all of the responsibilities of a Country on their own. The 'constitutional considerations' clause of Article 73(e) would probably no longer apply in such a situation, and it could be argued that the Kingdom should decide to resume its reporting obligation.[182] There is one prece-

---

[182] The Antillean islands of Bonaire, St Eustatius and Saba recently declared that they thought the Kingdom should resume reporting on them once the Netherlands Antilles had been abolished

dent for such a decision. When the UK retracted the autonomy of Malta in 1959, it also recommenced transmitting reports to the UN under Article 73(e).[183] Since the UK's decision to stop transmitting information on Malta in 1949 was based on similar arguments as the Dutch decision of 1951, this precedent seems particularly relevant. To avoid this situation, it could of course also be decided to create a relationship with these islands that would comply with the criteria for integration of Resolution 1541. In that case, the Kingdom government could transmit a copy of the new arrangement to the UN, in conformity with GA Resolution 222 (III), and consider the decolonization of these islands complete, at least with respect to international law.

6.3.8 Conclusion

The status of the Netherlands Antilles and Surinam remained unclear after the GA Resolution of 1955. There existed fundamental disagreement among states on the application of Chapter XI of the UN Charter to Surinam and the Netherlands Antilles. A majority of states seemed to think that the Dutch territories had not really acquired a full measure of self-government.

Opinions on the form of government of the Kingdom differed widely, from a colonial power administering two colonies, to a type of confederation, association, integration, or a construction *sui generis*. Many representatives did not even attempt to characterize the structure of the Kingdom, and there appeared to be a consensus that it was hard to fathom.

The representatives were reluctant to decide whether the Netherlands Antilles and Surinam had exercised their right to self-determination. It appears most states were satisfied that the populations did not openly disapprove of the new status, and that the representatives of the Countries were very happy with it. It was also accepted that the Netherlands would probably not block a wish for independence, if it was expressed by the population of one of the Caribbean Countries. It was also clear that the Countries had obtained self-government in the areas on which the Administering state should report (economic, social and educational conditions). These three factors were sufficient to warrant the decision that the Netherlands no longer needed to report on the Countries, but the GA refused to declare that the Netherlands Antilles and Surinam had achieved a full measure of self-government, and the Resolution also did not state that the

---

and the three islands would have 'direct ties' with the Netherlands (*see* the closing statement of the summit meeting of the islands on constitutional structures in Philipsburg, St Maarten, on 13 and 14 March 2006, reproduced on <http://curacao-gov.an>).

    [183] *See* GAOR (XIV), Fourth Committee, 981st Meeting, para. 43, or the *Repertory of Practice of the UN Organs*, Suppl. No. 2 (1955-59), Vol. 3, paras. 105-6.

right to self-determination had been exercised, nor that Chapter XI no longer applied.

This decision seems to conflict with the rule that Administering states should continue to report until the GA has declared that a full measure of self-government has been achieved, unless it is interpreted to mean that the obligation to report was suspended because the autonomy of the Countries makes it impossible for the Kingdom government to collect and transmit the information referred to in Article 73(e). The UN Charter and Resolution 1541 seem to create this possibility, and it is not inconsistent with the debate in the GA and the arguments presented by the Netherlands in defence of its decision. It would mean that Chapter XI probably continues to apply, and the Netherlands Antilles and Aruba would have an intermediate status between self-governing and Non-Self-Governing Territories.

The GA has failed to issue a clear statement on the status of the Netherlands Antilles and Aruba, but it probably remains authorized to do so in the future. The cases of Puerto Rico and New Caledonia have shown that, given the right circumstances, the UN is prepared to re-inscribe (former) NSGTs on the list. The GA would probably judge the status of the Netherlands Antilles and Aruba by the criteria for free association. As was concluded *above*, the Kingdom does not entirely comply with these criteria. This does not automatically mean, however, that the Countries are 'arbitrarily subordinated' in the sense of Resolution 1541 or that their decolonization is incomplete, as I will discuss in the next section.

6.4   'ARBITRARY SUBORDINATION'?

The term 'arbitrary subordination', while central to the question whether a full measure of self-government has been achieved, has been left very vague by the GA. Most of the arguments used in the GA in comparable cases do not really apply to the Kingdom.[184] The relations within the Kingdom are clearly not

---

[184] A few arguments could be applied analogously. Iraq, for instance, noted with regard to the Portuguese territories: 'The existence of economic subordination was proved by the fact that … the Constitution forbade the overseas provinces to negotiate loans in foreign countries.' (GAOR (XV) 4th Comm., 1036th Meeting, para. 16). The Kingdom Charter contains a similar provision (Article 29), which requires the Countries to secure the approval of the Kingdom government before negotiating foreign loans. But the Kingdom government is only allowed to withhold its approval if the interests of the Kingdom are at stake (Borman 2005, p. 190). The government has so far interpreted its authority very restrictively, and only looks at whether the foreign relations of the Kingdom as a whole might be negatively affected. The fact that the metropolis is able to promulgate legislation that applies in the overseas territories without their consent was recently proposed at a Regional Seminar of the Decolonization Committee as a litmus test for the absence

comparable to Portuguese rule in Angola, for instance, but they are not all that different from the relation between some of the current NSGTs, for instance Bermuda, with their mother country. It is therefore very difficult, or perhaps even impossible, to decide whether the Caribbean Countries are 'arbitrarily subordinated' purely on the basis of their constitutional position within the Kingdom.

As was argued in chapter 2, however, a correct reading of the right to decolonization should give precedence to the right to self-determination, in the sense of the freedom of choice of the population. This means that the opinion of the population concerned should be the decisive factor when determining whether a situation of 'arbitrary subordination' exists. As the GA has repeatedly recognized, 'all available options for self-determination are valid as long as they are in accordance with the freely expressed wishes of the peoples concerned.'[185]

This might mean that an overseas people is kept in a situation of 'arbitrary subordination' when the metropolis does not give it the freedom to determine its own political status. Any status that has been freely chosen by the population, with full awareness of the possible consequences of that choice, can hardly be considered 'arbitrary subordination', especially if the people retains the freedom to choose another status at a later date.[186]

It is therefore important to take a closer look at the way in which the present status of the Caribbean Countries has been determined, and whether the population has freely chosen that status.

6.4.1 Have the Netherlands Antilles and Aruba Freely Chosen their Status?

The process leading up to the promulgation of the Kingdom Charter has been described by many authors, most fully by *Klinkers*.[187] As was described in chapter 4, the Netherlands opposed an explicit recognition of the right to self-determination of the Netherlands Antilles and Surinam in the Charter. Despite this, the process could be characterized as a form of self-determination if the populations of the Caribbean territories freely and voluntarily chose to accept the new legal order in the awareness of the consequences, and while there were other options.

---

of self-government (UN Doc. A/59/23 (2004), p. 41). The Kingdom has this power, but only with regard to a few subjects.

[185] GA Res. 59/134 (2004).

[186] *See* chapter 2, in the section on the freedom of choice.

[187] Klinkers 1999. This study formed the basis for Oostindie & Klinkers 2001a.

The first draft for the Kingdom Charter was written by the Dutch government, but it was modified on a number of points in the process of negotiations with representatives of Surinam and the Netherlands Antilles.[188] The final text was approved by the parliaments of the Countries, which had been elected on the basis of general suffrage. But as an exercise of the right to self-determination, the process was flawed in some crucial aspects.

Options such as independence or integration with the Netherlands were clearly not on the table, for various reasons. It is impossible to say how the population of the islands would have reacted had they been offered a choice between these or other options, but it is clear that there was not much freedom of choice.

The newspapers in the Netherlands Antilles reported on the negotiations and the ratification process, but it did not form an important issue in any elections in the Netherlands Antilles.

While the Charter was seen as a positive development in the Netherlands Antilles, it was not exactly what the Antillean government had desired,[189] nor was it the result of a free choice by the population. The debate in the UN in 1955 showed that many representatives did not consider the adoption of the Charter as an expression of the right to self-determination. An analogous application of the standards that the Dutch ministry of Foreign Affairs used in the case of Puerto Rico, should also lead to the conclusion that the procedure for the adoption of the Kingdom Charter did not truly represent an exercise of the right to self-determination.[190]

The Dutch government in a position paper of 1990 nonetheless stated that the promulgation of the new legal order of the Kingdom in 1954 represented a form of self-determination.[191] This opinion is still occasionally voiced in the

---

[188] The Constitution of 1948 declared that the relations with Surinam and the Netherlands Antilles would be reformed on the basis of consultations with representatives of the population of those territories (Article 208, renumbered as 215 in the Constitution of 1953).

[189] The Dutch pressure on the Antilles and Surinam to join in the defence of the Charter at the UN, created a fear that the Netherlands would force the Netherlands Antilles to declare at the UN that all of its constitutional wishes had been fulfilled by the Charter. The Netherlands might later use such a declaration in case the Netherlands Antilles would wish to change the Charter. *See* Oostindie & Klinkers 2001a, p. 304, note 27.

[190] The Dutch Ministry of Foreign Affairs in its report of the Eighth Session of the GA criticized the procedure by which Puerto Rico had obtained its new status in 1953. The plebiscites of 1952 could not be considered a real exercise of the right to self-determination, the report claimed, since the population of the territory did not have the possibility to choose independence or integration in those plebiscites. In the view of the ministry, the Puerto Rican general elections of 1948, at which status was an issue, and during which the political party that promoted commonwealth-status received 61 per cent of the votes, could not be put on a par with a plebiscite, as the outcome of these elections was undoubtedly influenced by other issues as well. *See* BuZa 1954b, p. 140.

[191] *Kamerstukken II* 1989/90, 21 300 IV, no. 9, '*Schets voor een gemenebestconstitutie*', p. 6.

Netherlands.[192] The process of 1954 did resemble an exercise of the right to self-determination because it led to the creation of a new relation with the Netherlands which also had the approval of the governments and the parliaments of the Netherlands Antilles and Surinam. But the population was not given the opportunity to make a free choice and it can therefore not really be established whether the Kingdom Charter enjoyed the support of the population of the Netherlands Antilles in 1954.

Aruba's Status Aparte

In 1986, when Aruba achieved its separate status under the condition that it would become independent in 1996, no referendum was held, nor when it was afterwards decided that Aruba would not become independent. In 1977, a referendum had been organized on the island, but this suffered from too many defects to represent an accurate gauging of popular opinion.[193]

While it was abundantly clear that most Arubans did not want independence, and did not want to be a part of the Netherlands Antilles either, it was (and is) far from clear what kind of relation with the Netherlands exactly had the preference of the population.[194] It is true that Aruba had experienced democratic self-government (as part of the Antilles) for over thirty years when it

---

[192] *See for instance* Hoogers 2005, p. 70.

[193] The referendum offered the population of Aruba a choice between independence as part of a federation of the Netherlands Antilles, or independence for Aruba on its own. The opposition party *AVP* boycotted the referendum because it considered that the option of a separate status within the Kingdom should also be offered. Another opposition party, *PPA*, called on its supporters not to vote. The turn-out was 70 per cent, which was only slightly lower than for the local elections of that same year, but 14 per cent of the votes were invalid. The vast majority of the votes cast (82 per cent) were in favour of independence separate from the Netherlands Antilles. Only 4 per cent of the votes were in favour of becoming independent as part of the Netherlands Antilles (*see* Van Benthem van den Bergh et al. 1978, p. 129 for the exact figures). The referendum has been widely criticized because it offered too little freedom of choice, the information provided on the options was vague and confusing, and because there were a number of flaws in the voting procedure (*see* Van Benthem van den Bergh et al. 1978, p. 28, Van Aller 1994, p. 381, and Van Rijn 1999, pp. 55-6). It is generally considered unlikely that a majority of the Aruban population was really in favour of independence in 1977. No research or opinion polls have ever shown a substantial portion of Arubans to be in favour of independence (*see* Oostindie & Verton 1998, p. 25 et seq). The vote was therefore interpreted to mean that a majority of Arubans wanted to be separated from Curaçao, but not from the Kingdom (Van Rijn 1999, p. 56, Oostindie & Verton 1998, p. 26, and Oostindie & Klinkers 2001c, p. 83).

[194] According to Verton 1990, p. 203, an opinion poll during the elections of 1985 on Aruba showed that 'a majority of those canvassed had voted affirmatively for separate status for Aruba within the Kingdom.' This is not entirely in line with the numbers *Verton* provides on p. 216: 37 per cent of the voters supported 'the relations as they are', while 50 per cent desired a closer relation with Holland as an overseas province, and 11 per cent would chose independence.

achieved its *status aparte*. But the negotiations between the Netherlands and Aruba on the continuation of the *status aparte* after 1996 were conducted on government level and the general public was not directly involved. It also remained unclear which options were actually available to the island, apart from independence. While it may be accepted that Aruba's decision to remain part of the Kingdom, but not a part of the Netherlands Antilles, did not appear to against the wishes of the population, it would go too far to say that the status of Aruba under the Kingdom Charter was created on the basis of a free and informed choice by the Aruban people.

Dissatisfaction with the Charter

Fifty years of the Kingdom Charter have witnessed much dissatisfaction with the legal order it has created, for very different reasons, and from many different corners. Nonetheless, there has never appeared to be a majority among the population of the Netherlands Antilles (as a whole) or Aruba in support of moving towards a fundamentally different relation with the Netherlands, by which I mean independence or complete integration with the Netherlands. The few political parties on the islands which campaigned for such a fundamentally different status never received much support during elections. Many parties are officially in favour of independence, but only at some very distant future date. It should be noted, however, that the party system on the islands does not so much revolve around issues, but around personalities and client relations.

Opinion polls and research such as *Ki sorto di Reino?* ('What Kind of Kingdom?') indicate that most islanders would like to see some changes to the relations with the Netherlands that are not supported by most of the political parties represented in the Caribbean parliaments.[195] This is of course not uncommon in a system of representative democracy, but in the context of self-determination, it means that regard should be had to the risk that a parliament may not always adequately represent the will of the 'peoples' when it comes to changes to the territory's political status,[196] which was clearly shown by the referendums of 1993 and 1994.

The Referendums

The referendums that have been held on the Netherlands Antilles since 1993 were organized to decide whether the Country should stay together, or whether

---

[195] *Ki sorto di Reino* revealed that there existed substantial majorities on the islands in favour of closer relations with the Netherlands and more involvement by the Netherlands government, whereas political parties on the islands are generally opposed to that (Oostindie & Verton 1998).

[196] *See also* chapter 3 in the section on popular consent.

each island should seek direct relations with the Netherlands, or become independent. They mainly concerned the relations of the islands to each other. Consequently, the outcome of these referendums only had limited value for determining the desired relation with the Netherlands. The only thing that really became clear in 1993 and 1994 was that the populations of the islands wanted to stick together, and that none of the islands wanted to become independent, at least not on its own, and not in the near future.

In the referendums of 2000, 2004 and 2005, the choice was again mainly between staying together as a Country, or breaking up the Netherlands Antilles. This time, a majority of the population on most islands chose to break up the Country. But again, it remained rather unclear what relation the islanders desired with the Netherlands. On Bonaire and Saba, a majority chose for 'direct relations' with the Netherlands, although it was not clear what form these relations should take. On Curaçao and St Maarten a majority chose a *status aparte*, which probably meant that the islanders desired a status comparable to that of Aruba. St Eustatius chose to keep the Netherlands Antilles together, creating a paradox that was built into the recognition of the right to self-determination of the individual islands in 1981.

The outcome of these referendums can be interpreted as a vote against full independence, since this option was on the ballot on all islands, and it received very few votes. But at the same time, the option of 'status quo' also attracted very few votes on most islands. These referendums can therefore hardly be taken as a free and voluntary acceptance of the legal order of the Kingdom. I will discuss them further in the context of the right to self-determination of the individual islands (*see* chapter 8).

The Right to Self-Determination Exhausted?

It is occasionally argued that the peoples of the Netherlands Antilles and Aruba have already exercised their right to self-determination, in 1954, and this proposition sometimes leads to the conclusion that the islands no longer have a right to self-determination, at least not in the sense of a right to decolonization under international law.[197] This conclusion is not valid, not only because the Charter was not intended to have this effect in 1954,[198] but also because it starts from

---

[197] This proposition was defended most recently in an editorial in *De Volkskrant* on 11 April 2005, as a reaction to the claim by the Referendum Committee of Curaçao that the outcome of the referendum would be binding on the Netherlands. *See also* Hoogers 2005.

[198] The Dutch minister, Kernkamp, in a letter to the Governing Council of Surinam, explained in 1952 that Surinam would not 'use up' its right to self-determination if the Charter referred to this right (Van Helsdingen 1957, p. 198). A majority of the members of the *Staten-Generaal* appeared to share this view. Senator Algra (*ARP*), for instance, stated that he did not

an implicit argument – namely that the right to self-determination cannot be exercised more than once – which is false. An exercise of the right to self-determination can only be considered final (in the context of decolonization) if it leads to independence, or perhaps when it leads to a complete form of integration (*see* chapter 3). Since the Kingdom relations currently most resemble a form of association, it should be assumed that the Caribbean populations have a continuing right to self-determination, as Resolution 1541 proclaims, and which was confirmed during the debates on the Cook Islands and the West Indies Associated States of the UK. The governments of the Countries and the Kingdom have consistently held that the populations of the Caribbean islands still have a right to self-determination, whether they have exercised it in 1954 or not.

6.4.2   Conclusion

The Kingdom Charter is not based on a free choice by the populations of the Caribbean Countries. It is clear that most islanders do not desire full independence in the near future, but what kind of relation they want with the Netherlands is not certain. Two series of referendums have been held on the question whether the Netherlands Antilles should stay together, but the populations have never been given the opportunity to make a free choice regarding their relations with the Netherlands.

6.5   CONCLUSION

The Kingdom order does not comply fully with any of the recognized forms of decolonization as defined by GA Resolution 1541. The Netherlands Antilles and Aruba are not integrated into the Netherlands, and the fact that they are an integral part of the Kingdom is not very meaningful for the application of Principles VIII and IX of Resolution 1541. The Kingdom relations are more similar to a form of free association, because the Countries are autonomous in most areas and the Charter mainly provides a structure for voluntary cooperation. A number of aspects of the Kingdom order do not, however, comply with the UN criteria for an acceptable form of free association. These mainly concern the

---

think the right to self-determination would be extinguished by the Kingdom Charter. He pointed out that territories such as Surinam could not be compared with regions such as Friesland. Only two right-wing members of the Lower House considered that the right to self-determination would be extinguished by the Charter. *See further* chapter 4.

powers of the Kingdom (i.e. the Netherlands) to intervene in the affairs of the Caribbean Countries without their consent.

That raises the question whether the Kingdom might be an *un*acceptable form of government under the law of decolonization, namely one based on 'arbitrary subordination', in which case the Netherlands Antilles and Aruba should perhaps be considered as Non-Self-Governing Territories under the UN Charter. The Kingdom Charter was discussed at length in the GA, but the representatives could not agree on the characterization of the Kingdom order, nor on the questions whether the Netherlands Antilles and Surinam remained NSGTs, whether they had exercised their right to self-determination, and whether the Caribbean Countries had achieved a full measure of self-government. A majority of states seemed to think that the answer to these last two questions should be 'no'. A Resolution was adopted which should probably be interpreted to mean that Chapter XI of the UN Charter continued to apply to the Netherlands Antilles and Surinam, even though the Kingdom was released from its obligation under Article 73(e).

It could be argued that the right to self-determination, defined as the freedom of choice, leaves open the possibility that a dependent people freely chooses a status that is not fully self-governing according to the standards of Resolution 1541, and which creates a subordinate position for that people. The essential criterion for the acceptability of such a status should be whether the population has truly made that choice in freedom and with due knowledge of the ramifications of its choice. In that case, the remaining elements of subordination could not be considered 'arbitrary', but should perhaps be seen as an acceptable side effect of continuing a constitutional relation between a European state and a distant island territory that considers itself too small to become independent.

The populations of the Netherlands Antilles and Aruba have never directly expressed their support for the political status that the Kingdom Charter has created for their islands. Neither independence nor complete integration into the Netherlands appears to have the support of a majority of the population on any of the islands. It is unclear what status *would* have the support of a majority of the population.

In view of all this, it would be hard to deny that Chapter XI of the UN Charter still applies to the Kingdom of the Netherlands, as well as the law of decolonization and self-determination as codified in GA Resolutions 1514, 1541 and 2625. This means that the political decolonization of the Dutch Caribbean is not yet complete under the terms of international law, and that there still exists an international obligation for the Kingdom under Article 73 of the UN Charter to strive towards the completion of the process of decolonization. Only when it becomes clear (preferably through a referendum) that each island has obtained a status that enjoys the support of the population could the Kingdom be considered a successful form of decolonization.

Chapter 7
IMPLICATIONS OF THE RIGHT TO DECOLONIZATION AND SELF-DETERMINATION FOR THE KINGDOM OF THE NETHERLANDS

In this chapter the implications of the law of decolonization for the Kingdom relations will be reviewed. The obligations that the Netherlands has undertaken under the UN Charter should not be taken lightly. If the Netherlands Antilles and Aruba do not yet have a full measure of self-government, the Kingdom of the Netherlands is under an international obligation to create a situation in which the population can freely and voluntarily choose another status that *does* comply with the criteria for full self-government.[1]

7.1 IMPLICATIONS OF THE UN CHARTER AND RESOLUTION 1541

Chapter XI of the UN Charter first of all creates a general obligation to promote 'the well-being of the inhabitants.' A number of more concrete obligations can also be derived from the Charter, and from the Resolutions by which the GA has interpreted Chapter XI, the advisory opinions of the ICJ, and customary law. For the Kingdom, the following obligations would appear to be relevant.

Promote Self-Government

Article 73(b) provides that the Administering States are obligated 'to develop self-government, to take due account of the political aspirations of the peoples, and to assist them in the progressive development of their free political institutions, according to the particular circumstances of each territory and its peoples and their varying stages of advancement.' The GA has interpreted 'self-government' to mean independence, free association, integration or any other option that is freely adopted by the population (*see* chapters 2 and 3).

---

[1] In a similar sense, *see* Kapteyn 1982, p. 22, Sap 2005, and Hoeneveld 2005, p. 63 et seq.

S. Hillebrink, The Right to Self-Determination and Post-Colonial Governance
© 2008, T·M·C·ASSER PRESS, *The Hague, The Netherlands and the Author*

The Declaration on the Granting of the Independence to Colonial Countries and Peoples (Resolution 1514), states that 'immediate steps shall be taken' to transfer 'all powers' to the people of the territory. It could be argued that the Netherlands has already complied with this part of Resolution 1514 by actively striving for the independence of the Netherlands Antilles and Aruba during the 1970s and 1980s. A more demanding interpretation of the right to self-determination and decolonization, which is defended *above* in chapter 2, would require that the populations of the islands are given an opportunity to make a free choice on their political status. It was argued in chapter 6 that the population of the Netherlands Antilles and Aruba have not really had this opportunity yet. Such an unconditional exercise of the freedom of choice does not entail that the Netherlands should accept the outcome as an overseas *diktat*, but merely that the Netherlands (and the other parts of the Kingdom) should try to realize it in good faith as far as possible. In chapter 8, I will discuss this question further, since this issue currently plays a large role with regard to the right to self-determination of the individual island territories of the Netherlands Antilles.

Since the 1960s it is no longer open to debate that the Caribbean parts of the Kingdom have the right to choose for independence, but it has remained controversial whether they could also choose another form of self-government – within the Kingdom. If one of the Caribbean populations would express a preference for entering into a free association with the Netherlands or the Kingdom, Resolution 1541 provides that the territory should be granted the right to determine its own constitution without outside interference. Any tasks that the Netherlands or the Kingdom would continue to perform for the associated territory would have to be based on a voluntary act by the territory. It is not certain which tasks the Netherlands would have to accept, nor under which conditions. An arrangement of free association could of course only come about through negotiations, in which the Netherlands would not have to accept any unreasonable demands.

A population that chooses integration would have to accept that the Netherlands legislature would become sovereign on its territory. It should obtain equal status under Dutch law with the inhabitants of the metropolitan territory for the integration to comply with Resolution 1541. Whether the international law of decolonization and self-determination means that the Netherlands would always have to accept a choice for integration is not certain, but it seems logical to assume that the burden of proof rests on the metropolitan government if it is not prepared to cooperate with realizing the outcome of a free choice by an overseas population.[2]

---

[2] *See* chapter 3 on the characteristics of free association and integration, and chapter 2 on freedom of choice.

So far, none of the Caribbean populations of the Kingdom have clearly chosen either free association or integration. The new status of the islands, which is currently being negotiated, might result in 'any other political status freely chosen by the people' – the fourth option enumerated by GA Resolution 2625 of 1970. The new Kingdom relations could be a realization of the right to self-determination of the islands' populations, if it is established with sufficient certainty that the new situation has their support.

Political Education

Information should be provided so that the population is aware of the ramifications of the status options contained in Resolution 1541, and so that it might be able to make an informed choice between them and/or other status options. The GA each year:

> reiterates its long-standing call for the administering Powers, in cooperation with the territorial Governments, to promote political education in the Territories in order to foster an awareness among the people of their right to self-determination in conformity with the legitimate political status options, based on the principles clearly defined in General Assembly resolution 1541 (XV).[3]

The UN organs could of course play a useful role as an impartial source of information. The GA each year asks its department of public information to disseminate information concerning decolonization, and the UNDP and the Electoral Division of the Secretariat also play a role in providing information.[4] In the Dutch Caribbean islands, information concerning the options open to them is not easily available (especially on the smaller islands), other than through the website of the UN and websites which support status change in other overseas territories, such as Puerto Rico. The governments of the Caribbean Countries and of the island territories clearly have a task in this area. In the referendum campaigns of 2004 and 2005 there was some information provided to the public on some of the islands, in the form of brochures and town hall meetings, which probably created some awareness of the options and certainly sparked debate. This must be considered as a positive development. One important flaw in these information campaigns was caused by the attitude of the Netherlands

---

[3] GA Res. 59/134 (2004).

[4] The UN Secretariat's Electoral Division has already observed several of the referendums on the islands of the Netherlands Antilles, and is also employed by the Decolonization Committee to supervise self-determination referendums and elections in the NSGTs. The UNDP is sometimes used by the Decolonization Committee to assist NSGTs with constitutional reform, for instance, in Tokelau.

government, which refused to state whether it would respect the outcome of the referendums, except on one occasion in 2000, when it announced beforehand that it would not realize the outcome of the referendum on St Maarten if the population chose for *status aparte* (*see* chapter 8).

Ascertain the Wishes of the Population

In the Plan of Action for the first and the second UN International Decade for the Eradication of All Forms of Colonialism, the GA formulated as one of the aims the 'holding of self-determination referendums preceded by adequate and unbiased campaigns of political education' in all of the territories.[5] This aim has been achieved on the islands of the Netherlands Antilles to some extent, but as I explained in the previous chapter, the referendums dealt mainly with the relations between the islands, and not so much with the relation with the Netherlands.

It would be an improvement on the current situation if the right to self-determination of the islands were codified in the Kingdom Charter. International law already demands that status changes require the explicit support of the population of the islands concerned, but it would be recommendable to make this more clear, and to determine how and when such approval should be obtained. The population should also have the right to initiate status changes.

Since the status issue will probably continue to occupy the minds of many people involved with the Kingdom relations, and seeing that the status debate has taken up much time and energy since the early 1970s, proceeding – and often receding – in a disorderly process, it should be considered as improvement if there existed a clear procedure for status change, in which the population of the islands should have the final say.

Respect the Wishes of the Population

As the GA has unanimously confirmed on countless occasions, 'it is ultimately for the peoples of the Territories themselves to determine freely their future political status.'[6] It is essential that the various governments of the Kingdom make clear that they will respect any choice that the island populations make and that they will do their utmost to realize that choice. This is not only because they are obligated under international law to do so, but also to remove the existing scepticism, cynicism, lack of interest or other factors that might pre-

---

[5] UN Doc. A/46/634/Rev.1. In more recent Resolutions, the GA has added that the wishes of the people can also be ascertained in other ways. *See for instance* GA Res. 59/134 (2004).

[6] GA Res. 59/134 (2004).

vent the Caribbean populations from participating in the process of constitutional reform, which could of course seriously undercut the chances of success of the whole operation, and render the right to self-determination meaningless.

Cooperate with Other Administering Powers and International Organizations

This obligation was already proclaimed by Article 73(d) of the UN Charter, and was initially realized by the creation of the Caribbean Commission of which the four Administering States of the Caribbean were members.[7] After the demise of this organization in 1965, the Kingdom has hardly cooperated with other metropolitan states in the region, at least not with the goal of decolonization. Perhaps it should make more of an effort to realize joint efforts with France, the UK and the US, because each of these states struggles with somewhat similar problems as the Kingdom in the Caribbean. It could be wondered, however, whether such cooperation could add to the already existing forms of international cooperation in the Caribbean, but this subject would require further study.

Does Article 73(d) also mean that the UN should be involved? One of the recurring recommendations of the GA is that the Decolonization Committee should supervise the process of decolonization. In cases of the integration or association of a territory with its mother country, such supervision is even considered obligatory by some writers. It could be wondered, however, whether a body like the Decolonization Committee, which has – or at least used to have – a very political agenda and which did not always seem to have the interests of the population at heart, is really the ideal organ to supervise or assist in the decolonization of the Caribbean Countries. Decolonization is no longer an issue that threatens world peace,[8] and it might be more effective – and less costly – to leave the assistance or supervision of the remaining decolonization processes to non-political bodies such as the Secretariat or specialized agencies.[9]

The division of power between the Countries and Kingdom sometimes makes it difficult to determine at which level of government these obligations and recommendations should be realized. Because the Caribbean Countries and the islands of the Netherlands Antilles are autonomous in many of the subjects concerned, their governments and legislators are the first in line to realize most of the goals listed *above*. But the Kingdom should guarantee that they are in-

---

[7] Oostindie & Klinkers 2001b, p. 63 et seq.

[8] The cases of Gibraltar, the Falkland Islands and the Western Sahara are exceptions in that they are still able to create considerable political tensions between states.

[9] The GA has recently requested a number of specialized agencies and other organizations to submit plans of action for the NSGTs, but most addressees did not respond. The Western states appear to be opposed to this GA initiative, and abstained from the vote on GA Res. 59/129 (2004).

deed realized, on the basis of Article 43, paragraph 2, and Articles 50 and 51 of the Kingdom Charter. Whether the Kingdom or the Country of the Netherlands should be considered as the 'Administering State' under Chapter XI of the UN Charter is uncertain, but in any case, the Kingdom should make sure that its international obligations do not fall through the cracks of its own constitutional checks and balances. What this means exactly is hard to say in the abstract, but should be determined in each concrete case.

7.2   CONCLUSION

The international law of decolonization and self-determination creates a number of obligations for the Kingdom, which should mostly be realized by the Countries and the islands of the Netherlands Antilles themselves, while the Kingdom should make sure that they are indeed realized. The Kingdom and its constituent parts should strive towards the achievement of 'a full measure of self-government' by the Caribbean parts of the Kingdom, either in the form of independence, free association, integration, or some other form of government that is freely chosen by the population. The population should be provided with some form of political education, in order to prepare them for such an act of self-determination. After the wishes of the population have been properly ascertained, the Countries and the Kingdom should respect them, and if necessary cooperate with other states and international organizations to realize the desired political status of the islands. It is recommended that the Kingdom Charter should contain a procedure through which the population of the islands would be able to express their opinion on status changes. The GA is of the opinion that the UN has to supervise these types of processes, but it could be wondered whether the Decolonization Committee could really play a useful role. Perhaps other UN organs could assist the Kingdom and the Caribbean governments in providing information on the status options and monitoring the process of decolonization.

Chapter 8
THE RIGHT TO SELF-DETERMINATION OF THE ISLAND TERRITORIES

Since the independence of Surinam in 1975, the discussions on the right to self-determination within the Kingdom have focused on the right of the individual island territories of the Netherlands Antilles to choose their political status, within the Kingdom or as independent states.

The unity of the Netherlands Antilles has always been under pressure from the forces of island separatism. The various origins of the lack of cohesion between the islands have been explained from historical, sociological and political perspectives by many authors.[1] The Netherlands Antilles is a Country made up of very diverse islands that have few economic ties and are located far apart. The Antilleans are not considered to form a nation. Hardly any attempts at nation building have been made in the past, and politicians and political parties have traditionally represented only their own islands. The centrifugal forces within the Netherlands Antilles became too strong to handle after the Netherlands decided in 1972 that Surinam and the Netherlands Antilles should become independent in the near future. Aruba forced its way out of the Netherlands Antilles, which left the Antilles economically and politically more unstable than before, with an increasing number of islands wishing to leave the sinking ship.

The Netherlands, the Netherlands Antilles and all the islands have explicitly recognized that the population of each island has a right to self-determination, but it remains a point of contention between The Hague and the islands what exactly this right to self-determination entails. Is it an absolute right that can be claimed by an island, and which needs to be respected unconditionally by the Netherlands and the other islands? Or are the choices of the islands subject to a right of veto by their partners in the Kingdom? May the Netherlands set conditions to the exercise of the right to self-determination of an island? And should

---

[1] *See* Oostindie & Klinkers 2001c and 2003 for Dutch policies during this period, Reinders 1993 for Antillean political developments, and Sluis 2004 for a review of the inter-island antagonism. *See also* Van Benthem van den Bergh et al. 1978 and Dalhuisen et al. 1997, p. 146 et seq.

S. Hillebrink, The Right to Self-Determination and Post-Colonial Governance
© 2008, T·M·C·Asser press, *The Hague, The Netherlands and the Author*

the international non-disruption principle be taken into account when breaking up the Netherlands Antilles?

8.1   THE RECOGNITION OF THE RIGHT TO SELF-DETERMINATION OF THE ISLANDS

The *Staten* of the Netherlands Antilles recognized the right to self-determination of the individual islands in 1973, but this decision did not lead to substantial status changes, since the opinion of the Netherlands – the 'silent and impotently ubiquitous common ruler'[2] – was considered crucial to any form of realization of the right to self-determination since the Netherlands could block the amendments to the Kingdom Charter that would have been necessary. In 1980, a Working Group – instituted by the Kingdom government to investigate the possible relations between the Netherlands Antilles and the Netherlands, and between the islands themselves – recommended that the right to self-determination of the individual islands should be recognized by the Netherlands, the Netherlands Antilles and all of the islands.[3]

The Report of the Working Group defines the right to self-determination as the right of the population of each island to determine its own political future. It considers this right to be derived from the principle of popular sovereignty, and connected to the free expression of the political will of a state's citizens. The Report refers to 'the many international regulations on that subject, of which the UN Charter can be considered as the most important.'[4]

The Report also listed the desired future status of the islands according to the members which represented the islands. The Aruban members opted for independence in 'a kind of commonwealth' with the Netherlands. The members from the other islands opted for continued constitutional relations with the Netherlands, either within or without the Netherlands Antilles. The Dutch members did not express an opinion, but did state that the Netherlands 'has the right to participate in a decision on its relations with those islands that prefer to maintain constitutional ties with the Netherlands.'[5]

---

[2] Laing 1974, p. 142 uses this phrase to describe the influence of the UK in the fragmentation of the British Caribbean.

[3] The report of the Working Group was published as: *Naar nieuwe vormen van samenwerking. Rapport van de Koninkrijkswerkgroep*, Staatsuitgeverij: 's- Gravenhage 1980. The Working Group was instituted by Royal Decree of 2 December 1978, No. 75 (*Stcrt.* 1978, no. 248 and *PB* 1979, no. 21).

[4] Report of the Kingdom Workgroup 1980, p. 45.

[5] Report of the Kingdom Workgroup 1980, pp. 16 and 45-7.

At the Round Table Conference of 1981 the Netherlands, the Netherlands Antilles and all six islands adopted the recommendations of the Working Group as 'preliminary points of consensus.'[6] It turned out to be impossible to reach a wider agreement on the issue of self-determination.[7] The two Countries and the six islands recognized that each island had the right to choose its own political status, based on the right to self-determination.[8]

The recognition of the right to self-determination of the island territories was probably the most important political event for the Netherlands Antilles since 1954. From the start it was perceived as a sword of Damocles hanging over the Country of the Netherlands Antilles. Others have compared the recognition to a Trojan horse, or a ticking time bomb.[9]

At the Round Table Conference of 1983 the Countries and the islands decided that Aruba would be allowed to secede from the Netherlands Antilles and become a separate Country within the Kingdom in 1986, in preparation for independence in 1996. Although the decision that Aruba would become independent was taken by mutual agreement, the general perception was that the Netherlands government had forced Aruba to accept it in exchange for being allowed to leave the Netherlands Antilles. The attitude of the Dutch government in these negotiations has been widely criticized.[10] *Nelissen & Tillema* recount with amazement how the Netherlands government in 1985 defended its refusal to discuss a postponement of the independence of Aruba with reference to paragraph 3 of GA Resolution 1514, which states that 'inadequacy of political, economic, social or educational preparedness should never serve as a pretext for delaying independence.' It was indeed rather opportunist that the

---

[6] '*Voorlopige punten van overeenstemming*' (preliminary points of consensus), *Kamerstukken II* 1980/81, 16 400 hoofdstuk IV, no. 25.

[7] Oostindie & Klinkers 2001c, p. 105.

[8] Point 1.1 of the '*voorlopige punten van overeenstemming*.'

[9] Janus 1990, p. 77, and Van Rijn 1999, p. 41. The Dutch government's 1990 proposal on the restructuring of the Kingdom claims that many Antilleans consider the right to self-determination of the islands as a 'time-bomb' (*Kamerstukken II* 1989/90, 21 300 IV, no. 9, '*Schets voor een gemenebestconstitutie*', p. 6). *Janus* considered, in another article of 1990, that the time bomb had been defused by Hirsch Ballin's recognition that the islands did not have to become independent (cited in Reinders 1993, p. 281). *Hoeneveld* describes the recognition of the right to self-determination of the islands as opening a door to the 'balkanization' of the Netherlands Antilles (Hoeneveld 2005, p. 65).

[10] *See for instance* Hirsch Ballin 1989, pp. 464-5, Croes & Moenir Alam 1990, p. 82. *See also* Oostindie & Klinkers 2001c, p. 138 who describe the position of the Netherlands on this issue as 'take it or leave it', and pp. 141-6 for an inventory of the opinion of a number of politicians on the condition of independence for Aruba. In the Senate of the Dutch parliament, a comparison was made by Senator Van der Jagt between the Dutch attitude towards self-determination and car manufacturer Ford's aphorism that his customers could choose any colour as long as it was black (*Handelingen I* 1984/85, p. 1314).

Dutch government defended its own policy on the basis of the anti-colonial insistence on independence at all costs, which it had always resisted at the UN.

There existed little doubt that the Arubans did not want independence, at least not in the near future. The date of independence was agreed upon because Aruba wanted to leave the Antilles, and the Netherlands wanted all of the islands to leave the Kingdom as soon as possible. The Netherlands government could therefore be accused of using the internal problems of the Antilles to realize its dream of completing the decolonization of the islands – against the will of the populations. In defence of this Dutch policy it could be said that Aruba had forced the issue to the brink of becoming an international problem,[11] but this does not change the conclusion that the solution chosen was not really acceptable from the perspective of the right to self-determination.

No referendums were held in the Netherlands Antilles during the 1980s, despite the fact that some Curaçaoan politicians had stated at the RTC of 1981 that the secession of Aruba should be approved by the population of the entire Country in a referendum.[12] The Island Council of Curaçao decided that a referendum should be held on the political future of Curaçao in 1985,[13] but such a referendum would not be held until 1993. The *status aparte* of Aruba was realized through an amendment to the Kingdom Charter, which also introduced a new Article providing that the Kingdom order would be terminated with regard to Aruba on 1 January 1996. The Aruban delegates from the *Staten* of the Netherlands Antilles that took part in the debates in the *Staten-Generaal* submitted two amendments to the proposals,[14] one of which would have provided for a referendum in which the people of Aruba would have the opportunity to give their opinion on the independence of the island. These proposals were rejected by the Dutch *Staten-Generaal*.[15]

Even though the Netherlands thus insisted that Aruba's *status aparte* could only be temporary, it yielded a few years later to Aruba's wish to remain part of the Kingdom. It was considered unrealistic to force Aruba to rejoin the Antilles, and the island was allowed to remain a separate Country within the Kingdom indefinitely, albeit with the promise that it would take more care to realize the principles of good government and the rule of law.[16]

---

[11] Verton 1978, pp. 776-7.

[12] *See* Report of the RTC 1981, for instance Elstak (p. 21), Martina (p. 22), and Lourens (p. 30).

[13] Oostindie & Klinkers 2001c, p. 157.

[14] The delegates have this right under Article 17, para. 4, even though they are not allowed to vote on such amendments. *See* Nap 2003a, pp. 79-80 and Borman 2005, pp. 124-5.

[15] *Kamerstukken I/II* 1984/85, 18 826 (R1275), nos. 13, 14 and 15. *See also* Croes 1992, pp. 18-19.

[16] On 21 October 1993, the Dutch and Aruban governments signed a Protocol in which a considerable number of measures were agreed upon to improve the government of Aruba, includ-

8.1.1 Legal Character of the Recognition of the Right to Self-Determination

The legal scholarship has never expressed any doubts about the legally binding character of the recognition of 1981 and 1983.[17] It is not really clear whether the conclusions of the RTCs should be seen as a collection of declarations, or as a *pactum de contrahendo*, as *Janus* has suggested.[18] But a more important question is what was recognized exactly in 1981, when the RTC agreed that the island populations had the right to self-determination. In the absence of evidence to the contrary, the assumption should probably be that the parties present at the RTC had in mind the right to self-determination as guaranteed by international law, which the Netherlands Antilles probably possessed as a whole before 1981.[19] The Report of the Kingdom Working Group referred to the UN Charter and international law, and the RTC formally approved the Report and copied large parts of it into its points of consensus.

It could be countered that the parties present at the RTC – or at least the Netherlands – might have intended to create a right to self-determination under the domestic law of the Kingdom, instead of recognizing the international right to self-determination. If the Netherlands government indeed intended to introduce such a novelty into the constitutional law of the Kingdom, it should have made this explicit. This is not a moot point, since the Netherlands made clear at the RTC that it aimed to limit the right to self-determination to a choice for independence, which would not be possible if the separate islands possessed a right to self-determination under international law.

As I argued in chapter 6, it should probably be assumed that the population of the Caribbean Countries retain the right to self-determination, in the sense of

---

ing amendments to the Kingdom Charter ('*Protocol ter invulling van het Resumé van de bilaterale gesprekken Aruba-Nederland*', *Kamerstukken II* 1993/94, 23 224, no. 5). This Protocol was partially implemented, but after the date of independence of Aruba was struck from the Kingdom Charter in 1995, the Protocol seems to have been forgotten, in spite of the opinion of the governments of the Netherlands and Aruba – and of the Lower House – that the Protocol was legally binding (*Kamerstukken II* 1994/95, 22 593 (R1433), no. 22).

[17] *See for instance* Kapteyn 1982, p. 29, Gorsira 1988, p. 60 et seq., Bongenaar 1991, Van Rijn 1999, p. 56, and Hoeneveld 2005, p. 64.

[18] Janus 1993, pp. 49 and 60-1. A *pactum de contrahendo* is an agreement which stipulates the basic principles for a definitive agreement to be reached at a later date. At the RTC of 1981, Dutch minister Van der Stee compared the conclusions of the RTC to an international agreement that needed to be ratified by the Netherlands parliament and by the Island Councils of the six islands (Report of the RTC 1981, p. 31).

[19] *Nelissen & Tillema* noted in this context that the Netherlands 'has made clear that it understands this right [to self-determination] as it has been elaborated upon in the context of the U.N. and the 1966 Human Rights Covenants. Therefore, *de iure* all the options, modalities, rights and duties as they exist in the strict colonial context, apply.' (Nelissen & Tillema 1989, p. 190).

a right to decolonization, until they have been allowed to make a free and in-formed choice on their political status. It is generally assumed by writers on international law that the right to self-determination of colonial peoples can change in content, but only after it has been exercised to achieve a full measure of self-government in the form of independence, free association or integra-tion. As the political status of the islands of the Netherlands Antilles (except Aruba) did not change after 1981, the conclusion should be that the right to self-determination has not changed in content, but only in its subject.

The Netherlands was not legally obligated to cooperate with transferring the right to self-determination of the Netherlands Antilles to the separate is-lands, but when the Netherlands decided to cooperate with this transfer, it should have realized that this procedure could not be used to limit the choices of the populations to independence. A choice for independence could only be made by the people(s) of the Netherlands Antilles, and until that choice had been made, all options for decolonization and self-determination should remain open.

In the legal literature, the freedom of choice of the island populations has been given precedence over the independence policy of the Netherlands gov-ernment. *Janus* writes that the Netherlands should cooperate with realizing such status options as integration with the Netherlands, association or any other option freely chosen by the population, because the essence of the right to self-determination is the need to pay regard to the freely expressed will of the people.[20] Up to this point, there is no disagreement in the legal literature. There also appears to be a consensus that the recognition of 1981/83 was not invali-dated by the fact that it was not supported by referendums or other forms of consultation of popular opinion, although this could well have been argued.[21] The scholarship is not in full agreement, however, on the delineation of this duty of the Netherlands and the islands to cooperate with realizing a desire for status change.

Borman thinks that integration or association with the Netherlands should not be an exclusive decision of an island population, but that such a status change would require an agreement with the Netherlands.[22] *Van Rijn* thinks the Netherlands could not refuse a Caribbean choice for closer or different ties with the Netherlands, although similar to *Janus*,[23] *Van Rijn* thinks that the

---

[20] Janus 1993, p. 49.

[21] I have deduced this consensus from the fact that none of the writers cited here consider that referendums should have been held.

[22] Borman 2005, pp. 29-30. The argument that 'what has been granted to Aruba, cannot be denied to the other islands' (*see Handelingen II* 1991/92, p. 849 et seq.) has some validity, but each case should be judged on the merits, according to *Borman*.

[23] Janus 1993, pp. 60-1.

modalities of such ties should be the subject of negotiations.[24] According to *Hoeneveld*, the Netherlands will have to accept a choice for another status by an island population, if – and to the extent that – such a status conforms to the criteria laid down in Resolution 1541, but unreasonable demands could be ignored.[25] *Nelissen & Tillema* note that self-determination is not an absolute right, and needs to be exercised in a reasonable manner, taking into account the legitimate interests of others. But 'the Dutch will not be entitled to require difficult conditions, like the ones formulated at the 1981-Round Table, to be met first, as this would in fact imply a denial of the Antillean right.'[26] *Gorsira* also emphasizes the freedom of choice of the Caribbean populations, but thinks that the Netherlands could nonetheless set conditions before it would be prepared to cooperate with a status change of the islands within the Kingdom, unless such conditions would amount to a repudiation of the islands.[27]

Despite the different approaches that these writers take to this issue, they seem to agree that the freedom of choice of the island populations should be respected, and that a new constitutional status within the Kingdom can only be realized through negotiations, in which the Netherlands are not obligated to accept unreasonable overseas demands. There is of course a fundamental difference between setting conditions to the right to remain a part of the Kingdom, as the Netherlands government appeared to do at the 1981 RTC, and setting conditions to the achievement of a new status within the Kingdom. There is probably little room for conditions of the first type, since the islands may not be pushed into independence against their will (*see* chapter 4), but conditions of the second type are not unreasonable *per se*.

The Netherlands and the islands have a long-standing difference of opinion on this subject. I will first describe the opinion of the Netherlands, and then describe the view of the islands as regards the unconditional nature of their right to self-determination.

8.1.2 Dutch Attitude towards the Self-Determination of the Islands

The Dutch government has made it a steady policy to acknowledge the right of each island to become independent unconditionally, but to reserve a right of veto, or at least of co-decision, on any other status options. This policy sometimes boiled down to a simple claim that the right to self-determination only

---

[24] Van Rijn 1999, p. 58.
[25] Hoeneveld 2005, pp. 37-8. It would be unreasonable, according to *Hoeneveld*, to demand from the Netherlands that it would drastically change its constitutional system.
[26] Nelissen & Tillema 1989, p. 191, cited with approval by Janus 1993, p. 61.
[27] Gorsira 1988, pp. 59-60.

means a right to independence. It has often been noted that this attitude towards self-determination is not consistent with the Dutch position at the UN.[28] It has been defended that the principle of *estoppel* precludes the Netherlands from using a different interpretation at home than the one it has consistently defended at the UN.[29] One could wonder whether the criteria for an *estoppel* have really been fulfilled here,[30] but it cannot be denied that the statements of the Netherlands at the UN can or should be used to interpret the intentions of the Netherlands when it recognized the right to self-determination of the island populations of the Netherlands Antilles, assuming that the international law of decolonization and self-determination still applied to the Netherlands Antilles in 1981 and 1983.[31]

If it is furthermore supposed that the right to self-determination of the Netherlands Antilles has devolved upon the populations of the separate islands, then the limitation put on the freedom of choice by the Netherlands cannot mean that the islands can only choose independence. GA Resolutions 1541 and 2625 clearly provide that a people can also choose for free association, integration or any other political status, and these resolutions must be considered to have the force of law (*see* chapter 2), including for the Netherlands since it has actively cooperated with the formulation of these Resolutions, and it has cited them (abroad and at home[32]) as containing the standards for self-determination and decolonization.

---

[28] *See for instance* Kapteyn 1982, p. 180, Tillema 1989, Croes & Croes 1989, Nelissen & Tillema 1989, pp. 182-4, and Sap 2005. It seems far-fetched to ascribe this difference to the legal fact that at the UN, the Netherlands represents the Kingdom as a whole, whereas in the debates on the future of the Caribbean Countries, it usually speaks as the Country. Politicians and diplomats rarely take account of the fact that there exists a difference between the Kingdom of the Netherlands and the Country of the Netherlands.

[29] Nelissen & Tillema 1989, p. 184.

[30] *See* Brownlie 2003, p. 615 for these criteria.

[31] The situation is somewhat comparable to promises that Administering states have made at the UN that they would not oppose the exercise of the right to self-determination by one of their (former) NSGTs, which are probably binding on them under international law. *See* Clark 1980, p. 45, note 264, who applies the doctrine derived from the *Nuclear Test Cases* to the statements of the US with regard to Puerto Rico.

[32] At the UN, the Netherlands has quite consistently defended the freedom of choice of overseas territories. When the GA wanted to set a date for the independence of the British territory of the Seychelles in 1971, the Netherlands stated: 'Inhabitants of dependent territories are entitled to several options in their exercise of the right to self-determination. We cannot force independence on them against their wishes. It is up to the people of those territories and only to them to determine their own destiny' (statement by the Netherlands on 13 December 1971 in the Fourth Committee of the GA, cited in Nelissen & Tillema 1989, p. 184, and Croes & Croes 1989, p. 32). This statement, and others similar to it, have repeatedly been cited in the discussions between the islands and the Netherlands. Elstak, one of the representatives of Curaçao at the RTC of 1981, reminded the Conference of a statement made by the Netherlands in the plenary debate

In this context, it is important to note that it has actually been more common for Dutch politicians to acknowledge that other options than independence also exist for the islands. During the debate on the ICCPR and ICESCR in the Lower House in 1978, it became clear that most MPs, as well as the Kingdom government, considered that the two Covenants granted a right to self-determination to the Netherlands Antilles, which – it was stressed – should not be equated to a right to independence. It also included the right to choose for free association or integration. Reference was made several times to GA Resolution 2625 (XXV).[33]

The Dutch government has recognized that 'self-determination can also be exercised in a meaningful manner in a constitutional relationship with the Netherlands.'[34] But such a form of self-determination can only be realized, according to the Dutch government, through the established procedures of the Kingdom Charter, which means that any substantial status changes will require the approval of the parliaments of Aruba, the Netherlands Antilles and the Netherlands, and of the Kingdom government.[35] It has often been repeated that the Netherlands, when it recognized the right to self-determination of the islands, reserved a 'right of co-decision' regarding any choice for continued ties with the Netherlands. This reservation could be interpreted to mean that the Netherlands could set conditions to the realization of the right to self-determination, and it has even been interpreted to mean that the Netherlands might veto a choice by an island population.

The most logical way of achieving conformity between the position of the Netherlands and international law, is by interpreting the phrase 'a right of co-decision' to refer to a right to participate in the decision-making process. In-

---

of the UN General Assembly in 1977, in which the Netherlands explained that 'if a territory, in a fully free and democratic decision, chooses to exercise its right to self-determination by opting for another solution than independence, that decision should be respected' (*see* Report of the RTC 1981, p. 21). This interpretation can also be found in the records of the *Staten-Generaal. See for instance* the government's explanation attached to the budget for Foreign Affairs of 1973 (*Kamerstukken II* 1972, 12 000 V, no. 2, p. 23) where it is stated that as a consequence of the right to self-determination, the international community must accept that some NSGTs will not become independent if the population concerned freely expresses itself in favour of maintaining ties with the mother country. *See also* the debate on the ICCPR and ICESCR *below.*

[33] *See for instance* the statement by Minister Van der Stee, *Handelingen II* 1978/79, p. 158.

[34] *Kamerstukken II* 1992/93, 22 593 (R 1433), no. 3, p. 1.

[35] *See for instance* the Memorandum on the right to self-determination of the islands attached to the letter of 27 October 2000 by the Secretary of State for Kingdom Affairs (De Vries) to the Lower House (reference CW00/82 274, reproduced in Hoeneveld 2005). The Memorandum was not included in the official records of the *Staten-Generaal*, and it was not discussed in parliament, but a delegation of the Lower House echoed its conclusions when it explained to the island government of St Maarten that the right to self-determination only meant a right to independence.

ternational law does not appear to prohibit the Netherlands (and the islands) from demanding that the concretization of the status option chosen by the population should be reasonable and should take account of its interests and of the Kingdom as a whole.

The Netherlands would thus have stated that the island territories have a right to choose another political status, but if that status involves continued constitutional relations with the Netherlands, the precise meaning would have to be negotiated between the island territory, the Netherlands and the other parts of the Kingdom.[36] This interpretation is not fundamentally at odds with the recent practice of the Netherlands government of leaving a choice regarding the future political status of the islands to the islands themselves, but at the same time insisting that any status other than independence can only come about through negotiations with the Netherlands. This interpretation leaves room for each island population to freely choose another political status, while the details of such a status can only be determined through negotiations with the other parts of the Kingdom.

In practice, the Dutch government has shown considerable deference to the wishes of the population of the islands.[37] In 1994, it abandoned its plans for a break-up of the Antilles after referenda on the islands showed the population to be clearly opposed to such a break-up. On the other hand, the Netherlands explicitly refused to realize the choice of the population of St Maarten in the 2000 referendum. This created some scepticism among the Antillean population about the usefulness of holding further referendums.[38] The Referendum Committee on Curaçao tried to remove these doubts by insisting that the Netherlands, as well as the authorities of Curaçao and the Netherlands Antilles, would be legally obligated to realize the choice of the Curaçaoans as an expression of the right to self-determination.[39]

---

[36] Members of the political parties *CDA* and *VVD* stated in the Lower House in 1992 that the islands had the right to choose to stay a part of the Kingdom, but that the way in which such a choice should be realized was a matter for negotiations (*Kamerstukken II* 1991/92, 22 593 (R 1433), no. 5, p. 4 and 9).

[37] The unanimously dismissive Dutch reactions to the outcome of the 2000 referendum on St Maarten were an exception. In this referendum, 69 per cent votes went to the option of *status aparte* for St Maarten. The Dutch Secretary of State for Kingdom Relations announced (before and after the referendum) that this option was simply out of the question. This opinion was supported by the Lower House (*Handelingen II* 2000/01, pp. 11-752 to 11-783) and continued by the Minister for Administrative Reform and Kingdom affairs that took office in 2003 (De Graaf, *see NRC Handelsblad*, 13 August 2003, '*Status aparte vinden wij geen optie*'). The Dutch newspaper *NRC Handelsblad* reported on the referendum under the headline: 'No status aparte for St Maarten', thereby giving precedence to the opinion of the Dutch government over the outcome of the referendum.

[38] *See* the report by the UN observer on Bonaire.

[39] *See* for example a press release issued on 16 February 2005 by the commission that organized the referendum on Curaçao, in which it explained that all of the authorities within the

Perhaps the claim of the Referendum Committee was stated too boldly, but as I explained in chapter 2, the freedom of choice which the right to self-determination aims to guarantee, means that the authorities should try to realize the wishes of the population as best they can. When a choice is made for one of the options of Resolution 1541, there should be exceptional and pressing reasons *not* to cooperate fully with realizing the freely expressed wishes of an overseas population. The view that the outcome of the referendum on Curaçao was binding is therefore defendable from the perspective of international law.

In 2005, after new referendums had revealed that the population (on four out of five islands) was now in favour of abolishing the Antilles as a single Country, the Dutch government re-opened the negotiations with the islands. The Minister for Government Reform and Kingdom Relations (Pechtold) stated in 2005 that he did not consider the outcome of the referenda binding on the Netherlands (as was claimed in the Netherlands Antilles), but that the government of the Netherlands respected them.[40] In a debate in the Lower House, Pechtold stated in response to one of the MP's concerns that Country status for St Maarten might be unwise (given its small size and the perception that the island was not ready for self-government):

> I share his concern, but we must be careful. At the end of the day, it was the referendum on St Maarten in 2000 which advocated this direction. Whether it is possible will have to be explored.[41]

Pechtold announced that the Dutch government would cooperate with a constitutional reform of the Netherlands Antilles, if the islands would cooperate with a joint solution to the financial and economic problems of the Netherlands Antilles, and cooperate with improving the level of law enforcement and gov-

Kingdom were obligated to realize the outcome of the referendum, since it was held on the basis of the right to self-determination of the people of Curaçao. *See* the website of the referendum committee: <http://www.referendum2005.an/updates_02.html>. The main advisory body of the government of the Netherlands Antilles, the *Raad van Advies*, in its report on the year 2004 also stated that the referendums on the islands were binding because they were an expression of the right to self-determination (*Jaarverslag 2004*, p. 36). In reaction to this discussion, Dutch senator Schouw (*D66*) noted to his dismay that on Curaçao 'there is talk of a right to self-determination', and stated that the outcome of a referendum on one single island could not have consequences for the constitution of the Kingdom. In his view, the Netherlands government should reject the outcome of the referendum, and look into only two options: independence or full integration into the Netherlands (*Handelingen I* 2004/05, p. 24-1029). *See also Amigoe* (10 and 15 February 2005), and the editorial of 11 April 2005 in *de Volkskrant*.

[40] *Handelingen I* 2004/05, p. 1035 (26 April 2005).

[41] In Dutch: '*Ik deel zijn zorg, maar wij moeten wel oppassen. Uiteindelijk is het het referendum op Sint Maarten in 2000 geweest dat die richting voorstaat. Of het mogelijk is, moet worden verkend.*' *See Handelingen II* 2005/06, p. 624 (12 October 2005).

ernance of the islands.[42] This proposal was accepted by the islands and formalized in an agreement of 22 October 2005, and confirmed at a Round Table
Conference on 26 November 2005.[43] The agreement states that the Netherlands respects the outcome of the referendums, but it does not refer to the right
to self-determination, because the Netherlands and the islands could not come
to an agreement about the meaning of this right.

8.1.3   The Interpretations of the Islands

Surinam and the Netherlands Antilles in 1952 defined the right to self-determination as follows:

> The right to self-determination gives the people the freedom to determine its rela-
> tion to other countries, whereby it has the right to choose between independence,
> association with the mother country or with another state, and incorporation.[44]

The Netherlands Antilles and all of the islands have since the 1970s quite consistently recognized that each island has the right to choose its own political
status, even if that means leaving the Netherlands Antilles. While the opinion
of the governments of the islands and the Netherlands Antilles has varied considerably on the most desirable future status of the Country and the islands, it
has never been denied, at least not since the *Staten* motion of 1973, that each
island determines its own political status in freedom.

During the 1980s, representatives of the islands mainly used the right to
self-determination to argue that the Netherlands was not allowed to push the
islands out of the Kingdom. Aruba, even while accepting independence as a

---

[42] Letter by the Minister for Government Reform and Kingdom Affairs (Pechtold) to the
Lower House, dated 26 May 2005 (*Kamerstukken II* 2004/05, 29 800 IV, no. 25).

[43] '*Hoofdlijnenakkoord tussen de Nederlandse Antillen, Nederland, Curaçao, St. Maarten,
Bonaire, St. Eustatius en Saba*', signed on Bonaire on 22 October 2005. This agreement was not
published in the records of the *Staten-Generaal*, but summarized in a letter of 7 November 2005
by the Minister for Government Reform and Kingdom Affairs to the Lower House (*Kamerstukken
II* 2005/06, 30 300 IV, no. 18). It was made available on several websites, for instance, on the
website of the island government of Curaçao <http://curacao-gov.an>. *See also* the '*Slotverklaring
van de start-Ronde Tafel Conferentie van het Koninkrijk der Nederlanden, gehouden op 26 november 2005 in Willemstad, te Curaçao.*' The Netherlands and the islands agreed to start a process that could lead to the realization of a new constitutional relation with the islands, but it will
demand that the governments of the islands meet with certain standards of good government – to
be defined jointly by the Netherlands and the islands – before the Netherlands Antilles can be
broken up.

[44] Statement by the Governing Council of the Netherlands Antilles and the Surinam mission,
cited in Van Helsdingen 1957, p. 197 (my translation, SH). According to *Van Helsdingen*, this
definition was derived from a statement by the US representative at the Sixth GA of the UN.

condition for its *status aparte*, continued to consider it a violation of international law to force the island to become independent against its will.[45]

After the Netherlands in 1990 abandoned its attempts to convince the islands to become independent, the islands started using the right to self-determination as a basis for claiming another position within the Kingdom. It was usually acknowledged that such a constitutional reform could not be achieved in complete freedom, but should take account of the interests of the parts of the Kingdom, and required an agreement with the Netherlands and the other islands. The government of St Maarten, for instance, claimed that the creation of an 'association' between St Maarten and the Netherlands 'is not necessarily a matter without encumbrance, but a form of co-operation by consent and on an equal basis.' The island government furthermore stated that the powers and authority of the Kingdom government would have to be determined by an agreement.[46]

A more radical view was expressed when the negotiations on the new status of the five islands were re-opened in 2005, and the Netherlands government announced that it would only cooperate with creating new entities within the Kingdom if certain conditions were met.[47] An Antillean committee that was installed to prepare a Round Table Conference in 2005 claimed, with reference to GA Resolutions 1514 and 2625, that the nature of the right to self-determination meant that a choice for an 'association' could not be made dependent on the fulfilment of conditions set unilaterally by the metropolitan state if those conditions would lead to the forced transfer of powers to that state. Otherwise, the right to self-determination would become 'completely hollow and illusory.' Any transfer of powers to the state should occur in complete freedom, whereby the associated territory could request guarantees or limitations to protect its identity.[48]

---

[45] The opinion of Aruba, or at least of the *AVP* (one of the major political parties of the island), on the right to self-determination is explained in detail in Croes & Croes 1989. Aruba's Prime Minister Eman interpreted the right to self-determination in a debate in the Lower House in 1993 as 'an exclusive right that belongs to an entity that is not yet independent to determine independently and in complete freedom its future political status, the exercise of which does not have to lead to independence at all. The population may decide on this issue in freedom, because this right cannot be made subject to conditions by the mother country' (*Handelingen II* 1993/94, p. 4338/39).

[46] The opinion of St Maarten was published in two booklets: 'Saint Martin Referendum June 23rd, 2000. Executing the Right of Self-Determination' (prepared by the Work Group for Constitutional Affairs, Sub-Group Constitutional Relations, February 2001), and 'Saint Martin as a Country within the Kingdom of the Netherlands' (prepared by the Work Group on Constitutional Affairs for the Island Council of the Island Territory of Saint Martin in 2002).

[47] Letter by the Minister for Government Reform and Kingdom Relations (De Graaf) to the Lower House, dated 17 December 2004 (*Kamerstukken II*, 2004/04, 29 800 IV, no. 18).

[48] Report of the Antillean committee of preparation for the Round Table Conference of 2005 ('*Toekomst in zicht*'), dated 12 August 2005, p. 8. The report was adopted by the government and

The prime minister of the Netherlands Antilles shortly thereafter published a legal advice on the right to self-determination which also claimed that the Netherlands could not set direct – or indirect – conditions for the exercise of the islands' right to self-determination.[49]

There are a number of flaws in the legal reasoning used to support the conclusion that the Netherlands should cooperate unconditionally with realizing the outcome of the referenda. First, it is not certain whether the current relation of the Netherlands Antilles with the Netherlands should be viewed as a form of free association in the sense of Resolution 1541 (*see* chapter 6) and it is even less certain whether the populations of Curaçao and St Maarten chose free association when they voted for the status of 'Country within the Kingdom' in the referenda of 2000 and 2005.[50]

Second, even if Country status is seen as a form of free association, international law does not prohibit the principal state from setting conditions before entering into a free association. Resolution 1541 limits the freedom of the principal state in (post-)colonial relations, but it does not obligate the principal state to accept unconditionally any form of free association that might be proposed by the overseas territory.

Third, the right to self-determination should be exercised in good faith. It would certainly not become completely hollow and illusory if it were exercised

---

the *Staten* of the Netherlands Antilles. Members of the *Staten* had defended a similar interpretation in 1992 during a meeting with members of the Dutch *Staten-Generaal* (*Kamerstukken II* 1991/92, 22 593 (R 1433), no. 5, p. 9).

[49] Legal advice of the directorate for Legislation and Legal Affairs of the Netherlands Antilles to the prime minister on the right to self-determination (undated). The advice was made public through various channels in September 2005. The prime minister communicated its conclusions in talks with Dutch ministers (*see Amigoe*, 1 September 2005). This interpretation may have been inspired by fears that the Netherlands would use the break-up of the Antilles (and its desperate financial situation) to increase its control over the governments of the individual islands. The new status of Curaçao and St Maarten would – it was feared – be less autonomous than the *status aparte* of Aruba. The Netherlands indicated that it would want a bigger say in the areas of law enforcement and the public spending of the new Countries. The prime minister of the Antilles stated that he would welcome the support of the Netherlands in these areas, but the current problems of the islands should not form a pretext for denying them their desired status (*Amigoe*, 1 September 2005). This interpretation of the right to self-determination (with regard to Curaçao) is also defended in Sap 2005.

[50] Both in the referendum in Curaçao (2005) and the referendum in St Maarten (2000), the option of free association was not included on the ballot for the referendum, despite requests to that end. The status of 'Country within the Kingdom' was generally interpreted to mean that the island would obtain the same *status aparte* as Aruba currently has under the Kingdom Charter. *See also* the Report of 12 August 2005, cited *above*, on p. 9, and the decision of the Island Council of Curaçao of 15 April 2005 which ratified the results of the referendum, and declared that Curaçao's new status should be 'at least the same as the *status aparte* of Aruba.'

while taking account of the rights and interests of the population of the metro-politan state, the other islands of the Netherlands Antilles, and Aruba.

Fourth, Resolution 1514 proclaims that an overseas territory should be al-lowed to take possession of all powers, but this means that an overseas territory should be free to become independent. Resolution 1514 does not proclaim that when a territory chooses *not* to become independent it can still unilaterally define its relation to the metropolitan state, nor has any other UN Resolution ever declared that the right to self-determination should be interpreted in this way.

The theory that the Netherlands cannot set any conditions to a new status for the islands therefore does not appear to hold water. The right to self-determina-tion of the islands guarantees a freedom of choice, but this freedom is not absolute and should be used in a reasonable manner, taking into account the interests of the other parts of the Kingdom, as has often been recognized in the islands. The question remains, however, what kind of conditions could be set to the realization of a choice by an island population, and which limits to the freedom of choice could be considered 'reasonable'.

8.1.4   Limits to the Freedom of Choice?

On the basis of GA Resolutions 1541 and 2625 the population of the islands must be considered free to choose a free association with the Netherlands, or to become an integral part of the Netherlands, or to choose some other status which might better suit their situation. The Netherlands cannot veto such a choice in itself but it can decide on how it will perform the tasks for which an island may request Dutch support, as long as this does not violate the legal principles which should guide the metropolitan states in the process of decolonization. In this sense the outcome of the referendum should be consid-ered as legally binding, unless it could be shown that it did not accurately gauge the opinion of the population – for instance because the turn-out was too low, or because the information provided to the population was inaccurate, biased or incomplete, or because the formulation of the options was flawed.[51]

Currently, the most important difference of opinion concerning the content of the right to self-determination revolves around the long-standing desire of Curaçao and St Maarten to obtain a *status aparte* as Countries within the King-dom, similar to Aruba. The referendums of 2000 and 2005 on St Maarten and Curaçao resulted in victories for the option of *status aparte*, and the islands therefore claimed that this status should be granted to them on the basis of their

---

[51] Some media reports indicated that the referendums on some of the islands were not per-fect, but to determine whether this is true would require further research.

right to self-determination. Country status for these two islands would inevitably lead to the end of the Country of the Netherlands Antilles, which would – at least potentially – create a number of problems for the three islands that would be left behind; Bonaire, St Eustatius and Saba. These three smaller islands would be affected by the disappearance of the Netherlands Antilles, because they certainly cannot take over all of the tasks of the central government, and they will have to find a way of making sure that the public services currently provided by the Netherlands Antilles are maintained at an acceptable level for their inhabitants.

In The Hague, it was feared that the break-up of the Netherlands Antilles would create a responsibility for the Netherlands to take care of the smaller islands, and it was moreover feared that the autonomous governments of Curaçao and St Maarten would be less effective than the current central government of the Netherlands Antilles, which may cause problems that could force the Kingdom (or in reality the Netherlands) to intervene in the internal affairs of the future Countries – a very unattractive perspective for most Dutch politicians.

It is recognized to some extent in The Hague that what has been granted to Aruba cannot be denied to Curaçao.[52] Seeing that Curaçao is larger than Aruba, and has been the administrative centre of the Dutch islands for a long time, it cannot reasonably be argued that Curaçao could not handle the responsibilities that have been attributed to Aruba, without calling into question the *status aparte* of Aruba, or in fact the basic framework of the Kingdom itself. But St Maarten is considerably smaller than Aruba, both in area and in population, and the challenges facing the island in the area of good government already forced the Kingdom to intervene during the 1990s. Doubts have therefore repeatedly been expressed in The Hague regarding the agreement to grant St Maarten Country status, because it might be incapable of taking on the responsibilities connected with that status.[53]

Perhaps it could be maintained that an island could be refused Country status if it is clearly not capable of exercising the tasks of a Country according to the criteria of the Kingdom Charter. But since there are a number of independent states that are equal in size, or even smaller than St Maarten,[54] it cannot be argued that it is impossible *per se* for such an island to perform the tasks of a Country within the Kingdom. Of course, the Kingdom may not want to be held internationally responsible for some of the situations that occur in existing

---

[52] *See for instance Kamerstukken II* 1992/93, 22 593 (R 1433), no. 8, p. 8.

[53] *See for instance* the remarks by member of the Lower House De Vries (*PvdA*) in 2005, *Kamerstukken II* 2005/06, 30 300 IV, no. 6, p. 2. The Dutch Minister for Government Reform and Kingdom Relations (Pechtold) stated that he shared these doubts about Country status for St Maarten, *see Handelingen II* 2005/06, p. 624.

[54] For example Tuvalu (11,000 inhabitants), San Marino (29,000), and Monaco (32,000).

microstates, and most microstates depend heavily on outside assistance of some sort.

To some extent, it will always remain an unattractive proposition for the Kingdom to be internationally responsible for a number of small islands located very far from the European part of the Kingdom, while it has hardly any say in the government of those islands. This situation was created in 1954 with the full consent of the Netherlands,[55] but this does not necessarily mean that the Netherlands is obligated to cooperate with granting Curaçao and St Maarten Country status, as well as accepting full responsibility for the orphaned islands of Bonaire, St Eustatius and Saba. The right to self-determination does not really provide a clear solution to this situation, except that there exists an obligation try and realize the choices of the populations in good faith.

This means that a reasonable solution should be sought, but what is reasonable will depend on the particulars of the case, and has to be determined on the basis of general principles and with regard to all the relevant facts and circumstances.[56] To prevent a situation where 'might equals right' – which is a real risk in an unequal relation – it should be possible to refer concrete conflicts regarding the interpretation of the Kingdom Charter or the political status of an island to an impartial and independent organ, for instance a constitutional court, which should have the authority – similar to the International Court of Justice – to settle conflicts (or recommend solutions) *ex aequo et bono* since conflicts between the Countries sometimes concern issues on which the law is vague, undeveloped or non-existent.[57] Aruba and the Netherlands already agreed in 1993 to create a new procedure in which conflicts between the governments of the Kingdom could be referred to the *Raad van State* of the Kingdom, but this agreement was never executed.[58]

In order to put an end to the 'difficult conferencing' of politicians on constitutional affairs, *Munneke* has proposed to codify the right to self-determination of the islands, and to create a procedure that would create a direct link between the population of each island and the metropolitan legislature. In his view, the population of each island should be allowed to choose (in a referendum) be-

---

[55] The Kingdom Charter has had to suffer much verbal abuse in the Netherlands for this reason. *See for instance* the letter by *Emmer* to the editor of *de Volkskrant* (15 September 2005) regarding the 'incredibly foolish Kingdom Charter' ('*het oliedomme Koninkrijksstatuut*'). *See also* Jansen van Galen 2004.

[56] *See* Brownlie 2003, pp. 25-6 for references to literature on the subject of the role of equity in international law.

[57] The authority to settle conflicts *ex aequo et bono* (i.e. on the basis of equity or fairness) has been attributed to the International Court of Justice in Article 38, para. 1 (c) of its Statute.

[58] '*Protocol ter invulling van het Resumé van de bilaterale gesprekken Aruba-Nederland*', *Kamerstukken II* 1993/94, 23 224, no. 5.

tween independence, association with the Netherlands, or accession to the legal order of the Netherlands. If an island would choose for association or accession, the Dutch legislature would regulate the tasks that should be performed by the Netherlands, but this legislation would not go into force until the population had confirmed its choice in a second referendum.

This proposal would create a constitutional guarantee that the people would have the final say on any status change.[59] From the point of view of self-determination this is obviously to be welcomed. But his proposal would also create a strong role for the Dutch legislature, which could design the new status as it saw fit, after which the population could only reject the proposal, presumably to return to the *status quo* which it had rejected in the first referendum. *Munneke* assumes that the Netherlands would claim a stronger role in law enforcement, securing the rule of law and good government, which – in his view – are much in need of improvement in the Caribbean Countries.[60] Since the Netherlands could bypass the local politicians by putting the newly designed status directly before the people, this procedure would offer the Netherlands government an opportunity to decrease the influence of the overseas politicians on the government of the islands, if the population would approve it.

Munneke also aimed to decrease the influence of Caribbean politicians in another way. He proposed to incorporate the procedure for self-determination in the Constitution of the Netherlands, and to abolish the legal order of the Kingdom Charter. In his view, the loss of equivalent status which the Charter formally guarantees, would be no more than a psychological disadvantage to the islands. The political status of the islands could – in the future – only be changed by the Dutch legislature with the approval of the population in a referendum, while in the current situation the *Staten* of the Caribbean Countries have a right of veto on amendments to the Kingdom Charter.

It is not certain whether this proposal, which is modelled on the French Constitution, would really be an improvement in every respect. The French Constitution has enabled the islands of Saint-Martin and Saint-Barthélémy to choose a new status, but this also involved a considerable amount of 'difficult conferencing' between Paris and local politicians on the details of the new status. Perhaps this should simply be accepted as an inevitable side effect of overseas relations. It seems to occur in every relation described in this study. It would be an improvement, however, if it were constitutionally guaranteed that the populations of the islands have to approve major status changes (*see* chapter 7).

---

[59] Munneke 1993, p. 858.
[60] *See* Munneke 1994 and Munneke 2001.

Aruba has a special position in this debate, because amendments to the Kingdom Charter require the consent of its *Staten*, while the Netherlands Antilles cannot be broken up without Charter amendments. Aruba recognized the right to self-determination of the islands of the Netherlands Antilles in 1981 and 1983, and it promised in 1993 that it would cooperate with Charter amendments if the Antilles would be dissolved.[61] It must be assumed that Aruba is under the same obligation as the Netherlands to cooperate with the exercise of the right to self-determination of the Antillean islands.

8.1.5 Conclusion

It must be assumed that the content of the right to self-determination of the six islands is the same as the former right to self-determination of the Netherlands Antilles as a whole, at least in relation to the Netherlands. The islands have not agreed to the limiting interpretation proposed by the Netherlands, and the freedom of choice of the island populations, which is guaranteed by international law, cannot be limited by a unilateral declaration of the Netherlands. The fact that the recognition of 1981/83 was not supported by referenda or other forms of consultation of popular opinion has not been considered by the governments of the Kingdom, nor in the legal literature, as invalidating this recognition. The referenda held between 2000 and 2005 showed a large part of the population of the Netherlands Antilles to be in favour of breaking up the Country and creating a separate status for each island.

The position of the Netherlands in negotiations concerning a new political status for an island depends on the choice of the island. A choice for integration would mean that the Netherlands should take on more responsibilities for the government of the island, in which case the Netherlands may determine to a large extent how it will perform its new tasks. At the other end of the scale, a choice for independence would mean that the Netherlands will be freed from all responsibilities for the government of the island, leaving it entirely to the island itself to determine how its government will be run. The islands currently seem only interested in status options that lie somewhere in between these extremes. The Netherlands seeks assurances that the responsibilities of the Kingdom in the Caribbean will be safeguarded after the dissolution of the Netherlands Antilles. General legal principles such as good faith, equity and proportionality should guide the authorities of the Kingdom, the Countries and the islands in the fulfilment of their obligation to realize as well as possible the 'free and genuine expression of the will of the people.' To this end, the King-

---

[61] *See* the Protocol cited in the previous footnote.

dom Charter should guarantee that the population is consulted when major status changes are contemplated.

8.2 The Non-Disruption Principle

It has often been wondered whether the non-disruption principle (or *uti possidetis*)[62] precludes the Kingdom from cooperating with the break-up of the Netherlands Antilles.[63] The principle of non-disruption in the context of decolonization could be seen as a corollary to the principle that only 'a people' as a whole has the right to self-determination. Several GA Resolutions emphasize that colonies should not be divided into smaller units before becoming independent. 'Colonies' here means the administrative units established by the colonial power, which may have no correspondence to the historical and ethnic realities which existed before, during and after the colonial era. The entities created by the colonial powers should perhaps be considered as states in an embryonic form, already possessing territorial integrity. Resolution 1514 (XV) of 1960 provides that: 'Any attempt aimed at the partial or total disruption of the national unity and the territorial integrity of a country is incompatible with the purposes and principles of the Charter of the United Nations.'[64]

It is far from certain to what extent this rule also applies to self-determination units which are not yet independent states, and which have no intention of becoming independent in the near future, such as the Netherlands Antilles. In practice, states and the UN organs have often co-operated with, or at least accepted, the division of dependencies if it was done with the approval of the territories themselves. In the history of the Trust Territories such divisions have been common practice. It happened only twice that a Trust Territory became independent within its colonial boundaries.[65] NSGTs more often became independent as a whole, without joining another territory or state, but here also, substantial changes were allowed to be made. In cases where there did not exist agreement among the different parts of the NSGT about a break-up, the GA has

---

[62] For the principle of *uti possidetis*, *see* Cassese 1995, p. 190 et seq.

[63] *See for instance* Kapteyn 1982, p. 28 et seq., and Gorsira 1988, p. 59.

[64] GA 2625 (XXV) of 1970 includes a similar provision in its section on self-determination: 'Every State shall refrain from any action aimed at the partial or total disruption of the national unity and territorial integrity of any other State or country.'

[65] Of the 11 Trust Territories, only Togoland (became Togo in 1960), Nauru (1968) and Western Samoa (became Samoa in 1962) have become independent states within the boundaries as they were administered as Trust Territories. The French Cameroons and Tanganyika at first also became independent within the colonial borders, but were soon thereafter joined with other territories. The other Trust Territories were either divided up or joined with other territories, in each case with the approval of the UN.

sometimes called on the administering state to ensure the integrity of territories that were on the verge of independence.[66]

A quick look at the first list of NSGTs of 1946 reveals that many of these territories have been broken up or joined with other territories. The Comoros were separated from Madagascar, and subsequently Mayotte from the Comoros; Niue was separated from the Cook Islands; Saint-Martin and Saint-Barthélémy from Guadeloupe; Aruba from the Netherlands Antilles; the Cayman Islands were separated from Jamaica, as were the Turks and Caicos Islands (which were subsequently adjoined to the Bahamas, from which they were again separated before that country became independent); the Leeward Islands were split up into St Kitts-Nevis-Anguilla (from which Anguilla was later separated), Antigua, Montserrat, and the British Virgin Islands;[67] the High Commission Terrritories of the Western Pacific became the Solomon Islands, Pitcairn and the Gilbert and Ellice Islands, which last colony was again broken up to become the independent states of Kiribati and Tuvalu; the British Indian Ocean Territory was created by separating the Chagos Archipelago from Mauritius in 1965; and the Cocos (Keeling) Islands and Christmas Island, which were administered by the UK as part of Singapore, were transferred to Australia.

During the first two decades after 1945, these separations were decided by the Administering states, although they were often desired by the islands themselves. The more recent separations were approved by the populations or the governments of the islands. None of these separations was explicitly approved by the UN, but only in the case of the separation of Mayotte from the Comoros,[68] and the Chagos Archipelago from Mauritius did the GA clearly object.[69] The Decolonization Committee was allowed to observe the referendum on the 'secession' of the Ellice Islands,[70] and closely followed the case of

---

[66] *See* Clark 1980, p. 79, and p. 80, note 423, with references to the cases of Fernando Poo (part of Equatorial Guinea), Mayotte, and Banaba (part of the Gilbert Islands). *See also* Buchheit 1978 for the cases of Bangladesh and Biafra. Administering states have also often resisted fragmentational tendencies without the interference of the UN, *see for instance* the cases of Rodrigues (forced by the UK to remain a part of Mauritius), Barbuda (*idem* in relation to Antigua), and Tobago (*idem* in relation to Trinidad). *See* Lowenthal 1980 on these cases. The Netherlands has also resisted the Aruban wish for a separate status for many decades, with Aruba making appeals to the UN, but in vain.

[67] The British Caribbean territories were all joined together to form the West Indies Federation in 1956, which was dissolved only two years later.

[68] *See* GA Res. 31/4 of 21 October 1976. In that same year, France was out-voted 14 to 1 in the Security Council on the issue of Mayotte, and was forced to use its veto to prevent the adoption of a condemning Resolution (S/PV. 1888 para. 247).

[69] *See* GA Res. 2066 (XX) of 1965, and Houbert 1980, p. 154, and De Smith 1968, pp. 611-612.

[70] *See* the Report of the UN Visiting Mission to the Gilbert and Ellice Islands, reproduced in the Report of the Decolonization Committee of 1974, Vol. V, Chapter XXI, Annex I (UN Doc. A/9623/Add.5). *See also* Macdonald 1982 and Drower 1992, p. 167 et seq.

Anguilla,[71] but in neither case did it recommend that the islands should stay together.

These examples show that the principle of non-disruption appears to have only limited meaning with respect to the right to self-determination and decolonization of small island territories, despite the apodictic language of paragraph 6 of Resolution 1514.

The example of the Comoros does suggest that states and UN organs consider that not only the population of the 'seceding' part of the territory has to agree to a break-up, but also the population of the rest of the territory. However, this rule is not clearly supported by other cases. It has been more common for the administering state to be led mainly by the desires of the dissident island(s), more or less forcing the other islands to agree to a break-up. The secession of Anguilla was criticized by some governments, since it was accomplished in the face of resistance by the government in St Kitts, but the criticism was far from unanimous, and not very strong.

The case of Aruba is somewhat comparable to that of Anguilla, and the reaction of the Netherlands was also somewhat similar to that of the UK. It could be argued that the secession of Aruba was inconsistent with the principle of non-disruption, because the break-up of the Country was not approved by the population in a referendum. The government of the Netherlands Antilles, and of the separate island territories agreed to the secession of Aruba, but no referendum was held (apart from the referendum of 1977 on Aruba[72]).

The application of the right to self-determination and decolonization to these cases would imply that a break-up of a territory that falls under GA Resolutions 1514 and 1541 cannot proceed without the consent of the entire population (or at least the majority), since such a break-up clearly affects the future political status of the territory. Resolutions 1514 and 2625 (and many others) moreover condemn actions that violate the national unity of a territory.

It seems logical to assume that when a people is entitled freely to determine its own political status, it should also be able to choose to end its existence entirely by dissolving into a number of new peoples and to attribute parts of its territory to each new people that is thus created. International law does not forbid this when it happens in an independent state, and it probably does not

---

[71] The Decolonization Committee heard petitioners from Anguilla in 1967 (UN Doc. A/AC.109/SC.4/SR.85-87, 24-25 August 1967). It expressed 'grave concern' about the deployment of British troops in Anguilla in 1969 (UN Doc. A/7623/Rev.1, Vol. IV, Chapter XXIII, para. 17). *See also* the statements by Hungary and Tanzania in the Fourth Committee, GAOR (XXIV) 4th Committee, 1851st Meeting, paras. 15-17 and para. 29. For the problem of Anguilla, *see* Fisher 1968, Brisk 1969, Barbier 1974, p. 619 et seq., De Smith 1974, p. 73, and Freymond 1980.

[72] *See* chapter 6 for this referendum.

either when it concerns a dependency, as long as the right to self-determination is not violated.[73]

UN-supervised referendums could be considered obligatory in cases such as these, as *Franck & Hoffman* write.[74] But the international practice outlined *above* shows that many break-ups of island territories were realized without referendums, and in those cases where a referendum was held, it was often only in the seceding part of the territory and not on all of the islands.[75]

8.2.1 The Non-Disruption Principle and the Break-Up of the Netherlands Antilles

Gorsira and *Hoeneveld* argue that the non-disruption principle no longer applied after the right to self-determination of the six islands had been recognized.[76] The problem with this argument is that the recognition of the right to self-determination of the separate island territories was not approved by the population.[77] *Kapteyn* considers that the non-disruption principle did apply to the secession of Aruba, but thinks that the Netherlands cannot be blamed for disrupting the 'national unity' of the Country of the Netherlands Antilles, because it consistently opposed the secession of Aruba for many decades.[78] This may be an acceptable interpretation of GA Resolution 1514. The Netherlands and other states are not allowed to undertake any attempt to disrupt 'the national unity and the territorial integrity' of a country, but this probably does not mean that the Netherlands Antilles itself is not allowed to undertake such attempts, seeing that the prohibition of 1514 is aimed at states and aims to protect the Netherlands Antilles. If the Country itself decides to forego this protection, it should be allowed to do so, but only with the support of the population, since the right to self-determination is clearly affected.[79]

---

[73] In a similar sense, *see* Clark 1980, pp. 78-83.

[74] Franck & Hoffman 1976, pp. 336-7.

[75] *See for instance* the cases of the Gilbert Islands, the Northern Mariana Islands, Aruba and Anguilla, where referenda on the issue of secession were held on the seceding islands, but not in the rest of the territory.

[76] Gorsira 1988, p. 59, and Hoeneveld 2005, p. 65.

[77] The Dutch government appears to think that the non-disruption principle still applies to the Netherlands Antilles. In 2004, the Dutch Minister for Kingdom Affairs wrote to the Executive Council of Bonaire that the non-disruption principle prohibited the Dutch government from involving itself with the planned referendum on the island and from providing a subsidy (which Bonaire had requested).

[78] Kapteyn 1982, p. 29.

[79] Franck & Hoffman 1976, pp. 336-7 also consider this the most important criterion. Clark 1980, pp. 80-83 is less certain, but also tends towards this conclusion. Crawford 2006, p. 620 states that the plebiscite of 1977 in Aruba was not permitted to justify its secession from the Antilles, but it is not clear from the text of the second edition of *Crawford*'s study whether the author was aware that Aruba achieved separate status in 1986.

This issue was debated in the Lower House in 1978, when the Kingdom legislature was preparing to approve the application of the UN Human Rights Covenants of 1966 (the ICCPR and ICESCR) to the entire Kingdom. The Kingdom government was of the opinion that the non-disruption principle meant that it could not cooperate with the independence of Aruba against the wishes of 'those concerned' – presumably the government and the *Staten* of the Netherlands Antilles, of which Aruba was then still a part.[80] According to Aruba, however, the non-disruption principle did not apply because the Netherlands Antilles did not represent a nation.[81] Representatives of Aruba submitted a proposal to the Lower House that would recognize this.[82] The Lower House instead adopted a statement declaring that Article 1 of the Covenant should not prejudge the negotiations on the new legal order of the Kingdom, as it was a up to the constituting parts of the Kingdom to take a sovereign decision on that matter.[83]

It was not considered necessary to ensure popular support in the five remaining islands. The right to self-determination and the principle of non-disruption nonetheless demand that the secession of an island should have the

---

[80] *Kamerstukken II* 1978/79, 13 932 (R 1037), no. 14, p. 2. The government made a somewhat inappropriate comparison between the situation of Aruba and that of New Guinea, and stated that it could not 'again' cooperate with the transfer of sovereignty – against the wishes of the population – to part of a country. According to a memorandum prepared by the Dutch Ministry of Foreign Affairs shortly before the debate in the Lower House on the Covenants, it was 'unthinkable' that the UN would accept a secession of Aruba from the Netherlands Antilles on the basis of the right to self-determination. The Netherlands Antilles were on their way to independence and had a government which represented the entire country. Encouraging the secession of one island from such a country would represent too dangerous a precedent for other countries with a federal or similar structure (Memorandum of 1 September 1977 (unpublished), cited in Oostindie & Klinkers 2001c, p. 482.)

[81] *Handelingen II* 1978/79, pp. 89-162. *See also* Hoeneveld 2005, pp. 57-8.

[82] Proposal submitted by Croes and Figaroa on 21 September 1978, *see Kamerstukken II* 1978/79, 13 932 (R1037), no. 16. It was later withdrawn by its sponsors when it became clear it did not enjoy majority support. Several members of the Lower House, as well as the Minister for Netherlands Antillean Affairs, considered that Aruba had 'a' right to self-determination. Some members also claimed that Article 1 would not prevent Aruba from exercising its right to self-determination because the Article did not refer to the principle of non-disruption. Others, however, thought that the Article *did* include that principle, and this appears to have been the opinion of the government as well.

[83] Proposal submitted by Roethof c.s. on 21 September 1978, *see Kamerstukken II* 1978/79, 13 932 (R1037), no. 17. The proposal was adopted without a vote, *see Handelingen II* 1978/79, p. 162. The Lower House thus declared that a decision on the status of Aruba fell within the domestic jurisdiction of the Kingdom. Apparently, the Netherlands parliament thought it could recognize the right to self-determination, ratify the Covenants, and at the same time bar the door to the influence of the Covenants to the relations with Aruba. This is obviously not possible. Once the Kingdom ratified the Covenants, the 'sovereign decision' that the Kingdom partners would take on Aruba had to conform with Article 1.

support of the population of the entire territory, although it is not clear from the international practice what form such popular support should take. In the absence of much visible or persistent protests in the other islands to the secession of Aruba, and seeing that the international practice contains other examples where secessions were realized in a similar way without provoking international censure, it should probably be assumed that international law was not violated.

If precedence is given to the freedom of choice of each separate island, however, a problem occurs when the populations of the islands express different preferences which cannot be reconciled with each other, as happened in 2005, when the population of one island (St Eustatius) chose to keep the Antilles together, while the referendums on the other islands had revealed a clear preference for breaking up the Antilles. It was obviously impossible to realize both these wishes, therefore the freedom of choice of either St Eustatius or the other islands had to be denied. If it is assumed that each island has the right to self-determination and decolonization, it would be unacceptable to deny the 'people' of one of the islands the right to determine its own constitutional future. In this case, precedence was given to the choice of the four islands who chose to break up the Antilles,[84] but this choice was not publicly motivated or defended, nor was it really challenged. Since the approximately 2,600 inhabitants of St Eustatius form only a small minority within the Netherlands Antilles (186,000 inhabitants), this choice was politically obvious, but still hard to reconcile with the idea that St Eustatius has the right to self-determination. This decision to some extent denied the right to self-determination of St Eustatius, but any other solution would have denied that right to the other four islands. It could therefore be defended as an equitable and reasonable solution, especially when the population of St Eustatius will be given the opportunity, at some point, to give its opinion on the new status that will be devised for that island.

In one respect, the outcome of this conflict is rather unusual in view of the practice within the Kingdom and abroad. Generally speaking, secession claims seem to be less readily acknowledged than the desire to maintain the status quo. This factor should have worked in favour of St Eustatius' wishes. Another factor which has strongly influenced some of these cases is the threat of violence,[85] but in 2005, there were no indications on any of the islands of the Netherlands Antilles that this threat existed. It seems that a third factor – the

---

[84] *See* the '*Slotverklaring van de start-Ronde Tafel Conferentie van het Koninkrijk der Nederlanden, gehouden op 26 november 2005 in Willemstad, te Curaçao.*'

[85] Brison 2005, p. 40 et seq. even concludes that constitutional changes in a 'colonial' context are never realized unless there exists a threat of violence. In his view, St Maarten should 'engage in creative violence' to realize its *status aparte.*

wishes of larger islands are often given precedence over smaller ones – was decisive in this case.

8.3   CONCLUSION

The recognition of the right to self-determination of the individual islands of the Netherlands Antilles in 1981 has thrown into doubt the application of the non-disruption to the Netherlands Antilles. It is not certain whether the population of the Netherlands Antilles as a whole should still be considered as a 'people' entitled to self-determination, nor is it clear whether the Country of the Netherlands Antilles is still an entity entitled to international legal protection of its unity on the basis of the principle of non-disruption (*uti possidetis*).

The international practice in comparable cases has not – at least not consistently – upheld the rule proclaimed by Resolution 1514 that states are not allowed to cooperate with the break-up of overseas territories. If there is popular support for a break-up of an overseas island territory, there has often been no clear international opposition to the secession of one or more islands from such a territory, even if it occurs shortly before independence is achieved. The practice does not reveal, however, what form this popular support should take. A referendum seems to be considered indispensable, but should such a referendum be held on all of the islands, or only on the seceding island(s)? This is uncertain, but it is certain that some form of consent of the territory as a whole is necessary. Absence of strong popular opposition has often been considered enough, as in the case of the secession of Aruba.

The current situation within the Netherlands Antilles is exceptional because separate referendums have been held on all of the five islands based on the right to self-determination. The outcome on St Eustatius – the Netherlands Antilles should remain a single Country – is not compatible with the outcome on the other four islands, which voted in favour of breaking up the Country. The Round Table Conference of 2005 decided to go ahead with the break-up of the Netherlands Antilles, which seems a reasonable decision if the population of St Eustatius is given the opportunity to express its opinion on the new status that will be devised for that island.

Chapter 9
THE RIGHT TO SELF-DETERMINATION IN RELATION TO THE EUROPEAN UNION

Most remaining overseas territories of European states maintain more or less close relations with the European Union. Twenty-one of them,[1] including the Netherlands Antilles and Aruba, belong to the category of Overseas Countries and Territories (OCT) of the European Union. The OCTs are a very diverse group, located in the Pacific, Indian, and Atlantic Oceans, in the Caribbean Sea and in Antarctica. They have almost no common characteristics apart from their OCT status and the fact that they are all islands[2] located far from their respective mother countries, Denmark, France, the Netherlands and the UK. Five OCTs have no – or a very small – permanent population, and the others have populations between 2,000 (Falklands) and 246,000 (French Polynesia).[3] Together they have a population of approximately one million. Their land area is small, if one does not count the ice covered areas of Greenland and Antarctica, but they have an exclusive economic zone that is much larger than the total area of the European Union.[4] All of the inhabited OCTs were originally

---

[1] Most sources count only 20 OCTs, because they do not include Bermuda, which is an OCT according to Annex II to the EC Treaty, but is not treated as such in OCT Decisions at its own request. The other OCTs are Anguilla, British Virgin Islands, Cayman Islands, Falkland Islands, Montserrat, Pitcairn, St Helena, Turks and Caicos Islands, British Antarctic Territory, the British Indian Ocean Territory, and the South Georgia and Sandwich Islands of the UK, Greenland of Denmark, Mayotte, New Caledonia, French Polynesia, the French Southern and Antarctic Territories, Saint-Pierre and Miquelon, Wallis and Futuna of France, and Aruba and the Netherlands Antilles of the Netherlands.

[2] Not counting the territorial claims of France and the UK on the continent of Antarctica, which are part of the OCTs French Southern and Antarctic Territories and the British Antarctic Territory.

[3] *See* the brochure published by the Overseas Countries and Territories Association (OCTA), 'Overseas Countries and Territories and the European Union: A shared history, a partnership for prosperity', December 2003.

[4] Geographical data on the OCT as a group are hard to find. I have added up the EEZ of the territories as listed on the website of Sea Around Us <www.seaaroundus.org>, which leads to roughly 15 million km². The land area of the EU is less than 4 million km². The total EEZ of the EU is some 5 million km², half of which belongs to the Ultra-Peripheral Territories of the EU

S. Hillebrink, The Right to Self-Determination and Post-Colonial Governance
© 2008, T·M·C·ASSER PRESS, *The Hague, The Netherlands and the Author*

NSGTs, and most of them still are. The other overseas territories of the EU member states are either Ultra-Peripheral Territories (UPTs), or have a special protocol-based relationship with the EU.

Their political and economic importance to the European Union is usually considered to be very limited. The general literature on the EU offers a familiar view to readers of literature on international law interested in overseas territories. Almost none of the studies on European law pay any substantial attention to the OCTs.[5] Those that do, often warn their readers that this subject has little importance,[6] or treat it as an annex to the EU-ACP association.

In recent years the question has been raised whether the Netherlands Antilles and Aruba should not become part of the EU as 'ultra-peripheral territories' (UPT) or obtain another relation with the EU. This question has become a part of the status debate in the Kingdom, since a choice for a different relation with the Netherlands may also require a different status in or outside of the EU. In some cases, the cooperation of the EU and its member states may be required to realize a process of decolonization and self-determination in the Kingdom of the Netherlands. For this reason it would be interesting to see whether the international law of decolonization also applies to the relations between the EU and its overseas territories. I will also discuss the differences between the status of OCT and UPT and how a choice between these options could be made.

9.1   Obligations for the EU Resulting from the Law of Decolonization?

As an organization that has its roots in international law, and as an international person, the EU is bound to respect international law.[7] General international law must be considered to be of a higher order than EU law, and the peremptory norms of international law, or *jus cogens*, form part of the legal order of the EU, both in its internal application and in relation to third states.[8] As the right to self-determination is considered to be part of *jus cogens*, the EU will therefore have to respect it. It has been argued that the EU is also bound by

---

(again based on the data of Sea Around Us). For some other geographical and demographic data on the OCTs and UPTs, *see* Ziller 1991, p. 178 et seq.

[5] A notable exception is Von der Groeben/Thiesing/Ehlermann 1999.

[6] *See for instance* Verhoeven 2001, p. 97.

[7] Schermers & Blokker 2003, para. 1335 and 1572 et seq., Bowett/Sands/Klein 2001, para. 14-034, and Vanhamme 2001, p. 96. *See also* the Advisory Opinion of the International Court of Justice on the interpretation of the Agreement of 25 March 1951, between the WHO and Egypt, *ICJ Reports* 1980, p. 73.

[8] Vanhamme 2001, p. 71 et seq. and p. 100, and Lawson 1999, para. 219-38.

treaties of which it is not a party, if it concerns a law-making treaty that codifies general principles of law.[9] Both the UN Charter and the UN Human Rights Covenants qualify for this criterion. Article 103 of the UN Charter furthermore provides that the obligations of the member states under the Charter prevail over their obligations under any other treaty. While this may not in itself create an obligation for the EU to adhere to the Charter, it does imply that the member states should make sure that the EU does not violate the Charter. Decisions of the UN General Assembly and the Security Council may also affect the EU, if they are binding on its member states.[10] Some of the GA resolutions discussed in the previous Chapters, mainly Resolution 1514, 1541 and 2625, which have determined the content of the right to self-determination and decolonization, are binding on the EU in that they provide evidence of peremptory norms of international law, and perhaps also because they constitute interpretations of the Charter that are binding on the member states. The EU must therefore be considered obligated to respect the right to self-determination of 'colonial countries and peoples' when exercising its powers.

The Preamble of the EC Treaty shows that the signatories were aware of this obligation in 1957, since it states:

INTENDING to confirm the solidarity which binds Europe and the overseas countries and desiring to ensure the development of their prosperity, in accordance with the principles of the Charter of the United Nations ...

Part IV of the EC Treaty, which deals with the OCT association, should therefore be read in the light of the UN Charter, most importantly Article 73,[11] which the founding states of the EEC had in mind when drafting Part IV (*see below*). It is not hard to see the similarities between these provisions. Both create an obligation to further the development of the territories, whereby the interest of the overseas populations should be paramount. Part IV, read in conjunction with the Preamble and Article 3 of the EC Treaty, can be seen as a partial attempt to realise the goals of Chapter XI of the UN Charter in the economic development of the NSGTs.

Through the substitution theory, as accepted by the Court in *International Fruit Company III*, it could be concluded that the EC (and the EU) are bound by Article 73 of the Charter 'in so far as under the EEC Treaty the Community has assumed the powers previously exercised by Member States' in the area

---

[9] Schermers & Blokker 2003, para. 1577. In a different sense, *see* Lawson 1999, paras. 198-218.

[10] Schermers & Blokker 2003, para. 1580.

[11] In a similar sense, *see* Vanhamme 2001, pp. 56-7, pp. 71-5, and p. 133.

governed by that Article.[12] In the *International Fruit Company* case, the treaty concerned was the GATT, to which the EEC was also not a party. The Court considered that since the EEC Treaty and the subsequent practice of the EEC organs showed that the EEC had been granted the authority to exercise the functions of its member states under the GATT, the EEC should also take on the obligations arising from that treaty.

This outcome cannot be simply copied to Article 73 of the Charter, because the member states have certainly not (yet) transferred entirely their authority to deal with their overseas territories to the EC or the EU. Through the European integration process and the establishment of the OCT association, the member states have lost some of their abilities to fulfil their obligations, notably with regard to economic measures. Most of the areas of the OCT Association concern subjects which can be handled by the EU or the member states, but with regard to the preferential trade, and to some extent the four freedoms, the EU has exclusive powers in relation to the OCTs. Paragraphs (a) and (d) of Article 73 state that the Administering States should further the economic development of the NSGTs. As regards the exclusive powers of the EU, the reference in Article 73 to 'the Administering States' should now presumably refer to the EU. [13] When it exercises its shared powers with regard to the OCTs, the EU is also obligated to strive towards the economic goals of Article 73, and as the European integration progresses, other areas of Article 73 might become of importance to the EU policies as well.

Should this mean that the interpretation of Article 73 by the General Assembly, and the customary law based on it, should be applied to the relations of the EU with the OCTs as well? Neither the EC nor the EU have co-operated with this development of Chapter XI, nor have they consented to it. Most of the EU member states have played an important role in developing the law of self-determination and decolonization at the UN, but normally this would only mean that the member states have adopted obligations under this law, and not the EC/EU. On the other hand, the explicit reference to the principles of the UN Charter in the EC Treaty could imply a wish to be bound by their subsequent development by the organs of the UN as well. The development of Article 73 had already come a long way in 1957, with the adoption of GA Resolution 742

---

[12] Judgment of the European Court of Justice of 12 December 1972 in Joined Cases 21/72 to 24/72 *International Fruit Company NV and others* v. *Produktschap voor Groenten en Fruit*, [1972] *ECR* 01219. For the substitution theory, *see* Lawson 1999, p. 55 et seq.

[13] A corollary of this reasoning is that the EU should report to the UN Secretary-General under Article 73(e) of the UN Charter on the OCTs that are still considered NSGTs, together with the Administering State. This practice is not followed, although the EU Presidency does sometimes speak on behalf of the EU member states in the debates in the Fourth Committee of the GA on decolonization, *see*, for example, the statement of 16 October 2001, UN Doc. A/56/23.

(VIII) in 1953. The Committee of Six which would draw up the Principles of GA Resolution 1541 (XIV) was established only one year after the EEC Treaty came into force, and included two of the current EU member states (the UK and the Netherlands). Also, a number of the Resolutions dealing with self-determination and decolonization are considered to reflect customary law, and perhaps even *jus cogens*, which is binding on the EU in any case. It must be assumed, therefore, that the content of such Resolutions as 1514, 1541 and 2625 is binding on the EU when it deals with the OCTs. The OCT group largely coincides with the list of NSGTs used by the GA, and the Netherlands Antilles and Aruba should probably be considered to fall under the application of the law of decolonization as well (*see* chapter 6).

The EU should therefore not frustrate an attempt by an OCT to become independent or to achieve some other political status in a process of decolonization and self-determination. It also means that the EU should not change the status of the OCTs without their consent. The Commission has recognised that it is not for the EU to unilaterally determine the future of the OCT association, and that major choices in this area can only be made by the overseas peoples themselves.[14] But the EU is not only obligated to allow the territories to exercise their freedom of choice with regard to their mother countries, it can – and in some cases must – play a role in the realization of these political choices.

Positive obligations for the EU can be construed in two areas, which will be discussed in the next sections. First, in the formulation of the content of the OCT Association, which is an exclusive competence of the Council of Ministers of the EU, and which may affect the measure of self-government achieved by the OCTs and the choices they have made with respect to their mother country. Second, the EU should, in certain circumstances, cooperate with status changes that are desired by an OCT, although this duty will in many cases dissolve into a duty for the member states because it will usually require an amendment of the EC Treaty.

9.2 OCT STATUS

9.2.1 History

The association with the OCTs was created at the request of France at the very end of the negotiations on the EEC in 1957. France still had substantial eco-

---

[14] Communication of 20 May 1999 by the Commission to the Council and the European Parliament, 'The Status of OCTs Associated with the EC and Options for "OCT 2000"' (COM (1999) 163 def).

nomic interests in its African territories, which were based on monopolies and trade preferences that would conflict with the economic community.[15] Full membership for these territories was out of the question, mainly because the Netherlands and Germany were not prepared to pay for the French '*mission civilatrice*' in Africa.[16] There also existed fears that the EEC could be accused of continuing or renewing colonial rule in Africa. The Soviet Union and some Third World countries denounced the proposals of France as colonial, and the issue was raised at the UN.[17] In the prospective OCTs, complaints were uttered about the fact that the overseas territories were not allowed to participate in the negotiations.[18]

After France threatened not to join the EEC, an agreement was reached that imports from the overseas territories would be allowed preferential access to the EEC, while similar imports from other tropical countries would become subject to high customs duties. Also, the EEC would contribute substantially to the development of the territories.[19] It seems Germany and the Netherlands agreed to this mainly because they wanted to keep France on board, but it was also expected that the association might have some political advantages. Many Western Europeans at the time hoped for the creation of 'Eurafrica', meaning that Africa would remain within the sphere of influence of Western Europe. The association would offer opportunities for companies from the other member states to venture into the French and Belgian territories, thereby perhaps contributing to the development of these territories. It was hoped the association would foster democracy in Africa after independence (which was expected to come soon). Africans would not mistrust the EEC as they did the French and Belgians. Thus, the new states might be prevented from becoming dependent on the Soviet Union or the USA.[20] According to *Nehring* this consideration was decisive in the end, but *Van Benthem van den Bergh* thought that Germany and the Netherlands were not receptive to this argument at all.[21] In any case, the member states decided to contribute the equivalent of US$ 581 million in

---

[15] *See* Van Benthem van den Bergh 1962b, p. 15 et seq. for the French economic relations with its TOMs in the 1950s and p. 45 et seq. for France's reasons why it needed a relationship between the EEC and the TOMs.

[16] Olyslager 1958, p. 13, Van Benthem van den Bergh 1962b, p. 48, Houben 1965, pp. 12-14, and Agarwal 1966, p. 19.

[17] *See for instance* the debate in the Committee on Information from Non-Self-Governing Territories, a fore-runner of the Decolonization Committee (UN GAOR (XIV), Supplement No. 15 (A/4111), pp. 8-9.

[18] Van Benthem van den Bergh 1962b, p. 51.

[19] Olyslager 1958, p. 11 et seq. and Van Benthem van den Bergh 1962b, p. 53 et seq.

[20] Agarwal 1966, pp. 19-20.

[21] Nehring 1963, p. 11, and Van Benthem van den Bergh 1962b, p. 48.

economic aid to the French, Dutch, Belgian and Italian territories that became OCTs in 1958.[22]

The Treaty provisions on the OCTs were intended to comply with Chapters XI and XII of the UN Charter.[23] All of the original OCTs were NSGTs or Trust Territories, and the Netherlands government considered that the association was only intended for such colonial territories.[24] The Administering States could use an organization as the EEC to realize their obligation under paragraph (d) of Article 73 of the UN Charter 'to co-operate with one another and, when and where appropriate, with specialised international bodies with a view to practical achievement of the social, economic, and scientific purposes set forth in this Article.' In a sense, Germany and Luxembourg – the only founding members of the EEC that were not Administering States – thus accepted part of the 'sacred trust' of Chapter XI to develop the NSGTs and Trust Territories towards self-government, and to 'promote the well-being of the inhabitants of these territories.' By creating the association with the OCTs the founding states wished to make clear that the relations with the overseas territories would not be characterized by Euro-centric economic exploitation, but by the desire to develop the territories in the interest of the overseas peoples. The EEC thus became a participant in the process of decolonization.

The initial fears about the negative political and economic consequences that the OCT association might have for the EEC were soon proven unfounded. In a debate in the European Parliament in 1960, the association was stated to be advantageous for both sides and a German study showed that there was no evidence of trade deflections.[25] Accusations of colonialism were silenced when most of the original OCTs became independent around 1960. Their preferential treatment was continued for the most part through the agreement of Yaoundé, which created an association with the independent African states, later widened to cover a number of Pacific and Caribbean former colonies as well, through the agreements of Lomé. The association with these African, Caribbean and Pacific (ACP) states was economically and politically much more important to the Community than the association with the remaining OCTs, which were few and small, especially before Denmark and the UK had joined the Community. For a short period around 1962, there were even hardly any OCTs left.[26] The

---

[22] Houben 1965, p. 14. The Dutch territory was Netherlands New Guinea. Surinam and the Netherlands Antilles became OCTs in 1962 and 1964, *see below.*

[23] Agarwal 1966, p. 23.

[24] *Kamerstukken II* 1956/57, 4725, no. 3, p. 42.

[25] Nehring 1963, p. 63 et seq.

[26] Only French Somaliland, the Comoros, New Caledonia, French Polynesia and a number of very small French territories remained. Surinam became an OCT in 1962, the Netherlands Antilles in 1964. A number of new OCTs were added after the UK entered the Community in

Council decisions which detailed the OCT association therefore did not take the trouble to create any specific measures for the OCTs, but merely copied the provisions of the development agreements with the ACP states.

The attitude of the E(E)C between 1962 and 1991 was characterized by the 'OUT' perspective, as EU Commissioner Pinheiro has termed it.[27] According to *Pinheiro*, the association's ambiguity and the member states' ambivalence towards it, was caused by two different perspectives which battled for dominance since 1957. On the one hand, the 'IN' perspective stressed that the OCTs belonged to member states and should therefore share as much as possible in the results of European integration. This perspective had been dominant in the formulation of Part IV of the EEC Treaty. On the other hand, the Council's policy of treating the OCTs similarly to the independent ACP states, stressed that the OCTs were not part of the EC, and were similar to third states. The case law of the European Court of Justice clearly supports this 'OUT' perspective. But the parallelism with the ACP states has become increasingly considered as a handicap for the OCTs.[28]

In 1991, the 'IN' perspective became prominent again by a concerted effort of the OCTs (especially the Netherlands Antilles) and their mother countries. In the Council, it was the Netherlands that convinced the other member states to stop treating the OCTs as if they were ACP states. The OCT Association has since developed into a *sui generis* form of association, with characteristics distinctly different from the relation EU-ACP and from associations with other third countries.

9.2.2 Terms of the Association

The OCTs are not part of the EC or the EU. According to the European Court of Justice, the OCTs are in a position towards the EC that is similar to third countries.[29] The provisions of the Treaties and the secondary legislation do not apply in the OCTs, unless the EC Treaty explicitly states otherwise.[30] Currently,

---

1973, and in 1986 the Danish territory of Greenland became an OCT. The Portuguese and Spanish overseas territories became UPTs upon the accession of their mother countries (*see below*).

[27] Pinheiro 1999, p. 11.

[28] De Bernardi 1998, p. 141. Pisuisse 1991, p. 327, thinks the OCTs actually benefit from the parallelism with the ACP states, because of the stronger position of these states, and because the 'development country-friendly' European Parliament has to consent to the ACP Conventions but not to the OCT Decisions, at least not formally.

[29] Opinion 1/78 of the European Court of Justice of 4 October 1979 in *International Agreement on Natural Rubber,* [1979] *ECR* 2871.

[30] Judgment of the European Court of Justice of 12 February 1992 in Case C-260/90 *Bernard Leplat* v. *Territory of French Polynesia* [1992] *ECR* I-00643.

probably only the provisions of Part IV of the EC Treaty and the secondary legislation based on Part IV are applicable to the OCTs. Even though the territory of the OCTs is not part of the EU, most of their inhabitants are European citizens, because they have the nationality of a member state.[31] For that reason, the Treaties and the legislation regarding European citizenship may also have application in the OCTs, although it is not yet certain to what extent. Whether Part II of the EC Treaty (Citizenship of the Union) applies in the OCTs in the same way that it applies in the EU, is a question that has been debated ever since the creation of European citizenship.[32] The European Court of Justice decided in 2006, in a case concerning the right to vote in elections for the European Parliament in Aruba, that the citizenship rights of Part II apply to European citizens who live in an OCT, as far as relevant.[33]

The secondary legislation under Part IV of the EC Treaty consists of the Council's OCT Decision, which is a 10-yearly decision *sui generis* based on unanimity between the member states, in which the terms of the association are detailed, and a small body of further Council and Commission legislation which implements the OCT Decision (mainly dealing with imports from the OCTs). No other EU legislation is applicable to the OCTs, a fact that appears sometimes to be overlooked in practice.[34]

The member states with OCTs have remained authorized to formulate separate policies for their OCTs, also in most areas where the EU has exclusive competence. For the Kingdom of the Netherlands this means that since only the Country of the Netherlands is member of the Community, the Kingdom may still represent the Netherlands Antilles and Aruba in foreign affairs independently of EU policies, and, for instance, conclude trade conventions that will only have application in one or both Caribbean Countries (*see below* in section 9.4.3).

---

[31] Article 17, para. 1 of the EC Treaty declares that all persons in possession of the nationality of a member state are European citizens. Only the inhabitants of the UK OCTs did not have the nationality of their mother country, but in 2001 they were granted the option to acquire UK nationality and since then most OCT citizens are also EU citizens.

[32] De Bernardi 1998, p. 153 et seq.

[33] Judgment in Case C-300/04 (*Eman & Sevinger*), *JO* 2006/C 281/09.

[34] Von der Groeben/Thiesing/Ehlermann 1999, p. 3/2096. The Netherlands government also considers that EU law as such does not apply to the Netherlands Antilles and Aruba, apart from Part IV of the EC Treaty, *see Kamerstukken II* 2003/04, 29 394, no. 6, p. 14. Article 183, para. 5 of the EC Treaty provides an exception in that it declares the EC's rules regarding freedom of establishment applicable to the OCTs. But this provision has been virtually annulled by the OCT Decision of 2001. Another exception is the Council Decision that introduced the euro as legal tender in Saint-Pierre and Miquelon and Mayotte (31 December 1998, 1999/95/EC). These territories (which are more integrated with France than the other French OCTs) used the French franc before, and France wished to maintain this parallelism.

Free Trade

The EC Treaty's provisions on the OCT association deal mainly with the establishment of an incomplete free trade area between the EC and the OCTs, with elements of a common market.[35] The OCTs are not part of the territory of the Community, but they have more free access to it than third countries. Article 3, paragraph 1 (s) of the EC Treaty lists the association with the OCTs as one of the activities the EC will undertake 'in order to increase trade and promote jointly economic and social development.' The purpose of the association is 'to promote the economic and social development of the countries and territories and to establish close economic relations between them and the Community as a whole.' Although, according to the Court of Justice, the EC takes 'a fundamentally favourable approach' towards the OCTs,[36] this does not mean that the EC Treaty intends to integrate the OCTs into the European market or the customs union. The Court of Justice has remarked that such an interpretation 'goes far beyond what was envisaged by the Treaty.'[37] Before the OCTs could be granted the same treatment as the European parts of the member states, the EC and the OCTs would first have to agree on common economic policies, which they clearly have not.[38] The OCT trade has therefore remained subject to several EU import restrictions, especially with regard to agricultural products.

Part IV clearly bears the traces of a hurried political compromise,[39] which means that the wording is rather vague and leaves many issues open to debate. An example is Article 183 of the EC Treaty (originally Article 132), which provides that member states shall apply to their trade with the OCTs the same treatment as they apply to trade with each other. In the doctrine, this provision was generally interpreted as laying down a concrete obligation for the member states. Until 1999, most authors thought that Article 183 did not merely lay down objectives, as the Article itself claims, but created obligations for the member states, the OCTs and the EC to take concrete measures.[40] This was probably an historical and textually correct interpretation of the Treaty and reflected the intentions of the founding states to let the OCTs share in the re-

---

[35] Lauwaars 1991, p. 27.

[36] Judgment of the Court (Sixth Chamber) of 26 October 1994 in Case C-430/92 *Kingdom of the Netherlands* v. *Commission* [1994] *ECR* I-05197, para. 22.

[37] Judgment of the Court of 22 April 1997 in Case C-310/95 *Road Air BV* v. *Inspecteur der Invoerrechten en Accijnzen*, [1997] *ECR* I-02229, para. 34.

[38] Judgment of the Court of 8 February 2000 in Case C-17/98 *Emesa Sugar (Free Zone) NV* v. *Aruba*. [2000] *ECR* I-00675.

[39] Van Benthem van den Bergh 1962b, p. 51.

[40] *See for instance*, Olyslager 1958, p. 27, Van Benthem van den Bergh 1962, p. 53 et seq, Lauwaars & Bronckers 1991, Martha 1991, Dekker 1998, and Von der Groeben/Thiesing/ Ehlermann 1999, p. 3/2105.

moval of trade barriers in Europe, but the Court of Justice decided otherwise in a series of rather poorly motivated judgments. The Court has decided that Article 183 merely lays down the objectives of the association, which are 'to be achieved by a dynamic and progressive process.'[41] The Court has also granted the Council an exceptionally wide margin of discretion to decide on the methods and the time-frame to be adopted, and has thereby left it to the Council to decide how and when these objectives are to be achieved.[42]

The Court has also rejected the notion that the Council should not be allowed to retrace its steps once it has provided a measure in furtherance of the objectives of the association. In spite of the Court's interpretation that the goals of Part IV should be achieved by a progressive process, this does not prohibit the Council from taking regressive steps. Part IV does not contain a 'locking mechanism', as a committee of experts had considered in an advisory opinion requested by the Kingdom of the Netherlands.[43] Although it may be assumed that a complete abolition of the preferential treatment of the OCTs would be incompatible with the Treaty,[44] the Court has not given an indication as to the extent that the OCTs may rely on their acquired rights.[45] The reasoning of the Court even suggests that the interests of the OCTs will always have to give way if the Common Agricultural Policy of the EU is disturbed, in which case the Council is authorized to take 'any measure' capable of removing the disturbance.[46]

---

[41] Judgment of 11 February 1999 of the Court in Case C-390/95 P *Antillean Rice Mills (and others)* v. *Commission* [1999] *ECR* I-00769. *See also* the annotation by C.T. Dekker to this judgment in *Sociaal-Economische Wetgeving*, 2000, pp. 184-6.

[42] Judgment of 22 April 1997 in Case C-310/95 *Road Air BV* v. *Inspecteur der Invoerrechten en Accijnzen* [1997] *ECR* I-02229 and judgment of 8 February 2000 in Case C-17/98 *Emesa Sugar (Free Zone) NV* v. *Aruba* [2000] *ECR* I-00675. *See* Oliver 2002 for a review of the Court's case law.

[43] 'Advies commissie van deskundigen inzake de juridische aspecten van Deel IV van het EG-verdrag en het Zesde LGO-besluit', 3 April 1997. The committee's membership consisted of H.C. Posthumus Meyjes, T. Koopmans (a former judge in the European Court of Justice), R.H. Lauwaars, and J.S. van den Oosterkamp. The advice had been requested by the Kingdom government in the sugar and rice conflict, *see below*.

[44] Van der Wal 2003, para. 39. *See also* the *Antillean Rice Mills* case, where the Court decided that products originating in the OCTs are to be treated preferentially in comparison to products from third countries.

[45] Oliver 2003, p. 350. In a similar sense, *see* Raad van State 2004, p. 33.

[46] In the *Emesa* case (para. 40), the Court stated that: 'the Council, after weighing the objectives of association of the OCTs against those of the common agricultural policy, was entitled to adopt, in compliance with the principles of Community law circumscribing its margin of discretion, *any measure* capable of bringing to an end or mitigating such disturbances, including the removal or limitation of advantages previously granted to the OCTs' [emphasis added]. The text of the judgment provides no support for Van der Wal's interpretation that the Court has formulated heavy conditions before the Council may revoke privileges (Van der Wal 2003, para. 39).

The OCTs in return also remain free to determine their own trade policies with regard to the EU. They are only obligated to treat the member states similarly to the way they treat their mother country. The OCTs are allowed to levy customs duties on imports from EU member states or other OCTs in order to promote their own development, as long as they do not exceed the customs duties levied on imports from the mother country.[47]

Sugar and Rice

The relatively vague Treaty provisions on the trade relations with the OCTs were clarified somewhat during a 10-year conflict between the EU and the Netherlands Antilles and Aruba over the imports of rice and sugar. In 1991, the Netherlands 'after months of heated debate' convinced the Council to open the European market to agricultural products originating in the OCTs.[48] This was not an important innovation in itself because most OCTs do not produce agricultural exports, but the Decision also created free access of goods that were produced in an ACP state or the EU, and imported into an OCT where they received some minor 'working or processing.'[49] The OCTs would now be able to profit from the substantial difference in prices for agricultural products in the ACP states and the EU.

These rules of 'cumulated origin' had already been proposed by the Netherlands Antilles in 1959, even before it became an OCT, because it was expected such rules might attract a whole new type of industry to the islands.[50] The new rules were quickly used in the Netherlands Antilles, Aruba, and some UK overseas territories, to start exporting rice and sugar to the EU that had been produced in ACP states and had only been milled or re-packaged in the OCT, or received some other marginal working. It seems that considerable profits were made by the producers in the ACP states and by the trading companies, at first mainly through the rice trade, the volume of which increased exponentially between 1991 and 1996.[51] Whether the economy of

---

See also Dekker 1998, p. 278, who considers (based on the Court's judgment in the *Road Air* case) that 'the common agricultural policy simply takes precedence' over the OCT association.

[47] Article 184 of the EC Treaty.

[48] Article 101, para. 1 of the 1991 OCT Decision. *See* COM(1999) 163 def, p. 17.

[49] Article 6, para. 2 of Annex II to the OCT Decision (91/482/EEC: Council Decision of 25 July 1991).

[50] Houben 1965, p. 17.

[51] The entire export to the EU of long grain rice produced in Surinam and Guyana was redirected through the Netherlands Antilles. The import of OCT/ACP rice into the EU through the Netherlands Antilles increased from 58,000 metric tons in 1991 to 224,280 metric tons in 1996. In that year, the rice trade accounted for 0.9 per cent of the GDP of the Netherlands Antilles. *See* Bekkers, Boot & Van der Windt 2003, pp. 26-7.

the Antilles and Aruba really profited from this trade has been a subject of debate.[52]

Italy, Spain and France soon called for safeguard measures. The imports from (mainly) the Netherlands Antilles were considered to frustrate the Community's Common Agricultural Policy (CAP) which at this time aimed to stimulate rice producers in southern Europe to switch to long grain rice, because there was a surplus on the market for other types of rice. Rice producers in Europe claimed that the prices for long grain rice had dropped considerably due to the ACP/OCT imports.[53] ACP states complained that the OCTs unfairly competed with the ACP states on the European market.[54] Allegations were also made of fraud and improper use of the rules.[55]

The EU was allowed, under the 1991 OCT Decision to take safeguard measures if there was evidence of trade deflections, or if a certain element in the OCT Decision did not benefit the sustainable economic development of the OCTs. The Commission and the Council therefore started from 1993 to take safeguard measures to protect the Community market from trade deflections, imposing minimum prices and creating quotas for the imports of rice and sugar of cumulated origin, professedly also because the new industries in the OCTs were not a form of sustainable economic development.[56] These measures and

---

[52] *See* Oostindie & Klinkers 2001c, p. 282 et seq. *Martha* claimed (Martha 1991a, p. 307) that the restrictive rules of origin of the OCT Decisions were one of the reasons why the investment climate in the OCTs did not improve. *Besselink* thinks that the rules of cumulated origin of 1991 had been 'much to the benefit of the economies of the overseas countries' (Besselink 2000, p. 177). However, Korthals Altes 1999, p. 206, note 144, claims that only a few entrepreneurs enjoyed the profits of this '*windhandel*' (speculative trade). This allegation was described as 'really not true' in a joint statement by the three parliaments of the Kingdom ('*Contactplan*') *see* *Kamerstukken I/II* 2000/01, 27 579, no. 1, p. 7. The EU Council of Ministers in 2001 considered that 'in view of the minimal, low value-added operations that currently suffice to obtain the status of a product originating in the OCTs in the sugar sector, the contribution of these exports to the development of the territories can only be small at best and, without a doubt, out of all proportion to the disruption caused to the Community sectors concerned' (2001/822/EC, para. 11 of the Preamble). Some authors think the trade never had much of a long-term future anyway, because of the developments at the WTO and the global trend towards the break-down of trade barriers. *See* Bekkers, Boot & Van der Windt 2003, p. 28 for an economic analysis of the preferential OCT trade.

[53] Bekkers, Boot & Van der Windt 2003, p. 26. The three parliaments of the Kingdom declared in a joint statement ('*Contactplan*') that these allegations were never supported by objective research, *see* *Kamerstukken I/II* 2000/01, 27 579, no. 1, p. 7. A study by the Netherlands Economic Institute commissioned by the Netherlands Antilles showed that the imports did not materially affect the European rice market, *see* IOB 2003, p. 141.

[54] COM (1999), 163 def., p. 30.

[55] Oostindie & Klinkers 2001c, p. 282. During the 1990s criminal proceedings were started in the Netherlands Antilles regarding a criminal conspiracy to commit fraud in the OCT sugar trade. At least one person, a leading figure of the political party 'Frente Obrero Liberashon 30 di Mei', was convicted in this case, *see* *Amigoe*, 14 August 2003.

[56] European Commission 1999, p. 24.

the 1997 revision of the OCT Decision, have been the subject of a long string of legal actions before the European Court of Justice, most of which involved the import of rice or sugar by companies based in the Netherlands Antilles and Aruba. The Court of Justice's digest of cases shows that since 1990 the majority of cases concerning the OCT association have dealt with safeguard measures by the Commission against imports from the OCTs.[57] Almost all of these cases were decided in favour of the Commission or the Council, which were allowed, according to the Court, to take safeguard measures to protect the CAP and to revoke trade preferences accorded to the OCTs.[58]

For the mid-term revision of the 1991 OCT Decision, which according to Article 136 (now 187) of the EC Treaty required unanimity, the Commission proposed to limit the rules of cumulated origin. The Netherlands Antilles and Aruba were against the proposal.[59] The Netherlands Antilles considered that the adoption of the decision fell within the category of economic and financial agreements by which it could not be bound without its consent, according to Article 25 of the Kingdom Charter. It therefore wished the Kingdom government to use its right of veto on the proposed decision in the Council of Ministers of the EU. The Netherlands government at first agreed, but when it became clear that all other member states supported the proposed Decision, it decided that the Kingdom should retract its opposition and accept the compromise that had been proposed. The compromise met a number of the objections of the Netherlands Antilles, but still established quotas for rice and sugar that effectively annihilated the new industry. Under considerable political pressure from the other member states,[60] the Netherlands agreed to the compromise. It considered (perhaps somewhat paternalistically) that the Caribbean Countries would not benefit from a continued opposition. A number of companies from the Netherlands Antilles and Aruba continued their opposition in the Dutch and European courts with little or no success.[61] I will discuss the conflict between the Netherlands and the Caribbean Countries on this subject *below*.

---

[57] *Répertoire de jurisprudence communautaire*, under heading B-17. In one of the cases before the Court of Justice, the French government even accused the Aruban company Emesa Sugar of conducting a juridical guerrilla campaign against the EU, *see* the Opinion of Advocate-General Ruiz-Jarabo Colomer in the case of *Emesa* v. *The Netherlands et al.* (C-17/98), note 4.

[58] *See* Oliver 2003 for a review of the most important cases.

[59] According to *Van Rijn*, the Caribbean Countries did not notify the Kingdom government early enough to enable the Kingdom to conduct a successful opposition against the Committee proposal (Van Rijn 2001, p. 135).

[60] *See* IOB 2003, p. 140. The European Parliament in 1997 debated the issue and called on 'the member state that caused difficulties' to cooperate with the adoption of the OCT Decision, and the Netherlands considered there was a clear threat that continued opposition would lead to repercussions in other areas, *see* *Kamerstukken II* 1996-97, 25 382, no. 1, p. 6.

[61] Mid-Term Revision of the 1991 OCT decision, 97/803/EC. For the final decision-making process in the Council of Ministers of the Kingdom, *see* *Kamerstukken II* 1997-98, 25 382, nos. 2 and 3, and Besselink et al. 2002, p. 202 et seq.

After 1997, the trade routes for rice from Surinam and Guyana took their old course again.[62] Experiments with importing other products through the Netherlands Antilles and Aruba to the EU were not very successful, and it is not generally expected that they will be in the near future.[63] It is widely expected that the EU's trade barriers for agricultural products from the Third World will disappear during the coming decades. At WTO meetings in 2004, the EU promised to remove such trade barriers, which would probably mean that the OCT trade preferences will lose most of their importance.

Future of the OCT Association

There exists some dissatisfaction with the functioning of the association, both in the EU and in the OCTs. The association does not appear to have been very successful, either as a form of development aid or as a means towards integrating the OCTs economically with the EU. The association has been described as an anachronism,[64] and its potential was certainly never fully realized. The Council and the OCTs appear to have had rather different views on how the association should develop. The OCTs want more free access to the European market, but the EU wants the OCTs to comply with European standards. This has created a stalemate during the past 45 years, but to say that the association is an empty shell goes too far. It has facilitated the development and maintenance of some economic relations, and the EDF has made a contribution to the development of the OCTs, albeit a modest one.

During the 1990s the association has been somewhat upgraded. The EU member states have indicated their readiness to renew the association. In a declaration annexed to the Treaty of Amsterdam all of the signatories stated that the difficult circumstances of the OCTs caused them to lag far behind, and that the special arrangements of 1957 could 'no longer deal effectively with the challenges of OCT development.' The Council was therefore requested to review the association in order to promote the economic and social development of the OCTs, and their relations with the EU, more effectively.[65]

---

[62] The import through the Netherlands Antilles dropped to 4,000 metric tons in 2002, *see* Bekkers, Boot & Van der Windt 2003, pp. 34-5.

[63] Bekkers, Boot & Van der Windt 2003, pp. 27-9. In 2004, the Commission granted the Netherlands Antilles the right to import dairy products into the EU, for which there exists no quota yet. A number of companies on Curaçao announced that they would use this opportunity to produce butter from milk fat imported from the US and Australia, which is then exported to the EU. This trade is expected to be profitable because the price of butter in the EU is kept artificially high. *See Amigoe*, 15 September 2004.

[64] Bernardi 1998, p. 134 et seq.

[65] Declaration no. 36, annexed to the Treaty of Amsterdam of 1997. The European Parliament supported this initiative, after hearing a number of representatives of the OCTs (PE 228.210 of 1 December 1998).

In 1999, the first real evaluation of the association by the Commission described the EU-OCT relations as ambiguous and ambivalent. The Commission noted that the debates in the EU showed that some member states thought the mother countries should pay for the development of their OCTs themselves, although this was never stated explicitly. At the same time, the EU had affirmed and reaffirmed its commitment to the development of the OCTs at numerous instances during the previous decades.

The Commission stressed that new approaches would be difficult to find. The 1990s showed that compromises between the 15 member states were difficult to achieve, and the growth of the EU with 10 new members was not expected to make things easier. Meanwhile, the Treaty text is open to more than one interpretation, and the compromises reached so far are of a fragile nature. This makes for a situation where states will not be readily inclined to reopen the negotiations.[66]

The difficult negotiations might be simplified if there were less participants. With a view to the interests that are most directly involved, it would seem logical to create a situation where the Commission negotiates directly with each OCT. This would mean that the member states, including the mother countries, would have to take a step back in favour of the OCTs and the Commission. This may seem politically unlikely, but it should be remembered that such a situation already exists between the EU and Greenland, which appears to function adequately (*see below* in the section on Greenland). Such a direct relation also does more justice to the OCTs right to self-determination, as will be explained in section 9.2.3.

9.2.3   Participation of the OCTs in the Formulation of the OCT Decisions

Part IV of the EEC Treaty was formulated in 1957 without consulting the prospective OCTs. As was explained in the previous sections, Part IV and the OCT Decisions deal mainly with development aid and preferential trade. These may be considered as 'gifts' to the OCTs. Whether trade and development policies may not in fact exercise a large and perhaps even undue influence on a country's internal affairs is an interesting question in this respect, but it falls outside the scope of this study and will be hard to answer anyway on the basis of legal arguments.

---

[66] Communication of 20 May 1999 by the Commission to the Council and the European Parliament, 'The Status of OCTs Associated with the EC and Options for "OCT 2000"' (COM (1999) 163 def).

But the OCT Decisions also contain a number of elements which take the form of legal obligations for the OCTs. Whereas the Decisions used to have the character of extensive subsidy schemes, mainly laying down obligations for the EC and the member states, and providing the conditions under which the OCTs could qualify for funding, the 1991 Decision was more akin to a form of legislation, instructing the OCTs to strive towards certain objectives, compelling them to prohibit certain activities, and calling on them to create 'overall, long-term policies' in an extensive area of public affairs.[67] In exchange, the OCTs were granted more access to the European market.

The 2001 OCT Decision has mitigated this development, which had not proven to produce the desired results.[68] The current Decision mainly lays down the conditions under which the Community shall assist and cooperate with the OCTs, but it also creates new obligations, such as the duty to implement 'efficient and sound competition policies', to protect intellectual property rights, and to guarantee the right to bargain collectively on labour conditions. These obligations are probably intended to function only in the sphere of the relations with the EU, but they are nonetheless laid down as general obligations for the OCTs.

It seems doubtful whether these obligations should be considered as legally binding on the OCTs. The Council's authority to provide legislation for the OCTs can only be derived from Article 187, which authorizes the Council to 'lay down provisions as regards the detailed rules and the procedures for the association.' Other forms of EU law are not binding on the OCTs because the OCTs are not part of the EU.[69] The OCT Decision therefore cannot create binding obligations outside the scope of Part IV of the EC Treaty, although the Council may take the other principles of the EC Treaty into account, according to the Court of Justice.[70]

As was outlined *above*, the scope of the association is potentially broad and somewhat vague. Its objectives are to promote the economic and social development of the OCTs and to establish close economic relations between them and the Community. The Council has used these objectives as a basis to deter-

---

[67] The OCT Decision of 1991 contained provisions on the protection of the environment, agriculture, food security, rural development, fisheries, commodities, mining, industrial development, manufacturing and processing, energy development, employment, encouragement of entrepreneurship, services and the trade in services, tourism, transport, communications, information technology, trade and economic development in general, and regional and international cooperation between OCTs and foreign states and organizations.

[68] Pinheiro 1999.

[69] Von der Groeben/Thiesing/Ehlermann 1999, p. 3/2096.

[70] Judgment of 11 February 1999 in Case C-390/95 P *Antillean Rice Mills (and others)* v. *Commission*, para. 37.

mine the areas of cooperation between the EU and the OCTs in the OCT Decisions. It has laid down a number of 'basic elements' which 'shall be common to the Member States and the OCTs linked to them.' These are liberty, democracy, respect for fundamental human rights and freedoms and the rule of law. Any form of discrimination based on sex, ethnicity, religion, age, etc. is entirely prohibited within the scope of the OCT association.[71] It could easily be argued that it is not necessary to lay down all of these principles in order to be able to promote the economic and social development of the OCTs, and that the Council has therefore stretched its authority beyond the limits of Article 187 by creating a quasi-constitutional regime for the OCTs, especially since this regime has been created without their formal consent. Any other interpretation of the EC Treaty would mean that the OCTs are at the mercy of the Council, which is inconsistent with their position outside of the EU.

The obligations that perhaps exist or may be created for the OCTs by the European Union remain to some extent uncertain. In order to shed some light on this unclear area of EU law, the OCTs and their mother countries have proposed to the Commission that lists could be drawn up of the EU rules that apply in each OCT, jointly by the OCT, the member state, and the Commission.[72]

Increased Participation by the OCTs in the Formulation of the OCT Decision

The provisions of Part IV of the EC Treaty, in the interpretation of the Court of Justice, have put the OCT in 'a very precarious position', as *Van der Burg* puts it.[73] The OCT Decisions are created without the formal consent of the OCTs, which are dependent on the 'patronage' of the metropolitan governments, which have many other interests to protect as well. This lack of direct representation of the overseas peoples cannot be blamed on any one single authority or factor, and has not been created purely in Europe. One of the reasons has probably been that many of the OCTs have for a long time simply not sent anyone to Brussels, either because they were not aware of the importance of the EC, or because they did not have adequate human and/or financial resources to become involved in European affairs, or perhaps because the metropolitan government did not allow it.

The association is based on the somewhat outdated principle that the OCTs fall completely under the sovereignty of their mother countries, and that the European organs can therefore not deal directly with the OCTs but only through

---

[71] Article 2 of the 2001 OCT Decision.

[72] Para. 1.2 of the Joint Position Paper signed by the OCTs and their mother countries on 4 December 2003 (available on <www.octassociation.org>).

[73] Van der Burg 2003, p. 195.

their mother countries. The UK and France retain full legislative powers over most of their OCTs, and can therefore probably invest the EU with the authority to take unilateral decisions with regard to these territories.[74] For the Dutch OCTs (and probably the Danish as well) this is not legally possible because the OCT decision mainly concerns subjects which are not Kingdom affairs but are within the autonomous realm of the Caribbean Countries. With regard to Greenland this problem was solved by providing that the fisheries agreement and the protocols to it are signed by 'the authority responsible for Greenland', which was interpreted by the Kingdom of Denmark to mean that the agreements should be signed by both Denmark and Greenland. The government of Greenland has thus obtained a separate position, and negotiates directly with the Commission on catch quota and corresponding compensation and development aid.[75]

The example of Greenland is of limited value to the other OCTs, because none of them has a bargaining chip comparable to Greenland's fish quota. But since the 1980s, there has been a steady development towards allowing the other OCTs to take part in the negotiations as well. This process was stimulated by a stronger presence of some of the OCTs in Brussels. The first notable result was the OCT decision of 1991, which ended to a certain extent the parallelism with the ACP regime and for the first time created provisions that were specifically tailored to the OCTs. Moreover, the concept of 'partnership' was introduced as a new foundation to the association, which meant that 'Community action shall be based as far as possible on close consultation between the Commission, the Member State responsible for a country or territory and the relevant local authorities of such countries or territories.'[76] The Council considered that 'the participation of the elected representatives of the population concerned should be stepped up' because there was an 'evident lack of democratic dialogue.'[77]

A consultation procedure was set up between the Commission, the OCTs and their mother countries, including working parties for regions with more than one OCT. This consultation procedure was used in the preparation of the mid-term revision of the 1991 Decision and the drafting of the 2001 Decision, and some of the recent new aspects of the OCT association can probably be attributed to the fact that the OCTs can now directly communicate their prob-

---

[74] The recently increased autonomy of New Caledonia and French Polynesia seems to have created the need to involve the authorities of those territories more directly with the EU, *see* De Bernardi 1998.

[75] *See* in section 9.5.2 the section on Greenland.

[76] Article 234 of the 1991 OCT Decision.

[77] Communication of the Commission to the European Parliament (COM (94) 538 of 21 December 1994).

lems and wishes to the Commission. The 2001 OCT Decision also created an EU-OCT Annual Forum at which the Commission and representatives of the OCTs and the member states are present.[78]

To be able to exercise a larger influence over the OCT Decision, representatives of the Netherlands Antilles, French Polynesia and the British Virgin Islands tried to coordinate their position during a series of meetings in 2000. According to the Netherlands ministry for Foreign Affairs, the OCTs were nevertheless unable to influence the negotiations, because of their diverse interests, and a lack of solidarity among them.[79] The initiative did lead to the establishment of the Association of Overseas Countries and Territories of the European Union (OCTA) in 2002, of which 14 OCTs became members.[80] The objectives of the OCTA are information sharing, and defending the collective interests of the OCTs *vis-à-vis* the institutions of the EU. In 2003, the OCTA formulated a Joint Position Paper on the future of the OCT association, that was also signed by the four metropolitan states of the OCTs.[81]

No progress was made in this area during the drafting of the constitutional treaty for the EU. The EU Constitution as it took form in August 2004 introduced no instruments for consultation of the OCTs on the OCT Decisions, nor did the Treaty of Lisbon.

Transforming the OCT Decision into an Agreement?

The language which the Council and the Commission currently use to describe the association, as well as the recent practice of consulting with the OCTs in different ways before adopting the OCT Decision, suggests that the relation is now to some extent based on mutual consent.[82] But the unilateral character of the OCT Decisions still formally exists, and combined with the fact that the OCTs have had participation in the formulation of Part IV of the EC Treaty

---

[78] Article 7, para. 2 of the 2001 OCT Decision.

[79] IOB 2003, p. 152.

[80] The seven OCTs which did not join the OCT had no – or a very small – permanent population, or were being prepared for UPT status (Mayotte), or did not want to be considered as an OCT (Bermuda).

[81] 'Joint Position Paper of the Governments of the Kingdom of Denmark, the French Republic, the Kingdom of the Netherlands, the United Kingdom, and the Overseas Countries and Territories on the Future of Relations between the Overseas Countries and Territories and the European Union', attached to the Final Declaration of the OCT-2003 Ministerial Conference, 4 December 2003 (*see* <www.octassociation.org>).

[82] It is probably for this reason that *The Courier ACP-EU* in 2002 mistakenly described the 2001 OCT Decision as an 'agreement' (Sutton 2002, p. 19.)

either, this means that the regime is still determined without the explicit approval of the OCTs.[83]

This does not necessarily mean that the association would have had a different form if it had been based on agreement with the OCTs, but the EU's professed need to create a 'democratic dialogue' with the OCTs, and the OCTs insisting on a right to fully participate in the decision-making process, indicates that the procedure provided by the EC Treaty is insufficient. It furthermore seems reasonable to assume that the OCTs will be more inclined to pursue the objectives and live up to the standards of the OCT Decisions if they have formally agreed to them, and this might make the whole scheme more effective.

The idea of giving the OCTs a say in the formulation of the rules governing the association has been proposed by such authors as *Vanhamme*, who considers that the EC Treaty rather bluntly denies the OCTs any right of participation in the formulation of their rights and duties under Part IV, which the author finds hard to reconcile with the principle of self-determination as guaranteed by the UN Charter,[84] and also by *De Bernardi* and other authors.[85] The idea was advocated in the Joint Position Paper of 2003 by the OCTs and the four member states with which they are associated.[86] The notion has always been an attractive one, at least for the Netherlands Antilles, which already asked to become associated with the EEC based on a special treaty under Article 238 in 1959, a request that was denied, also with respect to Surinam (*see below*). *Pisuisse* thinks the EU cannot enter into such agreements with the OCTs because they do not have international personality.[87] Whether this is correct, is uncertain. The EU does not consider it impossible to enter into agreements with OCTs *per se*, because it has done so with Greenland. Perhaps the best solution would be if the EC Treaty would provide that the consent of the OCT governments is required for the adoption of the OCT Decisions.

Direct communication between the EU and the OCTs – which already takes place to some extent – avoids the difficult trilateral relationship involving the metropolitan governments, which always has the potential of introducing all sorts of (post-) colonial attitudes and resentments into the relations. The recent creation of partnership meetings and the Annual Forum are a considerable im-

---

[83] The Netherlands Antilles and Surinam were allowed to decide whether they wanted to become OCTs (*see below*), but they were not allowed to participate in the negotiations on the formulation of part IV of the EEC Treaty itself, nor were any of the other OCTs.

[84] Vanhamme 2001, p. 72.

[85] De Bernardi 1998, p. 176 et seq and Van Benthem van den Bergh 1962a, p. 596.

[86] Para. 1.4 of the Joint Position Paper (*see above*).

[87] Pisuisse 1991, p. 321.

provement, and this could be developed into some form of permanent and separate representation at the EU, as *Van Benthem van den Bergh* already proposed in 1962.[88]

9.2.4 Conclusion

The OCT association was originally created as part of a process that led to the independence of most of the OCTs by 1962. The member states of the EEC wished to comply with the UN law of self-determination and decolonization, and considered Part IV of the EC Treaty as fulfilling their duties under Article 73 of the UN Charter with regard to their overseas territories. The EEC thereby accepted a (small) part of the 'sacred trust' to promote the well-being of the inhabitants of these territories, and to develop self-government. It must be assumed that GA Res. 1541 (XV), which gave an authoritative interpretation of Article 73, is also binding on the Community and the EU, as far as it is within the organization's powers to ensure its realization.

The main aspects of the association are development aid supplied by the EU, and an incomplete free trade area between the EU and the OCTs, wherein both parties are allowed to uphold considerable trade barriers. The rice and sugar conflict between the EU and the Netherlands Antilles and Aruba showed that the EU will give precedence to its common agricultural policy over the preferential imports from the OCTs.

Although most EU law should not apply in the OCTs, the Council of Ministers of the EU wishes to create certain legal standards for the OCTs through its OCT Decision, which is adopted without the consent of the OCTs. The participation of the overseas representatives has been increased in recent years, and this development should perhaps lead to the adoption of OCT agreements to (partly) replace the unilateral OCT Decision.

9.3 THE NETHERLANDS ANTILLES AND ARUBA AS OCTs

When the Netherlands joined the EEC in 1957, the Netherlands Antilles and Surinam did not become part of the Community. It is not clear whether the Caribbean Countries would have been allowed to join the EEC. This question simply was not discussed, as far as the historical sources show. The Netherlands government did inform the Caribbean Countries that it would be a good idea if they became OCTs. In 1957, it was not yet clear to the Netherlands

---

[88] Van Benthem van den Bergh 1962a, p. 596.

Antilles and Surinam what would be the consequences of becoming associated with the organization. The Kingdom therefore negotiated a protocol to the Treaty that recognized its right to ratify the Treaty only on behalf of the Country in Europe[89] and for Netherlands New Guinea, which would remain an OCT until it was handed over to Indonesia in 1963. The six prospective member states of the EEC declared that they would be prepared to enter into negotiations on treaties of economic association of the Netherlands Antilles and Surinam with the EEC.[90]

In 1959, the three Countries of the Kingdom agreed that Surinam and the Netherlands Antilles should become associated with the EEC based on a treaty of association under Article 238 (currently Article 310) of the EEC Treaty. Such an association agreement is concluded with the Community, which means that it does not require the ratification of the member states, and because Part IV does not apply to such associations, it would make it possible to take account of the circumstances of the Netherlands Antilles, which were quite different from the original OCTs that were all relatively undeveloped territories with little or no autonomy.[91] The Netherlands government considered that the OCT association was intended for Trust Territories and NSGTs only, and in light of UN GA Resolution 945 (X) of 1955, the Netherlands was of the opinion that the Netherlands Antilles were no longer a NSGT (*see* chapter 6).[92] A majority of the member states, however, thought that Article 238 of the EEC Treaty could not be used because it referred to treaties with third states, which the Netherlands Antilles was not.[93]

The member states rejected all of the other specific wishes of the Netherlands Antilles, because granting them was considered unfair towards the existing OCTs, and because their effects would be unclear and might be dis-

---

[89]   Van der Burg 2003, pp. 191-2 for this reason considers that the Country of the Netherlands is the member state of the EC, and not the Kingdom. Most other authors think the Kingdom is the member state, which seems to be more correct in view of the Kingdom Charter and the text of the EC Treaty which states that 'the Kingdom of the Netherlands' is a member of the EC. It should be recognized however, that the EC/EU usually distinguishes between OCTs and the 'member states that have special relations with these countries and territories.' The situation is therefore somewhat ambiguous, which has led to a rather inconsistent practice with regard to the ratification of the European treaties by the Kingdom. *See* on this subject Besselink et al. 2002, p. 192 et seq., and Raad van State 2003, p. 67.

[90]   For these negotiations, *see* Van Benthem van den Bergh 1962a, Houben 1965, and Oostindie & Klinkers 2001b. *See* Meel 1999 for the negotiations on Surinam.

[91]   Olyslager 1958, p. 19.

[92]   *Kamerstukken II* 1956/57, 4725, no. 3, p. 42.

[93]   Houben 1965, pp. 46-7. Olyslager 1958, p. 20 assumed that it had been the intention of the member states to conclude a treaty based on Article 238 EEC Treaty with the Netherlands Antilles and Surinam.

advantageous for the economies of the member states. The Kingdom government, after two years of unsuccessful negotiations, decided that the Netherlands Antilles would apply for normal OCT status. In exchange for the guarantee that oil products from the Netherlands Antilles would be considered as originating from that Country, the EEC *and* its member states gained the right to take safeguard measures against the importing of those products, and quotas were established that determined the maximum amounts of oil products to be imported per member state of the EEC. Because the right to take safeguard measures went further than Articles 115 and 226 of the EEC Treaty allowed, the agreement was laid down in a special oil protocol that was attached to the Treaty.[94] The normal procedure for amending the EEC Treaty needed to be followed for this, for which reason the member states also took the opportunity to place the Netherlands Antilles on Annex IV (now Annex II). This was not considered absolutely necessary to attain OCT status, as the procedure with regard to Surinam had shown (*see below*).[95]

Even though it had been expected that the association with the Netherlands Antilles would 'increase the strength of the EEC considerably',[96] the oil protocol does not appear to have had any measurable effect on trade between Europe and the Netherlands Antilles, nor did the OCT association as a whole before 1991.[97] The development aid provided through the European Development Fund has been of somewhat more importance. The funding provided is not very large[98] in comparison with the aid provided by the Netherlands, but it has played an independent role in the development of the islands. In rare cases the EDF has funded projects that were first refused by the Netherlands government, notably the extension of the landing strip of the airport on Bonaire, which appears to have been the main reason why tourism started to grow on the island after 1975.[99] The EDF focuses on infrastructural improvements, and in the Netherlands Antilles and Aruba it has been used to build and improve roads, harbours, etc., but also to build schools and provide housing. During the 1990s, the EDF has nonetheless suffered from considerable underspending – espe-

---

[94] Van Benthem van den Bergh 1962a, p. 595.

[95] Convention 64/533/EEC of 13 November 1962 amending the Treaty establishing the European Economic Community with a view to rendering applicable to the Netherlands Antilles the special conditions of association laid down in Part Four of that Treaty, *Journal Officiel* 1964, 150, p. 2414. These amendments to the EEC Treaty entered into force on 1 October 1964.

[96] Olyslager 1958, p. 20. It was expected that the oil refineries of Curaçao and Aruba could become important for the supply of oil products to Europe, which at this time had few oil refineries, but the Antillean refineries continued to deal mainly with the US and the region.

[97] Palm 1985, p. 148.

[98] The Netherlands Antilles is allocated some 20 million euro every five years, Aruba currently does not receive any funding. *See* IOB 2003, p. 151 and De Jong 2002, p. 246.

[99] Haan 1995, p. 197.

cially with regard to the funds available for the Netherlands Antilles. This was attributed by the Netherlands Antilles to the 'bureaucratic procedures' of the EDF, which was confirmed in a report by the Court of Auditors of the EU, and which the EU has promised to improve,[100] but the Court of Auditors also put the blame on 'the complex structure of the Netherlands Antilles, both geographically and in terms of the distribution of competences between the main actors in the decision-making process, and the absence of an overall development concept for the different islands which gave rise to numerous projects scattered both financially and geographically.'[101]

Loans from the European Investment Bank (EIB) have not played a large role in the Antillean and Aruba economies. These loans are available for projects in the OCTs under attractive conditions.[102] The EIB financed a few projects in the 1970s and 1980s, but the Countries never succeeded in obtaining the EIB's approval for enough projects to use up all the funding earmarked for them.[103] This problem persisted and has become even worse, so that at present there are no projects at all in the Netherlands Antilles and Aruba that are financed by the EIB.

9.3.1 Consequences of the Association for the Kingdom Relations

The EU membership of the Country of the Netherlands combined with the OCT status of the Netherlands Antilles and Aruba creates a constitutionally and politically complex situation within the Kingdom. It means that the members of the Council of Ministers of the Kingdom have to show loyalty to three different political entities: the EU, the Kingdom, and the Country to which they belong. During almost 50 years, these three loyalties have hardly ever seriously conflicted, and during this time the practice of decision making by consensus within the Kingdom Council of Ministers was firmly established. But in the rice and sugar conflict of the 1990s (*see above*) it became clear that this 'loyalty triangle' does have the potential to create serious problems between the three Countries, and between the Kingdom and the EU.

---

[100] Sutton 2002, p. 19.

[101] Special Report No 4/99, concerning financial aid to overseas countries and territories under the sixth and seventh EDF accompanied by the replies of the Commission (1999/C 276/01), p. 5. The Report is highly critical of the efficiency of the aid to the Netherlands Antilles, which suffers from poor planning by the local authorities and insufficient monitoring by the EU, *see* p. 8 of the Report. The aid relation with Aruba was considered satisfactory (De Jong 2002, pp. 93-4).

[102] *See* the brochure, 'Financing for the OCTs. The Overseas Association Decision of 27th November 2001. The Investment Facility and Loans from EIB's own resources: *Outline of Terms and Conditions*', available on <www.eib.org>.

[103] Haan 1995, p. 197.

· When the ministers of the Netherlands decided (as ministers of the Kingdom) that the Kingdom (as member of the EU) would agree to the revision of
the OCT Decision in 1997, they had to balance the interests of the EU's Common Agricultural Policy, the interests of the Country of the Netherlands, the
interests of the Kingdom of the Netherlands, and the interests of the Caribbean
Countries, all at the same time. The Kingdom Charter does not provide guide-
lines or special procedures in case of a conflict of interests, other than a form of
internal appeal, which is available to the ministers plenipotentiary against decisions of the Kingdom government (*see* chapter 4).

In the rice and sugar conflict, the Netherlands Antilles and Aruba claimed
that Article 25 of the Charter applied to the adoption of the mid-term revision
of the OCT Decision in 1997. Article 25 gives the Caribbean Countries a right
of veto on the application of an economic or financial agreement to their territories, if they expect it will negatively affect them. After the Dutch ministers
decided that the Kingdom should agree to the compromise on the mid-term
revision, internal appeal was instituted. The continued deliberations did not
lead to a different decision,[104] after which the Netherlands Antilles obtained a
court injunction that forbade the Dutch minister to vote in favour of the proposed OCT Decision in the Council of Ministers of the EU, and later to forbid
the government to cooperate with the execution of the OCT Decision, but this
judgement was overturned on appeal.[105]

In the meantime, several Antillean politicians publicly uttered their disappointment about the Netherlands' decision in no uncertain terms. The chairman
of the *Staten* of the Netherlands Antilles, which had sent a delegation to The
Hague to express its displeasure, considered that the Netherlands had chosen to
support European protectionism instead of its own Kingdom partners. This
showed, according to the chairman, that the Caribbean countries were still in a
'severely colonial situation.'[106]

According to *Oostindie & Klinkers* the Netherlands government did indeed
decide to give preference to its own interests in Europe over those of the Netherlands Antilles and Aruba.[107] A number of political parties in the Lower House
blamed the government for not properly protecting the interests of the Caribbean Countries, and some authors have considered that the Netherlands' deci-

---

[104] Contrary to Article 12 of the Kingdom Charter, the premiers of the Caribbean Countries
took part in the continued deliberations instead of the ministers plenipotentiary, *see* Oostindie &
Klinkers 2001c, p. 283 and IOB 2003, p. 142.

[105] The judgment of the *rechtbank* of The Hague was overturned by the *Gerechtshof
's-Gravenhage* (judgment of 20 November 1997, *JB* 1997, 272). The Dutch *Hoge Raad* confirmed this decision (judgment of 10 September 1999, *AB* 1999, 462).

[106] Mr L.A. George-Wout, cited in Oostindie & Klinkers 2001c, p. 284.

[107] Oostindie & Klinkers 2001c, p. 284.

sion was reprehensible.[108] The Netherlands government defended its decision by stating that it had been in the best interests of the Caribbean Countries, and also protected the interests of the Netherlands, which were at stake because of the severe political pressure of the other member states. Leaving aside the question whether a continued opposition to the OCT Decision could have led to a better result, this raises an issue of self-determination. Was the Netherlands allowed to decide this matter on behalf of the Caribbean Countries, or could it allow to let its own interests play a role in the decision? And more concretely, did the Netherlands Antilles and Aruba indirectly have a power of veto over the OCT Decision?

Veto Power for the Netherlands Antilles and Aruba on the OCT Decision?

It has been argued on legal grounds that the ministers of the Kingdom were not free to make a decision on the mid-term revision of the OCT Decision based on a balancing of the interests of the Countries, the Kingdom and the EU, but that the decision should have been based solely on the opinion of the governments of the Netherlands Antilles and Aruba. This argument rests on the assumption that either the OCT Decision should be considered as an international agreement to which Article 25 of the Kingdom Charter applies, or that the practice of the Kingdom before 1997 supported the conclusion that a customary rule had evolved which gave the Caribbean Countries the power of veto over OCT Decisions.

Martha considered that the intention of Article 25 of the Kingdom Charter – to prevent any disadvantageous effects for the Netherlands Antilles and Aruba from international economic or financial agreements concluded by the Kingdom – meant that it should be applied to the OCT Decision as well.[109] This interpretation was supported by the Netherlands Antilles government, by *Alkema, De Werd*, and by a research group of the University of Utrecht that was asked in 1997 to study this issue by the Netherlands Antilles government.[110] *Borman* on the other hand, considered that the Caribbean Countries cannot claim a right of veto analogously to Article 25, because that would make it impossible for

---

[108] *See Kamerstukken II* 1997/98, 25 382, no. 4, Besselink 1998, and Nap 2003b, p. 78.

[109] Martha 1991b, pp. 14-15.

[110] Martha 1991, p. 15 refers to a memorandum by the Netherlands Antilles government on this subject of 20 December 1990. *See also* Alkema 1995, p. 134, and De Werd 1997, p. 1851. Besselink 1998, p. 1295, note 23 refers to the report of the research group, which was not published, as far as I am aware. *Alkema* agreed with *Martha* that the Caribbean Countries should not be bound against their will by a decision of the member states on the OCTs, but also noted that the practice did not support this proposition.

the Kingdom government to balance the Dutch interests in the EU against the interests of the Caribbean Countries as OCTs.[111]

A fully analogous application of Article 25 to the OCT Decision is not possible, as *Nap* has pointed out.[112] Article 25 does not really create a right of veto with regard to the contested international agreement, but only with regard to the application of the agreement to the territory of the Country that opposes it. Paragraph 2 of Article 25 creates the possibility that a Country opposes the revocation or annulment of a treaty, but again only with regard to its own territory, leaving the Kingdom free to revoke the treaty for the other Country or Countries, if the treaty in question allows such a partial revocation.[113] It was obviously not possible for the Kingdom to agree to the proposed mid-term revision of the OCT Decision while leaving the 1991 Decision intact with regard to the Caribbean Countries. The OCT Decision is indivisible in this respect, which forces the Kingdom to take a decision as a whole.[114]

The Kingdom government in 1997 denied that Article 25 applied to the OCT Decisions, because the text of Article 25 only refers to international agreements and not to decisions of international organizations.[115] The doctrine after 1997 has accepted this interpretation, since the text of Article 25 is quite clear and the *travaux préparatoires* provide no support for a different interpretation.

Many authors nonetheless think the Kingdom government was not authorized to overrule the opposition of the Netherlands Antilles and Aruba to the revision of the OCT Decision in 1997 because they think there exists, or existed, a rule of customary constitutional law which states that the Kingdom may not agree to an OCT Decision if a Caribbean Country opposes it.[116] *Besselink* derives an *opinio juris* from two statements. The first was made by the Dutch Foreign Minister, Luns, in 1962 during the debate in the Lower House on the ratification of the EEC Treaty on behalf of Surinam. Luns explained that when 'typically Surinam interests' were involved, the Kingdom would speak

---

[111] Borman 2005, p. 154.

[112] Nap 2003b, p. 81.

[113] Van Helsdingen 1957, p. 411-12.

[114] Applying Article 25 to this situation would give the Caribbean Countries a 'chain veto', as *Nap* calls it, because a veto by the Country directly leads to a veto by the Kingdom as a whole. There is of course one situation in which a veto similar to Article 25 *could* be exercised by the Caribbean Countries without dragging the whole Kingdom along with it. If a Country expects that it will not benefit from a proposed OCT Decision, it can decide that it does not want to fall under the scope of the new Decision. The example of Bermuda has shown that this is possible. In such a case, the Kingdom could vote in favour of the OCT Decision, while still respecting the economic autonomy of the Caribbean Country.

[115] *Kamerstukken II* 1997/98, 25 382, no. 4, p. 14.

[116] Besselink 1998, p. 1295 (Besselink's publications of 2002 and 2003 contain similar passages on this subject), Hoogers & De Vries 2002, pp. 214-15, and Nap 2003b, p. 78 et seq.

in the Council of Ministers of the EEC with 'I do not want to say "his master's voice" – but still "Surinam's voice".'[117] The second statement is a declaration attached to the 1991 OCT Decision. It reads:

> The government of the Kingdom of the Netherlands draws attention to the constitutional structure of the Kingdom resulting from the Statute of 29 December 1954, and in particular to the autonomy of the countries of the Kingdom so far as concerns the provisions of the Decision and the fact that the Decision was, in consequence, adopted in cooperation with the Governments of the Netherlands Antilles and Aruba pursuant to the constitutional procedures in force in the Kingdom.[118]

Besselink claims this declaration aimed to inform the member states of the 'special veto power of the overseas countries', and that it stated 'that the decision needed the consent of the Netherlands Antilles and Aruba.'[119] 'Cooperation' does not mean exactly the same as 'consent', but it would be difficult to maintain that when a Caribbean Country votes against an OCT Decision in the Council of Ministers of the Kingdom it has 'cooperated' with the decision.[120]

The declaration also indicates that the Caribbean Countries are autonomous as regards *all* of the subjects covered by the OCT Decision. From 1964 until 1986, the Kingdom had issued similar declarations to the OCT Decisions, but these had referred to 'the autonomy of the non-European parts of the Kingdom so far as concerns *certain* provisions of the Decision' (emphasis added).[121] The words 'in consequence' furthermore suggest that the 'cooperation' of the Caribbean Countries was indispensable. It therefore seems hard to read the declaration of 1991 in any other way than to indicate that the Caribbean Countries had a decisive say over the position of the Kingdom with regard to OCT Decisions, although if the Kingdom government really wished to state this, it could have said so more clearly.

The *Raad van State* of the Kingdom interpreted the declaration as evidence that the Kingdom followed the practice of only agreeing to an OCT Decision if the governments of the Netherlands Antilles and Aruba did not object. The *Raad van State* considered that the Kingdom had treated the OCT Decision in practice as if they were economic agreements under Article 25, which the *Raad*

---

[117] *Handelingen II* 1961/1962, p. 1207.

[118] *See* Annex VIII to the 1991 OCT Decision (91/482/EEC).

[119] Besselink 2000, pp. 177-8. *See also* Besselink 1998, p. 1295, Besselink 2002, p. 201, and Besselink 2003.

[120] Vanhamme 2001, p. 72 interprets the declaration to mean that the Netherlands Antilles and Aruba have *consented* to the OCT Decision.

[121] *See for instance,* Annex VIII of the 1980 OCT Decision (80/1186/EEC, *OJ* 80/L.361) and Annex VIII of the 1986 OCT Decision (86/283/EEC, *OJ* 86/L.175).

van State considered to be in line with the purpose of Article 25, namely to prevent the Caribbean Countries from suffering negative consequences through international agreements concluded by the Kingdom.[122] The Kingdom government interpreted the opinion of the *Raad van State* to mean that 'in the end none of the countries of the Kingdom has the power to block the decision making process.' The government will in the future do its utmost to reach consensus, but failing that, the votes in the Council of Ministers of the Kingdom will decide the Kingdom's position on the OCT Decision, i.e., the Netherlands has the final say.[123] This interpretation is hard to reconcile with the text of the declaration attached to the OCT Decision in 1991, and the Kingdom has therefore not issued it anymore.

The argument that the decision to vote in favour of the mid-term revision of 1997 was in breach of a rule of customary law is hard to defend in the absence of clear evidence of a steady practice and an *opinio juris*. The declarations which the Kingdom government issued on the OCT Decisions before 1991 could not really be interpreted as giving the Caribbean Countries a right of veto over the OCT Decision as a whole, and the declaration of 1991 was issued only once. The doctrine before 1991 also does not support the conclusion that the Kingdom always followed the practice of only agreeing to an OCT Decision if the Caribbean Countries agreed to it, as *Besselink* claims.[124] Only one author discussed this problem, namely *Houben*.[125] He is cited by virtually all authors who have written on the rice and sugar conflict, and must be considered authoritative.

Houben differentiated between two types of situations. On the one hand there were cases in which clearly only the interests of one Caribbean Country were involved, such as a decision by the EU Council of Ministers to finance projects in that Caribbean Country, or when the Council deliberates on the trade policies of that Caribbean Country with respect to a third country. In such a case, the Kingdom's actions were guided by the opinion of the Country involved, Houben states. On the other hand, there are cases where the interests of two or three Countries are involved, for example, when the Council takes measures as part of the CAP or when it takes decisions on the trade policies of the

---

[122] Advice no. W01.98.0081 of 5 October 1998, published in the *Staatscourant* of 13 November 2001 (*Bijvoegsel Stcrt. no. 220*).

[123] Reaction by the Kingdom government (*'Nader Rapport'*) to the *Raad van State*'s advice (*Bijvoegsel Stcrt. no. 220*).

[124] Besselink 1998, p. 1295.

[125] Pisuisse in 1991 merely noted that the declaration of the Kingdom was issued to 'avoid problems', but that it would cause a problem if the Netherlands Antilles or Aruba refused to agree to an OCT Decision (Pissuisse 1991, p. 327). No other authors discussed this issue before 1991, as far as I am aware.

EEC with regard to the OCTs. In these cases, the Kingdom government itself takes the decision, by which Houben probably meant that the normal decision-making procedures were followed in which the Dutch ministers have a majority vote.[126] *Houben* does not state what practice was followed in case a decision (such as the OCT Decision) contained provisions which only concern a Caribbean Country, as well as provisions that fall in the second category. It seems logical to assume that since all three Countries have an interest in such a decision, the normal decision making process within the Kingdom would be followed. Only when the Council of Ministers of the EU deliberated on a certain element of the decision that only concerned one Caribbean Country, could that Country determine the Kingdom's position independently of the other Countries. When it came to a vote on the OCT Decision as a whole, the Caribbean Countries could probably not overrule the Netherlands.[127]

There is no evidence that the Kingdom government followed this practice after 1964, but neither is there any evidence that it did not. The negotiations on the OCT Decisions were probably conducted on the basis of consensus between the Countries, as in most other areas, there being no need (or no wish) to force the issue of who has the final say. But it seems unlikely that the Netherlands would ever have allowed a Caribbean Country to overrule it on the OCT Decision when its own interests were at stake as well.[128] The statement by Luns in 1962 should be interpreted to mean that Surinam determined the position of the Kingdom in the Council of Ministers of the EU when its 'typical' interests were under discussion, but it did not mean that when the Council discussed or decided issues that affected the other Countries as well, Surinam could have its own way at the cost of the other Countries, simply because its interests were involved.

Seeing that the conflict of 1997 concerned the trade policies of the EU towards the OCTs, as well as the CAP, the Caribbean Countries would probably not have had a right of veto if the early practice of the Kingdom (as described by *Houben*) had been followed. The interests of all three Countries were clearly involved in this Decision. The declaration issued by the Kingdom in 1991 was perhaps somewhat at odds with the practice, or reflected the wish to create a new practice whereby the Caribbean Countries would have a stronger say in the formulation of the OCT Decision. The situation has become legally somewhat uncertain because of the declaration, and the conflicting interpretations of

---

[126] Houben 1965, p. 98.

[127] *Houben* calls the declaration issued by the Kingdom government on the first OCT Decision 'superfluous' but he does not explain why. Apparently he did not think it was in conflict with the practice as described by him.

[128] *See* Alkema 1995, p. 134.

the Kingdom law as defended by the three Countries, the *Raad van State*, and the legal scholarship.

In view of these differing opinions and the absence of evidence that there exists a steady practice, it can only be concluded that the Countries are at least obligated to *try* to achieve consensus on OCT Decisions, because this obligation is supported quite unanimously. But the law should be clearer on the issue of who has the final say as long as the Kingdom has only one vote on the OCT Decision. The Countries' interests in the decisions of the Council may differ considerably, and this may lead to further conflicts if the constitutional law of the Kingdom does not stipulate how such conflicts of interests should be resolved.

Possible Solutions

The advice of the *Raad van State* recommends that the Countries should formulate an arrangement on how to exercise the right to vote in the Council of the EU on affairs that concern the Netherlands Antilles and Aruba. This recommendation was supported by many writers, such as *Besselink*, *Hoogers & De Vries* and *Nap*.[129] *Van Benthem van den Bergh* had already stressed the need for such an arrangement even before the first OCT Decision had been adopted.[130] Along with these authors, I think that such an agreement should ideally be laid down in a Kingdom act or in the Charter itself.

However, I do not think that under the current circumstances the rule should be that the Caribbean Countries have a right of veto on the OCT Decisions and other decisions of international organizations which affect them economically, similarly to Article 25 of the Charter. As long as the Kingdom only has one vote in the Council of the EU, and the OCT Decision has not been transformed into an agreement with the OCTs, the Kingdom has to take account of the legitimate interests of each Country and the Kingdom as a whole when using its vote in the Council. Under some circumstances this could mean that prevalence should be given to other interests than the economic or financial interests of one or both of the Caribbean Countries. A right of veto would moreover create potentially unsolvable situations, namely when the Caribbean Countries disagree with each other on a certain decision. If one of them expects economic advantages from it, while the other expects to be negatively affected, a right of veto would not provide a solution.

---

[129] Besselink 2002, pp. 205-6 and 216-17, Hoogers & De Vries 2002, p. 212 and Nap 2003b, p. 83.

[130] Van Benthem van den Bergh 1962a, pp. 595-6.

I agree that any rules on this subject should start from the economic autonomy of the Countries, which is one of the cornerstones of the Kingdom order. It reflects the reality that the Caribbean Countries are economically in a different position from the European part of the Kingdom, and this requires different policies. Based on the Kingdom Charter and the economic right to self-determination the Countries should be allowed to determine these policies for themselves. This does not mean, however, that other Countries, states, or international organizations can be forced to create or maintain beneficial arrangements for the Caribbean Countries.

The rule described by *Houben* would be a good basis for an arrangement between the Countries, since it does justice to the right to self-determination of the Caribbean Countries while not ignoring the interests of the Netherlands. The arrangement should provide that when only the interests of *one* Country is concerned, that Country decides the position of the Kingdom. The arrangement should also provide a way of resolving a deadlock which could be the result of a disagreement between the Caribbean Countries in a case where both their interests are at stake, while guaranteeing that the Kingdom will still be able to act effectively. These rules could perhaps also take their inspiration from the federal member states of the EU, for example Germany, a federation which allows its states (*Länder*) to represent Germany in the EU when only their interests are concerned.

The arrangement should also provide for a form of arbitration or judicial settlement of disputes on the interpretation of the arrangement, and especially to determine in concrete cases whether only the economic or financial interests of one Caribbean Country are involved, or whether the decision directly affects the interests of the other Countries or the Kingdom as a whole. This task could be attributed to the *Raad van State* of the Kingdom or to the Supreme Court, or to a constitutional court that could be established to resolve conflicts between the Countries.[131]

The three Countries have not come to any sort of agreement on this issue, nor taken steps towards such an agreement, perhaps because their interpretations of the Kingdom Charter appear to differ fundamentally on this point. If this is the case, it would provide an additional argument for transforming the OCT Decision into an agreement between the EU and the OCTs so that the Netherlands Antilles and Aruba will be able to defend their own interests in a direct relation with the EU, which would do more justice to their right to self-determination.[132]

---

[131] De Werd 1997.

[132] Article 28 of the Kingdom Charter, which opens the door to separate membership for the Caribbean Countries of international organizations, could perhaps accommodate a direct relation

This does not necessarily mean that the Caribbean Countries will lose their influence over the position of the Kingdom as the member state of the EU. The Kingdom government could decide that if the Netherlands Antilles and Aruba obtain a way of negotiating directly with the EU, it will only continue to represent the Country of the Netherlands in the EU.[133] In that case, the Caribbean Countries would have to decide whether they prefer to deal directly with the EU, or through the Kingdom and with the help of the Netherlands.

9.3.2 Conclusion

The Caribbean Countries expressed a desire to conclude separate agreements with the EEC, but the member states were only prepared to give them OCT status. Because of this, the Kingdom of the Netherlands has to use its vote in the Council to represent all three Countries, which creates the need for a way to settle differences of opinion and conflicts of interest between the Countries regarding the EU. Instead of creating such an arrangement, the Countries have chosen to strive towards consensus on each issue, which they appear to have achieved in all but one case. The rice and sugar conflict of the 1990s showed that the Countries differ in their opinions on the role of the Caribbean Countries in determining the Kingdom's position during the negotiations on the OCT Decisions. These differences have not yet been resolved, and the situation remains legally unclear.

The Kingdom Charter or a separate Kingdom act should provide rules to determine in which cases a Country can determine the position of the Kingdom independently, or jointly with another Country. In all other cases, the Kingdom Council of Ministers should decide the Kingdom's position via the normal procedure of trying to achieve consensus, since a Caribbean Country, in spite of its right to economic self-determination, cannot be allowed to overrule the other Countries when the interests of those Countries or the Kingdom as a whole are at stake as well. In these cases, the Dutch ministers will have a majority vote in the Kingdom Council of Ministers. Future conflicts could of course also be prevented if the OCTs were to gain a separate negotiating position on the formulation of the terms of their association.

---

between the EU and the Caribbean Countries. Van Benthem van den Bergh 1962a, p. 596 already proposed this. *See* Van Helsdingen 1957, p. 396 et seq. for the meaning of Article 28.

[133] Van Rijn 2001, p. 135.

9.4   Should the Netherlands Antilles and Aruba Remain OCTs?

Doubts and dissatisfaction about the OCT association are occasionally expressed, both in the EU and in the OCTs. In The Hague, it is often assumed that the Kingdom will disintegrate if the three Countries continue to have a different status with regard to the EU. For that reason, it has often been suggested that the Netherlands Antilles and Aruba should achieve another status within or outside of the EU, especially since the Treaty of Amsterdam created a special preferential position for the outermost regions of France, Spain and Portugal, called 'ultra-peripheral' status, which is considered by some to be an attractive alternative to OCT status.

9.4.1   Ultra-Peripheral Status

The ultra-peripheral territories (UPTs) consist of the French *départements d'outre-mer* (Martinique, Guadeloupe,[134] French Guyana, and Réunion), the Spanish autonomous community of the Canary Islands, and the Portuguese autonomous overseas regions of Madeira and the Azores. These territories are different from most OCTs, because they have substantially larger populations, and have traditionally more important economic ties with Europe.

Under Article 299, paragraph 2 of the EC Treaty, the UPTs fall entirely within the territorial scope of the Treaty, although the Council 'shall adopt specific measures' with regard to the application of EU law, 'taking into account the special characteristics and constraints of the outermost regions without undermining the integrity and the coherence of the Community legal order.' Under this provision, the UPTs have been granted a number of exceptions to the full application of EU law to their territories.[135] To what extent such exceptions are allowed is still somewhat uncertain.[136]

Since the 1970s, the fate of the UPTs has become inseparably linked with that of Europe,[137] and they have definitively moved through the 'IN' door, in the terminology of the Commission. The EU provides extensive funding to

---

[134] The UPT of Guadeloupe currently still includes Saint-Martin, which is the French half of the island which is called St Maarten on the Dutch half. The Netherlands Antilles therefore shares a land border with the EU. If Saint-Martin obtains a separate status in relation to France, it will probably continue to be a UPT, but this is still uncertain at the time of writing.

[135] *See* Brial 1998, p. 644 and Puissochet 1999. Since 1997, these exceptions can be created by the Council by a qualified majority of the votes, and no longer by unanimity (Article 299, para. 2 of the EC Treaty).

[136] Brial 1998, p. 658 and Puissochet 1999, p. 495.

[137] Brial 1998, p. 654.

improve the struggling economies of the UPTs, and to integrate them in Europe. For the period 1994–1999 the UPTs were granted 4.7 billion euro, and for the period 2000–2006 they were allocated 7.7 billion euro under the Structural Funds, representing the largest grant per capita anywhere in the EU.[138] The EU has also developed specific programmes for the UPTs, which concentrate on improving infrastructures, promoting productive sectors which generate jobs, and human resources development. There are also many other initiatives, which take account of the handicaps of these regions, such as their remoteness, insularity and reduced competitiveness.

For the Netherlands Antilles and Aruba, a change towards ultra-peripheral status would mean the incorporation of the entire *acquis communautaire*, unless the EU would be prepared to grant certain exceptions. It will involve a huge effort by the Countries, the Kingdom and the EU, but it seems to have been rather successful in the Azores, Madeira and the Canary Islands, which became part of the EEC in 1986 and have since become considerably integrated with the Community. This has resulted in a substantial growth of the GDP of these islands, which used to be much poorer than the Netherlands Antilles and Aruba. Whether the Netherlands Antilles and Aruba could profit from a similar development became a subject of much debate in 2003.[139]

The economic outcome of a change towards UPT appears to depend on a large number of factors, most of which cannot be controlled completely by the Caribbean Countries or the Kingdom. It cannot be determined beforehand, for example, which exceptions to EU law would be granted by the EU, or how much funds would be made available. It is also not possible to determine with any great amount of certainty the economic future of the OCT association. The only thorough economic comparison of both options published so far, conducted by researchers of the Erasmus University at the request of the Bank of the Netherlands Antilles, tentatively concluded that UPT status for the Nether-

---

[138] The UPTs are all classified in category no. 1 of the Structural Funds, which means that they are considered structurally underdeveloped. *See* Brial 1998, p. 648.

[139] During meetings in March 2003 of the biannual '*Contactplan*' of the three parliaments of the Kingdom, parliamentarians of the Netherlands Antilles and Aruba proposed that the Kingdom should investigate if the Caribbean Countries should opt for UPT status (*Kamerstukken I/II* 2002-03, 28 829, no. 1, pp. 4-5, '*Parlementair contactplan*', 24-28 March 2003). *See also* the position paper of the Aruban AVP of March 2003, 'Koninkrijks- en Europese verhoudingen; een appèl voor een nieuwe benadering', available on <www.fesca.org>. The Netherlands Minister for Kingdom Affairs requested the *Raad van State* of the Kingdom to provide information on this subject (*see below*). The Netherlands government did not wait for the outcome of this study, but announced that the Netherlands would strive towards the realization of the UPT status of the Caribbean Countries (*see* 'Hoofdlijnenakkoord' of 16 May 2003, *Kamerstukken II* 2002/03, 28 637, no. 19, p. 14). The governments of the Netherlands Antilles and Aruba protested that they had not been informed of this, and furthermore rejected the idea of becoming UPTs.

lands Antilles would produce 0.6 per cent more growth per year in comparison to OCT status.[140] Some have questioned whether the researchers started from the right assumptions,[141] or have dismissed the advantages of UPT status as 'purely theoretical.'[142]

From a legal point of view, the UPT status of a Caribbean Country would mean a considerable increase in the Kingdom's duty to guarantee the correct implementation of international obligations by the Caribbean Countries. In practice, this could lead to a decrease of the Caribbean Country's autonomy in relation to the Kingdom. Up till now, the risk of the Kingdom being held liable for a violation of international law in the Caribbean Countries has been relatively small,[143] and the Kingdom government rarely found it necessary to intervene in the autonomous affairs of a Caribbean Country for this reason.[144] But the obligations created by EU law are of a different nature, and are furthermore supervised by the EU organs, which may impose considerable penalties on the Kingdom if a Caribbean Country does not live up to the Kingdom's obligations. This will provide an incentive for the Netherlands to make sure that the Caribbean Countries correctly implement EU law, and will undoubtedly lead to a stronger Dutch involvement.

On the other hand, it has been suggested in Aruba that UPT status might increase Caribbean autonomy in a political sense, because the relationship with Europe, and the extra funding that might become available, creates new possibilities for Aruba to pursue its own culture and education policies and to strengthen its own identity in relation to the Netherlands.[145] This certainly seems possible, but much will depend on the Caribbean Country's ability to implement EU law and ensure its observance on the one hand, and on the other hand

---

[140] Bekkers, Boot & Van der Windt 2003.

[141] Van Beuge 2004. The Van Beuge committee has been criticized itself for implicitly choosing against UPT status based on the political outlook of a majority of its membership, see *Amigoe*, 17 July 2004. The Aruban opposition party *AVP* protested against the fact that it was not involved in the appointment of the members of the Committee, in spite of earlier promises.

[142] Rosaria 2003, p. 41.

[143] An isolated example can be found in the European Court of Human Rights' judgment in the case of *A.B.* v. *The Netherlands* (Application No. 37328/97) of 29 January 2002, in which the Court held that Article 8 had been violated in the Pointe Blanche prison of St Maarten (Netherlands Antilles) for which no effective remedies had been available (Article 13).

[144] An exception is the decision of the Kingdom government to confirm the decision of the Governor of the Netherlands Antilles (acting in his capacity as organ of the Kingdom) to quash two decisions of the government of Bonaire on the grounds that these decisions had violated the obligations of the Kingdom under an international treaty (the convention of Ramsar). *See* the royal decree of 11 December 2007 (*Stb.* 2007, 347).

[145] Alberts 2003. This report was the result of a fact-finding mission by FESCA, the think tank of the Aruban Christian-Democratic party (AVP), to Madeira and the Canary Islands in 2003.

the degree of trust that the Netherlands will have in the Country's ability to do so on its own.

9.4.2   Disintegration of the Kingdom

Apart from these issues of economics and autonomy, there is also the question whether the Kingdom does not face the threat of disintegration if the Countries continue to have a different relationship with the EU.[146]

The *Raad van State* of the Kingdom, in its advice on the future of the Netherlands Antilles and Aruba in relation to the EU, noted that the Netherlands currently has a double relationship, on the one hand with the EU and on the other hand with the Caribbean Countries. This creates 'competing commitments' which lead to tensions within the Kingdom which will only increase in the future, the *Raad van State* predicts.[147] The *Raad van State* also considers that it is far from certain the OCT association will be continued in the future, and concludes that the Netherlands Antilles and Aruba should probably choose between a closer relationship with the EU, either as UPTs or through some other arrangement, or accept that the integration of the Country of the Netherlands into Europe will gradually lead to the dissolution of the Kingdom (i.e., independence for the Netherlands Antilles and Aruba).[148]

The *Raad van State*'s arguments against the OCT status can be grouped into two categories. On the one hand, there is uncertainty about the future of the association, which is true, but it will not be ended any time soon. The EU Commission thinks major choices about the future of the OCT association can only be made by the overseas peoples, none of which have as yet expressed themselves in that sense.[149] The other arguments of the *Raad van State* are based on the notion of the incompatibility of the European integration with the Kingdom in its present form,[150] because the law of the Countries will increas-

---

[146] *See for instance* Hirsch Ballin 2003.

[147] Raad van State 2003. The advice lists a few examples of these frictions: most inhabitants of the Netherlands Antilles and Aruba are European citizens but they are not allowed to vote in the elections for the European parliament; the Kingdom is obligated to execute decisions of the Council regarding defence and foreign policy, even though these subjects are Kingdom affairs; and there is less concordance between the legislation of the Countries in non-Kingdom affairs because EU law generally does not apply in the Caribbean Countries.

[148] Raad van State 2003, especially pp. 22, 38, and 48-51.

[149] Except perhaps Mayotte, which in a referendum in 2000 approved a plan for closer ties with France, which had promised to attempt to realize more European funds for the island, which the French government interpreted as a choice for UPT status.

[150] This notion is endorsed by some authors, for example Hoeneveld 2004 and Alberts 2003, and denied by others, such as Van der Wal 2003 and Martha 1997.

ingly differ, and because the Kingdom will become bound to European decisions, also in Kingdom affairs such as defence and foreign affairs.

Whether the differences between the law of the Countries will in the future increase, depends for a large part on the Caribbean Countries' willingness to continue copying Dutch law. The fact that the Netherlands is increasingly bound to EU law does not really change this situation, because the Country of the Netherlands has never attached much consequences to its obligation under Article 39 of the Kingdom Charter to maintain legal concordance between the Countries in a number of important areas of the law. The Caribbean Countries still appear to be prepared to follow the legal developments in the Netherlands. Whether these are of European or Dutch origin does not really make a difference.

The Caribbean Countries are also occasionally requested to cooperate with implementing EU decisions in the entire Kingdom, for instance with regard to visa, and other measures in the 'wars' on drugs and terrorism.[151] But as OCTs, the Netherlands Antilles and Aruba cannot be compelled to adhere to EU law that is not based on Part IV of the EC Treaty, and the implementation of such law can therefore only be realised voluntarily by the Caribbean Countries.[152]

There exists another, perhaps stronger threat to the integrity of the Kingdom, however, namely the EU's growing capacity to represent its member states externally.

9.4.3 The Ability of the Kingdom to Represent the Caribbean Countries Externally

Alkema has wondered whether the Kingdom might not in the future lose its ability to represent the Netherlands Antilles and Aruba independently of the

---

[151] IOB 2003, p. 163 et seq. for visa, and p. 97 et seq. for the war on drugs. In these cases, an Aruban research group concluded, Aruba really has no choice but to implement EU law. *See* '*Aruba en de Europese Unie. Rapport van de Studiegroep Aruba-Europese Unie*', Oranjestad, 1 October 2003. This situation appears to exist in the other OCTs as well, *see* para. 1.2 of the Joint Position Paper signed by the OCTs and their mother countries on 4 December 2003 (available on <www.octassociation.org>).

[152] *Kamerstukken II* 2003/04, 29 394, no. 6, p. 14. The *Raad van State* has a long-standing difference of opinion with the Kingdom government on this subject, which is reflected in a number of advices concerning seagoing vessels (*see Kamerstukken II* 1999/00, 26 878, B for an overview). The *Raad van State* considers that all seagoing vessels with Dutch nationality, therefore including those registered in the Netherlands Antilles and Aruba, have to comply with EU (and other international) standards, because the safety of seagoing vessels is an affair of the Kingdom according to the Charter, and because nationality is indivisible under international law. The Kingdom government has consistently rejected the *Raad van State*'s position (*Kamerstukken II* 2003/04, 29 200 XII, no. 136, and *Kamerstukken II* 2003/04, 29 476, no. 4).

EU if the EU develops its own foreign policy. This problem has already led to conflicts when member states wished to represent their OCTs internationally while the Commission considered the member states should adhere to the common policies. In 1978, the European Court of Justice was asked to give an advisory opinion on the participation of the UK and France in an international conference on behalf of their overseas territories, even though the subject matter was within the exclusive competence of the EEC. The Court held that the UK and France (and by extension the Netherlands) had 'a dual capacity: on the one hand in so far as they are members of the Community and on the other hand in so far as they represent internationally certain dependent territories which are not part of the sphere of application of Community law.' This dual capacity means that the member states are allowed to act internationally on behalf of their OCTs independently of the EU.[153]

In 1989, the four states with OCTs and the Commission reached an agreement on the representation of overseas interests at international conferences, in order to 'resolve these problems in a pragmatic way without prejudging any legal positions.'[154] The member states and the Commission promised to consult each other on possible conflicts of interests between the EU and the OCTs and attempt to reach an agreement in each case before the start of the conference. Failing such an agreement, the member state will represent the interests of the OCT in the way it sees fit, but it will inform the Commission beforehand of its intentions. A similar declaration was annexed to the Final Act of Maastricht in 1992, which applies this principle to all instances of possible conflicts of interest between the EU and the OCTs.[155] As a result of this, the Kingdom has remained capable to represent the Caribbean Countries in international affairs, at least for the time being.

The Caribbean Countries are not fully satisfied with the way the Kingdom uses this ability, which is partly due to the fact that the ministries in The Hague seem to be increasingly focussed on European developments and policies, also in international affairs. While the Kingdom remains legally capable of representing the Caribbean Countries, the Netherlands ministers which represent the Kingdom may not be politically willing to do so, or even be aware of the possibility. *Van Rijn* considers that this development will lead to the Nether-

---

[153] Opinion 1/78 of the European Court of Justice of 4 October 1979, *International Agreement on Natural Rubber* [1979] *ECR* 2871. Similarly in Opinion 1/94 of 15 November 1994, *Competence of the Community to conclude international agreements concerning services and the protection of intellectual property* [1994] *ECR* I-05267.

[154] The text of the Declaration is annexed to Maurice 1991, pp. 247-9.

[155] Declaration (no. 25) on the representation of the interests of the overseas countries and territories referred to in Article 299 (former Article 227) (3) and (6) (a) and (b) of the Treaty establishing the European Community.

lands Antilles and Aruba being forced to develop their own foreign policies in a large number of fields.[156] An example of this tendency is that the Netherlands Antilles government has expressed a wish to obtain separate membership of the WTO.[157] Another solution might be that the EU organs assume the responsibility for the foreign affairs of the OCTs to the extent that the European integration incapacitates the metropolitan states to conduct the foreign affairs of their territories.[158]

9.4.4   Conclusion

It is controversial whether UPT status might be a realistic and attractive option for the Netherlands Antilles and Aruba. Their OCT status may in the future lead to the disintegration of the Kingdom, which might create a conflict with their right to self-determination. The OCTs may not be forced by the EU or the metropolitan states to move towards either independence or integration with the EU against their will. A choice to move in either direction must be left to the populations of the OCTs themselves. The EU Commission has taken this principle as a guideline for the future development of the OCT Association. As this principle does justice to the right to self-determination of the Netherlands Antilles and Aruba, the Kingdom should adopt it as well and not strive towards the termination of the OCT status of the Caribbean Countries, unless the populations of those Countries express a wish for another relation with Europe.

The Kingdom for the time being remains free to represent the Netherlands Antilles and Aruba externally independent of the EU, even in areas where a common foreign and security policy is realized. If this should change in the future, a solution will have to be found for the Netherlands Antilles and Aruba which does justice to their right to self-determination. Perhaps the EU should take on a greater role in representing the OCTs in external affairs to prevent the territories from becoming international orphans.

9.5   PROCEDURES FOR STATUS CHANGE

Seeing that the UPT status of a Caribbean Country would lead to substantial changes to the law and the international position of such a Country, such a

---

[156] Van Rijn 1999, p. 149.

[157] IOB 2003, p. 130.

[158] The European Commission may be venturing in this direction already with regard to Greenland. It wishes to participate on behalf of Greenland and the EU in various Arctic cooperation projects, *see* the communication to the Council and the European Parliament on Greenland of 3 December 2002 (COM(2002) 697 final).

status change should preferably be seen as an exercise of the right to self-determination in order to guarantee that the freedom of choice of the population of the Country is not undermined. If a Country chose to become a UPT, it would abdicate a number of its autonomous powers to the EU organs, and it would come to fall under the supervision of the Kingdom with regard to the correct implementation of, and abidance by, EU law. Politically and economically, the Country would become closer to Europe, which would represent a consequential change for the Netherlands Antilles and Aruba in their trade relations, monetary policies, and most of their other economic policies. For these reasons, the right to self-determination should be taken into account when determining which procedure to follow before a Dutch OCT could obtain another relationship with the EU.

9.5.1   Under European Union Law

Formally, the list of OCTs in Annex II to the EC Treaty determines whether a territory is an OCT or not. The Annex can only be amended through the procedure for amendments to the Treaty, of which it is an integral part.[159] The consent and ratification by all member states is therefore necessary for a territory to become an OCT, or to stop being an OCT under EU law. In practice some status changes have nonetheless been made without the explicit consent of the member states, and usually the Annex has not been amended to realize a status change.

UPT status can only be achieved through amendment of Article 299, paragraph 2, which lists the UPTs. An exception perhaps exists for France, which does not appear to need the consent of the other member states to create UPTs, because all of its DOMs are automatically UPTs, or so Article 299 suggests.[160] But the consent of the member states is indispensable to obtain the support of the EU needed to integrate the territory with the Union, and to realize exceptions to the application of EU law in a UPT.

The Treaty of Lisbon creates a procedure for status change which will allow UPTs to become OCT and vice versa. The new Article 311a, paragraph 6 of the EC Treaty (which will be renamed the Treaty on the Functioning of the European Union) will state that:

> The European Council may, on the initiative of the Member State concerned, adopt a decision amending the status, with regard to the Union, of a Danish,

---

[159] Von der Groeben/Thiesing/Ehlermann 1999, p. 3/2101-2, and Pisuisse 1991, p. 325.
[160] Ciavarini Azzi 2004, p. 7.

French or Netherlands country or territory referred to in paragraphs 1 and 2. The European Council shall act unanimously after consulting the Commission.[161]

Independent of whether the Treaty of Lisbon will come into force, any status change of the Dutch OCTs will, at least in the near future, require the consent of all member states. But the freedom of the member states to deny a request for status change is limited by the right to self-determination and decolonization. Through the EC Treaty all of the member states have adopted obligations towards the OCT, in the fulfilment of which they are bound to take the right to self-determination into account (*see above*). It is possible for the OCTs to invoke the right to self-determination when a significant change in their status is discussed, especially since most of the OCTs, including the Netherlands Antilles and Aruba, have not been able to make a really free choice on their relation with Europe in the past.

The obligations for the EU and the member states are probably most clear in a situation where a Caribbean Country exercises its right to self-determination in relation to the Netherlands, resulting in a full integration with the Netherlands. If the EU or one or more of the member states should oppose the application of the Treaties to that Caribbean Country, it would prevent or seriously frustrate a process of decolonization. EU law has become an important part of the law of the Netherlands, and any territory that would want to become fully part of the Netherlands would have to comply with the obligations arising from EU law. A refusal to accord such a territory the beneficial aspects of EU membership would seriously hinder the integration of the territory in the Netherlands.

In any case, if one of the Caribbean Countries or an island of the Netherlands Antilles chooses to become integrated with the Country of the Netherlands, such a choice should not be treated in the same way as the accession of a foreign state to the EU. Firstly, because the Kingdom is already a member of the EU, and will be responsible for the adherence to EU law in any part of its territory where the Treaties apply, and secondly because the EU already has a relation with the OCTs on the basis of the EC Treaty to which the right to self-determination and decolonization as laid down in the UN Charter applies. The freedom of choice, which is the essence of this right, should be respected by the EU and its member states.

This does not mean, however, that the Caribbean Countries could force the EU to accept them as UPTs, because this is not the same as merely extending

---

[161] The territories referred to in paras. 1 and 2, are the UPTs and the OCTs. I do not know why the British OCTs are excluded. The new procedure will also not apply to such territories as the Faeroe Islands, Gibraltar and the Åland Islands. For these territories the current procedure involving treaty amendment will stay in place.

the territorial scope of the Treaties to those Countries. UPT status creates the obligation for the EU to create beneficial measures for the territory. It would be hard to argue that such a preferential status could be chosen as a direct result of the exercise of the right to self-determination. Full integration with the Netherlands almost inevitably means that a Caribbean Country would have to become part of the EU, but UPT status would not be absolutely necessary. On the other hand, seeing that the historical, social and geographical circumstances of the Dutch OCTs are rather similar to those of the existing UPTs, and also that the application of EU law in the Dutch OCTs would probably lead to similar problems, a member state opposing the UPT status of the Netherlands Antilles or Aruba might find it difficult to present a convincing case.

The situation is less clear when a Caribbean Country would prefer to change its status in relation to the EU *without* changing its relation with the Netherlands. Such a change could take the form of a special protocol as in the case of the Åland Islands, or some other tailor-made status established through an agreement between the Kingdom and the other member states, or it could take the form of UPT status. These status changes could – at least in theory – be achieved without any major constitutional changes in the relation with the Netherlands. It therefore concerns status changes that can only be realised by the EU. The right to self-determination could certainly be used by a Caribbean Country presenting such a request, with reference to the Preamble of the EC Treaty's promise of adhering to the principles of the UN Charter, but it cannot be maintained that the member states would be obligated to grant such a request, at least not when it is purely based on the right to self-determination.

9.5.2 European Practice with Regard to Status Change

The European practice with regard to the status of overseas territories has been somewhat careless.[162] Many changes were realized during the 1970s and 1980s without updating Annex II of the EC Treaty. Annex II was finally updated in 1997[163] and has remained correct since. It may be expected that the EU will in the future insist on the adherence to the procedure of Treaty amendment before a territory can become OCT or UPT. An exception might still be made for territories which secede from an existing OCT.[164] The EU may probably not

---

[162] *See also* Martha 1991b, p. 9, who calls the EEC's practice disturbingly sloppy.

[163] *See* Vignes 1991, pp. 360-2 on the political reasons why some member states (especially France) refused to remove a number of independent states from Annex II.

[164] The practice shows that once a member state allows an island to secede from an overseas territory and become a separate overseas territory, the EU (as well as other international organizations) starts to treat this new territory on a similar footing as the entity of which it formerly was a

consider a territory as an OCT if such a recognition conflicts with international law.[165] This could occur when an OCT is broken up in violation of the principle of *uti possidetis* (*see* chapter 8).

The EU has accepted a number of status changes of overseas territories, notably that of Greenland, which chose to leave the EEC in a referendum. Other examples are Saint-Pierre and Miquelon, and Bermuda. Of course, Brussels has also respected the right to self-determination of the approximately 25 OCTs that have become independent states since 1958, but it did not really have a choice in these cases, since it was not considered possible to extend the application of Part IV to independent states.[166]

The EU Commission in 1999 stressed that 'it is not for the Commission or the Council to impose such options' as integration with the EU or joining the ACP Conventions. According to the Commission, such a decision is 'a political choice that only the peoples concerned can make within their own constitutional frameworks.'[167]

According to *Von der Groeben* a territory cannot change its status in relation to the EU simply through an expression of its (or its mother country's) will, but only through an amendment of Annex II to the EC Treaty.[168] Nonetheless, there have been many examples where this procedure was not followed. Obviously, all of the OCTs that have become independent have changed their status in relation to the EC through a unilateral act. Bermuda is another example, as it is not treated as an OCT at its own request, but still remains on Annex II to the

part. Thus, Mayotte was treated as an OCT from 1976, Anguilla from 1980, and the Council of Ministers also accepted Aruba's decision to leave the Netherlands Antilles and become a separate Country within the Kingdom in 1986. *Martha* in 1991 wondered whether Aruba had really become an OCT because it was not yet listed on the Annex to the EEC Treaty (Martha 1991b, p. 10). Other authors considered that Aruba inherited the rights and obligations of the Netherlands Antilles as a form of state succession (for instance Hoogers & De Vries 2002, p. 245).

[165] Such a problem exists with regard to the French and British claims to Antarctica, which are part of their OCTs. The Antarctica Treaty does not allow any actions which constitute a basis for claiming sovereignty over a part of the continent, for which reason some authors think that OCT status should not be interpreted as recognition of the international status of a territory. This conclusion is probably not correct. The recognition by the EU of a certain territory as an OCT of a member state would seem to indicate that the EU considers that the member state in question exercises sovereignty over that territory. The French and British Antarctic claims are exceptions, or more properly, the EU should make clear that these territories are not OCTs (*see in a similar sense* Vanhamme 2001, pp. 76-7). In all other instances, the OCT status of a territory means that the EU recognizes that one of its member state has 'special relations' with that territory, which should logically be interpreted to mean that the member state exercises sovereignty over that territory.

[166] The OCT Decisions do make it possible that the association is temporarily continued until the former OCT has been able to ratify the ACP convention.

[167] COM(1999) 163.

[168] Von der Groeben/Thiesing/Ehlermann 1999, p. 3/2101-2.

EC Treaty. *Von der Groeben*'s rule perhaps does apply when a territory wishes to become OCT or UPT. I will discuss three such cases in order to determine whether OCT or UPT status requires treaty amendment.

Surinam

After the Surinam government decided to request an association with the EEC,[169] the Commission of the EEC announced that it was in favour of Surinam becoming an OCT. Surinam's request to be allowed to send a representative to participate in the negotiations on its future status was denied, because according to France and Germany these negotiations were an internal affair of the EEC.[170] The Council of Ministers of the EEC asked a special legal working group to give advice on the proper procedure to be followed. It considered that the EEC Treaty needed to be amended in order to add Surinam to the list of OCTs in the Annex. The Commission rejected this advice because it thought such a partial amendment of the Treaty might inspire other member states to request Treaty changes as well. The Commission proposed that the Netherlands should ratify the EEC Treaty again, but this time for Surinam. The member states did not object, and the Netherlands seized this opportunity to quickly realize the OCT status of Surinam, even though an amendment to the Treaty was 'a legally more thorough form', according to the Netherlands government.[171] Surinam was not placed on the Annex to the Treaty, which strictly speaking meant that Surinam did not become an OCT, and the Treaty applied to the Country without restrictions.[172] But seeing that it had been the clear intention of the Netherlands and the other member states to create OCT status for Surinam, it was treated as such.[173]

Saint-Pierre and Miquelon

The status change of Saint-Pierre and Miquelon was part of an attempt by France during the 1970s to terminate the constitutional irregularity which represented

---

[169] Oostindie & Klinkers 2001b, p. 454, note 2. *See* Meel 1999, p. 281 et seq. and Houben 1965, p. 43 et seq. for (differing) accounts of the negotiations within the Kingdom and with the EEC.

[170] Meel 1999, pp. 296-7.

[171] *Handelingen II* 1961/62, p. 1200. The EEC Treaty was ratified for Surinam by the Kingdom statute of 19 July 1962, *Staatsblad* 1962, no. 285. For the debates in the Netherlands parliament, *see Kamerstukken II* 1961/62, 6701 (R 275), *Handelingen II* 1961/62, p. 1175 et seq., and *Handelingen I* 1961/62, p. 525 et seq.

[172] Maas 1962, p. 597.

[173] Houben 1965, p. 48. The OCT Decisions of 1964 until 1976 treated Surinam as an OCT. After Surinam became independent, it joined the group of independent ACP states.

the *territoires d'outre-mer* (TOM).[174] France thought that the remaining TOMs should either become independent or fully integrated into the republic in the form of *départements d'outre-mer.* Saint-Pierre and Miquelon, an archipelago located near Newfoundland, served as a test-case for the transformation of TOM into DOM. There existed no independence movement in the territory and it was considered to be very French already. The *Conseil général* (parliament) of the territory was opposed to the transformation, but the French legislature went ahead with the integration of the territory into the Republic in 1976 as a DOM.

The DOMs were (and are still) not listed in the text of the EEC Treaty, which thereby implicitly left it to France to decide which of its territories should be covered by Article 227, §2 (currently 299, § 2) of the Treaty. This represents an exception to the rule that the member states decide together on the territorial scope of application of the Treaty.[175] None of the organs of the EEC, nor the member states, either opposed or accepted France's decision to transform Saint-Pierre and Miquelon into a DOM and thereby bring it under the full application of EEC law.[176] France's choice was not without financial consequences for the EEC, however, because the DOMs qualify to receive funding which is not available to the OCTs.

The *départementalisation* quickly ran into legal and political difficulties due to the '*réalités locales*' as *Branchet* puts it,[177] and also because the French government apparently had not anticipated the Court of Justice's 1978 decision in the *Hansen* case, which meant that EEC law fully applied in the DOMs.[178] France came to the realization that the full integration of the territory into the EEC would be economically disadvantageous. Three-quarters (75 per cent) of the archipelago's imports came from Canada and the US, and would now fall under the import regulations of the EEC, which meant that these imports became considerably more expensive. To replace these with products from Europe was not an attractive option because of the costs of transportation.

Negative consequences were also expected in the area of fisheries, which is an important part of the islands' economy. The creation of a common European fisheries policy in 1983 meant that the EEC gained control over the access of

---

[174] Ziller 1991, p. 189. On the status changes of Saint-Pierre and Miquelon, *see* Branchet 1991.

[175] In this sense, *see* Ziller 1991 and Ciavarini Azzi 2004. Von der Groeben/Thiesing/Ehlermann 1999, p. 3/2101-2 thinks the member states have to agree to a TOM becoming a UPT, but this would be in contradiction to the text of the EC Treaty.

[176] Saint-Pierre and Miquelon remained on Annex IV to the EEC Treaty, but this Annex was never fully up-to-date until 1997. The French decision must perhaps be considered to have annulled or overridden the inclusion of Saint-Pierre in Annex IV. The archipelago was removed from the more accurate Annex to the OCT Decisions in 1980 (80/1186/EEC, *OJ* 1980, L.361).

[177] Branchet 1991, p. 300.

[178] Ziller 1991, p. 189.

foreign fleets to the fishing grounds of the islands. This threatened to worsen the longstanding territorial dispute with Canada, which refused to recognize Saint-Pierre's new status because it did not want to deal with the EEC in this matter, and furthermore feared the advent of the European fishing fleet.[179]

These difficulties, combined with the local opposition to the entry into the common market, led France to decide that Saint-Pierre and Miquelon should not be an integral part of the EEC after all. For this reason, the status of the islands under the French Constitution was changed. It became a *collectivité territoriale de la République française* in 1985, a category that had been created for Mayotte in 1976, and is somewhere in between TOM and DOM status. This time, the islands were in favour of the status change.[180]

The new status of 1985 meant that Saint-Pierre and Miquelon reverted to OCT status. Its inclusion in Annex IV was 'revived', since the member states had not yet taken the trouble of striking the name of the territory from it.[181] The OCT Decision of 1986 welcomed back Saint-Pierre and Miquelon by listing it as a 'territorial collectivity' in the Annex to the Decision without any comment.[182]

The Treaty of Lisbon aims to put an end to this French prerogative by listing all of the DOMs by name.[183] France's wish to change Mayotte into a UPT in the near future therefore had to be accommodated during the intergovernmental conferences of 2003 and 2004 by the adoption of a declaration that Mayotte may be added to the list of UPTs when France requests it.[184]

---

[179] Branchet 1991, pp. 303-4 and Ziller 1991, p. 189.

[180] Branchet 1991, p. 309, states that the choice was put to the voters of Saint-Pierre and Miquelon on 27 January 1985, but I have not found any other references to this consultation. Ziller 1991, p. 189 only states that the local assembly agreed to the new status. Maurice 1991, p. 228 claims that *both* status changes were at the request of the population, but he does not substantiate this claim.

[181] Ziller 1991, p. 190 doubts whether it was legally possible to revive an annulled provision by a unilateral act of a member state.

[182] Council Decision of 30 June 1986 (86/283/EEC, *OJ* 1986, L.175). Von der Groeben/Thiesing/Ehlermann 1999, p. 3/2102 claim that the Council issued an internal explanatory declaration in which it explicitly recognized the new status of the islands.

[183] The Treaty of Lisbon (*OJ* C.306 17 December 2007) had not yet been ratified at the time of writing of this study.

[184] *See* Declaration no. 43 of the Declarations concerning provisions of the Treaties which were issued with the Treaty of Lisbon: 'The High Contracting Parties agree that the European Council, pursuant to Article 311a(6), will take a decision leading to the modification of the status of Mayotte with regard to the Union in order to make this territory an outermost region within the meaning of Article 311a(1) and Article 299, when the French authorities notify the European Council and the Commission that the evolution currently under way in the internal status of the island so allows.' *See also* the French '*Accord sur l'avenir de Mayotte*' of 27 January 2000, *JO*, No. 32 of 8 February 2000.

Greenland

Greenland first became part of the EC in 1973 when it was still an integral part of Denmark. The accession referendum which had been held in the entire Kingdom of Denmark showed that 70 per cent of the Greenlanders did not want to join the EC, but as the majority of the Danish population as a whole voted in favour of accession, the Kingdom of Denmark became member of the EC as a whole. After Greenland achieved its Home Rule in 1979,[185] another referendum was held in 1982 on the question whether it should leave the EC. The Inuit population of Greenland resented the fact that European fishermen had obtained generous catch quotas in Greenland's fishing grounds, which were the mainstay of the island's economy, and were unhappy about the EC's decision to ban seal hunting.[186] Nonetheless, the opposition to the EC had become smaller since 1973, with only 52 per cent of the Greenlanders voting in favour of leaving the EC. Denmark respected the outcome of the referendum, and requested the other member states to cooperate in granting Greenland's wish.

Many member states were not keen on Greenland's departure, because the island's fishing grounds were of considerable importance to the EC. The Danish proposal to grant the island OCT status also met with opposition because the territory was considerably wealthier than the average OCT.[187] After 'a strenuous and time-consuming process',[188] an agreement was reached on a treaty of withdrawal for Greenland,[189] which states in its Preamble that, whilst OCT status is deemed to provide an appropriate framework, 'additional specific provisions are needed to cater for Greenland.' A new Article was added to Part IV of the EC Treaty which provides that Part IV applies to Greenland, subject to the Protocol on special arrangements for Greenland, annexed to the EC Treaty. This protocol guarantees that fishery products from Greenland will have completely free access to the EC, if the EC obtains a satisfactory amount of access to Greenland's fishing grounds.[190]

---

[185] The move towards Home Rule was inspired by the outcome of the referendum on the accession of Denmark to the EEC (Fægteborg 1989, p. 32). It was expected that Home Rule would enable Greenland to get out of the EC without becoming independent from Denmark, *see* Havel 1992, p. 122.

[186] Fægteborg 1989, p. 33

[187] Von der Groeben/Thiesing/Ehlermann 1999, p. 3/2118-9.

[188] Fægteborg 1989, p. 33 cites the president of the Home Rule Government of Greenland.

[189] Treaty amending, with regard to Greenland, the Treaties establishing the European Communities, *OJ* No. L 29/19, of 13 March 1984, which entered into force on 1 February 1985.

[190] Protocol on special arrangements for Greenland, attached to the Greenland Treaty, Article 1, para. 1. *See also* Council Regulation No. 223/85 of 29 January 1985, and Von der Groeben/Thiesing/Ehlermann 1999, p. 3/2120.

A ten-year fisheries agreement between the EC and 'the authority responsible for Greenland', which can be renewed for six-year periods, and the protocols to it, determine the access of the EC to the fishing grounds of Greenland, and also the funding provided to Greenland by the EU.[191] It also makes it possible for the EU to trade its catch quota with third countries such as Norway and Iceland, which is considered to be very important for the EU's fishery policies. Because the 'authority responsible for Greenland' is interpreted to mean both the governments of Denmark and of Greenland, this agreement and the subsequent protocols were signed by Denmark and Greenland. Greenland has negotiated directly with the Commission on these protocols.

The EU does not provide funds for Greenland through the EDF, but only through the protocols. If Greenland fell under the rules of the EDF, the Commission estimates it would receive only 10 per cent of the 42 million euro per year it receives currently as compensation for the EU's catch quota, and as development aid under the Fourth Protocol. The Commission has expressed its dissatisfaction with this situation because the real catches of European fishing vessels are worth less than half the amount paid as compensation, due to the near depletion of some species. But the renewed protocol of 2002 nonetheless granted roughly the same amount of financial aid as before.[192]

9.5.3 Under the Constitutional Law of the Kingdom of the Netherlands

The Netherlands and the other states maintaining 'special relations' with overseas territories generally seem to consult their territories before taking a decision on their relations with the EU, but the legal status of such consultations can be very different in each state.

In the Kingdom of the Netherlands the application of international economic and financial agreements such as the EC Treaty to the territories of the Netherlands Antilles and Aruba is constitutionally a matter for the governments of those territories, as Articles 25 and 26 of the Kingdom Charter stipulate. The overseas governments have a right of veto on the application and the termination of the application of such treaties to their territory,[193] and they may request the conclusion of such treaties, which the Kingdom will conclude if they only

---

[191] 'Agreement on fisheries between the European Economic Community, on the one hand, and the Government of Denmark and the local Government of Greenland, on the other' signed at Brussels on 13 March 1984, and annexed to Council Regulation (EEC) No. 223/85 of 29 January 1985.

[192] Communication of the Commission to the Council and the European Parliament of 3 December 2002, COM(2002) 697 (final), p. 8.

[193] Article 25 of the Kingdom Charter.

apply to (one of) the Caribbean Countries, 'unless this would be inconsistent with the partnership of the country in the Kingdom.'[194] The Kingdom therefore in 1957 left it to the Caribbean Countries to decide for themselves whether they wanted to become OCTs or not, although the initiative for the decision was taken by the Netherlands. It must be assumed that any future decision with regard to a change in the relation with the EU should also be taken by the Netherlands Antilles and Aruba themselves.[195] Presumably, this situation will not change by the adoption of the Treaty of Lisbon.[196]

It could be argued that it would not be wise for a Caribbean Country to seek another relationship with the EU against the will of the Netherlands – especially if it would be a closer relationship with the EU. While this may be true because of the political preponderance of the Netherlands within the Kingdom, it does not detract from the legal rule that the Caribbean Countries should be allowed to make an autonomous decision on their relation with the EU.

9.6   CONCLUSION

The law of decolonization and self-determination should be applied analogously as far as possible to the OCT association, because the OCTs were all, or are still, NSGTs, and the EEC in 1957 took on part of the 'sacred trust' towards these territories. In so far as the metropolitan states are no longer capable to take measures to realize the goals of Chapter XI of the UN Charter for their OCTs because of the European integration, these measures should be taken by the EU. The relations of the OCTs with the EU have gained some importance for the overseas territories, for which reason these relations should be considered part of the political status of those territories.

For EU law to conform to the right to self-determination of the OCTs, and their separate status under international law, the OCTs will have to be given a form of participation in the adoption of the OCT Decision under Article 187 of

---

[194] Article 26 of the Kingdom Charter.

[195] In a similar sense, *see* Martha 1991b, p. 9.

[196] The Treaty of Lisbon provides a new procedure for status changes of the OCTs and other overseas territories of France, Denmark and the Netherlands (Article 311a, para. 6). Such changes can be realized by a decision of the European Council, which means that the Treaty will no longer have to be amended in order to realize a status change. It would also seem to mean that Article 25 and 26 of the Kingdom Charter formally no longer apply, because those Articles only apply to international agreements, and not to decisions of international organizations (*see above*). That would mean that the same uncertainty surrounding the adoption of the OCT Decisions would also surround status changes of the Dutch OCTs. Perhaps to prevent this, the Kingdom issued a declaration which reads that a Kingdom decision to request a status change for the Netherlands Antilles and Aruba will be taken in conformity with the Kingdom Charter.

the EC Treaty, and the EU and the member states should not frustrate a legitimate exercise of the right to self-determination of an OCT, including the Netherlands Antilles and Aruba.

The EU Commission and the OCTs have been working on the modernization of the association for the last 15 years. The new view of the character of the association that is currently taken by all the parties involved should also be reflected by the EC Treaty, especially in its procedures for the adoption of the OCT Decision, and for status changes of the OCTs.

The consent of all member states is formally required under EU law for a status change of an OCT because the OCTs are listed in Annex II to the EC Treaty. But if such a status change is part of a self-determination process in relation to the mother country, the other member states should not frustrate that process. The EU and the member states cannot be forced, however, to grant the territory a preferential status as UPT. That would be a matter for negotiations between the Kingdom, the EU, and the other member states.

The application of the right to self-determination and decolonization to the relationship between the EU and overseas territories means that a status change can only be realized in agreement with the overseas people involved. Within the Kingdom of the Netherlands, Articles 25 and 26 of the Kingdom Charter entail that the Caribbean Countries determine the Kingdom's position with regard to the Treaty amendments needed to change from OCT to UPT or another status.

Chapter 10
CONCLUSION

In this study, I have looked at the international law concerning self-determination in the context of decolonization. I have tried to determine at which point international law considers a process of decolonization completed and whether there are criteria for a legitimate exercise of the right to self-determination, in order to determine whether this area of the law is still relevant to the constitutional relations between the Netherlands, the Netherlands Antilles and Aruba. In this final chapter, I will summarize the results of my research, and review the implications of the international law of decolonization and self-determination for the Kingdom of the Netherlands.

10.1   THE INTERNATIONAL LAW OF DECOLONIZATION AND SELF-DETERMINATION

In the view of the UN and the legal scholarship, there still exists a separate category of 'colonial peoples' which can claim a right to decolonization and self-determination. This category of 'peoples' is not so much defined by their subordination to a system of colonial government, traditionally defined as a repressive system of exploitation and discrimination, but simply on the basis of the list of overseas territories of the Western states that were known to be 'of the colonial type' in 1945. The UN General Assembly has claimed the authority to classify these territories as 'Non-Self-Governing Territories' under Chapter XI of the UN Charter, as long as they have not yet become independent, and as long as their relation with the mother country is characterized by 'arbitrary subordination', or does not otherwise comply with the Principles laid down in GA Resolution 1541 (XV) of 1960. These Principles provide that territories remain NSGTs until the population makes an informed and democratic choice to become an independent state, a freely associated territory of an independent state, or an integrated part of an independent state.

It has also been established that the choice of one of these status options can be considered as an exercise of the right to self-determination, and has to com-

S. Hillebrink, The Right to Self-Determination and Post-Colonial Governance
© 2008, T·M·C·Asser press, *The Hague, The Netherlands and the Author*

ply with the standards laid down for the self-determination of colonial peoples, most importantly the Declaration on the Granting of Independence to Colonial Countries and Peoples (GA Resolution 1514 (XV) of 1960). The International Court of Justice has confirmed that the dependent peoples have a right to self-determination in the form as developed by the organs of the UN, which it has defined as the need to pay regard to the freely expressed will of the people.

A problematic situation arises when a population also does not wish to achieve one of the accepted forms of full self-government. Based on the right to self-determination, peoples should have freedom of choice. It could be argued that the right to self-determination, defined as the freedom of choice, leaves open the possibility that a dependent people freely chooses a status that is not fully self-governing according to the standards of Resolution 1541, and which creates a subordinate position for that people. The essential criterion for the acceptability of such a status should be whether the population has made that choice in freedom and with due knowledge of the ramifications of its choice. In that case, the remaining elements of subordination should perhaps be seen as an acceptable side effect of continuing a constitutional relation between a European state and a distant island territory that considers itself too small to become independent.

All states have explicitly or implicitly recognized the UN's authority in the area of decolonization, but difference of opinion still exists on the extent of this competence. Opinions also vary on the work of the Decolonization Committee. It seems to be appreciated in most of the remaining territories, and most of the metropolitan states have relinquished some of their opposition to the Committee's involvement with their territories. At present, criticism of the Committee focuses on its supposed lack of effectiveness, and it is argued by the metropolitan states that their remaining NSGTs are no longer colonies and should therefore not be discussed by the Committee.

10.2   STATUS OPTIONS

The UN has formulated two alternatives to independence; free association and integration. The possibility of other options that could qualify as full self-government was recognized in GA Resolution 2625 of 1970, but in practice such options are viewed at the UN with even more suspicion than free association and integration, and are only accepted as temporary solutions at best.

Free association can be a satisfactory form of decolonization for small territories, if the metropolitan state is prepared to relinquish its legislative and administrative control over the territory, and to actively promote the territory's capacity to enter into international relations independently. The population of a territory should be aware that the option of free association often ends up being very close to independent statehood. While the US and New Zealand have provided their associated states with substantial financial aid, they are not obligated to do so under international law, nor does international law compel the principal states to extend their nationality to the inhabitants of associated states.

International law also recognizes the possibility of integrating overseas territories into the mother country as a form of complete decolonization. Most metropolitan governments have not been willing to discuss this option since the 1960s because of the fear that it would entail huge costs and cut off the road to independence for the territories. The few territories that have been allowed to integrate completely into the metropolis seem to be happy with it, however.

The UN is generally rather suspicious of integration as a form of decolonization. It has re-listed a number of cases of incomplete integration as NSGTs. It should probably be assumed that a status which does not represent complete integration, but does continue to grant some jurisdiction to the metropolitan state in the internal affairs of the overseas territory, may authorize the UN to consider that Chapter XI of the UN Charter and GA Resolutions 1514 and 1541 continue to apply.

The cases of Puerto Rico and New Caledonia, while hugely different in most respects, share at least one common characteristic: their current political status is somewhere in between association and integration. To some extent this 'in-betweenity' of their status causes problems, because it creates a real or imagined responsibility of the metropolis for the internal problems of the territory, which is resented by some, and considered insufficient by others. When there exists internal disagreement both in the territories and in the metropolis on the political future of the overseas relations, a stalemate situation arises, which may hamper the political development of the territory and which can occasionally even lead to violence, as happened in New Caledonia. In this territory, a solution was found by explicitly placing the decision on the future of the territory in the hands of the population. A decisive referendum will be organized between 2013 and 2018 on the political future of the territory.

10.3 Self-Government under the Charter for the Kingdom

According to the Charter for the Kingdom, the Netherlands, the Netherlands Antilles and Aruba have voluntarily chosen to create a structure in which a number of affairs are handled jointly on the basis of equivalence. They form three separate Countries which are autonomous in all affairs, except those which are listed in the Charter as affairs of the Kingdom (most importantly, foreign affairs, nationality and defence). The Kingdom has very limited powers to intervene in the autonomous affairs of the Countries.

The Kingdom is a somewhat ambiguous structure, since the Kingdom is often identified with the Country of the Netherlands, while the islands are part of the *Kingdom* of the Netherlands, but not of the *Country* of the Netherlands. The islands have the right to leave the Kingdom, based on the right to self-determination – which has been recognized by all of the Countries of the Kingdom and the islands – but the Netherlands does not have the right to terminate the relations unilaterally.

During the first decades after 1954, the self-government of the Caribbean Countries remained virtually unchallenged in the expectation that the Countries would achieve independence in the foreseeable future. Surinam became independent in 1975, but the Netherlands Antilles and Aruba chose to stay part of the Kingdom. In 1990, the Netherlands government accepted this, but the realization that the ties with the Caribbean Countries would not be severed anytime soon caused the Netherlands to become more involved with the internal affairs of the Netherlands Antilles and Aruba, especially in the areas of law enforcement and public spending. Aruba left the Netherlands Antilles in 1986 to form a separate Country within the Kingdom. In 2005, negotiations were started to dismantle the Netherlands Antilles entirely, after referendums on the islands showed that four out of five islands were in favour of obtaining a position outside of the Netherlands Antilles, but within the Kingdom.

10.4 CHARACTERIZATION OF THE KINGDOM IN CONSTITUTIONAL THEORY

The Kingdom is not a nation state in the traditional sense. There have so far been few indications of the development of a trans-Atlantic community of interests that could lead to the birth of a nation. The Charter is an expression of this reality. The federal and unitary traits that the text of the Charter exhibits, have turned out to be no more than constitutional make-up. The Kingdom functions more like a confederation, but it is different in that it is not based on a treaty, the Countries are not independent states, and the organs of the Kingdom do have some – albeit very limited – power over the citizens of the Countries. The structure of the Kingdom does not fit any of the other traditional forms of government. In the Dutch literature on constitutional law, it is usually called a construction *sui generis*, but it has also been described as a 'constitutional association' or a 'cooperative structure governed by constitutional law.'

The constitution of the Kingdom is substantially different from the other overseas forms of government discussed in this study, except perhaps the former

British West Indies Associated States, which were considered by some to be freely associated with the UK, but by others – including the UN – to be NSGTs.

Because of the large difference in size between the Netherlands and the Caribbean Countries, combined with the firm desire to change as little as possible the constitution of the Kingdom as it existed before 1954, the drafting of the Charter resulted in a structure that was not a radical breach with the colonial era, but offered a pragmatic way of realizing some of the most important wishes of the governments of the Netherlands, Surinam and the Netherlands Antilles at the time. Even though the Charter was intended to create a flexible system that could accommodate the constitutional development of the Caribbean Countries, it has chained the three Countries together in a relationship that currently creates considerable dissatisfaction, particularly in The Hague.

10.5   CHARACTERIZATION OF THE KINGDOM ORDER UNDER INTERNATIONAL LAW

The Kingdom Charter was discussed at length in the UN General Assembly, but the representatives could not agree on the characterization of the Kingdom order, nor on the questions of whether the Netherlands Antilles and Surinam remained NSGTs, whether they had exercised their right to self-determination, and whether they had achieved a full measure of self-government. A majority of states seemed to think that the answer to these last two questions should be 'no'. A Resolution was adopted by which the GA accepted that the Netherlands would no longer report on the Netherlands Antilles and Surinam, but which left the other issues intentionally undecided.

The international status of the Netherlands Antilles (and Aruba) was thus left somewhat unclear. Based on the debates of 1955 it cannot be excluded that the UN could at some point decide to test the Kingdom Charter against Chapter XI of the UN Charter. The UN has interpreted the provisions of Chapter XI in a number of Resolutions, the most pertinent in this case is Resolution 1541 of 1960. The Principles annexed to this Resolution were defined with the active participation of the Netherlands, and have been generally accepted as a legally binding interpretation of the UN Charter provisions. The UN would probably test the Kingdom order against this Resolution if the need arose, as it has done in the cases of New Caledonia and Puerto Rico.

The Kingdom order does not comply fully with the forms of decolonization as defined by Resolution 1541. The Netherlands Antilles and Aruba are not integrated into the Netherlands, and the fact that they are an integral part of the Kingdom is not very meaningful for the application of Principles VIII and IX of Resolution 1541. The Kingdom relations are more similar to a form of free association, because the Countries are autonomous in most areas and the Charter mainly provides a structure for voluntary cooperation. A number of aspects of the Kingdom order do not, however, comply with the criteria for free association. These concern the powers of the Kingdom to intervene in the internal affairs of the Caribbean Countries without their consent, and the fact that the present status of the Caribbean Countries is not – at least not clearly – based on an act of free choice by the populations of the islands.

Since the majority of the UN member states thought that the status of Country within the Kingdom did not represent 'a full measure of self-government', and since that status also does not comply fully with the Principles of Resolution 1541, it could be argued that Chapter XI of the UN Charter still applies to the Netherlands Antilles and Aruba, or that the UN might decide that this is the case.

10.6 IMPLICATIONS FOR THE KINGDOM OF THE INTERNATIONAL LAW CONCERNING SELF-DETERMINATION AND DECOLONIZATION

If it is indeed assumed that Chapter XI of the UN Charter still applies to the Netherlands Antilles and Aruba, then there continue to exist a number of international obligations for the Kingdom as a whole. The obligation to respect the wishes of the populations is the central element of self-determination, as defined by the International Court of Justice. A completion of the decolonization process can probably only be achieved when the populations of the Netherlands Antilles and Aruba make a free choice for a status that complies with the international standards for full self-government.

The GA is of the opinion that the UN should supervise these types of self-determination processes. It could be wondered whether the Decolonization Committee could usefully play such a monitoring role, although much depends on the attitude of the Administering state in these cases. It has been suggested that other UN organs could assist the Kingdom and the Caribbean governments in providing information on the status options and monitoring the process of decolonization. This suggestion should receive serious consideration by the authorities of the Kingdom and the islands.

10.7   THE RIGHT TO SELF-DETERMINATION OF THE ISLAND TERRITORIES

The decolonization of the Netherlands Antilles has been complicated from the start due to the fact that the territory consisted of very diverse islands that are located far apart. In 1981, it was decided by the Countries and the six islands that the choice of its political future would be for each island to decide for itself, based on the right to self-determination. In 1986, Aruba left the Antilles to become a separate Country within the Kingdom. One final attempt by the five remaining islands to make the Antilles work failed during the 1990s. Referendums were held between 2000 and 2005, which showed that the populations of four of the islands were now in favour of breaking up the Country entirely.

In the legal literature the question has been raised whether the break-up of the Antilles does not violate the *uti possidetis* or non-disruption principle, which provides that states should not cooperate with the secession of parts of dependent territories which are on their way to independence. Leaving aside the question whether the Netherlands Antilles is still – or ever was – on its way to independence, it could be wondered whether this principle is really a part of international law when it concerns small dependent island territories.

The international practice with regard to such territories suggests that it is allowed to cooperate with the secession of islands. As long as there was popular support for it, and as long as the metropolitan government did not actively promote, there has often been no clear international opposition to the secession of one or more islands from a dependent archipelago, even if it occurred shortly before independence. The practice does not reveal, however, what form the popular support should take. A referendum is considered indispensable by some writers, but should such a referendum be held on all of the islands, or only on the seceding island(s)? Absence of strong popular opposition on the other islands has sometimes been considered sufficient, as in the case of the secession of Aruba.

At present, it is uncertain whether the populations of the remaining Antilles still form one 'people' for the purpose of self-determination and the application of the non-disruption principle. Possibly the recognition of the right to self-determination of the separate islands in 1981 should be interpreted to mean that the Antillean people no longer exists, and that the population of each island constitutes a separate people.

The current situation within the Netherlands Antilles is exceptional because separate referendums have been held on all of the five islands based on the right to self-determination, while the outcome on St Eustatius – that the Netherlands Antilles should remain together as a single Country – is not compatible with the outcome on the other four islands, which voted in favour of breaking up the Country. The Round Table Conference of 2005 decided to go ahead with the break-up of the Netherlands Antilles, which seems a reasonable decision as long as the population of St Eustatius is given the opportunity to approve the new status that will be devised for that island.

10.8   THE RIGHT TO SELF-DETERMINATION IN RELATION TO THE EUROPEAN UNION

An additional question, which currently has some relevance, is whether the law of decolonization and self-determination might also have implications for the European Union in its relations with the Netherlands Antilles and Aruba. I answered this question in the affirmative, because the EEC in 1957 took on part of the 'sacred trust' of Chapter XI of the UN Charter towards the overseas territories of the member states. In so far as the metropolitan states are no longer capable to take measures to realize the goals of Chapter XI for their OCTs because of the European integration, these measures should be taken by the EU.

For EU law to conform to the right to self-determination of the OCTs, and their separate status under international law, the OCTs will have to be given a formal say in the shaping of the association which exists between them and the EU. Also, the EU and the member states should not frustrate a legitimate exercise of the right to self-determination of an OCT, including the Netherlands Antilles and Aruba. The EU Commission and the OCTs have been working on the modernization of the association for the last 15 years. The view of the character of the association that is currently taken by all the parties involved should also be reflected by the EC Treaty (or the EU Constitution).

At present, the consent of all member states is required for a status change of an OCT, because the OCTs are listed in Annex II to the EC Treaty. But if such a status change is part of a self-determination process in relation to the mother country, the other member states should not frustrate that process by refusing a territory to enter or exit the EU. The EU and the member states cannot be forced, however, to grant the territory a preferential status as UPT. That would be a matter for negotiations between the Kingdom, the EU, and the other member states.

The application of the right to self-determination and decolonization to the relationship between the EU and overseas territories means that a status change can only be realized in agreement with the overseas people involved. Within the Kingdom of the Netherlands, Article 25 of the Kingdom Charter provides a veto right for the Caribbean Countries with regard to the Treaty amendments needed to change their status from OCT to UPT or another status.

10.9   EPILOGUE

The results of the referendums that were held on all of the Antillean islands between 1993 and 2005 and the results of the general elections in those islands and Aruba indicate that the populations are mainly interested in status options that lie somewhere in between independence and integration with the Netherlands. The ties with the Netherlands are considered important, and for the time being independence is clearly rejected. The Netherlands government has accepted this reality, but at the same time seeks to create more effective tools for the Kingdom to realize its responsibilities in the Caribbean, especially in the new entities that will be created after the dissolution of the Netherlands Antilles, but also in Aruba where the rule of law is sometimes under pressure due to the small scale of the society.

The Netherlands set conditions before cooperating with realizing the *status aparte* of Aruba in 1986, and before it agreed to an indefinite continuation of that status after 1996. It has also set conditions to its cooperation with realizing the outcome of the referenda on the other islands of the Netherlands Antilles. This is not unreasonable in itself, since the Kingdom to a large extent revolves around the assistance offered to the Caribbean islands by the Netherlands. In case a conflict arises concerning these conditions, general legal principles such as good faith, equity and proportionality should guide the authorities of the Netherlands, the other Countries and the islands in the fulfilment of their obligation to realize as well as possible the 'free and genuine expression of the will of the people.'

The Caribbean populations should be aware of the consequences of the options open to them, in order for their choice to be considered a proper exercise of the right to self-determination. In preparation of the various referendums on the islands, considerable amounts of information were distributed, and debates were held on the issues of self-determination and the political future of the islands. This should be seen as an important step towards exercising the right to self-determination.

The status debate is sometimes denounced as unimportant, and diverting attention away from really important issues such as the economy. If that is true, it provides an additional argument to bring this debate to a speedy and satisfactory conclusion. In view of the remarkable nature of the Kingdom relations – some might call it a freak of history – spanning the Atlantic Ocean and crossing considerable cultural differences, the status debate will not simply disappear, but needs to be resolved in a satisfactory manner.

The principle that the overseas populations should have the final say on their own political future has been recognized to an increasing extent in the practice of the Netherlands and other metropolitan governments during the twentieth century. The declining international interest in decolonization, however, especially when it concerns small islands which are unlikely to cause serious international conflicts, has meant that it often takes territories a long time and much persistence to obtain metropolitan agreement to status changes, unless it is independence that the territory wants.

The right to self-determination of small overseas territories has a distinctly do-it-yourself character in the eyes of the metropolitan governments, including the Netherlands. It cannot be denied that the overseas populations should decide for themselves, this is what self-determination means,[1] but especially in the smallest and least developed territories, the metropolitan government should not take lightly its obligations under Chapter XI of the UN Charter to ensure that the population has access to information concerning its rights under international law, and the opportunity to express an informed opinion on its political future. Ultimately, the Kingdom cannot hide behind the autonomy of the Caribbean Countries and the Antillean island governments.

At the time of writing, work is underway to transform the general direction which the referendums have indicated into concrete proposals for a new status of the five islands of the Netherlands Antilles. Bonaire, St Eustatius and Saba have chosen to become part of the Netherlands, and Curaçao and St Maarten want to become Countries within the Kingdom. Before these proposals are implemented, the authorities concerned should make sure that the proposals really reflect the wishes of the populations, so that the new situation can be seen as a realization of the right to self-determination.

The position of Aruba is somewhat different from the islands of the Netherlands Antilles, because it – or at least a majority of its politicians – do not want its status changed. Aruba is prepared to cooperate with the Charter amendments that will be required for the break-up of the Antilles, as long as its *status aparte* remains unchanged. This position does justice to the right to self-determination of the Antillean islands.

Aruba's current status was achieved as a result of a long and persistent struggle against the dominant position of Curaçao within the Netherlands Antilles. But while it may be accepted that Aruba's decision to stay a part of the Kingdom as

---

[1] A headline in the *Amigoe* newspaper of 6 May 2004 accurately summarized a lecture that I gave at the University of Aruba as '*Zelfbeschikkingsrecht moet je zelf doen*' ('Self-determination means do-it-yourself').

a separate Country did not go against the wishes of the population, it would perhaps go too far to say that the status of Aruba under the Kingdom Charter was the result of a free and informed choice by the Aruban people. The decision to leave the Netherlands Antilles clearly enjoyed the support of many Arubans, but it is not certain how the Aruban people would view alternatives to its current status. Most political parties on Aruba continue to defend the current definition of *status aparte* fervently, but the referendums on the Antillean islands have shown that unanimity among politicians on constitutional status does not necessarily always reflect the wishes of the population. In view of the sometimes difficult political relations between Aruba and the Netherlands, Aruba should perhaps wonder whether further steps could not be taken in its process of decolonization, obviously with due regard for the wishes of the population.

BIBLIOGRAPHY*

Abdullah 1991
F. Abdullah, 'The Right to Decolonization', in: Mohammed Bedjaoui (ed.), *International Law: Achievements and Prospects*, Paris: Unesco 1991, pp. 1205-17.

Agarwal 1966
Jamuna Prasad Agarwal, *Die Assoziierung der überseeischen Staaten und Gebiete mit der Europäischen Wirtschaftsgemeinschaft und die Auswirkung dieser Assoziierung auf die Ausfuhr der nichtassoziierten Entwicklungsländer in diese Gemeinschaft* (Kieler Studien, No. 77), Tübingen: J.C.B. Mohr (Paul Siebeck) 1966.

Agniel 1997
Guy Agniel, 'L'expérience statutaire de la Nouvelle-Calédonie. Ou de l'étude du mouvement du yo-yo au service de l'évolution institutionelle d'un territoire d'outre-mer', in: Jean-Yves Faberon (ed.), *L'avenir statutaire de la Nouvelle-Calédonie. L'évolution des liens de la France avec ses collectivités périphériques* (colloquium organized by the Centre de recherches et d'études administratives de Montpellier, also published in *Notes et études documentaires* No. 5053-5, 16 June 1997), Paris: La documentation Française 1997, pp. 41-57.

Albaharna 1968
Husain M. Albaharna, *The Legal Status of the Arabian Gulf States. A Study of their Treaty Relations and their International Problems*, Manchester: Manchester University Press 1968.

Alberts 2003
A.J. Alberts (ed.), *Fact-finding mission Madeira en Canarische eilanden. Studie naar de praktische werking van de Ultraperifere status binnen de Europese Unie*, Aruba: Fundacion Estundionan Social Christian 2003.

Aldrich 1993
Robert Aldrich, *France and the South Pacific since 1940*, Basingstoke: Macmillan 1993.

Aldrich 1997
Robert Aldrich, 'France in the Indian Ocean: Declining Independence in Mayotte', in: Robert Aldrich & Isabelle Merle, *France Abroad. Indochina, New Caledonia, Wallis and Futuna, Mayotte*, [Sydney, NSW]: University of Sydney 1997, pp. 99-168.

Aldrich & Connell 1992
Robert Aldrich & John Connell, *France's Overseas Frontier. Départements et Territoires d'Outre-mer*, Cambridge: Cambridge University Press 1992.

Aldrich & Connell 1998
Robert Aldrich & John Connell, *The Last Colonies*, Cambridge: Cambridge University Press 1998.

Alkema 1984
E.A. Alkema, 'Wat betekenen de Europese mensenrechten voor de Antilliaanse rechtspraktijk?', 5 *Tijdschrift voor Antilliaans recht* (1984) pp. 1-12.

---

* Note: 'De Jong' is found under 'D' and 'Van Aller' is found under 'V'.

Alkema 1995

E.A. Alkema, 'Nederland een verander(en)de Koninkrijkspartner?', *Tijdschrift voor Antilliaans recht-Justicia* (1995), no. 4, pp. 132-42.

Arangio-Ruiz 1979

Gaetano Arangio-Ruiz, *The Declaration on Friendly Relations and the System of the Sources of International Law*, Alphen aan den Rijn: Sijthoff 1979.

Asamoah 1966

Obed Y. Asamoah, *The Legal Significance of the Declarations of the General Assembly of the United Nations*, The Hague: Martinus Nijhoff 1966.

Autin 1997

Jean-Louis Autin, 'L'avenir statutaire de la Nouvelle-Calédonie', in: Jean-Yves Faberon (ed.), *L'avenir statutaire de la Nouvelle-Calédonie. L'évolution des liens de la France avec ses collectivités périphériques* (colloquium organized by the Centre de recherches et d'études administratives de Montpellier, also published in *Notes et études documentaires* No. 5053-5, 16 June 1997), Paris: La documentation Française 1997, pp. 261-71.

Baker 1929

Noel Baker, *The Present Juridical Status of the British Dominions in International Law*, London: Longmans 1929.

Barbier 1974

Maurice Barbier, *Le Comité de Décolonisation des Nations Unies*, Paris: Librairie Générale de Droit et de Jurisprudence 1974.

Barsh 1984

Russel Lawrence Barsh, 'The International Legal Status of Native Alaska', *Alaska Native News*, July 1984, p. 35 et seq.

Bekkers, Boot & Van der Windt 2003

H. Bekkers, A. Boot & N. van der Windt, *Nederlandse Antillen. LGO of UPG?*, Rotterdam: SEOR 2003.

Belinfante & De Reede 1997

A.D. Belinfante & J.L. de Reede, *Beginselen van het Nederlandse Staatsrecht*, Alphen a/d Rijn: Samson H.D. Tjeenk Willink 1997.

Belle Antoine 1999

Rose-Marie Belle Antoine, *Commonwealth Caribbean Law and Legal Systems*, London: Routledge Cavendish 1999.

Bergamin & Van Maarseveen 1978

R.J.B. Bergamin & H.Th.J.F. van Maarseveen, 'Constitutional and Administrative Law', in: D.C. Fokkema et al. (eds.), *Introduction to Dutch Law for Foreign Lawyers*, Deventer: Kluwer 1978, pp. 381-434.

Berman 1998

Alan Berman, 'Future Kanak Independence in New Caledonia: Reality or Illusion?', 34 *Stanford Journal of International Law* (1998) pp. 287-346.

Bernier 1973

Ivan Bernier, *International Legal Aspects of Federalism*, London: Longman 1973.

Besselink 1998

Leonard F.M. Besselink, 'Suiker en rijst uit de West. Over Europees recht en de Koninkrijks-verhoudingen', *NJB* (1998) pp. 1291-96.

Besselink 2000

Leonard F.M. Besselink, 'Community Loyalty and Constitutional Loyalty', 6 *European Public Law* (2000) No. 2 pp. 169-82.

Besselink 2003
Leonard F.M. Besselink, 'Commentaar bij de voorlichting van de eerste afdeling van de Raad van State over de verhouding van de Nederlandse Antillen en Aruba tot de Europese Unie, verzonden door de Raad van State van het Koninkrijk op 9 september 2003' (not published, but available on the website of the author at the University of Utrecht <http://www.uu.nl>), [s.n.]: [s.n.] [2003].

Besselink 2004
Leonard F.M. Besselink, *Kingdom of the Netherlands. Charter and Constitution*, Nijmegen: Ars Aequi 2004.

Besselink 2007
Leonard F.M. Besselink, 'Nederlands postkoloniaal kiesrecht: het Europees Parlement en de Tweede Kamer', *Nederlands tijdschrift voor Europees recht* (2007) pp. 64-71.

Besselink et al. 2002
Leonard F.M. Besselink et al., *De Nederlandse Grondwet en de Europese Unie*, Groningen: Europa Law Publishing 2002.

Bijkerk 2003
M. Bijkerk, 'We tillen de Antillen ... met een paardensprong', *NJB* (2003) p. 1862.

Blaustein/Raworth 2001a
Philip Raworth (ed.), 'Netherlands Dependencies', in: Albert P. Blaustein, Eric B. Blaustein and Philip Raworth (eds.), *Constitutions of Dependencies and Territories* (Release 2001-1), Dobbs Ferry, New York: Oceana 2002.

Blaustein/Raworth 2001b
Philip Raworth (ed.), 'New Zealand Dependencies. Cook Islands', in: Albert P. Blaustein, Eric B. Blaustein and Philip Raworth (eds.), *Constitutions of Dependencies and Territories* (Release 2001-1), Dobbs Ferry, New York: Oceana 2001.

Blaustein/Raworth 2001c
Philip Raworth (ed.), 'New Zealand Dependencies. Commentary', in: Albert P. Blaustein, Eric B. Blaustein and Philip Raworth (eds.), *Constitutions of Dependencies and Territories* (Release 2001-1), Dobbs Ferry, New York: Oceana 2001.

Blaustein/Raworth 2002
Philip Raworth (ed.), 'Introduction', in: Albert P. Blaustein, Eric B. Blaustein and Philip Raworth (eds.), *Constitutions of Dependencies and Territories* (Release 2002-3), Dobbs Ferry, New York: Oceana 2002.

Blérald 1989
Alain Philippe Blérald, 'Le bilan économique et social de la départementalisation. Une autre dépendance?', in: Jean-Claude Fortier (ed.), *Questions sur l'administration des DOM. Décentraliser outre-mer?*, Paris: Economica 1989, pp. 251-69.

Blok et al. 1982
D.P. Blok et al. (eds.), *Algemene geschiedenis der Nederlanden. Deel 15: Nieuwste tijd*, Haarlem: Fibula-Van Dishoeck 1982.

Boerefijn 1999
Ineke Boerefijn, *The Reporting Procedure under the Covenant on Civil and Political Rights: Practice and Procedure of the Human Rights Committee*, Antwerp: Intersentia 1999.

Boneparth & Wilkinson 1995
Ellen Boneparth & M. James Wilkinson, 'Terminating Trusteeship for the Federated States of Micronesia and the Republic of the Marshall Islands: Independence and Self-Sufficiency in the Post-Cold War Pacific', 18 *Pacific Studies* (1995) pp. 61-77.

Bongenaar 1987
K.E.M. Bongenaar, *Kurasón Kurasoleño?*, Curaçao: [s.n.] 1987.
Bongenaar 1991
K.E.M. Bongenaar, 'De Schets van een gemenebestconstitutie voor het Koninkrijk der Nederlanden. Enig commentaar op de nota van minister Hirsch Ballin', in: E.L. Joubert et al. (eds.), *Uní ku UNA. Noten bij Van der Grinten* (opstellen aangeboden aan prof. mr. W.C.L. van der Grinten ter gelegenheid van zijn afscheid als gastdocent aan de Universiteit van de Nederlandse Antillen), Zwolle: W.E.J. Tjeenk Willink 1991, pp. 1-21.
Borman 1986
C. Borman, 'Aruba land in het Koninkrijk', 35 *Ars Aequi* (1986) pp. 361-69.
Borman 1988
C. Borman, 'Na grondwetsherziening ook statuutsherziening?', in: M.M. den Boer et al. (eds.), *Gegeven de Grondwet* (bundel ter gelegenheid van het 25-jarig bestaan van de stafafdeling Constitutionele Zaken en Wetgeving van het Ministerie van Binnenlandse Zaken), Deventer: Kluwer 1988, pp. 3-18.
Borman 2005
C. Borman, *Het Statuut voor het Koninkrijk*, Deventer: W.E.J. Tjeenk Willink 2005.
Bos 1976
Maarten Bos, 'Surinam's Road from Self-Government to Sovereignty', 7 *NYIL* (1976) pp. 131-55.
Bowett/Sands/Klein 2001
Philippe Sands & Pierre Klein, *Bowett's Law of International Institutions*, London: Sweet & Maxwell 2001.
Branchet 1991
Bernard Branchet, 'Saint-Pierre-et-Miquelon: Un statut particulier', in: Emmanuel Jos & Danielle Perrot (eds.), *L'outre-mer et l'Europe communautaire. Quelle insertion? Pour quel développement?* (Journées d'études du Centre de recherche sur les pouvoirs locaux dans la Caraïbe de l'Université des Antilles-Guyane, October 1991), Paris: Economica 1991, pp. 297-311.
Breillat 1993
D. Breillat, 'La France ultra-marine', in: D. Breillat et al., *Naar een nieuwe structuur van het Koninkrijk* (Staatsrechtconferentie 1993. Publikaties van de Staatsrechtkring, no. 6), Zwolle: Tjeenk Willink. 1993, pp. 1-32.
Brial 1998
Fabien Brial, 'La place des régions ultrapériphériques au sein de l'union européenne', 34 *Cahiers de droit européen* (1998) pp. 639-59.
Brierly 1955
J.L. Brierly, *The Law of Nations. An Introduction to the International Law of Peace*, Oxford: Clarendon 1955.
Brisk 1969
William J. Brisk, *The Dilemma of a Ministate: Anguilla* (Studies in International Affairs, No. 7), Columbia NY: Institute of International Studies 1969.
Brison 2005
Denicio Brison, 'The Kingdom's Charter (Het Statuut): Fifty years in the wilderness', in: Lammert de Jong & Douwe Boersema (eds.), *The Kingdom of the Netherlands in the Caribbean: 1954-2004. What Next?*, Amsterdam: Rozenberg Publishers 2005, pp. 35-43.
Broderick 1968
Margaret Broderick, 'Associated Statehood – A New Form of Decolonisation', 17 *ICLQ* (1968) pp. 368-403.

Broek & Wijenberg 2005
Aart G. Broek & Jan J. Wijenberg, 'Het roer moet om. Naar ongedeeld Nederlanderschap voor Antillianen en Arubanen', 44 *Civis Mundi* (2005) pp. 178-86.
Brown 1991
Jonathan Brown (ed.), 'Australian Practice in International Law 1984-1987', in: D.W. Grieg (ed.), *Australian Year Book of International Law* (Vol. 11), Canberra: The Australian National University 1991, pp. 179-84.
Brownlie 2003
Ian Brownlie, *Principles of Public International Law*, Oxford: Oxford University Press 2003.
BuZa 1952a
Suriname en de Nederlandse Antillen in de Verenigde Naties (Uitgaven van het Ministerie van Buitenlandse Zaken, No. 28), The Hague: Staatsdrukkerij- en Uitgeverijbedrijf 1952.
BuZa 1952b
Verslag over de zesde Algemene Vergadering van de Verenigde Naties (Uitgaven van het Ministerie van Buitenlandse Zaken, No. 29), The Hague: Staatsdrukkerij- en Uitgeverijbedrijf 1952.
BuZa 1953
Verslag over het eerste gedeelte van de zevende Algemene Vergadering van de Verenigde Naties (Uitgaven van het Ministerie van Buitenlandse Zaken, No. 32), The Hague: Staatsdrukkerij- en Uitgeverijbedrijf 1953.
BuZa 1954a
Verslag over de achtste Algemene Vergadering van de Verenigde Naties (Uitgaven van het Ministerie van Buitenlandse Zaken, No. 34), The Hague: Staatsdrukkerij- en Uitgeverijbedrijf 1954.
BuZa 1954b
Suriname en de Nederlandse Antillen in de Verenigde Naties II (Uitgaven van het Ministerie van Buitenlandse Zaken, No. 36), The Hague: Staatsdrukkerij- en Uitgeverijbedrijf 1954.
BuZa 1955
Verslag over de negende Algemene Vergadering van de Verenigde Naties (Uitgaven van het Ministerie van Buitenlandse Zaken, No. 39), The Hague: Staatsdrukkerij- en Uitgeverijbedrijf 1955.
BuZa 1956a
Suriname en de Nederlandse Antillen in de Verenigde Naties III (Uitgaven van het Ministerie van Buitenlandse Zaken, No. 41), The Hague: Staatsdrukkerij- en Uitgeverijbedrijf 1956.
BuZa 1956b
Verslag over de tiende Algemene Vergadering van de Verenigde Naties (Uitgaven van het Ministerie van Buitenlandse Zaken, No. 43), The Hague: Staatsdrukkerij- en Uitgeverijbedrijf 1956.
BuZa 1961
Verslag over het eerste gedeelte van de vijftiende Algemene Vergadering van de Verenigde Naties (Uitgaven van het Ministerie van Buitenlandse Zaken, No. 67), The Hague: Staatsdrukkerij- en Uitgeverijbedrijf 1961.
Cabranes 1978
José A. Cabranes, 'Puerto Rico: Out of the Colonial Closet', *Foreign Policy* (1978-1979) No. 33, Winter.
Carr 1984
Raymond Carr, *Puerto Rico: A Colonial Experiment*, New York: New York University Press 1984.

Cassese 1979
Antonio Cassese, 'Political Self-Determination – Old Concepts and New Developments', in: Antonio Cassese (ed.), *UN Law / Fundamental Rights: Two Topics in International Law*, Alphen aan den Rijn: Sijthoff & Noordhoff 1979, pp. 137-66.

Cassese 1981
Antonio Cassese, 'The Self-Determination of Peoples', in: Louis Henkin (ed.), *The International Bill of Rights: The Covenant on Civil and Political Rights*, New York: Columbia University Press 1981, pp. 92-113.

Cassese 1995
Antonio Cassese, *Self-determination of peoples: A legal reappraisal*, Cambridge: Cambridge University Press 1995.

Cassese 2001
Antonio Cassese, *International Law*, Oxford: Oxford University Press 2001.

Castañeda 1969
Jorge Castañeda, *Legal Effects of United Nations Resolutions*, New York: Columbia University Press 1969.

Castanha 1996
Anthony Castanha, *The Hawaiian Sovereignty Movement. Roles of and Impacts on Non-Hawaiians* (dissertation, University of Hawai'i), 1996 (published on the internet at <http://www.hookele.com/non-hawaiians/index.html>, visited on 5 February 2004).

Castellino 2000
Joshua Castellino, *International Law and Self-Determination: The Interplay of the Politics of Territorial Possession with Formulations of Post-Colonial 'National' Identity*, The Hague: Martinus Nijhoff 2000.

Chenal 1976
A. Chenal, 'Le Territoire Français des Afars et des Issas', *Annuaire du tiers monde* (1976) pp. 327-32.

Chapman 1982
Terry M. Chapman, et al., *Niue. A History of the Island*, [s. l.]: Institute of Pacific Studies & The Government of Niue 1982.

Churchill 2002
Ward Churchill, 'The Right of Hawai'i to be Restored to the United Nations List of Non-Self-Governing Territories', 1 *DES: A Scholarly Journal of Ethnic Studies* (2002) (published on the internet at <http://www.colorado.edu/EthnicStudies/ethnicstudiesjournal/> visited 5 February 2004).

Ciavarini Azzi 2004
Giuseppe Ciavarini Azzi, 'Mayotte et l'Union européenne: Entre PTOM et RUP', European Commission, 20 July 2004.

Clark 1980
Roger S. Clark, 'Self-Determination and Free Association: Should the United Nations Terminate the Pacific Islands Trust?', 21 *Harv. ILJ* (1980) pp. 1-86.

Clark & Roff 1984
Roger S. Clark and Sue Rabbitt Roff, *Micronesia: The Problem of Palau* (Minority Rights Group, Report No. 63), [s.l.]: Minority Rights Group 1984.

Connell 1970
D.P. Connell, *International Law*, London: Stevens 1970.

Connell 1987
John Connell, *New Caledonia or Kanaky? The Political History of a French Colony* (Pacific Research Monograph No. 16), Canberra: National Development Studies Centre 1987.

Connell & Aldrich 1992
John Connell & Robert Aldrich, 'Europe's Overseas Territories: Vestiges of Colonialism or Windows on the World?', in: Helen M. Hintjens & Malyn D. D. Newitt (eds.), *The Political Economy of Small Tropical Islands. The Importance of Being Small*, Exeter: University of Exeter Press 1992, pp. 30-41.

Connell 1994
John Connell, 'Britain's Caribbean Colonies: The End of the Era of Decolonisation?', 32 *Journal of Commonwealth and Comparative Politics* (1994), pp. 87-106.

Constant 1992
Fred Constant, 'Alternative Forms of Decolonisation in the East Caribbean. The Comparative Politics of the Non-Sovereign Islands', in: Helen M. Hintjens & Malyn D. D. Newitt (eds.), *The Political Economy of Small Tropical Islands. The Importance of Being Small*, Exeter: University of Exeter Press 1992, pp. 51-63.

Corbin 2000
Carlyle Corbin, 'What Future for the United Nations' Decolonisation Process?', *Indigenous Affairs* (2000) No. 1, pp. 4-13.

Corbin 2006
Carlyle Corbin, 'Decolonisation and Self-Government in the Netherlands Antilles', *Overseas Territories Report*, Vol. V, No. 3 (June 2006), pp. 1-13.

Crawford 1979
James Crawford, *The Creation of States in International Law*, Oxford: Clarendon Press 1979.

Crawford 1988
James Crawford (ed.), *The Rights of Peoples*, Oxford: Clarendon Press 1988.

Crawford 1989
James Crawford, 'Islands as Sovereign Nations', 38 *ICLQ* (1989) pp. 277-98.

Crawford 1996
James Crawford, *Democracy in International Law*, Cambridge: Cambridge University Press 1994.

Crawford 1997
James Crawford, 'State Practice and International Law in Relation to Unilateral Secession' (published on the website of the Canadian Justice Department: <http://canada.justice.gc.ca/>, visited on 21 December 2003).

Crawford 2001
James Crawford, 'The Right of Self-Determination in International Law: Its Development and Future', in: Philip Alston (ed.), *Peoples' Rights*, Oxford: Oxford University Press 2001, pp. 7-67.

Crawford 2002
James Crawford, *The International Law Commission's Articles on State Responsibility. Introduction, Text and Commentaries*, Cambridge: Cambridge University Press 2002.

Crawford 2006
James Crawford, *The Creation of States in International Law*. Second Edition, Oxford: Clarendon Press 2006.

Crocombe & Tuainekore Crocombe 1996
Ron Crocombe & Marjorie Tuainekore Crocombe, 'The Cook Islands', *The Contemporary Pacific* (1996) pp. 174-82.

Croes & Croes 1989

A.G. Croes & R.R. Croes, *Doño di nos proprio destino. Aruba en haar recht op zelfbeschikking* (memorandum on behalf of the Aruban political party *AVP*), [s.l.]: [s.n.] [1989].

Croes 1992

A.G. Croes, 'Op de grenzen van het Statuut' (part one, published in two parts), *A.J.V. Nieuwsbrief* (1992) no. 4, pp. 18-23.

Croes 2005

A.G. Croes, 'De "reinvention" van het Koninkrijk' in: Lammert de Jong & Douwe Boersema (eds.), *The Kingdom of the Netherlands in the Caribbean: 1954-2004. What next?*, Amsterdam: Rozenberg Publishers 2005, pp. 65-80.

Croes 2006

A.G. Croes, *De herdefiniëring van het Koninkrijk*, Nijmegen: Wolf Legal Publishers 2006.

Croes & Moenir Alam 1990

Robertico Croes & Lucita Moenir Alam, 'Decolonization of Aruba within the Netherlands Antilles', in: Betty Sedoc-Dahlberg (ed.), *The Dutch Caribbean: Prospects for Democracy*, New York: Gordon and Breach 1990, pp. 81-102.

Croese 1998

Koen Croese, *Interventie op afspraak: Nederlandse Mariniers op Curaçao*, Zutphen: Walburg Pers 1998.

Dahm 1958

Georg Dahm, *Völkerrecht. Band I*, Stuttgart: Kohlhammer 1958.

Dalhuisen et al. 1997

Leo Dalhuisen, Ronald Donk, Rosemarijn Hoefte & Frans Steegh (eds.), *Geschiedenis van de Antillen. Aruba, Bonaire, Curaçao, Saba, Sint-Eustatius, Sint Maarten*, Zutphen: Walburg Pers 1997.

Davies 1995

Elizabeth W. Davies, *The Legal Status of British Dependent Territories: The West Indies and North Atlantic Region*, Cambridge: Cambridge University Press 1995.

Daws 1974

Gavan Daws, *Shoal of Time. A History of the Hawaiian Islands*, Honolulu: University of Hawaii Press 1974.

De Bernardi 1998

Corine de Bernardi, *L'Applicabilité du droit international et du droit communautaire dans les territoires d'outre-mer français*, Paris: Ellipses 1998.

Dekker 1998

Cees T. Dekker, 'The Ambit of the Free Movement of Goods under the Association of Overseas Countries and Territories', 23 *European Law Review* (1998) pp. 272-78.

De Deckker 1996

Paul de Deckker, 'Decolonisation Processes in the South Pacific Islands: A Comparative Analysis Between Metropolitan Powers', 26 *Victoria University of Wellington Law Review*, (1996) pp. 355-71.

De Deckker 1997

Paul de Deckker, 'Evolutions statutaires dans le Pacifique insulaire: la manière anglo-saxonne', in: Jean-Yves Faberon (ed.), *L'avenir statutaire de la Nouvelle-Calédonie. L'évolution des liens de la France avec ses collectivités périphériques* (colloquium organized by the Centre de recherches et d'études administratives de Montpellier, also published in *Notes et études documentaires* No. 5053-5, 16 June 1997), Paris: La documentation Française 1997, pp. 82-98.

De Gaay Fortman 1947
B. de Gaay Fortman, *Schets van de politieke geschiedenis der Nederlandsche Antillen in de twintigste eeuw (Curaçao)*, The Hague: Van Hoeve 1947.

De Jong 2002
Lammert de Jong, *De werkvloer van het Koninkrijk. Over de samenwerking van Nederland met de Nederlandse Antillen en Aruba*, Amsterdam: Rozenberg Publishers 2002.

Dempsey 1976
Guy Dempsey, 'Self-determination and Security in the Pacific: A Study of the Covenant between the United States and the Northern Mariana Islands', 9 *New York University Journal of International Law and Politics* (1976) pp. 277-302.

De Smith 1968
S.A. de Smith, 'Mauritius: Constitutionalism in a Plural Society', 31 *MLR* (1968) pp. 601-22.

De Smith 1970
S.A. de Smith, *Microstates and Micronesia: Problems of America's Pacific Islands and Other Minute Territories*, New York: New York University Press 1970.

De Smith 1974
S.A. de Smith, 'Exceeding Small', in: *International Organization: Law in Movement: Essays in Honour of John McMahon*, London: Oxford University Press 1974, pp. 64-78.

De Werd 1996
Marc de Werd, 'Parlementaire zeggenschap bij rijksregelgeving', *NJB* (1996) pp. 1452-58.

De Werd 1997
Marc de Werd, 'Een Rijkshof voor het Koninkrijk', *NJB* (1997) pp. 1851-52.

De Werd 1998
Marc de Werd, 'Nogmaals: een Rijkshof voor het Koninkrijk', *NJB* (1998) pp. 1870-72.

Dip 2004
C.E. Dip, *Verzamelde Geschriften van Carlos Elias Dip*, Amsterdam: SWP 2004.

Dobbin & Hezel 1998
Jay Dobbin & Francis X. Hezel, 'Sustainable Human Development in Micronesia', *Micronesian Counselor*, No. 21 (March 1998) (reproduced on <http://micsem.org>, last visited on 13 April 2008).

Doehring 2002
Karl Doehring, 'Self-Determination', in: Bruno Simma et al. (eds.), *The Charter of the United Nations: A Commentary*, Oxford University Press 2002, pp. 47-63.

Dormoy 1997
Daniel Dormoy, 'Le droit international et les possibilités d'évolutions statutaires', in: Jean-Yves Faberon (ed.), *L'avenir statutaire de la Nouvelle-Calédonie. L'évolution des liens de la France avec ses collectivités périphériques* (colloquium organized by the Centre de recherches et d'études administratives de Montpellier, also published in *Notes et études documentaires* No. 5053-5, 16 June 1997), Paris: La documentation Française 1997, pp. 109-14.

Drower 1992
George Drower, *Britain's Dependent Territories. A Fistful of Islands*, Aldershot: Dartmouth 1992.

Duursma 1996
Jorri Duursma, *Fragmentation and the International Relations of Micro-States. Self-Determination. Self-Determination and Statehood*, Cambridge: Cambridge University Press 1996.

Duzanson 2000
Louis Duzanson, *An Introduction to Government. Island Territory of St. Maarten*, Philipsburg, St Maarten: House of Nehesi 2000.
El-Ayouty 1971
Yassin El-Ayouty, *The United Nations and Decolonization: The Role of Afro-Asia*, The Hague: Martinus Nijhoff 1971.
Ellis, Gorsira & Nuyten 1954
J.W. Ellis, M.P. Gorsira & F.C.J. Nuyten, *De zelfstandigheid der eilandgebieden: een bijdrage tot herziening der eilandenregeling Nederlandse Antillen*, Willemstad: Het eilandgebied Curaçao 1954
Emerson 1971
Rupert Emerson, 'Self-Determination', 65 *AJIL* (1971) pp. 459-75.
Engers 1956
J.F. Engers, *Hoofdstuk XI van het Handvest van de Verenigde Naties: oorsprong, ontstaan en toepassing van de verklaring betreffende niet-zelfbesturende gebieden*, Amsterdam: Noord-Hollandsche Uitgevers Maatschappij 1956.
Ermacora 1991
Felix Ermacora, 'Beschwerde von Einzelpersonen unter Berufung auf Selbstbestimmungs-recht für unzulässing erklärt / Südtirol-Fall', 18 *Europäische Grundrechte Zeitschrift* (1991) No. 8/9 pp. 158-60.
Ermacora 1992
Felix Ermacora, 'Colonies and Colonial Régime', in: Rudolf Bernhardt (ed.), *Encyclopedia of Public International Law*, Volume One, Amsterdam: North-Holland 1992, pp. 662-66.
European Commission 1999
European Commission, *The European Union and the overseas countries and territories*, Luxembourg: Office for Official Publications of the European Communities 1999.
Fægteborg 1989
Mads Fægteborg, 'Between Global Politics and Local Politics: The Dilemma of Greenlandic Home Rule', 1 *North Atlantic Studies* (1989) No. 2 pp. 32-8.
Fastenrath 2002
Ulrich Fastenrath, 'Chapter XI. Declaration Regarding Non-Self-Governing Territories', in: Bruno Simma et al. (eds.), *The Charter of the United Nations: A Commentary*, Oxford University Press 2002, pp. 1089-97.
Fernandes Mendes 1989
H.K. Fernandes Mendes, *Onafhankelijkheid en parlementair stelsel in Suriname: Hoofdlijnen van een nieuw en democratisch staatsbestel*, Zwolle: W.E.J. Tjeenk Willink 1989.
Fisher 1968
Roger Fisher, 'The Participation of Microstates in International Affairs', *Proceedings of the American Society of International Law* (1968) p. 166.
Forbes 1970
Urias Forbes, 'The West Indies Associated States. Some Aspects of the Constitutional Arrangements', 19 *Social and Economic Studies* (1970) pp. 57-88.
Fortuyn 2002
Pim Fortuyn, *"At your service". De laatste 32 columns*, [s.l.]: [s.n.] [2002].
Frame 1987
A. Frame, 'The External Affairs and Defence of the Cook Islands: The "Riddiford Clause" Considered', 17 *Victoria University of Wellington Law Review* (1987) pp. 141-51.

Franck 1985
Thomas M. Franck, *Nation against Nation. What Happened to the U.N. Dream and What the U.S. Can Do about it*, New York: Oxford University Press 1985.

Franck & Hoffman 1976
Thomas M. Franck and Paul Hoffman, 'The Right of Self-Determination in Very Small Places', 8 *New York University Journal of International Law and Politics* (1976) pp. 331-86.

Freymond 1980
Jean F. Freymond, *Political Integration in the Commonwealth Caribbean*, Geneva: Institut Universitaire de Hautes Etudes Internationales 1980.

Galindez 1954
Jezus de Galindez, 'Government and Politics in Puerto Rico – New Formula for Self-Government', 30 *International Affairs* (1954) pp. 331-41.

Gastmann 1964
Albert L. Gastmann, *The Place of Surinam and the Netherlands Antilles in the Political and Constitutional Structure of the Kingdom of the Netherlands* (dissertation, University of Columbia, NY) 1964.

Gastmann 1968
Albert L. Gastmann, *The Politics of Surinam and the Netherlands Antilles*, Rio Pedras, Puerto Rico: Institute of Caribbean Studies 1968.

George 2003
Norbert George, *Koninkrijksbeleid fataal voor Curaçao. Aan de leden der Staten-Generaal en de Raad van State*, Amsterdam: Thela Thesis 2003.

Gilmore 1982
William C. Gilmore, 'Requiem for associated statehood?', 8 *Review of International Studies* (1982) pp. 9-25.

Goesel-Le Bihan 1998
Valérie Goesel-Le Bihan, 'La Nouvelle-Calédonie et l'Accord de Nouméa, un processus inédit de décolonisation', 44 *Annuaire français de droit international* (1998) pp. 24-75.

Gohin 1997
Olivier Gohin, 'L' indépendance des Comores et le précédent de Mayotte', in: Jean-Yves Faberon (ed.), *L'avenir statutaire de la Nouvelle-Calédonie. L'évolution des liens de la France avec ses collectivités périphériques* (colloquium organized by the Centre de recherches et d'études administratives de Montpellier, also published in *Notes et études documentaires* No. 5053-5, 16 June 1997), Paris: La documentation Française 1997, pp. 67-81.

Goodrich, Hambro & Simons 1969
Leland M. Goodrich, Edvard Hambro & Anne Patricia Simons, *Charter of the United Nations. Commentary and Documents*, New York: Columbia University Press 1969.

Gorsira 1988
M.P. Gorsira, 'Zelfbeschikkingsrecht en Status Aparte: Enige beschouwingen over de toekomstige relatie tussen Nederland en het Caraïbisch deel van het Koninkrijk', in: M.Ph. van Delden (ed.), *Het oog van de meester: opstellen aangeboden aan mr. C.E. Dip*, [Willemstad]: Stichting Wetenschappelijke en Culturele Publicaties Curaçao 1988, pp. 51-64.

Grieco 2003
Elizabeth M. Grieco, 'The Federated States of Micronesia: The "Push" to Migrate', *Migration Information Source*, July 2003 (published on <http://www.migrationinformation.org>).

Haan 1998
Edo Haan, *Antilliaanse instituties. De economische ontwikkeling van de Nederlandse Antillen, 1969-1995*, Capelle aan de IJssel: Labyrint 1998.

Hannum 1996
Hurst Hannum, *Autonomy, Sovereignty, and Self-Determination: the Accommodation of Conflicting Rights,* Philadelphia: University of Pennsylvania Press 1996.

Hasan Ahmad 1974
S. Hasan Ahmad, *The United Nations and the Colonies*, Bombay: Asia Publishing House 1974.

Havel 1992
Jean E. Havel, 'Kalaali Nunaat/Groenland: Décolonisation Hésitante', 49 *Europa Ethnica* (1992) pp. 119-24.

Henderson 1994
John Henderson, 'Micro-states and the Politics of Association: The Future of New Zealand's Constitutional Links with the Cook Islands and Tokelau', in: Werner vom Busch et al. (eds.), *New Politics in the South Pacific*, Rarotonga, Cook Islands: University of the South Pacific 1994, pp. 99-112.

Higgins 1963
Rosalyn Higgins, *The Development of International Law through the Political Organs of the United Nations*, Oxford: Oxford University Press 1963.

Hillebrink 2003
S. Hillebrink, 'Het Nederlandse zelfbeschikkingsrecht: een recht op verstoting?', *NJB* (2003) pp. 1816-18.

Hillebrink 2005
S. Hillebrink, 'Constitutional In-Betweenity: Reforming the Kingdom of the Netherlands in the Caribbean', in: Lammert de Jong & Douwe Boersema (eds.), *The Kingdom of the Netherlands in the Caribbean: 1954-2004. What Next?*, Amsterdam: Rozenberg Publishers 2005, pp. 101-12.

Hillebrink & Loeber 2006
S. Hillebrink & L.H.M. Loeber, 'De Kieswet onder vuur vanuit Aruba', *NJB* (2007) no. 11, pp. 615-18.

Hillebrink & Nap 2002
S. Hillebrink & M. Nap, 'Een paardenmiddel tegen de zelfstandige maatregelen van rijksbestuur', *RegelMaat* (2002) pp. 99-112.

Hinck 1990
Jon Hinck, 'The Republic of Palau and the United States: Self-Determination Becomes the Price of Free Association', 78 *California Law Review* (1990) pp. 915-71.

Hintjens 1997
Helen M. Hintjens, 'Governance Options in Europe's Caribbean Dependencies. The End of Independence', *The Round Table* (1997) pp. 533-47.

Hirsch Ballin 1989
Ernst H.M. Hirsch Ballin, 'Het Koninkrijk in de Caribische Zee', 11 *Christen Democratische Verkenningen* (1989) pp. 463-71.

Hirsch Ballin 2003
E.M.H. Hirsch Ballin, 'De Koninkrijksgemeenschap' (lecture at the University of the Netherlands Antilles, 27 May 2003), *Tijdschrift voor Antilliaans recht-Justicia* (2003) no. 2 pp. 87-96.

Hoeneveld 2004
A. Hoeneveld, 'De reikwijdte van het zelfbeschikkingsrecht van de Nederlandse Antillen en Aruba', *Openbaar Bestuur* (2004) October, pp. 21-5.

Hoeneveld 2005
A. Hoeneveld, *De reikwijdte van het volkenrechtelijk zelfbeschikkingsrecht van de Nederlandse Antillen en Aruba* (thesis Open Universiteit), The Hague: Ministerie van Binnenlandse Zaken en Koninkrijksrelaties 2005.

Hoeneveld 2007
A. Hoeneveld, 'Het hoger toezicht van de Gouverneur ingevolge de Eilandenregeling', *Tijdschrift voor Antilliaans recht-Justicia* (2007) no. 4.

Hoogers 1998
H.G. Hoogers, 'Het Statuut voor het Koninkrijk der Nederlanden en Aruba's zelfbeschikkingsrecht', *Aruba Iuridica* (1998) no. 3 pp. 7-40.

Hoogers 2005
H.G. Hoogers, 'Opheffing van de Nederlandse Antillen ondoordacht', *Christen-Democratische Verkenningen* (2005), pp. 68-73.

Hoogers & De Vries 2002
H.G. Hoogers & F. de Vries, *Hoofdlijnen Arubaans staatsrecht*, Zutphen: Walburg Pers 2002.

Hoogers & Nap 2005
H.G. Hoogers & M. Nap, 'Het Statuut, de Grondwet en het internationale recht', in: L.J.J. Rogier & H.G. Hoogers (eds.), *50 jaar Statuut voor het Koninkrijk der Nederlanden. Bijdragen voor het congres 50 jaar Statuut voor het Koninkrijk der Nederlanden, 3 december 2004*, [s.l.]: Erasmus Universiteit Rotterdam 2005, pp. 53-86.

Houben 1965
P.-H.J.M. Houben, *De associatie van Suriname en de Nederlandse Antillen met de Europese Economische Gemeenschap*, Leiden: Sijthoff 1965.

Houbert 1980
Jean Houbert, 'Réunion I: French Decolonisation in the Mascareignes', 18 *The Journal of Commonwealth and Comparative Politics* (1980) pp. 145-71.

Igarashi 2002
Masahiro Igarashi, *Associated Statehood in International Law*, The Hague: Kluwer Law International 2002.

Ince 1974
Basil Ince, 'The Decolonization of Grenada in the U.N.', in: Bernard Coard et al. (eds.), *Independence for Grenada: Myth or Reality? Proceedings of a Conference on the Implications of Independence for Grenada sponsored by the Institute of International Relations and the Department of Government, the University of the West Indies, St. Augustine 11th – 13th January 1974*, St. Augustine, Trinidad: Institute of International Relations 1974, pp. 43-51.

IOB 2003
Inspectie Ontwikkelingssamenwerking en Beleidsevaluatie van het Ministerie van Buitenlandse Zaken, *Behartiging van de buitenlandse belangen van de Nederlandse Antillen en Aruba. Een evaluatie van de rol van het Ministerie van Buitenlandse Zaken* (IOB evaluaties, no. 295), The Hague: Ministry of Foreign Affairs 2003.

Islam 1989
Rafiqul Islam, 'The Status of New Caledonia and the Right of its Peoples to Self-Determination', 29 *The Indian Journal of International Law* (1989) pp. 1-23.

Jacobs 1974
Richard Jacobs, 'The Movement towards Grenadian Independence', in: Bernard Coard et al. (eds.), *Independence for Grenada: Myth or Reality? Proceedings of a Conference on the Implications of Independence for Grenada sponsored by the Institute of International Relations and the Department of Government, the University of the West Indies, St. Augustine 11th – 13th January 1974*, St. Augustine, Trinidad: Institute of International Relations 1974, pp. 21-33.

Janus 1990
J.A.B. Janus, 'Staatsrechtelijke ontwikkelingen in de jaren tachtig', *Tijdschrift voor Antilliaans recht-Justicia* (1990) pp. 77-91.

Janus 1993
J.A.B. Janus, 'Het Statuut voor het Koninkrijk der Nederlanden: Terugblik en perspectief', in: D. Breillat et al., *Naar een nieuwe structuur van het Koninkrijk* (Staatsrechtconferentie 1993. Publikaties van de Staatsrechtkring No. 6), Zwolle: W.E.J. Tjeenk Willink 1993, pp. 33-92.

Janus 1994
J.A.B. Janus, 'Een terugblik op 1993: De Toekomstconferentie en het Curaçaose referendum', 1 *Tijdschrift voor Antilliaans recht-Justicia* (1994) pp. 1-23.

Jessurun d'Oliveira 2003a
H.U. Jessurun d'Oliveira, 'Nederlandse secessie uit het Koninkrijk. Oftewel: Fifty Ways to Leave your Lover(s)', in: J.L. de Reede & J.H. Reestman (eds.), *Op het snijvlak van recht en politiek. Opstellen aangeboden aan prof. mr. L. Prakke*, Deventer: Kluwer 2003, pp. 111-30.

Jessurun d'Oliveira 2003b
H.U. Jessurun d'Oliveira, 'Naschrift', *NJB* (2003) p. 1819.

Jonkers 1955
A. Jonkers, 'De nieuwe rechtsorde in het Koninkrijk der Nederlanden' (radio speech of 14 December 1954), *Schakels* No. 84 (1955), pp. 52-6.

Jonkers 1960
A. Jonkers, 'De nieuwe rechtsorde in het Koninkrijk der Nederlanden', *Marineblad* (1960) pp. 1316-27.

Kagie 1982
R. Kagie, *De laatste kolonie: De Nederlandse Antillen: Afhankelijkheid, belastingprofijt en geheime winsten*, Bussum: Het Wereldvenster 1982.

Kapteyn 1982
P.J.G. Kapteyn, 'De Nederlandse Antillen en de uitoefening van het zelfbeschikkingsrecht', *Mededelingen der KNAW, afd. Letterkunde, nieuwe reeks*, deel 45, no. 6, 1982.

Karamat Ali 1988
E.I. Karamat Ali, 'De Nederlandse Antillen en Aruba en de onafhankelijkheid', in: M.Ph. van Delden (ed.), *Het oog van de meester. Opstellen aangeboden aan mr. C.E. Dip*, [s.l.]: SWCP 1988.

Kasteel 1956
Annemarie C.T. Kasteel, *De staatkundige ontwikkeling der Nederlandse Antillen*, The Hague: Van Hoeve 1956.

Keitner & Reisman 2003
Chimène I. Keitner & W. Michael Reisman, 'Free Association: The United States Experience', 39 *Texas International Law Journal* (2003) pp. 1-63.

Kelsen 1950
Hans Kelsen, *The Law of the United Nations: A Critical Analysis of its Fundamental Problems,* New York: Frederick A. Praeger 1950.

Kircher 1986
Ingrid A. Kircher, *The Kanaks of New Caledonia* (Minority Rights Group Report No. 71), London: Minority Rights Group 1986.

Kirchschläger 1961
Rudolf Kirchschläger, 'Kolonien', in: Hans-Jürgen Schlochauer (ed.), *Wörterbuch des Völkerrechts. Begründet von Professor Dr. Karl Strupp. Zweiter Band*, Berlin: Verlag Walter de Gruyter 1961, pp. 256-59.

Klinkers 1999
Inge Klinkers, *De weg naar het Statuut. Het Nederlandse dekolonisatiebeleid in de Caraïben (1940-1954) in vergel?kend perspectief* (Ph.D. thesis Utrecht), [s.l.]: [s.n.] 1999.

Kolff 1965
John Kolff, 'The Economic Implications of Self-Government for the Cook Islands', 74 *Journal of the Polynesian Society* (1965) pp. 119-24.

Korthals Altes 1999
Theo E. Korthals Altes, *Koninkrijk aan zee: De lange vlucht van de liefde in het Caribisch-Nederlands bestuur*, Zutphen: Walburg Pers 1999.

Kortmann 2007
C.A.J.M. Kortmann, 'Tweederangs Nederlanders? Afdeling bestuursrechtspraak Raad van State 21 november 2006', *Ars Aequi* (2007) pp. 456-59.

Kranenburg 1930
R. Kranenburg, *Het Nederlandsch staatsrecht. Tweede deel*, Haarlem: H.D. Tjeenk Willink 1930.

Kranenburg 1955
R. Kranenburg, *De Nieuwe Structuur van ons Koninkrijk*, Tjeenk Willink 1955.

Kranenburg 1958
R. Kranenburg, *Het Nederlands staatsrecht*, Haarlem: H.D. Tjeenk Willink 1958.

Kuyper & Kapteyn 1980
P.J. Kuyper & P.J.G. Kapteyn, 'A Colonial Power as Champion of Self-Determination: Netherlands state practice in the period 1945-1975', 3 *International Law in The Netherlands* (1980), pp. 149-218.

Laing 1974
Edward A. Laing, 'Crown Indivisibility, Governmental Liability and Other Problems in the West Indies Associated States', 23 *ICLQ* (1974) pp. 127-42.

Laing 1979
Edward A. Laing, 'Independence and Islands: the Decolonization of the British Caribbean', 12 *New York University Journal of International Law and Politics* (1979) pp. 281-312.

Lake 2000
Joseph H. Lake, Jr., *The Republic of St. Martin*, Philipsburg: House of Nehesi 2000.

Lauwaars 1991
R.H. Lauwaars, 'De Associatie van de Landen en Gebieden Overzee onder Deel IV van het EEG-Verdrag', in: *Met het oog op Europa. De Europese Gemeenschap. De Nederlandse Antillen en Aruba*, Willemstad: Stichting Tijdschrift voor Antilliaans Recht-Justicia 1991, pp. 22-33.

Lauwaars & Bronckers 1991
R.H. Lauwaars & M.C.E.J. Bronckers, 'Passen Communautaire origineregels in het handelsverkeer met Landen en Gebieden Overzee?', in: *Met het oog op Europa. De Europese Gemeenschap. De Nederlandse Antillen en Aruba*, Willemstad: Stichting Tijdschrift voor Antilliaans Recht-Justicia 1991, pp. 34-50.

Leibowitz 1976
Arnold H. Leibowitz, *Colonial Emancipation in the Pacific and the Caribbean. A Legal and Political Analysis*, New York: Praeger Publishers 1976.
Leibowitz 1989
Arnold H. Leibowitz, *Defining Status. A Comprehensive Analysis of United States Territorial Relations*, Dordrecht: Martinus Nijhoff Publishers 1989.
Logemann 1952
J.H.A. Logemann, 'Het komende statuut voor het Koninkrijk', *NJB* (1952) pp. 309-19.
Logemann 1955
J.H.A. Logemann, 'The Constitutional Status of the Netherlands Caribbean Territories' in: J.H.A. Logemann et al. (eds.), *Developments towards Self-Government in the Caribbean: A Symposium held under the Auspices of the Netherlands Universities Foundation for International Cooperation at The Hague, September 1954*. The Hague: Van Hoeve 1955, pp. 46-72.
Lopez-Reyes 1996
Ramon Lopez-Reyes, 'The Re-Inscription of Hawaii on the United Nations List of Non-Self-Governing Territories' *Peace Research* 1996, pp. 71-95.
Lowenthal 1980
David Lowenthal, 'Island Orphans: Barbuda and the Rest', 18 *Journal of Commonwealth and Comparative Politics* (1980) pp. 293-307.
Luard 1982
Evan Luard, *A History of the United Nations. Volume 1: The Years of Western Domination, 1945-1955*, London: Macmillan 1982.
Luard 1989
Evan Luard, *A History of the United Nations. Volume 2: The Age of Decolonization, 1955-1965*, London: Macmillan 1989.
Luiten 1983
W.A. Luiten, *Een inleiding tot het Antilliaanse staatsrecht*, Willemstad: Universiteit van de Nederlandse Antillen 1983.
Maas 1962
H.H. Maas, 'Wetgevingskroniek. Europa', *SEW* (1962) pp. 596-604.
Macdonald 1981
J. Ross Macdonald, 'Termination of the Strategic Trusteeship: Free Association, the United Nations and International Law', 7 *Brooklyn Journal of International Law* (1981) pp. 235-82.
Macdonald 1982
Barrie Macdonald, *Cinderellas of the Empire. Towards a History of Kiribati and Tuvalu*, Canberra: Australian National University Press 1982.
Maestre 1976
Jean-Claude Maestre, 'L'Indivisibilité de la République Française et l'exercise du droit d'autodétermination', 92 *Revue du droit public et de la science politique en France et á l'étranger* (1976) pp. 431-61.
Malanczuk 1997
Peter Malanczuk, *Akehurst's Modern Introduction to International Law*, London: Routledge 1997.

Mani 1993
V.S. Mani, *Basic Principles of Modern International Law. A Study of the United Nations Debates on the Principles of International Law Concerning Friendly Relations and Co-operation among States,* New Delhi: Lancers Books 1993.

Martha 1991a
R.S.J. Martha, 'Toepassing van het gemeenschappelijk origine begrip op het goederenverkeer met de landen en gebieden overzee', 5 *SEW* (1991) pp. 298-319.

Martha 1991b
R.S.J. Martha, 'Gevolgen van de Europese integratie voor het Koninkrijksverband – Enkele discussiepunten', in: *Met het oog op Europa. De Europese Gemeenschap. De Nederlandse Antillen en Aruba,* Willemstad: Stichting Tijdschrift voor Antilliaans Recht-Justicia 1991, pp. 5-21.

Martha 1997
R.S.J. Martha, 'De harmonie tussen Koninkrijks- en Gemeenschapstrouw' (lecture during the Round Table Session of the T.M.C. Asser Instituut on 'Suikerimport uit de Nederlandse Antillen: Koninkrijks- versus Gemeenschapstrouw' held on 26 November 1997. Published on <www.asser.nl/conf/rtsuiker.htm>).

Matos 2002
Nancy A. Matos, 'The Netherlands: A Federal Narcostate?', 3 *Griffin's View on International and Comparative Law* (2002) No. 2, pp. 63-70.

Maurice 1991
Pierre Maurice, 'Mayotte et la Communauté économique européenne', in: Emmanuel Jos & Danielle Perrot (eds.), *L'outre-mer et l'Europe communautaire. Quelle insertion? Pour quel développement?* (Journées d'études du Centre de recherche sur les pouvoirs locaux dans la Caraïbe de l'Université des Antilles-Guyane, October 1991), Paris: Economica 1991, pp. 227-50.

McGoldrick 1991a
Dominic McGoldrick, *The Human Rights Committee: Its Role in the Development of the International Covenant on Civil and Political Rights,* Oxford: Clarendon 1991.

McGoldrick 1991b
Dominic McGoldrick, 'Canadian Indians, Cultural Rights and the Human Rights Committee', 40 *ICLQ* (1991) pp. 658-69.

McCorquodale 1995
Robert McCorquodale, 'The Right to Self-Determination', in: David Harris and Sarah Joseph (eds.), *The International Covenant on Civil and Political Rights and United Kingdom Law,* Oxford: Clarendon 1995, pp. 91-119.

McCorquodale 2000
Robert McCorquodale (ed.), *Self-Determination in International Law,* Aldershot: Ashgate 2000.

Meel 1999
Peter Meel, *Tussen autonomie en onafhankelijkheid: Nederlands-Surinaamse betrekkingen 1954-1961,* Leiden: KITLV 1999.

Merry 2000
Sally Engle Merry, *Colonizing Hawai'i. The Cultural Power of Law,* Princeton NJ: Princeton University Press 2000.

Miclo 1989
François Miclo, 'Les contours du principe constitutionnel d'adoption', in: Jean-Claude Fortier (ed.), *Questions sur l'administration des DOM. Décentraliser outre-mer?,* Paris: Economica 1989, pp. 101-7.

Mortelmans & Temmink 1991

K.J.M. Mortelmans & H.A.G. Temmink, 'Het vrije personenverkeer tussen de Nederlandse Antillen en Aruba en de Europese Gemeenschap', in: *Met het oog op Europa. De Europese Gemeenschap. De Nederlandse Antillen en Aruba*, Willemstad: Stichting Tijdschrift voor Antilliaans Recht-Justicia 1991, pp. 51-90.

Munneke 1990

H.F. Munneke, 'Een gemenebestconstitutie voor het Koninkrijk der Nederlanden', *Tijdschrift voor Openbaar Bestuur* (1990) pp. 348-52.

Munneke 1993

H.F. Munneke, 'Deugdelijk bestuur en zelfbeschikkingsrecht in het Caraïbisch Koninkrijks-deel', *NJB* (1993) pp. 857-59.

Munneke 1994

H.F. Munneke, *Ambtsuitoefening en onafhankelijke controle in de Nederlandse Antillen en Aruba. Juridische en beheersmatige controle als waarborg voor deugdelijk bestuur*, Nijmegen: Ars Aequi 1994.

Munneke 1999

H.F. Munneke, 'Gevangenen op de Nederlandse Antillen. Recht op geweldloze behandeling?', *NJCM-Bulletin* (1999), no. 5, pp. 614-22.

Munneke 2001

H.F. Munneke, *Recht en samenleving in de Nederlandse Antillen, Aruba en Suriname. Opstellen over recht en sociale cohesie*, Nijmegen: Wolf Legal Publishers 2001.

Musgrave 1997

Thomas Musgrave, *Self-Determination and National Minorities*, Oxford: Oxford University Press 1997.

Nap 2003a

M. Nap, *Wetgeving van het Koninkrijk der Nederlanden*, Zutphen: Walburg Pers 2003.

Nap 2003b

M. Nap, 'Koninkrijksaspecten van de Europese integratie', in: J.W.L. Broeksteeg et al., *De Nederlandse Grondwet en de Europese Unie* (Publikaties van de Staatsrechtkring, no. 22), Deventer: Kluwer 2003, pp. 75-92.

Nehring 1963

Alfred Nehring, *Die Assoziierung überseeischer Länder mit dem gemeinsamen Markt* (Studien zum internationalen Wirtschaftsrecht und Atomenergierecht, Vol. 13), Göttingen: Georg Erler 1963.

Nelissen & Tillema 1989

Frans A. Nelissen and Arjen J.P. Tillema, 'The Netherlands Antilles and Aruba, an Embarrassing Legacy of the Dutch Colonial Era? Dutch Duties Revisited', 2 *LJIL* (1989) pp. 167-93.

Ninčić 1970

Ninčić, Djura, *The Problem of Sovereignty in the Charter and in the Practice of the United Nations*, The Hague: Martinus Nijhoff 1970.

Northey 1965

J.F. Northey, 'Self-Determination in the Cook Islands', 74 *Journal of the Polynesian Society* (1965) pp. 112-18.

Nowak 1993

Manfred Nowak, *UN Covenant on Political and Civil Rights: CCPR Commentary*, Kehl: Engel 1993.

Ntumy & Adzoxornu 1993
Michael A. Ntumy & Isaacus Adzoxornu, *South Pacific Islands Legal Systems*, Honolulu: University of Hawaii Press 1993.

Ofuatey-Kodjoe 1970
Wentworth B. Ofuatey-Kodjoe, *Self-Determination in International Law: Towards a Definition of the Principle* (Ph.D. dissertation Columbia University, New York), 1970.

Ofuatey-Kodjoe 1995
W. Ofuatey-Kodjoe, 'Self-Determination', in: Oscar Schachter & Christopher C. Joyner (eds.), *United Nations Legal Order.* Volume 1, Cambridge: Grotius Publications 1995, p. 349-389.

Oliver 2003
Peter Oliver, 'Case Law', 39 *Common Market Law Review* (2002) pp. 337-51.

Olyslager 1958
P. Olyslager, *De Associatie van de overzeese gebieden met de Europese Ekonomische Gemeenschap*, Leuven: Katholieke Universiteit te Leuven 1958.

Ooft 1972
Cornelis Desiré Ooft, *Ontwikkeling van het constitutionele recht van Suriname*, Assen: Van Gorcum 1972.

Oostindie 1994
Gert Oostindie, *Caraïbische dilemma's in een 'stagnerend' dekolonisatieproces*, Leiden: KITLV 1994.

Oostindie 1999
Gert Oostindie (ed.), *Dromen en littekens. Dertig jaar na de Curaçaose revolte, 30 mei 1969*, Amsterdam: Amsterdam University Press 1999.

Oostindie 2005
Gert Oostindie, *Paradise Overseas. The Dutch Caribbean: Colonialism and Transatlantic Legacies*, Oxford: Macmillan Caribbean 2005.

Oostindie & Klinkers 2001a
Gert Oostindie & Inge Klinkers, *Knellende Koninkrijksbanden. Het Nederlandse Dekolonisatiebeleid in de Caraïben, 1940-1975. Deel I, 1940-1954*, Amsterdam: Amsterdam University Press 2001.

Oostindie & Klinkers 2001b
Gert Oostindie & Inge Klinkers, *Knellende Koninkrijksbanden. Het Nederlandse Dekolonisatiebeleid in de Caraïben, 1940-1975. Deel II, 1954-1975*, Amsterdam: Amsterdam University Press 2001.

Oostindie & Klinkers 2001c
Gert Oostindie & Inge Klinkers, *Knellende Koninkrijksbanden. Het Nederlandse Dekolonisatiebeleid in de Caraïben, 1940-1975. Deel III, 1975-2000*, Amsterdam: Amsterdam University Press 2001.

Oostindie & Klinkers 2003
Gert Oostindie & Inge Klinkers, *Decolonising the Caribbean. Dutch Policies in a Comparative Perspective*, Amsterdam: Amsterdam University Press 2003.

Oostindie & Verton 1998
Gert Oostindie & Peter Verton, *Ki sorto di Reino? – What kind of Kingdom? Visies en verwachtingen van Antillianen en Arubanen omtrent het Koninkrijk*, Den Haag: Sdu 1998.

Oppenheim 1905
L. Oppenheim, *International Law. A Treatise. Volume I, Peace*, London: Longmans 1905.

Oppenheim/Lauterpacht 1955

L. Oppenheim/H. Lauterpacht (eds.), *International Law. A Treatise. Volume I, Peace*, London: Longmans 1955.

Oppenheim/Jennings & Watts 1992

Robert Jennings & Arthur Watts, *Oppenheim's International Law. Volume I, Peace*, Harlow: Longman 1992.

Oud 1967

P.J. Oud, *Het constitutioneel recht van het Koninkrijk der Nederlanden* (deel I), Zwolle: W.E.J. Tjeenk Willink 1967.

Oversteegen 1994

J.J. Oversteegen, *Gemunt op wederkeer: Het leven van Cola Debrot vanaf 1948*, Amsterdam: Meulenhoff 1994.

Pakaukau 2004

Ka Pakaukau, 'Reinscription. The Right of Hawai'i to be Restored to the United Nations List of Non-Self-Governing Territories', in: Ward Churchill & Sharon H. Venne (eds.), *Islands in Captivity. The Record of the International Tribunal on the Rights of Indigenous Hawaiians*, Cambridge, Massachusetts: South End Press 2004, pp. 303-21.

Palm 1985

J. Ph. de Palm (ed.), *Encyclopedie van de Nederlandse Antillen*, Zutphen: De Walburg Pers 1985.

Pappa 1996

Christopher Pappa, *Das Individualbeschwerdeverfahren des Fakultativprotokolls zum Internationalen Pakt über bürgerliche und politische Rechte*, Bern: Stämpfli 1996.

Paula 1986

A.F. Paula, *Het Statuut voor het Koninkrijk der Nederlanden: De rapportage-kwestie*, Willemstad: Centraal Historisch Archief 1986.

Paula 1989

A.F. Paula, *Hoofdmomenten uit de staatkundige ontwikkeling van de Nederlandse Antillen 1865-1986*, Willemstad: Centraal Historisch Archief 1989.

Pietersz 1993

Frithjof (Choy) Pietersz, 'Referendum onderstreept Antilliaanse democratie. Volksuitspraak verrast alle politici', *Diálogo*, No. 3, December 1993.

Pikeur & Lamers 2005

Wyrnus Pikeur & Peter Lamers, 'Antillen als provincie van Nederland', *VNG-magazine*, 14 January 2005, pp. 10-11.

Pimont 1992

Yves Pimont, 'La Nouvelle-Calédonie et le droit constitutionel', *Revue du droit public et de la science politique en France et à l'étranger* (1992) No. 6, pp. 1687-1705.

Pinheiro 1999

João de Deus Pinheiro, *The Status of OCTs Associated with the EC and Options for "OCT 2000". Communication from Mr. Pinheiro to the Commission*, 23 April 1999.

Pisuisse 1991

C.S. Pisuisse, 'Nogmaals de handelsrelatie tussen de landen en gebieden overzee en de gemeenschap', 5 *SEW* (1991) pp. 320-27.

Pomerance 1982

Michla Pomerance, *Self-Determination in Law and Practice. The New Doctrine in the United Nations*, The Hague: Martinus Nijhoff 1982.

Post & Van der Veen 1980
H.H.G. Post and J.H. van der Veen, 'Discussieverslag', in: H. Meijers (ed.), *Volkenrechtelijke aspecten van Antilliaanse onafhankelijkheid*, [?]: [?] Tjeenk Willink 1980, pp. 154-56.

Prince p1989
Harry G. Prince, 'The United States, the United Nations, and Micronesia: Questions of Procedure, Substance, and Faith', 11 *Michigan Journal of International Law* (1989), pp. 11-89.

Puissochet 1999
Jean-Pierre Puissochet, 'Aux confins de la Communauté européenne: Les régions ultrapériphériques', in: Gil Carlos Rodríguez Iglesias et al. (eds.) *Mélanges en hommage à Fernand Schockweiler*, Baden-Baden: Nomos 1999, pp. 491-509.

Quane 1998
Helen Quane, 'The United Nations and the Evolving Right to Self-Determination', 47 *ICLQ* (1998) pp. 537-72.

Raad van State 2004
De Raad van State van het Koninkrijk, *Verdieping of geleidelijk uiteengaan. De relaties binnen het Koninkrijk en met de Europese Unie*, The Hague: Raad van State 2004.

Ramsoedh 1993
Hans Ramsoedh, 'De geforceerde onafhankelijkheid', 12 *Oso: Tijdschrift voor Surinaamse Taalkunde, Letterkunde, Cultuur en Geschiedenis* (1993), pp. 43-62.

Rapoport et al. 1971
J. Rapoport et al., *A UNITAR Study. Small States and Territories. Status and Problems*, New York: Arno Press 1971.

Reinders 1993
Alex Reinders, *Politieke geschiedenis van de Nederlandse Antillen en Aruba 1950-1993*, Zutphen: Walburg Pers 1993.

Reisman 1975
W. Michael Reisman, *Puerto Rico and the International Process: New Roles in Association*, Studies in Transnational Legal Policy, No. 6, Washington DC: The American Society of International Law 1975.

Report of the RTC 1981
Conferentie van de Nederlandse Antillen, de eilanden van de Nederlandse Antillen en Nederland: Stenografisch verslag van de eerste zitting, gehouden van maandag 16 t/m woensdag 25 februari 1981 te 's Gravenhage, The Hague: [Staatsuitgeverij] 1981.

Report of the Kingdom Working Group 1980
Naar nieuwe vormen van samenwerking: Rapport van de Koninkrijkswerkgroep ingesteld bij Koninklijk Besluit van 2 december 1978, nr. 75, 30 augustus 1980, The Hague: Staatsuitgeverij 1980.

Rigo Sureda 1973
A. Rigo Sureda, *The Evolution of the Right of Self-Determination. A Study of UN practice*, Alphen a/d Rijn: Sijthoff 1973.

Ritchie 1998
Harry Ritchie, *The Last Pink Bits. Travels Through the Remnants of the British Empire*, London: Sceptre 1998.

Roberts-Wray 1966
Kenneth Roberts-Wray, *Commonwealth and Colonial Law*, London: Stevens 1966.

Roland-Gosselin 1997
Yves Roland-Gosselin, 'Situation de la Nouvelle-Calédonie au regard du droit communautaire', in: Jean-Yves Faberon (ed.), *L'avenir statutaire de la Nouvelle-Calédonie. L'évolution des liens de la France avec ses collectivités périphériques* (colloquium organized by the Centre de recherches et d'études administratives de Montpellier, also published in *Notes et études documentaires* No. 5053-5, 16 June 1997), Paris: La documentation Française 1997, pp. 133-141.

Roman 1998
Ediberto Roman, 'The Alien-Citizen Paradox and other Consequences of U.S. Colonialism', *Florida State University Law Review*, vol. 26, no. 1 (1998), p. 1017.

Rosaria 2003
Alex Rosaria, *Notitie inzake Regionale Handelsbetrekkingen in het Westelijk Halfrond: mogelijke implicaties voor de Nederlandse Antillen*, Willemstad: [s.n.] 2003.

Šahović 1972
Milan Šahović, 'Codification of the Legal Principles of Coexistence and the Development of Contemporary International Law', in: Milan Šahović, *Principles of International Law Concerning Friendly Relations and Cooperation,* New York: Oceana 1972, pp. 9-50.

Sap 2005
Jan Willem Sap, 'Het volk van Curaçao heeft recht op zelfbeschikking', *Christen-Democratische Verkenningen* (2005) Winter, pp. 60-7.

Schermers & Blokker 2003
Henry G. Schermers & N.M. Blokker, *International Institutional Law*, Boston, Massachusetts: Martinus Nijhoff 2003.

Shaw 1994
Dorian Shaw, 'The Status of Puerto Rico Revisited: Does the Current U.S.-Puerto Rico Relationship Uphold International Law?', 17 *Fordham International Law Journal* (1994) pp. 1006-61.

Simma & Alston 1992
Bruno Simma & Philip Alston, 'The Sources of Human Rights Law: Custom, Jus Cogens, and General Principles', 12 *Australian Year Book of International Law* (1992) pp. 82-108.

Sloan 1991
Blaine Sloan, *United Nations General Assembly Resolutions in Our Changing World*, New York: Transnational Publishers 1991.

Sluis 2004
Miriam Sluis, *De Antillen bestaan niet. De nadagen van een fictief land*, Amsterdam: Bert Bakker 2004.

Sondaal 1986
H.H.M. Sondaal, *De Nederlandse verdragspraktijk*, The Hague: Asser Instituut 1986.

Spackman 1975
Ann Spackman, *Constitutional Developments of the West Indies, 1922-1968. A Selection from the Major Documents*, St. Lawrence, Barbados: Caribbean University Press 1975.

Spits 1951
A.I. Spits, 'Het toezicht van de Verenigde Naties op niet-zelfstandige gebieden', 5 *Indonesië* (1951-1952), No. 3, pp. 251-69.

Spits 1952a
A.I. Spits, 'Het toezicht van de Verenigde Naties op niet-zelfstandige gebieden', 5 *Indonesië* (1951-1952), No. 4.

Spits 1952b
A.I. Spits, 'Het toezicht van de Verenigde Naties op niet-zelfstandige gebieden', 6 *Indonesië* (1952-1953), No. 3.

Spits 1953
A.I. Spits, 'Het toezicht van de Verenigde Naties op niet-zelfstandige gebieden', 7 *Indonesië* (1953-1954), No. 2.

Spits 1954
A.I. Spits, 'Het toezicht van de Verenigde Naties op niet-zelfstandige gebieden', 7 *Indonesië* (1953-1954), No. 6.

Spits 1955
A.I. Spits, 'Het toezicht van de Verenigde Naties op niet-zelfstandige gebieden', 8 *Indonesië* (1954-1955), No. 5.

Spits 1956
A.I. Spits, 'Het toezicht van de Verenigde Naties op niet-zelfstandige gebieden', 9 *Indonesië* (1955-1956).

Stone 1965
David Stone, 'Self-Determination in the Cook Islands: A Reply', 74 *The Journal of the Polynesian Society* (1965), No. 3, pp. 360-74.

Stone 1966
David Stone, 'Self-Government in the Cook Islands 1965', 1 *The Journal of Pacific History* (1965), pp. 168-78.

Sutton 2002
Gail Sutton, 'The Overseas Countries and Territories: renewed partnership with the Community', *The Courier ACP-EU*, January-February 2002, pp. 19-20.

Tanoh-Boutchoue 2001
Bernard Tanoh-Boutchoue, 'The Special Committee on decolonization', *UN Chronicle*, December 2001.

Taylor 2000
David Taylor, 'British Colonial Policy in the Caribbean. The Insoluble Dilemma – The Case of Montserrat', *The Round Table* (2000) issue 355, pp. 331-44.

Te Beest 1988
Joset te Beest, *Nederland voor het internationale forum. Het staken van rapportage over Suriname en de Nederlandse Antillen aan de Verenigde Naties, 1951-1955* (undergraduate thesis, University of Nijmegen), 1988.

Thomas 1987
A. Thomas, *Associated Statehood in the Leeward and Windward Islands: A Phase in the Transition to Independence* (dissertation, City University of New York), 1987.

Thürer 1976
Daniel Thürer, *Das Selbstbestimmungsrecht der Völker. Mit einem Exkurs zur Jurafrage*, Bern: Stämpfli 1976.

Tillema 1989
A.J.P. Tillema, *The Netherlands Antilles and Aruba. A Study in Self-Determination*, The Hague: Institute of Social Studies 1989.

Touboul 1997
Frédéric Touboul, 'Le cadre juridique fonctionnel des relations extérieures des TOM', in: Jean-Yves Faberon (ed.), *L'avenir statutaire de la Nouvelle-Calédonie. L'évolution des liens de la France avec ses collectivités périphériques* (colloquium organized by the Centre de

recherches et d'études administratives de Montpellier, also published in *Notes et études documentaires* No. 5053-5, 16 June 1997), Paris: La documentation Française 1997, pp.115-32.

Townend 2003
Andrew Townend, 'The Strange Death of the Realm of New Zealand: The Implications of a New Zealand Republic for the Cook Islands and Niue', 34 *Victoria University of Wellington Law Review* (2003), pp. 571-607.

Trías Monge 1997
José Trías Monge, *Puerto Rico: The Trials of the Oldest Colony in the World*, New Haven, Connecticut: Yale University Press 1997.

Van Aller 1994
H.B. van Aller, *Van kolonie tot koninkrijksdeel. De staatkundige geschiedenis van de Nederlandse Antillen en Aruba (van 1634 tot 1994)*, Groningen: Wolters-Noordhoff 1994.

Van Aller 1996
H.B. van Aller, 'Puerto Rico en de overzeese delen van het Koninkrijk, een vergelijking', 1 *Spes Victoriae: Studentijdschrift* (1996) No. 1, April.

Van Benthem van den Bergh 1962a
G. van Benthem van den Bergh, 'De associatie van Suriname en de Nederlandse Antillen met de E.E.G.', *SEW* (1962) pp. 594-96.

Van Benthem van den Bergh 1962b
G. van Benthem van den Bergh, *De associatie van Afrikaanse Staten met de Europese Economische Gemeenschap*, Leiden: Sijthoff 1962.

Van Benthem van den Bergh et al. 1978
G. van Benthem van den Bergh, O. Braun, J.G.M. Hilhorst & A.J.M. van de Haar, *Aruba en onafhankelijkheid. Achtergronden, modaliteiten en mogelijkheden; een rapport in eerste aanleg*, The Hague: Institute of Social Studies 1978.

Van Beuge 2004
Banden met Brussel. De betrekkingen van de Nederlandse Antillen en Aruba met de Europese Unie (Rapport van de Commissie ter bestudering van mogelijke toekomstige relaties van de Nederlandse Antillen en Aruba met de Europese Unie), 1 July 2004.

Van der Burg 2003
F.H. van der Burg, *Europees gemeenschapsrecht in de Nederlandse rechtsorde*, Deventer: Kluwer 2003.

Van der Hoeven 1959
J. van der Hoeven, 'Koninkrijksrecht en nederlands constitutioneel recht', *Rechtsgeleerd Magazijn Themis* (1959) pp. 375-89.

Van der Pot 1946
C.W. van der Pot, *Handboek van het Nederlandse staatsrecht*, Zwolle: W.E.J. Tjeenk Willink 1946.

Van der Pot-Donner/Prakke et al. 2001
L. Prakke, J.L. de Reede & G.J.M van Wissen, *Van der Pot-Donner. Handboek van het Nederlandse staatsrecht*, Deventer: W.E.J. Tjeenk Willink 2001.

Van der Wal 2003
G. van der Wal, *Nederlandse Antillen en Aruba als ultraperifeer gebied in de zin van art. 299 lid 2 EG-Verdrag?* (Memorandum), Brussels: Houthoff Buruma 2003.

Van der Wal & Van Zandvoort 1992
H.A. van der Wal & M.J.M. van Zandvoort, 'Rapportage bij het BuPo-verdrag', *Tijdschrift voor Antilliaans recht-Justicia* (1992) No. 2, pp. 89-99.

Vanhamme 2001
Jan Vanhamme, *Volkenrechtelijke beginselen in het Europees recht. Gelding als hogere bron van EG- en EU-recht, inroepbaarheid en afdwinging in rechte*, Groningen: Europa Law Publishing 2001.

Van Haersolte 1988
R.A.V. baron van Haersolte, *Inleiding tot het Nederlandse staatsrecht*, Zwolle: W.E.J. Tjeenk Willink 1988.

Van Helsdingen 1956
W.H. van Helsdingen, *De Staatsregeling van de Nederlandse Antillen van 1955. Historische toelichting en praktijk*, 's-Gravenhage: Staatsdrukkerij- en Uitgeverijbedrijf 1956.

Van Helsdingen 1957
W.H. van Helsdingen (m.m.v. Th. J. van der Peyl), *Het Statuut voor het Koninkrijk der Nederlanden. Wordingsgeschiedenis, commentaar en praktijk*, 's-Gravenhage: Staatsdrukkerij- en Uitgeverijbedrijf 1957.

Van Panhuys 1958
H.F. van Panhuys, 'The International Aspects of the Reconstruction of the Kingdom of The Netherlands in 1954', 5 *NTIR* (1958) pp. 1-31.

Van Rijn 1999
A.B. van Rijn, *Staatsrecht van de Nederlandse Antillen*, Deventer: W.E.J. Tjeenk Willink 1999.

Van Rijn 2001
Arjen van Rijn, 'Brussel, Den Haag en de landen en gebieden overzee', in: Rolf de Groot, Elies Steyger & Ronald van den Tweel (eds.), *Onze Keus. Pirouettes in het Gemeenschapsrecht*, The Hague: Pels Rijcken & Droogleever Fortuijn 2001, pp. 126-36.

Van Rijn 2004
A.B. van Rijn, 'Vijftig jaar Statuut: hoe verder?', *NJB*, (2004), No. 44, pp. 2276-83.

Van Rijn 2005a
A.B. van Rijn, 'De plaats van Nederland en de Caribische partners in de buitenlandse betrekkingen en de verdragsrelaties van het Koninkrijk', in: L.J.J. Rogier & H.G. Hoogers (eds.), *50 jaar Statuut voor het Koninkrijk der Nederlanden. Bijdragen voor het congres 50 jaar Statuut voor het Koninkrijk der Nederlanden, 3 december 2004*, [s.l.]: Erasmus Universiteit Rotterdam, Rijksuniversiteit Groningen, Ministerie van BZK [2005], pp. 87-107.

Van Rijn 2005b
A.B. van Rijn, 'De buitenlandse betrekkingen van een Caribische provincie', *Christen-Democratische Verkenningen* (2005) Winter, pp. 155-63.

Van Vollenhoven 1934
C. van Vollenhoven, *Staatsrecht overzee*, Leiden: Stenfert Kroese 1934.

Verton 1977
P.C. Verton, *Politieke dynamiek en dekolonisatie. De Nederlandse Antillen tussen autonomie en onafhankelijkheid*, Alphen aan den Rijn: Samsom 1977.

Verton 1978
P.C. Verton, 'Aruba en de dekolonisatie van de Nederlandse Antillen', 32 *Internationale Spectator* (1978) No. 2, December, pp. 771-78.

Verton 1990
Peter C. Verton, 'The Dutch decolonization: independence for the Netherlands Antilles', in: Betty Sedoc-Dahlberg (ed.), *The Dutch Caribbean: Prospects for Democracy*, New York: Gordon and Breach 1990, pp. 203-18.

Vignes 1991
Daniel Vignes, 'Intervention (in the debate on 'Les statuts non "domiens"')', in: Emmanuel Jos & Danielle Perrot (eds.), *L'outre-mer et l'Europe communautaire. Quelle insertion? Pour quel développement?* (Journées d'études du Centre de recherche sur les pouvoirs locaux dans la Caraïbe de l'Université des Antilles-Guyane, October 1991), Paris: Economica 1991, pp. 360-64.

Von der Groeben/Thiesing/Ehlermann 1999
Peter Gilsdorf & Andreas Zimmerman, 'Assoziierung der überseeischen Länder und Hoheitsgebiete', in: Hans von der Groeben, Jochen Thiesing & Claus-Dieter Ehlermann, *Kommentar zum EWG-Vertrag. Band 3. Artikel 102a-136a EGV*, Baden-Baden: Nomos 1999, p. 2091-2120.

Wainhouse 1964
David W. Wainhouse, *Remnants of Empire. The United Nations and the End of Colonialism*, New York: Harper & Row 1964.

Werkstuk 1952
Werkstuk door de gemachtigden van Nederland, Suriname en de Nederlandse Antillen aan de Regering aangeboden, bestemd om te dienen als basis van bespreking op de eerlang te houden Conferentie Nederland-Suriname-Nederlandse Antillen tot opstelling van een ontwerp van een Statuut voor het Koninkrijk, 11 February 1952.

Wesel 1999
Reinhard Wesel, 'Colonialism', in: Javier Perez de Cuellar & Young Seek Choue (eds.), *World Encyclopedia of Peace*, Seoul: Seoul Press 1999, pp. 241-44.

Wohlgemuth 1963
Patricia Wohlgemuth, 'The Portuguese Territories and the United Nations', *International Conciliation* (1963) No. 545, November, pp. 1-68.

Ziller 1991
Jacques Ziller, 'Les pays et territoires d'outre-mer (PTOM) associés à la Communauté économique européenne: Une alternative statutaire pour les "regions ultra-périphériques"?', in: Emmanuel Jos & Danielle Perrot (eds.), *L'outre-mer et l'Europe communautaire. Quelle insertion? Pour quel développement?* (Journées d'études du Centre de recherche sur les pouvoirs locaux dans la Caraïbe de l'Université des Antilles-Guyane, October 1991), Paris: Economica 1991, pp. 173-92.

INDEXES

LEGISLATION

TABLE OF CASES

International Court of Justice (ICJ)
East Timor (Portugal v. Australia), *ICJ Reports* (1995) 90, 173
Interpretation of the Agreement of 25 March 1951, between the WHO and Egypt
   (Advisory Opinion), *ICJ Reports* (1980) 73, 294
Namibia (Advisory Opinion), *ICJ Reports* (1971) 47, 37, 39, 47
Nuclear Tests (Australia v. France), *ICJ Reports* (1974) 253, 167, 274
Nuclear Tests (New Zealand v. France), *ICJ Reports* (1974) 457, 167, 274
Western Sahara (Advisory Opinion), *ICJ Reports* (1975) 12, 19, 22, 37-8, 44, 171, 173

European Court of Human Rights (ECHR)
A.B. v. The Netherlands, Judgment of 29 January 2002 (Application no. 37328/97), 329
Mathew v. The Netherlands, Judgment of 29 September 2005 (Application no. 24919/
   03), 135
Py v. France, Judgment of 11 January 2005 (Application no. 66289/01), 95, 133, 201
Sevinger and Eman v. The Netherlands, Decision of 6 September 2007 as to the admissi-
   bility (Applications nos. 17173/07 and 17180/07), 154-5
Tyrer v. UK, Judgment of 25 April 1978 (Application no. 5856/72), 200

Court of Justice of the European Communities
Antillean Rice Mills, Judgment of 11 February 1999 (Case C-390/95 P), *ECR* I-00769,
   303
Competence of the Community to conclude international agreements concerning services
   and the protection of intellectual property, Opinion 1/94 of 15 November 1994, *ECR* I-
   05267, 332
Eman and Sevinger, Judgment of 12 September 2006 (Case 300/04), 154, 212, 301
Emesa Sugar, Judgment of 8 February 2000 (Case C-17/98), *ECR* I-00675, 302
International Agreement on Natural Rubber, Opinion 1/78 of the Court of 4 October 1979,
   ECR 2871, 300, 332
International Fruit Company III, Judgement of 12 December 1972 (Cases 21/72 to 24/72),
   ECR 01219, 296
Leplat, Judgment of 12 February 1992 (Case C-260/90), *ECR* I-00643, 300
Kingdom of the Netherlands v. Commission, Judgment of 26 October 1994 (Case C-430/
   92), *ECR* I-05197, 302
Road Air, Judgment of 22 April 1997 (Case C-310/95), *ECR* I-02229, 302, 303, 304

Hoge Raad (Supreme Court of the Netherlands)
Harmonisatiewet, Judgement of 14 April 1989, *AB* 1989, 207, 159, 200
Emesa, Judgement of 10 September 1999, *AB* 1999, 462, 152, 318
Matos v. The Netherlands Antilles, Judgement of 21 November 2000, *NJ* 2001, 376, 152
Nederlands-Antilliaans Uitleveringsbesluit, Judgement of 7 November 2003, *NJ* 2004/99,
   m.n. Koopmans, 159, 201
Oduber and Lamers, Judgment of 13 April 2007, *RvdW* 2007, 394, 152

Afdeling bestuursrechtspraak van de Raad van State (Council of State of the Netherlands)
Judgement of 21 November 2006, Cases 200607567/1 and 200607800/1, 154, 212
Judgement of 21 November 2006, Cases 200404446/1 and 200404450/1, 154, 212

GENERAL INDEX